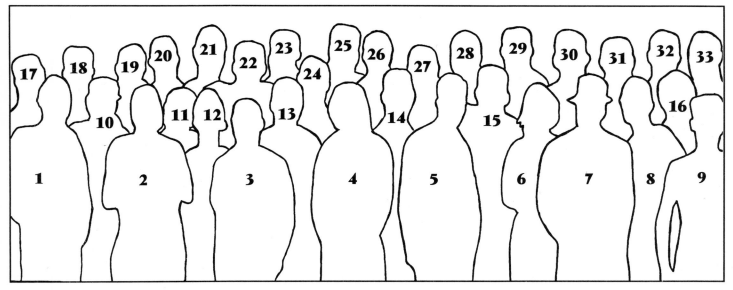

1– Lou Henson, 2– Red Grange, 3– Robert Zuppke, 4– Mary Eggers, 5– George Huff, 6– Renee Heiken, 7– Ray Eliot, 8– Craig Virgin, 9– Bob Richards, 10– Lou Boudreau, 11–Karol Kahrs, 12– Nancy Thies, 13– Dike Eddleman, 14– Andy Phillip, 15– Jim Grabowski, 16– Tonja Buford, 17– Jonelle Polk, 18– Chuck Carney, 19– Deon Thomas, 20– Harold Osborn, 21– Johnny "Red" Kerr, 22– Dick Butkus, 23– George Halas, 24– Steve Stricker, 25– Darrin Fletcher, 26– Derek Harper, 27– Dana Howard, 28– Jon Llewellyn, 29– Eddie Johnson, 30– Kendall Gill, 31– Alex Agase, 32– Buddy Young, 33– Art Schankin

ILLINI
LEGENDS, LISTS & LORE

100 Years of Big Ten Heritage

by Mike Pearson

Foreword by Dike Eddleman
Epilogue by Jim Turpin

SAGAMORE PUBLISHING
Champaign, Illinois

Interior design: Michelle R. Dressen
Editor: Susan M. McKinney
Dustjacket design: Jack W. Davis
Proofreader: Phyllis L. Bannon

Library of Congress Catalog Number: 95-70431
ISBN: 1-57167-018-1

We have made every effort to trace the ownership copyrighted photos. If we have failed to give adequate credit, we will be pleased to make changes in future printings.

Printed in the United States

To my loyal wife, Laura, who has taught me some of life's most important lessons

To my children, who make me smile

To my parents, who taught me the virtues of being a good person

And, to the spirit of George Huff, Ray Eliot and Chief Illiniwek

---

THANK YOU

to the following sponsors for their generous support

ILLINI PRIDE SPONSORS

Crouse Printing
English Brothers Construction Company
EMP Insurance
Illini Union Bookstore
JCPenney Company
Jerry's IGA
Kam's
Prairie Gardens & Jeffrey Alans
Professional Impressions Media Group, Inc.
University of Illinois Alumni Association

LOYALTY SPONSORS

Atlas Travel/Carlson Travel Network
Blossom Basket
Busey-Carter Travel
Follett's U of I Bookstore
Greater Champaign-Urbana Economic Partnership
Pages for All Ages Bookstore
Scantech Color Systems
TGI Friday's
United Graphics, Inc.
Waldenbooks, Inc.

CENTENNIAL SPONSORS

Herriott Group, Inc.
Illini FS Farmtown
Jillian's Billiard Club of Champaign, Inc.
Jon's Colorfilm Lab, Inc.
Market Place Shopping and Convenience Cente
Ramshaw-Smith Company
TIS Bookstore
Schumacher's Sportswear, Inc.
UpClose Printing & Copies
WDAN/WDNL

Table of Contents

Acknowledgments

Any author, particularly one writing his first book, will tell you that it's nearly impossible to thank everyone who has offered a helping hand along the way.

From the people who actually assisted in my research of the last 100 years of Fighting Illini history, to those who simply offered insight or encouragement, please accept my undying gratitude. My only regret is that I could not have included all of the stories I wanted to, but space limitations prevented me from doing so.

Early in my life, I came to the realization that if I was to have a career in athletics it would have to take place in the confines of an office building rather than on the playing fields. Through the sage advice of legendary Detroit sportswriter Joe Falls, I was directed to my first mentors, Fred Stabley and Nick Vista of Michigan State University's outstanding sports information office. Their thoughtfulness and leadership provided me with a firm base for success.

My friendships at the University of Illinois began with my comrade, the late Tab Bennett. Tab was a talented individual who, like the Alma Mater statue in front of Altgeld Hall, welcomed me to Champaign-Urbana with the warmth of an old friend. He taught me how to be a creative thinker and stay one step ahead of the competition.

My second tour of duty with the Illini is indebted to the man who hired me, former Athletic Director and Head Football Coach John Mackovic, and his staff of Bob Todd, Dana Brenner, Karol Kahrs, Tom Porter, Terry Cole, Rick Allen, Tim Tracy, Mike Hatfield, Al Martindale, Andy Dixon, and others.

Ron Guenther, John's successor as AD, has instilled new life and Illini spirit into the program since taking over in 1992. I am grateful to him for allowing me the opportunity to work on this book, and I look forward to helping him accomplish his dreams.

To the terrific Illini coaching staff with whom I have served, a heartfelt thank you. People such as Lou Henson, Lou Tepper, Gary Wieneke, Paula Smith, Yoshi Hayasaki, Jennifer Roberts, Lee Eilbracht, Don Sammons, and others have demonstrated the true meaning of *Illinois Loyalty*.

I've been blessed with a wonderful Sports Information staff as well. The list of people includes my proofreader Kent Brown, Dave Johnson, Dick Barnes, Janice Revell, Julie Dalpiaz, Louann Wilcock, Marty Kaufmann, Nancy Herpstreith, Robin Loughran, Kevin Nordquist, Kelly Willis, Steve Reaven, Natalie Doom, Sara Garman, Dal Bristow, Frank Reed, Erika Amstadt, Lisa Nelson, and a bevy of talented student assistants. Thanks in part to their efforts, the University of Illinois' athletic program has enjoyed tremendous visibility throughout the Land of Lincoln and beyond.

The five men who have preceded me as UI's Sports Information Director played as big a role as any in assembling the treasure chest of information for this book. Mike Tobin, the nation's first SID, Chuck Flynn, Charlie Bellatti, Norm Sheya, and Tab went to painstaking efforts to record Illinois' tremendous athletic heritage. A thank you goes also to Lani Jacobsen, Tom Boeh, and Mary Fowler who have coordinated news about women's athletics for the Illini.

To the multitude of athletes who I have served during my 10 years at Illinois, please accept my humble gratitude. I've enjoyed watching your special talents from the sidelines. I consider myself fortunate to have been able to attach the special word "friend" to such Illini legends as Ray Eliot, Dike Eddleman, Alex Agase, and Jim Grabowski. It was also a great thrill each of the three times I had the opportunity to share time with Red Grange and his lovely wife, Muggs.

The staff at University Archives, directed by the incomparable Maynard Brichford, opened their files to me and answered every question I asked. Thanks, also, to the people at the Urbana and Champaign Public Libraries for their assistance.

If pictures are indeed worth a thousand words, then a great deal of the praise must go to the photographic genius of Mark Jones, Phil Greer, Curt Beamer, and others. Also thanks to the artistry of designer Jack Davis for his magical work on the cover of this publication and for many of the posters that are contained within these pages.

To the media who have covered the Illini during my years at Illinois, I express my appreciation. Loren Tate, Jim Turpin, Gary Childs, Mark Tupper, Fowler Connell, Dave Dorr, Ed Sherman, Jim Ruppert, Steve

Batterson, Dick Martin, Herb Gould, Chris Owens, Dave Loane, Dan Roan, Chris Widlic, Dan Swaney, Ron Rector, Bob Logan, Randy Kindred, Ed Bond, Jim Sheppard, Mike Haile, Nolan Hurt, Lorraine Kee, Dave Dickey, Jim Benson, Andy Bagnato, Andy Gottesman, Sam Rickelman, Jim Wildrick, John Supinie, John Mayo, Scott Musgrave, Scott Andresen, and many, many others have all been valued friends of the University of Illinois.

To the people of Champaign-Urbana, particularly those special friends from First Christian Church, thank you for your encouragement while working on this book.

I also salute the good people at Sagamore Publishing for their incredible support. Joe and Peter Bannon, Michelle Dressen, and Jude Lancaster have been especially inspiring during the past three years.

Finally, I want to acknowledge the people who are dearest to my heart, my family. Included are my loving wife, Laura, who endured more loneliness during my marathon sessions in the office than I'll ever be able to replace; my children, Tony, Tom, Paige, and Parker; my parents, Glenn and Ruby Pearson; and my five sisters and their families. Thanks for being there when I've needed you most.

Foreword

As a high school senior, I had offers to attend a number of universities including Georgetown, Notre Dame, William and Mary, Indiana, and Kentucky. I chose the University of Illinois, not only because it is one of the finest educational institutions in the world, but because of its distinguished roster of sports legends. With such famous alumni as George Halas, Red Grange, Bob Zuppke, Ray Eliot, and George Huff, Illinois was the best choice for a young athlete eager for world-class competition.

God must have made my blood orange and blue, because from the first time I stepped onto the hardwood of Huff Gym, I knew that the University of Illinois was where I wanted to compete. Every boy in Illinois dreamed of playing in the State Basketball Tournament in Champaign-Urbana. Having participated in that tournament three of my four years at Centralia High School, I felt comfortable making the state's foremost university my collegiate home.

More than any other single factor, it was the Illini tradition that attracted me to this university, instilling in me the virtue of Illinois loyalty. It was my high school coach and history teacher, Arthur L. Trout, who taught me that our rich heritage at Illinois was named for the Illini Indians. A proud people, they were skilled hunters and fighters who demonstrated a generous nature whether at war or at peace. Among neighboring tribes, the Illini were best known for their fighting spirit and their great heart. The Illini were individualists who allowed their children the freedom to grow up as they desired, provided they demonstrated bravery and self-sacrifice.

Perhaps there is no greater tribute to our namesake than the men and women of Illinois athletics. Representing a diversity of racial and ethnic backgrounds, there have been a galaxy of colorful athletes who have broken records by the score. Overwhelming victories earned the unstinted praise of the nation's sportswriters. As you will discover in the pages of this book, throughout the annals of Illini sports, both athletes and coaches have been characterized by patience, perseverance, sacrifice, and spirit.

As I reflect on the past 100 years of Illinois sports, I feel gratified to have been a part of its glory. Through seniority alone, some consider me to be an Illini sports historian, having been involved in Illinois sports for half a century. I applaud Mike Pearson for accomplishing a monumental task in the writing of this book. I believe the following legends, lists, and lore will serve as a valuable reference for anyone who has ever played, coached, or cheered for the Illini. Possibly by what is written here, you can relive your own college days. Hopefully, it will inspire a new field of Illini legends.

Dike Eddleman
(Illinois '49)

The News-Gazette

SECTION
B
Saturday

AS ILLINI AS MEMORIAL STADIUM

Sports B-1-6
Scoreboard B-4
Outdoors B-6

Throughout history, *The News-Gazette* and *WDWS-AM 1400* have been leaders in Illini sports coverage—right down to the exciting play-by-play broadcasts by *The News-Gazette*'s Loren Tate and *WDWS*' Jim Turpin. Nobody knows the hometown team like *The News-Gazette* and *WDWS-AM 1400*.

NewsTalk 1400
WDWS-AM

The News-Gazette®

"No other individual had the esteem and affection of so many alumni, students, and friends than George Huff. He stood for everything that was right and honorable, not only in his administration and direction of athletics, but in all of his activities. His personal code of honor and of sportsmanship was based upon a philosophy of life that should inspire any man or woman. The influence of his career on all who knew him and the ideals he has left us will be a cherished heritage."

— A.C. Willard
President, University of Illinois,
upon the death of George Huff

1895-1904

1895-96

I·L·L·I·N·I M·O·M·E·N·T

The Palmer House, Chicago, Illinois, late 1800s.

FORMATION OF THE BIG TEN CONFERENCE:

The date was February 8, 1896. At the Palmer House in Chicago, Illinois, seven men were meeting to establish standards and regulations for the administration of intercollegiate athletics. These faculty representatives from seven of the Midwest's finest universities designated themselves as the "Intercollegiate Conference of Faculty Representatives." Professor Henry H. Everett represented the University of Illinois. Today, the organization is known as the "Big Ten Conference," although its bulky original label is still the official title. The seven charter members of the Conference included the Universities of Illinois, Chicago, Michigan, Minnesota, Wisconsin, plus Northwestern University and Purdue University. Indiana and Iowa were admitted in 1899, and Ohio State gained entrance in 1912. Chicago formally withdrew from the Conference in 1946 due to its inability to "provide reasonable competition," reducing the Big Ten to the Big Nine. Three years later, it was once again the Big Ten when Michigan State was admitted by the membership. Most recently, in 1989, an invitation to Big Ten membership was made to and accepted by Penn State.

ILLINI BIRTHDAYS

OCTOBER 1895
2– Clarence Ems, football

NOVEMBER 1895
11– Eugene Smith, football

FEBRUARY 1896
2– George Halas, football/basketball/baseball
2– Ralf Woods, basketball
2– Ray Woods, basketball
21– Dan Elwell, basketball

MARCH 1896
29– Reynold Kraft, football

MAY 1896
9– Edward Kurtzrock, wrestling
27– Julian Mee, basketball
27– Kenneth "Tug" Wilson, basketball and track

30– Craig Ruby, basketball coach

JUNE 1896
23– John McGregor, football
28– Norton Hellstrom, basketball

JULY 1896
8– Robert Doepel, football

AUGUST 1896
9– Harold Hoffman, wrestling

Senior catcher and soon-to-be Illini baseball coach George Huff took a relaxed pose in this 1895 team picture.

(Left to right) Harry Hadsall, Harvey Sconce, and Paul Cooper each earned varsity letters in both football and baseball.

ILLINI ITEM

A TOTAL OF 40 MEN won varsity letters for the University of Illinois' three athletic teams (football, baseball, and track) during the 1895-96 season. Three men—Harry Hadsall, Paul Cooper, and Harvey Sconce—earned letters in both football and baseball. It should be noted that the "I" letters weren't officially awarded to those men until November 3, 1923.

ILLINI LISTS

ILLINI FOOTBALL SUCCESS
(DECADE BY DECADE)

Decade	W	L	T	PCT
1890-1899	45	26	8	.620
1900-1909	61	27	6	.681
1910-1919	49	15	7	.739
1920-1929	55	19	3	.734
1930-1939	38	39	5	.494
1940-1949	38	49	5	.440
1950-1959	48	37	6	.560
1960-1969	36	59	1	.424
1970-1979	38	67	4	.367
1980-1989	63	48	4	.565
1990-1994	32	26	1	.551
TOTAL	503	412	50	.547

Illinois' first football team

ILLINI LEGEND:
GEORGE HUFF

When George Huff entered the University of Illinois as a student in 1887, he had no idea how much of an impact he would make upon his hometown of Champaign over the next half century. Not only was "G" a member of the school's first football team in 1890, he also molded the lives of hundreds of other young men through his roles as Fighting Illini coach and director of athletics. The rotund Huff lettered twice in football as the team's center and three times as a multi-position player in baseball. As head coach of the Fighting Illini football team from 1895-1899, "G" was only mildly successful (21-16-3). However, as skipper of the Illini baseball squad, Huff dominated his opponents, winning nearly 70 percent of the 544 games he coached from 1896-1919. "G" directed the Illini nine to a record 11 Big Ten championships. As UI's athletic director from 1901-36, Huff's contributions were monumental. He had a knack of hiring outstanding coaches (Bob Zuppke, Carl Lundgren, Craig Ruby, and Harry Gill). He helped build a phenomenal athletic plant (Memorial Stadium and Huff Gymnasium). But George Huff will be best known as a man who devoted his life to the honor and glory of the University of Illinois with honesty and fair play. On October 1, 1936, uremic poisoning claimed the life of the "Father of Fighting Illini Athletics" at the age of 64.

Illini Lore

During the 1895-96 school year, the University of Illinois had nine instructional buildings and 84 faculty members. Of President Andrew Draper's 855 total students, nearly 80 percent were males, and nearly a third of the student body majored in either English or Electrical Engineering.

1896-97

America's Time Capsule

- **July 7, 1896:** *The city of Chicago hosted the Democratic National Convention, nominating William Jennings Bryan as its candidate.*
- **Oct. 1, 1896:** *The Federal Post Office established rural free delivery.*
- **Nov. 3, 1896:** *William McKinley won the U.S. presidency in a landslide.*
- **March 17, 1897:** *Bob Fitzsimmons defeated "Gentleman Jim" Corbett for the world heavyweight boxing title.*
- **April 19, 1897:** *John McDermott won the first Boston Marathon in a time of two hours, 55 minutes, and 10 seconds.*

I·L·L·I·N·I M·O·M·E·N·T

Amos Alonzo Stagg directed the University of Chicago to a victory in Illinois' first Big Ten football game.

ILLINOIS' FIRST CONFERENCE FOOTBALL GAME—OCTOBER 31, 1896: "It not infrequently happens," reported the University of Illinois' student newspaper, *The Illini*, "that a team which is manifestly superior to that lined up against it, comes out the loser. If there ever was a game in which the weaker of the two elevens gained the victory, it was in the contest between Chicago and Illinois on Marshall Field when Stagg's aggregation of hirelings managed to win, 12 to 0. The rotten state of athletics at Chicago is well known and her name has become synonymous for corruption in that branch of college life." What made this game particularly momentous was that it was the Fighting Illini football team's very first Conference game. Coach Amos Alonzo Stagg's Maroons defeated Illinois that afternoon, with an alleged "professional," Frederick Nichols, directing the Maroons to two touchdowns (worth four points each), and two goals after touchdown (two points each).

ILLINI BIRTHDAYS

SEPTEMBER 1896
5– Robert Knop, football
13– Ralph Lanum, football

DECEMBER 1896
26– Bryan Doolen, basketball
29– Ernest McKay, basketball

FEBRUARY 1897
17– Leonard Charpier, football

MARCH 1897
13– Earl Anderson, basketball

JULY 1897
5– Merwin Mitterwallner, football
24– Stuyvesant Smith, football

Illinois Field served as the home of Fighting Illini football teams beginning in 1891 until the last game on October 13, 1923.

I

Captain William Fulton hit .302 for the 1897 Illini baseball team.

ILLINI ITEM

THREE FIGHTING ILLINI baseball players—second baseman William Fulton, shortstop Hugh Shuler, and centerfielder Harry Hadsall—were selected to the 1897 All-Western team by *Harper's Weekly*. Fulton (.302) and Shuler (.304) both hit well, but Hadsall batted just .160 for the year.

ILLINI LISTS

ILLINI ATHLETIC DIRECTORS

- 1892-1894   Edward K. Hall
- 1894-1895   Fred H. Dodge
- 1895-1898   Henry H. Everett
- 1898-1901   Jacob K. Shell
- 1901-1936   George A. Huff
- 1936-1941   Wendell S. Wilson
- 1942-1966   Douglas Mills
- 1967-1972   E.E. (Gene) Vance
- 1972-1979   Cecil N. Coleman
- 1979   Ray Eliot (interim)
- 1980-1988   Neale R. Stoner
- 1988   Ronald E. Guenther (interim)
- 1988   Dr. Karol A. Kahrs (interim)
- 1988-1991   John Mackovic
- 1991-1992   Robert Todd (interim)
- 1992-   Ronald Guenther

Edward Hall was UI's first director of athletics

ILLINI LEGEND:

HENRY EVERETT

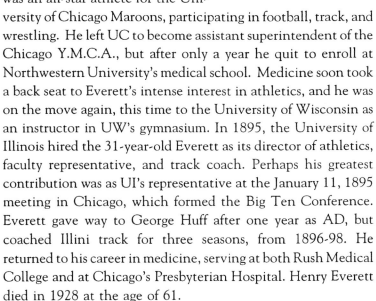

The University of Illinois' third athletic director and first faculty representative was Henry Houghton Everett. A native of Chicago, Everett was an all-star athlete for the University of Chicago Maroons, participating in football, track, and wrestling. He left UC to become assistant superintendent of the Chicago Y.M.C.A., but after only a year he quit to enroll at Northwestern University's medical school. Medicine soon took a back seat to Everett's intense interest in athletics, and he was on the move again, this time to the University of Wisconsin as an instructor in UW's gymnasium. In 1895, the University of Illinois hired the 31-year-old Everett as its director of athletics, faculty representative, and track coach. Perhaps his greatest contribution was as UI's representative at the January 11, 1895 meeting in Chicago, which formed the Big Ten Conference. Everett gave way to George Huff after one year as AD, but coached Illini track for three seasons, from 1896-98. He returned to his career in medicine, serving at both Rush Medical College and at Chicago's Presbyterian Hospital. Henry Everett died in 1928 at the age of 61.

Illini Lore

Dedicated June 8, 1897, the University of Illinois library—renamed Altgeld Hall in 1940—served students for nearly 30 years as the campus's main resource center. The original structure cost $380,000 and featured a distinctive 132-foot tower, from which a daily chimes concert emanates. Additions to the building were made in 1914, 1919, 1926, and 1956. After its service as the home of the library, it became the headquarters for the College of Law for 28 years, and in 1955 was assigned to the Department of Mathematics.

1897-98

America's Time Capsule

- **Sept. 21, 1897:** *In response to a letter from young Virginia O'Hanlon, a New York Sun editorial declared, "Yes, Virginia, there is a Santa Claus."*
- **July 2, 1897:** *A coal miners' strike put 75,000 men out of work in Pennsylvania, Ohio, and West Virginia.*
- **Feb. 15, 1898:** *An explosion destroyed the battleship Maine, as 260 crew members perished.*
- **April 24, 1898:** *The United States declared war on Spain, and the Spanish-American War began.*
- **June 1, 1898:** *Congress passed the Erdman Arbitration Act, making government mediation in railroad disputes legitimate.*

I·L·L·I·N·I M·O·M·E·N·T

SCENE AT THE COLISEUM DURING THE INDIAN-ILLINOIS GAME.

ILLINOIS' FIRST INDOOR FOOTBALL GAME—NOVEMBER 20, 1897: The University of Illinois' first night game and its first game played indoors came against the Carlisle Indians at the old Chicago Coliseum. The contest, called by one journalist "hair raising in its recklessness," pitted East (Carlisle) against West (Illinois) on a gridiron of sand and sawdust. Though the great Jim Thorpe had already graduated, Carlisle remained a power-house team. The Fighting Illini began like a prairie whirlwind, scoring the first touchdown after a series of rushes down the field. Halftime's intermission saw Illinois ahead, 6-5, but that lead evaporated in the second half as the Indians tallied three unanswered touchdowns. After the game, the two teams traveled together by train to Champaign-Urbana, where the Carlisle squad stayed until the following Wednesday as the guests of the University.

ILLINI BIRTHDAYS

SEPTEMBER 1897
9– Floyd Larimer, football
23– Neal Leitch, football
25– George Koch, football

OCTOBER 1987
2– Jesse Kirkpatrick, football
10– John Probst, basketball

NOVEMBER 1897
23– Richard Reichle, baseball

FEBRUARY 1898
2– Ben Mittelman, basketball
15– Philip Durant, football

MARCH 1898
9– Lawrence Walquist, basketball/football

APRIL 1898
25– Fred Corray, Illini broadcaster

JUNE 1898
23– William Kopp, football/basketball

AUGUST 1898
12– Bob Emery, track
29– Burt Ingwersen, football/basketball

Four members of the 1917-18 Illinois basketball team were born during the 1897-98 season. They included Ben Mittleman (second row, far left), Burt Ingwersen (second row, fourth from left), William Kopp (third row, third from left), and John Probst (third row, fourth from left).

J.K. Hoagland was Illinois' first individual conference track champion.

ILLINI ITEM

ILLINOIS' TRACK AND FIELD team placed fifth among five teams at the first Indoor Western Intercollegiate meet, held in Chicago. J.K. Hoagland of Illinois won the 880-yard walk to become the school's first individual conference track champion.

ILLINI LISTS

ILLINI SINGLE-SEASON FOOTBALL SHUTOUTS

- 1900 — 8 (in 12 games)
- 1902 — 8 (in 13 games)
- 1910 — 7 (in 7 games)
- 1901 — 7 (in 10 games)
- 1904 — 7 (in 12 games)
- 1917 — 6 (in 8 games)
- 1903 — 6 (in 14 games)

The 1900 Illini football team posted eight shutouts in 12 games.

ILLINI LEGEND:

FRED SMITH

During the infancy of college athletics in the late 1800s, it was very common for one individual to hold more than one position within the athletic department. Such was the case with athletic director/baseball coach/football coach George Huff. "G" decided that the multiple responsibilities were diluting his efficiency and affecting his health, so in 1900 he submitted his resignation as the Illini grid mentor. Huff chose former Illini assistant coach Fred Smith as his successor in 1900, a man who had performed the bulk of the head coaching duties for Huff in 1897 and '98. Smith starred as a quarterback at Princeton, directing the Tigers to a 10-0-1 record and the mythical national championship. During his lone season as Illinois' official head coach, Smith guided the Illini to a very respectable 7-3-2 record, including a victory over Purdue. Altogether, Illinois registered eight defensive shutouts in 12 games, a mark that equals the most in Illinois football history during a single season. Smith eventually settled in New York City, where he doubled as an engineer with the Department of Public Works and as head football coach at Fordham College. He died in 1923 at the age of 50.

 Illini Lore

In April of 1897, Charles W. Spalding, treasurer for the University of Illinois, was charged with embezzling University funds of $460,000. About 95 percent of that total had been secretly invested by Spalding in land deals in the state of Idaho. Two months after he had been caught, the Illinois state legislature appropriated money to cover the deficit caused by Spalding's actions. On December 1, 1897, Spalding was sent to the state penitentiary to begin a four-year sentence.

1898-99

FOOTBALL TEAM 1898

I·L·L·I·N·I M·O·M·E·N·T

ILLINI'S 11-10 FOOTBALL WIN AT MINNESOTA— NOVEMBER 24, 1898:

Coach George Huff's Illini limped into Minnesota with a three-game losing streak, so no one gave the visitors much of a chance that cold and snowy Thanksgiving Day. Only a day after being shutout by the Carlisle Indians, the Illinois party set off on its exceedingly long and tedious trip to the Land of 10,000 Lakes. The first-ever match-up between the two schools began predictably, as Minnesota jumped off to a 10-0 first-quarter lead. Illinois battled back, scoring a five-point touchdown just before the whistle sounded to trail 10-5 at the intermission. In the final 25 minutes, the Illini successfully navigated the treacherous field by rushing the ball. All-star fullback A.R. Johnston, the Illini captain, scored the game-tying TD, then kicked the point after for the eventual 11-10 victory.

ILLINI BIRTHDAYS

SEPTEMBER 1898
15– Bernard Oakes, football

NOVEMBER 1898
20– Sam Hill, football

DECEMBER 1898
15– Ralph Fletcher, football/basketball
23– Walter Crawford, football
30– Don Peden, football

JANUARY 1899
6– John Depler, football
20– Richard Lifvendahl, football
25– Milt Olander, football

MARCH 1899
3– Paul Taylor, basketball

APRIL 1899
13– Harold Osborn, track

JUNE 1899
8– Jack Crangle, football

JULY 1899
2– Russell Linden, football
4– Earl Greene, football
30– Hubert Tabor, football/basketball

AUGUST 1899
6– Stephen Coutchie, football
9– Jerome Jordan, baseball

Arthur Hall earned letters in football and baseball from 1898 to 1900. He later coached the Fighting Illini football team from 1907-12.

This "I" sweater from 1898 belonged to Illini player and later head football coach, Arthur Hall.

ILLINI ITEM

IN DECEMBER OF 1898, the UI's Athletic Association began issuing blue sweaters with the orange block "I" to members of the Illini football, baseball, and track teams who either won a contest or individual event against teams representing the universities of Chicago, Michigan, Wisconsin, or Minnesota, or to Illini who won a point in the annual field meet of the Western Intercollegiate Athletic Association.

ILLINI LISTS

JUSTA LINDGREN'S ALL-TIME ILLINI FOOTBALL TEAM (chosen in 1943)

- Ends: Chuck Carney and Claude Rothgeb
- Tackles: Walter Crawford and Butch Nowack
- Guards: Ralph Chapman and Jim McMillin
- Center: Bob Reitsch
- Quarterback: Potsy Clark
- Halfbacks: Red Grange and Harold Pogue
- Fullback: Jack Crangle

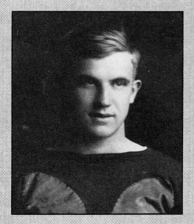

George "Potsy" Clark was the quarterback on Justa Lindgren's all-time Illini football team.

ILLINI LEGEND:

JUSTA LINDGREN

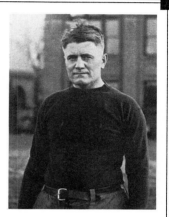

For 40 consecutive years plus a few more, the name Justa Lindgren was synonymous with Fighting Illini football. "Lindy," as he was known to the legion of players he coached and his many friends, first joined the University of Illinois as a freshman lineman from Moline in 1898. Four letter-winning seasons later, he graduated from the UI and was contacted by Cornell College in Mt. Vernon, Iowa, to become the school's head football coach. After only two seasons in Iowa, Lindgren returned to Urbana-Champaign as one of four graduates in George Huff's alumni coaching system. He served for one season as the Illini's head coach, 1906, but the conservative, detail-minded Lindgren felt more comfortable as an assistant, serving as line coach under Arthur Hall, Bob Zuppke, and Ray Eliot through 1943. Lindgren developed seven All-America players at Illinois during that span and was an integral member of eight Big Ten championship teams. He died in 1951 at the age of 72.

Illini Lore

On May 5, 1899, the University of Illinois' Board of Trustees decided to erect a $150,000 agriculture building. The facility, which opened for use September 10, 1900, eventually came to be known as Davenport Hall, in honor of the College of Agriculture's dean, Eugene Davenport.

1899-00

America's Time Capsule

- **Oct. 14, 1899:** *William McKinley became the first President to ride in an automobile.*
- **Nov. 21, 1899:** *Vice President Garret Hobart died. New York Governor Theodore Roosevelt was nominated as Hobart's replacement. Roosevelt first declined the nomination, but later relented at the Republican National Convention.*
- **March 14, 1900:** *Congress standardized the gold dollar as the unit of monetary value in the United States.*
- **May 14, 1900:** *Carrie Nation began her anti-liquor campaign.*
- **July 4, 1900:** *The Democratic Party nominated William Jennings Bryan of Nebraska as its presidential candidate.*

I·L·L·I·N·I M·O·M·E·N·T

CONFERENCE CHAMPIONS 1900
COACH HUFF CAPT JOHNSTON FALKENBURG STEINWEDELL MGR. MARTIN LOTZ
WILDER McCOLLUM SWITZER ABSIT COOK
MILLER DEVELDE B. FULTON MATHEWS LUNDGREN

ILLINOIS' FIRST WESTERN CONFERENCE TITLE:

The beginning of the 20th century trumpeted the arrival of the University of Illinois' very first Western Conference title. Coach George Huff's 1900 baseball squad returned most of its members from the 1899 Big Ten runner-up, and began its preseason with a series of exhibition games against the Chicago White Sox. After winning three and tying one of the nine games, Huff knew he had the makings of a championship club. His standout players included pitchers Carl Lundgren and Harvey McCollum, second baseman Billy Fulton, third baseman Carl Steinwedell, and centerfielder Jimmy Cook—all members of Huff's all-time Illinois baseball team. The Illini won seven of their first eight conference games, winding up with an 11-2 record.

ILLINI BIRTHDAYS

SEPTEMBER 1899
28– Charles Vail, basketball

OCTOBER 1899
3– Henry Hughes, football
11– Albert Mohr, football
26– Otto Vogel, football/baseball

NOVEMBER 1899
20– Charles Lovejoy, football
23– Glenn Potter, basketball

FEBRUARY 1900
1– Joseph Sternaman, football
28– Robert Fletcher, football

JULY 1900
26– David Wilson, football

AUGUST 1900
25– Chuck Carney, football/basketball

The only four-generation Illini family was completed in 1981 when gymnast David Peterson (bottom right) earned a varsity "I." His father, Waldo (bottom left) was a track letterman in 1954. His grandfather, David Wilson, (top right) was captain of the 1922 Illini football team. And his great-grandfather, Fred Thompson (top left) earned baseball letters in 1895 and '96.

ILLINI ITEM

JUNE 9, 1900: The University of Illinois lost nearly all of its historical athletic records as well as its championship banners and trophies on June 9, 1900, when fire destroyed the UI woodshops, the second floor of which was occupied by the Men's Gymnasium.

ILLINI LISTS

ALL-TIME BIG TEN BASEBALL VICTORIES
(Through 1995 Season)

- Michigan (1896)   779
- ILLINOIS (1896)   777
- Minnesota (1906)   671
- Ohio State (1913)   602
- Wisconsin (1896)   565
- Iowa (1906)   546
- Indiana (1906)   472
- Purdue (1906)   443
- Northwestern (1898)   436
- Michigan State (1951) 375
- Chicago (1896)   221
- Penn State (1992)   41

George Huff coached the Illini baseball program from 1896 to 1919.

ILLINI LEGEND:

CARL LUNDGREN

The immortal George Huff called him "the greatest of all college baseball coaches." An early sports magazine, *Athletic World*, praised him as "the peer of all college baseball instructors." In any case, the name Carl Leonard Lundgren is permanently linked with University of Illinois success on the baseball diamond. As a pitcher on the Fighting Illini nines of 1899-1902, "Lundy" led Illinois to Big Ten championships his sophomore and senior seasons. The esteem in which he was held by his fellow students was displayed by his election to the baseball team's captaincy, but also to the presidency of UI's senior class. Lundgren went directly from Illinois into professional baseball, pitching, for the Chicago Cubs for seven seasons. Twice the Cubbies were world champs, due in great part to his spectacular pitching which accounted for 92 career victories. After leaving the Cubs, he began his brilliant coaching career at Princeton as freshman coach, then went to Michigan as varsity coach, where he coached future Hall of Famer George Sisler. Huff lured Lundgren back to Champaign to coach the Illini in 1921, directing Illinois to five conference titles in 12 seasons. Lundgren died on August 24, 1934, of a heart attack at the age of 54.

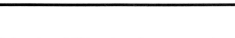

Illini Lore

On September 20, 1899, the University of Illinois' student-operated newspaper, the *Illini*, began publishing on a tri-weekly basis. For the previous five years, the *Illini* was printed just once per week. The newspaper expanded to printing five times per week during the 1902-03 school year.

1900-01

America's Time Capsule

- **Sept. 8, 1900:** *A hurricane ravaged Galveston, Texas, killing 6,000 people and causing property damages of $20 million.*
- **Nov. 6, 1900:** *William McKinley won the presidency for a second term.*
- **Jan. 10, 1901:** *A well near Beaumont, Texas, brought in oil, the first evidence of oil from that region.*
- **March 3, 1901:** *The United States Steel Corporation was incorporated in New Jersey.*
- **June 15, 1901:** *Willie Anderson won the U.S. Open golf tournament.*

I·L·L·I·N·I M·O·M·E·N·T

Second baseman Jimmy Cook led the Illinois effort against the Chicago Cubs.

ILLINOIS VS. THE CUBS—APRIL 3-16, 1901:

Before the days of spring-training sites in warm climates, major league baseball teams frequently would hook up for a series of practice games against teams from the local universities. Such was the case in 1901, when manager Tom Loftus brought his Chicago Cubs to Champaign-Urbana for a nine-game series. The Cubbies featured future Hall of Famer Frank Chance, he of the famous baseball triumvirate "Tinker-to-Evers-to Chance." Coach George Huff's Illini surprisingly won four games against the National League club, paced by the hitting of second baseman Jimmy Cook and catcher Jake Stahl. Illinois used the exhibition series as a springboard to a second-place finish in the Big Ten, but the Cubs ultimately finished 37 games behind the Pittsburgh Pirates in the N.L. race.

ILLINI BIRTHDAYS

SEPTEMBER 1900
10– Henry Reitsch, basketball
15– Henry McCurdy, baseball

OCTOBER 1900
9– Vivian Green, football

DECEMBER 1900
16– Horatio Fitch, track

JANUARY 1901
2– Franklin Johnson, track
23– Clarence "Stub" Muhl, football

FEBRUARY 1901
7– Rial Rolfe, golf

MAY 1901
18– John Happenny, football/baseball
23– Cecil Hollopeter, basketball

JULY 1901
14– Cordon Lipe, basketball
19– Richard Wagner, football

AUGUST 1901
8– George Dawson, football
14– Emil Schultz, football
29– Clarence Drayer, football

The 1924 United States Olympic team was represented by five former Illini athletes. From left to right, the quintet included Franklin Johnson (born January 2, 1901), Horatio Fitch (born December 16, 1900), Avery Brundage, Dan Kinsey, and Harold Osborn.

ILLINI ITEM

ROBERT "RED" MATTHEWS, the nation's first acrobatic cheerleader, served as the University of Illinois' first cheerleader from 1899-1900. Said Matthews later, "I just busted out on the sidelines like the measles, and started hollering with my head up, my arms waving, and my legs jumping." Matthews was an institution at the University of Tennessee from 1907-49, serving on the Engineering faculty and initiating UT's first cheerleading program. At age 95, he attended Illinois' 1973 Homecoming game and joined the Illini cheerleading squad on the sidelines. Matthews died in 1978 at the age of 99.

ILLINI LISTS

ALL-TIME BIG TEN CHAMPIONSHIPS
(Men's and Women's Sports)
(Through 1994-95 season)

1.	Michigan	271
2.	**Illinois**	**205**
3.	Ohio State	141
4.	Indiana	139
5.	Wisconsin	128
6.	Minnesota	111
7.	Iowa	83
8.	Chicago	72
9.	Michigan State	56
10.	Purdue	55
11.	Northwestern	50
12.	Penn State	7

ILLINI LEGEND:

DR. JACOB SHELL

Dr. Jacob Kinzer Shell's tenure as the University of Illinois' athletic director from 1898-1901 was generally accented by achievement. Though football and track successes were minimal, the baseball team won a Western Conference (Big Ten) championship in 1900, the school's first ever. Shell also had a hand in welcoming Indiana and Iowa into the conference, and he helped establish the Urbana-Champaign campus as the training quarters for the Chicago Cubs. During his undergraduate days at the University of Pennsylvania in the early 1880s and during his graduate career at Swarthmore College, Shell was a fantastic athlete. "Doc" starred in football, baseball, gymnastics, track, lacrosse, boxing, and won America's middleweight wrestling championship. Shell resigned his post as UI's director of athletics on May 29, 1901, opening the door for his successor, George Huff. He was one of the founders of the American Athletic Union, serving 34 years for the AAU in numerous capacities. Shell died on December 10, 1940, at the age of 78.

 Illini Lore

University of Illinois seniors first wore caps and gowns at commencement exercises on June 12, 1901. The procession of students marched up Burrill Avenue to the old Armory. After diplomas were received, the seniors marched back to the lawn south of Green Street, where they sang "Auld Lang Syne." A total of 174 degrees were issued at the Urbana-Champaign campus in 1900-01, the most in the history of the University.

1901-02

FOOTBALL TEAM 1901

I·L·L·I·N·I M·O·M·E·N·T

1901 ILLINOIS-CHICAGO FOOTBALL GAME—OCTOBER 19, 1901:

Coach Edgar Holt's Illini were unstoppable through the first four games of the season, rolling up 135 points. Their defensive play was particularly impressive, allowing nary a single opponent to penetrate their end zone. But now came the real test, against Coach Amos Alonzo Stagg's University of Chicago club, on the Maroons' home field. Nearly half of the crowd of 7,000 cheered on the Illini from the east bleachers. Though the first half was scoreless, the Orange and Blue controlled play with a steady ground game that ultimately accounted for 560 total yards by game's end. Illinois continued its dominance in the second half, with Jake Stahl following the blocks of lineman Justa Lindgren for UI's first two scores. The Illini won the game, 24-0, chalking up their fifth consecutive shutout. On the following Monday evening, the team was honored with a parade and a 24-gun salute, and was presented with a key to the city of Urbana.

ILLINI BIRTHDAYS

SEPTEMBER 1901
4— John Mauer, basketball

OCTOBER 1901
1— Morris Robison, football
13— Robert Clark, football
17— Louis Slimmer, football
29— Harold Woodward, football

NOVEMBER 1901
7— Edward Richards, football
11— Leonard "Ted" Haines, basketball

JANUARY 1902
6— Robert Barnes, baseball
22— Dan Kinsey, track
29— Jack Lipe, basketball

FEBRUARY 1902
14— Fred Major, baseball

MARCH 1902
4— Roland Popken, basketball
9— Edward Mieher, cross country
31— Glenn Law, wrestling coach

MAY 1902
30— Ernest Chatten, football

JUNE 1902
9— Lee Dunham, baseball

JULY 1902
19— Harold "Hek" Kenney, wrestling & wrestling coach

AUGUST 1902
28— Wally Roettger, basketball/baseball

Harold "Hek" Kenney, one of Illinois' legends in the sport of wrestling, was born on July 19, 1902.

- 16 -

Center Fred Lowenthal earned All-Western honors in 1901.

ILLINI ITEM

ILLINOIS' 1901 FOOTBALL TEAM posted seven shutouts in 10 games, allowing an average of less than four points per game. Against Western Conference competition, Coach Edgar Holt's squad won four of six league games, allowing just 39 total points. Guard Jake Stahl and center Fred Lowenthal won All-Western honors for the Fighting Illini.

ILLINI LISTS

ILLINOIS' ALL-TIME SINGLE-SEASON BATTING AVERAGES

1. Darrin Fletcher, 1987   .497
2. Ben Lewis, 1933   .473
3. Boyd Bartley, 1943   .460
   John Toncoff, 1933   .460
5. Jerry Jordan, 1926   .447
6. Jake Stahl, 1903   .444
7. Jake Stahl, 1901   .443
8. Fred Major, 1926   .441
9. Larry Sutton, 1991   .434
10. Ruck Steger, 1950   .429

Ben Lewis' .473 average in 1933 stood as Illinois' single-season record for 54 years.

ILLINI LEGEND:

GARLAND "JAKE" STAHL

During his era, Garland "Jake" Stahl was a man among boys at the University of Illinois. He was an All-American tackle in football, leading the Illini to 25 victories in his last three seasons on the gridiron. As a catcher on the baseball team, Stahl played a level above his teammates, averaging well over .400 from the plate the last three years. His 400-foot, bases-loaded home run against Michigan, May 9, 1903, off the tree in deep right center field at Illinois Field remains as one of the most legendary single plays in Illini baseball history. Stahl's senior-year batting average of .444 stood as a school record for 23 seasons. But, as it turned out, that was only the beginning. Stahl took his act into major league baseball, enjoying a magnificent career. Included among the highlights of his eight-year career were two World Series championships with the Boston Red Sox (1903 and 1912), the last one as the manager, and an American League-leading 10 home runs in 1910. Stahl died on September 18, 1922, at the age of 43.

Illini Lore

On April 6, 1902, University of Illinois president Andrew Sloan Draper was seriously injured when he was thrown from his horse-drawn carriage. Three days later, doctors amputated his leg. President Draper didn't return to the university until October 1.

1902-03

I·L·L·I·N·I M·O·M·E·N·T

ILLINOIS-OHIO STATE FOOTBALL GAME—NOVEMBER 15, 1902:
Tying a game, it has been said, is like kissing your sister. But Illinois' 0-0 stalemate with Ohio State in the first-ever engagement between the sister institutions was more like a spat. The Buckeyes had not yet become a member of the Big Ten, though they regularly played against conference schools. The Illinois contingent traveled to Columbus expecting an easy victory, since OSU had been pummeled by Michigan earlier in the year by an 86-0 count. Several times during the game, Illinois threatened the Buckeye endzone, but fumbles and two failed field goals did in the Illini. Coach Edgar Holt's Illini squad wound up the season with a 10-2-1 record, placing fourth in the conference behind Michigan's famous point-a-minute team.

ILLINI BIRTHDAYS

SEPTEMBER 1902
28– Donald Karnes, basketball

OCTOBER 1902
5– Harry Hall, football
11– Frank Rokusek, football
16– Leland "Slim" Stilwell, basketball & team physician
23– Jim McMillen, football

JANUARY 1903
16– Forrest Greathouse, football
20– Wallace McIllwain, football
31– Russell Daugherity, football/basketball

FEBRUARY 1903
1– Roy Miller, football
17– Hollie Martin, basketball

MARCH 1903
17– Ray Gallivan, football
31– Don Garner, football

APRIL 1903
18– Leonard Umnus, football

MAY 1903
12– George Wickhorst, football
26– Bernie Shively, football/track/wrestling
28– Dwight Follett, football

JUNE 1903
6– Richard Hall, football
13– Harold "Red" Grange, football

JULY 1903
5– Earl Britton, football
9– Curtis Parker, basketball

AUGUST 1903
12– Gilbert Roberts, football

Garland "Jake" Stahl, shown at bat, connected on one of the most famous home runs in Illini history, May 9, 1903. With the bases loaded, Stahl's grand slam belt was estimated to be hit approximately 400 feet, into a tree in deep right center field.

Four-year-old Red Grange

ILLINI ITEM

ON A SEASONABLY MILD DAY—June 13, 1903—at their home in Forksville, Pennsylvania, Sadie Grange gave birth to a bouncing baby boy named Harold Edward Grange. Little did she know that the youngster would grow up to revolutionize the sport of football.

ILLINI LISTS

MOST BIG TEN CHAMPIONSHIPS BY A SCHOOL IN A SINGLE SPORT
(Through 1994-95 season)

1.	Michigan (football)	37
2.	Michigan (men's tennis)	35
3.	Illinois (men's fencing)	30
	Michigan (baseball)	30
	Michigan (men's outdoor track)	30
	Wisconsin (men's cross country)	30

1951 Big Ten Championship fencing team.

ILLINI LEGEND:

EDGAR HOLT

Before the turn of the century, it was Harvard and Princeton who were two of the kingpins of college football. So, thought Illini athletic director George Huff, why not hire an Eastern coach to turn the sluggish Illinois football program into a winner? Huff's choice was Edgar Garrison Holt, a product of both the Harvard and Princeton systems. Holt had toiled as a lineman during his playing days, so he spent the bulk of his time tutoring UI front-line players such as "Jake" Stahl, Fred Lowenthal, and Justa Lindgren. In two seasons, 1901 and '02, Holt guided Illinois to its first two winning records in Big Ten play and a cumulative record of 18-4-1. Holt died April 19, 1924 at the age of 49.

 Illini Lore

The University of Illinois' new $289,000 Chemical Building opened to students September 28, 1902. At that time, the 165,000 square-foot facility was said to be the largest building in the country devoted exclusively to chemistry. An addition was made to the structure in 1916, and, on May 13, 1939, the laboratory was named in honor of longtime department head William Noyes.

1903-04

I·L·L·I·N·I M·O·M·E·N·T

(Seated, far right) Frank Pfeffer pitched a two-hitter in Illinois' title clincher against Chicago.

ILLINI "9" CAPTURES CONFERENCE TITLE:

Nobody gave Coach George Huff's 1904 Fighting Illini baseball team much of a chance to defend the Big Ten title it had won the season before. After all, how would Illinois ever replace such stalwarts as Jake Stahl and Jimmy Cook, both .400 hitters in 1903? Huff's club played a very ambitious non-conference schedule, but lost just one of 13 games. In conference play, the Illini battled Wisconsin for the top spot, ultimately out-distancing the Badgers with an impressive 11-3 record. The title clincher came on May 28th when Illinois defeated the University of Chicago, 11-0, behind the two-hit pitching of Frank Pfeffer and two home runs by Captain Roy Parker. The leading Illini hitters in 1904 were left fielder Claude Rothgeb at .351 and third baseman R.L. Pitts at .350.

ILLINI BIRTHDAYS

OCTOBER 1903
6– Marshall Cooledge, football
31– Fred Fisher, football

NOVEMBER 1903
5– Oliver Langhorst, football
20– Charles Kassel, football

APRIL 1904
2– Joe Sapora, wrestling
22– Forrest "Frosty" Peters, football

MAY 1904
15– Buel "Pat" Patterson, wrestling coach

JUNE 1904
20– Louis Muegge, football
29– Allie Morrison, wrestling

JULY 1904
28– Cecil Perkins, football

AUGUST 1904
6– Marion Leonard, football
6– Albert "Butch" Nowack, football
28– Frank Purma, track

Football star Forrest "Frosty" Peters (left) and long-time wrestling coach Buel "Pat" Patterson were born during the 1903-04 season.

I

ILLINI ITEM

HARRY GILL, who debuted as the Fighting Illini track and field coach in 1904, was America's premier decathlon performer in 1900. A native Canadian, Gill defeated three-time United States champion Ellery Clark in a one-on-one contest in New York to earn that distinction.

ILLINI LISTS

MULTIPLE LETTERWINNERS (1878-1925)

- A.W. Merrifield — 11 letters (baseball & track)
- Claude Rothgeb — 10 letters (football, baseball, & track)
- Burt Ingwersen — 9 letters (football, basketball, & baseball)
- James Cook — 8 letters (football & baseball)
- Don Sweney — 8 letters (football & track)
- Charles Carney — 7 letters (football & basketball)
- Ira Carrithers — 7 letters (football, baseball, & track)
- George Huff — 7 letters (football & baseball)
- Arthur Johnston — 7 letters (football & baseball)
- Garland "Jake" Stahl — 7 letters (football & baseball)
- Lawrence Walquist — 7 letters (football & basketball)

A.W. Merrifield earned 11 varsity letters in baseball and track.

ILLINI LEGEND:

CLAUDE ROTHGEB

One way to gauge the accomplishments of an athlete is to measure the success of his teams. During the 1903-04 season, the most successful Fighting Illini teams were found over at Illinois Field. The Illinois football teams, though they never were champions, racked up a cumulative record of 44 victories, 15 losses, and four ties from 1900 through 1904. In baseball, the 1904 and '05 clubs were 37-9. The sparkplug of those teams was a talented young man named Claude Rothgeb. As an end for the football squad, Rothgeb lettered four times and served as captain of the 1903 team. So outstanding was he that during his senior year he became only the third Illini gridder to earn All-America honors. As the left fielder for George Huff's baseball team, Rothgeb was the leading hitter (.351) for the 1904 Big Ten champs and the captain of the 1905 conference runner-up. Rothgeb also lettered four times for the Illini track team as a sprinter and shot putter, winning a Big Ten individual title in the latter event.

Illini Lore

On August 23, 1904, Dr. Edmund James, president of Northwestern University, was elected to the University of Illinois presidency. James replaced President Andrew Draper who resigned in January to accept a position as Commissioner of Education for the state of New York. By 1909, James had become a national figure, and by 1916, he was being discussed as a candidate for the presidency of the United States.

1904-05

America's Time Capsule

- **Oct. 8, 1904:** *Automobile racing as an organized sport began with the Vanderbilt Cup race on Long Island, New York.*
- **Oct. 27, 1904:** *The first section of New York City's subway system was opened to the public.*
- **Nov. 8, 1904:** *Theodore Roosevelt was reelected president of the United States, defeating Alton Parker by nearly two million votes.*
- **April 17, 1905:** *The Supreme Court found a New York state law that limited maximum hours for workers unconstitutional, ruling that such a law interfered with the right to free contract.*
- **May 5, 1905:** *Boston's Cy Young threw baseball's first-ever perfect game, retiring 27 consecutive Philadelphia Athletic batters.*

I·L·L·I·N·I M·O·M·E·N·T

ILLINI TIE STAGG'S MAROONS:
Illinois' 1904 football team was coached by Justa Lindgren, Arthur Hall, Fred Lowenthal, and Clyde Mathews who led the Illini to a perfect record through their first seven games. On October 29th, hundreds of Illini fans filled UC's Marshall Field to witness the Illini vs. Coach Amos Alonzo Stagg's Chicago Maroons. The Illini clearly outplayed their hosts in the first half, but neither team was able to score. In the third quarter, Illinois made its only mistake of the game as quarterback William Taylor fumbled the ball on his own 27-yard line. Chicago's left tackle, Glenn Parry, gathered up the loose pigskin and, with an extra-point kick, gave the Maroons a 6-0 lead. On the ensuing kickoff, Illinois' Claude Rothgeb ran the ball back to Chicago's 20-yard line. Charles Fairweather then scored a five-point touchdown and Charles Moynihan kicked the point for a 6-6 final score. Illinois continued its aggressive play against the highly favored Maroons, but time ran out and the game ended in a tie. Back in Champaign, Illini fans frolicked in the streets until midnight. In their eyes, this tie was definitely not like kissing their sisters.

ILLINI BIRTHDAYS

SEPTEMBER 1904
3– Edward Howell, wrestling

OCTOBER 1904
10– Blair French, football

DECEMBER 1904
18– Ermel McElwee, cross country

JANUARY 1905
18– Ernest Schultz, football
29– John Sittig, track

FEBRUARY 1905
4– Charles Jenks, football
5– Clarence Ringquist, football
6– John Ritz, wrestling

MARCH 1905
1– Clyde Knapp, football

APRIL 1905
12– Ed Tryban, baseball
21– Earl Drew, basketball

MAY 1905
1– Leonard Grable, football
2– Royner Greene, basketball
21– Wendell "Weenie" Wilson, football/ athletic director

JUNE 1905
5– Arthur D'Ambrosio, football
13– Ray Eliot, football/ football coach/ baseball

AUGUST 1905
3– William Green, football
25– Kenneth Reynolds, basketball

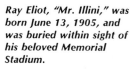

Ray Eliot, "Mr. Illini," was born June 13, 1905, and was buried within sight of his beloved Memorial Stadium.

ILLINI ITEM

COACH GEORGE HUFF'S Fighting Illini baseball team got only one hit against Wisconsin, May 27, 1905, but they made the most of it and defeated the Badgers, 1-0, at Illinois Field. In the second inning, clean-up hitter Claude Rothgeb smacked a curve ball far into right field. By the time the Badger fielders retrieved it from the bleachers and could relay it home, Rothgeb had rounded the bases, crossed the plate, and was sitting on the bench. The victory secured second place in the Big Ten standings for Illinois behind eventual champion Michigan.

ILLINI LISTS

POINTS SCORED BY HARRY GILL'S ILLINI TRACK TEAMS IN BIG TEN OUTDOOR MEETS (1904-29)

• **ILLINOIS**	**914 pts**
• Michigan	587 1/3 pts
• Chicago	541 1/2 pts
• Wisconsin	514 1/2 pts
• Iowa	328 pts
• Ohio State	211 pts
• Minnesota	186 1/3 pts
• Northwestern	151 1/2 pts
• Purdue	136 1/3 pts
• Indiana	101 1/2 pts

ILLINI LEGEND:

HARRY GILL

It was a Canadian who brought the University of Illinois to prominence as an American collegiate track power. During a 29-year coaching career at Urbana-Champaign from 1904-29, then again from 1931-33, Harry Gill's Fighting Illini churned out an amazing 19 Big Ten championships—11 titles outdoors and eight indoors. On the national scene, Gill's teams won NCAA titles in 1921 and 1927, plus three Spalding Cups, at an annual invitational meet that attracted the nation's top colleges. The height of Gill's coaching career came in 1924 when his Illinois athletes—Harold Osborn, Dan Kinsey, and Horatio Fitch—scored more track and field points in the 1924 Summer Olympic Games than any other nation. In addition to those stars, Gill developed all-time greats Avery Brundage, longtime president of the International Olympic Federation, and "Tug" Wilson, former Olympic performer and Big Ten commissioner. Gill died in 1956 at the age of 80. The Harry Gill Company, a sporting goods manufacturer specializing in track equipment, remains in Urbana.

Illini Lore

Around 1894, University of Illinois students began displaying their individual class colors by wearing ribbons on their shirts around campus. There was great disdain for the lowly freshmen, especially from the sophomores. Consequently, the two classes engaged in an annual physical battle called the "class rush." The reigning champions defended a greased flagpole from which a flag of their class colors flew. As many as 300-400 students locked arms and encircled the pole, while the challengers used any means to remove their opponent's flag. University officials eventually channeled the students' energy toward a game called push-ball, which only resulted in more injuries than the color rush. Another contest, called the sack rush, was then instituted, but eventually in 1914, Illinois students discontinued these dangerous traditional rivalry games.

That was then.

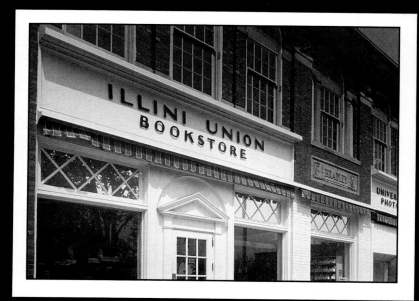

You should see us now!

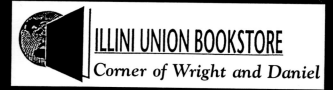

1905-06

I·L·L·I·N·I M·O·M·E·N·T

ILLINOIS' FIRST BASKETBALL GAME:
The first official intercollegiate basketball game occurred at the University of Illinois some 15 years after it was introduced in Springfield, Massachusetts by Dr. James Naismith. Three hundred twenty-five fans, many of whom were probably watching the game for the very first time, saw their Fighting Illini defeat Indiana, 27-24. When a goal was made, a spectator had to retrieve the ball out of the closed basket so that the game could resume. The Illini starting lineup featured Roy Riley at the center position, Floyd Talmage and V.C. Kays at the forwards, and E.G. Ryan and Arthur Ray at the guards. Indiana jumped off to a 5-0 lead, before Talmage finally scored Illinois' historic first basket. Talmage continued his sharp-shooting, scoring seven field goals and two free throws for 16 of UI's 27 total points.

ILLINI BIRTHDAYS

SEPTEMBER 1905
4– William Roush, football
11– Robert McKay, basketball
19– Lester Marriner, football

DECEMBER 1905
2– Garland Grange, football

JANUARY 1906
11– Robert Reisch, football

FEBRUARY 1906
2– Leroy Wietz, football

MARCH 1906
20– George Buchheit, football

APRIL 1906
20– Herb Hill, basketball
25– Russ Crane, football

MAY 1906
5– Keston Deimling, football/basketball

JUNE 1906
5– Andrew Solyom, basketball
11– Edgar Nickol, football
15– Dwight Stuessy, football
29– Everette Olson, basketball
29– James "Bud" Stewart, football/baseball
29– John How, basketball

JULY 1906
1– Webber Borchers, Chief II
15– Lou Gordon, football
19– Ralph Webster, wrestling

AUGUST 1906
13– John O'Grady, baseball

17– Clifton Hyinck, football
23– Verne McDermont, track
25– William Short, football
28– Judson Timm, football

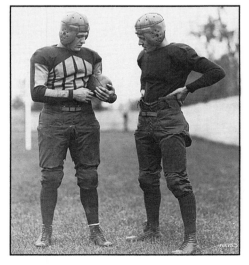

Garland Grange, (right) born December 2, 1905, gets a tip from his famous brother, Harold.

ILLINI ITEM

THE UNIVERSITY OF ILLINOIS' WATER POLO TEAM (later called water basketball) made its debut on February 17, 1906, by defeating the University of Chicago, 2-1. For the next 33 years, the Illini dominated the sport in the Midwest, winning 10 Big Ten championships and registering a dual-meet record of 95-39-3. The sport discontinued competition at Illinois during the war years of 1941-46, and was never resumed.

ILLINI LISTS

MARCHING ILLINI BAND HIGHLIGHTS

- June 6, 1872: The UI band performed for the first time
- February, 1892: UI Military Band presented its first annual concert
- March 3, 1906: "Illinois Loyalty" first performed
- Fall, 1910: Debut of "Oskee-Wow-Wow" and "Hail to the Orange"
- Oct. 15, 1910: Band first formed "Block I"
- Oct. 15, 1921: Band sang "Hail to the Orange" a capella for first time
- Nov. 4, 1922: First mass bands performance at Illinois
- Nov. 3, 1923: Band first formed the word "Illini"
- Oct. 30, 1926: First performance of Chief Illiniwek
- Sept. 11, 1943: Idelle Stitch became first female to portray Chief Illiniwek
- Sept. 1, 1948: Austin Harding, director of bands, retired, ending 43-year career at UI
- Jan. 1, 1952: UI band's first performance in Tournament of Roses Parade
- September, 1970: First female members of Marching Illini
- June, 1976: Everett Kissinger ended 27-year career as director of Marching Illini; succeeded by Gary Smith
- Fall, 1976: Debut of Illinettes, Big Ten's first women's dance team
- September 1977: Deborah Soumar became first female drum major in Big Ten
- Winter, 1980: First collegiate band to use a giant school flag

ILLINI LEGEND:

THATCHER GUILD

It's a name even the most avid Fighting Illini fan doesn't know. But, if the University of Illinois ever establishes an athletic Hall of Fame, Thatcher Howland Guild's name needs to be included. Guild didn't score any touchdowns or hit any home runs, but his contribution to the University—"Illinois Loyalty"—has been sung thousands of times at every home Illini football and basketball game for nearly 90 years. Much like Schubert's "Unfinished Symphony," Guild brought the lyrics and melody to the Urbana-Champaign campus with him from his alma mater, Brown University. His original first line ran: *We're Loyal to You, Men of Brown.* A newly hired English instructor, Guild took his tune to UI's longtime band director Austin Harding, and the two men refined the now legendary melody. After more than six months of work, "Illinois Loyalty" was finally performed before the UI student body at Harding's First Anniversary Concert on March 3, 1906. Guild died at the tender age of 35 in 1914 from a heart attack, during a hot summer's day tennis match.

Illini Lore

On October 16, 1905, the University of Illinois' Women's Building was dedicated. Designed by the celebrated architectural firm of McKim, Mead, and White, it became a stately element along the University's principal mall. The $330,000 structure, now known as the English Building, features a central colonnade and twin-domed towers.

1906-07

I·L·L·I·N·I M·O·M·E·N·T

Wilbur Burroughs (third row, second from right) led the Illini to the 1907 Western Conference track title.

ILLINOIS' FIRST BIG TEN TRACK & FIELD TITLE:
The University of Illinois track and field team had traveled a rocky road during the first three seasons of the Harry Gill coaching era, finishing no higher than fifth in the Western Conference championship outdoor meet. So, on that cold first day of June, 1907, the Illini could only be cautiously optimistic about what would ultimately turn out to be the greatest day in the history of the sport at Illinois. Illini football star Wilbur Burroughs was the star of the day, capturing individual titles in both the shot put and the hammer throw and accounting for nearly one-third of the team's points. Billy May finished first in the 100-yard dash and second in the 220-yard dash, which gave the Illini eight more valuable points, allowing Illinois to edge host Chicago, 31-29, for the school's very first conference championship in track and field.

ILLINI BIRTHDAYS

SEPTEMBER 1906
4– Walter Jolley, football
5– William McClure, football
12– G.O. Minot, wrestling
26– Tracy "Kewpie" Barrett, baseball

OCTOBER 1906
15– John Tarwain, basketball

NOVEMBER 1906
21– Arnold Wolgast, football
29– Theodore Hesmer, wrestling

DECEMBER 1906
7– Carl Bergeson, football/basketball

JANUARY 1907
9– Harry Richman, football

FEBRUARY 1907
18– Evert Nelson, football

APRIL 1907
1– Lester Leutwiler, Chief Illiniwek I
11– Forrest Lindsay, basketball

MAY 1907
23– Jim Lymperopoulos, baseball
23– Norm Gundlach, baseball
25– Fred "Fritz" Humbert, football
30– Franklin Lanum, football

JUNE 1907
10– Robert "Zack" Hickman, football

Left fielder Ira Carrithers helped Illinois' 1907 baseball team to a perfect 7-0 record in Western Conference action.

Louis Cook filled in as Illini baseball coach during George Huff's brief stint with the Boston Americans.

ILLINI ITEM

THE ILLINI BASEBALL TEAM won its second consecutive Western Conference title in 1907, capturing all seven of its league games. On April 14, just three days before the regular season was to begin, Coach George Huff accepted an offer from the Boston Americans to manage that professional club, so Louis Cook hastily took over for Huff to direct Illinois to its fourth conference baseball title in the last five years. After only 13 days in Boston, Huff sent a telegram to UI President Edmund James, stating "Have received my release. Will be back Saturday. This is final and positive."

ILLINI LISTS

ILLINI COACHES WITH THE LONGEST REIGNS (through 1994-95 season)

- Ed Manley, swimming — 33 years (1920-52)
- Bob Zuppke, football — 29 years (1913-41)
- Gary Wieneke, cross country — 28 years (1967-94)#
- Leo Johnson, track — 28 years (1938-65)
- Max Garret, fencing — 27 years (1941-72)*
- Lee Eilbracht, baseball — 27 years (1952-78)
- Harry Gill, track — 26 years (1904-29)
- George Huff, baseball — 24 years (1896-1919)
- Don Sammons, swimming — 23 years (1971-93)
- Ralph Fletcher, golf — 23 years (1944-66)
- Leo Johnson, cross country — 23 years (1938-60)

*UI did not sponsor fencing from 1943-46 and Garret did not coach in 1970
#Still active as UI coach

"G" Huff directed the Illini baseball program for 24 years.

ILLINI LEGEND:

AVERY BRUNDAGE

He was best known for his 20-year reign as the controversial president of the International Olympic Committee (IOC), but few know that Avery Brundage's career in the world of sports began at the University of Illinois as an athlete. Brundage, a native of Detroit, earned varsity letters with the Fighting Illini basketball team and track squads. He was the center for the 1908 basketball squad that won 20 of 26 games, and an outstanding shot putter and discus thrower for the Illini thinclads, winning an individual title in the latter event at the 1909 Western Conference track meet. Brundage competed in the 1912 Olympic decathlon with the legendary Jim Thorpe. In 1916 and 1918, he won the national all-around decathlon championship. Brundage served as president of the Amateur Athletic Union from 1928-35 and for the U.S. Olympic Committee from 1929-33. As the IOC's most famous administrator, he fought a fierce battle to maintain the Olympic ideals of amateurism. A longtime member of the UI President's Club, he established a scholarship bearing his name in 1974. Brundage died of a heart attack May 8, 1975, at the age of 87. His papers in the University Archives continue to attract scholars from around the world.

Illini Lore

On May 18, 1907, the last saloon in Champaign-Urbana closed. The editor of the University of Illinois' *Alumni Quarterly* applauded the move. "Though it cannot be expected that the closing of the saloons will put an end to drinking in the two cities," the *Quarterly* said, "it must, in a large degree, mitigate the effect. With the saloons gone, Champaign and Urbana are undoubtedly safer places for young men than they have previously been."

1907-08

I·L·L·I·N·I M·O·M·E·N·T

Pitcher Ernie Ovitz starred on the mound and at the plate.

ILLINI DEFEAT MINNESOTA TO WIN TITLE:
Winning Western Conference baseball titles had become commonplace for the University of Illinois, but the game that clinched the Illini's 1908 championship was one of the most decisive victories ever registered at Illinois Field. Minnesota, which eventually wound up as the conference's runner-up, was the Illini victim on that 23rd day of May. To say that Illinois merely "won" that day would be an understatement, for the 16-0 romp over the Gophers was never competitive. Pitcher Ernie Ovitz not only blanked Minnesota on the mound, allowing just one hit, he also scored runs in all four of his official times at the plate. The deadly combination of 14 Illini hits and nine Gopher errors resulted in an average of two runs every inning and the most lopsided shutout victory in four conference seasons.

ILLINI BIRTHDAYS

NOVEMBER 1907
11– Ernest Dorn,
　　basketball
12– Charles Hall, football
28– Edwin Winsper,
　　football

22– Charles Harper,
　　basketball
29– William Adams,
　　wrestling

FEBRUARY 1908
5– Harold Groh,
　　swimming
13– John Evans, football

MARCH 1908
9– Doug Mills,
　　basketball/football/
　　coach/athletic director

MAY 1908
8– John Ovelman,
　　football
13– Frank Walker, football

AUGUST 1908
8– Lloyd Burdick,
　　football/wrestling

The 1908 Fighting Illini baseball team won 11 of 14 conference games, en route to its third consecutive league title.

Coach Fletcher Lane

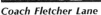

ILLINI ITEM

TWENTY VICTORIES in a season is the benchmark of success for collegiate basketball teams, and it only took the University of Illinois basketball program three years to reach that plateau. The 1907-08 Illini squad, coached by Fletcher Lane, accumulated a 20-6 record that season, a feat that wasn't again accomplished until 41 years later when Harry Combes' 1948-49 team went 21-4.

ILLINI LISTS

ILLINOIS' MOST DOMINANT FOOTBALL TEAMS

- 1910   7-0-0, outscored its opponents 89-0
- 1914   7-0-0, outscored its opponents 224-22
- 1915   5-0-2, outscored its opponents 183-25
- 1923   8-0-0, outscored its opponents 136-20
- 1927   7-0-1, outscored its opponents 152-24
- 1951   9-0-1, outscored its opponents 220-83

(Left to right) Ray Eliot, Arthur Hall, and Bob Zuppke were architects of the six most dominant football teams in Illini history.

ILLINI LEGEND:
ARTHUR HALL

The architect of the University of Illinois' first-ever Big Ten football title was Coach Arthur Hall, an Illini athlete himself from 1898-1900. Hall's greatest season came in 1910 when his Fighting Illini team became only the second conference team, and only the 13th in college football history, to be undefeated **and** unscored upon. In six seasons at Illinois from 1907-12, Hall coached the Illini gridders to a record of 27-10-3. Incredibly, coaching football wasn't Hall's only profession. His "day" job was practicing law in Danville, Illinois. At the end of the 1912 season, Hall decided that the pace was too hectic, so he resigned his position at the University of Illinois and went into law full time. Athletic Director George Huff replaced Hall with the immortal Bob Zuppke. Artie Hall served as Vermilion County (Illinois) probate court judge until his retirement in 1954. He also was instrumental in developing the state of Illinois' "hard road" system. Hall died in 1955 at the age of 86.

 Illini Lore

On November 4 and 5, 1907, the University of Illinois dedicated its new $152,000 auditorium, which provided an adequate place for convocations, lectures, concerts, and other large gatherings. Constructed of brick and Indiana limestone, the facility was remodeled in 1915 to correct its accoustical deficiencies. The structure was rededicated as the Foellinger Auditorium April 26, 1985, named for benefactor Helene Foellinger ('32). Among those who have performed or lectured at the auditorium are John Phillip Sousa (1909), Amelia Earhart (1935), Duke Ellington (1948), and Eleanor Roosevelt (1956).

1908-09

I·L·L·I·N·I M·O·M·E·N·T

Roger Stephenson's first-place finish in the broad jump helped Illinois win its second Western Conference title in three years.

GILL'S MEN ROMP AWAY WITH TRACK TITLE:

On June 5, 1909, at Chicago's Marshall Field, Coach Harry Gill directed the University of Illinois track and field squad to its second Western Conference title in three years. Though it was the official conference meet, non-conference schools such as Stanford, Michigan Agricultural College, and Notre Dame also participated in the festivities. Illinois won three individual firsts, including Roger Stephenson in the broad jump (22'6 ¼"), Lud Washburn in the high jump (5'10"), and Avery Brundage in the discus throw (43'2 ½"). The meet was clinched by the Illini mile relay team. Altogether, Illinois athletes scored in 11 of the 15 events, claiming four firsts, four seconds, and four thirds.

ILLINI BIRTHDAYS

SEPTEMBER 1908
10– James Lewis, football
18– Boyd Owen, basketball

NOVEMBER 1908
4– Richard Martin, golf
6– Olaf Robinson, football
22– Pete Yanuskus, football

DECEMBER 1908
30– Elbridge May, basketball

FEBRUARY 1909
1– Kenneth Fields, football
3– Thielen Huddleston, football

MARCH 1909
26– Otto Hills, football
29– Robert Horsely, football

APRIL 1909
17– Henry Schumacher, football

MAY 1909
18– Glen Orth, wrestling

JUNE 1909
5– Arthur Schultz, football
9– John Snook, football

JULY 1909
15– George Fencl, basketball

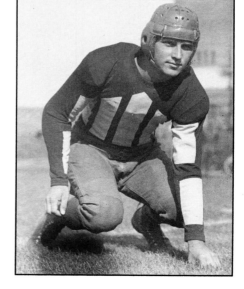

Pete Yanuskus, born November 22, 1908, won football letters in 1929, '30, and '32.

ILLINI ITEM

THOUGH PURDUE denied Illinois its fourth consecutive Western Conference baseball title, the 1909 season was nevertheless considered a grand success. The Boilermakers' 7-2 conference record was just a few percentage points better than the Illini's 9-3 league mark. Coach George Huff issued a challenge to Purdue to determine a true champion, but the Boilermakers reportedly refused.

ILLINI LISTS

BEST ILLINI DEFENSIVE PERFORMANCES (VS. BIG TEN BASKETBALL OPPONENTS)

- 1909   Illinois 30, Indiana 2
- 1909   Illinois 35, Northwestern 4
- 1913   Illinois 35, Iowa 9
- 1915   Illinois 27, Purdue 8
- 1916   Illinois 21, Ohio State 10
- 1920   Illinois 41, Michigan 14
- 1921   Illinois 17, Wisconsin 9
- 1926   Illinois 17, Minnesota 8
- 1993   Illinois 52, Michigan State 39
- 1994   Illinois 84, Penn State 59

1921 Basketball Team

ILLINI LEGEND:

FOREST VAN HOOK

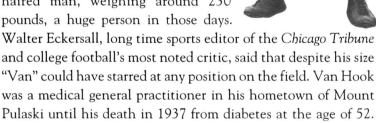

Forest Van Hook, captain of the 1908 Illini football team, was the first University of Illinois athlete to earn All-Western honors each of the three seasons he lettered. An outstanding guard for coach Arthur Hall, Van Hook and his teammates had their best performance in 1908 during his senior season. The 5-1-1 Illini lost their only game, 11-6, at the University of Chicago and eventually placed second in the Western Conference standings to the undefeated Maroons. Van Hook was a burly, dark-haired man, weighing around 230 pounds, a huge person in those days. Walter Eckersall, long time sports editor of the *Chicago Tribune* and college football's most noted critic, said that despite his size "Van" could have starred at any position on the field. Van Hook was a medical general practitioner in his hometown of Mount Pulaski until his death in 1937 from diabetes at the age of 52.

 Illini Lore

T he University of Illinois observed the 100th anniversary of the birth of Abraham Lincoln on February 8, 1909, with a campus-wide celebration. The exercises included a convocation, an exhibit of Lincolniana, and addresses on several aspects of Lincoln's service as U.S. president.

1909-10

America's Time Capsule

- **Oct. 16, 1909:** *The Pittsburgh Pirates defeated the Detroit Tigers in the sixth World Series.*
- **Feb. 6, 1910:** *The Boy Scouts of America organization was chartered by Chicago publisher William Boyce.*
- **March 16, 1910:** *Auto racer Barney Oldfield set a land speed record of 133 miles per hour.*
- **June 19, 1910:** *Spokane, Washington became the first city to celebrate Father's Day.*
- **July 4, 1910:** *Jack Johnson successfully defended his world heavyweight boxing championship against Jim Jeffries.*

I·L·L·I·N·I M·O·M·E·N·T

ILLINI "9" BEATS CHICAGO IN 17-INNING MARATHON:
The May 20, 1910, baseball match-up between the Universities of Illinois and Chicago was described by the UI campus newspaper as "...the most brilliant game ever played on Illinois Field." When the three-hour-and-twenty-minute marathon ended, Coach George Huff's Illini won their 10th consecutive game, a streak that would eventually climax at 14-0 and result in a Western Conference championship. Illinois' John Buzick went the entire distance on the mound, as did his counterpart, UC's Pat Page. With the score tied at one run apiece, Page lost the game in the bottom of the 17th inning when Illinois' Ray Thomas led off with a double, moved to third on a sacrifice by E.B. Righter, then scored when Page uncorked a wild pitch. The Illini went on to win their final four games and wound up as the first conference baseball team in history to finish with an unblemished overall record.

John Buzick pitched all 17 innings in Illinois' baseball marathon vs. Chicago.

ILLINI BIRTHDAYS

SEPTEMBER 1909
8– Sam Gorenstein, football
9– Max Pike, baseball
15– Robert Conover, football
18– Bernon Perkins, football
19– Earl Jackson, football
21– Harry Palmer, football
24– Elbert Kamp, basketball

OCTOBER 1909
13– Edward Kawal, football

NOVEMBER 1909
5– James "Scotty" Reston, golf

DECEMBER 1909
17– Robert Kamp, basketball

JANUARY 1910
21– Stanley Jensen, football

FEBRUARY 1910
10– Roy Guttschow, basketball
20– Henry Steinman, football

MARCH 1910
7– Lee Sentman, track

APRIL 1910
17– Joseph Van Dyke, football
30– Clark Root, football

MAY 1910
18– Edward Schalk, football

JUNE 1910
16– Wilbur Dooley, wrestling

26– Edwin Kolfenbach, football
28– Bob Emmons, wrestling

JULY 1910
20– William Fuzak, basketball
28– Paul Chervinko, baseball

AUGUST 1910
13– Donald Munch, football
28– William Theobald, basketball

Lee Sentman, born March 7, 1910, won several Big Ten individual track and field titles, and set the world's record in the 70-yard high hurdles (:08.5) in 1930.

- 34 -

Frank Murphy pole vaulted to a height of 12'4⅞" at the 1910 conference meet and was the only Illini athlete to win an event.

ILLINI ITEM

THE FIRST WESTERN CONFERENCE outdoor track and field meet held at a site other than Chicago came on June 4, 1910, at Champaign. Though Illinois was the top-finishing conference team, it placed third behind Notre Dame and Stanford. It wasn't until 1926 that only conference teams were allowed to participate in the outdoor championship meet.

ILLINI LISTS

HOMECOMING THRILLERS

- Oct. 15, 1910 — Illinois 3, Chicago 0 (UI's first-ever Homecoming game, the nation's first of its kind)
- Nov. 3, 1923 — Illinois 7, Chicago 0 (UI's first-ever game at Memorial Stadium; Red Grange scores touchdown)
- Oct. 18, 1924 — Illinois 39, Michigan 14 (Dedication game of Memorial Stadium)
- Nov. 4, 1939 — Illinois 16, Michigan 7 (UI beat UM and future Heisman Trophy winner Tom Harmon)
- Oct. 27, 1956 — Illinois 20, Michigan State 13 (UI beat ninth-ranked Spartans)
- Oct. 26, 1968 — Ohio State 31, Illinois 24 (No. 2 Buckeyes score winning TD with 1:30 left)
- Oct. 15, 1983 — Illinois 17, Ohio State 13 (Illini beat No. 6 Buckeyes)
- Oct. 20, 1990 — Illinois 15, Michigan State 13 (Doug Higgins kicks game-winning field goal with :42 left)

Goal-line action from the very first Homecoming game.

ILLINI LEGEND:

CLARENCE WILLIAMS & ELMER EKBLAW

Clarence Williams (left) and Elmer Ekblaw (right) aren't familiar names to even the most ardent Fighting Illini fans, but their accomplishment back in 1910 definitely earns them a niche in University of Illinois history. Williams—better known as "Dab"—and Ekblaw—the editor of the *Daily Illini*—conceived the very first Homecoming during the fall of 1909. They presented the idea to Shield and Trident, a senior honorary society, then called upon UI President Edmund James and Dean Thomas Arkle Clark. A year later, during that first Homecoming weekend—October 14-16, 1910—more than 1,500 UI graduates returned to campus, nearly one-third of the school's alumni. The culmination of the inaugural Homecoming weekend was a 3-0 victory by the Illini football team over the University of Chicago. Illinois' Otto Seiler kicked a field goal to provide the final margin.

Illini Lore

On August 10, 1909, the cornerstone of Lincoln Hall was laid. President William Abbott of the Board of Trustees presided. Three-and-a-half years later on February 12, 1913, the 104th anniversary of Abraham Lincoln's birth, Lincoln Hall was dedicated by the University of Illinois.

1910-11

I·L·L·I·N·I M·O·M·E·N·T

1910 BIG TEN FOOTBALL CHAMPIONS:

The University of Illinois football team's unbeaten, unscored upon season of 1910 is a feat that's been duplicated only 19 times in the history of college football. Though Coach Arthur Hall's squad wasn't an offensive juggernaut, averaging just 13 points a game, it was an immovable force when it came to playing defense. In fact, their opponents rarely crossed Illinois' 50-yard line the entire season! The Illini opened their campaign with easy non-conference victories over Millikin and Drake before the school's historic first Homecoming game on October 15th, a 3-0 win over Chicago. Two weeks later, Illinois shut out Purdue, then blanked Indiana and Northwestern on consecutive Saturdays to wrap up the school's very first Western Conference title. Otto Seiler kicked his third game-winning field goal of the year in the season finale at home against Syracuse to give the Illini a perfect 7-0 record.

ILLINI BIRTHDAYS

SEPTEMBER 1910
22– Mark Swanson, football

NOVEMBER 1910
2– Harold Line, cross country
3– Vernon Moore, basketball
21– Thomas Wilson, football

DECEMBER 1910
5– Lindley Murray, football

JANUARY 1911
1– Bob Minsker, football
4– Chuck Bennis, football
30– Kenneth Berry, wrestling

FEBRUARY 1911
19– Linden Piatt, football

MARCH 1911
2– Dick O'Neill, football
21– Gil Berry, football

APRIL 1911
16– Floyd Wrobke, baseball
26– William Hedtke, football

MAY 1911
9– Al Klingel, swimming coach
12– Albert Kamm, basketball

JUNE 1911
3– Robert Green, football
4– Robert May, football
29– Robert Woolsey, cross country/track

JULY 1911
15– Thomas Straw, football

AUGUST 1911
25– Fred Frink, football/baseball

Chuck Bennis, born January 4, 1911, earned honorable mention All-America honors in 1934.

Harry Geist (far left), R.J. Roarke (second from left), Edward Hollman (fourth from left), and Edward Styles (far right) all won individual titles in 1911.

ILLINI ITEM

THE UNIVERSITY OF ILLINOIS won its first men's Western Conference gymnastics title on April 22, 1911 over host Chicago, 1104.50 to 1016.25. Illinois' Edward Styles, R.J. Roarke, Edward Hollman, and Harry Geist all captured individual championships.

ILLINI LISTS

FOOTBALL GAMES WON IN FINAL MINUTE BY A FIELD GOAL

- Oct. 15, 1910: Illinois 3, Chicago 0 — Otto Seiler, 38 yards (exact time not available)
- Nov. 5, 1910: Illinois 3, Indiana 0 — Otto Seiler (exact distance and time not available)
- Nov. 22, 1919: Illinois 9, Ohio State 7 — Bob Fletcher, 20 yards, :12 remaining
- Oct. 30, 1926: Illinois 3, Pennsylvania 0 — Frosty Peters, 14 yards (exact time not available)
- Sept. 13, 1980: Illinois 20, MSU 17 — Mike Bass, 38 yards, :00 remaining
- Oct. 23, 1982: Illinois 29, Wisconsin 28 — Mike Bass, 46 yards, :03 remaining
- Oct. 5, 1985: Illinois 31, Ohio State 28 — Chris White, 38 yards, :00 remaining
- Oct. 17, 1987: Illinois 16, Wisconsin 14 — Doug Higgins, 34 yards, :54 remaining
- Oct. 20, 1990: Illinois 15, MSU 13 — Doug Higgins, 48 yards, :59 remaining
- Oct. 22, 1991: Illinois 10, Ohio State 7 — Chris Richardson, 41 yards, :36 remaining

Otto Seiler kicked a pair of final-minute, game-winning field goals for Illinois in 1910.

ILLINI LEGEND:

GLENN BUTZER

The premier performer during the 1910-11 athletic season at the University of Illinois was a young man whose teams tasted defeat only twice in 27 contests. Not only did Glenn Butzer captain Illinois' greatest football team ever in 1910, he also was the leading hitter on the 1911 Western Conference champion baseball team. On the gridiron, the Hillsdale, Illinois, native was a Walter Camp All-American as one of the game's finest linemen. The 1910 Illini football squad posted a perfect 7-0 record and never allowed its opponents to score a point. On the diamond, Butzer batted .350 as an outfielder. Although a large man, he possessed exceptional speed. The Illini "9" cruised to the Western Conference title, beating runner-up Purdue by five full games with a 14-1 league record. Following his athletic career at Illinois, Butzer served as city superintendent of highways of Livingston County and also for several years as city engineer in Pontiac, Illinois. He died of cancer November 13, 1935, at the age of 46.

Illini Lore

United States President William Howard Taft visited the University of Illinois on February 11, 1911. Taft arrived at 8:50 a.m. and was driven to Illinois Field, where he reviewed the cadet regiment. He then took a tour of the campus grounds, made a five-minute address at the Illinois Central Station, and left for Springfield, all in less than an hour.

1911-12

I·L·L·I·N·I M·O·M·E·N·T

This 1911 trophy was presented to Coach Ed Manley's Fighting Illini swimming team.

ILLINOIS WINS ITS FIRST SWIMMING TITLE:

The University of Illinois' men's swimming program had traditionally languished at or near the bottom of the Big Ten standings. But, for the first three seasons of conference meets from 1911-13, Coach Ed Manley's Illini set the standard of excellence. Perhaps Illinois' greatest team was its 1912 squad, winner of the Western Conference championship by 17 points over second-place Northwestern. The Illini weren't a one-man team that year, but it would be difficult to overlook the monumental contribution by Captain Bill Vosburgh. The Illini junior accounted for four individual titles—at 40, 100, 220, and 440 yards—and was the anchor of Illinois' championship relay squad. Vosburgh also took third place in a since-discontinued event called "plunge for distance."

ILLINI BIRTHDAYS

SEPTEMBER 1911
2– Earl Jansen, football
25– Hudson Hellmich, basketball
28– Elbert Gragg, football

OCTOBER 1911
11– William West, cross country
12– Arthur O'Keefe, football

DECEMBER 1911
8– Les Lindberg, football
16– Bill Waller, football
27– Caslon Bennett, football/basketball
28– Jacques Dufresne, cross country/track

JANUARY 1912
1– David Cook, football
2– Tony Blazine, football coach
14– James Theodore, football

24– Julius Hoeft, football
29– Barney Cosneck, wrestling

FEBRUARY 1912
6– John "Red" Pace, assistant baseball coach

MARCH 1912
5– Edwin Snavely, football

APRIL 1912
5– Fred Fencl, basketball
7– George Legg, ticket manager
30– Matthew Tischler, football

MAY 1912
6– Everett Kisinger, marching band director
12– John Toncoff, basketball

30– Ed Dancisak, baseball

JUNE 1912
4– John Fischer, football
6– Frank Froschauer, football/basketball

JULY 1912
7– Hunter Russell, football
9– Andrew Dahl, wrestling
12– Ivan Schustek, football
21– Forest Craven, football
21– William Newton, Chief III
30– Crain Portman, football

AUGUST 1912
12– Michael Orlovich, track
15– Ben Lewis, baseball

Long-time ticket manager and Varsity "I" director George Legg was born April 7, 1912.

EDWARD STYLES won his second consecutive individual all-around championship on April 13, 1912, leading the University of Illinois gymnastics squad to its second straight team title, 1174.75 to 957.25, over Wisconsin.

ILLINI LISTS

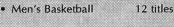

ILLINOIS' BIG TEN MEN'S TEAM TITLES
(through 1993-94)

- Fencing — 30 titles
- Men's Outdoor Track — 28 titles
- Baseball — 26 titles
- Men's Gymnastics — 22 titles
- Men's Indoor Track — 22 titles
- Wrestling — 16 titles
- Football — 14 titles
- Men's Basketball — 12 titles

Long-time track coach Harry Gill (left) and baseball coach George Huff won a total of 31 Big Ten titles during their distinguished careers.

ILLINI LEGEND:
ED MANLEY

For 41 years, the name Ed Manley was synonymous with University of Illinois swimming. He was lured to Champaign-Urbana by UI athletic director George Huff in 1912 from Springfield, Missouri, where he served as an aquatic instructor. Manley's Illini swimming teams captured Western Conference titles his first two years at Illinois, and placed among the top five in the league 24 times. He also developed 20 conference champions in the sports of water polo and water basketball, and directed those teams to dual-meet victories nearly 75 percent of the time. Manley called 1930's performer Chuck Flachmann his greatest single performer. The veteran coach was honored posthumously in 1975 when the University named the historic Huff Gym natatorium the Edwin Manley Memorial Pool. Manley died in 1962 at the age of 75.

Illini Lore

In response to a request from the athletic department that its needs be given more consideration in future planning of the campus, Professor James White, supervising architect of the University of Illinois, submitted a new campus scheme to the Board of Trustees on October 5, 1911. Extensive additions to the University's land holdings were proposed, with particular view to providing playgrounds to compensate for the utilization of the area south of the Auditorium for building sites. White suggested that the entire tract of land between the campus and the Illinois Central railroad be acquired. Less than 10 years later, a portion of that tract was reserved for the construction of Memorial Stadium.

1912-13

I·L·L·I·N·I M·O·M·E·N·T

Front row (left to right) Elston, Gage, Lansche, Simison, Meyers. Back row (left to right) Jones, Brunkow, Colombo, Leichsenring, Schroeder, Featherstone.

ILLINOIS WINS CONFERENCE WRESTLING CHAMPIONSHIP:
Illinois and Minnesota shared the title at the first-ever Western Conference Wrestling Championship, held April 19, 1913, at Madison, Wisconsin. Junior lightweight G.W. Schroeder, Illinois' captain, was his team's only individual winner, defeating Albert Gran of Iowa. Illini wrestlers M.F. Leichsenring, a middleweight, and J.B. Colombo, wrestling in the "special" division, both were runners-up at their weights. It was the final season of Illinois coach Alexander Elston's brief two-year career. The Illini wrestling program went on to dominate the conference through the 1930s, capturing 13 team titles, more than any other school.

ILLINI BIRTHDAYS

SEPTEMBER 1912
14– Kenneth Carpenter, wrestling
29– Harry Temple, gymnastics

OCTOBER 1912
3– Paul Gibbs, basketball
22– C.G. Swikle, baseball

NOVEMBER 1912
30– Vincent VanMeter, football

DECEMBER 1912
8– LaRue Morris, football
14– Scott Marriner, football
23– Allen Sapora, wrestling
29– Frank Bell, football

MARCH 1913
24– A.F. Citron, wrestling
25– John Theodore, football

APRIL 1913
16– Fred Kasch, baseball
17– Albert Spurlock, track

MAY 1913
18– Steve Polaski, football

JUNE 1913
3– Bob King, assistant football coach
21– Charles Flachmann, swimming
28– George Frederick, football

AUGUST 1913
29– Robert Grieve, football/track

Al Sapora, born December 23, 1912, became a Big Ten and NCAA wrestling champion for the Fighting Illini in the late 1930s.

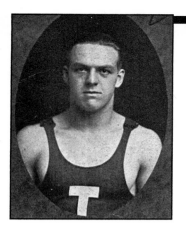

ILLINI SWIMMER BILL VOSBURGH wrapped up his sensational career at the 1913 Western Conference Championships by capturing three individual titles and anchoring the first-place UI relay squad. During his three years at Illinois, Vosburgh claimed 10 individual conference championships and swam on two relay winners, an all-time record at that time.

ILLINI LISTS

WINNINGEST MARGINS BY ILLINOIS FOOTBALL TEAMS

- 84 pts — Illinois 87, Ill. Wesleyan 3 (10/5/12)
- 80 pts — Illinois 80, Iowa 0 (11/27/02)
- 79 pts — Illinois 79, Ill. College 0 (10/19/1895)
- 73 pts — Illinois 79, Ill. Normal 6 (9/16/44)
- 68 pts — Illinois 75, Rolla Mines 7 (10/9/15)
- 67 pts — Illinois 67, Butler 0 (10/3/42)
- 66 pts — Illinois 66, Northwestern 0 (11/3/1894)
- 66 pts — Illinois 70, Knox 4 (10/10/1896)
- 64 pts — Illinois 64, Knox 0 (11/12/1897)
- 64 pts — Illinois 64, Rush 0 (10/10/03)

1915 football team

ILLINI LEGEND:

RALPH CHAPMAN

His parents presented him with the distinguished appellation of Ralph Dwyer Clinton Chapman. His classmates knew him best as "Slouie." And Bob Zuppke, the legendary coach of the Fighting Illini, touted him as one of the greatest players he ever coached. Whatever you called him, it would be difficult not to call Ralph "Slouie" Chapman the University of Illinois' best athlete of his day. A native of Vienna, Illinois, the 180-pound Chapman was named by the legendary Walter Camp as a consensus All-America performer following his sensational senior season in 1914. The captain of Illinois' first national championship club was known for his speed, aggressiveness, and fighting spirit. Following his graduation in 1915, Chapman answered the call to arms when the United States entered World War I. He was wounded in action and underwent a series of operations. Upon his discharge, Chapman entered the brokerage business in Chicago, and he once served as vice-president of the UI Foundation. Chapman died in 1969 at the age of 77.

Illini Lore

Ground was broken September 18, 1912, for the University of Illinois' Armory. Completed in 1915 at a cost of $702,000, the 98-foot-high roof is supported by 14 three-hinged arches. The outer section of military offices and classrooms was not completed until 1927. The Armory has been the site of Fighting Illini track meets since 1916.

1913-14

America's Time Capsule

- **Oct. 11, 1913:** *The Philadelphia Athletics defeated the New York Giants to capture the 10th annual World Series.*
- **Dec. 23, 1913:** *President Woodrow Wilson reformed the American banking system by establishing the Federal Reserve System.*
- **April 22, 1914:** *Mexico severed diplomatic relations with the United States.*
- **May 7, 1914:** *A congressional resolution established the second Sunday in May to be celebrated as Mother's Day.*
- **Aug. 15, 1914:** *Australia defeated the United States to win the Davis Cup tennis challenge.*

I·L·L·I·N·I M·O·M·E·N·T

Fred Henderson (second row, second from right) helped the 1914 Illini track team win the conference title.

MEN'S TRACK TEAM DOMINATES CONFERENCE MEETS:
The University of Illinois track and field program had become a dominant force in the Western Conference under Coach Harry Gill. It was a rare occasion when the talented Illini lost a dual meet, and equally rare when they failed to win the conference title. During the 1914 season, Illinois performed at a level that allowed the team to cruise to both the indoor and outdoor conference championships. The Illini were a superbly balanced outfit, scoring points in nearly every event. Indoors at Evanston, Illinois waltzed to a nine-point victory over Wisconsin. Outdoors at Chicago, the Illini's winning margin was 22 points, led by Fred Henderson's victories in the 440- and 880-yard runs. "You have a wonderful track team," wrote Cornell coach John Moakley to Gill. And who could argue with that?

ILLINI BIRTHDAYS

SEPTEMBER 1913
6– Joseph Puerta, wrestling
11– John Duffner, baseball
12– Ernie Cavallo, baseball
14– Eugene Dykstra, football
17– Ellsworth VanOrman, football
18– Ralph Epstein, fencing
28– Irving Seeley, track

OCTOBER 1913
6– Bob Haefler, baseball
22– August Kowalski, football
22– Russell Doyle, baseball

NOVEMBER 1913
3– George Ledbetter, wrestling

14– Jim Vopicka, basketball
20– William Huth, wrestling

FEBRUARY 1914
15– John Ginay, wrestling
21– Ed Gryboski, football
14– Barton Cummings, football

MARCH 1914
20– Ralph Silverstein, wrestling
21– Clifton Gano, football

APRIL 1914
1– Murray Franklin, baseball
23– Charles Andrews, wrestling

MAY 1914
13– Joe Klemp, football
20– Frank Seamans, football

24– Edward Weber, baseball

JUNE 1914
21– Martin Markworth, basketball
29– Culver "Coke" Mills, basketball

JULY 1914
12– William Gates, basketball
23– John Callahan, baseball

AUGUST 1914
30– William "Buster" Fuzak, baseball

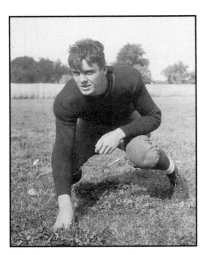

Bart Cummings, born February 14, 1914, was an Illini football star from 1932-34 and the 1972 "I" Man of the Year.

ILLINOIS' BASEBALL TEAM defeated league-leading Chicago, 4-3, on May 29, 1914, to win the conference title for the first time in three years. Illini pitcher Walt Halas, the older brother of football immortal George Halas, went the distance on the mound in a driving rainstorm.

ILLINI LISTS

ILLINI FOOTBALL COACHES' FIRST CONTRACTS

- Bob Zuppke
  $1,500 (1913)
- Ray Eliot
  $6,000 (1942)
- Pete Elliott
  $18,000 (1960)
- Jim Valek
  $18,500 (1967)
- Bob Blackman
  $25,000 (1971)
- Gary Moeller
  $35,000 (1977)
- Mike White
  $50,000 (1980)
- John Mackovic
  $70,000 (1988)
- Lou Tepper
  $120,000 (1992)

Bob Zuppke's first UI coaching contract was less than one one-hundredth the size of Lou Tepper's.

ILLINI LEGEND:

BOB ZUPPKE

Robert Carl Zuppke was introduced to the world in 1879, just 10 years after college football's very first game in New Brunswick, New Jersey. Thirty-five years later, the native of Berlin, Germany, would establish the University of Illinois as the home of the 1914 national football champions. By the time he retired in 1941, Zuppke's 29 teams captured three more national titles—1919, 1923, and 1927—and seven Big Ten crowns. He was football's most innovative coach, being credited with such originations as the huddle, the screen pass, and the "flea flicker." Among the stars Zuppke tutored were consensus All-Americans Chuck Carney, "Red" Grange, and Bernie Shively. He was honored in 1951 by being selected a charter member of college football's Hall of Fame. Zuppke died in 1957 at the age of 78. On November 12, 1966, Memorial Stadium's playing field was named in his honor.

Illini Lore

Edward A. Doisy, a 1914 graduate of the University of Illinois, shared the Nobel Prize in medicine in 1943 for isolating and determining the composition of vitamin K. This vitamin stimulates the production of prothrombin as a major element in blood clotting. Seventeen years earlier in 1926, Doisy isolated estrone, a sex hormone. He died October 23, 1986, at the age of 92.

1914-15

America's Time Capsule

- **Oct. 13, 1914:** *The National League's Boston Braves completed their sweep of the Philadelphia Athletics to win baseball's World Series.*
- **Jan. 25, 1915:** *Alexander Graham Bell placed the first successful transcontinental telephone call from New York City to San Francisco.*
- **Feb. 8, 1915:** *D.W. Griffith's famous motion picture, "Birth of a Nation," opened in Los Angeles.*
- **April 5, 1915:** *Jess Willard defeated Jack Johnson in 23 rounds to win the world heavyweight boxing title.*
- **May 7, 1915:** *A German submarine sank the British steamship Lusitania and nearly 1,200 drowned.*

I·L·L·I·N·I M·O·M·E·N·T

Coach Ralph Jones' 1915 squad achieved the only perfect record (16-0) in Illini basketball history.

ILLINI BASKETBALL TEAM NIPS CHICAGO:

On March 6, 1915, Illinois' undefeated basketball team faced its biggest challenge of the season, a game at the University of Chicago against the second-place Maroons. Coach Ralph Jones' Illini trailed by a score of 11-9 at the halftime intermission, and the teams traded baskets for most of the second half, with the lead going back and forth. Only a minute remained when Chicago star George Stevenson threw in a field goal, and the Maroon fans began to celebrate the apparent upset victory over their downstate rivals. However, the Illini regained the lead 30 seconds later when senior Frank Bane weaved through the Chicago defense for the game-winning basket. Illinois' 19-18 triumph improved its league record to 11-0 and clinched the school's first-ever Western Conference basketball title. Their 16-0 overall record that season marks the only time in Illini history that perfection has been achieved.

ILLINI BIRTHDAYS

SEPTEMBER 1914
6– Harold Swanson, baseball
21– Chuck Galbreath, football

OCTOBER 1914
7– Bob Wright, football/track/track coach
19– Tony Maze, football
20– Cliff Kuhn, football

NOVEMBER 1914
2– Victor Hinze, baseball
22– Billy Jones, swimming
22– Ken Nelson, football

DECEMBER 1914
12– Andy Glosecki, football
28– Anthony Daukus, baseball

JANUARY 1915
7– William Chiprin, fencing

24– Wilbur Henry, football/basketball/baseball
24– John Kanosky, football

MARCH 1915
3– Harry Combes, basketball
14– Howard Berg, baseball

APRIL 1915
1– Charles Farrington, baseball
18– Harold Shapiro, basketball

MAY 1915
17– Daniel Blum, wrestling
19– Frank Stewart, football
31– William Bennis, football

JUNE 1915
11– Elvin Sayre, football

JULY 1915
12– John Worban, football
22– Howard Carson, football

AUGUST 1915
11– Charles Lutz, wrestling
12– Edward Kalb, Chief IV
21– Don Christiansen, baseball
30– Edward Skarda, football

Chuck Galbreath, (left) born September 21, 1914, eventually became Coach Bob Zuppke's Fighting Illini football captain in 1935.

ILLINI ITEM

EDWARD WILLIFORD, the leading scorer of the 1915 Fighting Illini basketball team, was the University of Illinois' first Big Ten Conference Medal of Honor recipient. The award has been given annually since that year at each conference institution to the student-athlete who demonstrates proficiency in scholarship and academics.

ILLINI LISTS

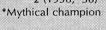

ILLINOIS' NATIONAL CHAMPIONS (TEAMS)

- Men's Gymnastics
  9 (1939, '40, '41, '42, '50, '55, '56, '58, '89)
- Men's Track & Field
  5 (1921, '27, '44, '46, '47)
- Football
  4* (1914, '19, '23, '27)
- Fencing
  2 (1956, '58)
*Mythical champion

1914 National Champion football team

ILLINI LEGEND:

PERRY GRAVES

At 5'6" and 148 pounds, Perry Graves looked more like a gymnast than an All-America football player. Even back when he played in 1913 and 1914, Graves was small by Big Ten standards, but all who went against him quickly realized he was a powerhouse. During his senior season, Coach Bob Zuppke's Fighting Illini posted a perfect 7-0 record, won the Big Ten championship, and shared the national title with Army. A native of Rockford, Graves played freshman ball at the University of Pittsburgh, but returned to his home state to compete for Illinois. He also played baseball for Coach George Huff's Illini, starring as a shortstop and a third baseman as Illinois went on to win the Big Ten title. Graves was the owner and operator of the Robinson (Illinois) Lumber & Coal Company for several years, and served as a Big Ten football official for 22 seasons. He died in 1979 at the age of 89.

 Illini Lore

During the summer of 1915, the west addition of what is now known as the Henry Administration Building was completed. The $1.45 million office space served as home of the registrar and dean of men on the first floor, the architect and the comptroller on the second floor, and as headquarters for President Edmund James and the Alumni Association on the third floor.

Building an Illini Tradition

Beautiful Memorial Stadium was completed in 1924 by English Brothers Company. They are proud to be a part of the rich Illini tradition and continue to support the Fighting Illini.

July 7, 1923

October 1922 — R. Zuppke and G. Huff — Observe

R. C. English — at jobsite

October 1924 — Memorial Stadium — the dream is reality.

English Brothers Company
Founded 1902 Builders of Memorial Stadium

ATHLETICS

1915-1924

1915-16

I·L·L·I·N·I M·O·M·E·N·T

"RED" GUNKEL'S NO-HITTER:
Coach George Huff's 1916 Fighting Illini pitching staff was nearly flawless during its Western Conference slate, allowing a total of just 10 runs in nine league games. The strongest arm belonged to a wiry, red-headed senior named Woodward "Red" Gunkel. Red's finest game came on May 5, 1916, at Illinois Field when he no-hit the Ohio State Buckeyes, 4-0. Gunkel pitched to only 28 men in his nine innings of work, striking out 12 batters, while notching his third of four consecutive shutouts. The Illini wound up taking the conference title that season with an 8-1 record.

"Red" Gunkel no-hit Ohio State in 1916, pitching to only 28 men in nine innings.

ILLINI BIRTHDAYS

SEPTEMBER 1915
7– Jack McIlvoy, wrestling
10– Robert Zuppke, football

NOVEMBER 1915
28– Charlie Pond, gymnastics coach

JANUARY 1916
2– Charles Stotz, football
12– James Brennan, wrestling/baseball

FEBRUARY 1916
20– Willard Cramer, football

MARCH 1916
6– Warren Overman, swimming

APRIL 1916
29– Pete Pakutinsky, wrestling

MAY 1916
6– Carl Davies, football
18–Paul Fina, gymnastics
21– Jack Berner, football

JUNE 1916
1– Tom Riggs, football
6– David Strong, football
15– Carl Knox, football

JULY 1916
2– Harold Swanson, basketball/baseball

AUGUST 1916
1– George Wardley, football/basketball
7– Lowell Spurgeon, football
13– George Lowe, swimming
26– Robert Castelo, football

Harold Pogue was an All-Big Ten selection in football during his Illini career from 1913-15 and also was an outstanding sprinter for the UI track team.

Illinois' 1915-16 basketball team was part of the longest winning streak in Illini history.

ILLINI ITEM

ILLINOIS' BASKETBALL TEAM won 25 games in a row from February 21, 1914, through February 9, 1916, a record that still stands. Included in the streak were 17 consecutive Western Conference victories, in which Illinois' competition averaged less than 14 points per contest.

ILLINI LISTS

LONGEST ILLINI MEN'S BASKETBALL WINNING STREAKS IN CONFERENCE PLAY

- 17 February 21, 1914 thru February 9, 1916
- 15 January 20, 1951 thru February 2, 1952
- 14 March 7, 1942 thru January 3, 1944
- 13 February 23, 1924 thru February 21, 1925
- 13 February 26, 1955 thru February 20, 1956
- 9 February 24, 1941 thru February 7, 1942

The 1951-52 Illini basketball team built up a 15-game conference winning streak.

ILLINI LEGEND:

RAY WOODS

Nowadays, Ray Woods' name is out-shown by such basketball luminaries as George Mikan, Bill Russell, and Oscar Robertson. But in 1917, the spotlight was on him, when he was recognized as America's greatest college basketball player. As a three-year Fighting Illini letterman under Coach Ralph Jones from 1915-17, Woods became the University of Illinois' very first first-team All-American. Though he never led his team in scoring or shooting as did his twin brother Ralf, no one was a better all-around ball-handler or defender or leader than Ray Woods. The crafty guard from Evanston led the Illini to a cumulative record of 42 victories against only six losses in three seasons. Two of those three teams—1915 and 1917—were Western Conference champions, while the 1916 club finished as the league runner-up. Woods died in Berwyn, Illinois in 1965 at the age of 70.

Illini Lore

On April 14, 1916, former University of Illinois regent Thomas J. Burrill died of pneumonia, 11 days short of his 77th birthday. He served on the UI faculty from 1868 to 1912, rising from a position as a horticulture instructor to acting head of the University in just 11 years. Burrill served as the official regent (president) from 1891-94, establishing the UI's graduate school during that tenure.

1916-17

America's Time Capsule

- **Sept. 30, 1916:** *The New York Giants' 26-game winning streak, baseball's longest ever, was halted by the Boston Braves.*
- **Nov. 7, 1916:** *Woodrow Wilson was reelected president of the United States.*
- **Feb. 3, 1917:** *The United States severed diplomatic relations with Germany due to increased submarine warfare.*
- **March 2, 1917:** *The Jones Act made Puerto Rico a U.S. territory.*
- **April 2, 1917:** *President Wilson requested a declaration of war against Germany.*

I·L·L·I·N·I M·O·M·E·N·T

THE ILLINI UPSET MINNESOTA'S "PERFECT TEAM":
The November 5th edition of the *Chicago Record-Herald* screamed out in bold type: "HOLD ON TIGHT WHEN YOU READ THIS!" And for good reason. In one of the greatest upsets in college football history, Coach Bob Zuppke's undermanned Illinois club had handed Minnesota's "perfect team" its only loss of the 1916 season, 14-9. The Illini led 14-0 at halftime on first-quarter touchdowns by Bart Macomber and Ren Kraft. Minnesota narrowed the gap in the third quarter by scoring a touchdown and adding a safety, but Zuppke's men hung on in the final stanza for the victory at Minneapolis. Just how good were the Gophers? Well, other than its loss to Illinois that year, Minnesota compiled a flawless 6-0 record by outscoring its opponents, 339-14.

ILLINI BIRTHDAYS

SEPTEMBER 1916
22– Frank Conley, baseball

OCTOBER 1916
19– Harry Chanowitz, tennis
25– David Turnbull, football

NOVEMBER 1916
17– Paul Podmajersky, football
22– Amo Bessone, hockey/ baseball

DECEMBER 1916
6– Charles Phillips, basketball
13– David Helman, wrestling
17– James Hodges, football
31– Tom Nisbet, basketball

JANUARY 1917
6– Milt Hopwood, swimming

8– Joe Giallombardo, gymnastics
23– Robert Harris, wrestling

MARCH 1917
28– Herbert Young, football

APRIL 1917
7– Florian Surdyk, footbal
16– Frank Battaglia, wrestling
18– Maxwell Garret, fencing coach
27– Albert Lundberg, football

MAY 1917
14– Robert O'Neill, football
15– Henry Stillwell, faculty representative
23– Ken Zimmerman Sr., football

24– Don Kienlen, swimming

JUNE 1917
28– Jim McDonald, football
29– Richard Fay, football

JULY 1917
6– Kimbrell Hill, wrestling
13– John Kirschke, football
17– Lou Boudreau, basketball/baseball
27– Merlyn "Bo" Burris, football
27– Robert Thomases, football

AUGUST 1917
2– James Birkhimer, wrestling
7– Edward Dillon, wrestling
14– James Emmons, wrestling

14– Robert Schwarz, tennis
22– Ralph Hathaway, football
31– Chuck Purvis, football

Walter Becker not only captured the Big Ten's tennis singles title in 1917, he also teamed with Ernest McKay for the conference doubles crown.

Illinois' 1916-17 men's basketball team.

ILLINI ITEM

ILLINOIS SHARED the Western Conference basketball title with Minnesota in 1917, with each team recording a mark of 10-2. Coach Ralph Jones' squad won its last six games of the season, including an 18-17 victory over the co-champion Gophers on February 10 at Urbana.

ILLINI LISTS

GEORGE HALAS CHRONOLOGY

1895—Born February 2 in Chicago
1918—Graduated from University of Illinois
1919—Named player of the game in the 1919 Rose Bowl, playing for Great Lakes
1919—Baseball career ends with New York Yankees (replaced by Babe Ruth)
1920—Organized the American Professional Football Association, forerunner of the NFL, which involved his Decatur Staleys
1925—Signed Red Grange from the University of Illinois
1933—Led Bears to NFL championship
1940—Coached Bears to 73-0 massacre over Washington in NFL title game
1963—Won his final NFL championship, 14-10, over New York Giants
1968—Retired permanently as coach of Bears
1983—Succumbed to cancer on October 31

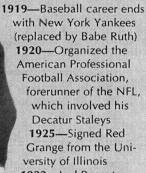

ILLINI LEGEND:

GEORGE HALAS

George Halas became famous by his moniker "Papa Bear", but his athletic career at the University of Illinois spanned much further than just the football field. He lettered in baseball, basketball, and football for the Illini from 1916-18, starring in each sport. Halas was graduated from the UI in 1918 with a degree in civil engineering, but his life took a detour when he enlisted in the Navy for service in World War I. When the war ended, he played major-league baseball for a season with the New York Yankees. However, an injury ended his baseball career, and Halas turned to his first love—football. He was a driving force in giving birth to the National Football League in 1920, and brought credibility to the league five years later when he signed Illini running back "Red" Grange to a $100,000 Chicago Bears contract. During his 40-year coaching career with the Bears, Halas won more games (326) than any other NFL coach in history. He died October 31, 1983, at the age of 88.

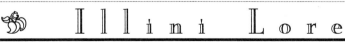

Illini Lore

Nearly five million Americans served their country during World War I, including 9,442 faculty, staff, and students from the University of Illinois. Of about 117,000 Americans who died, 183 men and one woman from the Urbana-Champaign and Chicago campuses lost their lives. The names of those 184 individuals are memorialized on the columns of Memorial Stadium.

1917-18

America's Time Capsule

- **Oct. 15, 1917:** *The Chicago White Sox defeated the New York Giants to win the World Series.*
- **Nov. 3, 1917:** *U.S. forces engaged in their first World War I battle in Europe.*
- **Dec. 18, 1917:** *The U.S. Constitution's 18th amendment was passed, outlawing the manufacture and sale of alcoholic liquors.*
- **May 15, 1918:** *Airmail service began between New York City and Washington, D.C.*
- **June 25, 1918:** *American forces halted the Germans in the Battle of Belleau Wood in France.*

I·L·L·I·N·I M·O·M·E·N·T

FIGHTING ILLINI ATHLETICS AND WORLD WAR I:

World War I put a crimp in the University of Illinois' athletic program during the 1917-18 season, as only football, basketball, baseball, and track were among the teams that competed on a varsity level. None of the four squads were conference champions, though baseball and outdoor track both finished runners-up to Michigan. Illinois' other sports—gymnastics, wrestling, tennis, cross country, and fencing—were all suspended during the war years, with most not reinstated for competition until the 1919-20 season. Among Illinois' most famous World War I servicemen was three-sport star George Halas, who enlisted in the Navy in January of 1918. The University would later honor its war dead with the construction of Memorial Stadium.

ILLINI BIRTHDAYS

SEPTEMBER 1917
6– Harry Siebold, football

OCTOBER 1917
6– Al Kirkland, swimming
7– Wes Leverich, wrestling

NOVEMBER 1917
5– Ebon Jones, tennis
20– Ralph Palmer, football

DECEMBER 1917
2– William Lenick, football
16– Richard Kucera, baseball
19– Ray Poat, baseball
29– John Patterson, football

JANUARY 1918
20– Harry Lasater, football/basketball

23– Charles Mettler, hockey
26– Bill Hapac, basketball/baseball

FEBRUARY 1918
6– Harold Weingartner, fencing
15– Lou Kachiroubas, wrestling
17– Bob Wehrli, football
17– William Usinger, golf
19– Alan Grant, baseball

APRIL 1918
3– Wesley Martin, football
19– Ralph Bennett, football

MAY 1918
25– Jesse Boyd, wrestling

JUNE 1918
17– Vic Wukovits, basketball
27– Howard Cronk, basketball

JULY 1918
17– Bob Blackman, football coach
21– Joe Frank, basketball

AUGUST 1918
15– Robert Finn, baseball
21– John Hughes, wrestling

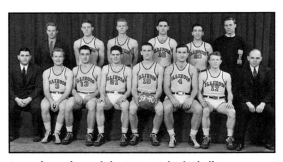

Several members of the 1939-40 basketball team were born during the 1917-18 season, including Bill Hapac (front row, fifth from left), Vic Wukovits (front, fourth from left), Joe Frank (front, seventh from left), and Howard Cronk (back, second from left).

TWO FIGHTING ILLINI letter-winning athletes died in service of their country during World War I. They were Homer Dahringer, who lettered for the basketball team in 1912 and '13, and Edward Wallace, a 1911 baseball letterwinner. The names of these men are engraved on two of the 200 columns that support the east and west sides of Memorial Stadium.

ILLINI LISTS

BOB ZUPPKE'S CONSENSUS ALL-AMERICA FOOTBALL PLAYERS

- 1914   Ralph Chapman, G
- 1914   Perry Graves, E
- 1915   Bart Macomber, HB
- 1918   John Depler, C
- 1920   Charles Carney, E
- 1923   Jim McMillen, G
- 1923-25 Harold "Red" Grange, HB
- 1926   Bernie Shively, G

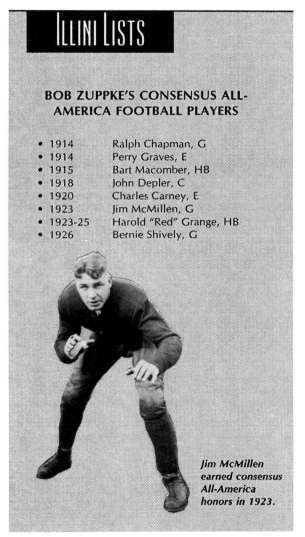

Jim McMillen earned consensus All-America honors in 1923.

ILLINI LEGEND:

JOHN DEPLER

One of the premier football players at the University of Illinois during the war years was a center from Lewistown, Illinois, named John Depler. Depler's All-American career with Coach Bob Zuppke's Illini was dotted with success, having been a key member of the 1918 and 1919 Western Conference champions. Illini teams won 14 of 17 conference games during his playing career. Following his graduation in 1919 from UI, Depler coached for eight seasons at Columbia University. In 1930, he organized and was co-owner of the Brooklyn Dodgers professional football team. Depler spent several years of his life in operating hotels and restaurants. Upon his retirement, he wrote a newspaper column for the *Fulton County* (Illinois) *News* and was presented with the Illinois State Historical Society's "Individual Award for Regional History Writing." Depler died in 1970 at the age of 71.

Illini Lore

I n the November 15, 1917, edition of the *Alumni Quarterly*, the University of Illinois announced that "plans for an elaborate celebration of the 50th birthday of the University have been abandoned," due to World War I. The celebration was to have centered around a "great pageant" to depict the history of the institution, that opened for business March 2, 1868. Instead, the UI was asked to raise $20,000 as its share in the state of Illinois' effort to collect $3 million for support of American servicemen.

1918-19

I·L·L·I·N·I M·O·M·E·N·T

A capacity crowd at Illinois Field saw the Illini beat Ohio State, 13-0, for the Big Ten football title.

ILLINI GRIDDERS CLAIM CONFERENCE TITLE:
Just five days after the Germans surrendered to end World War I, University of Illinois students had cause to celebrate another major event. On November 16, two-time defending Big Ten champion Ohio State came to Illinois Field to face Coach Bob Zuppke's Fighting Illini. Illinois took charge immediately, marching down the field for a touchdown on its first possession. That 7-0 halftime lead was increased to the eventual final score of 13-0 in the third quarter. The Illini wrapped up a perfect 4-0 Big Ten season (all four wins coming by shutouts) the following Saturday with a 29-0 win over Chicago. Zuppke wanted to play undefeated Michigan for an unscheduled winner-take-all game on December 7, but the proposed playoff game was vetoed by UI's Council of Administrators. Ohio State coach Jack Wilce told the press afterwards, "We met both Illinois and Michigan, and there is no comparison. Illinois is, by far, the better."

ILLINI BIRTHDAYS

SEPTEMBER 1918
7– Ted Purvin, wrestling
30– John Sabo, football/ basketball

OCTOBER 1918
15– Mel Brewer, football
24– Paul Govedare, wrestling
25– John Grable, Chief V
26– Robert Riegel, basketball

NOVEMBER 1918
6– George Rettinger, football
12– Archie Deutschman, wrestling
25– Colin Handlon, basketball

DECEMBER 1918
6– Frank Richart, golf
11– Ralph Ehni, football
11– Robert Campbell, football

13– Louis Fina, gymnastics

JANUARY 1919
17– Cliff Peterson, football

FEBRUARY 1919
13– Joe Alexander, baseball

MARCH 1919
3– Leon Lipson, fencing
3– Jim Wollrab, swimming
10– Joe Pawlowski, football
20– Duane Fultz, football
25– Don Elting, football

APRIL 1919
28– Henry Holquist, swimming

MAY 1919
14– Leonard Kallis, baseball

JUNE 1919
15– George Bernhardt, football
17– Peter Kurlak, swimming
22– James Phillips, football
24– Stan Stasica, football

JULY 1919
5– Leo Hartman, swimming
19– Russ Drechsler, baseball

AUGUST 1919
27– Robert Tapscott, golf

Mel Brewer, born October 15, 1918, was an Illini football letterwinner from 1937-39. He later served as an assistant on Ray Eliot's football staff from 1947-59. Following nearly eight years as an assistant athletic director, Brewer resigned from the Illinois staff in 1966, after he allegedly turned over a set of records that implicated the Illini athletic department in what would be known as the "slush fund" scandal.

1918 Illinois football team

ON OCTOBER 26, 1918, Illinois hosted the Municipal Pier football team in a game at Illinois Field in Urbana. The Fighting Illini lost the game, 7-0, but no one complained. That's because the game was played behind closed gates, due to an influenza epidemic in Champaign-Urbana.

ILLINI LISTS

WINNINGEST ILLINI MEN'S BASKETBALL COACHES (BY PERCENTAGE)
(7 or more seasons, through 1994-95 season)

	W	L	Pct.
• Ralph Jones (1913-20)	85	34	.714
• Doug Mills (1937-47)	151	66	.696
• Harry Combes (1948-67)	316	150	.678
• Lou Henson (1976-95)	405	211	.657
• Craig Ruby (1923-36)	148	97	.604
• Harv Schmidt (1968-74)	89	77	.536

Ralph Jones' .714 winning percentage is tops among Illini men's basketball coaches.

ILLINI LEGEND:
KENNETH "TUG" WILSON

Kenneth "Tug" Wilson admitted that it was a long way from Atwood to Antwerp, but that's exactly where his athletic career led him. Born in Atwood, Illinois, a little town 30 miles south of the University of Illinois, Wilson enrolled at the UI in the fall of 1916 after two years of teaching at a country school near his home. He was a fantastic athlete, winning five varsity letters in basketball and track and field. On the hardwood, Wilson led the Illini in scoring as a junior and was the team's captain his senior year. Athletically, his greatest accomplishment came in the summer of 1920 when he was a member of the United States Olympic team, competing at Antwerp, Belgium, in the javelin and discus. Wilson began his career in athletic administration at Illinois under George Huff, then spent three years at Drake, and 21 years at Northwestern as athletic director. In 1945, he resigned from NU to become Major John Griffith's successor as Commissioner of the Big Ten Conference. Tug Wilson died February 1, 1979, at the age of 82.

🐘 Illini Lore 🐘

An entertaining part of campus life at the University of Illinois during the first three decades of the 20th century was the annual Interscholastic Circus. The 1919 version of the circus, described by UI's *Alumni Quarterly* magazine as "a roaring furnace of farce," attracted more than 7,000 students, faculty, and staff. Highlights of the May 31st festivities included clowns, acrobats, and swimming coach Ed Manley's "plunge from a dizzy height of 50 feet into a shimmering, seething tank of fiery water."

1919-20

I·L·L·I·N·I M·O·M·E·N·T

Bob Fletcher (third row, far left) came off the bench to kick the first field goal of his career.

FLETCHER FIELD GOAL BEATS OHIO STATE:

The Illini traveled to Ohio State for the 1919 season finale with both the Big Ten championship and the national title on the line. Coach Bob Zuppke's men trailed the Buckeyes, 7-6, with just five minutes left in the game. Quarterback Lawrence Walquist and end Chuck Carney connected for three pass completions, putting the Illini deep into Ohio State territory. With only 12 seconds remaining in the game and Illinois placekicker Ralph Fletcher out of the game with an ankle injury, Coach Zuppke called upon Ralph's younger brother, Bob, to kick a game-winning 25-yard field goal—*the first field goal he'd ever attempted in a game!* The 9-7 victory gave Illinois its second national championship.

ILLINI BIRTHDAYS

SEPTEMBER 1919
13– Paul Milosevich, football
15– Jim Reeder, football
19– Robert Richmond, basketball

OCTOBER 1919
7– Henry Sachs, basketball

NOVEMBER 1919
23– Ken Cheeley, football
28– James Smith, football
29– Elmer Engel, football

DECEMBER 1919
31– William Kolens, football

JANUARY 1920
8– Isaiah "Ike" Owens, football
24– Robert Falkenstein, football

27– Maurice Gould, football

FEBRUARY 1920
10– Sam Zatkoff, football

MARCH 1920
5– Bert Piggott, football
14– Richard Good, football

APRIL 1920
20– David Dillon, football
20– Alex Aloia, wrestling
22– Jim Easterbrook, football

MAY 1920
18– Landis Hurley, football

JUNE 1920
2– Donald Kindy, wrestling
18– Nate Johnson, football

JULY 1920
19– Bob Scharbert, football
23– Jim Wilson, assistant track coach

AUGUST 1920
15– Alphonse Anders, football
17– Matthew Smerdel, football
30– George Bujan, football

The 1920 Illini wrestling team was the Big Ten champion. Two UI wrestlers, heavyweight H. A. Whitson and 175-pounder H. L. Hoffman, captured individual titles.

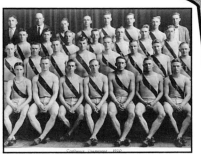

Captain Bob Emery (front row, fourth from left) was a member of the mile-relay unit that gave Illinois the conference title.

ℐLLINI ℐTEM

ON MARCH 20, 1920, Illinois' mile-relay team of Phil Donohoe, John Prescott, Phil Spink, and Bob Emery set an indoor conference record of 3:29 in the final event, giving the Illini track team the conference title over Michigan, 31⅝ to 27½.

ILLINI LISTS

LONGEST CONTINUOUS TENURES AS ILLINI ASSISTANT FOOTBALL COACH

- Justa Lindgren   40 years (1904-43)
- Ralph Fletcher   22 years (1942-63)
- Burt Ingwersen   20 years (1946-65)
- Leo Johnson   15 years (1942-56)
- Mel Brewer   13 years (1947-59)
- Robert King   11 years (1947-57)
- Milt Orlander   11 years (1924-34)
- Gene Stauber   11 years (1960-70)
- J.C. Caroline   10 years (1967-76)

Justa Lindgren's (right) career as an assistant coach at Illinois stretched over a span of five decades.

ILLINI LEGEND:

BURT INGWERSEN

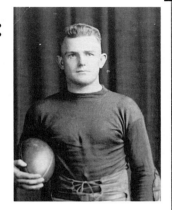

Burt Ingwersen was, literally, a man for all seasons at the University of Illinois. After the Fighting Illini football season was completed, he'd lace up his sneakers for duty with Coach Ralph Jones' basketball team. And after the basketball stopped bouncing, Ingwersen would race back out to Illinois Field to play first base for Coach George Huff's Illini baseball squad. He earned nine varsity letters altogether from 1917-20, earning all-star acclaim in football. Following graduation, Ingwersen joined the UI coaching staff, handling the freshmen football and baseball squads. In 1924, Ingwersen succeeded Howard Jones as Iowa's head football coach, compiling a record of 33-27-4 in eight seasons as the Hawkeye mentor. After Iowa, he made assistant coaching stops at Louisiana State and Northwestern. In February of 1943, Ingwersen was commissioned a lieutenant commander in the U.S. Navy, serving as head football coach. Two years later, he was transferred to the Naval Air Technical Training Center in Chicago, where he also served a brief stint as athletic director. Ingwersen rejoined Coach Ray Eliot's UI football staff in the fall of 1945, retiring in 1965. He died on July 17, 1969, at the age of 70.

🐎 Illini Lore 🐎

Bob Zuppke (left) was a key member of George Huff's athletic teaching school.

Formal instruction in athletic coaching began during the fall of 1919 as a regular department in the University of Illinois' College of Education. Athletic Director George Huff had been running successful coaching sessions for several summers, but up until this time, students in those classes never received actual course credit. Out of 136 credit hours that were required for graduation, students enrolled in the athletic curriculum had to complete studies in 34 hours of practical coaching and physical education. Among the graduates were: Floyd "Shorty" Stahl, who went on to coach basketball at Ohio State; Otto Vogel, head baseball coach at Iowa; and Bernie Shively, athletic director at Kentucky for 30 years.

1920-21

- **Sept. 28, 1920:** *Eight members of the Chicago White Sox were indicted on charges of having taken bribes to throw the 1919 World Series.*
- **Nov. 2, 1920:** *Warren Harding was elected U.S. president by a landslide margin.*
- **Nov. 2, 1920:** *Radio station KDKA in Pittsburgh broadcast the results of the presidential election, the first time that happened.*
- **June 29, 1921:** *Elizabeth Ryan and Bill Tilden claimed Wimbledon tennis titles.*
- **July 2, 1921:** *Jack Dempsey successfully defended his heavyweight boxing title against Georges Carpentier.*

I·L·L·I·N·I M·O·M·E·N·T

George Huff (front row, far right) and Bob Zuppke (second row, third from left) were members of the Stadium Committee.

FUND DRIVE FOR NEW STADIUM:
The old gym annex looked like the Chicago Coliseum during the Republican convention on that 25th day of April, 1921. Every seat was filled, as bands played and horns tooted. On the platform were University executives and distinguished Illini athletes and coaches. President David Kinley first spoke to the masses, then Athletic Director George Huff followed. When the ovation ceased, Huff said, "I want to see a great Stadium at the University of Illinois. The Stadium will be many things—a memorial to Illini who have died in the war, a recreational field, and an imposing place for our varsity games. But it will also be an unprecedented expression of Illinois spirit." Then football coach Bob Zuppke spoke, his hands rigidly clasped begind his back. After a few minutes, Zup ended with his request for voluntary donations of $1,000 for the Stadium. Finally, following a few seconds of silence, a Latin-American student named R.L. Cavalcanti shouted out, "I will give, sir!" Within 10 minutes, more than $700,000 of the $2.5 million needed to build the great structure had been pledged by the undergraduate body.

ILLINI BIRTHDAYS

SEPTEMBER 1920
- 1– Alton Shirley, basketball
- 1– Joe Turek, football
- 17– Ken Clapper, tennis
- 21– Glenn Holthaus, Chief VI
- 23– Clifford Niedzielski, football

OCTOBER 1920
- 3– John Drish, basketball/baseball

JANUARY 1921
- 9– Art Marlaire, football

FEBRUARY 1921
- 1– George Balestri, baseball
- 8– Walter "Hoot" Evers, baseball
- 11– Boyd Bartley, baseball

- 23– Lavere (Liz) Astroth, football
- 23– Jim Lothrop, tennis

MARCH 1921
- 1– William Hocking, basketball
- 8– Tom McCullough, football
- 11– Alexander Prokopis, football

APRIL 1921
- 4– Tony Butkovich, football
- 21– Steve Sucic, assistant football coach

MAY 1921
- 24– Ken Parker, basketball

JUNE 1921
- 23– Tom Hull, baseball

JULY 1921
- 6– Robert Wilson, football
- 7– Albert Scharf, baseball
- 28– Robert Wallin, football

AUGUST 1921
- 12– Wes Tregoning, football
- 19– Fred Steers, tennis
- 31– Stan Fronczak, basketball

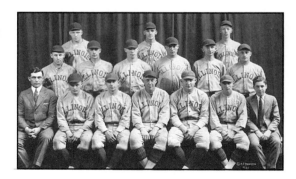

The 1921 Fighting Illini baseball team captured the Big Ten crown with a 10-1 conference mark.

Dad's Day has been celebrated at Illinois since 1920.

ILLINI ITEM

FIRST DAD'S DAY GAME: The University of Illinois hosted intercollegiate football's first "Dad's Day" on November 20, 1920. Unfortunately, Coach Bob Zuppke's Illini dropped a 7-0 decision to Western Conference champion Ohio State at Illinois Field.

ILLINI LISTS

ILLINI NCAA TRACK AND FIELD TEAM CHAMPIONSHIPS

Illinois won the NCAA's very first outdoor track and field championship on June 18, 1921, even though it didn't win a single individual title.

YEAR	CHAMPION	RUNNER-UP	SITE
1921	Illinois, 20¼ pts	Notre Dame, 16¼ pts	Chicago
1927	Illinois, 35⅗ pts	Texas, 29 ½ pts	Chicago
1944	Illinois, 79 pts	Notre Dame, 43 pts	Milwaukee
1946	Illinois, 78 pts	Southern Cal, 42⁸⁵/₁₀₀ pts	Minneapolis
1947	Illinois, 59⅔ pts	Southern Cal, 34⅙ pts	Salt Lake City

Illini track and field action from 1921.

ILLINI LEGEND:

CHUCK CARNEY

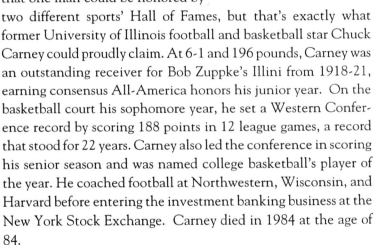

The greatest of athletes are honored following their careers by being selected to their particular sport's Hall of Fame. It's inconceivable that one man could be honored by two different sports' Hall of Fames, but that's exactly what former University of Illinois football and basketball star Chuck Carney could proudly claim. At 6-1 and 196 pounds, Carney was an outstanding receiver for Bob Zuppke's Illini from 1918-21, earning consensus All-America honors his junior year. On the basketball court his sophomore year, he set a Western Conference record by scoring 188 points in 12 league games, a record that stood for 22 years. Carney also led the conference in scoring his senior season and was named college basketball's player of the year. He coached football at Northwestern, Wisconsin, and Harvard before entering the investment banking business at the New York Stock Exchange. Carney died in 1984 at the age of 84.

Illini Lore

President David Kinley surveys the construction at Memorial Stadium.

President David Kinley began his 10-year term at the University of Illinois September 1, 1920. The 60-year-old Scottish-born professor of economics was vice president and dean of the graduate school during the term of his predecessor, Edmund James. The Kinley period was highlighted by the completion of several projects begun by James. Among the facilities constructed in Kinley's decade of service were Memorial Stadium, Smith Music Hall, the Library, and McKinley Hospital.

1921-22

America's Time Capsule

- **Sept. 8, 1921:** *Margaret Gorman of Washington, D.C. won the title of the first Miss America.*
- **Nov. 11, 1921:** *The "Unknown Soldier" of World War I was buried at Arlington National Cemetery.*
- **Feb. 21, 1922:** *An explosion of the airship Roma killed 34 of its 45-man crew.*
- **May 30, 1922:** *The Lincoln Memorial, designed by UI student Henry Bacon, was dedicated in Washington, D.C.*
- **July 15, 1922:** *Gene Sarazen won the U.S. Open golf tournament.*

I·L·L·I·N·I M·O·M·E·N·T

Illini third baseman Harry McCurdy

CROWD OF 15,000 SEES ILLINI "9" BEAT MICHIGAN:
The boisterous crowd of 15,000 that gathered to watch their heroes at Illinois Field that 20th day of May, 1922, totally encircled the baseball diamond. And Coach Carl Lundgren's Illini didn't disappoint the faithful throng, pounding three Michigan hurlers for 12 hits en route to a 7-3 victory over the conference leaders. Third baseman Harry McCurdy was the hitting star for the Illini that afternoon, drilling two of Illinois' seven doubles. Wally Roettger relieved UI starter C.L. Jackson on the mound in the seventh inning, shutting out the Wolverines the rest of the way. Illinois clinched its second consecutive Western Conference title three days later at home, defeating Purdue, 5-3.

ILLINI BIRTHDAYS

SEPTEMBER 1921
17– Norm Anthonisen, wrestling
24– John MacArthur, football

OCTOBER 1921
11– Charles Campbell, baseball

NOVEMBER 1921
18– Louie Donoho, football
28– James McCarthy, football
30– Ray VonSpreckelsen, tennis

DECEMBER 1921
18– Don Greenwood, football
20– Les Joop, football

JANUARY 1922
7– John Wrenn, football

22– Dominic Mattiazza, football

FEBRUARY 1922
5– Ed Bernardoni, wrestling
10– John Genis, football
13– Ray Grierson, football

MARCH 1922
4– Peter Lukas, wrestling
7– Andy Phillip, basketball/baseball
21– Clarence Tohn, football
27– Alex Agase, football

APRIL 1922
9– William Brekke, swimming
13– Joe Garcia, wrestling
16– Charles Schunk, tennis
20– Edwin Parker, basketball/baseball

MAY 1922
5– Stan Patrick, basketball
10– Idelle Stith, Princess Illiniwek
17– Achille "Chick" Maggioli, football

JUNE 1922
1– Theron Bradley, football
8– Mac Wenskunas, football
17– Irv Kagen, wrestling
20– Roger Downs, tennis

JULY 1922
5– Stanley Lee, wrestling
10– Herb McKenley, track
23– Walter Correll, football
28– Charles Fowler, basketball

George Chandler, who for many years portrayed Uncle Petrie on the popular Lassie TV series, was an Illini track letterman in 1922.

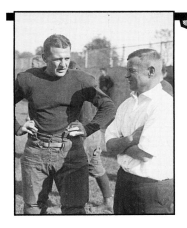

ILLINI ITEM

BOB ZUPPKE first met Red Grange on May 20, 1922, when Grange was on the University of Illinois campus participating in a high school track meet. After witnessing Grange win the 220-yard dash, Zuppke commented to the youngster, "I think you have a chance to make our team."

ILLINI LISTS

ZUPPKEISMS

Illinois' Bob Zuppke was a master of memorable aphorisms. Here are some of his best:

- The hero of a thousand plays becomes a bum after one error.
- All quitters are good losers.
- A man has to lose before he can appreciate winning.
- If the team wins all of its games, the alumni are loyal.
- Victory in football is 40 percent ability and 60 percent spirit.
- I don't care how big or how strong our opponents are, as long as they're human.
- My definition of an All-American is a player who has weak opposition and a poet in the press box.
- Never prophesy a great football future for any back until he has gained his first yard and taken his first bump.
- No athletic director holds office longer than two unsuccessful football coaches.
- Never let hope elude you. That is life's biggest fumble.

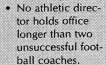

ILLINI LEGEND:

PAUL PREHN

The most prosperous University of Illinois coach in terms of Big Ten success was wrestling mentor Paul Prehn. During his coaching career from 1920-28, Prehn's Fighting Illini grapplers dominated the sport in conference action. Illinois won Big Ten titles seven times in nine seasons, and had an impressive dual-meet record of 42-5. Among Prehn's individual stars were Illini wrestling legends Allie Morrison and Hek Kenney. When he left Illinois, Prehn began a highly successful restaurant business in Champaign-Urbana. He also served as chairman of the Illinois Athletic Commission for four years, a period that included the Jack Dempsey-Gene Tunney "Battle of the Century" boxing match in Chicago. Prehn also served as the state director for Illinois' Republican Party for 10 years. The World War I veteran from Mason City, Iowa, died on May 10, 1973, at the age of 80.

Illini Lore

In the spring of 1922, a 400-watt transmitter using the call letters WRM went into operation in the University of Illinois' Electrical Engineering Laboratory. The listeners' favorite programming included the bands, the glee clubs, and the scores of Fighting Illini athletic teams, but the few alumni who owned radio sets asked for more. In 1926, Boetius Sullivan, a wealthy UI alumnus, presented the University a radio station in memory of his father. The station was larer shifted to 890 KC, and the call letters were changed to WILL.

1922-23

America's Time Capsule

- **Oct. 4, 1922:** *Famed sportswriter Grantland Rice reported the first radio play-by-play coverage of the World Series.*
- **Oct. 8, 1922:** *John McGraw's New York Giants won their second consecutive World Series title against the New York Yankees.*
- **March 13, 1923:** *Motion pictures with sound were first demonstrated in New York City.*
- **July 15, 1923:** *Golf amateur "Bobby" Jones won the U.S. Open.*
- **Aug. 2, 1923:** *President Warren Harding died of an embolism while recovering from an attack of ptomaine poisoning.*

I·L·L·I·N·I M·O·M·E·N·T

Big Ten medalist Rial Rolfe (far right) led Illinois to its first-ever conference golf championship.

ILLINOIS' FIRST CONFERENCE GOLF TITLE:
The first of seven all-time Big Ten golf championships for the University of Illinois was registered by Coach George Davis' team on June 19, 1923. Evanston Golf Club was the site for Illinois' five-stroke victory over defending champ Chicago, 643 to 648. The Maroons whittled nine strokes off the Illini's first-day, 14-stroke lead, but the one-two punch of UI's Rial Rolfe and John Humphreys was ultimately too much to overcome. Rolfe, a product of Chicago Senn High School, also captured Illinois' first-ever individual title, defeating teammate Gustav Novotny by four strokes.

ILLINI BIRTHDAYS

SEPTEMBER 1922
1– Joe Astroth, baseball
10– Robert Rehberg, track
26– Eddie McGovern, football
26– John Kopka, baseball

OCTOBER 1922
2– Ken Menke, basketball
4– Don Lenhardt, baseball
14– Eugene Kwasniewski, football
15– Don Griffin, football

NOVEMBER 1922
20– Mike Kasap, football

DECEMBER 1922
22– Jack Smiley, basketball
27– Dwight "Dike" Eddleman, football/basketball/track

FEBRUARY 1923
6– Ray Florek, football
12– Robert O'Neal, basketball
13– Al Glassgen, wrestling
20– Albert Widner, football
22– Al Mastrangeli, football
25– Gene Vance, basketball/athletic director

MARCH 1923
24– Melvin Randoll, tennis
30– Robert Bitzer, Chief Illiniwek IX

APRIL 1923
4– Lou Levanti, football
6– Julius Rykovich, football
7– John Hazelett, football
19– John Bartley, wrestling
25– William Heiss, football

MAY 1923
27– Gordon Hortin, basketball

JUNE 1923
9– Robert Schroeder, golf
14– Richard Cashmore, baseball
19– Bill Huber, football
22– Joe Buscemi, football
26– Stanley Green, football

JULY 1923
13– Art Mathisen, basketball
21– Art Dufelmeier, football

AUGUST 1923
23– Jim Gates, tennis

Julius Rykovich, born April 6, 1923, rushed for 103 yards against UCLA in Illinois' 1947 Rose Bowl victory.

Illinois' 1923 track and field team

ILLINI ITEM

ILLINOIS' TRACK AND FIELD SQUAD lost the Western Conference outdoor meet to host Michigan on June 2, 1923, 57 ½ to 57. Despite a victory by the Illini in a conference-record time of 3:20 in the mile relay, the meet's final event, the referee ordered the race re-run when a misplaced hurdle caused a Michigan runner to miss a step and fall. Coach Harry Gill's Illini refused to run again, and the referee eventually canceled the event altogether, handing Michigan the team championship.

ILLINI LISTS

ILLINI TRACK & FIELD
OLYMPIC GOLD MEDALISTS

1912   Ed Lindberg, 1,600-meter relay (second leg), 3:16.6
1924   Harold Osborn, High jump, 6'5 ¹⁵/₁₆"
        Harold Osborn, Decathlon, 7710.755 points
        Dan Kinsey, 110-meter hurdles, :15.0
1952   Bob Richards, Pole vault, 14'11 ¼"
        Herb McKenley*, 1,600-meter relay (second leg), 3:03.9
1956   Bob Richards, Pole vault, 14'11 ½"
        *Member of Jamaican Olympic team

Dan Kinsey (left in white uniform) won an Olympic gold medal in 1924.

ILLINI LEGEND:

HAROLD OSBORN

Just how outstanding a track and field athlete was the University of Illinois' Harold Osborn? He was so good that he was one of 26 persons selected as charter members of the National Track and Field Hall of Fame, joining such greats as Ralph Boston, Bob Mathias, Wilma Rudolph, and Jesse Owens. Osborn is the only competitor in Olympic history ever to win an individual-event gold medal (the high jump), as well as the gold medal in the decathlon, registering a world record in both events! While a member of the Illini track team, Osborn led Illinois in indoor and outdoor Western Conference crowns in 1920, '21, and 22. From 1922 to 1933, Osborn was a coach and teacher at Champaign High School. He was an osteopathic physician in Champaign from 1939 until his retirement. Osborn died in 1975 at the age of 75.

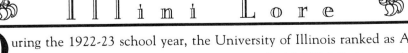

Illini Lore

During the 1922-23 school year, the University of Illinois ranked as America's third-largest institution of higher learning. A total of 9,285 full-time students were enrolled at Illinois, a total higher than any other U.S. university except the University of California (14,061) and Columbia University (10,308). The Universities of Michigan and Minnesota ranked fourth and fifth. At the time, Illinois had more architecture students than any other (237) and ranked second in the country in terms of its number of commerce students (2,044).

1923-24

America's Time Capsule

- **Sept. 14, 1923:** *Jack Dempsey retained his heavyweight boxing crown with a second-round knockout of Luis Angel Firpo, the "Wild Bull of the Pampas."*
- **Oct. 15, 1923:** *The Yankees won the World Series over the Giants in an all-New York City showdown.*
- **Jan. 25, 1924:** *The first Winter Olympics were held in Chamonix, France, as the Americans finish fourth in the unofficial team standings.*
- **June 30, 1924:** *The Teapot Dome oil leasing scandal indicted several oil company presidents on charges of bribery and conspiracy to defraud the United States.*
- **July 21, 1924:** *Life sentences were given to Nathan Leopold and Richard Loeb for the highly publicized murder of Bobby Franks.*

I·L·L·I·N·I M·O·M·E·N·T

A crowd of 60,632 jammed into not-yet-completed Memorial Stadium on November 3, 1923.

MEMORIAL STADIUM MAKES ITS DEBUT:
Illinois' football team made its debut at Memorial Stadium a successful one, defeating the University of Chicago, 7-0, November 3, 1923. Construction of the stadium, begun just 14 months before, was not totally completed, but athletic director George Huff had pledged that the imposing structure would be ready for the Illini Homecoming game of 1923. Red Grange—who else—scored the first and only touchdown in that inaugural game, rushing 24 times on the muddy field for 101 yards. It rained hard all afternoon, and because the stadium's walkways weren't yet completed, several hundred of the 60,632 fans were forced to abandon their shoes and boots in the mud. Tickets, priced at $2.50 each, yielded record gate-sale receipts of more than $132,000 to the UI Athletic Association.

ILLINI BIRTHDAYS

SEPTEMBER 1923
7– Leo Gedvillas, basketball
7– Ken Siegel, football
8– Warren Sullivan, fencing

OCTOBER 1923
19– William Krall, football
26– Charles Turnbow, golf
27– Chuck Gottfried, football
28– Robert Wakefield, baseball

NOVEMBER 1923
10– Oliver Shoaff, basketball
23– Fred Green, basketball

DECEMBER 1923
5– Lawrence Forst, football

23– Ken Hanks, Chief VIII

JANUARY 1924
10– Herb Siegert, football
24– Robert Hughes, wrestling
21– Vern Seliger, football
27– Bill Butkovich, football/baseball

FEBRUARY 1924
9– Don Maechtle, football

MARCH 1924
4– John Brittin, baseball
22– Lee Eilbracht, baseball
30– Robert Eads, baseball

APRIL 1924
11– Edward Bower, wrestling
12– Cecil Coleman, athletic director
15– Hal Craig, basketball

26– Donald Delaney, basketball
29– Peter Perez, football

MAY 1924
1– Thomas Gallagher, football
6– Arthur Archer, football
21– Ray Ciszck, football

JUNE 1924
30– Willard Franks, football

AUGUST 1924
2– Lou Agase, football
19– Roy Gatewood, basketball

Illinois miler Melvin Hall set a Big Ten record with a time of 4:23.6 at the conference's indoor meet, March 15, 1924.

- 64 -

ILLINI ITEM

COACH CRAIG RUBY'S Illini basketball team clinched a tie for the Western Conference title on March 10, 1924, with a 31-19 victory over Minnesota. Senior Leland "Slim" Stilwell, in the final game of his career, was blanked from the field, but converted 11 free throws. Stilwell later returned to the University of Illinois to serve as the school's team physician.

ILLINI LISTS

MEMORIAL STADIUM CONSTRUCTION STATISTICS

- 2,700 tons of steel
- 800 tons of reinforcing bars
- 4.8 million bricks
- 50,000 barrels of cement
- 7,200 tons of cut stones
- 404 miles of lumber
- 17 miles of seats, covered by 21 acres of paint

George Huff (right) and friends in front of the Memorial Stadium skeleton.

ILLINI LEGEND: HAROLD "RED" GRANGE

Those who call Harold Edward "Red" Grange the greatest college football player of all time have plenty of facts to back up their braggadocio. They'll point out that he was the very first winner of the *Chicago Tribune's* Silver Football Award as the Big Ten's Most Valuable Player. They'll mention that he was a charter member of both college and professional football's Hall of Fame. And they'll conclude that the Galloping Ghost was a unanimous selection on the all-time All-America team. So talented was Grange that the number 77 he wore on his back during his career at Illinois from 1923-25 was immediately retired by the university. So recognizable was his name that, in his very first game as a pro, Grange turned a normal Chicago Bears' gathering of less than 5,000 into a standing-room only crowd of 36,000. Upon Grange's death in January of 1991 at the age of 87, UI athletic director John Mackovic summed up Grange's life by saying, "Red Grange has been, and will always be, one of the largest legends in the game of football. His presence will continue to be felt as long as the game is played."

 Illini Lore

The cornerstone for the University of Illinois' new McKinley Memorial Hospital was laid May 10, 1924. The original structure, completed in the fall of 1925 at a cost of $225,000, didn't include its current wings on the north and south sides. Senator W.B. McKinley, a student at the UI in the 1870s, was the benefactor of the campus' first health facility. Each student that joined the hospital association that first year paid fees of $3 per semester, and was afforded a maximum of 28 days of free care.

America's Time Capsule

- **Oct. 10, 1924:** *The Washington Senators, led by pitcher Walter Johnson, defeated the New York Giants, four games to three, in the World Series.*
- **Nov. 4, 1924:** *Calvin Coolidge was re-elected president of the United States, defeating Democrat John Davis.*
- **Jan. 5, 1925:** *Mrs. William B. Ross was inaugurated governor of Wyoming, becoming the first woman governor in U.S. history.*
- **July 21, 1925:** *Tennessee teacher John Scopes, a former University of Illinois student, was convicted for teaching the theory of evolution to his students.*
- **Aug. 24, 1925:** *Helen Wills and Bill Tilden successfully defended their singles titles at the U.S. Lawn Tennis championships.*

I·L·L·I·N·I M·O·M·E·N·T

THE WHEATON ICEMAN GALLOPS OVER MICHIGAN:

October 18, 1924, is, quite understandably, the most memorable single day in University of Illinois sports history. Not only was it the afternoon the university's imposing Memorial Stadium was officially dedicated, but it also was the day when one of America's greatest football legends—Red Grange—was christened. During the first 12 minutes of the game, the Wheaton Iceman scored touchdowns the first four times he touched the ball, on runs of 95, 67, 56, and 44 yards. He later returned to score a fifth TD on an 11-yard run, and also threw for a sixth Illini score. When the final gun sounded, Grange had piled up 276 yards of total offense and had 126 yards in kickoff returns. Illinois beat mighty Michigan by the unlikely score of 39-14.

ILLINI BIRTHDAYS

SEPTEMBER 1924
3– Walter Kirk, basketball

OCTOBER 1924
20– Lyle Button, football

NOVEMBER 1924
9– Orville Hall, football
20– John Kane, football
21– Lou Baker, assistant football coach
30– Ben Migdow, tennis

DECEMBER 1924
1– Murney Lazier, football
19– George DeLong, wrestling
21– Pete Gotfryd, baseball
29– Jim Seyler, basketball

JANUARY 1925
23– George Dimit, football
30– Tom Zaborac, football

FEBRUARY 1925
12– William Mann, swimming
14– Robert Phelps, track
14– Ralph Serpico, football
16– Howard Judson, basketball/baseball

MARCH 1925
15– Robert Malley, baseball
27– Walter Linden, baseball
29– Chris Pagakis, football

APRIL 1925
2– Denman Bassett, baseball
10– Roy Wiedow, baseball
15– William Willis, football

MAY 1925
3– Robert Bischoff, Chief X

7– James Helbling, football
11- Robert Morton, basketball
13– Clyde Perkins, football
17– Phil Abramovich, wrestling
17– Joe Hayer, football
23– Aldo Martignago, football
27– Robert Bohannon, wrestling

JUNE 1925
11– George Mullins, swimming
20– Robert Branch, swimming
27– Ray Ward, football
29– Robert Menke, basketball

JULY 1925
12– Robert Burwell, wrestling
23– Dale Smith, golf

AUGUST 1925
16– Charles Leistner, football
26– Jerry Cies, football

Earl Britton, a letter winner in both football and basketball, kicked the very first 50-yard field goal in Illinois history.

Red Grange won the Big Ten's first-ever Silver Football Trophy.

THE *CHICAGO TRIBUNE* AWARDED the very first Silver Football Trophy to the University of Illinois' Red Grange following the 1924 season, honoring him as the Big Ten's Most Valuable Player. Grange rushed for a career-high 743 yards on only 113 carries and scored a school record 13 touchdowns.

ILLINI LISTS

ILLINI WHO PLAYED (OR COACHED) IN THE WORLD SERIES

- Fred "Cy" Falkenberg (1903, Pittsburgh)
- Garland "Jake" Stahl (1903, 1912-manager, Boston)
- Carl Lundgren (1906, 1907, 1908, Chicago)
- Frank Pfeffer (1910, Chicago)
- Wally Roettger (1928, St. Louis)
- Lou Boudreau (1948, Cleveland)
- John Brittin (1950, Philadelphia)
- Lou Skizas (1959, Chicago)
- Tom Haller (1962, San Francisco)
- Ed Spiezio (1964, 1967, 1968, St. Louis)
- Ken Holtzman (1972, 1973, 1974, Oakland)

Lou Skizas played with the Chicago White Sox in the 1959 World Series.

ILLINI LEGEND:

WALLY ROETTGER

Like George Huff and Carl Lundgren before him, the University of Illinois' Wally Roettger became the third consecutive Fighting Illini baseball coach to return to his alma mater. Roettger was an outstanding player at Illinois from 1922-24, with a career batting average over .300. As a junior in 1923 he hit .409, the fifth-best single-season average ever at that time. Major league scouts quickly noticed Roettger and, in six big-league seasons for his hometown St. Louis Cardinals, the New York Giants, and the Cincinnati Reds, he batted a respectable .277 in 468 games. Roettger also helped the Cardinals win the World Series title over the Philadelphia Athletics. He retired from the majors following the 1932 season to coach the baseball and basketball teams at Illinois Wesleyan. In 1934, Roettger's life changed dramatically when Carl Lundgren, his mentor at Illinois, died suddenly of a heart attack. It didn't take long for Fighting Illini athletic director George Huff to choose Lundgren's successor. In the next 17 years, Roettger won four Big Ten titles and finished among the top three eight other times; his record with the Illini baseball team was 212-111-7. However, all was not well with Roettger, and in 1951, he took his own life at the age of 49.

Illini Lore

In the fall of 1924, the University of Illinois' Alumni Association conducted a random survey of its graduates, polling them regarding their occupations, their incomes, and their spending habits. Of the 264 people who responded, the survey concluded that the alumnus' average annual income was $7,031. Graduates who went on to become manufacturers led the way with an average yearly salary of $27,100, followed by architects ($14,960), physicians ($13,831), and bankers ($12,014). One-hundred-eight of the 264 respondents owned their homes, while 86 were renters. Those who owned automobiles preferred Fords (47), a choice nearly three times the total of the second-most preferred cars, Buicks and Dodges (17 each).

60 YEARS OF ILLINI TRADITION

KAM'S

Yesterday & TODAY

The meeting place for students and alumni!

FOOTBALL
UNIVERSITY OF ILLINOIS

MEMORIAL
STADIUM

Oct. 3 - Nebraska $2.

Oct. 10 - Butler $2.
(No reserved seats)

Oct. 24 - Michigan $2.50
(Homecoming)

Nov. 7 - Chicago $2.50
(Dads Day)

Nov. 14 - Wabash $1.50
(No reserved seats)

Grange

Mail orders to Football Ticket Office, Urbana
Tickets in Chicago at The Hub

C. B. Bradbury

1925-1934

1925-26

- **Sept. 3, 1925:** *The U.S. Army dirigible Shenandoah was wrecked in a storm near Ava, Ohio, killing 14 people.*
- **Oct. 15, 1925:** *Baseball's World Series was won by the Pittsburgh Pirates in seven games over the Washington Senators.*
- **March 7, 1926:** *The American Telephone and Telegraph Company successfully demonstrated the first transatlantic radiotelephone conversation between New York City and London.*
- **May 9, 1926:** *Rear Admiral Richard Byrd made the first successful flight over the North Pole.*
- **Aug. 6, 1926:** *Nineteen-year-old Gertrude Ederle of New York City became the first woman to swim the English Channel.*

I·L·L·I·N·I M·O·M·E·N·T

Red Grange (about to cross the 40-yard line) quieted his Eastern critics with a 237-yard performance against Pennsylvania.

ILLINI GRIDDERS VICTORIOUS AT PENN:

Red Grange's most famous college football game, of course, was his 1924 dismantling of Michigan at Memorial Stadium. But just as impressive was his performance on October 31, 1925, against the powerful University of Pennsylvania, gridiron rulers of the East. Bolstered by the 160-man UI marching band who had made the cross-country trip to Philadelphia, Coach Bob Zuppke's Illini handed their hosts a stunning 24-2 loss. The muddy Franklin Field turf didn't slow down Grange, who rushed for 237 yards on 28 carries, the best performance of his career. Besides scoring three touchdowns, Grange returned two kickoffs for 79 yards and caught two passes for 35 yards. Wrote Walter Eckersall of the *Chicago Tribune* afterwards, "Whatever doubt there was in the minds of Eastern gridiron critics and coaches regarding the quality of Red Grange was settled once and for all today."

ILLINI BIRTHDAYS

SEPTEMBER 1925
4– Arthur Gerometta, football
22– John Johns, baseball

OCTOBER 1925
7– Chester Sainai, football
9– Tommy Stewart, football
18– Dick Foley, basketball
21– George Leddy, basketball
31– Jack Curry, football

NOVEMBER 1925
1– Herschel Kearney, football
24– Tony Klimek, football

DECEMBER 1925
2– Burt Schmidt, football
4– Eddie Bray, football
6– Henry Anderssohn, baseball
26– Alfred Parfitt, football

JANUARY 1926
5– Claude "Buddy" Young, football/track
6– Stan Sprague, football
9– Joe Fina, gymnastics
12– Bernie Krueger, football
20– Ralph Bassey, football

FEBRUARY 1926
3– Les Bingaman, football
4– Walt Versen, football
13– Tom Hoffman, baseball
15– Robert Hinkle, football
20– Bob Richards, track
23– Wallie Mroz, basketball

MARCH 1926
4– John Brittin, baseball
16– Russell "Ruck" Steger, football/baseball

APRIL 1926
12– Louis Possehl, baseball
14– Gordon Gillespie, baseball

MAY 1926
16– Jack Pierce, football

JUNE 1926
14– Paul Furimsky, football
26– Robert Cunz, football

JULY 1926
8– Cirilo McSween, football
26– Robert "Bunker" Jones, football
28– Donald Janssen, football
29– Don Pittman, football

AUGUST 1926
4– Perry Moss, football

9– Albert Zimmerman, football
26– Jim Marks, basketball
27– Charles Smith, football

During his distinguished career, Cirilo McSween helped lead the Fighting Illini track team to six Big Ten titles. Born on July 8, 1926, McSween sprinted his way to 33 first-place finishes. He's now a successful entrepreneur in Chicago.

TWO DAYS AFTER his final game with the University of Illinois football team—November 23, 1925—"Red" Grange signed a $100,000 contract to play football for Coach George Halas' fledgling Chicago Bears. Including his royalties for endorsements, Grange was reportedly making thousands of dollars per week during his peak, but he asked his agent, C.C. Pyle, to limit him to a drawing account of a flat $100 a week.

Promoter C.C "Cash & Carry" Pyle helped turn Red Grange into one of sports' first successful endorsers.

IF ILLINI ATHLETES WERE KNOWN BY THEIR MOTHER'S MAIDEN NAME

- Red Sherman (Grange)
- Dike Snyder (Eddleman)
- Craig Putt (Virgin)
- Lou Faulconer (Henson)
- Lou Deglau (Tepper)
- Ray Bulgin (Nusspickle), later changed name to his middle name, Eliot

Eliot was actually Ray Nusspickle's middle name.

ILLINI LEGEND:

TIM O'CONNELL

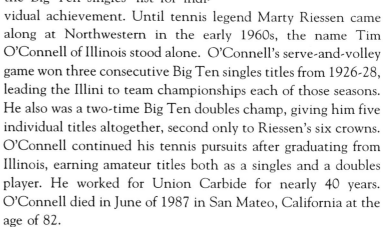

The University of Illinois' tennis program has enjoyed only moderate team success during its history, but one Fighting Illini player still tops the Big Ten singles' list for individual achievement. Until tennis legend Marty Riessen came along at Northwestern in the early 1960s, the name Tim O'Connell of Illinois stood alone. O'Connell's serve-and-volley game won three consecutive Big Ten singles titles from 1926-28, leading the Illini to team championships each of those seasons. He also was a two-time Big Ten doubles champ, giving him five individual titles altogether, second only to Riessen's six crowns. O'Connell continued his tennis pursuits after graduating from Illinois, earning amateur titles both as a singles and a doubles player. He worked for Union Carbide for nearly 40 years. O'Connell died in June of 1987 in San Mateo, California at the age of 82.

Illini Lore

The University of Illinois' "New Gymnasium," later to be known as Huff Gym, opened for business with a basketball game between the Illini and Butler, December 12, 1925. The building was completed at a cost of $500,000—20 cents per cubic foot. A $225,000 south wing, which included a swimming pool, was added a year later. Huff Gym had a capacity of 7,000, double the size of its predecessor, the Men's Old Gym Annex. From 1925 through 1963, when the Assembly Hall opened, Illini basketball teams compiled a record of 339 victories against only 121 losses at Huff Gym.

RED GRANGE: An Original Superstar

*T*he legend of Harold "Red" Grange and his contributions to the University of Illinois and American society are almost larger than life. Here are some rarely seen photographs of the most famous Fighting Illini athlete of all time, along with some of the people he touched during his 87 years.

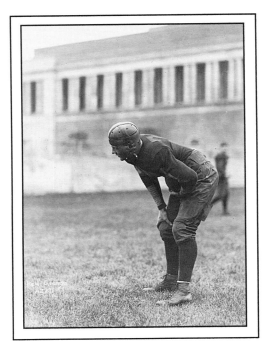

Red Grange, shown here on the practice field east of Memorial Stadium, was one of the heroes of America's Golden Era of Sports.

Centerfielder Red Grange batted a paltry .091 for Coach Carl Lundgren's 1924 Illinois baseball team.

The famed Wheaton Iceman struck this pose for a 1920s publicity photo.

Resplendent in the garb of the 1920s, this was one of the final photos taken of Red Grange as a University of Illinois student. He served as a member of the University's Board of Trustees from 1951-55.

Babe Ruth (right) met Red Grange for the first time in a New York City hotel room during the Chicago Bears' 1925-26 barnstorming tour. The Bambino said, "Kid, I want to give you two pieces of advice: Don't pay any attention to what they say or write about you. And don't pick up too many checks."

Red Grange worked in the broadcast booth for 29 years, including several seasons with his long-time partner Lindsey Nelson.

A memorial to Illinois' Galloping Ghost, dedicated in 1994, stands at the north end of Zuppke Field.

The Red Grange Archives are featured at the DuPage County Heritage Gallery in Wheaton, Illinois.

Red Grange visited Champaign and his old Illini coach, Bob Zuppke (right), in this 1948 photograph.

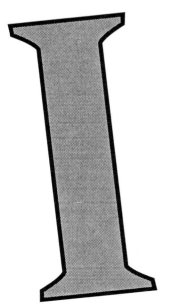

Red Grange, shown here at his Florida home, on his 77th birthday, June 13, 1980.

1926-27

I·L·L·I·N·I M·O·M·E·N·T

CHIEF ILINIWEK DEBUTS:

The first appearance of the University of Illinois' symbol, Chief Illiniwek, was October 30, 1926, at Memorial Stadium. UI assistant marching band director Ray Dvorak is credited with starting the tradition, which officially began at halftime of the 1926 Illinois-Pennsylvania football game. Sophomore Lester Leutwiler, a UI student interested in Indian lore, was selected as the first Chief. In his recollection of that first performance, Leutwiler wrote, "As the band marched into the formation (spelling out the word "Penn"), the Chief ran from a hiding place north of the Illinois stands and led the band with his frenzied dance. The band stopped in the center of the field and played 'Hail Pennsylvania' while the chief saluted the Penn rooters. William Penn, impersonated by George Adams (the Illinois drum major), came forward and accepted the gesture of friendship. Together, we smoked the peace pipe and walked arm in arm across the field to the Illinois side, amidst a deafening ovation." Leutwiler's performance was so well received that he was asked to continue his performances at Fighting Illini football games.

ILLINI BIRTHDAYS

SEPTEMBER 1926
24– Donald Johnson, football
29– Pete Elliott, football coach

OCTOBER 1926
15– Emil Tomanek, football

NOVEMBER 1926
3– Roland Harkness, wrestling
4– Frank Dolan, gymnastics
8– Walt Kersulis, football & basketball

DECEMBER 1926
12– Frank Hurtte, football
20– Robert Dwyer, wrestling
23– Jack Burmaster, basketball

JANUARY 1927
5– Jim Kilbane, baseball
23– Robert Malinsky, football
27– Rudy Macchione, football

FEBRUARY 1927
28– Victor Twomey, track

MARCH 1927
27– Roger Little, tennis

APRIL 1927
19– Pete Fletcher, golf
19– Gerry Kaires, baseball

MAY 1927
13– Sam Piazza, football

JUNE 1927
10– Johnny Orr, football/basketball
27– Gene Buwick, tennis

JULY 1927
27– Gil Gaumer, wrestling

AUGUST 1927
4– Jim Moses, tennis
6– Paul Patterson, football
19– Amos Jones, football
29– Bob Anderlik, baseball
30– Don Ellis, football

Johnny Orr, born June 10, 1927, lettered in both football and basketball, and played baseball at Illinois. He became better known as a successful basketball coach at Michigan and Iowa State.

ILLINI ITEM

ILLINI LISTS

CHIEF ILLINIWEK FACTS

- Total number of Chief Illiniweks: 31 (as of 1994-95)
- First Chief Illiniwek: Lester Leutwiler, 1926
- First Chief to appear in authentic American Indian regalia: Webber Borchers, 1930
- First female Chief (Princess): Idelle Stith, 1943
- First brothers to perform as Chief: John Forsyth, 1957-59 & Ben Forsyth, 1960-63
- First father-son to perform as Chief: Robert Bitzer, 1945-46 & John Bitzer, 1970-73
- Most common home states of Chiefs: Illinois (25 times) & Missouri (four times)

Chief Mike Gonzalez met UI's first Chief Illiniwek, Lester Leutwiler, September 25, 1976.

ILLINI LEGEND:

BERNIE SHIVELY

When a list of the University of Illinois' finest all-around athletes is compiled, the name Bernie Shively always appears. Perhaps most famous as a guard running interference for the immortal Red Grange, Shively was selected as the Fighting Illini's eighth consensus All-America football player following the 1926 season. He was inducted into the College Football Hall of Fame in 1982. The former prep star from Paris, Illinois, also excelled on the wrestling mat, grappling to a draw with his heavyweight opponent from Indiana in the 1926 Big Ten championship match, but losing on a coin toss. Shively also was a three-time letterwinner for the UI track and field squad, placing twice in conference championship competition as a hammer thrower. Altogether, he won eight varsity letters at Illinois. Following his graduation in 1927, Shively began a distinguished career at the University of Kentucky, culminating in a 30-year career as director of athletics. He died in 1967 at the age of 64.

Illini Lore

 amed sculptor Lorado Taft laid the cornerstone for the new $500,000 University of Illinois architecture building, November 16, 1926. In Taft's remarks at the ceremony, he paid homage to Professor Nathan C. Ricker, the father of Illinois architecture. The structure, located at the south end of the campus, brought together the instructors of not only architecture, but also of art, design, sculpture, and other branches of the fine arts. The site of the three-story structure was formerly an apple orchard.

1927-28

America's Time Capsule

- **Sept. 30, 1927:** *Babe Ruth slugged his record-setting 60th home run for the New York Yankees.*
- **Oct. 6, 1927:** *The world's first talking motion picture—The Jazz Singer—using the sound-on-film process was released. The movie was based on a play by Illinois alumnus Samson Raphaelson.*
- **Nov. 13, 1927:** *The Holland Tunnel, America's first underwater tunnel, was opened to traffic, linking New Jersey with Manhattan. Its ventilation system was designed by Illinois professor Arthur Willard.*
- **May 25, 1928:** *Amelia Earhart became the first woman to fly an airplane across the Atlantic.*
- **July 30, 1928:** *George Eastman demonstrated the world's first color motion pictures at Rochester, New York.*

I·L·L·I·N·I M·O·M·E·N·T

ILLINI GRIDDERS CLAIM THE NATIONAL CHAMPIONSHIP:
A rock-ribbed defense was the hallmark of Coach Bob Zuppke's 1927 University of Illinois national championship football team. In five of its eight games, the Fighting Illini defensive unit had shutout efforts, while in two other games, it yielded only a single touchdown. A 12-12 tie with Iowa State was Illinois' only flaw. The stars of Zuppke's team included All-America linemen Bob Reitsch, Russ Crane, and "Butch" Nowack. Among the key performers on the steady but unspectacular offensive team were backs Doug Mills, Frank Walker, and Fred Humbert, and end Jud Timm. Illinois' 5-0 Big Ten Conference record was good for first place ahead of 3-0-1 Minnesota.

ILLINI BIRTHDAYS

SEPTEMBER 1927
- 1– Robert Lunn, football
- 3– Art Schankin, fencing
- 11– Richard Loewe, wrestling
- 12– Robert Doster, basketball
- 15– Don Scherwat, swimming
- 18– Fred Ballantine, baseball

OCTOBER 1927
- 8– Arthur Wyatt, golf
- 14– Merle Schlosser, football
- 17– Louis Stuebe, fencing
- 18– Marv Rotblatt, baseball
- 23– Cal Luther, assistant basketball coach
- 25– John Marks, basketball

NOVEMBER 1927
- 1– John Gugala, baseball

- 17– Richard Weik, baseball

DECEMBER 1927
- 21– Robert Prymuski, football

JANUARY 1928
- 23– Herbert Agase, baseball
- 25– Ray McClure, basketball
- 25– Jim Valek, football
- 27– John Karras, football

MARCH 1928
- 2– Dwight Humphrey, basketball
- 15– Gene Kenney, wrestling

MAY 1928
- 24– Stan Feldman, baseball

JUNE 1928
- 9– Al Brosky, football
- 14– Herb Plews, baseball
- 19– Charles Brown, football
- 25– Harold Smith, golf
- 30– Dick Raklovits, football

JULY 1928
- 6– Walt Osterkorn, basketball
- 14– Dick Campbell, assistant basketball coach
- 30– Leo Cahill, football

Illinois' Dave Abbott was a two-time NCAA track champion in 1928 and '29 in the two-mile run.

All-America lineman "Butch" Nowack and his coach, Bob Zuppke

ILLINI ITEM

THE FIGHTING ILLINI FOOTBALL TEAM made a trip to Evanston, Illinois, October 22, 1927, to take on the Northwestern Wildcats at NU's brand-new Dyche Stadium. Illinois defeated Northwestern, 7-6, on a Bud Jolley touchdown and "Butch" Nowack's successful point after touchdown. The Illini victory snapped a seven-game Wildcat winning streak.

ILLINI LISTS

ILLINI ATHLETES WHO LATER BECAME UI ATHLETIC DIRECTORS

	Years as UI athlete	Years as UI A.D.
George A. Huff	1890-93	1896-1935
Wendell S. Wilson	1924-26	1936-41
Douglas R. Mills	1926-30	1941-66
E.E. (Gene) Vance	1942-47	1967-72
Raymond Eliot (interim)	1929-31	1979
Ronald E. Guenther	1963-66	1992-present

Athletic Director Gene Vance

ILLINI LEGEND:

ALLIE MORRISON

One of the University of Illinois' greatest athletes in the sport of wrestling was Allie Morrison, the gold medalist at 135 pounds at the 1928 Olympic Games in Amsterdam. A native of Marshalltown, Iowa, Morrison was unbeaten as a 135-pound Fighting Illini wrestler from 1928-30, compiling a perfect 22-0 record. He also won three consecutive national AAU individual titles. Team-wise, his three Illini squads won two Big Ten championships (1928 and '30) and finished second once (1929). He began a long coaching career immediately afterwards. Among his coaching stops were Penn State and Doane College, then at the high school level in Omaha, Nebraska, where he produced four state titles in five years. A member of the Helms Foundation Amateur Wrestling Hall of Fame, Morrison died in 1966 at the age of 62.

Illini Lore

During the fall of 1927, St. John's Catholic Church was completed at the corner of Sixth Street and Armory Avenue. The church accommodated a congregation of between 1,500 to 2,000 and featured marble altars from Italy and stained glass windows from Germany. UI band leader Ray Dvorak served as the church's organist and choir director. Two additional residence halls, comprised of 180 rooms for 360 male students, were attached to the church. The Reverend Monsignor Edward Duncan has served as chaplain to the Catholic students and director of the Newman Foundation since October, 1943.

1928-29

• **Oct. 9, 1928:** *The St. Louis Cardinals were swept in four straight games by the New York Yankees at the World Series.*

• **Nov. 6, 1928:** *In a landslide Republican victory, Herbert Hoover defeated Alfred Smith for the presidency of the United States.*

• **Feb. 14, 1929:** *The mass murder known as the St. Valentine's Day Massacre took place on Chicago's North Side.*

• **May 16, 1929:** *"Wings" was selected as the best picture at the first Academy Awards.*

• **June 30, 1929:** *Bobby Jones won the U.S. Open golf tournament over runner-up Al Espinosa.*

Illini quarterback Frosty Peters scored UI's only touchdown vs. Ohio State in 1928.

I·L·L·I·N·I M·O·M·E·N·T

ILLINI CLINCH BIG TEN FOOTBALL TITLE WITH VICTORY OVER OHIO STATE:

November 24th, 1928, was a day when Illinois' football team needed all the "ifs" to come true, and that's exactly what happened. Coach Bob Zuppke's Fighting Illini and Ohio State entered the 1928 season finale at Memorial Stadium with identical 3-1 conference records, one-half game behind undefeated Wisconsin. The combatants would not only need a victory over the other, but also a win by Minnesota over the league-leading Badgers. After the dust had settled, the unlikely scenario played out perfectly to the Illini's advantage, as Illinois beat OSU, 8-0, and the Gophers beat Wisconsin, 6-0. That combination of results allowed Illinois to finish atop the Western Conference standings with a 4-1 record, its second consecutive league title. "Frosty" Peters scored the only Illini touchdown of the afternoon late in the first half on a quarterback sneak.

ILLINI BIRTHDAYS

SEPTEMBER 1928
22– Burdette Thurlby, basketball

OCTOBER 1928
31– Bob Nicollette, trainer

DECEMBER 1928
21– Thomas Murphy, football

JANUARY 1929
13– Charles Fox, football
17– Chuck Studley, football
26– Gerald Johnson, track

FEBRUARY 1929
4– Donald Smith, football
5– Bob Gambold, assistant football coach
7– Charles Reitsch, swimming

13– Robert Forsythe, fencing

APRIL 1929
7– Paul Douglass, football
26– Ted Beach, basketball
30– Marshall Smith, football

MAY 1929
17– Bill Vohaska, football
21– Don Laz, track
22– Ron Heberer, baseball

JUNE 1929
4– Ron Clark, football
20– Fred Major, football

AUGUST 1929
10– Lynn Lynch, football
23– John Vayda, baseball

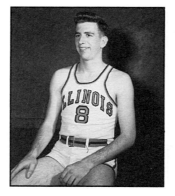 

Ted Beach (left), born April 26, 1929, and Chuck Studley, born January 17, 1929, went on to become prominent athletes at the University of Illinois.

*I*LLINI *I*TEM

Joe Sapora was one of Illinois' first two NCAA wrestling champions.

UNIVERSITY OF ILLINOIS WRESTLERS Joe Sapora and George Minot won individual titles at the second annual NCAA championship, held in Columbus, Ohio. Sapora, a 115-pounder, and Minot, at 135 pounds, were Illinois' first two NCAA wrestling champs.

ILLINI LISTS

ILLINOIS' SPORTS INFORMATION DIRECTORS

1922-43	L.M. "Mike" Tobin
1943-56	Charles "Chuck" Flynn
1956-70	Charles "Charlie" Bellatti
1970-74	Norm Sheya
1974-89	Tab Bennett
1980-85	Lani Jacobsen (women's SID)
1985-87	Tom Boeh (women's SID)
1987-89	Mary Fowler (women's SID)
1989-present	Mike Pearson

Former Sports Information Directors (left to right) Charlie Bellatti, Chuck Flynn, and Tab Bennett

ILLINI LEGEND:

L. M. "MIKE" TOBIN

The greatest of Fighting Illini fans can easily recite the legends of "Red" Grange and the "Whiz Kids," but nary a one probably knows L.M. "Mike" Tobin, the man whose diligent work made those athletes household names. The Danville, Illinois, native was the first full-time collegiate athletic publicitor in the country, and it was his initial task to spread the word about a red-headed youngster from Wheaton who became the most famous collegiate football player ever—Red Grange. For more than 20 years from his tiny office in Huff Gymnasium, Tobin pounded out thousands of stories about the Illini on his manual typewriter. Every sportswriter in the Midwest relied upon Tobin to supply them with information about the nationally prominent University of Illinois athletic program. Upon Tobin's death in 1944 at the age of 64, Bob Zuppke said that Illinois had lost "its most loyal of loyal friends. We owe him more than we ever could have repaid."

 Illini Lore

Lorado Taft's Alma Mater Statue, the $25,000 gift of the University of Illinois classes from 1923-29, was formally dedicated June 12, 1929. Originally located just south of the Auditorium, the statue was moved to the Altgeld Hall lawn in August of 1962. The central figure of the three-figure bronze, inspired by Daniel Chester French's "Alma Mater" at Columbia University, welcomes visitors to the Urbana-Champaign campus. The figures at the rear, their hands clasped, represent learning and labor. Inscribed at the statue's granite base are the words, "To thy happy children of the future, those of the past send greetings."

1929-30

I·L·L·I·N·I M·O·M·E·N·T

Fred Siebert (second from left), Otto Haier (sixth from left), and "Doc" Gross (second from right) all won Big Ten fencing titles in 1930.

"PERFECT" ILLINI WIN BIG TEN FENCING CHAMPIONSHIP: Everything went "perfectly" for Coach H.W. Craig's Fighting Illini fencing team at the Western Conference's 1930 fencing championships in Chicago. Not only did Craig's squad capture the team title, all three of the young men who accompanied him on the trip to Chicago came home individual champions. Shattering all conference records as well as their own, the Illini fencing triumvirate of Otto Haier, Fred Siebert, and Chalmer "Doc" Gross recorded the league's first perfect score—a 15. Captain Haier won the foil title, his second consecutive crown in that weapon; Siebert was king of the epeeists, and Gross finished first among the sabremen. It was the second in a string of five consecutive team titles for the Illini fencers.

ILLINI BIRTHDAYS

SEPTEMBER 1929
5– Richard Jenkins, football
9– Richard Mueller, football

OCTOBER 1929
6– Phil Krueger, assistant football coach

NOVEMBER 1929
15– Betsy Kimpel, women's golf coach
23– Laurence Stevens, football
29– Norton Compton, wrestling
30– Wayne Gaumer, wrestling

DECEMBER 1929
14– Chuck Ulrich, football
20– Don Sunderlage, basketball
28– Marvin Berschet, football

28– Vince D'Orazio, fencing

JANUARY 1930
1– Rod Fletcher, basketball
17– Herb Neatherly, football
20– Floyd McAfee, football

FEBRUARY 1930
4– Don Gnidovic, football
6– Dick Tamburo, assistant athletic director
22– Ralph Valentino, football

MARCH 1930
4– Bob Rylowicz, football
8– Chuck Boerio, football
10– Dan Peterson, football
17– Louis Krantz, baseball

28– William Hug, Chief XII

APRIL 1930
14– Jorge Quiros, fencing
18– Donald Clooney, swimming

MAY 1930
27– Mack Follmer, basketball

JUNE 1930
1– Jim Schuldt, basketball
6– Al Tate, football
20– Sammy Rebecca, football

JULY 1930
20– Bernie Elsner, football
20– John Vukelich, football
24– Richard Reynolds, track

AUGUST 1930
4– Joe Brewer, baseball
18– Gene Bartow, basketball coach
29– Bruce Sublette, fencing

Sammy "The Toe" Rebecca, born June 20, 1930, scored Illinois' only points in his team's 3-0 victory over Northwestern in 1951, a win that clinched UI's berth in the 1952 Rose Bowl. Rebecca went on to a successful career in administration at his alma mater.

Illinois captain Russ Crane shakes hands with the Army captain before the 1929 match-up.

ILLINI ITEM

ON NOVEMBER 9, 1929, underdog Illinois up-ended powerful Army, 17-7, before a crowd of nearly 70,000 in the first match-up between the two teams. Illinois' Arnold Wolgost scored the eventual game-winning touchdown on a 75-yard dash from scrimmage, while the Illini defense completely corralled Army's future Hall of Famer "Red" Cagle.

ILLINI LISTS

ILLINOIS' FIRST AFRICAN-AMERICAN MALE ATHLETES

- 1904   Football (Roy Young)
- 1904   Track & Field (Hiram Hanibal Wheeler)
- 1929   Tennis (Douglas Turner)
- 1947   Swimming (Ralph Hines)
- 1950   Fencing (John Cameron)
- 1951   Basketball (Walt Moore)
- 1963   Wrestling (Al McCullum)
- 1965   Baseball (Trenton Jackson)
- 1982   Gymnastics (Charles Lakes)

Roy Young (left) was Illinois' first African-American football player, while Ralph Hines was UI's first African-American swimmer.

ILLINI LEGEND:

DOUG MILLS

The 40-year athletic career of Doug Mills at the University of Illinois must be discussed in three different chapters: as an athlete, as a coach, and as an administrator. From 1927-30, Mills' career as a football and basketball athlete was highlighted by both individual and team success. He was a two-time all-conference basketball player and a three-year letterman on the gridiron, leading his teammates to a pair of Big Ten football titles. As a coach, Mills guided the Illini cagers to three conference championships in 11 seasons. Illini basketball reached its peak with Mills shortly before World War II, when four in-state athletes—Gene Vance, Ken Menke, Andy Phillip, and Jack Smiley—formed the nucleus of a team that was known simply as the "Whiz Kids." Following the 1946-47 season, Mills "retired" from the coaching ranks to devote his time full-time as Illinois' athletic director, a job he inherited in 1941 at the age of 33. The last years of Mills' administration were marred by a Big Ten investigation, and he gave up his post in November, 1966. He died on August 12, 1983, at the age of 75.

Illini Lore

The University of Illinois' Library Building was dedicated October 18, 1929. The library was constructed in three sections and cost a total of $1.75 million. At that time, the facility contained more than 758,000 volumes and nearly 157,000 pamphlets. In 1994-95, the library houses nearly nine million volumes.

1930-31

America's Time Capsule

- **Sept. 27, 1930:** *Bobby Jones became the first player to capture golf's Grand Slam when he won the U.S. Amateur tournament.*
- **Dec. 11, 1930:** *The powerful Bank of the United States closed in New York City, due to the deepening economic crisis.*
- **Jan. 7, 1931:** *The President's Emergency Committee for Unemployment Relief announced that between four and five million Americans were out of work.*
- **March 3, 1931:** *President Herbert Hoover signed a congressional act making "The Star Spangled Banner" the USA's national anthem.*
- **May 1, 1931:** *The Empire State Building, the world's tallest building, opened in New York City.*

I·L·L·I·N·I M·O·M·E·N·T

Coach Zuppke (left) and running back Gil Berry.

A "BERRY" GOOD PERFORMANCE:

A young sophomore halfback from Abingdon, Illinois, wearing the number "7" on his back, stole the show for Illinois' football team on October 11, 1930, reminding fans of a redhead named Grange who had galloped the Memorial Stadium turf just five years before. Though he didn't wind up his career with as much acclaim as his famous predecessor, Gilbert Berry—for one game, at least—showed ghost-like moves on that cool autumn afternoon. His touchdown runs of 60 and 80 yards led the Fighting Illini to a 27-0 shutout of Butler. Berry touched the ball only 19 times for 227 yards of total offense. Rushing-wise, he averaged better than 20 yards per carry, gaining 183 yards on nine attempts. The Illini victory would turn out to be one of only three for Coach Bob Zuppke's club that season.

ILLINI BIRTHDAYS

SEPTEMBER 1930
8– Al Dierkes, baseball
13– Frank Bare, gymnastics
26– Tommy O'Connell, football

OCTOBER 1930
6– Dan Sabino, football
7– Robert Bennorth, tennis
21– Ted Flora, assistant baseball coach
23– Joe Vernasco, football

NOVEMBER 1930
4– Elie Popa, football
7– George Kasap, football
14– Dale Smith, football
18– Irv Bemoras, basketball

DECEMBER 1930
7– Jim Pendleton, swimming

16– Joe Cole, football
17– Donald Engels, football
22– Marshall Dusenbury, football
29– Pete Bachouros, football
30– Frank Wodziak, football

JANUARY 1931
6– Allen Mills, fencing
26– Bob Weddell, football

FEBRUARY 1931
17– Jim Catlin, football
20– Steve Nosek, football

MARCH 1931
6– Carl Ahrens, baseball
11– Jerry Baranski, baseball
13– Nicholas Szluha, fencing
26– Percy Oliver, football

APRIL 1931
20– Elry Falkenstein, football

MAY 1931
24– Max Baumgardner, basketball

JUNE 1931
11– Stacey Siders, track
12– Arthur Andrew, wrestling
23– Richard Broerman, football

JULY 1931
20– Bob Twardock, track

Junior cager Elbert "Babe" Kamp led Illinois to a 35-28 victory over Northwestern, February 16, 1931. Kamp's 15-point effort helped the Illini hand the Wildcats their only loss of the 1931 Big Ten season.

ILLINI ITEM

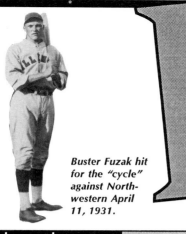

Buster Fuzak hit for the "cycle" against Northwestern April 11, 1931.

COACH CARL LUNDGREN'S Fighting Illini baseball team won its Big Ten season opener April 11, 1931, crushing Northwestern, 15-4, at Illinois Field. The hitting star for the Illini was senior Buster Fuzak, who hit for the cycle against the Wildcats. Fuzak connected for a single, a double, two triples, and a home run, while scoring three runs himself.

ILLINI LISTS

ILLINI CODE OF SPORTSMANSHIP

In 1930, George Huff, Director of Athletics at the University of Illinois, instituted the Illini Code of Sportsmanship.

A true Illini sportsman ...
1. Will consider all athletic opponents as guests and treat them with all of the courtesy due to friends and guests.
2. Will accept all decisions of officials without question.
3. Will never hiss or boo a player or official.
4. Will never utter abusive or irritating remarks from the sideline.
5. Will applaud opponents who make good plays or show good sportsmanship.
6. Will never attempt to rattle an opposing player.
7. Will seek to win by fair and lawful means, according to the rules of the game.
8. Will love the game for its own sake and not for what winning may bring him.
9. Will 'do unto others as he would have them do unto him.'
10. Will 'win without boasting and lose without excuses.'

UI Athletic Director George Huff instituted the Illini Code of Sportsmanship in 1930.

ILLINI LEGEND:

DICK MARTIN

While Walter Hagen and Bobby Jones were dominating professional golf, the kingpin of the Big Ten Conference was Illinois' Dick Martin. A letterman for Coach J.H. Utley's Fighting Illini from 1929-31, Martin captured conference medalist honors as a junior in 1930 at Westmoreland Country Club in Evanston, winning by one stroke, and leading his teammates to the Big Ten title. As senior, he again was the Big Ten medalist, but he had to come from behind to do so. Martin entered the final round five strokes behind Ohio State's Johnny Florio. He played through a continual downpour to pass Florio on the 12th hole, then had birdies on his final two holes to pull away. Once again, the Illini won the team title, by five strokes over host Michigan. Both years, Illinois placed fifth at the NCAA Championships. Martin probably would have won three consecutive Big Ten titles, but Illinois did not compete in the conference meet his sophomore year due to finals scheduled on the day of the meet. Martin has been "lost" in the Alumni Association's records since graduation.

 Illini Lore

Dr. Harry Woodburn Chase assumed duties as the sixth president of the University of Illinois, July 5, 1930, taking over from David Kinley. He came from the University of North Carolina where he had served as president from 1919-30. Chase was called to take over administration at the Urbana-Champaign campus during a time that a major construction program was ending. Construction on campus during his tenure included Freer Gymnasium, the Ice Skating Rink, and the president's residence. Chase resigned July 1, 1933, to become chancellor of New York University.

1931-32

I·L·L·I·N·I M·O·M·E·N·T

Cas Bennett (front row, left) and Red Owen (front row, fourth from left) were the Illini heroes in a 1932 victory over Purdue.

ILLINI CAGERS DERAIL BOILERMAKERS:

Purdue ruled Big Ten basketball during the 1930s, but the Fighting Illini teams of Coach Craig Ruby always seemed to have the Boilermakers' number. Such was the case on January 9, 1932, when Illinois beat Purdue, 28-21, at the New Gym (soon to be called Huff Gym). Ward "Piggy" Lambert's Boilers showed a perfect 6-0 record coming into the game, relying on a fast-break style of play. However, Illinois' defense applied the breaks to the Boilermaker express in the first half, claiming a 19-5 lead at halftime. Purdue All-American Johnny Wooden, who later became college basketball's most dominant coach at UCLA, led a strong comeback by scoring a game-high 10 points. However, the Illini held on to win, behind the sterling play of Cas Bennett and "Red" Owen. The loss would turn out to be the only blemish in 18 games for Purdue that season, ending with a 17-1 record.

ILLINI BIRTHDAYS

SEPTEMBER 1931
1– Dick Kohlagen, football
9– Bill Tate, football
12– Willie Williams, track
20- Peter Palmer, football

OCTOBER 1931
1– Clive Follmer, basketball/baseball
11– Milton Brown, track
22– Jim Bredar, basketball
27– Jack Chamblin, football

NOVEMBER 1931
15– Stan Wallace, football
30– Ken Nordquist, wrestling

JANUARY 1932
5– Rex Smith, football
10– Lou Henson, basketball coach
21– John Cameron, fencing

FEBRUARY 1932
9– Robert Lutz, wrestling
25– Cliff Waldbeser, football

MARCH 1932
11– John Bauer, football
14– Bob Lenzini, football
20– Baird Stewart, football
25– Don Stevens, football

APRIL 1932
14– Ronald Ultes, baseball
24– Max Hooper, basketball/baseball

MAY 1932
2– James Baughman, football

JUNE 1932
2– Lou Skizas, baseball
2– Walter Vernasco, football
2– Emil Diewald, wrestling

6– Don Sammons, swimming coach
14– Herb Borman, football
25– Ken Swienton, football

JULY 1932
1– Joe Saban, football
5– John "Rocky" Ryan, football
12– Paul Luhrsen, football
17– John Kerr, basketball
19– Robert Clemons, swimming
22– Robert Bishop, football
22– Bruce Frazier, baseball
23– Ken Miller, football
23– Austin Duke, football
24– Jim Wright, basketball

AUGUST 1932
16– Conrad Woods, tennis
26– Clarence "Bud" DeMoss, football

28– Robert Kramp, swimming

Joe Puerta won a Big Ten wrestling title at 123 pounds in 1932.

Eddie Lejeck (fourth from left) won the Big Ten singles title, and he teamed up with Fred Hands (second from left) as doubles finalists.

ILLINI ITEM

ILLINOIS' 1932 MEN'S TENNIS TEAM shared the 1932 Big Ten Conference championship with Indiana in a showdown at Bloomington, Indiana, on May 18. Illini senior Eddie Lejeck beat Ohio State's Carl Dennison for the singles title, while he and Fred Hands were runners-up in doubles competition.

ILLINI LISTS

ILLINOIS' TOP TEN CAREER BASEBALL HITTERS

1.	Darrin Fletcher, 1985-87	.392
2.	Dave Payton, 1984-87	.374
3.	Tim Richardson, 1980-83	.372
4.	Herb Plews, 1947-50	.367
5.	Ed Tryban, 1930-32	.365
6.	Sean Mulligan, 1989-91	.364
7.	Ben Lewis, 1933-35	.361
8.	Mike Murawski, 1967-69	.356
9.	Larry Sutton, 1989-92	.351
10.	Bubba Smith, 1989-91	.343

Ed Tryban had a .365 career batting average from 1930-32 at Illinois.

ILLINI LEGEND:

CRAIG RUBY

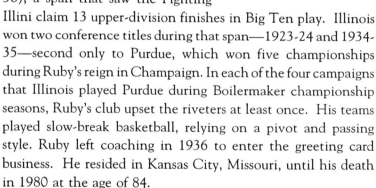

Known as one of the great basketball strategists of his time, Craig Ruby directed University of Illinois' basketball team for 14 years (1923-36), a span that saw the Fighting Illini claim 13 upper-division finishes in Big Ten play. Illinois won two conference titles during that span—1923-24 and 1934-35—second only to Purdue, which won five championships during Ruby's reign in Champaign. In each of the four campaigns that Illinois played Purdue during Boilermaker championship seasons, Ruby's club upset the riveters at least once. His teams played slow-break basketball, relying on a pivot and passing style. Ruby left coaching in 1936 to enter the greeting card business. He resided in Kansas City, Missouri, until his death in 1980 at the age of 84.

Illini Lore

James "Scotty" Reston, a 1932 graduate of the University of Illinois, is one of the school's most influential alumni. The native of Scotland worked as a student assistant in UI's sports information office and competed in varsity golf and soccer. Reston moved to the *New York Times* in 1939 following a seven-year stint with the Associated Press, becoming one of America's most noted journalists. *Time Magazine* said in a 1960 edition, "Politicians and other newsmen watch Reston's tone and are influenced by it." Reston won two Pulitzer prizes for national reporting. He retired as vice president of the *Times* in December of 1974.

1932-33

- **Oct. 2, 1932:** *The Chicago Cubs were swept in four straight games by the New York Yankees at the 29th annual World Series.*
- **Nov. 8, 1932:** *In a landslide victory over Herbert Hoover, Franklin Roosevelt was elected president of the United States.*
- **March 13, 1933:** *United States banks began to reopen across the country, following a prolonged depression.*
- **May 27, 1933:** *Chicago's Century of Progress Exposition began, in honor of that city's centennial celebration.*
- **July 6, 1933:** *Babe Ruth hit a home run at major league baseball's first all-star game, as the American League defeated the National League, 4-2, at Chicago's Comiskey Park.*

I·L·L·I·N·I M·O·M·E·N·T

Coach Zuppke (left) and quarterback Jack Beynon.

ILLINOIS GRIDDERS WIN DOUBLEHEADER:

The only football doubleheader in University of Illinois history was played at Memorial Stadium on October 1, 1932. Coach Bob Zuppke divided his squad into two entirely separate units, one playing the first half of both games and one playing the second half of both. In game one, Illinois cruised to a 20-7 victory over Miami of Ohio, thanks to a pair of touchdown passes from quarterback Jack Beynon to halfback Dave Cook. The "nightcap," which began at 3 p.m., resulted in a 13-0 shutout by the Fighting Illini over Coe College. Though they were blanked, Coe proved to be the tougher adversary of Illinois, shutting out their hosts for most of the first half. Pete Yanuskus' touchdown just before halftime proved to be the only score the Illini would need. The biggest disappointment was that only 4,568 fans showed up on that beautiful, 70-degree fall afternoon, causing the UI Athletic Association to incur a $3,600 loss after expenses.

ILLINI BIRTHDAYS

SEPTEMBER 1932
18– Jim Bell, fencing
18– John Greenleaf, tennis

OCTOBER 1932
7– Don Ernst, football
20– Ellis Rainsberger, football

NOVEMBER 1932
1– Vince Feigenbutz, baseball
24– Charles Fort, baseball
29– Gene Cherney, football

DECEMBER 1932
1– Dean Willmann, football
16– Robert Peterson, basketball
27– Richard Miller, football

JANUARY 1933
7– Victor Locascio, wrestling
17– J.C. Caroline, football
19– Marvin Graves, baseball

FEBRUARY 1933
16– Robert Gongola, football

MARCH 1933
31– Morris Sterneck, basketball

APRIL 1933
9– Bob Scott, football
25– Will Thomson, track

MAY 1933
5– Ed Makovsky, basketball

JUNE 1933
24– Jim Flynn, baseball
28– Steve Hill, tennis

JULY 1933
27– Harold Stafford, tennis

AUGUST 1933
12– Joe Fitzgerald, baseball
19– Frank Kastor, wrestling

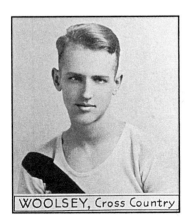

WOOLSEY, Cross Country

Illinois' Dean Woolsey won the individual title at the 1932 Big Ten cross country meet. Unfortunately, Indiana runners finished second, third, and fourth, and the Hoosiers edged the Illini for the team championship.

COACH HARRY GILL directed the Fighting Illini track and field squad for his 30th and final season in 1932-33. During those three decades, Gill directed Illinois' program to 11 Big Ten outdoor team championships and eight indoor titles.

ILLINI LISTS

MULTIPLE BIG TEN FENCING CHAMPIONS

Robert Tolman	3 titles (Foil: 1920-21; Sabre: 1921)
Ralph Epstein	3 titles (Foil: 1932-33-34)
Francis VanNatter	2 titles (Sabre: 1916; Epee: 1916)
Otto Haier	2 titles (Foil: 1929-30)
Fred Siebert	2 titles (Epee: 1930; Foil: 1931)
E. Perella	2 titles (Sabre: 1932-33)
William Chiprin	2 titles (Foil: 1935-42)
Herman Velasco	2 titles (Foil: 1954-56)
Larry Kauffman	2 titles (Epee: 1955-56)
Art Schankin	2 titles (Foil: 1957; Sabre: 1958)
Nate Haywood	2 titles (Epee: 1972-73)
Mark Snow	2 titles (Foil: 1981-82)
Eric Schicker	2 titles (Foil: 1986-87)

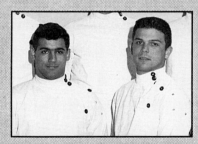

Herman "Pete" Velasco (left) and Larry Kauffman won two titles each in the mid 1950s.

ILLINI LEGEND:

RALPH EPSTEIN

The only fencer in Fighting Illini history to win Big Ten individual titles in three consecutive seasons was Ralph Epstein. The foil specialist from Chicago won championships in 1932, '33, and '34, leading Illinois to team honors during his sophomore and junior seasons. Epstein also was a standout in the classroom, becoming the 20th Illini athlete to be honored as the UI's Big Ten Conference Medal of Honor winner. As a serviceman in World War II, he helped the United States Air Corps design this nation's very first jet airplane. After the war, Epstein returned to the Chicago architectural engineering firm of Epstein & Sons International, where he retired as president. He died on August 11, 1986, at the age of 72.

 Illini Lore

On December 26, 1932, President Chase announced that the University of Illinois would reduce its legislative request for operating expenses by a million dollars, as compared to its last appropriation. Salaries of UI faculty and administrative staff were reduced by 10 percent, and deans and department heads were asked to boil down their budgets as never before. Ultimately, the state's appropriation to the University was reduced much more severely than expected. UI's $11.3 million budget during the 1931-32 and '32-33 school years was cut to $7.8 million during 1933-34 and '34-35, a reduction of 31 percent.

1933-34

I·L·L·I·N·I M·O·M·E·N·T

(Left to right) Fred Fencl, Chin Kamm, and Huddie Hellmich helped the Illini spoil Purdue's championship season.

ILLINI SPOIL BOILERS' CHAMPIONSHIP SEASON:

Coach "Piggy" Lambert's Purdue Boilermakers had wrapped up their Big Ten championship a few days before with a home-court victory over Indiana. So, perhaps they had little more than pride to play for when they came to Champaign on March 5, 1934, for the season finale against Illinois. The Illini, however, had a different outlook toward the game, hoping to send out their senior quartet of Huddie Hellmich, Fred Fencl, and Chin and Jake Kamm on a winning note against the 17-2 Boilermakers. The game was nip-and-tuck all the way, and came down to the final hair-raising 20 seconds. With the Illini ahead by one point, UI's Hellmich fouled Purdue All-American Ray Eddy. Fortunately, for Illinois, the Big Ten's individual scoring champion missed both of his free throws, allowing the Illini to escape with a 27-26 win.

ILLINI BIRTHDAYS

SEPTEMEBER 1933
- 2– Dale Foster, football
- 17– Jan Smid, football
- 18– Ray Essick, swimming
- 18– Ken West, golf
- 20– Rex Berry, baseball

OCTOBER 1933
- 2– Don Tate, football

NOVEMBER 1933
- 22– Merle Dunn, wrestling
- 28– George Gfoerer, swimming

DECEMBER 1933
- 12– George Gilmore, tennis
- 13– George Walsh, football
- 21– Roger Wolf, football
- 29– Bill Burrell, football

JANUARY 1934
- 15– Jim Dammann, fencing
- 15– Leroy Hunt, basketball coach
- 31– Larry Kauffman, fencing

FEBRUARY 1934
- 2– Bill Ridley, basketball
- 3– Charles Butler, football
- 24– Frank Schwartz, baseball
- 26– Bob Reitsch, golf
- 28– Arnold Cajet, swimming

MARCH 1934
- 1– Abie Grossfeld, gymnastics
- 9– Bruce Brothers, basketball
- 15– Jim Dutcher, basketball
- 19– Ron Yochem, football

APRIL 1934
- 10– Paul Judson, basketball/baseball
- 10– Phil Judson, basketball/baseball
- 13– Don Grothe, football
- 28– Larry TenPas, wrestling

MAY 1934
- 3– Jim Bickhaus, baseball
- 7– Dan Dudas, baseball
- 21– Bill Frentz, baseball

JUNE 1934
- 13– L.T. Bonner, football
- 17– Melvin "Mickey" Bates, football
- 29– Elmer Koestner, baseball

JULY 1934
- 8– Pete Velasco, fencing

AUGUST 1934
- 9– Herbert Badal, football
- 15– Rudy Siegert, football
- 31– Bob DesEnfants, football

Four members of Coach Harry Combes' 1954-55 basketball team were born during the 1933-34 season. Among the four were Bill Ridley (front, left), Bruce Brothers (back, left), Paul Judson (back, second from left), and Phil Judson (back, third from left).

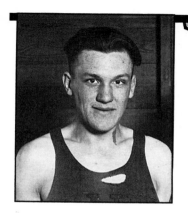

ILLINI ITEM

DR. LELAND "SLIM" STILWELL was named team physician for the University of Illinois' Athletic Association in 1933. A basketball letterman for the Fighting Illini from 1922-24, he was known to UI student-athletes as "Doc" Stilwell for 35 years. He was named UI's Varsity I Award winner in 1971.

ILLINI LISTS

FAMOUS ILLINI "33's"

- Kenny Battle, men's basketball
- Dee Dee Deeken, women's basketball
- Bill Erickson, men's basketball
- Chris Green, football
- Eddie Johnson, men's basketball
- Ken Norman, men's basketball
- Lonnie Perrin, football
- Harv Schmidt, men's basketball
- John Valente, baseball

Captain Bill Erickson wore jersey number 33.

ILLINI LEGEND: FRANK FROSCHAUER

From September of 1932 through March of 1935, the name Frank Froschauer dominated the sports pages at the University of Illinois. As a member of Coach Bob Zuppke's Fighting Illini football team, the Lincoln, Illinois, native was a prominent contributor from his halfback position. With Coach Craig Ruby's basketball squad, Froschauer led the team in scoring for three consecutive years, averaging eight points per game in an era when the entire team only scored 30 points a game. He also paced the Big Ten in scoring his senior season. Froschauer served as a coach and athletic director for 37 years in the south suburban Chicago area. He was involved with football, swimming, and golf at Thornton of Harvey over a period of 25 years and became Thornridge's first athletic director in 1960, serving until 1972 when he was succeeded by Ron Ferguson. Froschauer died April 28, 1985, at the age of 75.

Illini Lore

Arthur Cutts Willard took over as the ninth president of the University of Illinois July 1, 1934, succeeding Arthur Daniels. He had been head of the UI's Mechanical Engineering department and acting dean of the College of Engineering. In 1921, Willard had received international recognition for his research work, which provided engineering principles for the ventilation system of the Holland Tunnel under the Hudson River connecting Manhattan, New York, with Jersey City, New Jersey. After 12 years of service, during a period when a depressed economy gripped his campus and the rest of America, Willard retired.

1934-35

America's Time Capsule

- **Oct. 9, 1934:** *Dizzy Dean and the St. Louis Cardinals won the World Series over the Detroit Tigers.*
- **Dec. 9, 1934:** *The Chicago Bears lost the NFL championship game to the New York Giants, 30-13.*
- **May 6, 1935:** *The Works Progress Administration (WPA) began operation, giving jobs to millions of Americans.*
- **May 24, 1935:** *More than 20,000 fans at Cincinnati's Crosley Field watched their Reds beat the Philadelphia Phillies in baseball's first-ever night game.*
- **Aug. 14, 1935:** *President Roosevelt signed the Social Security Act, establishing payment of benefits to senior citizens.*

I·L·L·I·N·I M·O·M·E·N·T

Bob Reigel scored nine points in Illinois' 36-22 victory over Michigan.

ILLINI CAGERS BEAT MICHIGAN, CLAIM BIG TEN TITLE:
Illinois athletic teams traveled to Ann Arbor three times during the 1934-35 season, returning each time with a victory. In football, the Illini beat Michigan, 7-6. In baseball, Illinois triumphed, 1-0, at Ferry Field. But, perhaps, its most satisfying conquest in Michigan came on March 4, when the Illini basketball team beat their hosts, 36-22, to claim a share of the Big Ten title. Illinois exploded out of the blocks, scoring the first 15 points of the game, behind Captain Frank Froschauer who ended the contest with nine points. Bob Riegel (nine points), Harry Combes (eight), and Roy Guttschow (seven) tallied 24 of the remaining 25 points. Illinois wound up tying for the title with Purdue and Wisconsin, all finishing with 9-3 league records.

ILLINI BIRTHDAYS

SEPTEMBER 1934
9— Harry Jefferson, football
12— Roger Bielefeld, tennis
21— Bob Wiman, football

OCTOBER 1934
2— Cliff Roberts, football

NOVEMBER 1934
6— Dean Renn, football
23— Darrel DeDecker, football

DECEMBER 1934
8— Robert Baietto, football
14— Jake Grossman, swimming

JANUARY 1935
2— Bob Graeff, football
20— Larry Pasko, football

FEBRUARY 1935
1— Jim Minor, football

15— Abe Woodson, football
17— John Paul, basketball
20— Robert Shoptaw, baseball
23— Ralph Nelson, football
24— Clement Ryan, football

MARCH 1935
27— Harry Brandt, tennis
29— David Sterrett, swimming

APRIL 1935
21— Jim Slothower, golf
25— Richard Gunn, baseball

MAY 1935
1— Vito Iovino, football
3— Jim Frillman, baseball
10— Hiles Stout, football/basketball
25— Wayne Williams, assistant football coach

JUNE 1935
6— Bobby Mitchell, football/track
9— Rolla McMullen, football
12— Gary Francis, football
12— Jim VanTine, tennis
13— David Fricker, wrestling
22— Robert Delaney, football

JULY 1935
1— George BonSalle, basketball
10— Bill Altenberger, basketball

AUGUST 1935
9— Jon Weiss, tennis
27— Em Lindbeck, football/baseball
25— Ted Caiazza, basketball

Coach Hartley Price led the 1935 Fighting Illini gymnastics team to the 1935 Big Ten Championship at a meet held in Champaign.

ON OCTOBER 20, 1934, when Illinois squared off against Michigan's football team at Ann Arbor, Illini team members didn't realize that they were lining up against a future president of the United States. Wolverine center Gerald Ford became president 40 years later in 1974, when he succeeded Richard Nixon.

ILLINI LISTS

NCAA WRESTLING CHAMPIONS

1929-30	Joe Sapora, 115 pounds
1929	George Minot, 135 pounds
1932	Joe Puerta, 121 pounds
1935	Ralph Silverstein, 175 pounds
1938	John Ginay, 165 pounds
1938	Allen Sapora, 126 pounds
1939	Archie Deutschman, 136 pounds
1946	David Shapiro, 165 pounds
1956	Larry TenPas, 157 pounds
1957-58	Bob Norman, heavyweight
1991	Jon Llewellyn, heavyweight
1995	Steve Marianetti, 150 pounds
1995	Ernest Benion, Jr., 158 pounds

Ralph "Ruffy" Silverstein won the 175-pound NCAA championship in 1935.

ILLINI LEGEND:

CHARLES FLACHMANN

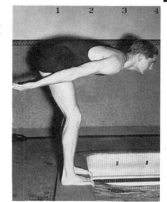

One of Illinois' most brilliant athletes during the mid-1930s was swimmer Charles Flachmann. Lettering for the Fighting Illini from 1934-35 for Coach Ed Manley, Flachmann dominated the freestyle events in Big Ten championship competition. He swept the 50- and 100-yard races both years, and also captured the 220-yard event his junior year. Nationally, Flachmann also won titles in all three events. Following his athletic career at Illinois, he served as a captain in the Army during World War II. When Flachmann returned to civilian life, he worked as an insurance broker in St. Louis, and also was an amateur artist. Flachmann died in 1983 at the age of 69.

Illini Lore

O n February 9, 1935, the University of Illinois' Board of Trustees approved the formation of the UI Foundation, to encourage the giving of more gifts to the University, not only by alumni but by citizens in general. An organization called the Alumni Fund, the predecessor to the Foundation, managed to raise only $48,000 since it came into being in 1921. Over the past 60 years, the UI Foundation has accepted more than $1.4 billion in gifts and contributions.

We're Loyal to You, Illinois!

Patrick F. Daly, Vice President; Roger L. Plummer, President; William L. Blake, Past President; Louis D. Liay, Executive Director

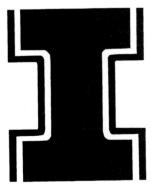

The University of Illinois Alumni Association has been a proud supporter of Illinois athletics for more than a century. Organized in 1873 to give alumni a voice, the U of I Alumni Association is one of the largest in the world. Our fight song, "We're Loyal to You Illinois" says it all.

All Alumni join me in congratulating the alumni who have represented their University as student athletes. We're proud of you and we're proud to be a part of the Fighting Illini team.

GO ILLINI!

The University of Illinois Alumni Association
Urbana-Champaign • Chicago • Springfield

1935-1944

1935-36

I·L·L·I·N·I M·O·M·E·N·T

Lowell Spurgeon's 31-yard field goal beat Michigan in 1935.

ILLINI BURY WOLVERINES IN MUD:

The Michigan "Football Express" roared into Illinois' Memorial Stadium on a four-game winning streak, but the combination of a stingy Illini defense and a muddy field buried the Wolverines in their tracks, November 9, 1935. The mud-encrusted right foot of Illini kicker Lowell Spurgeon accounted for the only score of the day, a 31-yard field goal in the second quarter, as Illinois beat Michigan, 3-0. The Wolverine offense never got started; in fact, it never carried the ball as far as the middle of the field. Gaining only 16 total yards, the only first down Michigan managed the entire afternoon was courtesy of an Illini penalty. The mud didn't seem to bother Illini quarterback "Wib" Henry, though, as he rushed for a net gain of 123 yards.

ILLINI BIRTHDAYS

SEPTEMBER 1935
8– Carl Johnson, football
16– Gerald Wood, football
20– George Brokemond, football
25– Allan Rubenstein, swimming
25– Harv Schmidt, basketball

OCTOBER 1935
11– David Walker, football

NOVEMBER 1935
11– Rod Hanson, football
24– Donald Tonry, gymnastics
27– David Williams, baseball

DECEMBER 1935
7– Don Kraft, football
11– John Gremer, football
23– Joseph Bellephant, football

27– John Garland, swimming

JANUARY 1936
3– Louis Landt, basketball
3– Mike White, football coach
6– Richard Vorreyer, baseball
17– Dick Hendrickson, football

FEBRUARY 1936
26– Bill Bolk, baseball

MARCH 1936
31– Richard Perez, football

APRIL 1936
14– Richard Newell, football
15– Rock Sharer, swimming
18– Don Ohl, basketball

JUNE 1936
8– Dan Wile, football
13– John Voyda, golf
19– John Kating, baseball
19– Larry Breyfogle, basketball

JULY 1936
10– Paul Adams, football
15– Carl Noble, tennis
17– Ronald Kaiser, Chief XIV
21– John Bozich, baseball

AUGUST 1936
1– James Cvik, baseball
6– Richard Nordmeyer, football
14– Al Holtmann, tennis
16– Robert Hunt, swimming
23– Rich Kreitling, football
29– John Jurasevich, baseball

Gymnast Art Fisher won the Big Ten tumbling title for the second consecutive year in 1936. He also was awarded the Big Ten Conference Medal of Honor.

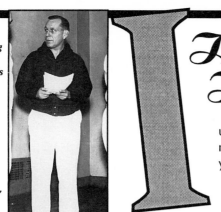

Thirty-nine-year-old Craig Ruby announced his resignation in 1936, saying, "I do not choose to face the prospect of coaching basketball at 50 or 60 years of age."

ILLINI ITEM

BASKETBALL COACH CRAIG RUBY concluded his 14-year career at the University of Illinois, announcing his resignation on February 7, 1936. "My reason for resigning," said the 39-year-old Ruby, "is that I believe it is unwise for my family and myself to depend upon the game of basketball entirely in the later years of my life. I do not choose to face the prospect of coaching basketball at 50 or 60 years of age."

ILLINI LISTS

HEISMAN AWARD WINNERS WHO PLAYED AGAINST ILLINOIS
(Performances in the year they won the award)

- Jay Berwanger of Chicago (11/23/35)
  26 rushes for 106 yards, 1 TD
- Tom Harmon of Michigan (10/19/40)
  21 rushes for 58 yards, 1 TD, 1 FG
- Bruce Smith of Minnesota (10/11/41)
  Yardage unavailable, 2 TD
- Angelo Bertelli of Notre Dame (10/23/43)
  5 of 7 passes for 82 yards, 1 TD pass
- Les Horvath of Ohio State (11/18/44)
  22 rushes for 109 yards, 2 TD
- Vic Janowicz of Ohio State (11/18/50)
  21 rushes for 90 yards, 5 of 12 passes for 59 yards, 1 TD
- Howard Cassady of Ohio State (10/8/55)
  18 rushes for 95 yards, 2 TD
- Archie Griffin of Ohio State (11/2/74)
  20 rushes for 144 yards, 2 TD
- Archie Griffin of Ohio State (11/8/75)
  23 rushes for 127 yards, 1 TD
- Desmond Howard of Michigan (11/16/91)
  7 catches for 80 yards, 1 TD

ILLINI LEGEND:

HARRY COMBES

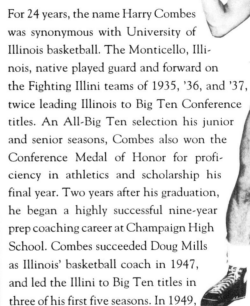

For 24 years, the name Harry Combes was synonymous with University of Illinois basketball. The Monticello, Illinois, native played guard and forward on the Fighting Illini teams of 1935, '36, and '37, twice leading Illinois to Big Ten Conference titles. An All-Big Ten selection his junior and senior seasons, Combes also won the Conference Medal of Honor for proficiency in athletics and scholarship his final year. Two years after his graduation, he began a highly successful nine-year prep coaching career at Champaign High School. Combes succeeded Doug Mills as Illinois' basketball coach in 1947, and led the Illini to Big Ten titles in three of his first five seasons. In 1949, '51, and '52, UI basketball clubs finished third at the NCAA tournament each year. Combes' 20-year coaching record at Illinois was 316 wins and 150 losses, a mark that stood as the Illini record until it was broken by Lou Henson. He died November 13, 1977, at the age of 62.

 Illini Lore

In December of 1935, after four months of negotiations, the State of Illinois approved an appropriation of $1.2 million to the University of Illinois for a major addition to the Medical Center on Polk Street in Chicago. For a time, the depression halted progress on the Center's east tower. But finally, in 1937, construction was eventually completed through the federal Public Works Administration.

1936-37

I·L·L·I·N·I M·O·M·E·N·T

Hale Swanson's tip-in salvaged the Illini comeback against Purdue.

ILLINI CAGERS SNAP 14-YEAR JINX AT PURDUE:

In one of the most raucous basketball battles ever played between Illinois and Purdue, it took a rebound basket by Illini reserve center Hale Swanson with just five seconds left to secure a 38-37 victory. The January 18, 1937, win was Illinois' first at West Lafayette in 14 seasons and moved the Illini into a first-place tie in the Big Ten standings. Trailing 23-11 early in the second half, Illinois steadily whittled away at the Boilermaker advantage and took the lead with six minutes remaining. Purdue regained the lead in the final minute, but fouled Illini star Lou Boudreau with just five seconds left in the game. Boudreau missed both free-throw attempts, but Swanson's tip-in salvaged the Illini comeback. Illinois went on to win six of its last seven games to tie Minnesota for the Big Ten title.

ILLINI BIRTHDAYS

SEPTEMBER 1936
1– Ken Sutter, football
12– Bruce Beckmann, football
15– Charles Schrader, football
24– William Gabbard, wrestling

DECEMBER 1936
3– Mike Bouchard, swimming
12– Ladd Pash, golf coach
19– Bill Offenbecher, football
19– Casey Barszcz, baseball
25– Harold Brownstein, wrestling
29– Ray Nitschke, football

JANUARY 1937
27– Lee Sentman, fencing
30– Roger Taylor, basketball

FEBRUARY 1937
9– Jim Brown, football
19– Gerald Patrick, football
22– Anthony Danosky, football

MARCH 1937
1– Govoner Vaughn, basketball
2– Bruce Dollahan, football
9– Robert Allen, football
13– Don Yeazel, football
15– Jack Delveaux, football/baseball
20– David Ash, football
20– David Stewart, football

APRIL 1937
10– John Fix, swimming

MAY 1937
1– Don Saunders, football

5– Tom Walker, swimming
19– George Utz, football
22– Joe Hunsaker, swimming

JUNE 1937
23– Tom Haller, football/ basketball/baseball
25– William Gawron, baseball

JULY 1937
21– Owen Ackerman, swimming

AUGUST 1937
1– Charles Dickerson, football
2– Donald Tjarksen, track

Fighting Illini wrestler John Ginay won the 195-pound Big Ten title in both 1937 and '38, leading Illinois to the team championship as a junior.

ILLINI ITEM

WENDELL "WEENIE" WILSON, Illinois varsity football letterwinner in 1925 and '26, was officially appointed director of athletics February 27, 1937, replacing the late George Huff. Only 31 years old at the time of his appointment, Wilson became the Big Ten's youngest athletic director.

ILLINI LISTS

ALL-TIME COLLEGE BASEBALL "DREAM TEAM"
(As selected in 1990 by *Collegiate Baseball*)

- Lou Boudreau, Illinois
- Mickey Cochrane, Boston U.
- Jackie Robinson, UCLA
- George Sisler, Michigan
- Eddie Collins, Columbia
- Joe Sewell, Alabama
- Frankie Frisch, Fordham
- Thurman Munson, Kent State
- Mike Schmidt, Ohio U.
- Harvey Kuenn, Wisconsin
- Ethan Allen, Cincinnati
- Tony Gwynn, San Diego State
- Lou Gehrig, Columbia
- Reggie Jackson, Arizona State
- Carl Yastrzemski, Notre Dame
- Dave Winfield, Minnesota
- Christy Mathewson, Bucknell
- Eddie Plank, Gettysburg

Illinois' Lou Boudreau was a member of college baseball's Dream Team

ILLINI LEGEND:

LOU BOUDREAU

The folks at Harvey Thornton High School probably knew that Lou Boudreau would end up in the Hall of Fame. However, they figured it would be the sport of basketball, not baseball, where their favorite son would make his greatest impression. Boudreau did enjoy great success on the hardcourts at Illinois, earning All-America honors as a junior, averaging nearly nine points per game. However, the major league baseball scouts also liked what they saw of Boudreau in 1937, hitting .347 while leading the Illini to the Big Ten title. The very next spring, he joined the Cleveland Indians. Four years later at age 24, Boudreau was named player-manager of the Indians. His greatest success on the baseball diamond came in 1948 when he guided Cleveland to the World Series title, while earning American League MVP honors. During his 15-year major league career with Cleveland and the Boston Red Sox, Boudreau hit .295 with 68 home runs and 789 RBI. In addition to managing Cleveland, he also was the skipper for the Red Sox, the Kansas City Athletics, and the Chicago Cubs. He served as a television and radio announcer for the Cubs for more than two decades, and was inducted into Baseball's Hall of Fame in 1970. The University of Illinois retired baseball jersey number five in his honor on April 18, 1992. Boudreau currently lives in Dolton, Illinois.

Illini Lore

"If every professor on the campus were as good in his line as Illini Nellie is in hers," the *Illinois Alumni News* said in a June, 1937 story, "what a University we would have!" The dairy department's super-cow was the world's record holder for production, setting seven marks during a 12-month period. Nellie produced 1,200 pounds of butterfat and 29,569 pounds of milk, as compared to the average cow (161 pounds of butterfat). The nine-year-old, pure-bred brown Swiss cow's average daily diet consisted of 25 pounds of hay, 15 pounds of grain, 20 pounds of beet pulp, and five pounds of silage.

1937-38

I·L·L·I·N·I M·O·M·E·N·T

FIGHTING ILLINI BATTLE IRISH TO STANDSTILL:
The scoreboard at the end of the game read Illinois-0, Notre Dame-0, but none of the 45,000 fans in attendance at Memorial Stadium that mild afternoon of October 9, 1937, went home disappointed. They'd just seen one of the most magnificent defensive efforts ever by their Fighting Illini, holding Coach Elmer Layden's Irish juggernaut to little more than 100 total yards. Jack Berner, who punted 10 times for an average of 35 yards, was also a bulwark on defense, lending a hand in stopping almost every Notre Dame run. Mel Brewer missed what would have been the game-winning field goal, a 14-yarder, in the first quarter, but the Illini never generated another true scoring threat. Notre Dame wound up the season with a 6-2-1 record, while Illinois finished at 3-3-2.

ILLINI BIRTHDAYS

SEPTEMBER 1937
2– Forest Devor, wrestling
5– Wayne Lanter, baseball
12– Ed Jerzak, football
13– Gene Carr, football
15– Tony Yates, assistant basketball coach
19– William Henderson, football
20– Robert Breckenridge, tennis
23– Werner Holzer, wrestling
28– Tom Gabbard, wrestling
28– Jim Williamson, fencing

OCTOBER 1937
21– Ron Nietupski, football
26– Robert Becker, fencing

NOVEMBER 1937
13– Gary Wieneke, track and cross country coach
22– Richard Eberhardy, swimming

DECEMBER 1937
18– Joe Krakoski, football
27– Bobby Klaus, baseball

JANUARY 1938
2– Ken Kraml, wrestling
7– George Jurinek, wrestling
24– Martin Kramer, fencing
30– Richard McDade, football

FEBRUARY 1938
6– Augie Garrido, baseball coach
9– Bob Lansford, tennis
11– Robert Hickey, football

13– Bruce Bunkenberg, basketball
13– John Wessels, basketball
13– Edward Perry, basketball
14– DeJustice Coleman, football
21– Ernie McMillan, football

MARCH 1938
1– Joe Wendryhoski, football
12– Vern Altenmeyer, basketball

MAY 1938
16– Richard Fletemeyer, swimming
28– Doug Wallace, football

JUNE 1938
1– Thurman Walker, football

20– Alan Gosnell, basketball
22– Robert Madix, baseball
29– Bill Brown, football

JULY 1938
11– Lee Frandsen, basketball
13– Phil Catalano, baseball
16– Bob Burda, baseball

AUGUST 1938
1– Terry Gellinger, baseball
2– Joe Epkins, tennis
10– Abbey Silverstone, fencing

Pitcher Ray Poat compiled a perfect 10-0 record for the Illini baseball team in 1937 and '38.

ILLINI ITEM

ILLINI LISTS

Pat Harmon, historian of the National Football Foundation and College Football Hall of Fame, worked as a sportswriter and later served as sports editor of the *Champaign News-Gazette* from 1934 to 1947. Here's his list of the 10 most memorable Illini athletes of that period:

1. **Dike Eddleman** ... won 11 letters in football, basketball, and track.
2. **Lou Boudreau** ... a star in baseball and basketball.
3. **Ralph "Ruffy" Silverstein** ... a colorful showman for the Illini wrestling team.
4. **Alex Agase** ... a football All-American.
5. **Andy Phillip** ... the best basketball player of his era.
6. **Buddy Young** ... super-star of Illini football and track.
7. **Harry Combes** ... one of Illini basketball's greatest leaders.
8. **Lee Eilbracht** ... Illinois' best in baseball.
9. **Herb McKenley** ... the nation's best in the 440-yard dash.
10. **Wib Henry** ... a three-sport star in football, basketball, and baseball.

ILLINI LEGEND:

HEK KENNEY

Harold Eugene "Hek" Kenney is remembered as the man for whom Kenney Gym on the University of Illinois campus was named. However, it was his accomplishments in the sport of wrestling that gained him his initial fame. A two-time wrestling captain during his Illini career from 1924-26 under Coach Paul Prehn, Kenney succeeded his mentor as coach of UI grappling in 1929. For the next 15 years, he guided the Illini to a dual-meet record of 91-28-2 and four Big Ten titles. It was not uncommon for Kenney's teams to wrestle before crowds of more than 3,000 fans. Among his standout pupils were the Sapora brothers, Joe and Al, Ralph "Ruffy" Silverstein, and Archie Deutschman. So respected was Kenney that he served two terms as president of the National Wrestling Coaches and Officials Association. He was a member of UI's physical education faculty until his retirement in 1967. Two years later, he was honored as the first recipient of the College of Physical Education's "Distinguished Alumnus Award." Kenney died in 1972 at the age of 69. On April 25, 1974, the building in which he had toiled for most of his life was renamed in his honor.

Illini Lore

On March 11, 1938, the 70th anniversary of the opening of the University of Illinois, workers began razing Old University Hall. The facility, completed in 1873 at a cost of $150,000, represented 65 years of history to UI alumni and there was much resistance from them towards tearing it down. However, building experts indicated that the cost of leveling the structure would run as much as constructing a new classroom. Salvaged from the historic building was the Memorial Clock, a gift from the Class of 1878, which today graces the cupola of the Illini Union.

1938-39

I·L·L·I·N·I M·O·M·E·N·T

Coach Hartley Price

NATIONAL CHAMPS:

Coach Hartley Price's University of Illinois gymnasts were on top of the world during the 1938-39 season. They roared through their dual-meet schedule unbeaten, then hosted the Western Conference Meet at the Old Gym on March 11. The Fighting Illini didn't disappoint their hometown fans that day, outdistancing runner-up Minnesota by 22 points, 111.5 to 89.5. A month later came the national meet at the University of Chicago, and Illinois again wound up on top, claiming their first-ever NCAA title. Leading the way for the Illini was junior All-American Joe Giallombardo, who won the individual all-around championships at both the conference and national meets. Other UI stars included Paul Fina, Marvin Forman, and Harry Koehnemann.

ILLINI BIRTHDAYS

SEPTEMBER 1938
7– Lindell Lovellette, football
11– Warren Danzer, fencing
23– Howard Tippett, assistant football coach
27– Russ Martin, football/baseball

OCTOBER 1938
18– John Kruze, football
20– Dennis Gould, football
28– Larry Lavery, football

NOVEMBER 1938
1– John Stapleton, football

JANUARY 1939
3– Ken Chalcraft, football
25– Paul Foreman, track
26– Joe Rutgens, football

FEBRUARY 1939
16– Bruce Kriviskey, fencing
28– John Counts, football

MARCH 1939
6– Marshall Starks, football
18– Dave Gantt, baseball
21– Joe Huyler, swimming
23– Jim Riley, tennis
31– Bill Bonk, baseball

APRIL 1939
20– Joe Mota, football

JULY 1939
5– Jerry Curless, basketball
13– Paul Arneson, baseball
17– John Easterbrook, football
20– Jimmy Warren, football

29– Gary Hembrough, football

AUGUST 1939
2– Tony Parrilli, football

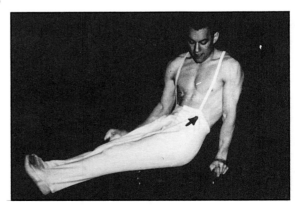

Pommel horse specialist Harry Koehnemann won his first of three consecutive titles in that event in 1939.

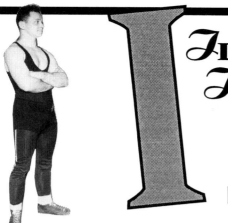

ILLINI ITEM

FIGHTING ILLINI WRESTLING CAPTAIN Archie Deutschman was a two-way star during the 1938-39 season. On the wrestling mat for Coach Hek Kenney, he won both the Big Ten and NCAA titles at the 136-pound classification. As a reward for his proficiency in the classroom, Deutschman was honored as Illinois' Big Ten Conference Medal of Honor winner.

ILLINI LISTS

ILLINI WHOSE NUMBERS HAVE BEEN RETIRED IN PROFESSIONAL SPORTS

No. 5	Lou Boudreau,	Cleveland Indians
No. 7	George Halas,	Chicago Bears
No. 22	Buddy Young,	Baltimore Colts
No. 51	Dick Butkus,	Chicago Bears
No. 66	Ray Nitschke,	Green Bay Packers
No. 77	Red Grange,	Chicago Bears

The Cleveland Indians retired Lou Boudreau's No. 5.

ILLINI LEGEND:

JOE GIALLOMBARDO

At first glance, Joe Giallombardo could hardly be mistaken as being a dominant athlete. However, packed inside his stocky five-feet-four-inch, 155-pound frame were tightly wound, spring-loaded muscles. While Jesse Owens, his Cleveland East Tech High School classmate, was making headlines as a track man, Giallombardo became the premier athlete in the sport of gymnastics. During his three years at the University of Illinois from 1938-40, "Little Joe" won every individual title there was to win. He was a three-time all-around champion in the Big Ten, helping the Fighting Illini win the 1939 team title. Among his record seven NCAA titles were three all-around crowns, three tumbling championships, and a first-place finish on the rings. Giallombardo coached gymnastics at New Trier and New Trier West high schools from the time he graduated until his retirement in 1975. He now lives in Wheeling, Illinois.

Illini Lore

The cornerstone of Gregory Hall was laid June 10, 1939, by Alfred Gregory, son of the man for whom the memorial was being made—John Milton Gregory, first president of the University of Illinois. The structure originally housed the College of Education, the School of Journalism, and classrooms for students enrolled in Liberal Arts and Science. A copper box containing, among other items, the photograph and biography of President Gregory was placed inside the cornerstone.

1939-40

America's Time Capsule

- **Sept. 3, 1939:** *The nations of France and Great Britain declared war on Germany, while President Roosevelt said that the United States would remain neutral.*
- **Dec. 10, 1939:** *The Green Bay Packers defeated the New York Giants, 27-0, to win the NFL championship.*
- **March 30, 1940:** *Indiana won its first NCAA basketball title, beating Kansas, 60-42.*
- **May 6, 1940:** *John Steinbeck won a Pulitzer prize for his book* The Grapes of Wrath.
- **May 15, 1940:** *The first successful helicopter flight in the United States took place.*

I·L·L·I·N·I M·O·M·E·N·T

Illini fans celebrated their heroes' upset of Michigan.

ILLINOIS SHOCKS MICHIGAN:

Winless Illinois wasn't given much hope against Coach Fritz Crisler's Michigan Wolverine football squad, starring eventual Heisman Trophy winner Tom Harmon. Michigan came to Champaign averaging 41 points per game, but on that seasonably mild November 4th afternoon, the Wolverines managed only a single touchdown. Though Harmon did net 72 yards rushing, his performance was stymied by a brilliant effort from Coach Bob Zuppke's defensive unit. Illinois' two touchdowns were scored by George Rettinger following a 48-yard pass and by Jim Smith on a three-yard run. One of the unsung heroes for the Illini was lineman Mel Brewer, who dedicated the game to his mother who had died earlier that week. The nation's sportswriters later selected the game as the biggest upset of the 1939 season. Illinois wound up the year with a 3-4-1 record as compared to Michigan's 6-2 overall mark.

ILLINI BIRTHDAYS

SEPTEMBER 1939
- 6– Dan Mesch, tennis
- 7– Jerry Parola, football
- 28– Thad Harshbarger, wrestling

NOVEMBER 1939
- 4– Max Crotzer, baseball
- 15– Pat Murphy, football
- 20– Jerry Colangelo, basketball/baseball

DECEMBER 1939
- 18– Sam Leeper, basketball
- 26– Mike Toliuszis, golf

JANUARY 1940
- 4– Tony Zeppetella, football
- 5– Lou Ryniec, baseball
- 13– Charlie Younger, swimming
- 14– Ernie Kumerow, baseball
- 20– Jay Lovelace, basketball

FEBRUARY 1940
- 7– Ed Searcy, basketball
- 14– Steve Thomas, football
- 23– Ray Hadley, gymnastics
- 28– Norm Willis, football

MARCH 1940
- 4– Francis "Bud" Felichio, baseball
- 8– Gary Brown, football
- 8– Mel Romani, football
- 13– Gary Kolb, football/baseball
- 31– Doug Mills, football/basketball/baseball

APRIL 1940
- 4– Robert Mountz, football
- 19– Stan Yukevich, football

MAY 1940
- 3– Dave McGann, football

12– Lloyd Flodin, baseball
18– Jim Hicks, baseball
21– Ed O'Bradovich, football
26– Peter Stelton, swimming

JUNE 1940
- 11– Laura Golden, women's basketball coach
- 19– Tom Boatman, tennis
- 21– Joe England, golf

JULY 1940
- 5– Pat Kelly, wrestling
- 22– Dick Bickhaus, baseball
- 24– Ethan Blackaby, football/baseball

AUGUST 1940
- 2– Lew Hankenson, wrestling
- 7– Mel Meyers, football
- 16– Bruce Stafford, tennis
- 31– Steve Heller, tennis

Bill Hapac takes his turn during batting practice of the 1940 Illini baseball team.

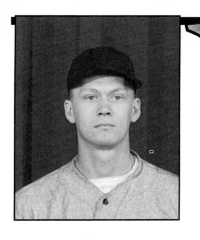

ILLINI ITEM

SOPHOMORE WALTER "HOOT" EVERS was the most versatile Fighting Illini athlete of 1939-40, lettering in basketball, baseball, and track. On the hardcourts, "Hoot" was Illinois' second-leading scorer. As a centerfielder in baseball, Evers hit a cool .353 in Big Ten play. Illini track coach Leo Johnson pulled Evers off the baseball diamond to compete in the Big Ten outdoor meet as a javelin thrower. Despite practicing only a week, "Hoot" placed second in the conference meet. At the end of the season, Evers received numerous offers to quit college and play professional baseball, which he turned down. However, in mid-term of the 1940-41 school year, Evers failed a history course and was declared ineligible for college athletics. He signed with Detroit and went on to a long and successful career in the major leagues.

ILLINI LISTS

EFFICIENCY RANKING OF ILLINOIS' GREATEST COACHES

A rating system was developed to determine which all-time Fighting Illini men's coaches had the most success during their careers. Coaches were awarded three points for every NCAA title they won, two points for each NCAA runner-up finish, one point for each Big Ten title, and one-half point for each conference runner-up placing. Their total points were then divided by the total number of seasons they coached, resulting in their efficiency rating.

1. 1.360—Charlie Pond, gymnastics (34 points in 25 seasons)
2. 1.079—Hartley Price, gymnastics (20.5 points in 19 seasons)
3. .952—Maxwell Garrett, fencing (29.5 points in 31 seasons)
4. .750—Paul Prehn, wrestling (6 points in 8 seasons)
5. .690—Bob Zuppke, football (20 points in 29 seasons)
6. .627—Harry Gill, track & field (32 points in 51 seasons)
7. .589—George Huff, baseball/football (16.5 points in 28 seasons)
8. .588—Hek Kenney, wrestling (10 points in 17 seasons)
9. .519—Leo Johnson, cross country/track & field (41 points in 79 seasons)
10. .464—Carl Lundgren, baseball (6.5 points in 14 seasons)

ILLINI LEGEND:

BILL HAPAC

Quick now—what does former Illinois basketball star Bill Hapac have in common with Andy Phillip, Terry Dischinger, Jimmy Rayl, Dave Schellhase, and Rick Mount? If you guessed that they all once set the Big Ten single-game scoring record, you get the grand prize. Hapac's night in the spotlight came against Minnesota on February 10, 1940, when he scored a then unheard-of 34 points. The Cicero, Illinois, native was the conference's leading scorer his senior year, averaging nearly 14 points per game. Besides lettering three times in basketball, Hapac also earned three varsity monograms in baseball. Twice, he scored five runs in a game, a mark that's still a school record. Hapac served as an officer in the Air Corps during World War II, then played pro basketball for several years. A consensus basketball All-American at Illinois, he coached the sport at Morton East High School until his death in 1967 at the age of 49.

Illini Lore

The world's first betatron, an atom-smasher for high-energy physics exploration into the nucleus of the atom, was introduced in 1940 by University of Illinois physicist Donald Kerst. Kerst's first betatron was 19 inches long, 20 inches high, eight inches thick, and weighed 200 pounds. It produced x-rays with an energy of two-and-one-half million electron volts. The electrons reached their energy by spinning around many times within a doughnut-shaped vacuum tube.

1940-41

I·L·L·I·N·I M·O·M·E·N·T

(Left to right) Captain Alex Welsh, John Holmstrom, John Buzick, Bill Usinger, Dick Wolfley, and Ross Reed

ILLINI GOLFERS CAPTURE BIG TEN CROWN:
When Coach Winsor Brown's Fighting Illini golf team captured its second consecutive Big Ten championship on June 19, 1941, it helped the University of Illinois to become the winningest conference school ever in the sport at that time. Led by individual medalist Alex Welsh, the Illini outdistanced runners-up Ohio State and Michigan for their sixth all-time team crown. Besides Welsh, other members of the team included John Holmstrom, John Buzick, Dick Wolfley, and Bill Usinger. A week later, the Illini golf squad traveled to to the NCAA championship meet and placed fourth. Since 1941, Illini golfers have won only one Big Ten team title.

ILLINI BIRTHDAYS

SEPTEMBER 1940
25– Bill Burwell, basketball

OCTOBER 1940
15– Tony Eichelberger, baseball

DECEMBER 1940
6– Neal Anderson, football
21– Tom Beck, assistant football coach
27– Tom Porter, wrestling coach

JANUARY 1941
26– Gary Moeller, football coach

FEBRUARY 1941
2– Michael Summers, football
2– George Galla, baseball
19– Jim Plankenhorn, football

APRIL 1941
3– Frank Lollino, football
6– Lyman Larson, track
21– Harold Holmes, gymnastics
23– Joe Sommer, swimming

MAY 1941
7– William Shriner, swimming
8– Robert Cravens, football
12– John Wheatland, football
19– Jerry Renner, basketball
31– Ronald Fearn, football
31– Joel Hirsch, golf

JUNE 1941
19– Jon Brannan, wrestling

JULY 1941
26– Mike Taliaferro, football

AUGUST 1941
14– Stuart Cohn, fencing

The Fighting Illini gymnastics team captured the Big Ten team championship behind the efforts of Lou Fina (left) on the rings and Caton Cobb on the horizontal bar.

Coach Vic Heyliger (back row, far left) led the Fighting Illini to college hockey's mythical national championship.

ILLINI ITEM

ILLINOIS WAS THE UNOFFICIAL national champion of college ice hockey in 1941, recording a mark of 17-3-1. In competition against Big Ten foes, the Illini were 6-1-1. The stars of coach Vic Heyliger's team were Norbert Sterle, Aldo Palazarri, and Amo Bessone. Bessone later became a successful coach at Michigan State, leading the Spartans to the 1966 NCAA title.

ILLINI LISTS

ILLINI MEN'S ATHLETIC TRAINERS

—— to 1913	William "Willie" McGill
1913-26	Dr. Samuel Bilik
1916-47	David M. "Matt" Bullock
1947-51	Elmer "Ike" Hill
1951-57	Richard Klein
1957-69	Robert Nicollette
1969-73	Robert Behnke
1973-83	John "Skip" Pickering
1983-present	Al Martindale

ILLINI WOMEN'S ATHLETIC TRAINERS

1975-78	Dana Gerhardt
1978-80	Ellen Murray
1980-present	Karen Iehl-Morse

Matt Bullock served as Illinois' head athletic trainer from 1916-47.

ILLINI LEGEND:

LEO JOHNSON

If the measure of success of a coach is quantified in championships, then long time University of Illinois coach Leo Johnson was a giant of his era in the sport of track and field. From the time he was hired as coach of the Illini in 1938 until his retirement at age 70 in 1965, Johnson guided Fighting Illini teams to 17 Big Ten titles and three national championships. Since 1944, when Johnson's Illini won the NCAA title, he is one of only four coaches outside the sun-belt states to win a national championship. His athletes captured 27 individual NCAA titles and 158 conference firsts during his 28 years at Illinois. A member of numerous track and field Halls of Fame, Johnson was also known in Illini football history as one of the game's finest scouts. A college football and track star at Millikin College in Decatur, Johnson served as a lieutenant in World War I. When the war ended, he played pro football briefly with George Halas' Decatur Staleys, then became head coach of all sports at Millikin in 1923. Johnson died in 1982 at the age of 87.

Illini Lore

The Illini Union officially opened its doors at the University of Illinois on February 8, 1941. Interest in building a facility intensified in 1934 when A.C. Willard was inaugurated as president of the University. One of the president's first official acts was to appoint a committee to investigate construction of a Union building. When the UI decided to raze University Hall—the site on which the Illini Union was built—the decision of the committee was unanimous. An addition to the $1.2 million structure was completed at a cost of nearly $7 million in 1963. More than 40 volumes of illustration of colonial architecture were used in preparing the preliminary drawings of the Illini Union. The distinctive feature of the building is a 30-foot open-arched cupola and its 11-foot bronze weather vane. In the belfry of the cupola is the University's historic chapel bell and, at its base, is the 117-year-old clock that once stood in University Hall.

1941-42

America's Time Capsule

- **Dec. 7, 1941:** About 3,000 Americans lost their lives when the Japanese attacked Pearl Harbor, Hawaii.
- **Dec. 11, 1941:** Germany and Italy declared war against the United States.
- **Dec. 21, 1941:** The Chicago Bears won the NFL championship, defeating the New York Giants, 37-9.
- **Jan. 9, 1942:** Joe Louis successfully defended his world heavyweight boxing title for the 20th time, knocking out Max Baer in the first round.
- **April 18, 1942:** American bombers, under the command of Maj. Gen. James Doolittle, conducted a successful air raid on Tokyo.

The Whiz Kids, coached by Doug Mills (left), were comprised of (l. to r.) Art Mathisen, Jack Smiley, Gene Vance, Ken Menke, and Andy Phillip.

I·L·L·I·N·I M·O·M·E·N·T

WHIZ KIDS:

Doug Mills, coach of the University of Illinois' most famous basketball team, placed his "Whiz Kids" in a class of their own. "Of all the players I ever coached," Mills recalled later, "only Lou Boudreau could have played with them. That's how good they were." Four finely tuned athletes, all around 6-foot-3, formed the heart of the "Whiz Kids." In three seasons together, the quartet of future Hall of Famer Andy Phillip, Jack Smiley, Gene Vance, and Ken Menke, along with two-year Whiz Kid Art Mathisen, fashioned a cumulative Big Ten record of 33-6 in 1942, '43, and '47, winning two conference titles and finishing second as seniors. The 1943 club finished the year with an overall record of 17-1 and was undefeated in conference play (12-0), but didn't play in the national tournament because of service in World War II. "Uncle Sam had our draft rights," said Vance, and the war took precedence over the five-year-old NCAA championship playoffs. "I'm 99 percent sure we would have won," said Menke. When the group reunited for the 1946-47 campaign, all four players returned to starting positions for Mills, but it wasn't quite the same. "The war had taken something out of them," recalled Mills. "They had gone through terrible war experiences, and they had changed." Still, in the history of Fighting Illini basketball, there has never been a team quite like the "Whiz Kids."

ILLINI BIRTHDAYS

SEPTEMBER 1941
3– Bill Small, basketball
21– Glenn Glauser, football
29– Howard Cianciarulo, wrestling

OCTOBER 1941
9– Norm Parker, assistant football coach
11– Bruce Singman, football
23– Dick Dooley, swimming
25– Cecil Young, football
28– Dave Downey, basketball
31– Ed Spiezio, baseball

NOVEMBER 1941
1– John Collins, football
26– William Pasko, football
28– Ken Zimmerman Jr., football/fencing

DECEMBER 1941
9– John DeAno, wrestling
17– Donald Simon, golf
21– Jack Wainwright, football
21– Ronald O'Neal, football

JANUARY 1942
1– Elroy Morand, assistant football coach
19– Jim Spreitzer, swimming
24– Cliff Dammers, fencing

FEBRUARY 1942
3– Dwain Painter, assistant football coach
9– Robert Easter, football
17– Arthur McCaskill, football
19– Bill Harper, football
27– Ken Jacobson, wrestling
28– Trenton Jackson, football/baseball

MARCH 1942
6– Lynn Snyder, assistant athletic director

APRIL 1942
2– Larry Moss, tennis
17– Dave Krom, wrestling
20– Dave Ryniec, baseball

MAY 1942
4– Mannie Jackson, basketball

JUNE 1942
28– Tom Fletcher, baseball
30– Gregg Schumacher, football

JULY 1942
1– Michael Dundy, football
28– Frank Noble, tennis
29– Allen Carius, cross country/track
20– Ben Forsyth, Chief XVI

John Adkins captured his second consecutive Big Ten tumbling title as the Fighting Illini gymnastics team won the conference championship.

I

ON NOVEMBER 17, 1941, five days before his team's season finale at Northwestern, veteran Fighting Illini football coach Bob Zuppke announced his retirement. Under pressure from alumni and the University of Illinois' Board of Trustees, Zuppke stepped down "for the good of Illinois." Unfortunately, Zuppke's teams ended the season on a sour note, losing to the Wildcats, 27-0.

ILLINI LISTS

RECIPIENTS OF THE VARSITY "I" AWARD

1970	Claude "Buddy" Young ('46)	Football/Track
1971	Leland Stilwell ('24)	Basketball
1972	Barton Cummings ('35)	Football/Track
1973	Ray Eliot ('32)	Football/Baseball
1974	Robert Wright ('36)	Football/Track
1975	Willard Franks ('49)	Football/Track
1976	Perry Graves ('15)	Football/Baseball
1977	George Halas ('18)	Football/Basketball/Baseball
1978	Charles Bennis ('35)	Football
1979	Charles Carney ('22)	Football/Basketball
1980	Duane Cullinan ('37)	Track
1981	Wayne Paulson ('66)	Football
1982	Cirilo McSween ('54)	Track
1983	Dwight "Dike" Eddleman ('49)	Football/Basketball/Track
1984	Thomas Stewart ('50)	Football
1985	Russell "Ruck" Steger ('48)	Football/Baseball
1986	Willard Thomson ('55)	Track
1987	Louis Boudreau ('87)	Basketball/Baseball
1988	David Downey ('63)	Basketball
1989	Thomas Riggs ('41)	Football
1990	Richard Butkus ('65)	Football
1991	Thomas Haller ('59)	Football/Basketball/Baseball
1992	William Butkovich ('47)	Football/Baseball
1993	Jerry Colangelo ('93)	Basketball/Baseball
1994	Bobby Mitchell ('58)	Football/Track
1995	Tal Brody ('65)	Basketball

ILLINI LEGEND:

ANDY PHILLIP

The magnificent career of Fighting Illini basketball star Andy Phillip can be summed up in just two words: record-setting. Besides setting University of Illinois basketball records for points in a game, in a season, and in a career, the Granite City, Illinois, native also put his name in the record book beside several Big Ten marks. Following the 1945 season, he was named first-team All-America and was honored as the Big Ten's Most Valuable Player. Phillip and his "Whiz Kids" teammates won back-to-back Big Ten titles in 1942 and '43, compiling an unbelievable 25-2 record in conference play over that span. After the end of the '43 season, Phillip was called to active duty with the Marine Corps for three years. When World War II ended, he returned to Illinois with three other "Whiz Kids" (Jack Smiley, Gene Vance, and Ken Menke) in 1947, when they settled for a second-place finish in the conference. For the next 11 years, Phillip played professional basketball in the National Basketball Association, including two with the World Champion Boston Celtics. A five-time NBA all-star, he was named to the Basketball Hall of Fame in 1961. Phillip has spent all of his post-basketball life in California, retiring in 1987 after 24 years as supervising officer for the Riverside County Probation Department. He currently resides in Rancho Mirage, California.

 Illini Lore

During its first 12 months of operation, the $1.7 million Abbott Power Plant in 1941-42 proved to be more efficient than University of Illinois officials hoped it would be. The new plant was built adjacent to the Illinois Central railroad tracks, just northwest of Memorial Stadium, and close to the expanding University. A comparison of the facility's performance in 1941-42 to 1932-33 showed that nearly 10 percent less coal was burned and that 13 percent more cubic feet of space was heated.

1942-43

I·L·L·I·N·I M·O·M·E·N·T

Lineman Alex Agase scored two touchdowns for the Illini to beat defending national champion Minnesota.

ILLINI END MINNESOTA'S 18-GAME WINNING STREAK:

The 24,000 fans who attended Illinois' 32nd annual Homecoming Game witnessed one of the greatest Illini football upsets ever. First-year coach Ray Eliot inspired his troops with a pregame pep talk and snapped defending national champion Minnesota's 18-game winning streak. The unlikely Illini hero that afternoon was junior guard Alex Agase who scored two of his team's three touchdowns. With the score tied 13-13 late in the fourth quarter, Agase scored the game-winning TD by pouncing on an errant Gopher snap in the end zone. Illinois' 20-13 victory was its first over a Big Ten foe since 1939.

ILLINI BIRTHDAYS

SEPTEMBER 1942
4– George Donnelly, football
6– Jerry Olefsky, tennis
13– William Gabbett, football
20– Greg Gwin, swimming

OCTOBER 1942
1– Sam Price, football
2– Bob Shineflug, tennis
20– David Pike, football
24– John Jeffery, wrestling
29– Jim Holbrook, swimming

NOVEMBER 1942
2– Archie Sutton, football
3– Jerry Baker, baseball
14– Phil Karafotas, swimming

DECEMBER 1942
8– Bill Edwards, basketball
9– Dick Butkus, football

JANUARY 1943
5– Bob Belsole, baseball
20– Clayton Beattie, wrestling
29– Ed Washington, football

FEBRUARY 1943
2– Wayne Paulson, football
27– Brian Duniec, football

MARCH 1943
15– Joel Jonas, baseball
18– Bruce Capel, football
18– Gerald Smith, golf
27– Larry Bauer, basketball

APRIL 1943
5– Duane "Skip" Thoren, basketball

MAY 1943
7– Bogie Redmon, basketball
8– Craig Bell, fencing

23– Bill Langdon, wrestling
29– Dave Powless, football

JUNE 1943
4– John Sisson, tennis
8– Ted Harvey, baseball
17– Bill Schlueter, baseball
30– Tom McCollum, tennis

JULY 1943
16– William Minor, football

AUGUST 1943
21– Wylie Fox, football
26– Dick Dorr, football
31– Tal Brody, basketball

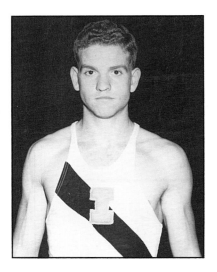

Illinois' Herb Matter won both the pole vault and the broad jump title at the 1943 Big Ten Indoor Track and Field Championships.

Andy Phillip scored 18 points in Illinois' rout of Northwestern.

ILLINI ITEM

ILLINOIS' "WHIZ KIDS" beat Northwestern, 86-44, at the Chicago Stadium on February 27, 1943, before a record crowd of 19,848. The triumph marked the school's largest margin of victory ever on the road, and was the 11th of 12 in a row as the Illini wrapped up a perfect record in conference play.

ILLINI LISTS

WHIZ KIDS' MOST MEMORABLE GAMES

In June 1994, the University of Illinois' famous Whiz Kids basketball team of the 1940s was surveyed to find out what they considered to be their most mem-orable games. Ken Menke, Andy Phillip, Art Mathisen, Gene Vance, and Jack Smiley were asked to rank their top 10 selections in order, with 10 points awarded for their first selection, nine points for their second choice, etc. Four of the five men selected Illinois' game vs. Great Lakes on December 19, 1942 as their most memorable game. In that contest, the "Whiz Kids" came from behind to beat a team of former pros, 57-53.

1.	12/19/42 vs. Great Lakes	48 pts
2.	2/27/43 at Northwestern	39 pts
3.	1/3/42 at Wisconsin	26 pts
4.	1/2/43 vs. Stanford	24 pts
5.	2/28/42 at Northwestern	23 pts
6.	3/1/43 vs. Chicago	17 pts
7.	2/23/42 vs. Wisconsin	16 pts
8.	1/11/43 at Wisconsin	13 pts
9.	1/13/47 vs. Ohio State	13 pts
10.	12/9/41 vs. Marquette	12 pts

Nearly 50 years after they had performed there as athletes, the Whiz Kids returned to Huff gym to participate in a 1990 re-dedication ceremony. Pictured here are (left to right) Andy Phillip, Ken Menke, Art Mathisen, Jack Smiley, and Gene Vance.

ILLINI LEGEND:

RAY ELIOT

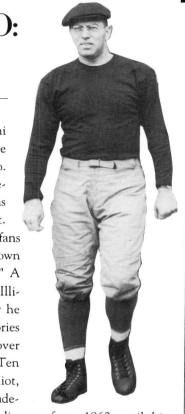

During his days as a Fighting Illini football player under Bob Zuppke in the 1930s, he was listed on the roster as No. 38, Ray Nusspickle. As Zuppke's replacement from 1942 to 1959, he was introduced as Head Coach Ray Eliot. However, to the thousands of loyal fans who grew to love him, he was best known by the simple moniker "Mr. Illini." A football and baseball letterwinner at Illinois, Eliot's greatest fame came after he coached the Illini to Rose Bowl victories in 1947 over UCLA and in 1952 over Stanford. Three times, he won Big Ten championships (1946, '51, and '53). Eliot, whose enthusiasm and vigor were trademarks, served as associate athletic director from 1960 until his retirement in 1973. He represented the Illini program in an honorary capacity after that, before being called upon in the spring of 1979 to become interim athletic director. Eliot was a dynamic speaker who was best known for his inspiring speech "The Proper State of Mind." He died on February 24, 1980, at the age of 75, and was buried in Mt. Hope Cemetery, across Fourth Street from Memorial Stadium.

 Illini Lore

The University of Illinois focused much of its efforts toward war-time preparedness during the 1942-43 academic year. About 1,100 persons, including the physical plant staff and several faculty members, were actively engaged in a program of war-time civilian defense. University enrollment dropped nine percent, but more than 2,000 Navy School trainees were on campus, using Newman Hall and the ice rink as barracks. The UI taught 42 special war courses, ranging from training in Red Cross and Civilian Defense to the structural design of airplanes. A total of 20,276 alumni served in the armed forces during World War II, with 29 former varsity athletes and 709 others with UI ties losing their lives in service.

1943-44

I·L·L·I·N·I M·O·M·E·N·T

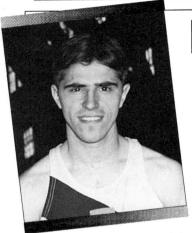

Track's Marce Gonzalez was one of only three letterwinners from 1942-43 who returned to compete in 1943-44 for Illinois.

ILLINI ATHLETICS DURING THE WAR:
World War II had a dramatic effect upon the University of Illinois' intercollegiate athletics program in 1943-44. Of the 81 men who earned varsity letters during the 1942-43 season, only wrestling letterman Robert Hughes and track and field monogram winners Marce Gonzalez and Robert Phelps returned to the '43-44 rosters. Among the more than 150 eligible athletes who left school to serve in the United States' armed forces were such Illini stars as basketball "Whiz Kids" Andy Phillip and Gene Vance, football's Alex Agase and Tony Butkovich, and baseball's Lee Eilbracht. The war forced the Athletic Association to totally drop its gymnastics and fencing programs from 1943-46, while ice hockey was eliminated from varsity status altogether. However, Athletic Director Doug Mills decided that "athletics in wartime should be carried on in as nearly pre-war fashion as possible. Certainly, material is not plentiful, coaches may feel their task at times is insurmountable, and gate receipts may decline seriously. But none of these factors should influence us from the conviction that the basic values of the athletic program must remain alive."

ILLINI BIRTHDAYS

SEPTEMBER 1943
29– Bill McKeown, basketball

OCTOBER 1943
1– John Mackovic, football coach/athletic director
4– Lynn Stewart, football
14– Tom Koenig, wrestling
25– Vic DeMarco, wrestling

NOVEMBER 1943
15– Richard Callaghan, football/baseball
22– Tony Kusmanoff, wrestling
27– Tom Branca, swimming

DECEMBER 1943
31– Fred Custardo, football

JANUARY 1944
4– Tony Parola, football
7– Mike Hebert, volleyball coach
24– Gary Eickman, football
26– Fred Cash, Chief XVII

MARCH 1944
3– John Tocks, fencing
21– Steve Kimbell, football

APRIL 1944
5– Tom Bauer, tennis
29– Ed Walsh, football
30– Fred Aprati, wrestling

MAY 1944
13– Jim Lehnerer, wrestling
17– Bob Brown, basketball
30– Gary Durchik, assistant football coach

JUNE 1944
7– Art Allen, baseball
14– Dick Kee, football

15– Jim Vopicka, basketball
27– Dan Jeffery, wrestling
29– Bob Lewke, tennis

JULY 1944
7– Mel Blackwell, basketball
13– Dale Greco, football
18– Don Freeman, basketball
24– Steve Simons, tennis

AUGUST 1944
7– Paul Koch, baseball
9– David Evans, fencing
20– Don Hansen, football
22– John "Skip" Pickering, athletic trainer
25– Al McCullum, wrestling

Illinois' talented Robert Kelley won the 880-yard run at both the Big Ten indoor and outdoor meets, and at the NCAA championship.

Illinois' 1943 football squad lost a heartbreaker at Ohio State.

ILLINI ITEM

ILLINOIS LOST ITS ONLY opportunity to salvage a dismal football season on November 13, 1943, when it traveled to Ohio State. When Buckeye quarterback Dean Sensenbaugher's last-play-of-the-game pass fell incomplete in Illinois' end zone, the two teams went disappointedly to their dressing rooms, tied at 26 all. However, a game official had signaled the Illini offsides and put two seconds back on the field. Both teams were brought back on the field, and OSU placekicker John Stungis kicked a 23-yard field goal to give the Buckeyes a 29-26 victory.

ILLINI LISTS

DAYS ON WHICH ONE ILLINI DIED AND ANOTHER WAS BORN

Jan. 15, 1974	Football's Charles Belting died (baseball's Brian McClure was born)
Feb. 15, 1952	Football's Louis Fischer died (football's Chuck Kogut was born)
Feb. 19, 1956	Baseball's Ray Demmitt died (football's Dan Bulow was born)
March 5, 1954	Track's Ike Durland died (basketball's Dennis Graff was born)
March 19, 1968	Football's Ralph Lanum died (football's Elbert Turner was born)
April 2, 1969	Football's Tom Straw died (track's Shayla Baine was born)
April 23, 1961	Basketball's Roy Gatewood died (volleyball's Chris Dowdy was born)
May 10, 1971	Basketball's Ted Haines died (swimming's Frank Niziolek was born)
July 3, 1969	Basketball's Jim White died (gymnastics' David Pearlstein was born)
Aug. 2, 1960	Baseball's Harry McCollum died (tennis' Dorothy Hogan was born)
Aug. 5, 1968	Football's Bob Fletcher died (golf's Tony Russo and Sue Winkelman were born)
Sept. 5, 1970	Football's Ken Bradley died (football's Brad Hopkins was born)
Sept. 19, 1960	Football's Fred Clarke died (basketball's Diane Ricketts was born)
Oct. 3, 1947	Football's Leonard Charpier died (wrestling's Dennis Rott was born)
Oct. 31, 1972	Track's Robert Ayres died (football's Tim McCloud was born)
Nov. 3, 1971	Football's Albert Mohr died (football's Drew Daniels was born)
Nov. 8, 1972	Football's George "Potsy" Clark died (football's Ken Blackman was born)

ILLINI LEGEND: CLAUDE "BUDDY" YOUNG

The University of Illinois' first nationally famous African-American athlete stood only five-feet-four-inches tall, but the legacy he established is immeasurable. Claude "Buddy" Young came to Champaign-Urbana from Chicago Phillips High School, where he was a state champion sprinter and an all-star halfback in football. In his very first competition with the Fighting Illini track team on February 5, 1944, Young won the 60-yard dash at New York's prestigious Millrose Games. He lost very few races that freshman year, tying the world indoor record of 6.1 seconds in the 60 and capturing two sprint titles at the NCAA outdoor meet. On the football field, little number 66 was equally magnificent. The 1944 season saw Young tie Red Grange's school record for touchdowns (13) and average nearly nine yards every time he rushed the ball. He served in the Navy in 1945, but was able to return to the Illini football team in 1946, winning MVP honors in the '47 Rose Bowl. Young left Illinois after that season to sign a football contract with the New York Yankees. His Hall of Fame career in pro football ended after 10 seasons, and he became the first Baltimore Colts player to have his jersey—No. 22—retired. In 1964, Young became the first black executive to be hired by the National Football League. He stayed at that post until his death in an automobile accident on September 4, 1983.

Illini Lore

On June 1, 1944, the University of Illinois' Board of Trustees approved a proposal to establish a College of Veterinary Medicine and Surgery. Twenty-five years earlier, in 1919, establishment of the college had been authorized by the Illinois General Assembly, but no appropriations followed. The first course in veterinary medicine was actually taught at the UI in 1870.

1944-45

I·L·L·I·N·I M·O·M·E·N·T

George Walker accounted for 15 of Illinois' 65½ points and led the Illini track and field team to the 1945 Big Ten outdoor championship.

WALKER LEADS ILLINI TO TRACK TITLE:

Scoring in 12 of the 14 events, Coach Leo Johnson's Fighting Illini track and field squad ended Michigan's two-year reign as Big Ten champions, May 26, 1945. Illinois' star performers included two veterans and a pair of freshmen. Junior captain Marce Gonzalez captured the 220-yard dash while grad student Bob Kelley repeated his conference outdoor titles in the 440- and 880-yard runs. Illini rookie George Walker accounted for 15 of his team's 65½ points, taking first place in the 100-yard dash, the 120-yard high hurdles and the 220-yard low hurdles. Fellow freshman Henry Aihara won the broad jump and tied for fourth in the high jump. Two weeks later at the NCAA meet in Milwaukee, the Illini placed second behind Navy, 62 to 57¾. Walker captured both hurdles events, Aihara won the broad jump, and Bob Phelps took top honors in the pole vault event.

ILLINI BIRTHDAYS

SEPTEMBER 1944
4– Earl Hoffenberg, baseball
8– Bill Hartman, track
9– Jim Grabowski, football
14– Bill Kroll, strength coach
16– Roger Garret, fencing

OCTOBER 1944
2– Dave Crouse, baseball
3– Ron Acks, football
25– Willis Fields, football

NOVEMBER 1944
8– Richard Fitzgerald, football
17– Bruce Burns, wrestling
28– Tom Smith, football
28– Bob Petkus, football

DECEMBER 1944
21– Alan Castator, swimming

JANUARY 1945
4– Deon Flessner, basketball
6– Alan Waters, football
11– Phil Knell, football
17– Preston Pearson, basketball

FEBRUARY 1945
7– Dick Stotz, football
7– Jim Stotz, football
12– Len Wislow, football
16– Bob Johansen, basketball

MARCH 1945
6– Bob Trumpy, football
6– Rick Wurtzel, tennis
10– Bo Batchelder, football
22– Dave Florio, swimming
31– Joe Domko, wrestling

APRIL 1945
6– Jerry Carbonari, football
13– Doug Harford, football
18– Jim Dawson, basketball

MAY 1945
21– Dan Humay, football/baseball

JUNE 1945
1– Ron Aufrecht, fencing
8– Fred Klemm, baseball
22– Terry Kasper, baseball
23– Gerry Schmidt, football
27– Andy Dystrup, baseball
27– Jerry Mettille, basketball

JULY 1945
2– Bob Bachman, swimming

6– Bill Mitchell, football
29– Tom Sawicki, swimming
30– Charles Harter, fencing

AUGUST 1945
3– Pete Bates, swimming
23– Bruce Sullivan, football

Illinois' Vic Twomey was the top finisher at the 1945 Big Ten cross country meet.

Buddy Young (66) rushed three times for 100 yards in his Illini football debut.

ILLINI ITEM

TO SAY THAT THE FOOTBALL debut of Buddy Young, September 16, 1944, was impressive would be a mammoth understatement. The nation's fastest halfback played nine and one-half minutes for Illinois against Illinois State, averaging more than 28 yards every time he touched the ball. Young lost four yards on his very first carry, then scored touchdowns of 22 and 82 yards on his next two attempts. He also ran 51 yards for a TD, only to have it called back by a clipping penalty. The final score: Illinois 79, ISU 0.

ILLINI LISTS

ILLINI FOOTBALL PLAYERS IN HEISMAN TROPHY BALLOTING

1944	Buddy Young, 5th
1951	John Karras, 6th
1953	J.C. Caroline, 7th
1959	Bill Burrell, 4th
1963	Dick Butkus, 6th
1964	Dick Butkus, 3rd
1965	Jim Grabowski, 3rd
1980	Dave Wilson, 10th
1982	Tony Eason, 8th
1989	Jeff George, 35th

Buddy Young finished fifth in the 1944 Heisman Trophy balloting.

ILLINI LEGEND:

WALTON KIRK

It was a star-studded cast of nominees for the *Daily Illini's* annual "Illini Athlete of the Year" award in 1944-45, but in the end, a junior basketball guard nicknamed "Junior" ran away from his competition. Unanimous All-Big Ten selection Walton "Junior" Kirk was the students' first choice, out-distancing two-sport standout Howie Judson by a two-to-one margin. The native of Mt. Vernon, Illinois, was the Most Valuable Player of Doug Mills' Illinois cagers, averaging nearly 11 points per game. His best effort of the '44-45 campaign came at Michigan in a 55-37 victory when he scored a season-high 21 points. Kirk went into the service at Fort Lewis in June of 1945, then returned to Illinois for the 1946-47 season. He then signed a $10,000 NBA contract with the Fort Wayne Pistons, joining teammates Jack Smiley and Ken Menke. Kirk scored 907 points during his 163-game NBA career with Fort Wayne, Tri-Cities, and Milwaukee. In 1952, he began a long high school coaching career, which saw him make stops at Harvard and Salem, Illinois, and at Dubuque, Iowa. Now retired, he and his wife reside in Dubuque.

 Illini Lore

George Stoddard (left) became UI's 10th president in 1945, replacing Arthur Willard (right).

George Dinsmore Stoddard was appointed as the University of Illinois' 10th president May 26, 1945, replacing Arthur Cutts Willard as the chief executive officer. Stoddard was the University's chief executive officer during a construction boom on campus, but he also found himself mired in controversy. UI's Board of Trustees and state legislators disapproved of Stoddard's frequent trips abroad and with his on-going debates with various members of the school's faculty. Stoddard resigned July 24, 1953, under pressure from the Board of Trustees following a 6-3 vote of "no confidence."

F. Dwyer Murphy, Jr. '48

*UI Varsity I-Man & co-founder of
Goodman-Murphy Insurance Agency (1948)*

George Huff '92
First UI Athletic Director

*Grandfather of Eisner-Murphy Insurance
Agency co-founder, F. Dwyer Murphy, Jr.*

Frank D. Murphy '12
1912 Olympic Pole Vaulter

*Grandfather of current EMP Insurance
Agency owners, Kathy & Tim Murphy*

Robert E. Eisner, Jr. '42

*UI Varsity I-Man & co-founder of
Eisner-Murphy Insurance Agency (1960)*

Illini Athletics...It's Really In Our Blood.

Our long-standing involvement in UI athletics continues...through our company's sponsorship of the
EMP/MVP program. Each year, an EMP/MVP is designated for every UI varsity basketball game and
a contribution is made to the UI school in which each MVP is enrolled.

emp INSURANCE

We've Got You Covered!

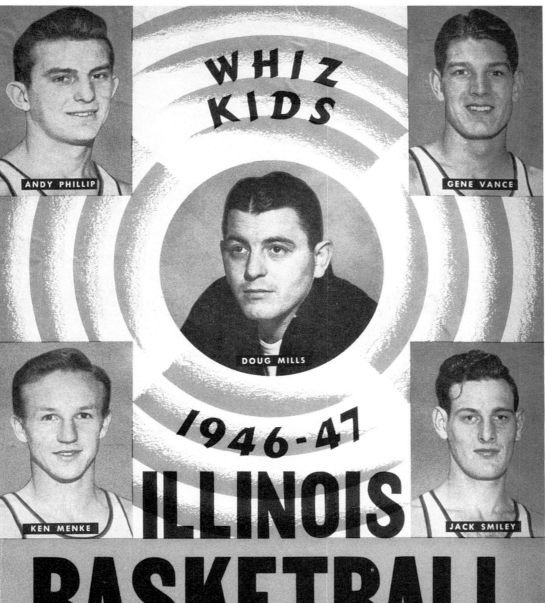

WHIZ KIDS

ANDY PHILLIP

GENE VANCE

DOUG MILLS

KEN MENKE

JACK SMILEY

1946-47

ILLINOIS
BASKETBALL

GAMES AT HOME
All Home Games at 7:28 p.m.

DEC. 6 .	CORNELL COLLEGE	JAN. 11 . .	NORTHWESTERN
DEC. 11 . . .	MARQUETTE	JAN. 13 . . .	OHIO STATE
DEC. 14 . . .	PITTSBURGH	JAN. 25 . . .	WISCONSIN
DEC. 28	NEBRASKA	FEB. 8	IOWA
JAN. 4 .	UNIV. OF MEXICO	FEB. 15 . . .	INDIANA
JAN. 6 . . .	MINNESOTA		

Mar. 20-22—Illinois State High School
Basketball Tournament

GAMES AWAY — Dec. 16—MISSOURI (at Kansas City); Dec. 20—CALIFOR-
NIA (at Berkeley); Dec. 21—CALIFORNIA (at Berkeley); Jan. 1—WISCONSIN (at Madi-
son); Feb. 1—OHIO STATE (at Columbus); Feb. 5—PURDUE (at Lafayette); Feb. 22—
NORTHWESTERN (at Chicago Stadium); Feb. 24—MICHIGAN (at Ann Arbor); Mar. 1—
INDIANA (at Bloomington).

1945-1954

1945-46

I·L·L·I·N·I M·O·M·E·N·T

The 1946 Illini tennis team won its first Big Ten title in 14 years. Pictured here (left to right) are Jim Gates, Fred Steers, Ben Migdow, Coach Howard Braun, Melvin Rondoll, Roger Downs, and Ray Von Spreckelsen.

ILLINI TEAMS WIN FOUR BIG TEN TITLES:
Though they finished second to Ohio State in the all-sports standings among Big Ten schools, Fighting Illini teams won more conference titles than any other conference member during the 1945-46 athletic season. Illinois took top honors in the sports of both indoor and outdoor track, wrestling, and tennis. The latter two were especially pleasing, since several years had lapsed in between championships. Nine years had passed since the Illini grapplers last won a title, and 14 years had gone by since the tennis squad ended up on top of the league standings. Coach Leo Johnson's track and field team made the biggest news, however. Not only did they sweep titles in both Big Ten seasons, they also took top honors nationally, outdoors, winning the NCAA title in Minneapolis.

ILLINI BIRTHDAYS

SEPTEMBER 1945
7– Lou Tepper, football coach

OCTOBER 1945
3– Ron Guenther, football and athletic director
13– Stan Catlett, wrestling
30– James Hoffman, football

NOVEMBER 1945
3– Ken Holtzman, baseball
29– Joel Stellwagen, football

JANUARY 1946
9– Dean Volkman, football
11– John Wright Sr., football

13– Jay Walters, football
14– Ken Kmiec, football

FEBRUARY 1946
19– Kit Werremeyer, swimming
20– Ben Louis, basketball

MARCH 1946
5– David Holden, tennis

APRIL 1946
11– Frederick "Fritz" Harms, football
19– Don Kahon, wrestling
27– David Tomasula, football
28– Bill Allen, football

JUNE 1946
18– Dick Tate, football
26– Walter Kummerow, wrestling

JULY 1946
9– Ron Bess, football
18– Gary Simpson, Chief XIX
27– Rich Erickson, football

AUGUST 1946
25– John Davis, football
25– Gregg Gregory, baseball

Les Bingaman, a second-team All-Big Ten guard at Illinois, went on to an outstanding career in the NFL, including seven seasons with the Detroit Lions.

ILLINI ITEM

THE VERY FIRST "FLYING ILLINI" team took to the airways November 16, 1945, when Coach Ray Eliot's football squad chartered a flight from Willard Airport to Ohio State. Eliot and 19 of his top players departed Savoy at 1 p.m., landing an hour and a half later in Columbus in their TWA airliner. It was the first large passenger take-off from the new airport, dedicated just three weeks before. Illinois' starting left tackle Bill Kolens, a navy fighter pilot, voluntarily gave up his seat on the plane to let someone else experience his first flight. The balance of the Illini football team rode a New York Central train for seven hours to the Ohio capital city. The entire squad returned to Champaign via the railways following their 27-2 loss.

ILLINI LISTS

MULTIPLE ILLINI BIG TEN INDIVIDUAL MEN'S TRACK CHAMPIONS (since 1945)

- Charlton Ehizuelen — 12 titles (includes one relay title)
- George Walker — 10 titles
- Mike Durkin — 9 titles
- Herb McKenley — 9 titles (includes three relay titles)
- Willie Williams — 9 titles
- Tim Simon — 8 titles (includes four relay titles)
- George Kerr — 7 titles (includes two relay titles)
- Don Laz — 7 titles
- Willard Thomson — 6 titles
- Cirilo McSween — 6 titles (includes three relay titles)

George Kerr won seven Big Ten track titles during his career from 1958-60.

ILLINI LEGEND:

HERB McKENLEY

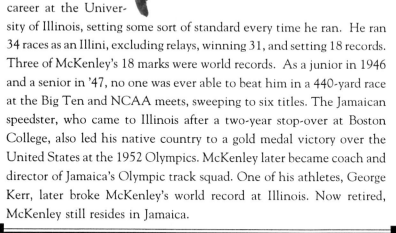

His coach, Leo Johnson, once compared Herb McKenley to "a golf ball bouncing down a concrete road." That statement probably doesn't do justice to how good Illinois' greatest quarter-miler actually was. McKenley rarely met defeat during his two-year track career at the University of Illinois, setting some sort of standard every time he ran. He ran 34 races as an Illini, excluding relays, winning 31, and setting 18 records. Three of McKenley's 18 marks were world records. As a junior in 1946 and a senior in '47, no one was ever able to beat him in a 440-yard race at the Big Ten and NCAA meets, sweeping to six titles. The Jamaican speedster, who came to Illinois after a two-year stop-over at Boston College, also led his native country to a gold medal victory over the United States at the 1952 Olympics. McKenley later became coach and director of Jamaica's Olympic track squad. One of his athletes, George Kerr, later broke McKenley's world record at Illinois. Now retired, McKenley still resides in Jamaica.

Illini Lore

Less than four years after President Arthur Willard first addressed the University of Illinois' Board of Trustees about securing an appropriation of $200,000 for the purchase of land in Savoy, the University's new airport was dedicated October 26, 1945. The 762-acre airport featured three mile-long, concrete runways, making it the nation's foremost university-owned facility. It was renamed UI Willard Airport on October 18, 1961, after the former President.

1946-47

Quarterback Tommy Stewart (#21) sets down the Illini offensive team during a practice at the Rose Bowl stadium.

I·L·L·I·N·I M·O·M·E·N·T

ILLINI SMELL THE ROSES:

The road to Pasadena was a long and winding one for the University of Illinois. Illini players traveled familiar highways through such Midwestern cities as Bloomington, Ann Arbor, and Iowa City, but had also detoured through much less familiar sites such as Germany and Okinawa before that. Nearly 300 men, most of whom were returning from military duty in World War II, turned out for Coach Ray Eliot's opening practice in 1946. The Illini split their first four games, but stepped on the gas at the end. Illinois consecutively disposed of Wisconsin, Michigan, Iowa, Ohio State, and Northwestern to wind up with a 6-1 Big Ten record and a berth in the Rose Bowl. It marked the first game in the pact between the Big Ten and the Pacific Eight conferences. Though it marked UI's first-ever trip to Pasadena for the New Year's Day classic, the Illini weren't greeted with open arms. California's media didn't respect the 11-point underdogs, predicting a huge victory by third-ranked UCLA. The Bruins led, 7-6, after the first quarter, but it was all Illinois during the final three periods. Illini running backs Julius Rykovich and Buddy Young rushed for 103 yards apiece, and seven different players each scored a touchdown. The final score: Illinois 45, UCLA 14.

ILLINI BIRTHDAYS

SEPTEMBER 1946
23– Fred Lukasik, golf

OCTOBER 1946
20– Bob Loffredo, wrestling
20– Mike Schroeder, fencing
31– Ed Halik, track

NOVEMBER 1946
3– Jim Marinangel, football
9– Art Stark, swimming
13– Cyril Pinder, football/track
26– Bart Macomber, wrestling

DECEMBER 1946
2– Ron Dunlap, basketball
5– Richard Binder, baseball
17– John Townsend, assistant football coach

21– Paul Shapin, gymnastics
24– Bob Robertson, football
26– Herschel Johnson, football
27– Rich Jones, basketball

JANUARY 1947
3– Steve Levenson, tennis
24– Terry Cole, assistant athletic director
28– Ed Thompson, tennis

FEBRUARY 1947
5– Michael Walker, fencing
6– Carson Brooks, football
10– Bill Huston, football
11– Larry Holton, assistant football coach
11– Jim Whiteside, football

13– Tom Crum, football
13– Lloyd Gussis, baseball
14– Les Busboom, basketball
15– John Lamoreux, track
23– Jim DeBord, swimming

MARCH 1947
1– Gerald Line, football
9– Bob Naponic, football
18– Kip Pope, swimming
19– Jodie Harrison, basketball
22– Jim Brubaker, track
26– Bill Nowak, football

APRIL 1947
11– Karl Fretz, fencing
21– Ron Ingrum, baseball
29– Dennis Pace, basketball

MAY 1947
1– Rodney Roberts, fencing
19– Randy Rodgers, football

JUNE 1947
3– Kerry Anderson, wrestling
15– Phil Cochran, baseball
23– Larry Smiley, swimming
26– Tony Pleviak, football

JULY 1947
7– Michael Elbl, tennis

AUGUST 1947
6– Paul Jacob, wrestling
19– Jed Hertz, tennis

Jack Smiley was the defensive whiz of the 1947 "Whiz Kids."

Bob Rehberg was the Big Ten mile champion indoors.

ILLINI ITEM

IN ADDITION to the Fighting Illini football team, four other Illinois athletic teams finished on top of their respective Big Ten standings. Coach Leo Johnson's track team swept to titles both indoors and out, led by Bob Rehberg, Bob Richards, John Twomey, Bill Mathis, Herb McKenley, Dike Eddleman, and George Walker. The Illini baseball team, coached by Wally Roettger, got big seasons from pitcher Marv Rotblatt and catcher Lee Eilbracht, winning their conference race by one game over Ohio State. Finally, the Illinois wrestling squad saw Dave Shapiro and Lou Kachiroubas successfully defend their Big Ten titles, en route to the team championship.

ILLINI LISTS

ILLINI FOOTBALL PLAYERS WHO WERE BIG TEN MVPs

The *Chicago Tribune* has awarded the Silver Football award to the Big Ten's Most Valuable Player each year since 1924. Here are the six Illinois gridders who've been so honored:

1924	Harold "Red" Grange,	halfback
1946	Alex Agase,	guard
1959	Bill Burrell,	guard
1963	Dick Butkus,	linebacker
1965	Jim Grabowski,	fullback
1983	Don Thorp,	defensive tackle

Dick Butkus was selected as the Big Ten's Most Valuable Player in 1963.

ILLINI LEGEND:

ALEX AGASE

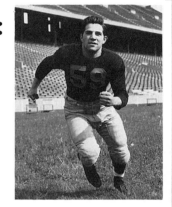

In 1990, to commemorate the 100th anniversary of Walter Camp's first All-America football team, the *New Haven* (Connecticut) *Register* selected a 24-member All-Century Team. Among the two dozen players chosen, the University of Illinois led the way with three honorees. Two were predictable—Red Grange and Dick Butkus—but the third Illini—Alex Agase—was probably a surprise to some. However, when one considers that the 205-pound guard from Evanston, Illinois was the only college player to be a three-time All-American for two different teams—Illinois and Purdue—his selection makes perfect sense. In addition to earning MVP honors at Illinois in 1946, Agase also was selected as the Big Ten's top player, leading the Illini to the 1947 Rose Bowl championship. Following a pro football career in Chicago, Cleveland, and Baltimore, Agase entered the coaching ranks. He served as head coach for both Northwestern and Purdue, earning "Coach of the Year" honors in 1970. Agase is now retired and lives in Ann Arbor, Michigan.

 I l l i n i   L o r e

The University of Illinois received the largest gift in its history in June of 1946, when wealthy land owner Robert Allerton presented the UI with more than 6,000 acres of farm land, located just west of Monticello, Illinois. The gift more than doubled UI's land holdings. Allerton Park was eventually opened to the general public, with the exception of the mansion, which Allerton stipulated to be used for general University purposes. During the Bob Blackman Era, the Illinois football team stayed at Allerton House the night before home games.

1947-48

America's Time Capsule

- **Oct. 14, 1947:** *Captain Chuck Yeager piloted the world's first supersonic aircraft.*
- **Dec. 5, 1947:** *Heavyweight boxing champion Joe Louis earned a split decision over "Jersey Joe" Walcott.*
- **March 8, 1948:** *The Supreme Court ruled that religious education in public schools was a violation of the First Amendment.*
- **May 3, 1948:** *James Michener's* Tales of the South Pacific *and Tennessee Williams'* A Streetcar Named Desire *earned Pulitzer prizes.*
- **Aug. 16, 1948:** *Babe Ruth, baseball's greatest player, died of cancer.*

I·L·L·I·N·I M·O·M·E·N·T

Cadets of the U.S. Military Academy parade on the turf of Yankee Stadium before the 1947 game between Illinois and Army.

ILLINOIS & ARMY BATTLE TO SCORELESS TIE:

New York's historic Yankee Stadium, the site of many of baseball's greatest games, hosted one of college football's top battles, October 11, 1947. The combatants were a powerful Army team, unbeaten in 30 consecutive games, and Illinois, looking for its third win in three outings. Coach Ray Eliot's Fighting Illini carried the fight through the entire game, out-gaining their highly favored opponents 212 yards to 162. Illinois' best opportunity to score came late in the first half when it moved the ball 51 yards from its own 27 to the Army 22. Illini placekicker Don Maechtle came in to try a field goal, but a low snap ruined UI's only chance to score all day. Army, which had only nine total first downs, never came close to denting the Illini end zone, and the game ended in a 0-0 tie.

ILLINI BIRTHDAYS

OCTOBER 1947
3– Dennis Rott, wrestling
21– Jeff Trigger, football
29– Gordon Brenne, wrestling

NOVEMBER 1947
8– Jeff McLellan, track
19– William Foss, baseball
24– Jimmy Collins, assistant basketball coach

DECEMBER 1947
9– Greg Jackson, basketball

JANUARY 1948
4– Tom Dunlap, tennis
17– William Abraham, fencing

FEBRUARY 1948
7– Doug Redmann, football

11– Terry Hite, volleyball coach

MARCH 1948
2– Bruce Kirkpatrick, wrestling
20– Carla Thompson, basketball and tennis coach
21– Bruce Erb, football

APRIL 1948
12– Dave Scholz, basketball

MAY 1948
26– Brad Matten, swimming

JUNE 1948
1– Tom Calza, baseball
21– Randy Crews, basketball/baseball

JULY 1948
6– Curt Cramer, swimming
10– Lee Carpenter, swimming
21– Flint Gregory, baseball
21– Terrill Rosborough, tennis
26– Bruce Layer, wrestling

AUGUST 1948
3– Linda Pecore, tennis coach

Illini baseball's Herb Plews ended his career with an all-time best average of .367, then went on to a four-year stint in the majors with Washington and Boston.

Coach Doug Mills and guard
Jack Burmaster

THE 1947-48 BASKETBALL SEASON marked the first of 20 years in the saddle for Illinois hoops coach Harry Combes. Combes, who'd spent the year before as head coach at Champaign High School, won his first seven games as the Illini mentor. His Illini were nearly perfect in contests at Huff Gym that season, winning 11 of 12 games, losing only to eventual Big Ten champion Michigan.

ILLINI LISTS

ILLINOIS' GREATEST STRIKE-OUT PITCHERS (CAREER)
(through 1995 season)

1.	Marv Rotblatt (1946-48)	286
2.	John Ericks (1986-88)	210
3.	Carl Jones (1984-87)	196
	Greg McCollum (1984-87)	196
5.	Jeff Innis (1981-83)	178
6.	Bubba Smith (1989-91)	171
7.	John Oestriech (1992-95)	169
8.	Mark Dressen (1989-92)	162
9.	Rich Capparelli (1986-89)	161
10.	George Mills (1930-32)	159

George Mills set an Illini
record for strikeouts
from 1930-32

ILLINI LEGEND:

MARV ROTBLATT

Perhaps the most nearly perfect pitching performance in Fighting Illini baseball history belonged to a five-foot-seven-inch southpaw named Marv Rotblatt. Relying on his wicked curve ball, Rotblatt set a plethora of records in 1947 and '48, many of which still stand. In six Big Ten appearances during the '47 campaign, the lefty from Chicago's Von Steuben High School compiled a perfect 6-0 record, striking out 49 batters in 54 innings. Rotblatt's finest single-game effort was an 18-strikeout gem against Purdue on April 30, 1948. Career-wise, from 1945-48, he won 25 of 29 decisions for the Illini and registered a school-record 286 K's. Rotblatt signed with the Chicago White Sox for a $3,000 bonus, and pitched in the major leagues for three seasons. Nowadays, he lives in Chicago.

 Illini Lore

During the 1947-48 academic year, Professor Albert Austin Harding completed 43 years as director of University of Illinois bands. A 1906 UI graduate, Harding helped "Illinois Loyalty" composer Thatcher Howland Guild arrange the school's fight song. Harding was widely acclaimed for his work with university bands, and, due to his admiration of Harding's work, famed "March King" John Philip Sousa donated his massive band collection to the University.

1948-49

- **Nov. 2, 1948:** *In a major political upset, Harry Truman defeated Thomas Dewey for the U.S. presidency.*
- **Dec. 15, 1948:** *Former State Department official Alger Hiss was indicted by a federal grand jury on two counts of perjury.*
- **April 4, 1949:** *NATO was formed when the North Atlantic Treaty was signed in Washington, D.C.*
- **April 20, 1949:** *The discovery of cortisone, the hormone promised to bring relief to sufferers of rheumatoid arthritis, was announced.*
- **June 22, 1949:** *Ezzard Charles defeated "Jersey Joe" Walcott to become the new heavyweight boxing champion.*

I·L·L·I·N·I M·O·M·E·N·T

Fred Green (#48) was the hero of Illinois' double-overtime victory at Indiana.

ILLINI NEED TWO OVERTIMES TO BEAT HOOSIERS:

Fred Green needed nearly 50 minutes to score his only basket of the game, but it proved to be the biggest one of his career and the biggest shot of the 1948-49 Illini basketball season. Playing before a sellout crowd in Bloomington January 8, 1949, Illinois and Indiana battled back and forth through a 37-37 tie at regulation time and 40-all at the end of the first overtime. With 14 seconds left in the second OT and the ball belonging to the Illini out-of-bounds under Indiana's goal, Bill Erickson slowly brought the ball down the court and shot a pass into Green, deep in the lane. The 6-7 senior from Urbana wheeled to his left and shot with his right hand, threading the ball through the hoop with just four seconds remaining. Illinois' 44-42 victory was its second of what would eventually be a league-leading 10 wins that season, enough for the school's first Big Ten title in six years.

ILLINI BIRTHDAYS

SEPTEMBER 1948
11– Mike Price, basketball

OCTOBER 1948
9– Bob Bess, football
9– Clyde Kuehn, baseball
23– Chris Accornero, volleyball coach
27– Jeffrey Cook, tennis
29– Neil Baskin, football

DECEMBER 1948
1– Peter Trobe, fencing
2– John Fregeau, wrestling
10– Bob Levine, swimming
28– Bob Wintermute, football

JANUARY 1949
16– Rich Brennan, football
23– Rick Howat, basketball

FEBRUARY 1949
8– Tim Kerestes, wrestling
12– Doug Dieken, football
14– Joe Howard, fencing
24– Tony Clements, football
28– Alan Fritz, baseball

APRIL 1949
14– Bob Burns, football

MAY 1949
1– Dan Rotzoll, football
17– John Bitzer, Chief XX
22– Dean Tjaden, fencing
27– Bev Mackes, gymnastics coach

JUNE 1949
12– Ken Howse, track
20– Tim McCarthy, football
28– George Voss, tennis

JULY 1949
5– Tom Jones, football

AUGUST 1949
20– Dan Darlington, football
24– Greg Johnson, wrestling coach

Jim Valek, head coach of the Fighting Illini from 1967-70, was Illinois football's Most Valuable Player in 1948.

THOUGH IT WAS THE ONLY time in his first dozen seasons that he didn't win the Big Ten title, Charlie Pond made his debut as head coach of the University of Illinois gymnastics team in 1948-49. Pond's success with the Illini was accentuated by 11 conference championships and four NCAA titles.

ILLINI LISTS

LONGEST ILLINI PUNTS

88 yards	Dike Eddleman vs. Iowa, 11/6/48	
86 yards	Bill Butkovich vs. Michigan, 10/27/45	
85 yards	Phil Vierneisel vs. Michigan State, 10/19/74	
74 yards	Dike Eddleman vs. Iowa, 11/6/48	
71 yards	Chad Little vs. Northwestern, 9/1/84	
70 yards	Bill Tate vs. Wisconsin, 10/4/52	

Dike Eddleman's 88-yard punt vs. Iowa is the longest in Illini football history.

ILLINI LEGEND:

DIKE EDDLEMAN

In the fall of 1992, the University of Illinois honored the greatest all-around athlete in its history by naming its "Athlete of the Year" award after the incomparable Dike Eddleman. No other man can claim the amazing feats accomplished by the pride of Centralia, Illinois, during his Illini career. Not only was Eddleman a member of Illinois' first Rose Bowl championship team in 1947 and the leading scorer on UI's first Final Four basketball team in 1949, he also won a silver medal as a high jumper in the 1948 Olympic games. Dike's 11 varsity letters at Illinois also stands as a record. He starred in the classroom as well, being awarded the Big Ten Conference Medal of Honor as an Illini senior. Following his graduation, Eddleman played in the NBA with the Tri-City Blackhawks and the Fort Wayne Pistons. In 1970, Dike returned to Illinois as the executive director of the Athletic Association's Grants-in-Aid program, retiring in 1992. He suffered a near fatal heart attack in the spring of 1995, but recovered. Eddleman resides in Champaign, with his wife, Teddy.

Illini Lore

Professor Joseph Tykociner, developer of sound-on movies, retired in 1949 after 27 years at the University of Illinois. He was born in Russian Poland in 1877 and studied in German technical institutes before coming to the United States in 1920. Following a year with Westinghouse, Tykociner joined the UI staff and, a year later on June 9, 1922, gave his first public demonstration of movies with sound. The developmental budget for Tykociner was less than $1,000. By coincidence, the first full-length sound picture, *The Jazz Singer*, was written by UI alumnus Samson Raphaelson.

1949-50

America's Time Capsule

- **Oct. 9, 1949:** The New York Yankees beat the Brooklyn Dodgers to win baseball's World Series.
- **Oct. 24, 1949:** The United Nations headquarters were dedicated in New York.
- **Jan. 31, 1949:** President Truman authorized development of the hydrogen bomb.
- **April 23, 1950:** The Minneapolis Lakers, starring George Mikan, beat the Syracuse Nationals to win the first National Basketball Association championship.
- **June 27, 1950:** President Truman ordered U.S. armed forces to Korea to help South Korea repel the North Korean invasion.

I·L·L·I·N·I M·O·M·E·N·T

Johnny Karras was known as "The Argo Express."

THE ARGO EXPRESS:

Johnny Karras originally reported to the University of Illinois football camp in the fall of 1946, but he quickly discovered that his opportunity to be a first-team running back was limited by the presence of an abundance of returning war veterans, including Buddy Young and Paul Patterson. Karras decided to return to his hometown of Argo, Illinois, and enlist in the Army, spending 18 months in the service. It turned out to be one of the smartest decisions he ever made, for when he came back to Illinois in 1949 as a mature, 20-year-old sophomore, he exploded into prominence, earning first-team All-Big Ten honors. In nine games that season, the Argo Express averaged 6.5 yards per rush and 31 yards per kickoff return, scoring an Illini-high seven touchdowns. For that performance, he was named Illinois' "Most Valuable Player." Karras' success continued in 1950 and '51, eventually as he earned All-America laurels his senior year.

ILLINI BIRTHDAYS

SEPTEMBER 1949
6– Dan Haas, wrestling
17– Jerry Brackett, baseball
24– John Kelly, cross country/track
24– Fred Newport, diving coach
27– Mark Koster, track
29– Jessica Dragicevic, women's track coach

NOVEMBER 1949
1– Rick Wack, tennis
14– Kirk McMillin, football
17– Jim Welsh, football
28– Bob Bucklin, football

DECEMBER 1949
28– Dave Kaemerer, track

JANUARY 1949
3– Kathleen Haywood, volleyball coach
18– Thomas Heinrich, baseball

21– Joe Tanner, swimming
22– Lee LaBadie, track

FEBRUARY 1950
1– Glenn Collier, football
8– Terry Masar, football
12– Tom Jeske, football
12– Nick Conner, basketball
24– Rick Gross, cross country/track

MARCH 1950
10– Barry Maxwell, tennis
30– Donn Damos, football
30– Dave Kronenfeld, fencing

APRIL 1950
16– David Engle, baseball

MAY 1950
13– Michael Pickering, football
24– John Spiller, football
31– Jamie Dufelmeier, football

JUNE 1950
10– Darrell Robinson, football
24– Denver Beck, wrestling
29– Jerry Cole, football
29– Dan Lehmann, fencing
30– Gary Paetau, track

JULY 1950
15– Bob Quinn, football
20– Nick Weatherspoon, basketball
21– Steve Livas, football
29– Dick Doty, baseball
31– George Samojedny, football

AUGUST 1950
2– Dave Zochert, football
3– William Emerick, baseball
7– Moe Kelly, football
7– Larry Cobb, track
27– Jack Morscheiser, football

Walt "Ox" Osterkorn led the Fighting Illini basketball team in scoring with 15.1 points per game in 1950, earning team MVP honors.

I

ILLINI ITEM

DICK "ROCKY" RAKLOVITS was one of Illinois' most brilliant performers in the early 1950s, starring on both the football field and the baseball diamond. He and Ruck Steger are the only two Fighting Illini athletes in the last 50 years to earn first-team All-Big Ten honors in both of those sports in the same season (1950-51).

ILLINI LISTS

ILLINI ATHLETES WHO BECAME MEMBERS OF THE BOARD OF TRUSTEES

Name, Sport(s)	Service Years
*James W. Armstrong, football/track	1923-35
David J. Downey, basketball	1991-93
Harold E. Grange, football	1951-55
Wirt Herrick, track	1949-61
Robert Z. Hickman, football	1949-55
*Harold A. Pogue, football/track	1935-41
Russell W. Steger, football/baseball	1969-75
Frederick L. Wham, football	1925-27

*Served as president of UI's Board of Trustees

ILLINI LEGEND:

RUCK STEGER

Russell "Ruck" Steger was a born entertainer. As an athlete, he thrilled Fighting Illini fans with battering-ram runs and tape-measure clouts. Off the field, Ruck mesmerized his audience by strumming a guitar and singing "The Wabash Cannonball." In addition to combining brawn and charm, the native of St. Louis also had his share of brains, maintaining a "B" average in the classroom and eventually earning the Big Ten Conference Medal of Honor. Uncle Sam put the finger on Ruck for two years before he could begin his athletic career at the University of Illinois. But once he put on an Illini uniform, there was no holding him back. In football, Steger was a first-team All-Big Ten running back, leading Illinois rushers in 1947 and '48. As an outfielder for Wally Roettger's UI baseball squad, Ruck had a career .317 average, en route to winning all-conference and Illini Athlete of the Year honors in 1950. His success didn't stop there, as he enjoyed a prosperous career in insurance and other businesses. Steger also served as a member of UI's Board of Trustees, and is now semi-retired in Chicago.

This scene from 1948 shows workers dredging out a pond for the new golf course in Savoy.

 ## Illini Lore

The University of Illinois' new 18-hole golf course, built at a cost of $250,000 entirely from Athletic Association funds, opened May 13, 1950, in Savoy. Constructed on 170 acres of rich farmland donated by Hartwell Howard, the 6,884-yard course was designed and built by C.D. Wagstaff, a 1918 UI alumnus.

1950-51

I·L·L·I·N·I M·O·M·E·N·T

Rod Fletcher helped lead Illinois to the 1951 Big Ten basketball title.

FLETCHER'S HEROICS LEAD ILLINI TO BIG TEN TITLE:
Trailing by four points in the Big Ten season finale with only four-and-a-half minutes left on the Jenison Field House clock, Illinois' prospects for an undisputed conference basketball crown certainly didn't look very promising . . . that is, until Rod Fletcher stepped forward to put on a dazzling one-man show for the Illini. During the next 60 seconds, he picked the pocket of two Michigan State dribblers and cashed them into baskets, tying the score at 43-all. With 3:30 left, the back-court whiz from Champaign rose at the free-throw line to can a jumper, and a minute later tapped in a left-handed rebound to give Illinois a four-point lead, and its eventual 49-43 victory. Fletcher's heroics gave Harry Combes' troops a nearly perfect 13-1 record in Big Ten play, a half-game better than runner-up Indiana, sending them to the NCAA tournament. In post-season play, the Illini lost the opening-round game at New York's Madison Square Garden to Kansas State, then rebounded in game two to defeat Columbia. Illinois then beat North Carolina State, and lost to champion-to-be Kentucky by two points. The Illini salvaged third place in the Final Four by beating Oklahoma A&M at Minneapolis, giving them a final overall record of 22-5.

ILLINI BIRTHDAYS

SEPTEMBER 1950
- 8– Ben Dozier, track
- 24– Jim Krelle, basketball
- 27– Ken Barr, gymnastics

OCTOBER 1950
- 10– Mike Walker, football
- 13– Gary Stluka, swimming
- 15– Tom Baumgart, football
- 24– Enos Brownridge, wrestling

NOVEMBER 1950
- 7– Mike Levanti, football
- 9– Ann Pollok, swimming coach
- 13– Al Olive, fencing
- 18– John Blair, assistant volleyball coach

DECEMBER 1950
- 5– Bruce Shuman, tennis coach
- 7– Joe Burden, golf

JANUARY 1950
- 4– Gary Windy, football
- 6– Allen Kustok, football
- 20– Rob Mango, track
- 22– John McBride, basketball
- 23– Jed Foster, basketball
- 31– John Graham, football

FEBRUARY 1950
- 2– Galen Avery, football
- 9– Sid Milstein, fencing
- 16– Mike Dobrzeniecki, football
- 17– Larry Huisinga, football

MARCH 1951
- 5– Richard Wright, football

- 15– Mason Minnes, football
- 22– Willie Lee, football
- 24– Nick Janicki, baseball

APRIL 1951
- 2– Norm Cooper, football
- 4– John Bedalow, football
- 5– Jim DeDecker, basketball
- 10– Willie Osley, football
- 10– Tom Mullin, football
- 13– Larry Cohen, basketball
- 26– Mike Navarro, football
- 28– Dennis Driscoll, football

MAY 1951
- 2– John Wiza, football
- 13– Randy Cordova, baseball
- 25– Ken Fleischer, fencing

JUNE 1951
- 2– Larry Allen, football
- 10– Greg Fenske, gymnastics
- 10– Tony Sterba, swimming
- 15– Mike Bennett, baseball

- 18– Mike Wells, football
- 20– Scott Irving, assistant track coach

JULY 1951
- 5– Bruce Keswick, swimming
- 6– Dave Wright, football
- 15– Ron Phillips, track
- 17– Miles Harris, tennis
- 28– Jeff Dawson, basketball
- 28– Bob Cortesi, baseball

AUGUST 1951
- 7– Mike Alley, baseball
- 19– Jim Steffenson, swimming
- 27– Steve Ross, football

Frank Dolan, a gymnastics letterman from 1949-51, won Big Ten titles on the horizontal bar and the pommel horse.

ILLINI ITEM

ON MAY 25, 1951, Don Laz's unusual double victory in the pole vault and the broad jump led Illinois to the Big Ten Outdoor Track and Field Championships at Dyche Stadium in Evanston, Illinois. Laz's amazing feat marked the first time in the 51-year history of the conference championships that the same man had captured individual titles in those two events in the same meet.

ILLINI LISTS

ILLINI FOOTBALL'S GREATEST PERFORMANCES VS. NO. 1-RANKED TEAMS

- Nov. 5, 1955   Illinois 25, Michigan 6
- Nov. 18, 1950   Illinois 14, Ohio State 7
- Oct. 27, 1956   Illinois 20, Michigan State 13
- Oct. 30, 1948   Michigan 28, Illinois 20
- Oct. 1, 1966   Michigan State 26, Illinois 10
- Oct. 24, 1970   Ohio State 48, Illinois 29

Illinois upset the No. 1-ranked Ohio State Buckeyes in 1950.

ILLINI LEGEND:

DON SUNDERLAGE

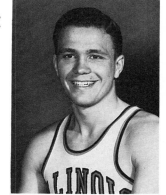

The 1951 Big Ten basketball season featured an abundance of stars, including Indiana's Bill Garrett and Minnesota's Whitey Skoog, but the league's Most Valuable Player that year was a senior guard from the University of Illinois named Don Sunderlage. The Illini captain led the conference in scoring with an average of 17.4 points per game. Many of Sunderlage's points came from the charity stripe, setting Illini records for both free throws made (171) and attempted (218). Those marks stood for 42 years at Illinois until Kiwane Garris broke them in 1993-94. Sunderlage wound up his college career as Illinois' all-time scoring leader, tallying 777 points in three seasons. He spent two seasons in the NBA, one year each with Milwaukee and Minnesota, averaging nearly eight points per game. Sunderlage was a member of the West squad in the 1954 NBA ALL-Star game. His life came to a tragic end at the age of 31 on July 15, 1961, when he and his wife, Janice, were killed in an automobile crash.

Illini Lore

The first coed cheerleaders for a University of Illinois athletic event appeared September 30, 1950, when the Fighting Illini football team hosted Ohio University at Memorial Stadium. The group included (left to right) Marilyn Lowe of Springfield, Dorothy Rich of Manteno, Mary Lou Schaeflein of Chicago, and Marilyn Berger of Chicago.

1951-52

I·L·L·I·N·I M·O·M·E·N·T

Illinois' defensive lineup for the 1952 Rose Bowl included (front row, left to right) Lawrence Stevens, Bob Weddell, Bob Lenzini, Don Ernst, Marvin Berschet, and Frank Wodziak; (back row, left to right) Stan Wallace, Elie Popa, Al Brosky, Chuck Boerio, and Herb Neathery.

MORE ROSES:

Coach Ray Eliot's 1951 squad is the last University of Illinois football team to be undefeated during an entire season. They won their first seven games of the campaign, then played to a scoreless tie at Ohio State. Illinois' Rose Bowl-clinching victory came in the regular-season finale at Northwestern, thanks to the toe of Sammy Rebecca, who kicked a 16-yard field goal. The New Year's Day showdown against Stanford, America's first college football game to be nationally telecast, proved to be a defensive struggle through the first half, with the Indians leading the Illini by a single point, 7-6. However, Illinois exploded for 34 unanswered points in the second half, capitalizing on a pair of Stan Wallace defensive interceptions and a strong running attack from game MVP Bill Tate (150 yards) and Johnny Karras. The 40-7 victory capped a 9-0-1 season and allowed the Illini to finish third in the national rankings.

ILLINI BIRTHDAYS

SEPTEMBER 1951
15– Tab Bennett, football
18– George Uremovich, football
19– Joe Lewis, football

OCTOBER 1951
7– Gary Grieshaber, wrestling
20– Jim Rucks, football/basketball/baseball
25– Jim Fieldhouse, swimming

NOVEMBER 1951
1– Ken Braid, football
9– Larry McCarren, football
24– Jack Groppel, tennis coach

DECEMBER 1951
2– Mitch Heinrich, football

JANUARY 1952
2– Palmer Klaas, wrestling
9– Kevin Morrey, tennis
10– Glenn Guth, baseball
12– Ken Panique, football
15– Gerry Sullivan, football
22– Bruce Dobson, football
23– John Wilson, football
27– Bob Dubrish, football
27– Billy Morris, basketball

FEBRUARY 1952
3– Lonnie Perrin, football
10– John Levanti, football
12– Mike Hinsburger, football
15– Chuck Kogut, football
25– Greg Colby, football/baseball/assistant football coach
26– Joe Irle, wrestling

MARCH 1952
13– Bud Kittler, football
20– Mark Coomes, assistant basketball coach

APRIL 1952
2– Gary Winckler, women's track coach
6– Garvin Roberson, football/basketball

MAY 1952
24– Tom McCartney, football

JUNE 1952
2– John Gann, football
13– Bob Standring, football
21– Carl Kemner, fencing

JULY 1952
8– Roger Coleman, football

AUGUST 1952
1– Marc Minkus, tennis
14– Willie Gartrell, football
16– Wayne Angel, track

13– C.J. Schroeder, basketball
18– Chip Castello, golf

Pitcher Gerry Smith compiled a perfect 5-0 record with a 1.40 earned-run average in 1952, leading the Illini baseball team to the Big Ten championship.

Illini pole vaulter Bob Richards

ILLINI ITEM

ON JANUARY 2, 1952, former University of Illinois pole vaulter Bob Richards was named winner of the Sullivan Award, symbolic of the nation's top amateur athlete. The 25-year-old preacher was the first choice on 174 of the 487 ballots cast by a nationwide panel of sports authorities, easily outdistancing teenage tennis sensation Maureen Connolly. Richards was the reigning Olympic champion in both the pole vault and the decathlon events, and the only two-time gold-medal winner in his event (1952 and '56) in Olympic competition. For several years, Richards was the spokesman for Wheaties cereal.

ILLINI LISTS

MOST BIG TEN MEN'S TEAM CHAMPION-SHIPS IN A SINGLE SEASON
(Through 1994-95 season)

- 8 Illinois, 1951-52
- 8 Michigan, 1943-44
- 6 Illinois, 1921-22
- 6 Michigan, 1922-23
- 6 Illinois, 1923-24
- 6 Michigan, 1960-61
- 6 Indiana, 1972-73
- 6 Indiana, 1973-74
- 5 Michigan, 8 times
- 5 Illinois, 6 times
- 5 Michigan State, 1 time

ILLINI LEGEND:

CHUCK BOERIO:

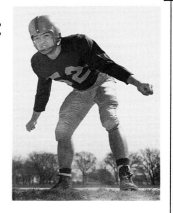

Linebacker Chuck Boerio typified the group of players who made up the University of Illinois' 1952 Rose Bowl team. At five-feet-11-inches and 190 pounds, Boerio was Coach Ray Eliot's star linebacker, earning first-team All-Big Ten honors. As the Illini's defensive signal caller, the Kincaid, Illinois, walk-on was the leader of a unit that allowed its six Big Ten foes an average of only five points per game during the 1951 campaign. Boerio, named Illini Athlete of the Year for 1951-52, was selected defensive captain of the 1952 College All-Stars in their game against the NFL champion Los Angeles Rams. His pro football career lasted only half a season with the Green Bay Packers, primarily due to his lack of size and speed. Boerio returned to the UI in 1956 and coached under Eliot for three seasons. He served as an assistant at the University of Colorado from 1959-61, helping guide the Buffaloes to the school's first Big Eight title that final year. Boerio was a teacher and coach in the Boulder, Colorado, school district for 28 years, retiring in 1990.

Illini Lore

Dennis Swanson, President of ABC-TV Sports, is a product of UI's School of Journalism.

The University of Illinois' School of Journalism celebrated its silver anniversary May 9, 1952. Among the individuals who have studied journalism at the UI are *Chicago Sun-Times'* movie critic Roger Ebert, *New York Times'* columnist and former Illini golfer, James "Scotty" Reston, *Sports Illustrated's* William Nack, the *Wall Street Journal's* Frederick Klein, and ABC-TV's President of Sports Dennis Swanson.

1952-53

America's Time Capsule

- **Sept. 23, 1952:** *Rocky Marciano won his 43rd consecutive bout without a loss, defeating "Jersey Joe" Walcott for the world heavyweight boxing title.*
- **Nov. 4, 1952:** *Dwight Eisenhower defeated Illinois governor Adlai Stevenson for the presidency of the United States.*
- **Jan. 2, 1953:** *Wisconsin senator Joseph McCarthy, known for his charges of communist infiltration in various organizations, was accused by a senate subcommittee of "motivation by self-interest."*
- **March 18, 1953:** *Baseball's Boston Braves moved to Milwaukee, Wisconsin.*
- **May 4, 1953:** *Author Ernest Hemingway was awarded a Pulitzer prize for his book,* The Old Man and the Sea.

I·L·L·I·N·I M·O·M·E·N·T

Willie Williams helped Illinois' track team dominate the Big Ten in 1952-53.

MORE TITLES IN 1952-53:

At no time in University of Illinois history was its athletic program prospering more than in the early 1950s under Athletic Director Doug Mills. In fact, from the 1950-51 season through the 1953-54 campaign, Fighting Illini teams captured 23 of the Big Ten Conference's possible 48 championships— nearly 50 percent! The 1952-53 athletic year saw Illinois ring up five titles. Lee Eilbracht's baseball team averaged only .223 at the plate in 13 conference games that season, but the strong pitching of Clive Follmer, Carl Ahrens, and Gerry Smith rung up a combined record of 9-2 on the mound as Illinois tied Michigan. Charlie Pond's Illini gymnastics team reigned as Big Ten champs for the fourth consecutive season and placed second in the NCAA meet, behind the consistent performances of Frank Bare, Jeff Austin, and Bob Sullivan. The Illini track teams, directed by Leo Johnson, once again dominated the conference cinders both indoors and out, thanks to sprinter Willie Williams, middle-distance star Stacey Siders, and high hurdler Joel McNulty. In fencing, it was business as usual, with Illinois winning its fourth consecutive Big Ten crown under Coach Max Garret. Sabreman John Cameron slashed his way to an individual title in his specialty.

ILLINI BIRTHDAYS

SEPTEMBER 1952
1– Al Ryniec, baseball
11– Octavius Morgan, football
13– Mike Wente, basketball
18– Tom Knotts, baseball

OCTOBER 1952
1– Rick Reinhart, football
5– Virgus Jacques, football
7– Dave Lundstedt, baseball
10– Ed Jenkins, football
24– Dean March, football

NOVEMBER 1952
6– Ty McMillin, football
11– Paul Hunt, gymnastics

DECEMBER 1952
9– Mike Gow, football
15– David Axelrod, track
18– Tom Hicks, football

JANUARY 1953
11– Kevin Lowe, football
16– Jeff Hollenbach, football
20– Roy Robinson, football

FEBRUARY 1953
4– Rod MacDonald, swimming
6– Stu Levenick, football
21– Mike Bridges, track
25– Mike Baietto, track
28– Mike Waller, football

MARCH 1953
4– Alan Acker, fencing
4– Lenny Willis, assistant football coach

20– Tom Feeheley, football
23– Mark Peterson, football
31– Brian Whalin, fencing

APRIL 1952
14– Mike Durkin, cross country/track
21– Nate Haywood, fencing
27– Ben App, track
27– Otho Tucker, basketball

MAY 1953
4– Dave Roberts, basketball
15– Bobby Johnson, football
18– Tom Carmichael, basketball
26– Randy Sulaver, wrestling

JUNE 1953
15– Bill Uecker, football
20– Howard Beck, gymnastics

JULY 1953
1– Paul Yadron, football
13– John Tanner, swimming
14– Chris Williams, football
14– Joe Hatfield, football
16– Joe Smalzer, football
17– Bill Kleckner, football
23– Neil Janota, swimming
31– Manuel Amaya, tennis

AUGUST 1953
26– Randy Chirico, wrestling
27– Tom Carpenter, swimming
27– Ed Murray, football

John Cameron, the first African-American fencer in Fighting Illini history, slashed his way to an individual Big Ten sabre title in 1953.

ILLINI ITEM

ILLINOIS' TOP TWO-SPORT ATHLETE of 1952-53 was basketball/baseball star Clive Follmer from Forrest, Illinois. Follmer averaged 11.8 points per game in hoops as a senior starter, helping the Illini to an 18-4 overall record and a second-place finish in the Big Ten. As a pitcher for the baseball team that season, he had a 6-1 overall record, striking out 51 batters in 68 innings, and allowing just more than two earned runs per outing. The current Urbana, Illinois, attorney was awarded five UI varsity letters during his career—three in basketball and two in baseball—and was a member of four Big Ten championship clubs.

ILLINI LISTS

ILLINI ON ALL-TIME PRO BASKETBALL SCORING LIST*
(through 1994-95 season)

17,658 points	Eddie Johnson (1982-94)
13,229 points	Derek Harper (1984-95)
12,480 points	John "Red" Kerr (1955-66)
12,233 points	Don Freeman (1968-76)
11,549 points	Don Ohl (1961-70)
8,349 points	Ken Norman (1988-95)
7,922 points	Rich Jones (1970-77)
7,168 points	Nick Anderson (1990-95)
6,384 points	Andy Phillip (1948-58)
5,808 points	Kendall Gill (1991-95)
4,086 points	Nick Weatherspoon (1974-80)
3,221 points	Dike Eddleman (1950-53)

*Includes NBA, ABA, NPBL

Don Ohl scored 11,549 points during a 10-year career in the NBA.

ILLINI LEGEND:
AL BROSKY

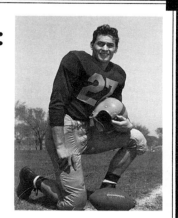

The record Al Brosky achieved as a defensive back for the Fighting Illini football team is difficult to measure accurately. It might be akin to Joe DiMaggio hitting safely in 56 consecutive games or Harry Broadbent's record of scoring a goal in 16 straight National Hockey League contests. However, Brosky's NCAA record of an interception in 15 consecutive games is significantly more impressive, in that opposing quarterbacks purposely threw their passes away from him, knowing his proficiency as a defender. The youngest of 12 children of immigrant Czechoslovakian parents, Brosky attended Harrison Tech High School in Chicago. Upon his graduation, Brosky enlisted in the Army and served for more than 15 months. He was discharged in 1948 and enrolled at St. Louis University, but left there after a semester and came to the University of Illinois. During the next three seasons, Brosky was simply amazing, developing into the greatest Illini pass defender ever. In 28 career games at Illinois, he picked off a national record 30 interceptions. Besides being captain and Most Valuable Player of the 1952 squad, Brosky also was an All-Big Ten and All-America selection. A severe back disorder as well as other complications never allowed him to pursue a career in professional football, so he went into business for himself. The last 10 years he's spent as a truck driver in Chicago. Nowadays, Brosky resides in Naperville.

✥ Illini Lore ✥

In February of 1953, the Federal Communications Commission assigned television channel 12, later to become WILL-TV, to the University of Illinois. Coordinated by the UI's new TV-Motion Picture unit, channel 12's original studio was located just inside Gate 24 on the west side of Memorial Stadium. Also located in the southwest tower of the stadium were the station's offices, control room, projection booth,s and film editing facility. Often, Fighting Illini fans who were unable to secure a ticket to sold-out basketball games at Huff Gym were given the opportunity to watch the events on closed-circuit TV inside the Great West Hall of the stadium. WILL-TV officially began TV broadcasts August 1, 1955, as the nation's 14th education station. The broadcasts were initially limited from 6:45 to 8:30 p.m., Monday through Friday.

1953-54

J.C. Caroline (left) and Mickey Bates were known as "Mr. Zoom and Mr. Boom."

I·L·L·I·N·I M·O·M·E·N·T

CAROLINE, BATES, & CO. JET PAST BUCKEYES:
One veteran Ohio sportswriter said that Illinois' October 10, 1953, performance against Ohio State was "the wildest first half in Ohio Stadium history, leaving Buckeye fans stunned." Though Illinois led by only one point at halftime, 21-20, it was all Illini in the second half, with the final score showing them on top, 41-20. Two jet-powered halfbacks, J.C. Caroline and Mickey Bates, combined for an unheard-of 339 yards rushing from scrimmage, 192 by Caroline and 147 by Bates. Afterwards, bewildered OSU coach Woody Hayes, said, "They just ran us to death, that's the whole story." Illinois continued its rampage through the Big Ten, with the No. 3-ranked Illini stumbling only at Wisconsin, and tying Michigan State for the Conference football title. Since the Illini and the Spartans hadn't faced each other in 1953, Big Ten athletic directors were forced to choose the league's Rose Bowl representative. Unfortunately, they picked MSU, and the Illini spent their holidays at home.

ILLINI BIRTHDAYS

SEPTEMBER 1953
- 7– Mike Washington, basketball
- 10– Revie Sorey, football
- 18– Ron Lapins, baseball
- 22– Donn Deputy, basketball
- 25– Dave Druz, swimming
- 28– Terry Ormsbee, football

OCTOBER 1953
- 1– Bruce Beam, wrestling
- 25– Dave Littell, tennis
- 30– Rick Schmidt, basketball
- 30– Mike Suppan, football

NOVEMBER 1953
- 30– Charlton Ehizuelen, track

DECEMBER 1953
- 2– Bill Rucks, basketball
- 7– Tom Stewart Jr., baseball
- 11– Brian Diedrich, football
- 24– Nate Williams, basketball

JANUARY 1954
- 21– Harris Kal, baseball
- 22– Wayne Morrison, tennis

FEBRUARY 1954
- 17– Jim Goss, baseball
- 23– Dan Ingram, baseball

MARCH 1954
- 3– Brian Ford, football
- 5– Dennis Graff, basketball
- 14– Jeff Cimack, baseball

- 20– Mark Bial, assistant basketball coach
- 25– Craig Klaas, wrestling
- 30– Don Hardin, assistant volleyball coach

APRIL 1954
- 19– Russ Meyer, swimming
- 23– Jim Hanlon, track

MAY 1954
- 1– Jim Kopatz, football/baseball
- 5– Jeff Chrystal, football
- 5– Jack Dombroski, football
- 17– Steve Greene, football

JUNE 1954
- 15– Doug Kuehl, wrestling
- 19– Doug Kleber, football/baseball

- 25– Brad Nedrud, swimming
- 28– Mark Bergren, wrestling

JULY 1954
- 8– Harvey Seybold, swimming
- 14– Ron White, football
- 21– Dave Weinstein, tennis
- 24– Bob Harold, baseball

AUGUST 1954
- 4– Jim Stauner, football
- 5– Dave Smith, basketball
- 8– Webb Hayne, tennis
- 10– Marty Friel, football
- 24– Ron Logeman, football
- 27– Scott Studwell, football

Football's Bob Lenzini was Illinois' 1954 winner of the Big Ten Conference Medal of Honor as well as the school's first Academic All-American.

Johnny "Red" Kerr was the Big Ten's basketball MVP in 1954.

ILLINI LISTS

ILLINOIS' FIRST-ROUND NFL/AFL DRAFT PICKS

1944	Tony Butkovich, RB, Los Angeles Rams, 11th pick
1954	Stan Wallace, DB, Chicago Bears, 6th pick
1954	John Bauer, G, Cleveland Browns, 12th pick
1959	Rich Kreitling, WR, Cleveland Browns, 11th pick
1961	Joe Rutgens, DT, Oakland Raiders, AFL, 4th pick
	Joe Rutgens, DT, Washington Redskins, 3rd pick
1965	Dick Butkus, LB, Chicago Bears, 3rd pick
1965	George Donnelly, DB, San Francisco 49ers, 13th pick
1966	Jim Grabowski, RB, Green Bay Packers, 9th pick
	Jim Grabowski, RB, Miami Dolphins, AFL 1st pick
1981	Dave Wilson, QB, New Orleans Saints, 1st pick*
1983	Tony Eason, QB, New England Patriots, 15th pick
1988	Scott Davis, DE, Los Angeles Raiders, 25th pick
1990	Jeff George, QB, Indianapolis Colts, 1st pick
1991	Henry Jones, DB, Buffalo Bills, 26th pick
1992	Brad Hopkins, OT, Houston Oilers, 13th pick

*Supplemental draft

ILLINI LEGEND:

J.C. CAROLINE

Though he played only for two seasons, J.C. Caroline made a tremendous impact on the college football scene, ultimately being honored as a Hall of Famer. The personable South Carolinian made headlines as a sophomore, rushing for a Big Ten record 1,256 yards in 1953, shattering Red Grange's Illini single-season mark. Of the myriad of stars Ray Eliot coached during his 18 years at Illinois, the veteran mentor rated Caroline at the very top. Having averaged six yards per carry from scrimmage—1,696 yards on 287 attempts—who can argue with Eliot's choice? Caroline's All-America career at Illinois ended when he dropped out of school before his senior season to sign with Montreal of the Canadian Football League. In 1956, coach George Halas of the Chicago Bears inked Caroline after only one year in the CFL, converting him into a defensive back. He retired as a player in 1965 after 10 seasons with the Bears, earning All-Pro honors and being a member of three championship teams. Caroline served as an assistant coach at Illinois from 1967-76, then coached briefly at Urbana High School. He continues to live in Urbana and works as a teacher in that city's school system.

Illini Lore

On February 1, 1954, Dr. Lloyd Morey became the seventh president and 11th chief executive officer of the University of Illinois. Morey had been appointed acting president five months earlier when President George Stoddard was forced to resign by UI's Board of Trustees. Morey had been on the staff for 42 years and held the position of comptroller at the time of his appointment.

1954-55

I·L·L·I·N·I M·O·M·E·N·T

Among the members of the 1955 Illini gymnastics team were (front row, l to r) Tony Hlinka, Charles Highsmith, Captain Tom Gardner, Coach Charlie Pond, Jeff Austin, and manager Larry Cross; (back row, l to r) Jon Culbertson, Dan Lirot, Richard Jirus, Eric Stattin, and Kenneth Stone.

ILLINI GYMNASTS CLAIM FIRST OF TWO CONSECUTIVE NATIONAL TITLES: Coach Charlie Pond's outstanding Illini gymnastics teams of the 1950s strung together a since-unmatched chain of 11 consecutive Big Ten crowns, but the pinnacle of their success came during the 1955 and '56 seasons when Illinois won back-to-back NCAA championships. The first of the two national titles in 1955 at Los Angeles was achieved without one single Illini gymnast winning an individual championship. Illinois placed at least two scorers in every event with the exception of the rings, with Jeff Austin coming the closest to a title with a runner-up finish on the trampoline. Illini captain Tom Gardner (fifth), Tony Hlinka (sixth), and Dick Jirus (seventh) all placed among the top seven all-arounders, as Illinois clipped second-place Penn State, 82.5 to 69, for the team crown. Pond's Illini traveled to Chapel Hill, North Carloina for the 1956 team title, nearly doubling runner-up Penn State's score, 123.5 to 67.5. Illinois' 56-point decision still is the second-biggest margin of victory ever for a gymnastics team in an NCAA championship meet. Don Tonry in the all-around and Dan Lirot in the tumbling event claimed individual championships that year.

WILLARD THOMSON of the Fighting Illini track team hurdled his way to three Big Ten championships during the 1954-55 season. Thomson won the 70-yard high hurdles indoors, then swept both the 120 highs and the 220 lows outdoors. Altogether during his career at Illinois, Thomson accounted for six individual conference hurdles titles.

ILLINI LISTS

TOP 10 RUSHING PLAYS AT MEMORIAL STADIUM

1. 89 yards Harry Jefferson of Illinois vs. Syracuse, 10/23/54
2. 84 yards Ray Nitschke of Illinois vs. Northwestern, 11/23/57
   84 yards Billy Taylor of Michigan, 11/8/69
4. 83 yards Emil Sitko of Notre Dame, 9/28/46
5. 80 yards Cyril Pinder of Illinois vs. Duke, 10/23/65
   80 yards Edgar Nichol of Illinois vs. Coe, 10/13/28
7. 78 yards Howard Griffith of Illinois vs. Utah, 9/17/88
   78 yards Keith Jones of Illinois vs. Nebraska, 9/20/86
9. 76 yards Rex Kern of Ohio State, 10/24/70
10. 75 yards Phil Colella of Notre Dame, 9/28/46

Harry Jefferson's 89-yard run vs. Syracuse in 1954 still ranks as the longest in Memorial Stadium history.

ILLINI LEGEND:

PAUL JUDSON:

Four different members of Clarence and Jesse Judson's family wore Fighting Illini basketball uniforms during a 36-year period, starting in 1944 with son Howard and ending in 1980 with grandson Rob. The Judson's twin boys, Paul and Phil, also lettered during the mid 1950s for Coach Harry Combes' Illini cagers, starring first on the University of Illinois campus in 1952 when they led tiny Hebron High to the state championship at UI's Huff Gym. Who was the best Judson athlete of them all? Well, Clarence and Jesse would never say, but objective observers would probably choose Paul. The 6-4 guard was Illinois' Most Valuable Player in 1955 as a junior and was later selected by the *Daily Illini* as the school's Athlete of the Year. During his career from 1954-56, Paul tallied 1,013 points, a total second only in Illini annals at the time to John Kerr. Though none of the three Illini teams with which Paul Judson played ever won a Big Ten championship, they did have a combined record of 52 victories against only 14 losses, a winning percentage of .788. Today, Paul lives in Florida, recently retired following a 30-year high school basketball coaching career at Dundee High School and a short stint as athletic director at Hampshire High School.

Illini Lore

On December 14, 1954, David Dodds Henry accepted an offer from the University of Illinois' Board of Trustees to succeed Dr. Lloyd Morey as the school's president. The 49-year-old Henry, a graduate of Pennsylvania State University, came to Champaign-Urbana from New York University, where he had served as that institution's vice chancellor since 1952. Henry began his appointment at the UI September 1, 1955, at a salary of $30,000.

1955-56

I·L·L·I·N·I M·O·M·E·N·T

Bobby Mitchell (#22) rushed for 173 yards vs. Michigan in 1955.

ILLINI GRIDDERS UP-END NO. 1 MICHIGAN:

Illini football fans who attended the November 5, 1955 match-up at Memorial Stadium between 3-3 Illinois and 6-0 Michigan probably were pessimistic about their hometown heroes' chances against the nation's No. 1-rated team. However, when the Illini battled the Wolverines on even terms after the first half, 6-6, there was a little more cause for optimism. A fake field-goal attempt that turned into a screen pass to Abe Woodson late in the third quarter gave the Illini a 12-6 lead. Then Illinois put its bag of tricks away to rely upon its fleet-footed halfback, Bobby Mitchell. The speedy sophomore from Hot Springs, Arkansas, who accounted for 173 rushing yards on only 10 attempts that afternoon, nailed the Michigan coffin shut with a 64-yard sprint to the end zone, giving the Illini an insurmountable lead and their eventual 25-6 upset win. Afterward, Illini coach Ray Eliot called his squad's effort "a great team victory. It best exemplified what is meant by the words Fighting Illini. Every kid did a magnificent job. They were all heroes."

ILLINI BIRTHDAYS

SEPTEMBER 1955
5– Lester Washington, track
9– William Kays, wrestling
10– Albert Young, football
20– Kevin Smith, football
22– Janice Kimpel, golf

OCTOBER 1955
16– Steve Borre, baseball
20– Kevin Pancratz, football/wrestling

NOVEMBER 1955
3– Scott Sommers, tennis
9– Jerry Finis, football
29– Bruce Dahlhein, baseball

DECEMBER 1955
9– Bruce Kandel, baseball
11– Kevin Puebla, wrestling
21– Bill Fritz, cross country
22– Rick Leighty, basketball

JANUARY 1956
3– Audie Matthews, basketball
14– Steve Yasukawa, gymnastics
15– Bob Scott, football
19– Brian Kingsbury, football
22– David Blakely, football
29– Rickie Mitchem, football

FEBRUARY 1956
7– Barbella Magas, basketball
18– Willie Young, football
19– Dan Bulow, football
22– Taylor Mason, football
24– Randy Taylor, football
28– Steve Gordon, football

MARCH 1956
4– Ray Estes, track
25– Ted Ahlem, swimming

APRIL 1956
16– Dale Hardy, football
16– Dennis Kleber, baseball
21– Fred Wich, swimming

MAY 1956
4– Kathy Lindsey, women's basketball coach

12– Ken Kellaney, golf

JUNE 1956
2– Charles Meurisse, tennis
6– Kurt Steger, football/baseball
14– Joel Hestrup, wrestling
14– Mary Paterson, swimming
20– Derwin Tucker, football
27– Brad Childress, assistant football coach

JULY 1956
1– Rich Adams, basketball
2– Mary Ellen Wilson, volleyball

17– Bill Cerney, football
18– Marty Kirby, baseball
31– Bill Callahan, assistant football coach

AUGUST 1956
1– Charlie White, cross country/track
1– Pat Ferrari, wrestling
3– Tim Smith, track
3– Tom Gerhardt, basketball
7– Gary Jurczyk, football
15– Jean Schlinkmann, volleyball
19– Mark McDonald, football
27– Jim Kogut, football
27– Bob McClure, football

ILLINI ITEM

EM LINDBECK was selected as the University of Illinois' Athlete of the Year for 1955-56, in the *Daily Illini*'s annual end-of-the-season contest. The native of Kewanee earned Most Valuable Player honors in both football and baseball. As a quarterback, Lindbeck led the Illini past No. 1-ranked Michigan, earning honorable mention All-Big Ten acclaim. On the baseball diamond, he batted .382 for the Illini, winning second-team All-Big Ten laurels as a centerfielder.

ILLINI LEGEND:

ART SCHANKIN

If you asked the man on the street to name the world's most famous fencer, you might end up with a blank stare. But if you asked a sports trivia expert about the greatest fencer in the history of the U of I, Art Schankin's name would probably be at the top of the list. Though toiling in relative anonymity, Schankin ruled the world of collegiate fencing from 1956 through 1958. He tied for fifth nationally in the sabre event as a sophomore, finished third in foil as a junior, and swept the NCAA sabre title as a senior, becoming the first intercollegiate fencer to win a national championship with an unbeaten mark. Schankin continued to compete in the sport after his graduation in 1958, being nationally ranked. In 1964, six weeks before his wedding day, he was in an automobile accident that ended his fencing career but began his highly successful coaching tenure with the Illini. From 1973-93, Schankin's UI teams amassed a dual-meet record of 391 wins and 51 losses, including seven Big Ten champions. In addition to being Illini fencing coach, he also was a sales supervisor for Collegiate Cap and Gown. Schankin resides in Champaign.

 Illini Lore

A pair of distinguished University of Illinois alumni—Dr. Vincent du Vigneaud and Dr. Polykarp Kusch—were awarded Nobel prizes in November of 1955. Dr. du Vigneaud, who received his bachelor's degree in 1923 and his master's in 1924 from the UI, won the $36,720 award for chemistry for his work on two hormones that assist in childbirth and keep a check on vital organs. He was on the staff of Cornell University's medical college at the time. Dr. Kusch, who earned his master's in 1933 and his Ph.D. in 1936 from the UI, split the Nobel physics award with Dr. W.E. Lamb of Stanford. Kusch, who then taught at Columbia University, won his prize for work in calculating the properties of the atom.

1956-57

America's Time Capsule

- **Oct. 8, 1956:** *Don Larsen of the New York Yankees hurled the first perfect game in World Series history.*
- **Nov. 4, 1956:** *Political demonstrations against Communist rule in Hungary led to a surprise attack by Soviet Armed forces, resulting in the death of 32,000 persons.*
- **Nov. 6, 1956:** *Dwight Eisenhower defeated Illinois governor Adlai Stevenson in the presidential election.*
- **Jan. 21, 1957:** *NBC carried the first nationally televised videotaped broadcast, a recording of the presidential inauguration ceremonies.*
- **July 12, 1957:** *Surgeon General Leroy Burney reported that a link between cigarette smoking and lung cancer had been established.*

I·L·L·I·N·I M·O·M·E·N·T

Coach Ray Eliot (front row, fifth from left) and his 1956 Illini stunned top-ranked Michigan State.

NO. 1 FALLS AGAIN TO ILLINI:

For the second consecutive season, a No. 1-rated football team from the state of Michigan was brought to its knees at Memorial Stadium, as Illinois beat top-ranked Michigan State, 20-13, on October 27, 1956. As big a thorn as Bobby Mitchell was to Michigan in 1955, so was Abe Woodson to the Spartans in 1956. Trailing 13-0 at halftime, prospects for another Fighting Illini upset looked bleak. But that's when the Austin Express got rolling. Woodson narrowed the margin to 13-6 midway through the third quarter on a two-yard touchdown. Then, in the fourth quarter, he tied the game with 1:42 gone on a 70-yard gallop around right end. Nine minutes later, Woodson scored the game winner when he grabbed a screen pass from sophomore quarterback Bill Offenbecher on the 18-yard line and dashed 82 yards. All told, Woodson touched the ball 20 times for 271 yards, marking an individual performance that ranks among Illinois' best ever.

ILLINI BIRTHDAYS

SEPTEMBER 1956
13– Mark Avery, track
16– Becky Beach, basketball/golf
19– Dorothy Carver, volleyball

OCTOBER 1956
1– John Sullivan, football
4– Diane Miller, golf

NOVEMBER 1956
19– Ed Kaihatsu, fencing
22– Ken Lavelle, fencing

DECEMBER 1956
11– Kevin Puebla, wrestling
18– Jeff Barnes, football

28– Rick Allen, assistant athletic director
29– Jim Shanel, swimming

JANUARY 1957
10– Dominic Forte, football
11– Carol Carmichael, basketball
19– Mike Priebe, football
23– Bob Noelke, football
25– Jim Cahill, baseball

FEBRUARY 1957
4– Kathy Walters, cross country/track
5– Mike Collins, football
10– Lawrence McCullough, football
12– Mark Furlong, wrestling

MARCH 1957
4– Tony Chiricosta, tennis
9– Dan Melsek, football
12– Robert Earl, tennis
14– Stanley Ralph, football
20– Kevin Westervelt, basketball
29– Ken Ferdinand, basketball

APRIL 1957
23– Lloyd Levitt, football

MAY 1957
3– Matt Meyer, basketball
12– Keith Burlingame, football
13– Mike McBeth, football

13– Kathy Gartland, volleyball
13– John Fillipan, baseball
21– Keith Potter, swimming
22– Dominic Borgialli, baseball
29– Janet Roberts, volleyball

JUNE 1957
2– Jim Eicken, track
4– Pete Froehlich, wrestling
6– Larry Will, track
6– Sandra Seyman, golf
10– Nancy Thies, gymnastics
11– Art Diamond, fencing
11– Larry Lubin, basketball

JULY 1957
8– Reno Gray, basketball
9– Doug Cozen, football
20– Mike Brzuszkiewicz, football
20– Tom Schooley, football
22– Charlie Weber, football

AUGUST 1957
10– Phil Quigley, swimming
21– Mary Pat Travnik, basketball
25– Levi Cobb, basketball

THE UNIVERSITY OF SAN FRANCISCO'S basketball team tasted defeat for the first time in more than two years on December 17, 1956, when Illinois beat the defending national champions, 62-33, at Huff Gym. Coach Harry Combes' Illini broke USF's national-record 60-game winning streak behind a strong defensive effort and 19 points from center George BonSalle.

ILLINI LISTS

GREAT ILLINI ROAD WINS

Charlie Bellatti served as Sports Information Director at the University of Illinois from 1956-70. Here's a list of the most memorable Fighting Illini road victories during the time he was SID.

1. 1/1/64 — Illinois 17, Washington 7 (Rose Bowl)
2. 12/19/64 — Illinois 91, Kentucky 86 (championship of Kentucky Invitational)
3. 11/28/63 — Illinois 13, Michigan State 0 (UI wins Big Ten football title)
4. 1/1/47 — Illinois 45, UCLA 14 (Rose Bowl)
5. 10/10/53 — Illinois 41, Ohio State 20 (J.C. Caroline and Mickey Bates emerge as national stars)
6. 12/29/62 — Illinois 92, West Virginia 74 (championship of Holiday Basketball Classic at New York's Madison Square Garden)
7. 11/3/62 — Illinois 14, Purdue 10 (Illinois breaks 15-game losing streak)
8. 11/6/66 — Illinois 28, Michigan 21 (Pete Elliott's only victory over his brother Bump)
9. 4/27/46 — Two different Illinois track mile relay teams win titles in the nation's two premier meets, the Drake and Penn Relays
10. 1/14/63 — Illinois 78, Northwestern 76 (Bob Starnes hits a 50-foot desperation shot at the buzzer)

ILLINI LEGEND:

ABE WOODSON

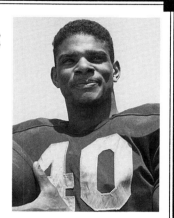

Abe Woodson had a lot to live up to when he inherited football jersey number 40 at the University of Illinois. The two men who wore those numerals before him were Dike Eddleman, Illinois' greatest all-time athlete, and Stan Wallace, a gridiron star in his own right at Illinois. Well, when Woodson's eligibility expired in 1956, the former star from Chicago's Austin High School proved that he was more than worthy. Woodson, of course, is best known for his role in Illinois' 1956 upset of No. 1-ranked Michigan State. He wound up his three-year career as the school's fifth leading rusher with 1,276 yards and twice led Illinois in pass receiving. Abe was also a terror on the track, winning two Big Ten titles as a 50-yard hurdler and tying the world's indoor mark twice in that event. After being selected as UI's Athlete of the Year in 1956-57, Woodson enjoyed a nine-year career in the National Football League with San Francisco and St. Louis. He hung up his cleats in 1967 and worked briefly for S&H Green Stamps. Woodson then began a 20-year career as a life insurance agent in the San Francisco area. In 1991, he enrolled as a student at the Southern California School of Evangelism. Today, Woodson is a Church of Christ minister in Las Vegas, Nevada, and has developed a prison ministry in Indian Springs, Nevada.

Illini Lore

The University of Illinois' John Bardeen was one of three American scientists to be awarded the 1956 Nobel prize in physics for their development of the transistor. Bardeen, a professor of electrical engineering and physics since 1951, perfected the micro-amplifiers with William Shockley of Pasadena, California and Walter Brattain of Murray Hill, New Jersey at the Bell Telephone Laboratories. In 1972, he again shared a Nobel prize for a theory on superconductivity.

1957-58

I·L·L·I·N·I M·O·M·E·N·T

Coach Garret (left) with his three star fencers, (left to right) Abbey Silverstone, Lee Sentman, and Art Schankin.

ILLINI FENCERS AND GYMNASTS WIN NCAA CROWNS:

University of Illinois athletes captured a pair of national team championships during the 1957-58 season, with Illini fencers and gymnasts bringing home top honors. Coach Mac Garret's swordsmen travelled all the way to Lubbock, Texas on March 21-22, edging Columbia, Yale, and Navy for the NCAA title. Illinois' fencers earned 47 points altogether, including 21 in sabre from individual champion Art Schankin, 14 in foil from Abbey Silverstone, and 12 in epee from Lee Sentman. The Illini gymnasts tied Michigan State for the national title on April 11-12, with each team scoring 79 points at MSU's Jenison Field House. Illinois got predicted individual championships in the horizontal bars and free exercise events from Abie Grossfeld, but it was a junior tumbler named Allan Harvey who provided the Illini with their biggest surprise. For the first time in his competitive career, Harvey executed the difficult double back somersault, a performance that netted him second place in tumbling. A shoulder injury suffered by UI's Bob Diamond on the first night of competition probably cost Illinois an undisputed team title, as Diamond was counted on to place well on the side horse.

ILLINI BIRTHDAYS

SEPTEMBER 1957
7– John Meyer, football
8– Carol Eaton, golf
13– Chris Tague, swimming
24– Anita Moyer, cross country/track
28– Bobby Smith, football

OCTOBER 1957
8– John Thiede, football
17– Nancy Maxwell, golf
17– Tom Tanner, swimming
21– Jean-Galan Ruleau, track
26– Eric Rouse, football

NOVEMBER 1957
1– Rudy Reavis, track

2– Larry Powell, football
22– Doug McConnell, swimming
24– Bud Mathieu, swimming
25– Cliff Hill, track

DECEMBER 1957
1– Kevin DeForrest, swimming coach
17– Tom Kolloff, football
20– Steve Schellenberger, track
21– Dave Stoldt, gymnastics
27– Mike Holmes, football

JANUARY 1958
13– Rob Judson, basketball
17– Mike Sherrod, football

27– Paul Marsillo, baseball
28– Steve Nowack, swimming

FEBRUARY 1958
3– Derek Holcomb, basketball
4– Chris Carr, football
11– Dave Kelly, football
14– Bruce Thornton, football
14– Jerry Ramshaw, football

MARCH 1958
9– Ralph Cortez, wrestling
13– Sally Pope, golf
28– Clarence Baker, football

APRIL 1958
2– Dan MacLean, football
10– Kathy Glynn, volleyball
15– Carooq Taylor, football
29– Gayle Fleischman, gymnastics

MAY 1958
1– Janae Hunziker, cross country/track
2– Jim Osness, fencing
8– Scott Doney, football
12– Pete Bihl, swimming
25– Dan Westerlind, football
28– Greg Dentino, football

JUNE 1958
1– Kevin Cawley, fencing
14– Joe Laws, fencing
28– Bob Hauser, football

JULY 1958
1– Steve Lanter, basketball
12– Ray Pavesic, football
31– Bruce Scheidegger, baseball

AUGUST 1958
5– Lois Haubold, tennis
8– Becky McSwine, swimming
11– Eric Priest, fencing

Ray Nitschke was inducted into the Pro Football Hall of Fame in 1978.

ILLINI ITEM

ILLINI IN PRO FOOTBALL HALL OF FAME
*Harold "Red" Grange	1963	1923-24-25
*George Halas	1963	1917
#Hugh "Shorty" Ray	1966	No letter in football
Ray Nitschke	1978	1955-56-57
Dick Butkus	1979	1962-63-64
Bobby Mitchell	1983	1955-56-57

*Charter members
#Supervisor of NFL officials

ILLINI LISTS

ILLINOIS' MULTIPLE BIG TEN WRESTLING CHAMPIONS

3—Jon Llewellyn, heavyweight (1989-90-91)
2—Joe Sapora, 115 pounds (1929-30)
2—Bob Emmons, 126 pounds (1932-33)
2—Lou Kachiroubas, 128 pounds (1946-47)
2—Archie Deutschman, 136 pounds (1938-39)
2—Norton Compton, 137 pounds (1952-53)
2—Jack McIlvoy, 145 pounds (1935-37)
2—Werner Holzer, 147 & 157 pounds (1957-58)
2—John Ginay, 165 pounds (1937-38)
2—Dave Shapiro, 165 pounds (1943-47)
2—Ralph Silverstein, 175 pounds & heavyweight (1935-36)
2—Bob Norman, heavyweight (1957-58)

Werner Holzer won Big Ten wrestling titles in both 1957 and '58.

ILLINI LEGEND:

BOB NORMAN

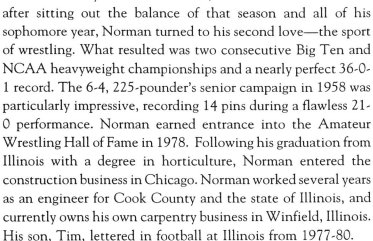

His dream was to play varsity football for the University of Illinois, but a knee injury during his freshman year never allowed Bob Norman to realize his boyhood ambition. So, after sitting out the balance of that season and all of his sophomore year, Norman turned to his second love—the sport of wrestling. What resulted was two consecutive Big Ten and NCAA heavyweight championships and a nearly perfect 36-0-1 record. The 6-4, 225-pounder's senior campaign in 1958 was particularly impressive, recording 14 pins during a flawless 21-0 performance. Norman earned entrance into the Amateur Wrestling Hall of Fame in 1978. Following his graduation from Illinois with a degree in horticulture, Norman entered the construction business in Chicago. Norman worked several years as an engineer for Cook County and the state of Illinois, and currently owns his own carpentry business in Winfield, Illinois. His son, Tim, lettered in football at Illinois from 1977-80.

Illini Lore

Details of a 10-year, $198.5 million building program for the University of Illinois were announced at a July 1957 meeting of the Board of Trustees. The previous comprehensive building program for the UI took place more than a quarter of a century earlier, when, during the 1920s, the University expanded its facilities to handle rising enrollments. Among the facilities planned were an education building, a physics building, an agronomy and plant sciences building, and a physical plant services building. More than $5 million of the 1957 request was for remodeling and renovation of existing structures.

1958-59

I·L·L·I·N·I M·O·M·E·N·T

Coach Harry Combes (left) and his starters—(left to right) Mannie Jackson, Al Gosnell, Govoner Vaughn, Roger Taylor, and John Wessels—upset first-place Indiana in 1959.

ILLINI RALLY DERAILS FIRST-PLACE HOOSIERS:

The odds seemed overwhelming that Illinois' basketball team would not derail league-leading Indiana at Bloomington, February 9, 1959. The ninth-place Illini, mired in the throes of a five-game losing streak, faced a Hoosier club that featured 6-11 center Walt Bellamy and an array of other talented sophomores. During the first four-and-a-half minutes, Indiana ran off to a 15-0 lead, and had visions of re-setting the single-game scoring record of 122 points that it had compiled one week before at Ohio State. The Hoosiers lost their momentum, however, and the Illini played on even terms for the balance of the first half. In the last period, Illinois rode the hot shooting of Govoner Vaughn to finally take the lead, 68-67. From that point on, Illinois never trailed, winding up with a come-from-behind 89-83 victory.

ILLINI BIRTHDAYS

SEPTEMBER 1958
- 2— James Griffin, basketball
- 13— Judy Kordas, basketball
- 20— Marty Schiene, golf
- 20— Mike Pacini, fencing
- 24— Steve Briggs, wrestling
- 24— Jeff Edwards, tennis
- 30— John Mulchrone, football

OCTOBER 1958
- 2— Kevin McBride, baseball
- 8— Carl DePaolis, baseball
- 9— Carey Westberg, tennis
- 12— Neil Bresnahan, basketball
- 25— Jim Werner, swimming

- 27— Nick Sowa, football
- 29— Mark Claypool, track
- 30— Dave Veatch, fencing

NOVEMBER 1958
- 3— Steve Lechner, gymnastics
- 5— John Gillen, football
- 16— Jim Graham, wrestling
- 19— Dennis Flynn, football
- 27— Tom Coady, football

DECEMBER 1958
- 3— John Kakacek, wrestling
- 16— John Scott, football
- 21— John Venegoni, football
- 26— Tim Fiorini, wrestling

JANUARY 1959
- 8— Mike Jones, basketball
- 10— Greg Boeke, football

- 10— Lee Boeke, football
- 13— Cliff Jones, football
- 18— Tyrone Worthy, football
- 19— Troy McMillin, football
- 19— Wayne Strader, football
- 23— Efrem Stringfellow, track
- 31— John Olszewski, cross country/track

FEBRUARY 1959
- 3— Dave Finzer, football
- 7— Kyle Jenner, track
- 15— Greg Foster, football
- 15— Bill Leigh, track
- 16— Jack Squirek, football

MARCH 1959
- 4— Mike Kramer, tennis
- 12— Earnest Adams, football

- 12— Julie Johnson, golf
- 13— Rusty Dardano, football
- 16— Dave Ayoub, track
- 21— Chip Bodicker, swimming

APRIL 1959
- 1— Dave Dwyer, football
- 6— Nick Zambole, golf
- 11— Virginia "Veegee" Elsen, cross country/track
- 19— Paul Heald, fencing
- 25— Amy Young, tennis
- 27— Dave Wilson, football

MAY 1959
- 1— Eddie Johnson, basketball
- 12— Chris Cosh, assistant football coach
- 12— Linda Wunder, basketball

- 13— Steve Stroker, swimming
- 13— Allen Tish, fencing
- 15— Tony Krainik, track
- 16— Mark Snow, fencing

JUNE 1959
- 16— Dave Wuethrick, baseball
- 22— Dave Peterson, gymnastics

JULY 1959
- 2— Dennis Bishop, football
- 3— Mark Schmidt, track
- 9— Tim McAvoy, football
- 10— Tim Norman, football
- 17— Linda Anderson, cross country
- 20— Martha Hutchinson, basketball
- 28— Rich Weiss, football
- 30— Ron Ferrari, football

Rich Kreitling caught touchdown passes of 83 and 64 yards at Minnesota.

ILLINI ITEM

THE FIGHTING ILLINI FOOTBALL TEAM beat Minnesota, 20-8, on October 18, 1958, recording their first victory on the Gophers' home field since 1919. Quarterback Bob Hickey and wide receiver Rich Kreitling combined for touchdowns of 83 and 64 yards, as Illinois won for the first time on the road in 12 tries.

ILLINI LISTS

ILLINOIS GYMNASTICS BIG TEN ALL-AROUND CHAMPIONS

E.B. Styles	1910-11-12
A.W. Ziegler	1920
Joe Giallombardo	1938-39
Frank Dolan	1950
Bob Sullivan	1952
Don Tonry	1956
Abie Grossfeld	1957-58-59
Ray Hadley	1960-62
Charles Lakes	1984-85
Dominick Minicucci	1988

Ray Hadley earned Big Ten all-around championships in 1960 and '62.

ILLINI LEGEND:

ABIE GROSSFELD

Abie Grossfeld was a Big Ten champion, a national champion and a two-time Olympian, but he said that being chosen as UI's Athlete of the Year marked one of the most special moments in his gymnastics career. "In 1959, when I received that award from the *Daily Illini*, I was the first person to win who wasn't a football or a basketball player. I was very proud to be picked as Illinois' Athlete of the Year." From 1957-59, Grossfeld won seven Big Ten titles and was a member of three conference championship teams. Grossfeld also earned the Big Ten Conference Medal of Honor as Illinois' top scholar-athlete. After earning his bachelor's and master's degrees at Illinois, Grossfeld entered the coaching world; he's been the head coach at Southern Connecticut State University since 1963. Grossfeld, currently the longest tenured collegiate gymnastics coach, directed SCSU to three national titles and 27 individual national titles. His greatest athlete at SCSU was Peter Kormann, a bronze medalist in the 1976 Olympics. Grossfeld was the head coach of the U.S. Olympic Gymnastics Team in 1972, '84 and '88, and was an assistant coach in 1964 and '68. Today, the gymnastics Hall of Famer resides in Woodbridge, Connecticut.

 Illini Lore

Charles "Chilly" Bowen stepped down from his post as executive director of the Alumni Association in June of 1959 following 17 years of service for the organization. A 1922 graduate of the University of Illinois, Bowen began his 32-year stint with the UI as ticket manager and business manager for the Athletic Association. In 1942, he was appointed as the Alumni Association's first executive director. Alumni membership grew from less than 3,000 to more than 19,000 during Bowen's time in that position.

1959-60

I·L·L·I·N·I M·O·M·E·N·T

The Ray Eliot era at Illinois ended in 1959 with a victory over Northwestern.

ILLINI END ELIOT ERA WITH VICTORY:

The Ray Eliot era at Illinois concluded with a storybook finish November 21, 1959, as the Fighting Illini football team swept past Northwestern, 28-0, at Memorial Stadium. Playing against the school that had inflicted so many thorns in his side during 18 years on the sidelines, Eliot and his charges were in control all the way, out-gaining the Wildcats 365 yards to 142. Three hundred forty-eight of Illinois' yards came on the ground as fullback Bill Brown (164 yards) and halfback Mel Counts (109 yards) averaged more than eight yards a carry. The Illini defensive unit, led by Bill Burrell, allowed Northwestern to penetrate the 50-yard line only once all day. When the final gun sounded, UI students rushed the field and, along with Illini players, hoisted the broad-smiling Eliot and carried him off the field.

ILLINI BIRTHDAYS

SEPTEMBER 1959
15– Bryan Castles, swimming
18– Doug Deckert, golf
22– Dan Unruh, wrestling
26– Mitch Stierwalt, baseball
29– Juan Causey, wrestling

OCTOBER 1959
1– Bruce Cochran, wrestling
8– Tony Eason, football
29– Mark Helle, football

NOVEMBER 1959
3– Joe Curtis, football
5– Mark Smith, basketball
7– Jim Haslett, fencing
21– Tab Carmien, football

DECEMBER 1959
8– Kenny Shaw, football

8– Mary Skudlarek, volleyball
11– Rich Antonacci, football
21– Bob Werner, swimming
25– Joseph Biel, baseball
28– William Jager, swimming
28– Margie Schwarz, volleyball

JANUARY 1960
1– Sukhoon Kim, fencing
2– Greg McMahon, assistant football coach
2– Vic Shockey, track
4– Pete Mulchrone, football
5– Gary Brozek, baseball
7– Calvin Thomas, football

21– Betsy Oberle, cross country/track
30– Ken Durrell, football

FEBRUARY 1960
18– Dave Rear, baseball
19– Lou Belmont, football
26– Liz Brauer, basketball
29– Trent Taylor, wrestling

MARCH 1960
8– Bonji Bonner, football
11– Mike Lehmann, track
11– Kim Lenti, volleyball
24– Mike Murphy, football
25– Jon Schmidt, cross country/track
27– Paul Palanca, fencing

APRIL 1960
3– Rick George, football
4– Ken Gillen, football
6– Bruce Irussi, wrestling

8– Kirk Bostrum, football
9– David Clapp, baseball
10– Debbie Taylor, basketball
11– Nick Leever, fencing
13– Cheryl Horvath, basketball
16– Andrew Barmes, track
21– Jeff Mitchell, gymnastics

MAY 1960
2– Gail Olson, track
11– Dan Shea, football
21– Chuck Salemo, gymnastics
27– John Lopez, football

JUNE 1960
1– Mike Bass, football
6– Robin Duffy, diving
17– Ed Brady, football
28– Anne Gatlin, swimming

JULY 1960
1– Denise Nitzel, swimming
2– Mike Weingrad, football
3– Kelvin Atkins, football
22– Perry Range, basketball
30– Butch Zunich, gymnastics

AUGUST 1960
2– Dorothy Hogan, tennis
5– Carrie Race, cross country/track
8– Raul Rodriguez, gymnastics
12– Jeanne Sullivan, volleyball
19– Jill Kuenne, track
20– Randy Conte, baseball

ILLINI ITEM

FIGHTING ILLINI BASKETBALL STAR Govoner Vaughn saved his best until last, scoring a career-high 30 points in his final game at Huff Gym, February 29, 1960. The senior forward from Edwardsville hit 14 out of 17 shots from the field, including all nine of his attempts in the second half, to lead Illinois to a 90-61 victory over Michigan.

ILLINI LISTS

LEO JOHNSON'S ALL-TIME ILLINI TRACK TEAM

Leo Johnson coached the University of Illinois track and field squad for 28 years, from 1938-65. Here, based on the Big Ten championship titles they won, is who Johnson might have chosen on his Fighting Illini outdoor track and field "Dream Team" (two men per individual event).

100-yard dash: Willie Williams and Claude "Buddy" Young
220-yard dash: Herb McKenley and Willie Williams
440-yard run: Cirilo McSween and Herb McKenley
880-yard run: Stacey Siders and George Kerr
One-mile run: Bob Rehberg and Jim Bowers
Two-mile run: Waldemar Karkow and Ken Brown
120-yard high hurdles: George Walker and Willard Thomson
220-yard low hurdles: George Walker and Willard Thomson
High jump: Dike Eddleman and Al Urbanckas
Pole vault: Don Laz and Bob Richards
Discus: Bogie Redmon and Marv Berschet
Shot put: Bill Brown and Norm Wasser
Long jump: Paul Foreman and Don Laz
One-mile relay team: Herb McKenley, Bob Rehberg, Cirilo McSween and Stacey Siders

ILLINI LEGEND:

BILL BURRELL

The 1959 Heisman Trophy balloting, long recognized as a barometer of individual greatness in college football, ranked Bill Burrell as the nation's fourth-best overall player and No. 1 defensive performer his senior year. He was named a consensus All-America linebacker and was a three-time first-team all-conference selection. The *Chicago Tribune* even named Burrell as Big Ten football's Most Valuable Player in 1959. But, today, despite all those laurels, Bill Burrell probably still doesn't receive the credit due him. Ray Nitschke, a teammate and one of the Illini linebackers ranked above Burrell, recently called him Illinois' "forgotten man." The fact that he was one of only a handful of blacks playing college football in the late 1950s lends credence to the charge that racism has robbed Burrell of his recognition. However, to his Illini teammates, it is impossible to masquerade No. 68 as anything less than the best UI player of his time. Today, Burrell lives in Rockford where he owns several commercial real estate properties.

Illini Lore

Nineteen eighty-eight presidential candidate Jesse Jackson was a member of the University of Illinois' freshman football team in 1959. Jackson, who departed the UI after two semesters for North Carolina A&T, maintained he left because racial prejudice prevented him from playing quarterback for Coach Ray Eliot's Fighting Illini. An article by Loren Tate in the December 24, 1987 Champaign-Urbana *News-Gazette* charged that an alleged plagiarism incident in a freshman English class during Jackson's spring semester in 1960 was the primary reason for his departure.

1960-61

America's Time Capsule

- **Sept. 26, 1960:** *Sen. John Kennedy and Vice-President Richard Nixon participated in the first of a series of televised presidential campaign debates.*
- **Oct. 13, 1960:** *Bill Mazeroski of Pittsburgh slammed a game-winning home run against the New York Yankees to give the Pirates the World Series championship.*
- **Nov. 8, 1960:** *John Kennedy was elected president of the United States in a narrow victory over Richard Nixon.*
- **April 17, 1961:** *Nearly 2,000 CIA-trained anti-Castro Cuban exiles landed at the Bay of Cochinos in Cuba, in what came to be known as the Bay of Pigs invasion.*
- **May 5, 1961:** *Alan Shepard made a successful flight aboard the Project Mercury capsule Freedom Seven to become the first American in space.*

I·L·L·I·N·I M·O·M·E·N·T

Quarterback John Easterbrook (#11) helped Illinois beat Indiana in 1960.

PETE ELLIOTT DEBUTS AS WINNER:

On September 24, 1960, just 10 months after the Eliot Era had concluded, the Elliott Era began at the University of Illinois' Memorial Stadium. And as Ray Eliot's career had ended, so, too, did Pete Elliott's career begin—with an Illini football victory. Illinois' victim on this warm September afternoon was Indiana, recently suspended from conference competition due to its violation of recruiting rules. For the first seven minutes of the game, Indiana appeared to be in complete control, marching for an 80-yard touchdown on the opening drive. Thereafter, it was all Illinois as Elliott's option attack punctured the Hoosier defense for two touchdowns and a field goal while the Illini defense limited IU to just two first downs the balance of the game. Illinois' individual star was Champaign senior quarterback Johnny Easterbrook who twice ran options around left end for TDs and led the team in rushing with 74 yards. The final score: Illinois 17, Indiana 6.

ILLINI BIRTHDAYS

SEPTEMBER 1960
- 3– Gilmarcio Sanches, gymnastics
- 8– Donna Crane, tennis
- 15– Archie Carter, football
- 18– Mike Carrington, football
- 18– Pete Burgard, football
- 19– Diane Ricketts, basketball
- 23– Lawrence Warshaw, fencing
- 24– Rich Hainsworth, fencing

OCTOBER 1960
- 1– Kevin Oltendorf, gymnastics
- 11– Lisa Robinson, basketball
- 11– Lynette Robinson, basketball
- 13– Tim Brewster, football
- 15– Becky Kaiser, track
- 17– Oliver Williams, football
- 19– Greg Domantay, cross country/track
- 21– Carie Nemec, volleyball
- 28– Mike DeOliver, football
- 31– Joe Daw, tennis

NOVEMBER 1960
- 2– Adam Lingner, football
- 5– Craig Tucker, basketball
- 7– Lisa Plummer, track
- 12– Bob Kopale, baseball
- 13– Pat Morency, basketball
- 14– Marianne Dickerson, cross country/track
- 14– Tom Henderson, tennis
- 18– Dave Goone, gymnastics
- 18– Mike Martin, football
- 28– Joyce Gallagher, basketball

DECEMBER 1960
- 6– Terry Dempsey, swimming
- 10– Jennifer Roberts, women's tennis/coach
- 10– Mitchell Brookins, football
- 18– Mike Chadwick, golf
- 22– Carles Choi, fencing
- 29– Brett Wilson, football

JANUARY 1961
- 1– Lance Hofer, football
- 1– Phil Rekitzke, baseball
- 4– Laurie Watters, volleyball

- 8– Pam York, swimming
- 18– Kevin Bontemps, basketball
- 19– Don Passmore, football
- 19– Dave Luyando, gymnastics
- 20– Scott Jennings, track
- 22– Cindy Stein, basketball/coach
- 31– Quinn Richardson, basketball

FEBRUARY 1961
- 6– Dan Gregus, football
- 7– David Tee, football
- 13– Brian Pangrle, gymnastics
- 16– Doug Hargis, baseball
- 23– Lisa Buchanan, tennis
- 25– Beth Zimmerman, cross country/track

MARCH 1961
- 7– Susan Westhoff, swimming
- 9– Rich Baader, track
- 14– Carolyn Wright, basketball
- 15– Tom Varrige, football
- 22– Craig Zirbel, football

- 28– Rick Filippo, baseball
- 29– Cullen Daniel, football

APRIL 1961
- 1– John Powers, wrestling
- 8– Kari Samsten, gymnastics
- 8– Clinton Haynes, football
- 11– Marty Finis, football
- 22– Chris Sigourney, football
- 23– Chris Dowdy, volleyball

MAY 1961
- 10– Samuel Clear, football
- 13– Arthur Bebak, fencing
- 13– Doug Jones, baseball
- 13– Mary Ellen Murphy, golf
- 14– Paul Golaszewski, football
- 15– Ken McDonald, football
- 22– Jim Erlandson, football
- 23– Harry Gosier, football

JUNE 1961
- 2– Mike Kraft, gymnastics
- 3– Liz Schwarz, volleyball
- 17– Tom Folts, swimming
- 21– Charles Armstead, football

- 23– Arnie Manaois, fencing

JULY 1961
- 1– Gayathri DeSilva, tennis
- 2– Ashley Plummer, football
- 5– Kevin McMurchie, gymnastics
- 8– Jane Murphy, golf
- 8– Vince Osby, football
- 8– Kevin West, football
- 11– Wally Duffy, cross country
- 16– Tim Damron, football
- 18– Jon Emrich, track
- 18– Kerry Krueger, football
- 18– Kurt Krueger, football
- 19– Mark Jones, football
- 21– Jeff Johnston, wrestling

AUGUST 1961
- 1– Dwayne Pugh, football
- 5– Frank Rosch, gymnastics
- 10– Nancy Redington, golf
- 12– John Scanlan, gymnastics
- 13– Jon Weisman, fencing
- 18– Keith Paloucek, wrestling
- 25– Amy Kopko, track

Bill Small's lay-up against Michigan State helped the Illini beat the Spartans.

ILLINI ITEM

ILLINOIS' BASKETBALL TEAM spotted Michigan State a 14-0 lead, but fought back to win, 93-92, at Huff Gym on January 30, 1961. Bill Small's lay-up with 21 seconds left gave the Illini their first lead of the game at 91-90, and two pressure-packed free throws by Dave Downey with eight seconds remaining provided Illinois with its final margin.

ILLINI LISTS

PETE ELLIOTT'S MOST UNDERRATED ILLINI PLAYERS

Pete Elliott, coach of the Fighting Illini football team from 1960-66, was asked to select his 10 most underrated players at Illinois. Here, in no particular order, are his choices and comments about those players:

- Ernie McMillan ... "an outstanding player in college and as a pro"
- Ed O'Bradovich ... "a standout later with the Chicago Bears"
- Mike Taliaferro ... "outstanding on Rose Bowl team and very good in pro ball"
- Jim Warren ... "excellent on offense and defense; became a fine pro defensive back"
- Dick Deller ... "captain of the Rose Bowl team"
- Ron Acks ... "a fine athlete who had an excellent pro career"
- Gregg Schumacher ... "a big, agile player who could do a lot of things"
- Bob Trumpy ... "later became a standout with the Cincinnati Bengals"
- Sam Price ... "a three-year starter and an excellent power halfback"
- Cyril Pinder ... "though he was plagued with injuries, he was one of Illinois' finest talents"

ILLINI LEGEND:

BILL BROWN

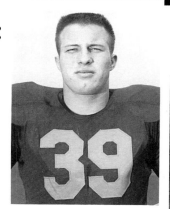

The term "battering ram" probably never more aptly described a football player than it did Illinois' Bill Brown. At 5-11, 210 pounds, the all-state fullback from Mendota, Illinois was never known as being a flashy player, but there were few who were more productive. From 1958-60, Brown grinded out a total of 1,269 yards to become Illinois' sixth-leading rusher of all-time. When his Illini offensive unit ran out of downs, Brown stayed on the field as a defensive linebacker. And when he wasn't playing offense or defense, Brown starred as a punter, winding up his career with a UI-record average of more than 40 yards per punt. When football season ended, Brown headed for the Armory to compete for Leo Johnson's track team as a shot putter. He lettered twice in track, holding the school's outdoor record in the shot put (54' 8 1/2") and winning the 1960 Big Ten indoor title. Brown was drafted by the NFL's Chicago Bears in 1961, but spent 12 of his 13 years in the pros with the Minnesota Vikings. He led the Vikings in rushing five times and played in three Super Bowls. After he hung up his cleats, Brown entered the insurance business for 10 years, but for the last 17 years has directed the sales force of John Roberts Printing Co. in Bloomington, Minnesota.

Illini Lore

On May 20, 1961, the University of Illinois' Krannert Art Museum was dedicated. Mr. and Mrs. Herman Krannert, benefactors of $430,000, were on hand to open the university's first real home for UI's permanent art collection. Previously, the Architecture Building was the campus site for art displays.

1961-62

America's Time Capsule

- **Oct. 1, 1961:** *Roger Maris of the New York Yankees hit his 61st home run, breaking Babe Ruth's single-season record.*
- **Feb. 10, 1962:** *Jim Beatty became the first American to break the four-minute mile indoors, registering a time of 3:58.9 in Los Angeles.*
- **Feb. 20, 1962:** *Astronaut John Glenn became the first American to orbit the Earth, circling the globe three times aboard Friendship 7.*
- **March 2, 1962:** *Wilt Chamberlain of the Philadelphia Warriors became the first NBA player to score 100 points in a game.*
- **Aug. 5, 1962:** *Actress Marilyn Monroe, 36, died in her Los Angeles home of an apparent overdose of sleeping pills.*

I·L·L·I·N·I M·O·M·E·N·T

Coach Lee Eilbracht and captain Tony Eichelberger

ILLINI BASEBALL TEAM IS UNDISPUTED CHAMPION:

Behind the flawless pitching of Tom Fletcher and Doug Mills and the timely hitting of Lloyd Flodin and Tony Eichelberger, Illinois' 1962 baseball team captured its first undisputed Big Ten title in 15 years. Only Indiana and Northwestern were able to hand the Fighting Illini losses in 15 Big Ten games, as Illinois finished a half-game better than runner-up Michigan. The clincher came on May 19 at Illinois Field when the Illini swept a doubleheader from Iowa, while the league-leading Wolverines were dropping a pair at Wisconsin. Fletcher and Mills both went to the mound five times during the Big Ten season, and each man recorded a perfect 5-0 win-loss mark. Illinois' top hitters were Flodin (.370), the team's catcher, and shortstop Eichelberger (.365). Right fielder Bud Felichio led the Illini in home runs and runs batted in during conference play, with two and 13, respectively. In NCAA tournament action, Coach Lee Eilbracht's troops beat the University of Detroit in their opening game (2-1), but lost their next two to Western Michigan (10-2) and Michigan (5-1) to be eliminated.

ILLINI BIRTHDAYS

SEPTEMBER 1961
- 1– Moe Bias, football
- 1– Melvin Keys, track
- 2– Craig Tiley, tennis coach
- 3– Greg Peterson, golf
- 9– Jackie Johnson, football
- 10– Dan Hamstra, baseball
- 24– Kirby Wilson, football

OCTOBER 1961
- 9– Gary Lee, football
- 11– Rita Hoppmann, tennis
- 13– Derek Harper, basketball
- 19– Jim Covington, football
- 24– Tony Scarcelli, football
- 31– Karen Collymore, volleyball

NOVEMBER 1961
- 4– Steve Franke, fencing
- 20– Greg Rogers, baseball

DECEMBER 1961
- 1– Maureen McNamara, tennis
- 2– Perry Carlini, football

- 2– Michael Yates, wrestling
- 5– Dwight Beverly, football
- 13– Ken Cruz, football
- 15– Diane Eickholt, basketball
- 17– Joe Miles, football
- 17– Rick Hogan, football
- 18– Debbie Stetson, cross country/track
- 24– Mike McQuinn, football
- 25– Tucker Jenkins, football
- 31– Mark Butkus, football
- 31– Gilberto Albuquerque, gymnastics

JANUARY 1962
- 4– Derrick Gentry, track
- 5– Mark Funk, swimming
- 7– Darryl Thompson, football
- 9– Barry Waddell, tennis
- 10– Tim Fritz, track
- 11– Don Pall, baseball
- 12– Jayne Glade, track
- 20– Randy Lewis, golf
- 31– Lisa Stevens, cross country/track

FEBRUARY 1962
- 5– Kris Jenner, football
- 6– Mike Stine, football
- 6– Tony Guercio, track
- 7– Cam Benson, football
- 14– Scott Somlar, football
- 16– Kent Helwig, swimming
- 21– Rhea Rogers, track
- 21– Christina Stoltz, cross country/track
- 28– Julie Lantis, cross country/track

MARCH 1962
- 2– Bob Miller, football
- 7– Jeff Lehmann, track
- 24– Terry Cole, football
- 26– Lori Hofer, basketball
- 27– Dave Birkey, football
- 31– David Edwards, football

APRIL 1962
- 3– Catherine McGlone, cross country/track
- 10– John Janata, football
- 11– Jeff Marczewski, track
- 18– Sara Olson, tennis

- 24– Mike Johnson, football
- 26– George Montgomery, basketball

MAY 1962
- 1– Steve Adamson, gymnastics
- 2– John Losito, tennis
- 6– Larry Coffey, baseball
- 9– David Goodman, tennis
- 16– Mike Giddings, football
- 17– Larry Mosley, football
- 20– Scott Brandt, swimming
- 24– Terrie Berto, golf
- 25– Scott Golden, football
- 29– Rob Pullen, baseball

JUNE 1962
- 1– Chris Babyar, football
- 5– Victor Bills, track
- 7– Mark Funkhouser, golf
- 9– Curtis Meyers, football
- 12– John Cyboran, golf
- 13– Karen Brems, gymnastics
- 17– Chris White, football
- 17– Nick Epps, football
- 26– Susan Homann, swimming

JULY 1962
- 1– Bob Stowe, football
- 5– Jeff Innis, baseball
- 5– Susan Lang, golf
- 7– Steve Nelson, football
- 10– Don Thorp, football
- 14– Kim Brombolich, basketball
- 21– Laurie Maybach, cross country/track
- 24– Victor Bowlay-Williams, football
- 25– Suzanne Yario, volleyball

AUGUST 1962
- 2– Richard Ryles, football
- 3– Ed Slattery, golf
- 6– Luke Sewall, football
- 6– Michele Vossen, basketball
- 14– Don Klusendorf, basketball
- 18– Chris Davis, wrestling
- 18– Tom Thomas, baseball
- 25– Teri Balzer, cross country/track

I

SENIOR MIKE TOLIUSZIS became the first University of Illinois golfer since 1942 to win medalist honors at the Big Ten Championships, May 18-19, 1962. Toliuszis trailed Purdue's Steve Wilkinson by five strokes after 36 holes, but pulled into a first-place tie after the third round. In the fourth and final round, the Illini star shot a 73 to wind up six strokes better than the second-place Wilkinson.

ILLINI LISTS

MOST POINTS BY BIG TEN BASKETBALL PLAYERS VS. ILLINOIS

49 pts	Glenn Robinson, Purdue (3/13/94)
49 pts	Gary Bradds, Ohio State (2/10/64)
48 pts	Mike Woodson, Indiana (3/3/79)
45 pts	Terry Dischinger, Purdue (1/8/62)
45 pts	Terry Dischinger, Purdue (2/17/62)
43 pts	Terry Dischinger, Purdue (1/11/60)
41 pts	Dave Schellhase, Purdue (2/6/65)
40 pts	Rick Lopossa, Northwestern (2/1/64)
40 pts	Joe Ruklick, Northwestern (3/8/58)
38 pts	Chris Pervall, Iowa (3/6/65)

Terry Dischinger

ILLINI LEGEND:

DOUG MILLS

Though he is no relation to his namesake, Douglas C. Mills had a lot in common with the long-time Illini athlete, coach and athletic director. Both men were multiple-sport stars as undergraduates, and both were huge successes after their playing days were through. The younger Mills, a native of Galesburg, lettered in football, basketball, and baseball during his career at the Urbana-Champaign campus, earning six monograms altogether. His greatest individual achievements came as a pitcher for Coach Lee Eilbracht's UI baseball squad, where he excelled as a pitcher. As a senior, Mills appeared on the mound five times in Big Ten play and won all five decisions, helping Illinois capture its first undisputed conference baseball title in 15 years. Though Mills' basketball and football performances were less spectacular, he did average nearly four points per game as a substitute guard for Coach Harry Combes. Illinois' 1962 Athlete of the Year has enjoyed a remarkable career in the banking industry, rising to his current position as Chairman of the Board of Urbana's First Busey Corporation.

Illini Lore

James Brady, former press secretary to President Ronald Reagan, earned a degree in journalism in 1962. The Centralia, Illinois native served as president of Sigma Chi fraternity as a University of Illinois student and also wrote for the *Daily Illini*. Just three months after his appointment as the presidential press secretary, Brady was critically injured in the March 1981 assassination attempt on the President. He received the UI Alumni Association's Alumni Achievement Award in 1991 and now serves as vice chairman of the National Organization on Disability in Washington, D.C.

1962-63

I·L·L·I·N·I M·O·M·E·N·T

Senior center Bill Burwell (25) puts up a shot in the first-ever game played at the Assembly Hall.

ILLINI CAGERS CLINCH BIG TEN TITLE AT NEW ASSEMBLY HALL: The 1962-63 basketball season was an unforgettable one for the University of Illinois. First, the Fighting Illini played their 38th and final season at Huff Gym, winning all nine of their games in that storied facility. Second, Illinois opened its futuristic new palace, the Assembly Hall, on March 4, 1963, with a nail-biting 79-73 victory over Northwestern. But the most thrilling chapter of 1962-63 came on March 9 when, in the regular-season finale at Champaign, Illinois defeated Iowa, 73-69, to claim a share of the Big Ten title and send it to the NCAA tournament for the first time since 1952. Illinois travelled up to East Lansing, Michigan for the Mideast Regional games, defeating Bowling Green in the opener, then losing to eventual champ Loyola in game two. The Illini heroes that season included starting forwards Bob Starnes and Dave Downey, center Bill Burwell, and guards Bill Small and Tal Brody. Skip Thoren, Bill Edwards and Bogie Redmon were valuable members of the team off the bench for Coach Harry Combes' 20-6 club.

ILLINI BIRTHDAYS

SEPTEMBER 1962
- 8– Jill Ittersagen, golf
- 9– Jack Trudeau, football
- 10– Cap Boso, football
- 11– Kent Knebelkamp, baseball
- 17– Tim St. Clair, track
- 30– Leslie Hawkins, cross country/track

OCTOBER 1962
- 1– Kathy Kewney, tennis
- 11– Dave Mingle, gymnastics
- 11– Mike Mingle, gymnastics
- 16– Mike Lawlor, football
- 29– Ron Hochstrasser, fencing

NOVEMBER 1962
- 14– Sue Hutchinson, tennis
- 15– Mark Tagart, football
- 29– Steve Maher, gymnastics

DECEMBER 1962
- 14– Karen Bruns, basketball

JANUARY 1963
- 13– Jeff Stevenson, football
- 16– Bonnie Bergsma, swimming
- 17– Brian Kennedy, golf
- 19– Cheryl Ward, cross country/track
- 21– Gary Borg, baseball
- 24– Rick Schulte, football
- 27– Curtis Clarke, football

FEBRUARY 1963
- 5– Keith Munson, fencing
- 18– Jay Daniels, basketball
- 26– David Boatright, football

MARCH 1963
- 1– Mark Arnold, track
- 10– Ann Henry, cross country/track
- 13– Ken Warmbier, baseball
- 21– Jeff Mauck, football

APRIL 1963
- 8– Kendra Gantt, basketball
- 10– Bob Sebring, football
- 15– Don Phillips, track
- 19– Steve Collier, football
- 22– Tim Hanson, wrestling

23– Phil Callahan, wrestling
27– Dana Anastasia, wrestling

MAY 1963
- 9– Al Ishu, fencing
- 25– Eric Wycoff, football
- 28– Kelly See, volleyball

JUNE 1963
- 1– Mike Patton, cross country/track
- 2– Randy Grant, football
- 4– Joe Olker, baseball
- 8– Joe Ledvora, gymnastics
- 10– David Williams, football
- 15– Pam McCloskey, golf
- 17– Mary Wylie, swimming

26– Cheri Hochhalter, swimming
27– Barbara Bareis, tennis

JULY 1963
- 1– Gretchen Grier, track
- 6– Ray Hairston, football
- 10– Mark Wieneke, track
- 19– Peter Bouton, tennis
- 27– Susan Arildsen, tennis
- 28– Jennifer Matz, tennis

AUGUST 1963
- 4– Per Ake Brinck, swimming
- 6– Kelly Rickard, tennis
- 11– Richard Chiao, fencing
- 17– Rachel Bass, track
- 17– Jerry Reese, football
- 20– Rolanda Conda, track
- 29– Tom Grossman, fencing

ILLINI ITEM

ON NOVEMBER 3, 1962, the University of Illinois football team broke the longest losing streak in modern Big Ten history—15 in a row—with a 14-10 upset victory over Purdue at West Lafayette, Indiana. Coach Pete Elliott's Illini shocked the Purdue Homecoming crowd when they took the lead on a 23-yard pass from Mike Taliaferro to Thurman Walker in the second quarter, and built the margin to 14-3 on a 30-yard gallop by Ken Zimmerman on the final play of the third period. When the team returned by bus from West Lafayette, it was greeted by thousands of fans lined up on Cunningham and Florida Avenues.

Illinois' Ken Zimmerman (20) grabs a pass as the Illini break a 15-game losing streak at Purdue.

ILLINI LISTS

PRO FOOTBALL HALL OF FAME

On January 29, 1963, the National Football League elected its charter class for the new Pro Football Hall of Fame in Canton, Ohio. Two men with Illini ties were among the group of 16:

- Sammy Baugh, QB
- Bert Bell, contributor
- Joe Carr, contributor
- "Dutch" Clark, QB
- **Harold "Red" Grange, RB**
- **George Halas, player/coach**
- Mel Hein, C
- Cal Hubbard, T
- Don Hutson, E
- "Curly" Lambeau, player/coach
- Tim Mara, contributor
- George Marshall, contributor
- Johnny "Blood" McNally, RB
- "Bronko" Nagurski, RB
- Ernie Nevers, RB
- Jim Thorpe, RB

ILLINI LEGEND:

DAVE DOWNEY

Dave Downey's association with the University of Illinois has seen him rise from the status of a student-athlete, to that of assistant coach, to a role as a color analyst on the Illini basketball telecasts, and, finally, to an appointment from the governor as a member of the UI's Board of Trustees. For Downey, the challenge of combining a career of athletics and academics was seemingly never difficult, as witnessed by his earning the prestigious Big Ten Conference Medal of Honor as a senior in 1963. He was best known for his Illini exploits on the basketball court, a three-year stretch from 1960-63 in which he was named team MVP every season. Downey set nearly every UI scoring record, including marks for a single game (53 points vs. Indiana on February 16, 1963) and for a career (1,360 points). A charter member of the Illinois Coaches Association High School Hall of Fame, the Canton, Illinois High School graduate earned All-Big Ten and All-America honors at Illinois. Downey was the recipient of the Varsity "I" Award in 1988, saluting his marvelous performance as an athlete and his successful career as president of Champaign's Downey Planning Services.

Illini Lore

A massive building program begun in 1958 at the University of Illinois saw the completion of numerous structures during the 1962-63 school year. Among the facilities opened to students included the $1.35 million Student Services Building, $1.96 million Entomology Building, the $2.3 million Physics Building, the $5.75 million Pennsylvania Residence Halls, the $6.9 million Illini Union addition, and the $8.3 million Assembly Hall.

The Assembly Hall begins to rise from the ground.

1963-64

I·L·L·I·N·I M·O·M·E·N·T

Senior quarterback Mike Taliaferro scrambles for yardage in Illinois' Rose Bowl-clinching victory at Michigan State.

PRESIDENT'S ASSASSINATION DELAYS ILLINI CHAMPIONSHIP:
For the University of Illinois football team, it was the worst of times and it was the best of times. Forced to postpone its season-ending showdown at Michigan State for five days due to the shocking assassination of President John Kennedy, Coach Pete Elliott's Illini made a second trip to East Lansing to play the fourth-ranked Spartans on Thanksgiving Day 1963. State's roster was stocked with All-Americans such as halfback Sherman Lewis, but the Illini countered with a stifling defense led by the incomparable Dick Butkus. In the end, Illinois' defenders were the difference, causing the Spartans to cough up three fumbles and throw four interceptions, resulting in a 13-0 Illini victory. UI's offensive attack was led by sophomore fullback Jim Grabowski, who rushed for 85 yards against the heretofore impenetrable Spartan defense. The triumph gave Illinois its 12th football championship and its third trip to the Rose Bowl.

ILLINI BIRTHDAYS

SEPTEMBER 1963
- 2– Greg Iavarone, baseball
- 4– George Arvanitis, football
- 6– John Ayres, football
- 6– Kent Koshkarian, fencing
- 7– Margaret Vogel, track
- 7– Michelle Vogel, cross country/track
- 10– Terry Wells, baseball
- 12– Bob Dombrowski, football
- 30– Deanna LaSusa, cross country/track

OCTOBER 1963
- 13– Jeanne Tortorelli, basketball
- 21– Brian McCracken, wrestling
- 21– Ruth Sterneman, cross country/track

NOVEMBER 1963
- 1– Rick Siler, football
- 9– Justin Dooley, gymnastics
- 14– James Finch, football

- 16– Tim Turner, golf
- 24– Rick Schulte, football
- 26– Thomas Rooks, football

DECEMBER 1963
- 4– Jim Kisner, football
- 9– Alec Gibson, football
- 12– Anthony Welch, basketball
- 12– Stephen Pierce, football
- 17– Holly Joesten, swimming
- 19– Efrem Winters, basketball
- 21– Jenny Middeler, basketball
- 22– Mike Meyer, tennis
- 25– Dave Aina, football
- 28– Mike Heaven, football
- 29– Nick Hrnyak, baseball

JANUARY 1964
- 3– Eddie Hungate, football
- 4– Scott Meents, basketball
- 7– Jim Russell, track
- 11– Todd Schertz, football
- 17– Doug Altenberger, basketball
- 23– Jay Lynch, football
- 25– Kathleen Dippel, volleyball

- 28– Steve Juengert, gymnastics

FEBRUARY 1964
- 2– Keith Massey, baseball
- 3– Rob Glielmi, football
- 3– Craig Swoope, football
- 5– Geraldine Dvorak, volleyball
- 7– Barb Hill, swimming
- 8– Darrin Brown, football
- 11– Tim Stanley, football
- 13– Bill Haubold, golf
- 16– Roosevelt Wardell, football
- 21– Doug Campoli, fencing
- 23– Pam Means, basketball
- 26– Toni Canino, swimming

MARCH 1964
- 11– Michael Bila, track
- 16– Stephanie Romic, basketball
- 19– Jim Orsag, baseball
- 29– Scott Hutchinson, track

APRIL 1964
- 4– David Moreno, fencing

- 9– Bruce Douglas, basketball
- 11– Todd Schertz, football
- 16– Matt Berger, wrestling
- 21– Brian Ward, football
- 29– Richard Canan, baseball

MAY 1964
- 2– William Mueller, swimming
- 7– Terry Travis, baseball
- 10– Guy Teafatiller, football
- 10– Mark Mathis, football
- 14– Michelle Campbell, golf
- 15– Jo Wickiser, tennis
- 22– Rita Schwarz, volleyball
- 31– Liz White, basketball
- 31– Reggie Woodward, basketball

JUNE 1964
- 3– Connie Borbeck, golf
- 3– Christy Flesvig, tennis
- 8– Ray Wilson, football
- 9– Yvonne Oldham, track
- 12– Renatta Schillmoeller, swimming

- 20– Chuck Sherline, track
- 26– Kim Dunlap, track
- 30– Dan Mota, wrestling

JULY 1964
- 12– Jeff Harp, wrestling
- 13– Mike McBain, football
- 16– Shane Lamb, football
- 26– Todd Avery, football
- 31– Richard Renfro, football

AUGUST 1964
- 3– Cathy Lawrence, basketball
- 3– Donell Whitehead, track
- 6– Charles Lakes, gymnastics
- 12– Molly Kissinger, volleyball
- 12– Chenise Whitehead, basketball
- 14– Derrick Williams, wrestling
- 14– Kirk Azinger, wrestling
- 17– Kevin Haime, golf
- 18– Shawn Jones, football
- 30– Andre Lambert, tennis

Illinois' 1964 Rose Bowl team was led by its rock-solid defense. The starters included Mike Summers (85), Ed Washington (66), Bill Minor (79), Archie Sutton (76), Wylie Fox (65), Bill Pasko (87), Mike Dundy (41), Don Hansen (32), Dick Butkus (50), George Donnelly (26) and Jimmy Warren (22).

ILLINI ITEM

THE FIGHTNG ILLINI FOOTBALL TEAM made it three Rose Bowl victories in a row on January 1, 1964, by defeating Washington, 17-7. In a game witnessed by nearly 97,000 fans, including former president and Tournament of Roses Grand Marshal Dwight Eisenhower, the Illini rebounded from a 7-0 deficit behind the methodical running of game MVP Jim Grabowski, who rushed for 125 yards.

ILLINI LISTS

NAISMITH AWARD WINNERS' PERFORMANCES VS. ILLINOIS

1971 Austin Carr, Notre Dame, 23 points on 1/30/71 (Illinois won, 69-66)

1973 Bill Walton, UCLA, 20 points on 12/30/72 (UCLA won, 71-64)

1976 Scott May, Indiana, 27 points on 1/17/76 (Indiana won, 83-55); and 6 points on 2/14/76 (Indiana won, 58-48)

1988 Danny Manning, Kansas, 28 points on 11/29/87 (Illinois won, 81-75)

1993 Calbert Cheaney, Indiana, 30 points on 1/16/93 (Indiana won, 83-79); and 29 points on 2/17/93 (Indiana won, 93-72)

1994 Glenn Robinson, Purdue, 49 points on 3/13/94 (Purdue won, 87-77)

Austin Carr, 1971's College Basketball Player of the Year, scored 23 points against the Illini.

ILLINI LEGEND:

PETE ELLIOTT

One of the most popular men to ever don Fighting Illini coaching apparel, Pete Elliott took his team from the brink of destruction to the pinnacle of success during his career from 1960-66. Elliott's initial years at the University of Illinois were clouded with failure, losing a modern Big Ten record 15 games in a row from November 19, 1960 to October 27, 1962. But in 1963, Elliott troops made Cinderella's story pale in comparison, capturing the 1963 Big Ten title and defeating Washington in the 1964 Rose Bowl. "We knew as we went through the losses that we didn't have a good team," Elliott told the Champaign-Urbana *News-Gazette* in 1977. "But we were confident because our athletes were devoted and they helped us recruit top prospects. They were tremendous emissaries for the school." On March 18, 1967, Elliott and basketball coach Harry Combes resigned from the UI staff as a result of the "slush fund" scandal. Elliott served as athletic director at the University of Miami for several years, and began his 17th year as executive director of the Pro Football Hall of Fame in 1995.

Illini Lore

Construction on the new University of Illinois Chicago Circle campus, located on 106 acres southwest of the Dan Ryan and Dwight Eisenhower expressways, continued during the 1963-64 academic year. Originally, a 119-acre site in the village of North Riverside was chosen for relocation of the Chicago undergraduate campus. Finally, in February of 1961, the UI's Board of Trustees settled on the present site, located at Harrison and Halsted Streets. Four years and $61 million later, the campus and its original 13 buildings opened February 22, 1965 with an enrollment of 5,300 students.

1964-65

America's Time Capsule

- **Sept. 27, 1964:** *The Warren Commission on the assassination of John Kennedy reported that there was no conspiracy and that Lee Harvey Oswald alone was responsible.*
- **Oct. 15, 1964:** *Bob Gibson and the St. Louis Cardinals defeated the New York Yankees for the World Series title.*
- **Nov. 3, 1964:** *Lyndon Johnson defeated Barry Goldwater in the presidential election.*
- **March 8, 1965:** *The first United States combat forces landed in South Vietnam to guard the U.S. Air Force base at Da Nang.*
- **June 5, 1965:** *Astronaut Edward White successfully completed a 20-minute walk in space, the first by an American.*

I·L·L·I·N·I M·O·M·E·N·T

Jim Grabowski (31) pounded out a Big Ten-record 239 yards vs. Wisconsin in 1964.

GRABOWSKI SETS BIG TEN RECORD:
Jim Grabowski is eternally grateful to men such as Archie Sutton, Ed Washington, Ron Acks and Dave Mueller, a few of the numerous teammates who opened the holes for his 239-yard rushing performance vs. Wisconsin, November 14, 1964. But the man to whom No. 31 owes the biggest debt of gratitude might be Illini publicity man Charlie Bellatti. It was Bellatti who sent word to his sideline spotters that Grabowski needed only 19 more yards in the final quarter to set a Big Ten record. "I wasn't going to put Jim back in the next series," head coach Pete Elliott told reporters afterwards, "but a man deserves a shot at a record like that." Badger coach Milt Bruhn, gracious despite Wisconsin's 29-0 defeat, praised Grabowski's ability to explode off the mark. "He keeps this head of steam up and blasts right through the man who is trying to tackle him," Bruhn said. Grabowski needed only 33 attempts to set the record, two of which resulted in touchdowns.

ILLINI BIRTHDAYS

SEPTEMBER 1964
- 2– Kelly McNee, cross country/track
- 3– Ron Bohm, football
- 3– Chris Carpenter, football
- 5– Ken Norman, basketball
- 10– Denise Fracaro, volleyball
- 10– Lane Lohr, track
- 12– Jim Juriga, football
- 20– Scott Kehoe, football
- 27– Keith Mosser, fencing
- 29– Colleen Hackett, cross country/track

OCTOBER 1964
- 7– Tony Wilson, swimming
- 10– Kenny Battle, basketball

NOVEMBER 1964
- 5– Andy Little, football
- 11– Adrienne Brooks, cross country/track
- 14– Carol Rumpel, volleyball
- 15– Carolyn Hamann, swimming
- 21– John Wine, swimming

DECEMBER 1964
- 1– Bonnie Moskovitz, volleyball
- 2– Brennon "Boo" Champagne, baseball
- 5– Paul Kivela, cross country
- 12– Sam Ellsworth, football
- 14– Dave Payton, baseball
- 21– Lisa Bradley, basketball
- 21– Keith Taylor, football
- 27– John Elliott, football
- 28– Nancy Shellander, basketball
- 30– Todd Searcy, football

JANUARY 1965
- 3– Darryl Usher, football
- 4– Jon Thanos, cross country
- 7– Jonelle Polk, basketball
- 17– Melvin Williams, football
- 18– Bill Howie, tennis
- 25– Steve Tyson, track
- 28– Tim Bourke, football
- 28– Jens Kujawa, basketball

FEBRUARY 1965
- 2– Kevin Brooks, track
- 7– John Jacobson, track
- 17– Jim Blondell, football

MARCH 1965
- 7– Tom Powers, baseball
- 16– Molly Terrien, basketball
- 17– Keith Erickson, swimming
- 17– Liz Grant, swimming
- 23– Mark Robinson, baseball
- 30– Steve Stammer, fencing
- 30– Darren Tee, football

APRIL 1965
- 3– Blake Schicker, fencing
- 3– Eric Schicker, fencing
- 7– Marty Sarussi, swimming
- 15– Mark Dennis, football
- 16– Terry Moore, track
- 19– Lesley Hudgins, basketball
- 22– Gordon Green, football

- 29– Tony Wysinger, basketball

MAY 1965
- 7– Jill Samuelson, volleyball
- 8– Sonya Costello, swimming
- 11– Heraldo Morrison, track
- 15– Renee-Claude Auclair, diving
- 16– Kelley Thomas, basketball
- 17– Tom Frei, tennis
- 19– Jessica Daw, tennis
- 26– Brenda MacConnachie, golf
- 29– Brad Leighty, golf

- 24– Andrew Lobb, tennis
- 25– Cheryl Arnholt, golf
- 30– Gabe dela Garza, football

JUNE 1965
- 1– Daren DePew, baseball
- 1– Angie Heitz, track
- 5– Greg McCollum, baseball
- 9– Scott Greenberg, tennis

JULY 1965
- 14– Terry Stoltz, cross country/track
- 17– Mike McGann, football
- 24– Chuck Fiser, golf
- 26– Carol Bruene, cross country
- 30– Alison Arnoff, swimming

- 16– Matt Scotty, swimming
- 16– Arael Doolittle, football
- 19– Doug Kane, baseball
- 21– Ed White, football
- 30– Anthony Williams, football

AUGUST 1965
- 2– African Grant, football
- 7– Scott Davis, football
- 7– Tom Schertz, football
- 10– Craig Moore, football
- 18– Darryl Humphrey, baseball
- 20– Deann Bercik, swimming
- 31– James Gordon, football

Skip Thoren led Illinois to a victory against defending national champion UCLA, Dec. 4, 1964.

I

ILLINI ITEM

COACH HARRY COMBES' Fighting Illini basketball team demolished defending national champion UCLA, 110-83, on December 4, 1964, severing the Bruins' 30-game-winning streak. Though UCLA guard Gail Goodrich tossed in a game-high 25 points, the Illini countered with a balanced attack that had six men score in double figures, paced by 20 points from center Skip Thoren.

ILLINI LISTS

LEADING SINGLE-GAME RUSHERS IN BIG TEN HISTORY

When Jim Grabowski broke the Big Ten's single-game football rushing record on November 14, 1964, he put his name atop a list that included many of the conference's greatest stars.

239 yards	**Jim Grabowski of Illinois, vs. Wisconsin, 1964**
216 yards	Bill Daley of Michigan, vs. Northwestern, 1943
212 yards	**Harold "Red" Grange of Illinois, vs. Michigan, 1924**
207 yards	Tony Butkovich of Purdue, vs. Illinois, 1943
205 yards	**J.C. Caroline of Illinois, vs. Minnesota, 1953**
200 yards	Alan Ameche of Wisconsin, vs. Minnesota, 1951
199 yards	Dick Gordon of Michigan State, vs. Wisconsin, 1964

Jim Grabowski (foreground) bested six other Big Ten greats, including legendary Red Grange (background).

ILLINI LEGEND:

DICK BUTKUS

Just how good was Illinois linebacker Dick Butkus? Consider the following:

- An award in his name is given annually to the nation's top college football linebacker.
- He was a two-time consensus All-America and All-Big Ten selection for the Fighting Illini from 1962-64.
- He was the Big Ten's Most Valuable Player in 1963.
- He finished third in the Heisman Trophy balloting as a senior, unheard of for a defensive player.
- His jersey number 50 was retired at Illinois alongside Red Grange's immortal "77."
- He's a member of every all-time all-star squad in existence, and was a first-ballot selection into the College and Pro Football Halls of Fame.
- During his nine-year career with the Chicago Bears, he was an All-Pro pick eight times.

George Halas, who coached Butkus with the Bears, says "Dick Butkus remains the standard for defensive players to strive for." Nowadays, in addition to being an analyst on the Bears' broadcasts, Butkus is a nationally acclaimed actor. He resides in Rancho Mirage, California.

Illini Lore

The College of Education dedicated its new $3.3 million building November 6-7, 1964, to an overflow group of students, alumni and other guests. The facility brought together departments that had been spread out over 27 campus locations. The education building was one of the first structures on campus to have extensive use of glass and to be fully air conditioned.

Illini Traditions Press Onward

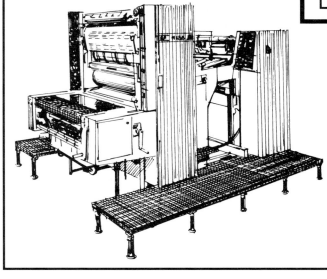

ILLINOIS
1965 HOME GAMES
KICKOFF 1:30 P.M. — $5.00

SEPT. 18 . . . . OREGON STATE
SEPT. 25 . . (H. S. Band Day) . . SOUTHERN METHODIST
OCT. 16 . . . . (Homecoming) . . . . INDIANA
OCT. 23 . . . . (Chicago Day) . . . . DUKE
OCT. 30 . . . . (Dad's "I" Men's Day) . . . . . . PURDUE
NOV. 6 . . . . MICHIGAN

OCT. 2—AT MICHIGAN STATE   NOV. 13—AT WISCONSIN
OCT. 9—AT OHIO STATE   NOV. 20—AT NORTHWESTERN

Mail Orders to Football Ticket Office, Assembly Hall, Champaign, Ill.

1965-1974

1965-66

America's Time Capsule

- **Oct. 28, 1965:** *Workers topped out the Gateway Arch in St. Louis, Missouri.*
- **Nov. 9, 1965:** *Millions of people in the Northeast were affected by a massive, 13-hour power blackout.*
- **Jan. 31, 1966:** *President Lyndon Johnson announced that American pilots had resumed their bombing raids on North Vietnam after a 38-day hiatus in hopes of furthering peace negotiations.*
- **April 28, 1966:** *The Boston Celtics beat the Los Angeles Lakers in game seven of the NBA championship series, enabling coach Red Auerbach to retire with his eighth successive title.*
- **June 8, 1966:** *The National and American football leagues merged, effective in 1970, setting up a Super Bowl game between the league champions.*

I·L·L·I·N·I M·O·M·E·N·T

COMBES WINS HIS 300TH IN ILLINI VICTORY OVER MICHIGAN:
Illinois' most memorable basketball victory of the 1965-66 season came on February 1, 1966, before a sellout crowd of 7,350 at Michigan's Yost Field House. The 99-93 triumph not only got Illinois back in the Big Ten race, it also marked UI's first win in Ann Arbor in 11 years and gave Coach Harry Combes his 300th win as the Illini coach. Trailing by three points at the half, Illinois shot a school-record .697 from the field in the second half (23 of 33) to create a three-team log-jam atop the conference standings. UI's offensive heroes were Don Freeman (33 points) and Rich Jones (31), while defensive kudos went to Preston Pearson who, despite playing the entire second half with four fouls, "held" Michigan's Cazzie Russell to 33 points.

Rich Jones' 31 points vs. Michigan helped Illinois give Coach Harry Combes his 300th Illini victory.

ILLINI BIRTHDAYS

SEPTEMBER 1965
- 3– Chad Little, football
- 5– Sheila Burns, tennis
- 9– Keith Healy, wrestling
- 10– Scott Murnick, football
- 12– Stacy Pfeifer, basketball
- 16– Steve Brazas, football
- 21– Mike Piel, football
- 27– Chris Bowe, track
- 30– Carl Jones, baseball

OCTOBER 1965
- 1– Kevin Arrison, swimming
- 3– Madhu Nair, tennis
- 15– Jenny Johnson, basketball
- 16– Tony Michalak, baseball
- 23– Dave Harbour, football
- 26– Ian Drury, wrestling
- 30– Lance Harkey, football
- 30– Anthony Williams, football

NOVEMBER 1965
- 1– Mike Scully, football
- 4– Tom Schaffer, basketball
- 16– Jeff Markland, football

DECEMBER 1965
- 1– Todd Mitter, baseball
- 6– Lori Anderson, volleyball
- 7– Eric Schantz, tennis
- 9– John Walewander, baseball
- 16– Stacey Knowles, tennis
- 18– Sandra Goern, tennis
- 31– Victoria Fulcher, track

JANUARY 1966
- 1– Jim Bennett, football
- 4– Mike Munson, baseball
- 5– Allison Johnston, golf
- 12– Shawn Turner, football
- 13– Joe Skubisz, football
- 14– Dwight Gilbert, cross country/track
- 15– Ken Thomas, football
- 19– Bridget Koster, cross country/track
- 20– Jane Richart, swimming
- 23– Reiner Kamper, fencing
- 28– Chris Lapriore, tennis

FEBRUARY 1966
- 2– Stan Fit, football
- 2– Scott Haffner, basketball

- 9– Meta Rose Torchia, swimming
- 9– Greg Turner, football
- 13– Cheryl Domitrz, swimming
- 13– Don Edwards, golf
- 15– Dan Hartleb, assistant baseball coach
- 18– Bobby Dawson, football
- 25– Elizabeth Binkley, volleyball

MARCH 1966
- 3– Disa Johnson, volleyball & assistant coach
- 4– Mike Small, golf
- 6– Roger Witek, football
- 10– John Mahon, golf
- 11– Shawn McGarris, football
- 13– Glynn Blackwell, basketball
- 14– Doug Foor, wrestling
- 20– Keith Jones, football
- 24– Troy Heitmeyer, track
- 26– Lou Campos, football

APRIL 1966
- 1– Eric Haake, baseball

- 3– Tod Jebe, fencing
- 3– Miles Phillips, fencing
- 3– Sean Lawlor, football
- 28– Jeff Martin, football
- 29– Scott Bishop, fencing

MAY 1966
- 1– Tim Powers, baseball
- 3– Lowell Hamilton, basketball
- 11– Andy Dillon, gymnastics
- 12– John Rubiner, wrestling
- 14– Mark Kelly, football
- 16– Tim Ryniec, baseball
- 18– Mark McGowan, football
- 22– Sally Grandcolas, swimming
- 23– Neil Wallner, football
- 27– Mike O'Brien, wrestling

JUNE 1966
- 4– Brad Wentz, baseball
- 17– Jon Burman, football
- 19– Erik Mueller, wrestling
- 28– Mike Bellamy, football
- 28– Paula Douglass, volleyball

JULY 1966
- 3– John Bisbikis, cross country
- 3– Steve Gillette, fencing
- 8– Dave Barbour, wrestling
- 13– David Halle, cross country/track
- 16– Ellen MacGregor, swimming
- 19– Jeanne Yoss, volleyball
- 25– Tony Ticknor, gymnastics
- 25– Tico Mkchyan, gymnastics

AUGUST 1966
- 1– Gail Huttenlocher, swimming
- 3– Greg Conradt, football
- 4– Mike Wolters, baseball
- 6– Dee Dee Deeken, basketball
- 7– Charlton Hamer, track
- 8– Stacey Kazarian, tennis
- 14– Ken Malmberg, swimming
- 18– Tim Hensley, fencing
- 27– Chris Michel, football
- 29– Debbie Smith, track

Don Freeman

ILLINI ITEM

CHICAGO STADIUM scoring records fell on January 28, 1966, when Illinois' basketball team defeated Notre Dame, 120-92. The Illini, led by Don Freeman's 33 points, just missed the school record of 121 points set twice a year before against Purdue and Michigan State. Illinois averaged more than 87 points per game that season, the fourth-highest average in its history.

ILLINI LISTS

TOP BIG TEN TITLE WINNERS AMONG ILLINI COACHES

20 titles	Harry Gill, track & field (1904-29 and 1931-33)
18 titles	Leo Johnson, cross country (1938-60) and track & field (1938-65)
17 titles	Maxwell Garret, fencing (1941-72)
12 titles	Gary Wieneke, cross country (1967-present) and track & field (1974-present)
11 titles	George Huff, baseball (1896-1919)
11 titles	Charlie Pond, gymnastics (1949-61 and 1962-73)
8 titles	Art Schankin, fencing (1973-93*)
8 titles	Gary Winckler, women's track and field (1986-95)
7 titles	Bob Zuppke, football (1913-41)
6 titles	Paul Prehn, wrestling (1921-28)
6 titles	Hek Kenney, wrestling (1929-43 and 1946-47)

*Fencing was discontinued as a Big Ten-sponsored sport following the 1985-86 season

Coach Leo Johnson (holding trophy) won 18 Big Ten championships as track and field coach at Illinois.

ILLINI LEGEND:

JIM GRABOWSKI

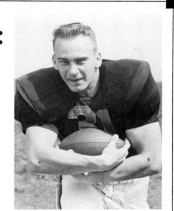

He broke nearly all of Red Grange's rushing records and played in the first two Super Bowls during a six-year career in the National Football League, but Jim Grabowski will be remembered for much more than just his prowess on the athletic field at the University of Illinois. The personable native of Chicago was an all-star in the classroom as well, earning Academic All-America acclaim in 1964 and '65 and the Big Ten Conference Medal of Honor in 1966. Grabowski was inducted into the Academic All-America Hall of Fame in 1993, joining such notables as Princeton's Bill Bradley, Notre Dame's Joe Theismann and Southern Cal's Pat Haden. No. 3 in the Heisman Trophy balloting of 1965, Grabowski finished his brilliant Illini career as the Big Ten's career rushing leader with 2,878 yards. He was the first-round pick of the Green Bay Packers in 1966, retiring after the 1971 season following a series of knee injuries. In January of 1995, Grabowski was selected to become a member of the College Football Hall of Fame. Currently, he is vice-president of Great Lakes Telecommunications Corporation. Grabowski has served as color commentator for the Illini Football Radio Network since the 1970s.

 Illini Lore

Early in 1966, wrecking crews began to remove the University of Illinois' temporary housing units known to their tenants as Illini Village and Stadium Terrace. The 41 one-story buildings, which once served as housing at an Indiana plant during World War II, provided housing for 762 families of married students. War veterans attending school on the G.I. bill, and many others over the next two decades, remember these hastily built structures as brutally hot in the summer and bone-chillingly cold in the winter.

1966-67

I·L·L·I·N·I M·O·M·E·N·T

UI President David Dodds Henry (left) at a football game.

SLUSH FUND SCANDAL ROCKS ILLINOIS:

March 19, 1967: *I have received today and have accepted the resignations of Pete Elliott, head football coach, Harry Combes, head basketball coach, and Howard Braun, assistant basketball coach.* With those 26 words, UI President David Dodds Henry brought an end to one of the darkest sagas in Fighting Illini athletic history. Henry's actions came three months after he had asked the Big Ten Conference to make an investigation of alleged irregularities in assistance to athletes. On December 23, 1966—two days before Christmas—Big Ten Commissioner Bill Reed announced confirmation that illegal funds did exist. "These funds were completely apart from the operation of the University's grants-in-aid program," Reed said. "They were created with the knowledge of the director of athletics (Doug Mills) and of the assistant director of athletics (Mel Brewer), and disbursements were made at the direction of the respective head coaches." Twelve Illini football and basketball athletes were identified by the Big Ten and suspended from any further intercollegiate competition. It would take Illinois 16 years to win its next Big Ten football title and 17 years to claim its next conference basketball championship.

ILLINI BIRTHDAYS

SEPTEMBER 1966
- 1– Lynn McClellan, football
- 1– Steve Hankenson, wrestling
- 8– Kevin Mottlowitz, wrestling
- 11– Tim Simon, track
- 11– Curtis Taylor, basketball
- 13– Mark Long, tennis
- 18– Ken Song, fencing
- 28– Mike Wilkerson, track

OCTOBER 1966
- 1– Juana Fernandez, track
- 3– Darrin Fletcher, baseball
- 8– Barb Scherschligt, tennis
- 14– Glenn Cobb, football
- 16– Brian Menkhausen, football

NOVEMBER 1966
- 5– Peter Freund, football
- 10– Susie Stout, tennis
- 14– Missi Wheeler, volleyball
- 20– Kathy Neil, tennis

- 21– William Townsell, wrestling
- 26– Theresa Gutteridge, swimming
- 29– Joyce Mathews, swimming

DECEMBER 1966
- 1– Chris McKee, gymnastics
- 8– Angie McClellan, basketball
- 11– Greg Boysaw, football
- 28– Jason Backs, baseball
- 28– Scott Mohr, football
- 28– Sandy Scholtens, volleyball
- 31– Mike Givot, swimming

JANUARY 1967
- 1– Steve Glasson, football
- 8– John Powers, cross country
- 9– Carrie Henderson, basketball
- 11– David Zeddies, gymnastics

- 12– Brad Hartmann, football
- 14– John Murray, tennis
- 17– Rodney Jones, basketball
- 22– Petra Laverman, volleyball
- 22– Manuel Velasco, tennis

FEBRUARY 1967
- 10– Richard Bianco, golf
- 14– Steven Williams, football
- 17– Judy Kats, swimming
- 23– Steve Stricker, golf
- 25– Earl Parham, track

MARCH 1967
- 3– Dan Donovan, football
- 13– Chris Schwarz, volleyball
- 14– Carrie Costigan, tennis
- 20– Lee Bridges, track
- 23– Neal Gassmann, cross country
- 27– Sharon Locascio, cross country/track
- 27– Karen Sundahl, swimming
- 28– Matt Pater, baseball

- 29– Mary Eggers, volleyball
- 31– Lisa Balagtas, track

APRIL 1967
- 5– Mike MacDonald, basketball
- 13– Dave Romero, gymnastics
- 14– Eric Ottoson, track
- 19– Chris Stapleton, swimming
- 28– Angela McClatchey, track

MAY 1967
- 3– Greg Kennett, tennis
- 6– Ann-Marie Beavis, diving
- 6– Ted Niezyniecki, baseball
- 10– Joel Tucker, gymnastics
- 23– Richard Seaman, swimming
- 25– Gary Richter, swimming
- 27– Tom Wessberg, swimming

JUNE 1967
- 3– Elizabeth Mackin, swimming

- 4– Renee Carr, track
- 7– Randy Lane, gymnastics
- 7– Joe Socolof, fencing
- 11– Rod Tolbert, track
- 11– Bob Oleson, track
- 13– Justi Miller, golf
- 17– Jeff Kaminski, wrestling
- 19– Dave Silva, football
- 27– Allison Gardiner, swimming

JULY 1967
- 16– Helen Mastoris, cross country/track
- 24– Brian Burchfield, football
- 26– Brian Junghans, football
- 29– Mark Shapland, basketball

AUGUST 1967
- 6– Rich Herr, football
- 9– Kevin Fairfield, golf
- 22– Howard Zavell, gymnastics
- 27– Stephen Jordan, football
- 29– Michael Barksdale, track

Fencing coach Mac Garret won 17 Big Ten titles during his distinguished career at Illinois.

ILLINI ITEM

LONG-TIME FIGHTING ILLINI fencing coach Maxwell Garret was inducted into the Helm's Fencing Hall of Fame on April 1, 1967. Garrett won 17 Big Ten titles and NCAA titles in 1956 and '58, serving as head coach from 1941-72, excluding three years when he was in the Army during World War II. His Illini teams finished in the top 10 of NCAA competition 19 times during his 27 years.

ILLINI LISTS

ILLINI WHO HAVE PLAYED IN THE SUPER BOWL

The first Super Bowl was played in January of 1967 between the Green Bay Packers and the Kansas City Chiefs. Two former Illini, Ray Nitschke and Jim Grabowski, played in that inaugural battle between the American and National Football Leagues. Here's a list of all the Illinois football players who have Super Bowl experience.

Ed Brady, Cincinnati - XXIII
Bill Brown, Minnesota - IV, VIII, IX
Darryl Byrd, L.A. Raiders - XVIII
Tony Eason, New England - XX
Jim Grabowski, Green Bay - I, II
Henry Jones, Buffalo - XXVI, XXVII, XXVIII
Jim Juriga, Denver - XXIV
Adam Lingner, Buffalo - XXV, XXVI, XXVII, XXVIII
Ray Nitschke, Green Bay - I, II
Preston Pearson, Baltimore - III; Pittsburgh - IX; Dallas - X, XII, XIII
Jack Squirek, L.A. Raiders - XVIII
Calvin Thomas, Chicago - XX

Former Illini basketball player Preston Pearson played in five Super Bowls during his NFL career.

ILLINI LEGEND:

JIM DAWSON

Jim Dawson's selection as the Big Ten most valuable basketball player in March of 1967 was a curious one. He wasn't the league's top scorer (25.5 points per game); that distinction belonged to Minnesota's Tom Kondla. He wasn't the conference's best rebounder or shooter; Ohio State's Bill Hosket easily won those titles. And he didn't lead his team to the Big Ten championship, as had Indiana's Butch Joyner. What earned Jim Dawson the MVP title was his ability to perform in the face of adversity, and no one endured more adversity than did the University of Illinois at that time. The "slush fund" scandal had brought about the ineligibilities of a trio of exceptional Illini players—Rich Jones, Steve Kuberski and Ron Dunlap—and stripped away Illinois' opportunity at a national title. Big Ten coaches clearly recognized the fact that, without Dawson, the 6 and 8 Illini might not have won a conference game. Following a one-year stint with the ABA's Indiana Pacers, the six-foot guard from Elmhurst York High School took that same approach in the business world, moving from New York's Wall Street to California, and, in 1992, to a management position with Victoria Investors in Winnetka, Illinois.

Illini Lore

The University of Illinois observed its Centennial celebration, beginning February 28, 1967. UI's Board of Trustees met at the Capitol in Springfield to witness the issuance of an executive proclamation by Governor Otto Kerner. On campus that morning, the Altgeld Hall chimes played a brief anniversary concert, followed by the band's performance of the *National Anthem* and *Illinois Loyalty*. A total of 3,567 UI students received degrees in June of 1967, as compared to 20 in the first senior class of 1872.

1967-68

America's Time Capsule

- **Oct. 2, 1967:** *Thurgood Marshall was sworn in as the United States' first black Supreme Court justice.*
- **Oct. 12, 1967:** *The St. Louis Cardinals won game seven of the World Series, defeating the Boston Red Sox.*
- **Jan. 23, 1968:** *North Korea seized the Navy intelligence ship U.S.S. Pueblo off its coast. Its crew of 83 was released on December 23.*
- **April 4, 1968:** *Dr. Martin Luther King Jr. was assassinated by a sniper at the Lorraine Motel in Memphis, Tennessee, setting off a week of rioting in several urban black ghettos.*
- **June 5, 1968:** *Presidential candidate Robert Kennedy was fatally shot in Los Angeles after delivering a speech to acknowledge his victory in the California primary.*

I·L·L·I·N·I M·O·M·E·N·T

VALEK WINS HOME DEBUT:

It would prove to be one of only four home-field victories he'd capture over the next four years, but new Fighting Illini football coach Jim Valek truly enjoyed his first appearance on the sidelines of Memorial Stadium, September 30, 1967. Valek's troops had lost their debut a week earlier at Florida, but this one belonged to the Illini from start to finish, defeating Pittsburgh, 34-6. Quarterback Bob Naponic directed Illinois to scoring drives of 46, 71 and 60 yards as the Illini beat Pitt for the sixth time in as many meetings. UI's work horse out of the backfield was junior fullback Rich Johnson who gained 116 yards in just 17 attempts. Illinois' defense, bolstered by interceptions from Ron Bess and Ken Kmiec, halted Panther runners to an average of less than two yards per try and allowed only eight of 23 passes to be caught. It would be more than a year later—November 16, 1968—before Illinois would win again at home.

ILLINI BIRTHDAYS

SEPTEMBER 1967
12– John Valente, baseball
16– John Ericks, baseball
20– Chris Siambekos, football
29– Astrid Eichner, tennis
29– Rich Kolasa, track
30– Philip Andrew, swimming

OCTOBER 1967
7– Phil Karnezis, fencing
9– Luke Petraitis, football
15– Peter Gruben, swimming
15– Richard Caparelli, baseball
15– Althea Thomas, track
18– Brian Williams, football
21– Loren Smolensky, tennis
23– Mike Lawrence, football
25– John Wachter, football

NOVEMBER 1967
3– Ervin Small, basketball
8– Ty Hawkins, assistant baseball coach
16– Kate DesEnfants, swimming
16– Josie Todd, basketball
17– Howard Griffith, football

20– Tom Prince, golf
27– Jason Guard, football

DECEMBER 1967
6– Shirley Bodden, track
6– Bannon Hayes, track
8– Jeff George, football
14– Brian Dillman, tennis
14– Lori Gremer, basketball
15– Frank Hartley, football
20– Rich Gianacakos, football
24– Bob Christensen, baseball
27– Robert Allen, swimming
27– Paul Ducato, wrestling
29– Leticia Beverly, track
29– Henry Jones, football

JANUARY 1968
8– Paul Staples, swimming
20– Nick Anderson, basketball
20– Amy Werkowski, track
23– Quintin Parker, football
26– Kerry VanHandel, basketball
27– Greg Dillman, swimming
31– Brian Haas, track

FEBRUARY 1968
2– Don Cuchran, baseball
4– Sandra Harris, basketball
5– Kristin Oostendorp, swimming
13– Wade Rome, wrestling
23– Heath Crawford, golf
23– Hugo Silva, fencing
24– Patrick Donnelly, football
25– Jeff Richards, baseball
26– Chris Green, football

MARCH 1968
2– Jin Kim, fencing
3– Bridgette Boyle, volleyball
6– Kurt Gregus, football
13– Elizabeth Kelleher, golf
19– Elbert Turner, football
26– Donna Russell, cross country/track
28– Doug Amaya, football
29– Dino Pollock, football

APRIL 1968
4– Doris Carie, basketball

4– Jenny Gullickson, swimming
5– Steve Bardo, basketball
11– Maura Corcoran, tennis
12– Audrey Cole, cross country/track
14– Tim Clancy, track
19– Patsy Sullivan, swimming
24– Dave Postmus, football
25– Scott Diamond, gymnastics

MAY 1968
14– Mark Dalesandro, baseball
14– Gary Pearne, tennis
16– Kristen Haynes, basketball
16– Jane Schofield, swimming
17– Jeff Finke, football
24– Errol Shavers, football
25– Kendall Gill, basketball
29– Mike Mershon, baseball

JUNE 1968
3– Jerry Hamner, football
4– Larry Smith, basketball
19– Michele Meriweather, swimming

24– Andy McVey, swimming
25– Melissa Straza, cross country
27– Steve Cyboran, golf
28– Shawn Wax, football
29– Denise Lamborn, gymnastics

JULY 1968
8– Hector Ortiz, tennis
28– Dave Zimner, cross country

AUGUST 1968
1– Jon Gustafsson, football
5– Tony Russo, golf
5– Sue Winkelman, golf
6– Celena Mondie-Milner, track
8– Emmitt Cohick, baseball
10– Moe Gardner, football
14– Kathleen McCarthy, swimming
19– Greg Woodcock, wrestling
21– Shellie Wood, golf
27– Leon Fisher, football

ILLINI LISTS

TATE'S TOP TEN

Loren Tate began his assignment as the Champaign-Urbana *News-Gazette*'s Illini beat writer in 1967. Here's a list of the 10 Illini athletes and coaches whom he considers to be his interview favorites. His list purposely excludes current coaches Lou Henson and Lou Tepper, who, Tate says, "are always friendly, honest, and willing to discuss anything."

- Tab Bennett, football — " ... was as open and friendly as any athlete. He gave us a lot of stories."
- Tim Brewster, football — " ... very open with interviewers ... a terrific recruiter now."
- Randy Crews, basketball and baseball — " ... he was always like talking to a good friend."
- Jim Dawson, basketball — " ... he kept Illinois' head above water during some very trying times."
- Bruce Douglas, basketball — " ... great insight ... like talking to a coach."
- Pete Elliott, football coach — " ...had the unique ability to make everyone feel like he was the most important person."
- Howard Griffith, football — " ... very receptive to anyone he talked to."
- Dana Howard, football — " ... always gave you flamboyant quotes that were fun for the readers."
- Deon Thomas, basketball — " ... evolved from being the most difficult to the easiest guy I ever interviewed."
- Dave Wilson — " ... a terrific interview who seemed to always be in the news."

ILLINI LEGEND:

JOHN WRIGHT

It was game five of his junior season, versus Indiana, that John Wright became the leading pass receiver in University of Illinois football history. From that point on, every time he caught a pass he set a record. During his three years at Illinois from 1965-67, the split end from Wheaton set Big Ten records of 159 catches for 2,284 yards, more than twice the previous UI record totals of Rex Smith (70 catches) and John "Rocky" Ryan (1,041 yards). To put his accomplishments even more into perspective, consider that during his three years at Illinois, Wright caught 28 more passes than all the rest of his teammates combined! Nationally, only four men—topped by all-time leader Howard Twilley from Tulsa (261 catches)—had more career receptions than did Illinois' No. 45. He also lettered twice in track as a hurdler. Academically, Wright grabbed even more honors, including Academic All-America laurels in 1966. Following college, he played for the NFL's Detroit Lions for three seasons, then began a highly successful career in insurance. Wright, whose father Bob and son John Jr. also played for the Illini, now lives near St. Joseph, Illinois.

Illini Lore

Jack Peltason (second from left) was one of three chancellors selected by UI president David Henry (left).

On June 15, 1966, the University of Illinois' Board of Trustees formally approved the establishment of the administrative post designated Chancellor of the Urbana-Champaign campus. Chosen as UIUC's first Chancellor was 43-year-old Jack Peltason, who previously served as Vice Chancellor for Academic Affairs at the University of California at Irvine. Peltason remained at Illinois until August of 1977, when he became President of the American Council on Education.

1968-69

I·L·L·I·N·I   M·O·M·E·N·T

Greg Jackson was a valuable member of Illinois' 19-5 basketball team in 1968-69.

ILLINI CAGERS BATTLE FOR BIG TEN CROWN:

Coach Harv Schmidt's 1968-69 basketball team fought to an impressive 19-5 overall record and a spot in the Top 20 national ranking, but could do no better than finish four games behind champion Purdue in the Big Ten standings. Illinois won its first 10 in a row before losing to Rick Mount's juggernaut at West Lafayette in game two of the conference season. The Illini turned a disappointing 4-4 conference start into a 9-5 final league record by winning five of its last six Big Ten games. UI's balanced attack was paced by senior forward Dave Scholz (19.1 points per game) and sophomore center Greg Jackson (16.4). Guards Mike Price (12.4) and Jodie Harrison (10.6) also were consistent scorers for the Illini. Illinois' 19 victories were the most since the 1962-63 season when that club won the Big Ten title with 20 overall wins.

ILLINI BIRTHDAYS

SEPTEMBER 1968
13— Joe Muti, football
14— Will Parsons, baseball

OCTOBER 1968
7— Ryan Nelligan, baseball
8— Barb Winsett, volleyball
9— Andy Kpedi, basketball
10— Nancy Brookhart, volleyball
13— Mike Craft, baseball
17— Kristen Klein, golf
19— Cynthia Lawrence, track
22— Curt Lovelace, football
25— Cam Pepper, football
26— Derrick Crenshaw, wrestling
27— Marcus Liberty, basketball
31— Jane Leishman, golf

NOVEMBER 1968
3— Brad James, football
9— Phil Kunz, basketball

16— Marty Black, baseball
16— Bob Carstenson, swimming
22— Mel Agee, football
26— Jon Llewellyn, wrestling

DECEMBER 1968
5— Bryan McGrone, football
7— Kim McClelland, basketball
11— Len Sitko, cross country/track
12— Marlon Primous, football
15— Gus Palma, football
17— Erin Roscetti, swimming
20— Michelle Hawkins, cross country/track
23— Bill Henkel, football
24— Rich Hyde, baseball
28— Darrick Brownlow, football
28— Mike Hopkins, football

JANUARY 1969
5— Glenn Schicker, fencing
10— Dominick Minicucci, gymnastics
10— Chris Lubeck, swimming
11— Bob Shank, track
11— Bob Palacio, baseball
24— Laurie Kane, tennis

FEBRUARY 1969
6— Tony Laster, football
15— Steve Nelson, football
17— Greg Eichorn, football
17— Jim Shaffer, football
22— Stephanie Dial, basketball
24— Kregg Ummel, cross country/track

MARCH 1969
5— Tim Simpson, football
7— Tim Thomas, baseball
11— Brian Samuels, football

15— Sadri Guecke, tennis
17— Sean Streeter, football
23— Matt Stern, football
27— Lisa Rakoski, swimming

APRIL 1969
2— Shayla Baine, track
5— Kameno Bell, football
8— Dan O'Brien, wrestling
8— Andy Small, baseball
18— Sarah Sharp, basketball
21— Trevor Beard, golf

MAY 1969
14— Mark Hoppenjans, tennis
22— Kirsten Gleis, volleyball

JUNE 1969
1— Romero Brice, football
1— Julyon Brown, football
2— Cully Welter, track

5— Reese Jones, swimming
7— Kristin Willey, tennis
8— Kevin O'Connor, baseball
9— Emilio Marrero, gymnastics
15— Julie Grumish, golf
16— Brian Kinkaid, track
17— Laura Bush, volleyball

JULY 1969
3— David Pearlstein, gymnastics
13— Joe Wall, football
17— Doug Higgins, football
21— Mary Charpentier, gymnastics

AUGUST 1969
16— Brian Roberts, baseball
22— Cynthia Chambers, tennis
23— Lynn Devers, gymnastics

ILLINI ITEM

AN INDOOR TRACK AND FIELD DUAL MEET against Wisconsin at the University of Illinois' Armory on February 22, 1969 was the site for a record-breaking performance by Illini pole vaulter Ed Halik. Halik cleared the bar at 16' 3/4", becoming the first Illinois vaulter and only the third Big Ten athlete to jump at a height beyond 16 feet.

IF ILLINI ATHLETES WERE KNOWN BY THEIR GIVEN FIRST NAMES

Nelison (Nick) Anderson
Theodore (Tab) Bennett
Casper (Cap) Boso
Burie (Shelly) Clark
George (Potsy) Clark
Talib (Ty) Douthard
Charles (Tony) Eason
Thomas (Dike) Eddleman
Walter (Hoot) Evers
Morris (Moe) Gardner
Harold (Red) Grange
Richard (Itch) Jones
Harold (Hek) Kenney
Duane (Skip) Thoren
Charles (Bubba) Smith
Ellis (Gene) Vance
Thomas (T.J.) Wheeler
Kenneth (Tug) Wilson
Claude (Buddy) Young

Mr. and Mrs. Boso named their baby son Casper, but he became better known as Cap to Illini and Chicago Bears fans.

ILLINI LEGEND:

DAVE SCHOLZ

Today, a humble Dave Scholz tells his friends that "I really didn't have the ability to play major college basketball." So how did the six-eighter from Decatur end up as the University of Illinois' all-time leading scorer? "I was on the receiving end of a lot of good passes," he says. Still, scoring a total of 1,459 points against such superstars as Lew Alcindor and Rudy Tomjanovich takes some coordination. In fact, of the nearly 400 men who've lettered in basketball at Illinois, only Scholz (20.5 points per game), Nick Weatherspoon (20.9), and Don Freeman (20.1) have averaged better than 20 points per contest. No. 40's biggest night came on February 24, 1968, when he drilled home 42 points against Northwestern, a single-game total second only to Dave Downey's 53-point masterpiece vs. Indiana. Following a brief tour of the pros, Scholz returned to the UI to obtain his master's degree in accountancy. In 1980, he began the first of six years in Saudi Arabia with the Arabian American Oil Co., then moved to Nashville, Tennessee, where he still resides.

 Illini Lore

The $21 million Krannert Center for the Performing Arts opened its doors to the University of Illinois community April 19-20, 1969. Donated to the UI by philanthropists Mr. and Mrs. Herman C. Krannert, Krannert Center was conceived with a two-fold purpose. First, it would provide the most up-to-date facilities for the training of UI students in the performing arts and it would also provide a modern cultural center for the community. The facility features three auditoriums: The Great Hall, seating 2,100, was designed for music presentations; the Festival Theatre, with a capacity of 965, was planned for singing performances; and the Playhouse, seating nearly 700, was designed specifically for acting.

1969-70

America's Time Capsule

- **Sept. 22, 1969:** *Willie Mays of the San Francisco Giants hit his 600th career home run, becoming only the second major leaguer other than Babe Ruth to reach that plateau.*
- **Nov. 16, 1969:** *More than 450 Vietnam villagers were slain by a U.S. infantry unit in what would be known as the My Lai massacre.*
- **March 18, 1970:** *The first major postal workers' strike began in the United States.*
- **April 29, 1970:** *U.S. and South Vietnamese troops invaded Cambodia.*
- **May 4, 1970:** *Four Kent State University students were killed by National Guard troops during an antiwar demonstration.*

I·L·L·I·N·I M·O·M·E·N·T

Rick Howat shot the lights out against Indiana, Jan. 6, 1970.

ILLINI SHATTER SHOOTING RECORD:

Coach Harv Schmidt's 1969-70 Fighting Illini basketball squad, known more for its defensive prowess, shot the proverbial lights out against Indiana on January 6, 1970 at the Assembly Hall. Illinois' .679 shooting performance from the field (40 of 59) obliterated its former high mark of .613, set against Iowa in 1967. Individually, the Illini outside shooters were paced by Rick Howat and Mike Price who hit 16 of their 24 long-bomb attempts. Inside, the triumvirate of Randy Crews, Fred Miller and Greg Jackson connected on nearly 71 percent of their shots. Illinois' 94-74 victory over the Hoosiers was the second of the young Big Ten season. Illinois went on to win three more games in a row to improve its record to 12-2. They couldn't keep up their momentum, however, winding up with an overall mark of 15-9.

ILLINI BIRTHDAYS

SEPTEMBER 1969
- 6– Michael Schwartz, fencing
- 6– John Wright Jr., football
- 9– Lisa Dillman, volleyball
- 15– Jacek Gorzowski, fencing
- 16– Chris Inch, track
- 17– Mike Poloskey, football
- 17– Greg Drake, swimming
- 19– Julyon Brown, football
- 21– Lia Biehl, golf
- 21– Kelly O'Brien, track
- 22– Michele Dixon, swimming
- 23– Todd Akers, track

OCTOBER 1969
- 17– Mike Ruth, baseball
- 24– Darren Boyer, football
- 24– Jodi Cathrall, tennis
- 27– David Hill, football
- 28– Jim Pesek, football
- 28– Mark Zitnik, football
- 29– Jason Moler, baseball
- 30– Chris Burke, fencing
- 31– Aaron Mobarek, track

NOVEMBER 1969
- 6– Kaili Salmon, swimming
- 7– Jim DeBeers, track
- 12– Jeff Kinney, football
- 12– Keith Bollman, wrestling
- 17– Andy Kaufmann, basketball
- 18– Steven Mueller, football
- 22– Michelle Donato, cross country/track
- 26– Loretta Withrow, cross country/track

DECEMBER 1969
- 4– Monica Cundiff, basketball
- 9– Scott Maddux, cross country/track
- 12– Mike Allen, golf
- 16– Alfred Pierce, football
- 17– Danielle Harpell, cross country/track
- 18– Charles "Bubba" Smith, baseball
- 20– Pat Wendt, football
- 23– Geoff Woodcock, wrestling

- 24– Linda Gates, tennis
- 28– Steve Mattison, football
- 28– Bill Zopf, gymnastics

JANUARY 1970
- 4– Kelly Taylor, swimming
- 11– Lorna Henderson, volleyball
- 11– John Martin, football
- 13– Brad Lawton, track
- 22– Tracy Shipman, volleyball
- 24– Mark Qualls, football
- 25– Mark Dressen, baseball
- 30– Arlena Roach, basketball

FEBRUARY 1970
- 25– Sharmella Walker, basketball

MARCH 1970
- 18– Davin Harris, basketball
- 22– Michelle Goecke, tennis
- 27– Steve Feagin, football
- 29– Martha Firnhaber, volleyball

APRIL 1970
- 1– Pam Trenda, swimming
- 3– Jason Verduzco, football
- 6– Padra Richter, swimming
- 14– Joyce Smith, volleyball
- 23– Scott Rush, fencing
- 25– Sean Mulligan, baseball
- 26– Art Slowinski, football

MAY 1970
- 14– Larry Sutton, baseball
- 18– Melissa Stone, track

JUNE 1970
- 1– Eileen Sampey, swimming
- 5– Debby Richards, swimming
- 6– Gavin Pearlman, football
- 7– Fred Cox, football
- 9– Matt Bernstein, wrestling
- 16– Matt Korfist, wrestling
- 22– Mark Scheirer, cross country
- 22– Terika Smith, track
- 22– Kevin Abel, fencing

JULY 1970
- 1– Jason West, track
- 6– Brian Pianfetti, fencing
- 20– Andy Homoly, cross country
- 22– Amy Carlisle, cross country/track
- 22– Paul Sullivan, wrestling

AUGUST 1970
- 8– Stephanie Bowers, volleyball
- 9– Kate Riley, basketball
- 12– Laura Simmering, cross country/track
- 17– Heather Oostendorp, swimming
- 17– John Redmond, gymnastics
- 18– Jill Doll, swimming
- 20– Mike Stonitsch, wrestling
- 25– Doug Clarida, basketball
- 27– Cindy Dilger, basketball
- 27– Tanja Nuhsbaum, track

Hall of Famer Lou Boudreau (right), joined by interim athletic director Bob Todd, had his jersey No. 3 retired at Illinois.

*I*LLINI *I*TEM

ON JULY 27, 1970, former Fighting Illini baseball and basketball standout Lou Boudreau was inducted into Cooperstown's Baseball Hall of Fame. Also included in Cooperstown's Class of 1970 with the former Cleveland Indians' star were pitcher Jess Haines and outfielder Earl Combs.

ILLINI LISTS

ILLINI FOOTBALL ACADEMIC ALL-AMERICANS
(first-team selections)

1952	Bob Lenzini, DT
1964-65	Jim Grabowski, FB
1966	John Wright Sr., E
1970	Jim Rucks, DE
1971	Bob Bucklin, DE
1980-81-82	Dan Gregus, DL
1991	Mike Hopkins, DB
1992	John Wright Jr., WR
1994	Brett Larsen, P

Jim Rucks of Illinois was an Academic All-America selection in 1970.

ILLINI LEGEND:

RANDY CREWS

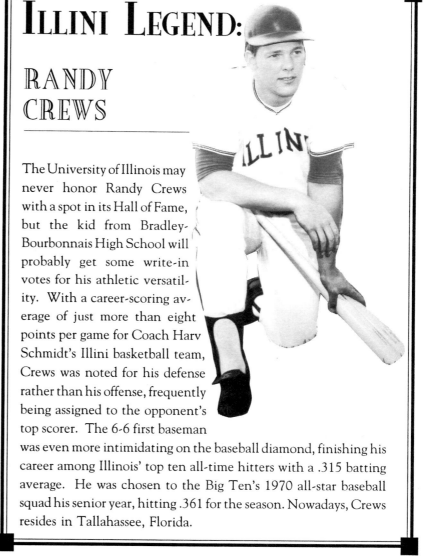

The University of Illinois may never honor Randy Crews with a spot in its Hall of Fame, but the kid from Bradley-Bourbonnais High School will probably get some write-in votes for his athletic versatility. With a career-scoring average of just more than eight points per game for Coach Harv Schmidt's Illini basketball team, Crews was noted for his defense rather than his offense, frequently being assigned to the opponent's top scorer. The 6-6 first baseman was even more intimidating on the baseball diamond, finishing his career among Illinois' top ten all-time hitters with a .315 batting average. He was chosen to the Big Ten's 1970 all-star baseball squad his senior year, hitting .361 for the season. Nowadays, Crews resides in Tallahassee, Florida.

---

*I*llini *L*ore

The month of May 1970, will be remembered by students and faculty as a period of great unrest at American universities. Stoked by President Nixon's announcement that American troops would be sent to Cambodia and ignited by the killing of four Kent State University students on May 4, UI students and thousands of others at campuses across the country called for a nationwide strike. A rally jammed the UI Auditorium on May 5, and action began the moment the gathering ended. The "trashing" of the campus business district and some University buildings soon began. UI Chancellor Jack Peltason denounced the violence and refused to close the university, but only 60 percent of the classes went on as scheduled. From May 5-10, police made 221 arrests, and damage totaled more than $26,000.

1970-71

I·L·L·I·N·I M·O·M·E·N·T

Quarterback Mike Wells (left) and tight end Doug Dieken (right) helped the Illini snap an 11-game Big Ten losing streak.

ILLINI GRIDDERS END LOSING STREAK:
It had been nearly two years since Illinois had won a Big Ten Conference football game, so the odds of coach Jim Valek's squad beating Purdue in PU's Homecoming game (October 31, 1970) would have tested even the bravest gambler. The Boilermakers jumped off to a 14-0 lead at halftime, thanks to a 62-yard touchdown pass from quarterback Gary Danielson to halfback Otis Armstrong. Illinois bounced back to take a 17-14 advantage early in the fourth quarter, but Purdue regained the lead, 21-17, with 4:01 remaining. Illini quarterback Mike Wells then engineered a game-winning, seven-play, 69-yard drive, combining his own passes to Doug Dieken with the brilliant running of Darrell Robinson. The 23-21 Illinois victory brought an end to the school's 11-game Big Ten losing streak. It would be the last win in Valek's Illini coaching career.

ILLINI BIRTHDAYS

SEPTEMBER 1970
1– Karl Johnson, fencing
5– Brad Hopkins, football
7– Aaron Rogers, track
15– Janos Pilenyi, fencing
27– John Frangos, baseball
28– Kraig Koester, football

OCTOBER 1970
3– David Nasser, tennis
4– Ben Bruce, golf
4– Ricardo Cheriel, gymnastics
4– Sonya Waters, basketball
10– Jeff Arneson, football
19– Mike Nichols, wrestling
23– David Cho, fencing

NOVEMBER 1970
3– Mike Cole, football
9– Mekelayaie Brown, track
12– Earl Jenkins, track

13– Aaron Shelby, football
22– Nick Baker, gymnastics

DECEMBER 1970
4– Dave Olson, football
4– Keith Toriani, baseball
8– Jeff Schwarzentraub, football
11– Doug Irwin, baseball
13– Tonja Buford, track
13– Wagner Lester, football
14– Matt Arrandale, baseball
24– Filmel Johnson, football

JANUARY 1971
1– Vuthik Chhay, gymnastics
6– Erik Foggey, football
11– Jill Estey, basketball
18– Greg Engel, football
20– Russ Maloney, swimming
26– Lance Pelton, wrestling

30– Derek Allen, football

FEBRUARY 1971
2– Ken Dilger, football
6– Anne Conway, volleyball
12– Matt Missey, track
22– Kara Corso, gymnastics
24– Mike Eberly, tennis
24– Deon Thomas, basketball
25– Robin Ramirez, fencing

MARCH 1971
1– Tom Michael, basketball
5– Tim Geers, basketball
11– Becky Gaa, gymnastics
13– Brooks Taylor, basketball
19– Todd Smiser, baseball
21– Forry Wells, football/baseball

26– Phil Rathke, football
31– Amanda Backwell, swimming

APRIL 1971
3– Connie Ruholl, basketball
10– Sean Henderson, gymnastics
12– Dave Seifert, baseball
22– Michelle Ciucci, swimming
30– Randy Bierman, football

MAY 1971
9– Mark Krajewski, tennis
10– Frank Niziolek, swimming
11– Clinton Lynch, football
17– Scott Woodcock, golf

JUNE 1971
1– Scott Bezella, fencing

3– Erik Hayes, football
26– Mike Jurack, baseball

JULY 1971
2– Derrick Rucker, football
5– John Sidari, football
10– Kimp Grant, gymnastics
22– Erich Baumann, fencing

AUGUST 1971
3– Dave Dziedzic, wrestling
14– Monica Heckert, swimming
20– Jennifer Tweedy, cross country/track
25– Tyrone Collins, football
29– Todd Leach, football

Tim McCarthy was recognized for his heroics at halftime of the 1981 football game between Illinois and Wisconsin.

ILLINI ITEM

TIM McCARTHY, who used to deliver hard hits as a safety on the Fighting Illini football team, took one for his country on March 30, 1981. The former walk-on from Chicago's Leo High School lettered for Illinois in both 1969 and 1970, but his greatest notoriety came as a Secret Service agent that afternoon in Washington, D.C. McCarthy stepped in front of a bullet aimed at President Ronald Reagan and was wounded in the abdomen. On January 11, 1982, the National Collegiate Athletic Association honored him with its Award of Valor.

ILLINI LISTS

ILLINOIS' FASTEST MILERS

1.	3:56.7	Mike Durkin, 1975
2.	3:58.8	Lee LaBadie, 1971
3.	4:00.4	Rick Gross, 1972
4.	4:00.56i	Len Sitko, 1991
5.	4:00.68i	Tom Stevens, 1982
6.	4:00.8	Jeff Jirele, 1976
7.	4:00.94i	Greg Domantay, 1983
8.	4:01.49i	Jon Schmidt, 1982
9.	4:02.30i	Mike Patton, 1985
10.	4:02.8	Craig Virgin, 1976

i — Indicates mark accomplished indoors

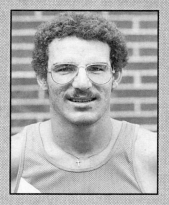

Mike Durkin ran an all-time Illini record 3:56.7 in the mile.

ILLINI LEGEND:

LEE LaBADIE

Though he won only one individual conference title during his three-year career at the University of Illinois, Lee LaBadie's name will always have a prominent place in Big Ten track and field lore. On May 11, 1971 in a dual meet against Southern Illinois, he became the first Big Ten Conference undergraduate to break the four-minute barrier in the mile run. LaBadie ran his first 440 yards in 60 seconds, but his pace slowed to 2:03 after the first half mile. Then he began to pour on the coals, touring the next quarter mile in :57.5. LaBadie ran the final 440 yards in :58.3, finishing in a record time of 3:58.8. He was also a key member of a world-record-tying two-mile relay squad at Illinois, a unit that won the 1972 NCAA indoor title. He served as cross country and track coach at Parkland College from 1976-85, and in 1985 LaBadie became head coach of Bowling Green State's women's cross country and track programs. From 1989-92, he was Ohio State's assistant men's cross country and track coach and helped Buckeye runner Mark Croghan to the NCAA steeplechase title. LaBadie left OSU following the 1992 season, joining his wife in a Westerville, Ohio real estate business, but he continues to coach Croghan in his bid for the 1996 games.

Illini Lore

On February 13, 1971, the Board of Trustees elected 46-year-old Dr. John Corbally as the 13th president of the University of Illinois, replacing the retiring David Henry. Corbally came to the Urbana-Champaign campus from Syracuse University where he served as president and chancellor. He remained at the UI until September 1, 1979.

1971-72

America's Time Capsule

- **Sept. 13, 1971:** *A prison riot at Attica State Correctional Facility in New York ended, an uprising that claimed 43 lives.*
- **Sept. 21, 1971:** *Baseball's Washington Senators announced that the franchise would move to Texas for the beginning of the 1972 season.*
- **Feb. 21, 1972:** *President Nixon began his historic visit to mainland China.*
- **May 26, 1972:** *Soviet secretary Leonid Brezhnev and President Nixon signed a treaty on antiballistic missile systems.*
- **June 17, 1972:** *Police arrested five men involved in a burglary of Democratic Party headquarters, beginning the famed Watergate affair.*

I·L·L·I·N·I M·O·M·E·N·T

BOB BLACKMAN HIRED:
The hiring of Bob Blackman as the Fighting Illini football coach December 23, 1970 was greeted with open arms by the Champaign-Urbana community and University of Illinois fans all around the state. The entire Illini athletic program had been submerged in the dregs of the infamous "slush fund," and Blackman's glowing 16-year record at Dartmouth was hoped to be the antidote that would cure the school's football ills. The Blackman era began slowly. After losing their first six games of 1971, including its first three by shutouts, the Illini bounced back to win their last five in a row. Again in 1972, Blackman's squad began poorly, losing its first seven games, before salvaging three of its last four contests. That mediocre trend continued for the balance of Blackman's six-year career at Illinois, with only 1974's 6-4-1 record breaking the sub-.500 pattern. There were several bright spots, however, during Blackman's reign. Despite going 0-12 against the Big Ten's "Big Two" of Michigan and Ohio State during his Illini career, Blackman's Illini amassed a cumulative record of 24-11-1 against the other seven conference opponents.

ILLINI BIRTHDAYS

SEPTEMBER 1971
18—Arvella Brooks, track
22—Terry Stevens, fencing
27—Gary Voelker, football

OCTOBER 1971
5— Rob Cordes, tennis
11— Samantha Gross, cross country/track
19— Christie Kestly, tennis
19— Jim Klein, football
19— Eric Larkin, fencing

NOVEMBER 1971
3— Drew Daniels, football
14— Mary Beth Williams, tennis
15— Steve Rusk, wrestling
23— Lori Richter, swimming
26— Sabine Ensslin, tennis

DECEMBER 1971
1— Chad Copher, football
9— Kevin Jackson, football
9— Matt White, gymnastics

11— Mary Piotrowski, cross country/track
12— Anthony Jones, track
15— Bernetta Jones, track
18— Gandy Pierre-Louis, track
20— Gene Cross, basketball
26— Adam Studebaker, baseball
30— Scott Pierce, basketball

JANUARY 1972
8— Ken Crawford, baseball
9— Pete Frew, baseball
10— Chris Richardson, football
17— Melvin Roberts, football
24— Kirsten Paulson, swimming
31— LeShawn Hawkins, baseball

FEBRUARY 1972
4— Jeff Hasenstab, football
4— David Eckburg, track

8— Kellie Hebeisen, volleyball
9— Marni Tobin, swimming
14— T.J. Wheeler, basketball
14— Robert Crumpton, football/track
17— Steve Marianetti, wrestling
20— Tsafrir Cohen, fencing
24— Mandy Cunningham, basketball
24— Jaimie Fairbanks, golf
25— Dana Howard, football
26— Scott Turner, football/track
26— Glen Howard, track
27— Jon Kerr, football
29— Pete Gabrione, football

MARCH 1972
6— Mike Suarez, football
7— Amy David, swimming
8— Kristi Meola, tennis
12— Bob Bodrogi, fencing
13— Charly Crawmer, tennis

17— Kristin Henriksen, volleyball
19— Andy Thompson, baseball
27— Ken Gerdes, wrestling

APRIL 1972
13— Rachel Kelleher, cross country/track
14— Jeff Teach, track
29— Dave Cable, golf

MAY 1972
7— John Holecek, football
12— Dan Lundine, baseball
17— Charles Gray, wrestling
17— Wendy Welch, cross country/track
28— Randy Briggs, golf

JUNE 1972
2— Renee Heiken, golf
10— Brian Stewart, wrestling
11— Jeff Thompson, swimming
11— Jason Schumaker, baseball

18— Stacey Pirk, golf

JULY 1972
9— Tony Spaulding, baseball
10— Brian Kobylinski, gymnastics
16— Merrill Mullis, volleyball
21— Amy Jones, volleyball
24— Matt Beary, track
28— Tina Rogers, volleyball

AUGUST 1972
11— Kyle Tate, football
14— Maurice Young, track
16— Tama Tochihara, track
20— Steve Roth, basketball
22— David Sullivan, wrestling
24— Mickey Chaudhuri, tennis
28— Jasper Strong, football
29— Vicki Klingler, basketball
30— Tom Moore, swimming

ILLINI ITEM

RICK GROSS concluded an outstanding career in cross country and track and field in 1972 at the University of Illinois. An All-American and 1971 Big Ten runner-up in cross country, Gross set Illini varsity records in the steeplechase (8:41.8) and in the 10,000-meter run (29:17.4), and nearly broke the magic four-minute barrier in the mile run (4:00.4).

ILLINI LISTS

DIKE EDDLEMAN'S FAVORITE ATHLETES
Illinois' greatest athlete of all-time chooses his favorite Illini.

- Alex Agase, football
- Kenny Battle, basketball
- Dick Butkus, football
- Dave Downey, basketball
- Tony Eason, football
- Jill Estey, basketball
- Darrin Fletcher, baseball
- Jim Grabowski, football
- Abie Grossfeld, gymnastics
- Renee Heiken, golf
- Dana Howard, football
- Lou Kachiroubas, wrestling
- John "Red" Kerr, basketball
- Herb McKenley, track
- Bob Norman, wrestling
- Ken Norman, basketball
- Andy Phillip, basketball
- Bob Richards, track
- Tina Rogers, volleyball
- Steve Stricker, golf
- Nancy Thies, gymnastics
- Deon Thomas, basketball
- Willard Thomson, track
- Buddy Young, football & track

Dike Eddleman, namesake of UI's annual award to its men's and women's Athletes of the Year.

ILLINI LEGEND:
TAB BENNETT

To become a college football All-American, it is almost always a necessity that one's team be ranked among the nation's elite. But that certainly wasn't the case in 1972 for Illinois' standout defensive end Theodore Anthony "Tab" Bennett. The Illini's 3-8 mark didn't draw attention to Bennett's individual talent as Nebraska's nearly perfect record had done for All-America middle guard Rich Glover, but it was difficult to disguise Bennett's outstanding abilities. The native of Miami, Florida lettered once under Coach Jim Valek and twice for Bob Blackman, and earned All-Big Ten honors both his junior and senior seasons. Bennett's 231 career tackles ranked second only to Dick Butkus at the time. An ankle injury prevented him from continuing his career in the NFL, so Bennett turned his sights toward a profession in college athletic administration at his alma mater. A meteoric rise saw him named as Illinois' Sports Information Director in 1974, becoming the Big Ten Conference's first-ever African-American SID. Bennett continued in that role until 1989, when a life-threatening automobile accident forced him to retire. He died March 13, 1994 at the age of 42.

Illini Lore

The $11.2 million Intramural-Physical Education Building opened for use at the University of Illinois during the fall semester of the 1971-72 academic year. UI students paid the major portion of the bill—$9.1 million—through an activity fee of $18 per semester. Highlighting the facility were four large gymnasiums, indoor and outdoor swimming pools, a three-court tennis complex, 23 handball courts and seven squash courts. Estimated usage by students that first year was more than 548,000, with a record 734,000 student usage in 1987-88.

1972-73

America's Time Capsule

- **Nov. 7, 1972:** *The Republican Party enjoyed its greatest landslide victory with the re-election of President Richard Nixon.*
- **Dec. 18, 1972:** *Paris peace negotiations reached an impasse and full-scale bombing of North Vietnam was resumed by American pilots.*
- **Jan. 22, 1973:** *An agreement to end the war in Vietnam was signed in Paris by representatives of the United States and North and South Vietnam.*
- **June 9, 1973:** *Secretariat, called the greatest race horse ever, won the Belmont Stakes and became the ninth Triple Crown winner.*
- **July 16, 1973:** *The existence of the Watergate tapes was revealed.*

I·L·L·I·N·I M·O·M·E·N·T

Lonnie Perrin put on a one-man show vs. Indiana in 1972.

PERRIN PUTS ON A SHOW AS ILLINI DAZZLE INDIANA:
November 11, 1972 marked one of the greatest individual performances in Fighting Illini football history, as Illinois' Lonnie Perrin set a Big Ten total offense record against the Indiana Hoosiers. The sophomore halfback from Washington, D.C. rushed 142 yards in 12 carries, completed two passes to Garvin Roberson for 94 yards, and grabbed three aerials from Mike Wells for an additional 35 yards. Perrin's 14 rushes and passes averaged 16.86 yards per play, erasing a four-year-old mark held by Iowa's Ed Podolak. The most exciting play in Illinois' 37-20 victory over the Hoosiers was Perrin's long, cross-field lateral to George Uremovich who sprinted down the west sideline to complete a 96-yard kickoff return. "I really didn't feel up for the game," said Perrin afterwards in the locker room, "but after my first play (a 16-yard gain) I was ready."

ILLINI BIRTHDAYS

SEPTEMBER 1972
4– Kim Thurmon, track
15– Bo Dailey, track
17– Chris Stelter, football
18– Shelly Clark, basketball
21– Scott Spiezio, baseball
22– Rod Boykin, football
28– Bill True, baseball
28– Jeff Turnbull, gymnastics
29– Doug Dossey, track
30– Tim Dobry, baseball

OCTOBER 1972
17– Theron Harris, football
18– Shane Fisher, football
18– Dave Wohlwend, baseball
30– Matt Sander, baseball
31– Tim McCloud, football

NOVEMBER 1972
2– Mikael Arneborn, fencing

3– Marko Koers, track
4– David Elkin, gymnastics
7– Jamison Hawthorne, tennis
8– Ken Blackman, football
8– Jeremy Sutter, tennis
15– Steve Rusk, wrestling
27– Jeremiah Landry, gymnastics
28– Steve Vasaune, fencing

DECEMBER 1972
2– Sara Marshack, tennis
8– Antwoine Patton, football
11– Rennie Clemons, basketball
11– Lissa Kimmel, tennis
15– Tom Sinak, baseball
16– Donnie Payne, baseball
19– Jay Scott, golf
26– Mike Russell, football

27– Marcus Jarboe, track
27– Jeremiah Landry, gymnastics
28– Carmel Corbett, track

JANUARY 1973
3– Jason Adkins, football
3– Julie Edwards, volleyball
5– John Oestreich, baseball
5– Steve Steinhaus, football
7– Lloyd Richards, football
8– Michael Kamin, track
21– Johnny Johnson, football
26– Ken Su, gymnastics
30– Charles Edwards, football

FEBRUARY 1973
17– Rey Puentes, tennis
21– Tyrone Washington, football

24– Christine Garrett, golf
25– Brett Hart, wrestling

MARCH 1973
1– Marc Davidson, basketball
1– Brett Larsen, football
2– Duane Lyle, football
4– Sean Williams, baseball
7– Mary Michal, cross country
20– Kristen Jones, tennis
20– Duane Dobko, swimming

APRIL 1973
6– Brian Schullian, baseball
8– Will Tuttle, basketball
13– Lou Angelo, track
22– Shawn Herzog, baseball

MAY 1973
18– Carl Myers, track

20– Dan Mazur, track
22– Jackie Hemann, basketball
25– Sue Nucci, volleyball
27– Ty Douthard, football
30– Jarrett Hansen, football

JULY 1973
2– John Curran, football
3– Kris Dupps, basketball
18– Sharon Plattner, swimming
20– Ryan Graff, golf
24– Kevin Hardy, football
31– Scott Benson, wrestling
31– Goncalo Macedo, gymnastics

AUGUST 1973
6– Charlie Kowalski, gymnastics
7– Lolita Platt, basketball
28– Becky Biehl, golf

Alan Acker (left) and Nate Haywood helped the Illini fencing team win the 1973 Big Ten title.

ILLINI ITEM

THE UNIVERSITY OF ILLINOIS' FENCING TEAM became the only Illini unit to win a Big Ten championship March 3, 1973, when Coach Art Schankin's swordsmen captured the conference title at East Lansing, Michigan. Led by epee champion Nate Haywood and sabre titlist Alan Acker, Illinois easily out-distanced second-place Ohio State, 37-25, to win its second consecutive team title.

ILLINI LISTS

GREATEST MEN'S BASKETBALL DEBUTS

Points
1. 30 pts. Jeff Dawson vs. DePauw, 12/2/72
2. 23 pts. Govoner Vaughn vs. Marquette, 12/2/57
3. 21 pts. Deon Thomas vs. American-Puerto Rico, 11/23/90
4. 20 pts. James Griffin vs. Texas-Arlington, 11/24/78
5. 19 pts. Nick Weatherspoon vs. Butler, 12/1/70

Rebounds
1. 13 rebs. Greg Jackson vs. Butler, 12/2/68
2. 12 rebs. Bill Burwell vs. Creighton, 12/1/60
3. 11 rebs. Dave Downey vs. Creighton, 12/1/60
   11 rebs. Don Freeman vs. Butler, 11/30/63
5. 10 rebs. Nick Anderson vs. Baylor, 11/27/87
   10 rebs. Efrem Winters vs. Vanderbilt, 11/26/82

Jeff Dawson scored 30 points in his Illini debut.

ILLINI LEGEND:

NICK WEATHERSPOON

Team-wise, Nick Weatherspoon's college basketball career at the University of Illinois was only moderately successful, but, individually, very few Fighting Illini basketball players were more proficient than "The Spoon." The former Ohio prep player of the year from Canton McKinley High School ruled Coach Harv Schmidt's Assembly Hall court from 1971-73, setting Illini records for points (1,481) and rebounds (806). His career averages of 20.9 points and 11.4 rebounds are still tops at Illinois. Weatherspoon seemed to peak when the Illini played Michigan, averaging nearly 26 points and 14 rebounds in his five career games against the Wolverines. "Spoon" was the 13th pick in the first round of the 1973 NBA draft, going to the Washington Bullets. His eight-year NBA career also included stints with the Seattle Supersonics, the Chicago Bulls and the San Diego Clippers. The 6'7" forward scored 4,086 points and grabbed 2,232 rebounds in 453 career NBA games. Today, Weatherspoon is semi-retired, but continues to direct his own insurance company in Bolingbrook, Illinois.

 Illini Lore

The Levis Faculty Center began operation during the 1972-73 academic year. Made possible by a $1.2 million gift from Mrs. Margaret Levis, a 1914 graduate, the center's primary purpose was to serve as an intellectual gathering place for the faculty and staff of the University of Illinois. The facility replaced the University Club on Oregon Street that UI faculty had previously used.

1973-74

I·L·L·I·N·I M·O·M·E·N·T

Illini basketball coach Harv Schmidt.

THE HARV SCHMIDT ERA ENDS:

Harv Schmidt's University of Illinois basketball coaching career ended in 1973-74 as stormily as it began. The former Illini standout from Kankakee was hired as his alma mater's head coach in 1967, taking over for Harry Combes who resigned in the aftermath of the infamous "Slush Fund." Schmidt's first team, headed by Dave Scholz, Randy Crews and Mike Price, managed only an 11-13 overall record. Illinois' success under Schmidt reached its zenith in 1968-69, streaking to a second-place finish in the Big Ten and a 19-5 season mark. The Illini fans fondly embraced their coach, rising to their feet at his mere appearance through the Assembly Hall tunnel. Harv's third Illini team in 1969-70 jumped off to a terrific 12-2 start, but managed only three more wins in its final 10 games that season. Despite that late-season slump, Illinois basketball fans turned out in record numbers during the '70-71 campaign, setting an NCAA-record attendance average of 16,128 per game. Schmidt's final four Illini teams from 1970-71 to 1973-74 compiled a sub-.500 mark of 44 wins and 50 losses, and he was replaced in 1974 by Gene Bartow.

ILLINI BIRTHDAYS

SEPTEMBER 1973
- 4– Andy Kortkamp, baseball
- 5– Becky Garrett, track
- 7– Eric Henson, track
- 9– Kyle Taylor, track
- 13– Nicole Ward, gymnastics
- 22– Jay Ford, wrestling
- 26– Mikki Johnson, football

OCTOBER 1973
- 10– Jennifer Pottgen, swimming
- 15– Scott Weaver, football
- 31– Dina Slomski, gymnastics

NOVEMBER 1973
- 4– Matt Jackson, baseball
- 13– Martin Jones, football
- 17– Dawn Riley, track
- 27– Kristen Rakoski, swimming

DECEMBER 1973
- 2– Brett Laurvick, baseball
- 3– Richard Keene, basketball
- 20– Chris Gandy, basketball

- 23– Matt McCully, baseball
- 24– Robert Bennett, basketball
- 31– Cindi Hanna, basketball

JANUARY 1974
- 1– Karla Peterson, gymnastics
- 15– Brian McClure, baseball
- 27– Ernest Benion, wrestling
- 27– Chris Koerwitz, football
- 31– Bridget Inman, basketball

FEBRUARY 1974
- 2– Josh Klimek, baseball
- 17– Kady Hackett, swimming
- 20– Chris McPartlin, football
- 24– Simeon Rice, football

MARCH 1974
- 15– Tim Kanke, wrestling
- 18– Seth Brady, wrestling

APRIL 1974
- 2– Adam Gilman, fencing
- 7– Jason Wollard, baseball

- 19– Megan Stettin, volleyball
- 24– Ron Weber, wrestling

MAY 1974
- 8– Tom McRae, fencing
- 14– Jeff Martin, baseball
- 15– Paul Preissner, wrestling
- 19– Ben Beyers, track
- 25– Dennis Stallings, football
- 26– Jason Dulick, football
- 29– Daren McDonough, track

JUNE 1974
- 10– Bill Antonacci, baseball
- 11– Kristie Mueller, swimming
- 14– Paul Marshall, football
- 14– Pharaoh Gay, track
- 15– Chris DeVore, tennis

JULY 1974
- 1– Jamie Lee, wrestling
- 2– Jason Provinse, wrestling
- 29– Eric Siebert, wrestling
- 30– David Manpearl, tennis
- 30– Laura Mindock, track

AUGUST 1974
- 5– Terra Crutchfield-Tyus, track
- 8– Raki Bogan, baseball
- 15– Michau Basson, tennis
- 23– Jessica Lee, volleyball

- 24– Hope Sanders, track
- 27– Natalie Forsthoefel, gymnastics

WOMEN'S MILESTONES

MAY 15, 1974:

The Board of Trustees of the University of Illinois, chaired by Earl Hughes, took action to put intercollegiate athletics for women under the auspices of the Athletic Association. Dr. Karol A. Kahrs became the UI's first assistant director for women's athletics on June 1, 1974.

ILLINI ITEM

ON SEPTEMBER 29, 1973, a red-headed Missionary's son from Africa began his assault on the University of Illinois football record book. Dan Beaver's 37-yard field goal against West Virginia was the first of 38 three-pointers he'd kick during his career from 1973-76. Two weeks later against Purdue, the soccer-style kicker booted a Big Ten-record five field goals. Beaver kicked four placements of 50 yards or more, including a conference-record-tying 57-yarder versus Purdue his junior year. He became Illinois' all-time leading scorer on November 20, 1976, breaking Red Grange's 51-year-old record with a four-year total of 198 points.

ILLINI LISTS

ILLINOIS' LONGEST FIELD GOALS
(in chronological order)

50 yards   by Earl Britton vs. Iowa, 10/23/23
51 yards   by Dan McKissic vs. Purdue, 11/4/67
52 yards   by Lonnie Perrin vs. Penn State, 10/7/62
57 yards   by Dan Beaver vs. Purdue, 10/18/75

OPPONENTS' LONGEST FIELD GOALS
VS. ILLINOIS
(in chronological order)

57 yards   by Pat O'Dea of Wisconsin, 11/11/1899
59 yards   by Tom Skladany of Ohio State, 11/8/75
61 yards   by Ralf Mojsiejenko of Michigan State, 9/11/82

Earl Britton kicked Illinois' first 50-yard field goal in 1923.

ILLINI LEGEND: CHARLTON EHIZUELEN

Twenty years have passed, but Big Ten track and field aficionados can still find Charlton Ehizuelen's name at the top of the conference's all-time lists in the long jump. The "kangaroo" from Benin City, Nigeria dominated the conference competition during his career from 1974-77 at Illinois. Ehizuelen missed the 1974 Big Ten meet due to a bout with malaria and was absent from the 1976 conference championships due to his suspension from the team. However, in the six Big Ten track meets in which he *did* compete, the amazing African captured 11 of a possible 12 conference titles. Ehizuelen also won four NCAA championships, including three long jump titles. After graduation in 1977, Ehizuelen held all-time Big Ten best performances in both the long jump (27-1¼ indoors, 26-10 outdoors) and the triple jump (54-9½ indoors, 55-2¼ outdoors), breaking Jesse Owens' record on one occasion. Though he performed for Coach Gary Wieneke, the 6-0, 160-pound Ehizuelen was actually recruited by Wieneke's predecessor, Bob Wright, who brought him to Champaign-Urbana with the help of Nigerian coach Awoture Eleyae, a UI post-graduate student. Today, Ehizuelen lives with his family in Los Angeles, California.

Illini Lore

A $1.65 million capital fund campaign "to keep Memorial Stadium beautiful for the next 50 years" was announced by the University of Illinois at a meeting of the UI Foundation in October of 1973. Priorities for the campaign were to replace Zuppke Field's natural grass with an artificial turf, to install lighting for night activities at the stadium, and to renovate the locker rooms and training facilities. Directing the "Golden Anniversary Fund Campaign" were chairman William Karnes and honorary chairman Harold "Red" Grange.

1974-75

I·L·L·I·N·I M·O·M·E·N·T

Red Grange returned to Memorial Stadium 50 years after galloping to glory against Michigan.

THE ICE MAN RETURNETH:

Fifty years to the day—October 18, 1974—Harold "Red" Grange returned to Memorial Stadium, the scene of his greatest triumph. A half century earlier, he'd galloped against Michigan, leading Illinois to a 39-14 victory. But on this afternoon, the 71-year-old football legend spoke to Coach Bob Blackman's 1974 Illini squad. "Football is a game that demands teamwork," Grange told the young Illini. "It is natural, I suppose, for the scorer to get all the publicity. But it isn't fair. At Illinois, I was just a cog in a good machine." That evening, the Galloping Ghost was feted by a packed house of nearly 700 fans at the Ramada Inn's Convention Center. George Halas, Grange's coach with the Chicago Bears, told the $20-a-plate crowd that "Red Grange had more impact on the game of football than any single individual in this century." The next day at Memorial Stadium, between halves of the Illinois-Michigan State game, which ended in a 21-21 tie, Grange was presented the UI Board of Trustees' highest award, the Trustee Medallion. Then the Wheaton Iceman addressed his adoring fans. "I've always said that this is the most beautiful stadium in the world and that Illinois fans are the most beautiful people in the world."

ILLINI BIRTHDAYS

SEPTEMBER 1974
14– Lindsey Durlacher, wrestling
20– Tracey Althans, gymnastics
24– Kiwane Garris, basketball

OCTOBER 1974
5– Tonya Williams, track
24– Anita Clinton, basketball
27– Anne Toth, swimming

NOVEMBER 1974
1– Jesse Katzman, gymnastics
12– William "Mo" Morris, football
20– Jon Vaughn, wrestling
20– Greg McGlaun, gymnastics
28– Aimee Smith, basketball

DECEMBER 1974
6– Norbert Aminzia, fencing

JANUARY 1975
13– Oscar Trujillo, gymnastics

28– Jessica Klapper, tennis
31– Jevon Herman, wrestling

FEBRUARY 1975
9– Melissa Neal, volleyball
13– Susanne Land, tennis

APRIL 1975
1– Brett Robisch, basketball
2– Jerry Turek, tennis
7– Jacqueline Rubin, golf
11– Jillian Randell, swimming
16– David James, football
23– Matt Redman, gymnastics
25– Nicole Ciccarelli, gymnastics
30– Kelly Scherr, volleyball

MAY 1975
3– Laura Rydberg, tennis
11– Stacy Redmond, gymnastics
29– Nora Weber, track

JUNE 1975
3– Justin Busche, baseball

JULY 1975
2– Matt Cushing, football
11– Jerry Hester, basketball
28– Brian Hecht, baseball
29– Kevin Koperski, gymnastics
31– Nicole Viernes, gymnastics

AUGUST 1975
12– Tricia Weygand, track
13– Jon Wasik, gymnastics
15– Kelly Hogan, gymnastics
22– Brian Johnson, basketball

Betsy Kimpel

WOMEN'S MILESTONES

JULY 7, 1974:

Betsy Kimpel became the first coach of the Fighting Illini women's fledgling varsity athletic program. She was hired by associate director of athletics Karol Kahrs at a 10-month salary of $2,900 to coach the women's golf team.

I

Charlton Ehizuelen wrapped up an Illini Big Ten track and field title with a 50'-6¼" triple jump.

ILLINI ITEM

THE UNIVERSITY OF ILLINOIS' 12-year drought without a Big Ten championship in any sport other than fencing ended on May 17, 1975, when the Illini track and field squad nipped runner-up Indiana by a point-and-a-half. Senior captain Mike Durkin paved the way with a double victory in the steeplechase and the 880-yard run. The meet was undecided heading into the triple jump finals, but Illini star Charlton Ehizuelen sewed up the team championship with a title-winning 50'-6¼" leap. Up to then—dating all the way back to a football title by the 1963 Illini—11 UI athletic teams, with the exception of the fencing squad, had entered 130 consecutive Big Ten championship competitions without a victory.

ILLINI LISTS

GARY WIENEKE'S ALL-TIME ILLINI TRACK & FIELD DREAM TEAM

Following is a list compiled by long-time Fighting Illini track and field coach Gary Wieneke of his all-time outdoor "Dream Team":

100 DASH:	Anthony Jones and Lester Washington
200 DASH:	Lester Washington and Rod Tolbert
400 DASH:	Tim Simons, Lee Bridges, and Scott Turner
800 RUN:	Ron Phillips, Charlton Hamer, and Marko Koers
1,500 RUN:	Mike Durkin and Len Sitko
3,000 STEEPLECHASE:	Tom Stevens, Mike Patton, and Jon Thanos
5,000 RUN:	Craig Virgin, Kerry Dickson, and Jeff Jacobs
10,000 RUN:	Craig Virgin, David Halle, and Rick Gross
110 HIGH HURDLES:	Jim Hanlon, Elbert Turner, and John Elliott
400 INTERMEDIATE HURDLES:	Wayne Angel, Ben Beyers, and Mark Koster
HIGH JUMP:	Gail Olsen
LONG JUMP:	Charlton Ehizuelen and Bannon Hayes
TRIPLE JUMP:	Charlton Ehizuelen and Bannon Hayes
SHOT PUT:	Mike Lehmann and Jeff Teach
DISCUS:	Jeff Lehmann and Kyle Jenner
JAVELIN:	Brad Lawton and John Kalmar
POLE VAULT:	Doug Laz and Dean Starkey
DECATHLON:	Bill Leigh and Matt Beary

ILLINI LEGEND:

KAROL KAHRS

When the United States Congress passed Title IX regulations in 1972, mandating equal opportunity for women, the face of intercollegiate athletics began to change at the University of Illinois. On June 1, 1974—just nine days after UI's Board of Trustees approved the Athletic Association's recommendation to include women's athletics—Dr. Karol Kahrs was hired by athletic director Cecil Coleman to oversee Illinois' seven-sport women's program. Kahrs' initial budget of $82,500 in 1974-75 grew slowly, but, in 1995-96, approached nearly $1.5 million. Women's athletics were incorporated into the Big Ten Conference during the 1981-82 season, and, since that time, Illini teams have won 12 league titles in three different sports. In 1988, Kahrs served as director of internal affairs for the AA, helping with its merger into the University in 1989 as the Division of Intercollegiate Athletics. In 1992, her contributions to intercollegiate athletes were recognized by the National Association of College Women Athletic Administrators when she was named NACWAA Administrator of the Year for District V.

Illini Lore

The operating budget for Director of Athletics Cecil Coleman and the Athletic Association in 1974-75 was $2.47 million, a 91 percent increase from the budget total of $1.29 million just 10 years earlier. The expenses rose 241 percent to $8.43 million from 1974-75 to 1984-85, and another 95 percent to $16.4 million from 1984-85 to 1994-95.

1975-76

- **Sept. 18, 1975:** A 19-month FBI search ended when Patricia Hearst was captured in San Francisco.
- **Oct. 1, 1975:** Heavyweight boxing champion Muhammad Ali defeated Joe Frazier in the "Thrilla in Manilla".
- **Feb. 13, 1976:** Dorothy Hamill won a gold medal in figure skating at the Winter Olympics in Innsbruck, Austria.
- **July 4, 1976:** The bicentennial of United States independence was celebrated.
- **July 20, 1976:** Viking I, launched 11 months earlier, landed on Mars.
- **Sept. 5, 1975:** President Gerald Ford escaped the first of two assassination attempts in a little more than two weeks. Lynette "Squeaky" Fromme was apprehended.

I·L·L·I·N·I M·O·M·E·N·T

Nate Williams' jump shot with 17 seconds left helped Illinois beat 14th-ranked Michigan.

ILLINI CAGERS UPSET MICHIGAN:

Fourteenth-ranked Michigan came to Champaign-Urbana with a nearly perfect 6-1 Big Ten record. Coach Johnny Orr's line-up included future NBA stars Phil Hubbard and Rickey Green, plus former Chicago prep star John Robinson. "I've never seen a line-up with the speed and quickness that Michigan has," said first-year Illini coach Lou Henson, who countered with blue-collar seniors like Nate Williams, Mike Washington and Otho Tucker. Despite a sub-par shooting performance, Michigan controlled play for the first 39 minutes, and led 75-72 following a Wayman Britt jumper with 55 seconds left. Illinois' Williams was fouled 17 seconds later when his 15-foot, turnaround jumper cut the Michigan lead to 75-74. And when he missed the free-throw attempt, 6-9 sophomore Rich Adams soared high to tip in the ball for what would ultimately be the winning goal. Orr's talented Wolverines had a flurry of attempts in the closing seconds, but a tip-in by Robinson came a split-second after the final buzzer. Michigan bounced back from that defeat to become an NCAA finalist, while Henson's Illini were limited to four victories in their last 10 games.

ILLINI BIRTHDAYS

SEPTEMBER 1975
5– Debbie Schwartz, swimming
9– Brian Atkinson, golf
25– Nicole Vasey, basketball

OCTOBER 1975
6– Natalie Adsuar, tennis
8– Trevor Starghill, football
8– Cody Salter, baseball
31– Ann Henderson, basketball

NOVEMBER 1975
9– Sean Bennett, baseball
14– Matt Gindler, golf
22– Kari Karubas, gymnastics

DECEMBER 1975
3– Currie Robertson, basketball
11– Robert Holcombe, football
11– Brady Blain, tennis
17– Kirsten Heck, swimming
26– Jerry Gee, basketball
27– Ashley Weber, golf

JANUARY 1976
25– Jennifer Sands, swimming

FEBRUARY 1976
6– Danny Rhodes, baseball
6– Dusty Rhodes, baseball
8– Amanda Weber, swimming
17– Heidi Coulter, volleyball

MARCH 1976
2– Lindy Mercer, swimming
20– Marchoe Dill, basketball

APRIL 1976
3– Krista Reinking, basketball
11– Karen Karmazin, golf
21– Kristin Montero, gymnastics
22– Sarah Fransene, swimming

MAY 1976
11– Corbin Archer, tennis
19– Jason Kimball, gymnastics

29– Kelli Farrar, gymnastics
30– Kevin Turner, basketball

JUNE 1976
5– Drew Parker, tennis
12– Dan Collins, wrestling

14– Kelly Bond, basketball
19– Bryant Notree, basketball
20– Christy Brown, swimming
26– Bret Scheuplein, football
30– Trisha Henry, swimming

AUGUST 1976
4– Lindsey Ward, swimming
8– Jennie Cook, volleyball
12– Jason Pero, wrestling

WOMEN'S MILESTONES

Coach Allison Milburn directed the Illini women's gymnastics team to the school's first-ever unofficial Big Ten title.

DECEMBER 4-5, 1975:

The University of Illinois women's gymnastics team, coached by Allison Milburn, won the first unofficial Big Ten women's championship in any sport. The Fighting Illini edged runner-up Michigan State, 102.55 to 97.10. Illinois' Nancy Thies not only won the all-around title, but also each of the other four events.

*I*LLINI *I*TEM

BECKY BEACH was one of the University of Illinois' premier female athletes during the infancy of women's intercollegiate athletics. Besides winning golf medalist honors at the 1976 Big Ten Championships, she also starred on the basketball court from 1976-78, finishing as the Illini's all-time leader in points, assists and rebounds. Nowadays, the daughter of former Illini basketball star Ted Beach is the golf professional at Lincolnshire Fields Country Club in Champaign.

ILLINI LISTS

LOU HENSON'S ALL-OPPONENT TEAM
(since 1975-76)

Starting Five:
G—Magic Johnson, Michigan State
G—Isiah Thomas, Indiana
C—Mychal Thompson, Minnesota
F—Glen Rice, Michigan
F—Glenn Robinson, Purdue

Bench:
Juwan Howard, Michigan
Jimmy Jackson, Ohio State
Ronnie Lester, Iowa
Shawn Respert, Michigan State
Jalen Rose, Michigan
Steve Smith, Michigan State
Chris Webber, Michigan

MSU's Magic Johnson

ILLINI LEGEND:

LOU HENSON

It took University of Illinois athletic director Cecil Coleman just three days to name a basketball coaching successor for Gene Bartow, and his April 5, 1975 announcement of Lou Henson stunned the media gathered that day at UI's Varsity Room. Among the names bandied about by the press were those of Bartow's assistants, Tony Yates and Leroy Hunt, plus Virginia Tech's Don Devoe and Kansas State's Jack Hartman, but never once mentioned was the 43-year-old head coach from New Mexico State. "Illinois is one of the top five or six basketball jobs in the United States," said Henson, "and I want to be here to see that develop." In 1975-76, Henson's first season as the Illini mentor, Illinois won its first five games en route to posting a 14-13 record. His first big year in Champaign-Urbana was 1978-79 when the Illini started out 15-0, including a two-point thriller over Magic Johnson and Michigan State. Henson's Illini made it to the semifinals of the NIT in 1979-80, while the '80-81 club qualified for the NCAA tournament for the first time in 18 years. Among Henson's other major accomplishments since coming to Illinois include an NCAA Final Four appearance in 1989, 11 seasons of 20 victories or more, and Big Ten Coach of the Year honors in 1993. Nobody calls him "Lou Who" anymore.

🐎 Illini Lore 🐎

The Medical Sciences building made its debut at the University of Illinois campus during a dedication ceremony, October 15, 1975. The ultra-modern, $10 million facility became the newest structure in the Life Sciences complex, joining Morrill and Burrill Halls. The School of Basic Medical Sciences, while located at the Urbana-Champaign campus, actually is a part of the College of Medicine at the Medical Center in Chicago.

1976-77

America's Time Capsule

- **Sept. 12, 1976:** *Jimmy Connors joined Chris Evert as U.S. Open tennis champion.*
- **Nov. 2, 1976:** *Jimmy Carter defeated incumbent Gerald Ford in the presidential election.*
- **Dec. 14, 1976:** *ABC-TV aired Barbara Walters' first special, featuring interviews with Jimmy Carter and Barbra Streisand.*
- **Jan. 17, 1977:** *A 10-year halt on capital punishment ended in the U.S. when Gary Gilmore was executed by a Utah firing squad.*
- **July 28, 1977:** *The trans-Alaska pipeline went into full operation.*
- **Aug. 10, 1977:** *New York City police arrested David Berkowitz as the Son of Sam killer.*

Doug Laz cleared 16'-6" at the 1977 NCAA Track and Field Championships in Champaign.

I·L·L·I·N·I M·O·M·E·N·T

ILLINI HOST 1977 NCAA TRACK MEET:

For five days in the spring of 1977, the University of Illinois' Memorial Stadium became the mecca for track and field fans. The 56th annual NCAA championship drew a talented field of competitors, including lightning-fast sprinters such as Harvey Glance of Auburn, Johnny Jones of Texas and Herman Frazier of Arizona State. Illinois native Gregory Foster, who wore the blue and gold uniform of UCLA, was the meet's most celebrated hurdler. Africans Samson Kimombwa and Henry Rono paced the distance runners, while five-foot-five-inch high jumper Franklin Jacobs of Farleigh Dickinson and pole vaulter Earl Bell of Arkansas State were premier performers in the field events. The Illini contingent was led by distance star Craig Virgin, who placed second in the 10,000-meter run and fourth in the 5,000; pole vaulter Doug Laz, who finished fourth with a respectable effort of 16'-6"; and Charlton Ehizuelen, who placed second in the long jump and third in the triple jump. Arizona State beat runner-up Texas-El Paso, 64-50, for the team title on June 4, before a crowd of between 15,000-20,000 at Memorial Stadium. Illinois meet officials so impressed their guests and NCAA officials that the meet was granted again to the UI in 1979.

ILLINI BIRTHDAYS

SEPTEMBER 1976
- 7– Aaron Nieckula, baseball
- 13– Matt Heldman, basketball
- 14– Lori Caraker, swimming
- 30– Sarah Hackler, swimming

OCTOBER 1976
- 31– Erin Borske, volleyball

NOVEMBER 1976
- 8– Kate Ryan, swimming
- 18– Ashley Berggren, basketball
- 26– Katie Hansmann, swimming

DECEMBER 1976
- 2– Cherie Sticha, swimming
- 9– Amy Hrischuk, volleyball

JANUARY 1977
- 12– Renee Gamboa, swimming

Coach Ann Pollock's Illini swimming team won the 1977 IAIAW state title.

WOMEN'S MILESTONES

FEBRUARY 25-26, 1977:

Coach Ann Pollock's Illini women's swimming team won the IAIAW state title, defeating Southern Illinois, 655 to 577. Mary Paterson led the way by winning individual titles in the 50-yard freestyle, the 50- and 100-yard butterfly and the 100-yard individual medley, as well as anchoring the 200- and 400-yard freestyle relay championships. Becky McSwine captured the 100- and 200-yard backstroke titles.

ILLINI ITEM

PERHAPS THE GREATEST FEMALE GYMNAST in University of Illinois history grew up in Urbana. Nancy Thies (Marshall), who made the United States Olympic team as a 14-year-old ninth grader, competed for the Fighting Illini gymnastics squad in 1976 and '77. She won the Big Ten's all-around title both years, as well as individual championships on the vault, the uneven parallel bars, the balance beam and the floor exercise. Thies also served as the UI's Homecoming Queen in 1978.

ILLINI LISTS

ILLINI BIG TEN CROSS COUNTRY CHAMPIONS

1928	David Abbott
1945	Victor Twomey
1962	Allen Carius
1963	Allen Carius
1973	Craig Virgin
1974	Craig Virgin
1975	Craig Virgin
1976	Craig Virgin

Allen Carius captured individual honors at the 1962 and '63 Big Ten Cross Country Championships.

ILLINI LEGEND:

CRAIG VIRGIN

It's shocking to learn that Craig Virgin, the University of Illinois' greatest distance runner ever, nearly never made it past age five. Following surgery for a bladder ailment, the young farm boy's condition worsened, affecting his kidneys. Doctors weren't optimistic, but, slowly, Virgin got stronger. As a scrawny high school freshman, his fame as a distance runner began to grow, luring Illini cross country coach Gary Wieneke to Virgin's hometown of Lebanon, Illinois. Virgin ultimately ended up at the UI, enjoying a four-year career that included every honor imaginable. He became the Big Ten's first four-time cross country champion from 1973-76, and captured the NCAA title in that sport his junior year. On the track, he became America's premier distance runner, setting the United States collegiate record for the 10,000-meter run in 1976 (27:59.4). Following his graduation from UI's College of Communications in 1977, Virgin continued to run. He was a member of the U.S. Olympic Team in 1976, 1980 and 1984, and competed for the U.S. International Cross Country Team from 1978-88, twice winning the world title. Virgin launched an unsuccessful campaign for the Illinois State Senate in 1992, and currently serves as president of Front Runner Inc., a sports marketing company.

 Illini Lore

James R. Thompson, a former student at the University of Illinois' Chicago Undergraduate Division at Navy Pier, became the first UI alumnus to win election as the state's governor, November 2, 1976. One other alumnus, Samuel Shapiro '29, advanced from lieutenant governor to the governorship when Gov. Otto Kerner resigned to become a federal judge in 1968.

1977-78

I·L·L·I·N·I M·O·M·E·N·T

Coach Gary Moeller (kneeling) and his prize recruits, Rich Weiss (left) and Wayne Strader.

MOELLER REPLACES BLACKMAN:

Just 13 days after Bob Blackman received word that his six-year reign as Illinois' head football coach had ended, the University of Illinois secured one of its arch enemies' brightest young assistants. On December 2, 1976, 35-year-old Michigan defensive coordinator Gary Moeller became Illinois' third coach in seven seasons. Illini athletic director Cecil Coleman interviewed eight men for the position, including Chuck Studley, Don James and Jim Young, but settled on Bo Schembechler's top assistant. "I want to have a winning program and see the players benefit from it," said Moeller at his introductory press conference. "We will throw the ball, if I feel we can do it successfully, but very few passing teams are consistent winners." Moeller's christening as a head coach came September 10, 1977, against Michigan and his former mentor. The Illini took a 3-0 lead that afternoon, but ended up losing, 37-9. Unfortunately, Moeller's luck at Illinois never changed as his teams struggled to consecutive records of 3-8, 1-8-2 and 2-8-1. On November 20, 1979, he was fired by athletic director Neale Stoner.

WOMEN'S MILESTONES

MAY 2, 1978:

Lisa and Lynette Robinson of Annawan, Illinois became the first women athletes in University of Illinois history to sign full scholarships. Four years later, they ended their careers as Illinois' top two career basketball scorers of all-time.

Lynette (#43) and Lisa (#34) Robinson

LINEBACKER JOHN SULLIVAN was Most Valuable Player of the 1977 and '78 Fighting Illini football team. He finished his career as Illinois' all-time leading tackler, breaking Dick Butkus' 14-year-old record. It should be pointed out, however, that Sullivan needed 36 games to break a mark that Butkus had established in just 26. Sullivan's record of 501 total stops was broken in 1994 by Dana Howard.

Illini Lists

TOP MEMORIAL STADIUM RUSHING PERFORMANCES

266 yards	Kent Kitzmann, Minnesota, 11/12/77
263 yards	Howard Griffith, Illinois, vs. Northwestern, 11/24/90
239 yards	Jim Grabowski, Illinois, vs. Wisconsin, 11/14/64
231 yards	Leroy Keyes, Purdue, 11/4/67
212 yards	Red Grange, Illinois, vs. Michigan, 10/18/24
208 yards	Howard Griffith, Illinois, vs. Southern Illinois, 9/22/90
205 yards	J.C. Caroline, Illinois, vs. Minnesota, 10/17/53
187 yards	Darrell Robinson, Illinois, vs. Ohio State, 10/24/70
186 yards	Jim Grabowski, Illinois, vs. Indiana, 10/16/65
186 yards	Keith Jones, Illinois, vs. Utah, 9/17/88

Minnesota's Kent Kitzmann rushed an NCAA-record 57 carries and a Memorial Stadium-record 266 yards against the Illini in 1977.

Illini Legend:

LEE EILBRACHT

From 1952 to 1978, 14 different men served as manager of the Chicago Cubs. During that same 27-year span, the University of Illinois had one baseball coach: Lee Eilbracht. Appointed acting head coach in 1952 following the death of Wally Roettger, Eilbracht's position was made permanent at the end of the season. "The Swami", as he was affectionately called by his players, recorded more coaching victories than any of his five Illini predecessors. His career record of 519-397-6 included Big Ten championships in 1952, '53, '62 and '63. Eilbracht coached two athletes to All-America honors, 12 to first-team All-Big Ten laurels, and 34 others to All-Star mention. Catcher Tom Haller and pitcher Ken Holtzman, who went on to major league fame, were two of his most famous pupils. Eilbracht earned three varsity letters at Illinois, and was named the Illini's Most Valuable Player in 1946 and '47. He hit .484 during the 1946 Big Ten season, the fourth-best average in conference history, and had a career average of .330. After his retirement following the 1978 season, Eilbracht served as the executive director of the American Association of College Baseball Coaches. Eilbracht and his wife, Euline, reside in Champaign.

Illini Lore

On his 48th birthday, September 9, 1977, William P. Gerberding was introduced as the new chancellor for the University of Illinois at Urbana-Champaign. He came from UCLA where he served for 16 years, first as a faculty member and then as executive vice chancellor. Gerberding left the UI in 1979 to become president at the University of Washington.

1978-79

- **Sept. 15, 1978:** *Muhammad Ali regained the heavyweight boxing title with a 15-round decision over Leon Spinks.*
- **Nov. 18, 1978:** *More than 900 people, including 211 children, were found dead in Guyana. Jim Jones, leader of a religious sect, led the group in a mass suicide by poison.*
- **March 26, 1979:** *Magic Johnson and Michigan State defeated Larry Bird and Indiana State in the NCAA basketball championship game at Salt Lake City.*
- **March 28, 1979:** *Three Mile Island, near Harrisburg, Pennsylvania, was the site of a nuclear near-disaster.*
- **May 25, 1979:** *An American Airlines DC-10 jet crashed shortly after takeoff in Chicago, killing all 272 passengers on board and three other people on the ground.*

I·L·L·I·N·I M·O·M·E·N·T

Eddie Johnson's jump shot nestles through the twine with just four seconds left to send Michigan State home with a 57-55 loss.

ILLINI VICTORY PROVES TO BE BETTER THAN MAGIC:

A record Assembly Hall crowd of 16,209 was on hand January 11, 1979 to watch their third-ranked Fighting Illini (14-0) against No. 1 Michigan State (9-1). The Johnson boys—MSU's Earvin and Illinois' Eddie—were their respective teams' stars, but despite his opponent's famous nickname, it was Eddie who was "magic" on this particular night. The Spartans vaulted off to a 24-13 lead after the first 10 minutes of play, but the Illini sizzled in the last 10 minutes, outscoring their guests, 19-4. The second half was like a see-saw, as the lead changed hands eight times. A Mike Brkovich jumper with 2:27 left pulled State even at 55-55, and Illini coach Lou Henson called a time out with just :37 left on the clock to set up his team's final shot. UI's Steve Lanter penetrated the lane, forcing MSU's Greg Kelser to abandon Eddie Johnson. Lanter then dished the ball out to the right baseline where No. 33 was in position for an uncontested 18-foot jumper. With six seconds left, Johnson set himself, flicked his wrist, and sent the ball arcing toward the hoop. Nothing but net! The 57-55 victory improved the Illini record to 15-0, but, unfortunately, that perfection would last only for another 36 hours.

WOMEN'S MILESTONES

FEBRUARY 23-24, 1979:

Illinois' women's gymnastics team stunned everyone by defeating perennial powerhouse Southern Illinois at the state championship meet, 130.95 to 130.70. It was the first defeat SIU had suffered at home in 11 years. Mary Charpentier led the way for the Illini, finishing first in the vault (8.80), second on the beam (8.55) and fourth in all-around competition (33.25).

Mary Charpentier's nearly flawless performance helped Illinois beat Southern Illinois for the state championship.

CECIL COLEMAN'S seven-year tenure as athletic director at the University of Illinois came to an end April 27, 1979 when the Athletic Association's board of directors voted to dismiss him. Hired in 1972 to improve the school's image with the NCAA and to balance a budget which had a $1 million deficit, Coleman achieved both of those objectives. He was often criticized for his hard-nosed approach, but he probably never received credit for a series of other accomplishments, including the hiring of basketball coach Lou Henson and the establishment of UI's women's athletic program. He died February 27, 1988.

ILLINI LISTS

ILLINOIS' GREATEST MEN'S BASKETBALL GAMES

During the 1994-95 season, a veteran panel of Fighting Illini sportswriters and broadcasters chose the greatest Illinois basketball games of all time. Here are games that made their Top Ten.

1. **March 26, 1989**   Illinois 89, Syracuse 86 "Flying Illini" qualify for the Final Four
2. **January 11, 1979**   Illinois 57, Michigan State 55 Eddie Johnson's jumper beats the eventual national champs
3. **December 4, 1964**   Illinois 110, UCLA 83 UI snaps defending national champion's 30-game winning streak
4. **March 4, 1989**   Illinois 70, Indiana 67 Nick Anderson hits a "miracle" three-pointer at Bloomington
5. **February 4, 1993**   Illinois 78, Iowa 77 Andy Kaufmann's last-second jumper beats No. 9 Hawkeyes
6. **January 22, 1989**   Illinois 103, Georgia Tech 92 17-0 Illini voted No. 1 next day
7. **March 24, 1989**   Illinois 83, Louisville 69 Illinois defeats Denny Crum's Cardinals for berth in NCAA's final eight
8. **January 14, 1963**   Illinois 78, Northwestern 76 Bob Starnes' 50-foot heave at the buzzer beats the Wildcats
9. **December 19, 1942** Illinois 57, Great Lakes 53 Voted by "Whiz Kids" as their most memorable game
10. **February 16, 1963**   Indiana 103, Illinois 100 Dave Downey scores Big Ten-record 53 points for Illini

ILLINI LEGEND:

MARK SMITH

Even though he was voted Most Valuable Player of the 1978-79 Fighting Illini basketball squad, Mark Smith could have easily developed a Rodney Dangerfield complex. Classmate Eddie Johnson got the bulk of the publicity during their four years together at Illinois from 1978-81, but Smith's accomplishments were nothing short of sensational. It's true that Eddie wound up as UI's all-time leading scorer with 1,692 points, but there was Mark with just 39 fewer points. Johnson was the Illini's career rebounding leader, but Mark averaged just one rebound less per game. Though Johnson was considered the better shooter, it was Smith who posted better percentages from both the field (.525 to .454) and at the free-throw line (.781 to .671). And when it came to passing the ball, the former Peoria Richwoods star had nearly twice as many career assists (350 to 209). During Smith's four years at Illinois, the Illini won nearly 62 percent of their games. After a brief career in international basketball, he now resides in his hometown.

Illini Lore

On May 4, 1979, John E. Cribbet was named interim chancellor at the Urbana-Champaign campus of the University of Illinois, replacing William Gerberding who had left to become president at the University of Washington. Seven months later, December 12, 1979, the dean of UI's College of Law was chosen from a field of 114 candidates to become the full-time chancellor.

1979-80

I·L·L·I·N·I M·O·M·E·N·T

STONER BEGINS INITIAL SEASON AS ATHLETIC DIRECTOR:

Californian Neale Stoner became athletic director of the University of Illinois, September 27, 1979, boldly proclaiming that "The '80s belong to the Illini." Stoner had extraordinary success as A.D. at Cal State-Fullerton, but rebuilding Illinois into an athletic power would be the most challenging task of his career. After less than three months on the job, he replaced Gary Moeller as head football coach with another Californian, Mike White. White's successful passing attack helped raise Illinois' average football attendance from 45,000 per game in 1979 to more than 76,000 in 1984. Grant-in-aid support rose from around $400,000 a year in the 1970s to between $2 million and $3 million in the mid-1980s. Other accomplishments during the Stoner era included a capital campaign that produced new offices for the football staff and new facilities for baseball and outdoor track and field. The beginning of the end for Stoner came during the summer of 1988 when media questioned his use of Athletic Association funds and his miscalculation of AA income and expenses, which resulted in a $1.45 million shortfall during the 1987-88 fiscal year. On July 12, 1988, Stoner submitted his resignation as UI's athletic director "so that accusations will no longer interfere with the effective operation of the Athletic Association."

Illini legend Ray Eliot (left) congratulates Neale Stoner on his appointment as Illinois' athletic director.

WOMEN'S MILESTONES

MARCH 7, 1980:

Long jumper Becky Kaiser became the University of Illinois' first female athlete to win All-America honors. The sophomore from Charleston, Illinois went 20'-5½" to place second at the Association of Intercollegiate Athletics for Women indoor track and field championship, held in Columbia, Missouri.

Illinois' 1979-80 senior class included (kneeling, left to right) Levi Cobb and Neil Bresnahan, and (standing, left to right) Kevin Westervelt, Reno Gray and Rob Judson.

ILLINI ITEM

ILLINOIS' MEN'S BASKETBALL TEAM reached the 20-victory plateau and qualified for post-season play for the first time in 17 years during the 1979-80 season. Coach Lou Henson's squad, led by junior forward Eddie Johnson, won 10 of its first 12 games and finished the regular-season portion of its schedule at 18-12. The Illini beat Loyola, Illinois State and Murray State in their first three games of the National Invitation Tournament, qualifying for a Final Four trip to New York City. Minnesota beat Illinois in the semifinals, 65-63, but Henson's Illini ended their season on an up note by defeating UNLV in the consolation game.

ILLINI LISTS

ILLINI MEN'S BASKETBALL SINGLE-GAME SCORING LEADERS

1.	53 points	Dave Downey at Indiana, 2/16/63
2.	46 points	Andy Kaufmann vs. Wisconsin-Milwaukee, 12/3/90
3.	42 points	Dave Scholz vs. Northwestern, 2/24/68
4.	40 points	Andy Kaufmann vs. Eastern Illinois, 12/1/90
	40 points	Andy Phillip at Chicago, 3/1/43
6.	39 points	Rich Adams vs. Arizona, 11/28/77
	39 points	Deon Thomas vs. Illinois-Chicago, 12/30/91
8.	38 points	John Kerr at Ohio State, 1/16/54
	38 points	Eddie Johnson vs. Long Beach State, 12/8/79
	38 points	Dave Scholz at Northwestern, 2/10/68

Rich Adams poured in 39 points vs. Arizona in 1977.

ILLINI LEGEND:

EDDIE JOHNSON

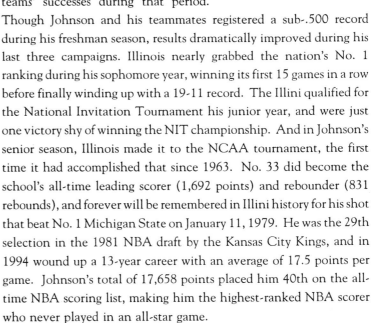

Much has been written about Eddie Johnson's record-breaking career at the University of Illinois from 1978-81, but much more could be written about his teams' successes during that period.

Though Johnson and his teammates registered a sub-.500 record during his freshman season, results dramatically improved during his last three campaigns. Illinois nearly grabbed the nation's No. 1 ranking during his sophomore year, winning its first 15 games in a row before finally winding up with a 19-11 record. The Illini qualified for the National Invitation Tournament his junior year, and were just one victory shy of winning the NIT championship. And in Johnson's senior season, Illinois made it to the NCAA tournament, the first time it had accomplished that since 1963. No. 33 did become the school's all-time leading scorer (1,692 points) and rebounder (831 rebounds), and forever will be remembered in Illini history for his shot that beat No. 1 Michigan State on January 11, 1979. He was the 29th selection in the 1981 NBA draft by the Kansas City Kings, and in 1994 wound up a 13-year career with an average of 17.5 points per game. Johnson's total of 17,658 points placed him 40th on the all-time NBA scoring list, making him the highest-ranked NBA scorer who never played in an all-star game.

Illini Lore

Forty-four-year-old Stanley O. Ikenberry began what was to become a 16-year term as the president of the University of Illinois, September 1, 1979. The University's 14th chief executive officer came from Pennsylvania State University where he had served for eight years as senior vice president. Ikenberry replaced Dr. John Corbally, who a year earlier, announced his resignation and a desire to return to teaching.

1980-81

I·L·L·I·N·I M·O·M·E·N·T

WILSON SETS NCAA PASSING MARK:

One Chicago sportswriter called it "the most incredible passing performance in collegiate history." That phrase, as well as any, accurately summed up the effort put forth by Illinois' senior quarterback Dave Wilson at Ohio State on November 8, 1980. In setting and tying 44 different Illini, Big Ten and NCAA records, Wilson completed 43 of 69 passes to 10 different receivers for an amazing 621 yards and six touchdowns, against a Buckeye team that had ranked first in the league in pass defense. Following Wilson's sixth TD pass with 11 seconds left that made the final score Ohio State 49, Illinois 42, Buckeye fans rose from their seats to give the Illini signal-caller a standing ovation. One loyal OSU fan even handed Wilson his Scarlet and Gray hat as a souvenir. "What makes it such a tremendous accomplishment," said Illini coach Mike White afterwards, "was that it came against a quick, aggressive Ohio State defense. Maybe Dave just plain wore them out." Completely overshadowed by Wilson's statistical extravaganza was Buckeye quarterback Art Schlichter, who completed all but four of his 21 pass attempts for 284 yards.

WOMEN'S MILESTONES

JANUARY 12-14, 1981:

The 76th annual NCAA convention at Miami, Florida featured the landmark decision to include women's athletic programs within the NCAA governing structure, sounding a death knell for the Association for Intercollegiate Athletics for Women. A prolonged debate on the constitutional amendment finally resulted in approval by nearly 70 percent of the record 551 delegates. Twenty-nine NCAA-sponsored championships for women were first conducted during the 1981-82 academic year.

Kevin McMurchie's second-place finish on the still rings helped Illinois win its first Big Ten gymnastics title in 21 years.

ILLINI ITEM

ILLINOIS' MEN'S GYMNASTICS TEAM won its first Big Ten Conference title in 21 years March 14, 1981 at Columbus, Ohio, outscoring five-time defending champion Minnesota by just one-tenth of a point, 539.50 to 539.40. Coach Yoshi Hayasaki's Illini built up a six-point lead during the first day's optional competition, behind the performances of Kevin McMurchie, Gilberto Albuquerque and Gilmarcio Sanches, who were respectively second in the still rings, vault and floor exercise. Kari Samsten was third in all-around and parallel bar competition, and Steve Lechner was third on the horizontal bar.

ILLINI LISTS

WOMEN'S BASKETBALL SINGLE-SEASON SCORING LEADERS

1. 658 points Lisa Robinson, 1980-81
   (31 games, 21.2 avg.)
2. 627 points Jonelle Polk, 1986-87
   (29 games, 21.6 avg.)
3. 624 points Jonelle Polk, 1985-86
   (30 games, 20.8 avg.)
4. 588 points Kendra Gantt, 1982-83
   (28 games, 21.0 avg.)
5. 505 points Lisa Robinson, 1981-82
   (30 games, 16.8 avg.)
6. 504 points Lynnette Robinson, 1980-81
   (31 games, 16.3 avg.)
7. 502 points Jonelle Polk, 1984-85
   (28 games, 17.9 avg.)
8. 495 points Dee Dee Deeken, 1988-89
   (29 games, 17.1 avg.)
9. 490 points Lisa Robinson, 1979-80
   (27 games, 18.1 avg.)
10. 485 points Sarah Sharp, 1990-91
    (27 games, 18.0 avg.)

Lisa Robinson (34) scored 658 points during a record-setting 1980-81 performance.

ILLINI LEGEND:

MIKE WHITE

On December 14, 1979, 43-year-old Mike White began his tempestuous career as head football coach at the University of Illinois. The San Francisco 49ers' assistant inherited a program that sorely needed an injection of adrenaline, and for the next seven years White provided plenty of excitement. Compared to the "vanilla" offensive system of his predecessor, Gary Moeller, White's style was strictly "neapolitan." In White's first season alone, 1980, Illinois had an 11-game passing yardage total of 3,227, compared to Moeller's 33-game total of 3,300 aerial yards. His best team was the 1983 Big Ten championship club, which registered 10 victories, including a record 9-0 mark against conference foes. For that performance, White was recognized as college football's Coach of the Year. His Illini appeared in the Liberty Bowl (1982), the Rose Bowl (1984), and the Peach Bowl (1985), but never won a postseason game. Attendance at Illini football games averaged nearly 69,000 during White's reign from 1980-88. However, despite all of the successes, Mike White's career was also marred by controversy with the NCAA. And on January 18, 1988, he tendered his resignation to Athletic Director Neale Stoner. "While I was unaware of the (NCAA) violations (that were taking place)," White said in his resignation statement, "I take full responsibility for the allegations in my capacity as the University of Illinois' head football coach." Today, White is head coach of the Los Angeles Raiders.

 Illini Lore

The Alma Mater sculpture made only its second journey in 52 years, August 11, 1980, when the campus landmark was removed from its base for a 10-day respite of restoration at the Physical Plant Services Building. Its first trip came in 1962 when the Alma Mater was transferred from a grove of evergreens south of the Auditorium to its present site north of Altgeld Hall. Nature's elements had rusted the iron bolts that secured the sections, so art professor Robert Youngman and his team of workers replaced what they could reach with stainless steel bolts and sprayed the remainder of the bronze sculpture with rust inhibitor. Physical Plant workers returned the refurbished Alma Mater by crane to her granite base on August 21, 1980.

1981-82

I·L·L·I·N·I M·O·M·E·N·T

Illinois' Diane Eickholt puts up a shot against Ohio State in UI's Big Ten home debut.

WOMEN'S ATHLETICS BEGIN IN BIG TEN:
Until May 15, 1974, women's athletics were under the auspices of the Department of Physical Education at the UI. At that time, the budget for the women's program amounted to $14,110. Nearly 26 months after the Equal Rights Amendment was passed by the U.S. Senate, the UI Board of Trustees placed intercollegiate athletics for women under the auspices of the Athletic Association. Seventeen days later, on June 1, Dr. Karol Kahrs was hired by the AA as the first assistant director for women's athletics. Immediately, the recruitment of part-time coaches began. There were no scholarships in the 1974-75 season, but steps were taken the following year to upgrade to tuition and fees. Finally, in May of 1978, the first full-scholarship athletes began to be signed. On August 1, 1981, after much discussion, the UI women's athletic program officially became part of the Big Ten Conference, and competition began in 1981-82. In March of 1982, the women's basketball team finished second in the conference standings and qualified for the first NCAA women's basketball championship. Through 14 seasons of Big Ten competition, Fighting Illini women's teams have won or shared 13 conference titles.

WOMEN'S MILESTONES

MARCH 31, 1982:

In a letter directed to Chancellor John Cribbet, the Office for Civil Rights of the U.S. Department of Education declared that the University of Illinois' intercollegiate athletic program complied with Title IX requirements for equal opportunities for women athletes. Cribbet praised the efforts of athletic director Neale Stoner and assistant director Karol Kahrs. "Illinois has been a leader in the Big Ten and nationally in promoting women's athletics," Cribbet said. "I am especially pleased that their hard work and commitment to excellence in women's athletics have been confirmed by the Department of Education."

ILLINI ITEM

FIGHTING ILLINI FIRST BASEMAN Tim Richardson amassed terrific statistics during his junior baseball season in 1982. Playing a record 72 games, he batted .400, becoming the first Illinois player since Ruck Steger in 1952 to crack that magic average. Additionally, Richardson stroked school-records for hits (104), triples (11) and total bases (163). At the end of the season, Big Ten coaches accorded him first-team all-conference honors.

ILLINI LISTS

MOST SUCCESSFUL ILLINI WOMEN'S SPORTS

Beginning with the 1981-82 season, Fighting Illini women's athletic teams were charted for their finish in the Big Ten standings or championship meet. If a team placed first in its particular sport's standings, it received the most possible points (first of 10 teams received 10 points). However, if a team finished last in its sport's standings, it received the fewest possible points (10th of 10 teams received one point). Here are the results of each sport's cumulative points from 1981-82 thru 1994-95.

1.	107.5 points	Outdoor Track and Field
2.	106.9 points	Volleyball*
3.	99.5 points	Indoor Track and Field
4.	81.6 points	Golf
5.	68.8 points	Gymnastics
6.	65.0 points	Tennis
7.	64.2 points	Cross Country
8.	59.2 points	Basketball
9.	38.1 points	Swimming

*Because volleyball was not involved in Big Ten competition in 1981-82, an average point total for the remaining 13 years was awarded for that season.

ILLINI LEGEND:

TONY EASON

The name Charles Carroll Eason IV sounds more as if it belongs to a Bostonian socialite than to a quarterback from Walnut Grove, California. However, the guy his Illini teammates called "Tony" was very much a quarterback, in fact, one of the greatest signal-callers in University of Illinois football history. Eason was recruited in 1980 by Coach Mike White along with another junior college QB, Dave Wilson. Wilson beat out Eason for the starting job that first season, but "Champaign Tony" was a smash hit in 1981, breaking nine Big Ten records by passing for 3,360 yards and 20 touchdowns. His senior season in 1982 was even more brilliant, accounting for 3,671 yards and earning first-team All-Big Ten honors for a second consecutive year as the Illini qualified for the Liberty Bowl. Named the Fighting Illini Player of the Decade for the 1980s, Eason enjoyed a successful career in the National Football League, quarterbacking the New England Patriots to a berth against the Chicago Bears in Super Bowl XX. He stayed with the Patriots for seven seasons (1983-89), ranking as that franchise's third-leading passer of all-time with 10,732 yards and 60 TD passes. Eason retired from the NFL following the 1990 season with the New York Jets. Eason has started a business called "Athletic Enhancements," training athletes to be more proficient. He is single and lives in San Marcos, California.

Illini Lore

The Big Ten Conference began one-year sanctions against the University of Illinois' intercollegiate football program, August 6, 1981. The original penalties, imposed in May, were partially a result of Illini quarterback Dave Wilson's legal struggle against the conference. The Big Ten faculty representatives voted to prohibit the Illini from playing in a post-season Bowl game in 1981 and denied the University a share of the conference receipts from televised football games. On September 3, Governor James Thompson signed into law a bill that created a special lottery that helped offset an estimated $500,000 loss in football TV revenue. The lottery, originally sponsored by State Senator Stanley Weaver of Urbana and State Representative Virgil Wikoff of Champaign, eventually netted UI's Athletic Association $850,000.

1982-83

America's Time Capsule

- **Sept. 29, 1982:** *Seven persons in the Chicago area died from cyanide placed in Tylenol capsules.*
- **Oct. 20, 1982:** *The St. Louis Cardinals won the seventh and deciding game of the World Series, defeating the Milwaukee Brewers.*
- **Dec. 2, 1982:** *Barney Clark was the first successful recipient of an artificial heart transplant. He died on March 23, 1983.*
- **March 2, 1983:** *More than 125 million viewers watched the final television episode of M*A*S*H.*
- **April 12, 1983:** *Democratic congressman Harold Washington became the first African-American mayor of Chicago.*

I·L·L·I·N·I M·O·M·E·N·T

Illinois' Mike White and Alabama's Paul "Bear" Bryant.

ILLINI GRIDDERS BATTLE THE BEAR:

The 1982 Fighting Illini football season will be remembered for many reasons. The year began with a highly successsful "Tailgreat" promotion and a big win over Northwestern in Memorial Stadium's first-ever night game. It was the season Tony Eason established an all-time record for passing proficiency. And it was the year that Illinois went "Bowling" for the first time in 19 years. The Fighting Illini met Alabama at the Liberty Bowl December 29th in Memphis, a game that would turn out to be the final one for the Crimson Tide's legendary Paul "Bear" Bryant. Bryant, who won more games than any coach in college football, announced his retirement two weeks before, making the otherwise second-rate Bowl game one of the season's top attractions. The night was clear, and the 34-degree weather favored Alabama's wishbone attack. Illinois trailed the Tide by a score of 7-6 at the half, as Alabama defenders repeatedly pummeled Eason with a ferocious pass rush. On three occasions, crushing Alabama tackles forced Eason from the game. "My eyes were bobbing up and down," the Illini quarterback said afterwards. "I couldn't even find the ground." Despite a record 423 yards passing by Eason, Illinois dropped a 21-15 decision, giving the Bear his 323rd and final collegiate victory.

WOMEN'S MILESTONES

SEPTEMBER 26, 1983:

Fighting Illini golfer Mary Ellen Murphy became the first UI female athlete to earn an NCAA Post-Graduate Scholarship. A two-time national qualifier and 1983 honoree as winner of the Big Ten Conference Medal of Honor, Murphy used the $2,000 scholarship prize to earn a degree in physical therapy at Northwestern University's Medical Center.

ILLINI ITEM

DISTANCE RUNNER Marianne Dickerson was the University of Illinois' Female Athlete of the Year for 1982-83. She set numerous records in cross country and track and field, and twice won All-America honors. During her Fighting Illini career, Dickerson recorded eight of the top 10 cross country marks, and set UI varsity records in the two- and three-mile runs and 5,000- and 10,000-meter runs. She also was an excellent student, graduating with a 4.5 grade-point average (on a 5.0 scale) in engineering.

ILLINI LISTS

ILLINI FEMALE ATHLETES OF THE YEAR

1982-83	Marianne Dickerson, track/cross country
1983-84	Karen Brems, gymnastics
1984-85	Kelly McNee, track/cross country
1985-86	Jonelle Polk, basketball
1986-87	Mary Eggers, volleyball
1987-88	Mary Eggers, volleyball
1988-89	Mary Eggers, volleyball
1989-90	Laura Bush, volleyball
1990-91	Renee Heiken, golf
1991-92	Renee Heiken, golf and Tonja Buford, track
1992-93	Tonja Buford, track
1993-94	Tina Rogers, volleyball
1994-95	Tonya Williams, track

Tonya Williams, 1994-95 Female Athlete of the Year.

ILLINI LEGEND:

DEREK HARPER

If Lou Henson is ever asked to select his all-time Fighting Illini defensive team, chances are that Derek Harper will be among his starting five. The 6-4 guard from West Palm Beach, Florida consistently shut down the Big Ten's premier perimeter scorers during his career from 1981-83. Harper led the conference in steals his sophomore and junior seasons, averaging more than two per game against such conference luminaries as Michigan State's Sam Vincent, Minnesota's Darryl Mitchell and Michigan's Mike McGee. Though he wasn't known as a shooter, Harper set a Big Ten record by making 19 consecutive field goal attempts during his final campaign in 1983. His best single effort was a 29-point outing against Michigan that season. During his three years at Illinois, the Illini averaged 20 victories per season and qualified twice for the NCAA tournament. Harper left Illinois following the 1982-83 season and was a first-round pick by the Dallas Mavericks in the 1983 NBA draft. He played in Dallas for nearly 11 seasons, winding up as the Mavericks' No. 3 all-time scorer (11,844 points), No. 1 all-time assist man (4,790) and No. 1 in career steals (1,459). He was traded to the New York Knicks late in the 1993-94 season and starred in the NBA finals against the eventual champion Houston Rockets. In regular-season NBA games from 1984-95, Harper scored 13,229 points.

Illini Lore

Following two years of intense debate and examination, the Circle and Medical Center campuses at Chicago began a unified effort during the 1982-83 academic year. University of Illinois President Stanley Ikenberry, in his recommendation to the Board of Trustees for acceptance of the consolidation, said the merger would give the new UI-Chicago "the ability to compete in the Chicago-area academic arena and contribute to the strengthening of the University as a whole."

1983-84

I·L·L·I·N·I M·O·M·E·N·T

Illinois fans packed the Rose Bowl for the 1984 game versus UCLA.

ILLINI FOOTBALL TEAM WINS BIG TEN:

Between 1896 and 1982, 50 of the first 87 Big Ten championship teams wound up unbeaten and untied. In 1983, Coach Mike White's Fighting Illini football team defied the odds by becoming the first Big Ten club to ever post victories over all nine of its conference foes. Game by game, momentum stayed in Illinois' corner. First, unbeaten Michigan State bit the dust (20-10), then fourth-ranked Iowa (33-0) and rugged Wisconsin (27-15). Sixth-ranked Ohio State battled the Illini tooth-and-nail at Memorial Stadium, before finally succumbing, 17-13. Illinois improved its conference mark to 5-0 with a 35-21 win at Purdue, setting up its showdown against unbeaten Michigan before a record crowd at Champaign. The bone-crushing Illini defense was at its best that day, holding the eighth-ranked Wolverines without a touchdown en route to a 16-6 victory. Now, all that separated Illinois from the Rose Bowl were a trio of conference doormats: Minnesota, Indiana and Northwestern. Despite a lackluster effort at the Metrodome, the Illini disposed of the Golden Gophers, 50-23, to improve their conference record to 7-0. On November 12, more than 73,000 fans were on hand at Memorial Stadium to see their Illini clinch their first Rose Bowl berth in 20 years with a convincing 49-21 triumph over Indiana. About 30,000 Illini faithful showed up at Northwestern's Dyche Stadium for the regular-season finale, and White's troops toyed with the Wildcats, 56-24, to post their Big Ten-record ninth victory. Before Illinois' Rose Bowl battle against Pac-10 champion UCLA, the team collected a bushel-full of accolades. Six Illini players earned first-team all-conference honors, including defensive tackle Don Thorp, who was named the Big Ten's Most Valuable Player. White was honored by nearly everyone as their Coach of the Year. On January 2, 1984, a lovely 84-degree day greeted the teams to Pasadena. Unfortunately, the weather was the high point of the day for Illinois. UCLA built up a 28-3 lead and wound up with a 45-9 victory over the fourth-ranked Illini, the most lopsided Rose Bowl score since 1960. An otherwise sweet season had been ruined by one very sour performance.

WOMEN'S MILESTONES

In 1983-84, University of Illinois women's gymnast Karen Brems became the first Fighting Illini athlete to be named as the school's Athlete of the Year and the Big Ten Conference Medal of Honor award winner in the same season. She's now a computer engineer in California and a world-class bicycle racer.

Bruce Douglas

ILLINI ITEM

ILLINOIS CLAIMED A SHARE of the Big Ten basketball title in 1983-84 by winning 15 of 18 conference games, including its last four in a row. Highlighting the regular season was a four-overtime victory at the Assembly Hall January 28 over Michigan, 75-66. Guard Bruce Douglas, a consensus first-team All-Big Ten selection, played all 60 minutes. The Illini won their first two games in NCAA tournament play, beating Villanova and Maryland, to advance to a quarterfinal showdown against powerful Kentucky at Lexington. The Wildcats had beaten Illinois in a Christmas Eve game at the Assembly Hall, 56-54, and the rematch was equally close, with the Illini finally losing by a score of 54-51. Illinois wound up the year with a 26-5 record, but were 0-2 against Kentucky.

ILLINI LISTS

ILLINOIS' TOP QUARTERBACKS

Using a formula that includes six different important variables, a rating system developed by *Sports Illustrated* magazine helps to identify the 10 greatest Fighting Illini quarterbacks since 1951. Among the elements included in the formula are: 1) yards per pass attempt; 2) yards per rush; 3) average yards per play; 4) pass completion percentage; 5) net touchdowns minus interceptions; and 6) winning percentage as a starter. Every player was ranked in each category, and each category was totaled. Here, including the 1994 season, are the results:

Player	Avg. Ranking
1. Jack Trudeau (1981-85)	2.8
2. Tony Eason (1981-82)	3.3
3. Tom O'Connell (1951-52)	4.4
4. Johnny Johnson (1993-94)	4.7
5. Jason Verduzco (1989-92)	5.3
6. Jeff George (1988-89)	5.5
7. Fred Custardo (1963-65)	6.5
8. Dave Wilson (1980)	6.8
9. Kurt Steger (1975-77)	7.2
10. Mike Wells (1970-72)	8.4

Tommy O'Connell, who lettered for the Illini from 1951-52, rates as Illinois' third-best quarterback ever.

ILLINI LEGEND:

DON THORP

As a youngster, Don Thorp attended Chicago Bears games with his father, idolizing their star linebacker, Dick Butkus. So, in 1983—exactly 20 years after Butkus was named the Big Ten's Most Valuable football player—the University of Illinois' defensive tackle from Buffalo Grove appropriately matched his hero's accomplishment, capturing the *Chicago Tribune's* Silver Football Award. Thorp easily outdistanced Iowa quarterback Chuck Long for the honor, garnering nine of the 14 first-place votes and placing second on two other ballots. Ever the big-play specialist, he registered 17 tackles-for-losses his senior year, bringing his career total to a school-record 37. Thorp, a member of Coach Mike White's first recruiting class at Illinois, was the stalwart for a defensive unit that was primarily reponsible for his team's perfect 9-0 Big Ten record. He was rewarded with first-team All-America laurels and, more importantly to him, Most Valuable Player honors from his teammates. Nowadays, Don Thorp is vice president and food broker for Greenfield Thorp Company in Chicago.

Illini Lore

William Warfield, University of Illinois professor of voice since 1973, was awarded a Grammy Award by the National Academy of Recording Arts and Sciences in April of 1984 for his narration of Abraham Lincoln in Aaron Copland's album, "A Lincoln Portrait." Warfield, a bass baritone, became nationally recognized for his role as Porgy in George Gershwin's "Porgy and Bess," and for his rendition of "Ol' Man River" in the 1951 movie "Showboat."

1984-85

I·L·L·I·N·I M·O·M·E·N·T

Efrem Winters scored a team-high 12 points in Illinois' victory over Indiana.

ILLINI BID BOBBY "GOOD KNIGHT":

Illinois took advantage of a freshman-dominated Indiana lineup January 27, 1985, and administered a 52-41 spanking to Coach Bobby Knight's young Hoosiers. The perfection-driven coach from Bloomington brought only 12 players with him on the bus to Champaign, leaving veterans Winston Morgan and Mike Giomi at home because he was so disgusted with their performance in a two-point loss at Ohio State a few nights before. Knight even left All-American Steve Alford on the bench all afternoon, underlining his slightly bizarre statement to his team. Fortunately, for the Illini, Knight's psychological ploy back-fired. So dominating was the Illini defensive effort that night at the Assembly Hall that Indiana managed only five baskets and two free throws in the first half. The final box score showed Efrem Winters and George Montgomery pacing Illinois with 12 and 10 points, respectively, while Anthony Welch grabbed 10 rebounds. Aside from 7-2 Uwe Blab, the six Hoosiers in the game were freshmen. Afterwards, Illini guard Doug Altenberger summed up the afternoon. "The game was just weird," he said. Was Illini coach Lou Henson disappointed he didn't get a chance to coach against Indiana's best? "It would suit me fine if they didn't play when we go over to Bloomington," he said. As it turned out, the Illini won again February 21 at IU, 66-50, propelling them to a second-place finish in the Big Ten in 1985.

WOMEN'S MILESTONES

OCTOBER 27, 1984:

The Fighting Illini women's cross country team placed second at the Big Ten Championship meet, its highest finish of all time. Illinois, directed by interim head coach Patty Bradley, was runner-up to defending champion Wisconsin, 27 to 79. Junior Kelly McNee earned All-Big Ten honors by placing sixth, individually. Three other Illini runners—Ruth Sterneman, Margaret Vogel and Colleen Hackett—all finished among the meet's top 17. McNee went on to represent Illinois at the NCAA championship, where she finished 21st of 150 runners and earned All-America honors.

Kelly McNee earned All-Big Ten honors, leading Illinois' cross country team to a second-place conference finish.

Ty Wolf paced the Illini cross country team to Illinois' only Big Ten team title in 1984-85.

ILLINI ITEM

FIGHTING ILLINI MEN'S TEAMS completed one of their finest overall seasons in school history during the 1984-85 campaign. Illinois outscored Michigan in total points, 87.5 to 84.5, based on a 10-9-8 points system for a 1st-2nd-3rd finish in the Big Ten's 12 championships. The Illini cross country squad was the only team to win a title, but four other sports—football, indoor track, fencing and basketball—placed second. Four Illinois teams placed among the NCAA's top 30 finishers—cross country, 14th; men's basketball, round of 16; fencing, 17th; and indoor track, 27th. The Illini men's gymnastics team was ranked among the nation's top 20, the baseball team won the Big Ten's West Division title, and the tennis team finished seventh in the National Invitation post-season tournament.

ILLINI LISTS

MIKE HEBERT'S VOLLEYBALL MVPs

1983	Laurie Watters
1984	Denise Fracaro
1985	Denise Fracaro
1986	Mary Eggers
1987	Mary Eggers and Nancy Brookhart
1988	Mary Eggers
1989	Laura Bush
1990	Petra Laverman
1991	Lorna Henderson
1992	Kirsten Gleis
1993	Tina Rogers
1994	Julie Edwards

Denise Fracaro was Most Valuable Player of the Illini volleyball team in 1984 and '85.

ILLINI LEGEND:

MIKE HEBERT

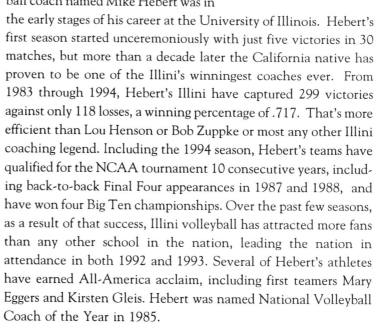

While the Fighting Illini football and men's basketball teams were winning Big Ten championships during the 1983-84 season, a 39-year-old volleyball coach named Mike Hebert was in the early stages of his career at the University of Illinois. Hebert's first season started unceremoniously with just five victories in 30 matches, but more than a decade later the California native has proven to be one of the Illini's winningest coaches ever. From 1983 through 1994, Hebert's Illini have captured 299 victories against only 118 losses, a winning percentage of .717. That's more efficient than Lou Henson or Bob Zuppke or most any other Illini coaching legend. Including the 1994 season, Hebert's teams have qualified for the NCAA tournament 10 consecutive years, including back-to-back Final Four appearances in 1987 and 1988, and have won four Big Ten championships. Over the past few seasons, as a result of that success, Illini volleyball has attracted more fans than any other school in the nation, leading the nation in attendance in both 1992 and 1993. Several of Hebert's athletes have earned All-America acclaim, including first teamers Mary Eggers and Kirsten Gleis. Hebert was named National Volleyball Coach of the Year in 1985.

Illini Lore

At a news conference May 22, 1984, President Stanley Ikenberry introduced Thomas Everhart, 52, as the chancellor-elect of the Urbana-Champaign campus. Everhart, dean of Cornell University's College of Engineering, succeeded John Cribbet who returned to teaching in UI's College of Law. "This is truly a great university," Everhart told the media, "one of the four or five premier public campuses in the country. The opportunity to assume the chancellorship of this distinguished campus is compelling." Everhart served the UI until 1988.

Outfitting the Illini Fan

1985-86

I·L·L·I·N·I M·O·M·E·N·T

Chris White (#8) is lifted to the shoulders of his Illini teammates after kicking a game-winning field goal vs. Ohio State.

CHRIS WHITE'S FIELD GOAL BEATS OHIO STATE:

Illinois coach Mike White called it "the sweetest victory I can remember in my coaching career," and none of the 76,343 Illini fans assembled at Memorial Stadium that windy October 5th afternoon could argue with his statement. Shouldering the burden of both a disappointing 1-2 start and a 28-14 second-half deficit to their guests from Ohio State, the Fighting Illini football team rose from the dead to register a stunning 31-28 win over the fifth-ranked Buckeyes. The decisive play came when the coach's son, Chris White, drilled a 38-yard field goal as the clock ran out. However, there were more Illini heroics prior to that, and quarterback Jack Trudeau was primarily responsible for the stunning rally. Completing 28 of his 40 passes, Trudeau relied on a short passing game against the wind. His quick shovel passes to fullback Thomas Rooks and timely catches by Stephen Pierce for 131 yards nickel-and-dimed the traditionally tough Buckeye defense to death. Chris White's game-winning kick came following a pair of timeouts, the second called by Ohio State in an attempt to unnerve the senior placekicker. "I've got a lot of faith in that son of mine," the elder White told the media afterwards. "His temperament is unbelievable. I don't think that ball was six inches off center."

WOMEN'S MILESTONES

MARCH 8, 1986:

Junior center Jonelle Polk became the first University of Illinois women's basketball player to earn first-team honors on the All-Big Ten squad. Polk led the conference in scoring with an average of 21.9 points per game and also ranked among the leaders in numerous other statistical categories. Despite being named Big Ten Player of the Week four times in 1985-86, Polk was edged out by Ohio State's Tracy Hall as league Player of the Year.

I

Illinois' plans for construction of new athletic facilities were unveiled in 1982 and begun in 1985.

ILLINI ITEM

AT A LATE JULY 1982 MEETING in Robinson, Illinois the Athletic Association's Board of Control approved Director Neale Stoner's long-range plan for construction of new athletic facilities. About 33 months later—April 15, 1985—construction began on $34 million worth of improvements. Of the total, $7 million was targeted toward upgrading football facilities, including the resurfacing of Zuppke Field, expansion of the football headquarters, and installation of an air-support structure that was eventually nicknamed "The Bubble." Construction on the new baseball and track stadiums began in June of 1985.

ILLINI LISTS

ILLINI MEN'S AND WOMEN'S BIG TEN GOLF MEDALISTS

1923	Rial Rolfe
1930	Richard Martin
1931	Richard Martin
1941	Alex Welsh
1942	James McCarthy
1962	Mike Toliuszis
1982	Mike Chadwick
1986	Steve Stricker
1988	Steve Stricker
1989	Steve Stricker
1991	Renee Heiken
1992	Becky Biehl
1993	Jamie Fairbanks
1993	Renee Heiken

Becky Biehl was the Big Ten's medalist at the 1992 women's golf championships.

ILLINI LEGEND:

DAVID WILLIAMS

The soft hands of All-America receiver David Williams were once described by a sportswriter as "bean bags used to catch bullets." During his illustrious career at the University of Illinois from 1983-85, Williams' hands caught 262 passes for 3,392 yards, mostly from the skillful arm of Illini quarterback Jack Trudeau. In the history of college football, only Tulsa's Howard Twilley was a more proficient receiver than the young man from Los Angeles, California. Season-wise, Williams' top effort came in 1984 when he became the first (and only) Illini receiver to catch more than 100 passes (101). Statistically, Illinois' No. 1 had his best individual game October 12, 1985 against Purdue when he set an Illini record with 16 catches for 164 yards. David was one of three Williams brothers who played for the Illini during the 1980s, including older brother Oliver (1981-82) and younger sibling Steven (1985-89). David, who was drafted in the third round of the 1986 NFL draft by the Chicago Bears, played with Tampa Bay and the Los Angeles Raiders his first two seasons as a pro. In 1988, he began a seven-year career in the Canadian Football League, playing with British Columbia, Ottawa, Toronto and Winnipeg. During that span in Canada, Williams played in 101 CFL games, catching 439 passes for 7,197 yards and 79 touchdowns. In the fall of 1995, he returned to the University of Illinois to complete his bachelor's degree.

Illini Lore

It wasn't a university-sponsored event, nor was it an athletic event, but probably the most noteworthy campus event of 1985-86 occurred at Memorial Stadium, September 22, 1985. The event's official name was "FarmAid," and it was undoubtedly one of the most diversified collections of musical talent to ever gather at the Urbana-Champaign campus. The 14-hour concert was marred by rain and cold temperatures, but that didn't much bother the 78,000 fans who filled the stadium. Among the more than 50 stars of rock and roll, blues and country who performed on the giant stage located at the north end of Zuppke Field were co-organizer Willie Nelson, Johnny Cash, Alabama, Billy Joel, the Beach Boys, Van Halen, B.B. King, and Kenny Rogers. More than $9 million in ticket sales, corporate donations and private pledges was eventually used for cash grants to needy farmers.

1986-87

I·L·L·I·N·I M·O·M·E·N·T

Disa Johnson won first-team All-Big Ten honors for the 1986 Fighting Illini volleyball team.

VOLLEYBALL WINS BIG TEN TITLE:

Perfection in an 18-match, round-robin format had never before been accomplished by a Big Ten volleyball team, but that all changed in 1986. Coach Mike Hebert's Fighting Illini sailed through the conference portion of the season, sweeping to victory an unprecedented 18 straight times, including three-games-to-none shutouts in 13 of those matches. During the regular season, the Illini dropped matches to only fourth-ranked San Jose and sixth-ranked Nebraska. Heading into the NCAA tournament with its 34-2 record, Illinois sported a 24-match winning streak. The Mideast Region's No. 2 seed easily disposed of Northern Iowa and Western Michigan in the first two rounds, but the Illini were eliminated in the semifinals by Nebraska in three consecutive games. Illinois athletes dominated the All-Big Ten squad as Player of the Year Mary Eggers, Disa Johnson, and Sally Rea all were named as first teamers. Eggers also won first-team All-America honors.

Leticia Beverly claimed a pair of Big Ten individual titles at the 1987 Women's Big Ten Track and Field championships.

WOMEN'S MILESTONES

MAY 23-24, 1987:

The Fighting Illini track team placed second to Purdue at the Big Ten Outdoor Track and Field Championships in Iowa City, Iowa, its highest finish ever to that point. Coach Gary Winckler's squad racked up a school-record 112 points, just three points behind the Boilermakers. Sophomore Leticia Beverly claimed two individual titles, winning the 100-meter hurdles and the long jump, as well as leading off the victorious 400-meter relay unit. Victoria Fulcher was the only other Illini athlete who captured an individual championship, winning the 400-meter hurdles.

ILLINI ITEM

ILLINOIS BASKETBALL STAR Ken "Snake" Norman had a marvelous season in 1986-87, earning first-team All-Big Ten and second-team All-America honors. The Fighting Illini MVP averaged nearly 21 points and 10 rebounds per game, leading the conference in the latter category.

ILLINI LISTS

WOMEN'S TRACK MULTIPLE BIG TEN INDIVIDUAL TITLISTS
(Through 1994-95 season)

25 titles Tonja Buford
(1990-93)
19 titles Celena Mondie-Milner
(1987-90)
15 titles* Tonya Williams
(1993-95)
14 titles Renee Carr
(1986-90)
9 titles Leticia Beverly
(1986-89)
9 titles Angela McClatchey
(1986-89)
8 titles Carmel Corbett
(1992-95)
7 titles Althea Thomas
(1989-90)
6 titles Victoria Fulcher
(1987-88)
6 titles Katherine Williams
(1991-94)

*Eligibility remained beyond 1994-95

Celena Mondie-Milner captured 19 Big Ten track titles during her Fighting Illini career from 1987-90.

ILLINI LEGEND:

DARRIN FLETCHER

If ever there was an All-American family at the University of Illinois, it was the Fletcher clan from tiny Oakwood, Illinois. Not only were dad Tom and son Darrin outstanding citizens and model student-athletes for the Fighting Illini, they were, quite literally, All-Americans in the sport of baseball. A first-team All-America selection as a pitcher in 1962, the elder Fletcher still holds the Illini records for lowest earned run average (0.38) and most shutouts (four). Darrin excelled as a catcher, but his greatest notoriety came as a batsman, hitting a school-record .392 from 1985-87, including a gaudy .497 average his junior year. Fletcher held eight UI marks altogether, and was named the 1986-87 Fighting Illini Male Athlete of the Year. He was chosen as the Big Ten's baseball player of the year, hitting .432 in conference play. Darrin was a sixth-round draft choice of the Los Angeles Dodgers in 1987, earning a spot on the parent club late in the 1989 season. He was traded to Philadelphia in 1990, and a year later was dealt from the Phillies to the Montreal Expos. The crowning moment of Fletcher's still-budding major league career came in 1994 when he was selected as a member of the National League all-star team.

 Illini Lore

On November 8, 1986, a gala ball at Lincoln Hall capped off a week of festivities that marked the 75th anniversary of the World Heritage Museum. The museum's early development occurred under curators Neil Brooks and Arthur Pease. Its first full-time director was Oscar Dodson in the 1960s. Among the museum's most notable pieces are an original fragment from the Bible's Book of James, a large display of medieval and Renaissance armor, a page from the Gutenberg Bible, and Olympic memorabilia from the collection of University of Illinois graduate and track star Avery Brundage.

1987-88

America's Time Capsule

- **Oct. 19, 1987:** *The worst stock crash in the recent history of the New York Stock Exchange occurred when the Dow Jones industrial average fell 508 points.*
- **Nov. 18, 1987:** *President Reagan was blamed for failing in his constitutional duty by the congressional committee report on the Iran-Contra affair.*
- **Feb. 5, 1988:** *A federal grand jury in Miami indicted Panamanian General Manuel Noriega in connection with illegal drug dealings.*
- **April 23, 1988:** *A ban on smoking in passenger planes went into effect.*
- **Aug. 8, 1988:** *The first night baseball game in the history of Chicago's Wrigley Field took place, though it was rained out.*

I·L·L·I·N·I M·O·M·E·N·T

John Mackovic replaced Mike White as the Illini football coach on Feb. 3, 1988.

WHITE OUT/MACKOVIC IN:

Just 16 days expired between the firing of Fighting Illini head football coach Mike White and the hiring of his replacement, John Mackovic. The furious chain of events began January 18, 1988, when White submitted his resignation to Director of Athletics Neale Stoner. An NCAA investigation into alleged recruiting violations prompted White's action. Said Interim Chancellor Morton Weir, "The Athletic Association's Board of Directors and I believe that Coach White has responded appropriately by tendering his resignation." The search for White's replacement began immediately, with the list of candidates including Illini defensive coordinator Howard Tippett, former Northwestern coach Dennis Green, Boston College's Jack Bicknell, and Stoner's personal choice, ex-Kansas City Chiefs coach John Mackovic. The AA's board convened for more than three hours on February 2 before arriving at the decision to hire Mackovic. The 44-year-old Wake Forest graduate immediately went about hiring a staff, and salvaging a nearly impossible recruiting scenario by signing eventual Illini standouts Brad Hopkins, Jason Verduzco, and John Wright.

WOMEN'S MILESTONES

MARCH 24-25, 1988:

Heather Singalewitch became the first Illinois women's athlete to be honored as the Big Ten Conference's Gymnast of the Year. She shared the honor with Minnesota's Marie Roethlisberger. The Illini sophomore tied Minnesota's Lisa Wittwer for the all-around championship with a 38.10 score, tied for second on the uneven bars (9.40), took third on the balance beam (9.60) and tied for third in the vault (9.50).

Illinois' Heather Singalewitch

Illini coach Ed Beard (right) and his star golfer, Steve Stricker.

ILLINI ITEM

ILLINOIS' MEN'S GOLF TEAM ended a 47-year championship drought May 16, 1988, when it defeated six-time Big Ten titlist Ohio State by 20 strokes. Illini junior Steve Stricker was named the conference's Player of the Year by firing a 72-hole total 279 to outdistance teammate Mike Small and OSU's Chris Smith by 14 shots. The triumph by Ed Beard's squad came at home on Savoy's Orange Course. Said Stricker afterwards, "I don't think you could ask for anything more than winning the Big Ten championship on your home course with your family and friends watching."

ILLINI LISTS

GREATEST FOREIGN ILLINI ATHLETES

Illinois' grand tradition in athletics has been bolstered by several athletes who were products of foreign shores. Here's a sampling:

Gilberto Albequerque, gymnastics, Brazil
Camille Baldrich, tennis, Puerto Rico
Darren Boyer, football, Canada
Carmel Corbett, track, New Zealand
Charlton Ehizuelen, track, Nigeria
Victor Feinstein, gymnastics, Israel
Kirsten Gleis, volleyball, Holland
George Kerr, track, Jamaica
Marko Koers, track, Holland
Andy Kpedi, basketball, Nigeria
Petra Laverman, volleyball, Holland
Graeme McGufficke, swimming, Australia
Herb McKenley, track, Jamaica
Cirilo McSween, track, Panama
Tigran "Tico" Mkchyan, gymnastics, Armenia
Lindsey Nimmo, tennis, England
Kari Samsten, gymnastics, Finland
Gilmarcio Sanches, gymnastics, Brazil

Nigeria's Andy Kpedi was co-MVP of the 1990-91 Illini basketball team.

ILLINI LEGEND:

MARY EGGERS

Wrote one sports journalist, Mary Eggers "stalks the court with an icy look of controlled violence that combines the cool of Star Trek's Mr. Spock with the rage of a pit bull." That analogy aptly described the woman who went on to become the most prolific player in University of Illinois volleyball history. From Big Ten Freshman of the Year in 1985 to conference MVP from 1986-88, no one individual dominated the court quite like Eggers. She led the nation in hitting percentage her sophomore and senior seasons, and set Fighting Illini career records for aces, blocks, kills and attack percentage. The four Illini teams on which she played had a cumulative record of 136 victories against only 17 losses for a winning percentage of .889. Eggers' crowning glory came following her senior season in 1988 when she earned the Honda Broderick Award, symbolic of the nation's top collegiate volleyball player. Following her graduation in 1991, she played professional volleyball in Europe. Currently, Mary Eggers Tendler is an assistant volleyball coach at Illinois State.

Illini Lore

Morton W. Weir, interim chancellor at the Urbana-Champaign campus since August of 1987, was unanimously approved as permanent chancellor by the University of Illinois' Board of Trustees, April 14, 1988. His appointment vacated the post left by former Chancellor Thomas Everhart, who left the UI to become president of Cal Tech. Weir also served as UI's acting chancellor between the terms of former chancellors Jack Peltason and William Gerberding. Among the previous positions held by Weir at the UI were head of the psychology department, vice chancellor of administrative affairs, and vice president of academic affairs.

1988-89

I·L·L·I·N·I M·O·M·E·N·T

THE FLYING ILLINI:

Nick Anderson (left), Coach Lou Henson, and Kenny Battle (right) triumphantly exit the Metrodome floor.

To many Illini fans, the 1988-89 men's basketball squad is the standard by which other Illini teams are measured. Coach Henson's athletes rolled through the regular season with a 27-4 record, including victories in their first 17 games. That 17th win, a 103-92 double-overtime victory against Georgia Tech at the Assembly Hall on January 22, catapulted the Illini to the top of the national rankings. Unfortunately, the bad news in that contest against the Yellowjackets was an injury to Kendall Gill, which triggered three Illinois losses in the next four games. Strong play by fellow All-Star Nick Anderson, co-captains Kenny Battle and Lowell Hamilton, and sophomore Marcus Liberty kept the Illini going until Gill returned with two games left in the regular season. The Illini beat Iowa and Michigan, finishing with a 14-4 conference record, and entered the NCAA tournament as the No. 1 seed in the Midwest Regional. There, they easily disposed of McNeese State and Ball State. In the third-round battle against Louisville, a strong effort by Liberty helped Illinois overcome an injury to Hamilton, and the Illini beat the Cardinals, 72-60. In the regional finals against Syracuse, Anderson came up with his most impressive game, scoring 24 points and grabbing 16 rebounds as Illinois beat the Orangemen, 89-86, to qualify for the Final Four in Seattle. The April 1 semifinal pitted the Illini against Michigan, a team they had already disposed of twice during the regular season. Unfortunately, the third time was a charm for the Wolverines and Michigan prevailed 83-81 to knock the Illini out of their chance to win a national title. After the season, Anderson, Illinois' most valuable player, announced that he was going to forego his final year of college eligibility to enter the NBA draft.

WOMEN'S MILESTONES

Illinois' women's track and field squad captured the 1989 outdoor title at IUPUI Track Stadium in Indianapolis with a record-setting 169 points, 31 more than any other previous champion had registered in the eight-year history of the meet. Fighting Illini athletes captured titles in 11 of the 19 events, including four by Celena Mondie-Milner (100- and 200-meter dashes, and 400- and 1,600-meter relays). Predictably, eight of the 16 athletes who earned All-Big Ten honors were Illini. Joining Mondie-Milner were Shayla Baine, Lisa Balagtas, Leticia Beverly, Renee Carr, Cindy Lawrence, Angela McClatchey, and Debbie Smith.

The quartet of (left to right) Angela McClatchey, Celena Mondie-Milner, Renee Carr, and Leticia Beverly combined to win the Big Ten's 400-meter relay title.

ILLINI ITEM

Shawn Wax's touchdown grab pulled the Illini within range of overtaking Indiana.

WITH ONLY THREE-AND-A-HALF MINUTES left in the game and Illinois trailing Indiana by 11 points, 20-9, Fighting Illini football fortunes looked hopeless at Memorial Stadium November 5, 1988. Coach John Mackovic's squad didn't give up though, narrowing the Hoosier lead to 20-15 on a spectacular shoestring grab by Shawn Wax from quarterback Jeff George with 1:27 remaining. On the first play of Indiana's final possession, Illini defensive back Chris Green knocked the ball loose from IU's Dave Schnnell and into the arms of linebacker Julyon Brown. George confidently directed the Illini drive down the field by mixing runs and passes, and, with just 26 ticks left on the clock, George threw a game-winning TD pass to Mike Bellamy. The Illini escaped with a one-point victory, 21-20.

ILLINI LISTS

JIMMY COLLINS AND DICK NAGY'S TOP TEN MEMORIES OF THE 1988-89 SEASON

Lou Henson's longtime assistants, Jimmy Collins and Dick Nagy, choose their top ten memories of the 1988-89 "Flying Illini."

1. March 26 vs. Syracuse: The Illini earn a spot in the Final Four.
2. December 19 vs. Missouri: Kenny Battle scores 28 as UI improves record to 8-0. The Illini overcame an 18-point deficit.
3. March 4 at Indiana: Nick Anderson hits a miracle three-pointer to beat Hoosiers.
4. March 24 vs. Louisville: Illinois wins its 30th game behind Anderson's 24 points.
5. January 22 vs. Georgia Tech: Illini earn No. 1 ranking with two-overtime win.
6. December 22 at LSU: Illini crush the Tigers by 27 points in Baton Rouge, scoring school-record 127 points.
7. March 11 at Michigan: UI wins school-record 27th game at Ann Arbor.
8. February 9 vs. Ohio State: Stephen Bardo holds Buckeye star Jay Burson to nine points.
9. January 25 vs. Indiana: Illini snap league-leading Indiana's 13-game victory streak.
10. March 8 vs. Iowa: Lowell Hamilton, Battle and Anderson play final home game. Kendall Gill returned to the line-up.

ILLINI LEGEND:

DAVID ZEDDIES

The most well-known individual athletic award presented to an intercollegiate athlete during any particular year is undoubtedly the Heisman Trophy, symbolic of the outstanding college football player in America. Perhaps, the least known single prize in college athletics might be the Nissen Award, emblematic of the top male gymnast. So, during the 1988-89 season, while Oklahoma State gridiron star Barry Sanders was picking up his hardware in New York City, Illinois gymnast David Zeddies was doing much the same April 12, 1989 in Lincoln, Nebraska. Zeddies, a native of Union Springs, New York, became the Illini's first Nissen Award winner since it was initially presented in 1966. He combined his marvelous athletic ability with sportsmanship and leadership, and also was an outstanding scholar. Zeddies excelled on the rings and the parallel bars, earning 1988 Big Ten Gymnast of the Year honors and helping to lead Coach Yoshi Hayasaki's Illini squad to the 1989 NCAA title. He currently is working on his doctorate at Northwestern University and serves as a research assistant in NU's neurology and physiology department.

Illini Lore

The Beckman Center was dedicated April 7, 1989, just two-and-one-half years after the ground-breaking ceremonies. The new home for the executive and scientific staffs of the National Center for Supercomputing Application had a $50 million price tag, $40 million of which was donated by philanthropist Arnold Beckman ('22). Located on University Avenue between Wright and Mathews Streets, the 310,000 square-foot facility is on the same site as Illinois Field, home of Illini football through most of 1923 and Illini baseball through 1987.

1989-90

I·L·L·I·N·I M·O·M·E·N·T

Illinois' stubborn 1989 defensive unit was anchored by the front line of (left to right) Mel Agee, Brian Williams, Sean Streeter and Moe Gardner.

ILLINI BOWL OVER VIRGINIA:

For the first time in more than a quarter of a century, Illinois' football team began its season with a win *and* ended it with a Bowl-game victory. At one time, the 1989 campaign was scheduled to begin several thousand miles away in Moscow with the first-ever Glastnost Bowl, but a last-minute change in plans placed the Fighting Illini instead at the Los Angeles Coliseum against highly ranked Southern Cal. A national television audience on Labor Day night witnessed one of the most exciting comebacks in UI history when quarterback Jeff George tossed a pair of fourth-quarter touchdowns to Shawn Wax and Steven Williams. The 14-13 triumph over the Trojans began a string of seven Illini successes in its first eight games, highlighted by Illinois' second straight win over Ohio State, George's triumphant return to Purdue, a miracle victory at Michigan State, and a decisive 31-7 pasting of the Iowa Hawkeyes at Kinnick Stadium. On November 11 at Memorial Stadium, Illinois hosted Michigan for the inside track to the Big Ten championship. However, for the second year in a row the Illini stumbled, forcing them to re-focus their sights on a second-place conference finish and a berth in the Florida Citrus Bowl. Mackovic's talented troops, led by a defensive unit that featured five future pros (Moe Gardner, Henry Jones, Mel Agee, Chris Green, and Darrick Brownlow), easily disposed of Indiana and Northwestern, and the Illini began packing for Orlando. The Illini climbed on the plane at Champaign, where the wind chill was a brutal 50 degrees below zero, and were similarly greeted by Florida's worst cold snap in years. But, like the weather, the Illini eventually warmed up to their task, defeating 10-1 Virginia by a score of 31-21. The pin-point passes of game MVP George to his trusty receiver, Mike Bellamy, ended a 26-year Bowl victory drought and lifted the Illini to 10th in the final national rankings with a 10-2 record. It would prove to be the final time that Jeff George would wear an Illini uniform, as he declared for the NFL draft and became the first overall pick by his hometown Indianapolis Colts.

WOMEN'S MILESTONES

March 23-24, 1990:

The Fighting Illini women's gymnastics team captured its first-ever official Big Ten title, nipping Michigan State and Minnesota in a championship where only four points separated the first and last place teams. Coach Bev Mackes' squad boasted four individual titlists, including Denise Lamborn in the vault, Peggy Pullman and Laura Knutson on the balance beam, and Heather Singalewitch in floor exercise. Mackes earned honors as Big Ten Coach of the Year.

ILLINI ITEM

ON JANUARY 19, 1990, the Fighting Illini men's swimming and diving team defeated Coach "Doc" Councilman's powerful Indiana Hoosiers, 60-53, marking Illinois' first dual-meet victory over IU since 1957. Illini coach Don Sammons got the most out of "Senior Night" at the IMPE Pool, as final-year swimmers Andy McVey (50- and 100-yard freestyle) and Jim Mackin (200-yard butterfly) had first-place finishes. McVey and Mackin also were key members of the winning 400-yard medley relay unit.

ILLINI LISTS

ILLINI WHO WERE FIRST-ROUND NBA DRAFT PICKS

1970	Mike Price, 17th pick, New York Knicks	
1973	Nick Weatherspoon, 13th pick, Washington Bullets	
1983	Derek Harper, 11th pick, Dallas Mavericks	
1987	Ken Norman, 19th pick, Los Angeles Clippers	
1989	Nick Anderson, 11th pick, Orlando Magic	
1989	Kenny Battle, 27th pick, Detroit Pistons	
1990	Kendall Gill, 5th pick, Charlotte Hornets	

Nick Anderson (left) and Kenny Battle were both first-round selections in the 1989 NBA draft.

ILLINI LEGEND:

KENDALL GILL

Kendall Gill joined Coach Lou Henson's Fighting Illini basketball team as the sleeper of Illinois' 1985 recruits, hidden behind the press clippings of fellow classmates Larry Smith and Steve Bardo. Four years later, he left as the Big Ten's scoring leader and a first-team All-American. You'd be hard-pressed to find a more beloved player in Illini basketball history than the charismatic kid from Matteson, Illinois. Gill proved to be one of the sparkplugs on Illinois' famed "Flying Illini" team of 1988-89. That squad glided to a 17-0 start and the nation's No. 1 ranking, but a broken bone in his foot sidelined him for 12 games, and the Illini juggernaut became just another team. Upon Gill's return to the lineup, the Illini quickly regrouped and rolled through Indianapolis and Minneapolis into the Final Four. During his sensational senior season at Illinois in 1989-90, Gill averaged 20 points per game and wound up his career as the school's seventh all-time leading scorer with 1,409 points. Selected in the first round of the 1990 National Basketball Association by the Charlotte Hornets, he was traded to Seattle in September of 1993, then back to Charlotte in 1995. In the spring of 1994, Gill generously donated $300,000 to the Cunningham Children's Home in Urbana.

Illini Lore

The 94-year-old University of Illinois Observatory earned the designation of a National Historic Landmark in the spring of 1990, placing it alongside the Brooklyn Bridge, Carnegie Hall and the Alamo. The Observatory's 12-inch refracting telescope, first used in 1896, is still being used by UI students for viewing the heavens and for instruction in general astronomy.

1990-91

I·L·L·I·N·I M·O·M·E·N·T

Among the players named to Illinois' All-Century Football Team were (front row, left to right) Alex Agase (#59), Johnny Karras (#48), J.C. Caroline (#26) and Al Brosky (#27), plus (back row, l. to r.) Mike Bass, Doug Dieken, Ed O'Bradovich, Dick Butkus, Dike Eddleman, Don Thorp, Jeff George and Jim Grabowski.

ILLINI FOOTBALL CELEBRATES ITS CENTENNIAL SEASON:

Coach John Mackovic's Fighting Illini shared the Big Ten football title with Iowa, Michigan and Michigan State in 1990, but that championship isn't what that season will be remembered for by most University of Illinois gridiron fans. The 1990 season was highlighted by the centennial celebration of Illini football, the largest athletic promotion ever staged at the Urbana-Champaign campus. The symbol of the event was a logo designed by UI student Rebecca Byrne, depicting a silhouette of Red Grange and the columns of Memorial Stadium. Among the key elements of the Centennial were:

- a traveling display of Illini football memorabilia that visited 44 locations around the state of Illinois;
- an historical book and video;
- banners on the street lights surrounding and leading to the stadium that featured each of the 100 years of Illini football;
- and a 25-man All-Century Team that was selected by more than 10,000 UI fans.

For each of the six home games in 1990, a different segment of Illini football was honored, with more than 500 former UI gridiron stars ultimately returning to their alma mater and being individually introduced to their adoring fans. Said one Illini football alumnus, "It was a thrill to once again walk onto the field, this time in the presence of my wife, son and daughter."

WOMEN'S MILESTONES

On September 4, 1990, the Fighting Illini volleyball team christened historic George Huff Hall as its new home. On hand for the festivities were the five men who provided the old gymnasium with its greatest basketball memories—Illinois' famed "Whiz Kids." The quintet of Jack Smiley, Ken Menke, Andy Phillip, Art Mathisen, and Gene Vance joined volleyball co-captains Barb Winsett and Laura Bush, and coach Mike Hebert at center court for the traditional ribbon-cutting. The Illini spikers then disposed of Southern Illinois in four games. Through the 1994 season, Illinois' volleyball team won 61 of 77 matches at Huff Hall.

The famed "Whiz Kids" participated in the ribbon-cutting ceremony at the rededication of Huff Hall. Shown here (left to right) are Jack Smiley, Ken Menke, Andy Phillip, Barb Winsett, Laura Bush, Art Mathisen, Gene Vance, and Mike Hebert.

ILLINI ITEM

THE APRIL 30, 1991 PERFORMANCE by Illinois' 28-17 baseball victory over UI-Chicago produced some awesome numbers, but none were more incredible than those generated by first baseman Bubba Smith. The junior from Riverside, California had seven official at-bats, hit safely a record-tying six times, including a record four home runs, scored a record-tying five times, drove home a record 10 RBIs, and accumulated a record 18 total bases.

ILLINI LISTS

HOWARD GRIFFITH'S NCAA RECORD EIGHT TOUCHDOWNS

On September 22, 1990, Illinois' Howard Griffith became the first player in NCAA Division I-A football to score eight touchdowns in a single game. He broke the record of seven TDs by Mississippi's Arnold Boykin, set against Mississippi State in 1951. Here's a score-by-score description of Griffith's explosion versus Southern Illinois at Memorial Stadium:

FIRST TD: 5-yard burst off right tackle, 10:06 left in 1st quarter
SECOND TD: 51-yard up-the-middle sprint, 8:50 left in 2nd quarter
THIRD TD: 7-yard up-the-middle run, 4:53 left in 2nd quarter
FOURTH TD: 41-yard dash off the left side, 3:10 left in 2nd quarter
FIFTH TD: 5-yard run off right tackle, 12:34 left in 3rd quarter
SIXTH TD: 18-yard, tackle-breaking zigzagger, 10:10 left in 3rd quarter
SEVENTH TD: 5-yard run off right tackle, 6:07 left in 3rd quarter
EIGHTH TD: 3-yard dive off right tackle, 1:25 left in 3rd quarter

ILLINI LEGEND:

JON LLEWELLYN

As a freshman wrestler at Hinsdale Central High School in suburban Chicago, Jon Llewellyn was a 98-pound weakling. But seven years later, he rose to the title of NCAA heavyweight champion. "I took my lumps as a 98-pounder," Llewellyn confessed, "I never dreamed of becoming a national champion. I put in my time lifting weights and working out. I would eat all the time, even when I didn't want to." From 1988-91, the 240-pound heavyweight was the only shining light in the Illini wrestling program. Three times—as a sophomore, junior, and senior—Llewellyn won the league title, setting an Illinois record in that weight class. His most glorious season came as a senior in '90-91 when he rolled through his competition with a perfect 33-0 record, boosting his career record to 97 wins against only 23 losses and three draws. Llewellyn's ultimate accomplishment came March 13, 1991 when he beat defending champion Kurt Angle of Clarion State, 6-3, at the NCAA championships in Iowa City, Iowa. Later that spring, he was honored as Illinois' Male Athlete of the Year, beating out two-time football All-American Moe Gardner. Today, Llewellyn and his family reside in Manteno, where he works as a structural engineer for the firm of Sargent and Lundy.

 Illini Lore

On November 7, 1990, despite finding Illinois not guilty of any of the original charges brought against the men's basketball program, the NCAA levied harsh penalties against the University of Illinois. Based on what it called "lack of institutional control" and a third appearance by the school in the previous six years before the infractions committee, the NCAA issued a three-year probation of Coach Henson's program. The coaching staff originally was accused of offering money and a car to recruit Deon Thomas, but was eventually exonerated of any unethical conduct. Chancellor Morton Weir acknowledged some procedural and administrative shortcomings in the basketball program, but was disturbed by the NCAA's labeling of "lack of institutional control." "Over the past five years or so," said Weir, "the University has taken extraordinary measures to ensure the integrity of intercollegiate athletics on this campus. Our record in recent years demonstrates that we do not hesitate to take the strongest actions when they are warranted."

1991-92

I·L·L·I·N·I M·O·M·E·N·T

Lou Tepper was introduced as Illinois' head football coach on Dec. 13, 1991.

TEPPER PROMOTED AFTER MACKOVIC LEAVES FOR TEXAS:
In a whirlwind 24-hour period, Illinois' football program lost one head coach and hired another. Rumors had constantly circulated around the status of athletic director/head coach John Mackovic, and, on December 12, 1991, the highly regarded Illini mentor was hired by the University of Texas. Quickly, Chancellor Morton Weir and interim AD Bob Todd promoted Lou Tepper the very next day as Mackovic's replacement. "We knew we had the right person right here on campus," said Weir. "Lou is a man of integrity, with a strong orientation toward the academic success of student-athletes." The 46-year-old Tepper pledged his long-term commitment toward the University, saying, "If I had just wanted to be a head coach, I could have done so several years ago. That was not my goal. My goal was to be a head coach at a prestigious institution and to be at one institution for a very long time." Tepper didn't need to wait the customary nine months to coach his first game, as he directed the Illini 18 days later in their December 31 John Hancock Bowl match-up against UCLA. The Illini lost to the Bruins by a score of 6-3.

WOMEN'S MILESTONES

SEPTEMBER 28, 1991:

The University of Illinois celebrated the 10th anniversary of women's athletics in the Big Ten Conference in grand style during the 1991-92 season, honoring a multitude of athletes at a reunion lunch at the Illini Union. All-Decade teams were chosen for each of the eight sports, and, from that group, a 20-person all-star team was selected. Each sport also celebrated the milestone season with its own individual reunion.

I

ILLINI ITEM

COACH GARY WINCKLER'S women's track team swept to Big Ten championships both indoors and out during the 1992 season. At the indoor meet February 28-29 at Columbus, Illinois out-lasted Wisconsin, 81-76, in a meet that went down to the final event, the 4 x 400-meter relay. Outdoors at Minneapolis, May 22-23, the Illini cruised to a 122-99 victory over the runner-up Badgers. Just as she had done indoors, junior Tonja Buford was selected as the Big Ten Athlete of the championship, again winning three individual events.

Coach Gary Winckler and women's track star Tonja Buford.

ILLINI LISTS

ILLINOIS' ALL-STAR ALL-DECADE TEAM

As part of the celebration of 10 years of women's athletics in the Big Ten Conference in 1991-92, the University of Illinois selected an all-star all-decade team for its entire women's program.

Leticia Beverly, track
Nancy Brookhart, volleyball
Tonja Buford, track
Laura Bush, volleyball
Robyn Duffy, swimming
*Mary Eggers, volleyball
Kendra Gantt, basketball
Renee Heiken, golf
Heidi Helmke, gymnastics
Disa Johnson, volleyball
Becky Kaiser, track

Denise Lamborn, gymnastics
Petra Laverman, volleyball
Celena Mondie-Milner, track
Mary Ellen Murphy, golf
Lindsey Nimmo, tennis
Jonelle Polk, basketball
Lisa Robinson, basketball
Lynette Robinson, basketball
Heather Singalewitch, gymnastics

*Athlete of the Decade

Diver Robin Duffy was a member of UI's Women's All-Star All-Decade Team.

ILLINI LEGEND:

RENEE HEIKEN

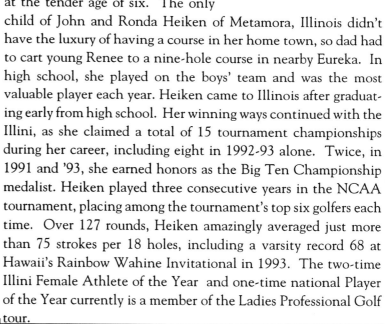

Renee Heiken, the greatest golfer in the 20-year history of women's athletics at the University of Illinois, began honing her skills on the links at the tender age of six. The only child of John and Ronda Heiken of Metamora, Illinois didn't have the luxury of having a course in her home town, so dad had to cart young Renee to a nine-hole course in nearby Eureka. In high school, she played on the boys' team and was the most valuable player each year. Heiken came to Illinois after graduating early from high school. Her winning ways continued with the Illini, as she claimed a total of 15 tournament championships during her career, including eight in 1992-93 alone. Twice, in 1991 and '93, she earned honors as the Big Ten Championship medalist. Heiken played three consecutive years in the NCAA tournament, placing among the tournament's top six golfers each time. Over 127 rounds, Heiken amazingly averaged just more than 75 strokes per 18 holes, including a varsity record 68 at Hawaii's Rainbow Wahine Invitational in 1993. The two-time Illini Female Athlete of the Year and one-time national Player of the Year currently is a member of the Ladies Professional Golf tour.

Illini Lore

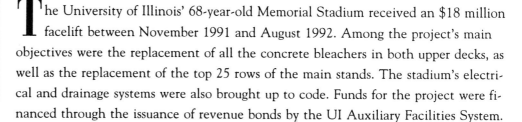

The University of Illinois' 68-year-old Memorial Stadium received an $18 million facelift between November 1991 and August 1992. Among the project's main objectives were the replacement of all the concrete bleachers in both upper decks, as well as the replacement of the top 25 rows of the main stands. The stadium's electrical and drainage systems were also brought up to code. Funds for the project were financed through the issuance of revenue bonds by the UI Auxiliary Facilities System.

1992-93

I·L·L·I·N·I M·O·M·E·N·T

Andy Kaufmann's dramatic shot vs. nationally ranked Iowa set off one of the wildest post-game scenes in Assembly Hall history.

KAUFMANN'S BUZZER BEATER UPSETS IOWA:

High-flying Iowa, led by lanky Acie Earl, invaded Illinois' Assembly Hall February 4, 1993 with soaring hopes, but a miracle shot by Andy Kaufmann instead sent the Hawkeyes home minus a few tail feathers. The Illini had not defeated an opponent ranked in the Top 10 in its last 12 tries, but this night belonged to the Orange and Blue. Freshman sharp-shooter Richard Keene kept Illinois close throughout the game by connecting on five three-pointers, but he saved the dramatics for his senior teammate from Jacksonville. After a fluke basket by Iowa with just two seconds left gave the Hawkeyes a two-point lead, Illinois immediately called time out. Illini coach Lou Henson drew up his team's last-gasp shot, calling for T.J. Wheeler to heave a three-quarters-court pass in the direction of the Illini basket. Kaufmann hauled in the pass in front of the Illinois bench, then spun, squared up and lofted a 23-footer toward the iron rim. The ball passed cleanly into the net as the buzzer sounded, sending a tumultuous throng of Illini fans onto the court in celebration of a 78-77 Illinois victory.

Volleyball's Kirsten Gleis (above) and tennis's Lindsey Nimmo dominated their sports in Big Ten action during the 1992-93 season.

WOMEN'S MILESTONES

A conference-record four University of Illinois women's stars earned Big Ten Athlete of the Year honors during the 1992-93 season, a feat that may never be duplicated. Volleyball All-American Kirsten Gleis dominated that sport in what would turn out to be her only season as an Illini. Tonja Buford ruled Big Ten track and field, winning nine indoor and outdoor conference titles altogether as a senior. Golfer Renee Heiken was the medalist in the 1993 conference championship, repeating as her sport's Player of the Year. Finally, on the tennis courts, no Big Ten player was better than Lindsey Nimmo. She captured Player of the Year honors.

Renee Heiken (left) and Jamie Fairbanks.

ILLINI ITEM

ILLINOIS GOLFERS scored a rare feat during the 1993 season, as individuals from both the men's and women's teams grabbed medalist honors in their respective Big Ten championship meets. From May 7-9 at Iowa City, senior Renee Heiken shot a 72-hole total of 300 to capture women's honors. Then, a week later at Bloomington, Indiana, junior Illini golfer Jamie Fairbanks averaged 71 strokes per round to win the men's conference tournament. That allowed Illinois to become only the second school in Big Ten history to sweep individual titles in both the women's and men's championships in the same season.

ILLINI LISTS

ILLINI BASEBALL CAREER HOME RUN LEADERS

1. 48— Scott Spiezio (1991-93)
2. 40— Sean Mulligan (1989-91)
3. 38— Darrin Fletcher (1985-87)
   38— Forry Wells (1991-94)
5. 33— Bubba Smith (1989-91)
6. 31— Tom Sinak (1992-95)
7. 26— Dave Payton (1984-87)
8. 25— Larry Sutton (1989-92)
   25— Brad Wentz (1985-88)
10. 23— Mark Dalensandro (1987-90)

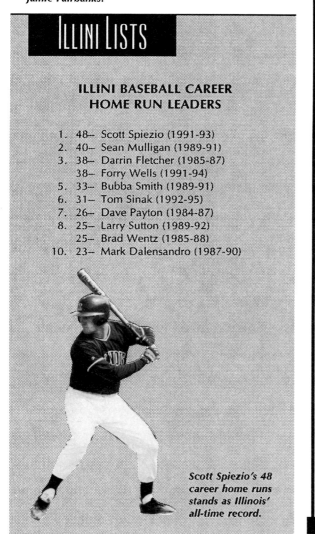

Scott Spiezio's 48 career home runs stands as Illinois' all-time record.

ILLINI LEGEND:

TONJA BUFORD

Tonja Buford's magnificent career at the University of Illinois is underlined by the fact that she not only won more individual Big Ten track titles than any other Illini athlete, but also more than any other women's or men's athlete in the history of the conference. Her total of 25 championships broke the record of 23 by Wisconsin distance star Suzy Favor, the namesake of the Big Ten's Female Athlete of the Year Award. From 1990-93, Buford dominated hurdles competition at league track and field meets. Buford's eight individual titles and two relay championships during her senior season may never be broken. She was a four-time Big Ten Track Athlete of the Year and was named Athlete of the Championship three times. The Dayton, Ohio native became the first Illini women's track runner to ever compete in the Olympic Games when she qualified for the 400-meter hurdles at the 1992 Summer Games in Barcelona, Spain. Buford shared Illinois' Female Athlete of the Year Award in 1992 and won it outright in 1993. Today, she competes on the professional track and field circuit.

Illini Lore

Michael Aiken, 60-year-old provost at the University of Pennsylvania since 1987, was chosen as chancellor for the University of Illinois at Urbana-Champaign in early February, 1993. The native of Arkansas and University of Mississippi graduate replaced Morton Weir, who stepped down to return to the classroom. "Though some board members had emphasized a search for women and minority candidates," said Board of Trustees President Judith Calder, "we were satisfied that Aiken's experience showed his commitment to equal opportunity."

1993-94

I·L·L·I·N·I M·O·M·E·N·T

Quarterback Johnny Johnson (#13) sets himself for his dramatic touchdown pass to Jim Klein.

ILLINI SURPRISE MICHIGAN:

Winning football games at Michigan has never been an easy chore for Illinois, so the Fighting Illini victory at Ann Arbor October 23, 1993 was especially gratifying for Coach Lou Tepper's troops. As had been the case so many times before in contests at mammoth Michigan Stadium, Illinois trailed the 13th-ranked Wolverines entering the fourth quarter. A Ty Douthard touchdown with 11:37 remaining narrowed the Illini deficit to 21-17, but Illinois' task appeared hopeless with just more than a minute remaining and Michigan in control of the ball. Suddenly, UI's Simeon Rice stripped the ball away from Maize and Blue running back Ricky Powers at the Michigan 44-yard line, and a confident Illini offense raced back onto the field. Quarterback Johnny Johnson methodically guided Illinois into the end zone in six plays, capped by a fourth-down, 15-yard touchdown pass to Jim Klein. The 24-21 Illini victory at Ann Arbor snapped a 27-year road jinx and presented Illinois with its most satisfying victory of the 1990s.

WOMEN'S MILESTONES

FEBRUARY 18-19, 1994:

Senior swimmer Jennifer Sadler set Illinois varsity records at the 1994 Big Ten Swimming and Diving Championships in Indianapolis. She first broke the Illini mark in the 50-yard freestyle (:23.62), then the 100-yard freestyle (:51.28).

I

Illinois' 1993-94 senior basketball players (front, left to right) Deon Thomas, Tom Michael, (back, left to right) T.J.Wheeler, and Gene Cross won 15 of 16 games at the Assembly Hall.

ILLINI ITEM

ONLY A 74-70 LOSS to 15th-ranked Michigan spoiled an otherwise perfect men's basketball season for Illinois at the Assembly Hall in 1993-94. Coach Lou Henson's Fighting Illini scored victories in 15 of 16 games on their freshly painted home court, including a shiny 8-1 mark in Big Ten contests. Among Illinois' highlights were a Super Bowl Sunday triumph over Indiana before a national television audience, UI's 13th-consecutive home-court win over a talented Wisconsin club, and a senior-night victory by Deon Thomas, T.J. Wheeler, and Tommy Michael over Minnesota.

ILLINI LISTS

ORIGINAL COSTS OF ILLINOIS' CURRENT ATHLETIC FACILITIES

*$40,000	Kenney Gym (1902)
$702,000	Armory (1915)
$2.5 million	Memorial Stadium (1923)
$725,000	Huff Hall (1925)
$250,000	Savoy Golf Course (1950, original 18 holes)
$8.35 million	Assembly Hall (1963)
$2.2 million	Outdoor Track & Field Stadium (1987)
$1.64 million	Illinois Field (1988)
$5.3 million	Atkins Tennis Center (1991)
$6 million	Bielfeldt Athletic Administration Building (1996)

*Estimated cost, due to the gymnasium being included in a bid of three different buildings

Kenney Gym cost $40,000 to build in 1902.

ILLINI LEGEND:

DEON THOMAS

The basketball career of Deon Thomas was a series of peaks and valleys. As a youngster, the soft-spoken Thomas survived the brutal experiences of growing up on the streets of Chicago's West Side to become one of the city's finest prep players at Simeon High School, ultimately earning academic eligibility and an athletic scholarship at the University of Illinois. Just a few months later, false allegations of NCAA recruiting violations, based on audio tapes obtained by an assistant coach at Iowa, turned Thomas' future down a road of great despair. He strongly considered leaving school, but, instead, stayed to prove his innocence. After sitting out his freshman season, Thomas began a brilliant career at Illinois during the 1990-91 campaign by averaging 15 points per game. His senior year, 1993-94, saw him break Fighting Illini records nearly every time he played. Not only did Thomas become the school's all-time leading scorer with 2,129 points, he also set UI marks for field goals, free throws, free-throw attempts and blocked shots, and ranked second-best in rebounds and field-goal percentage. Following his graduation from Illinois, Thomas was the first pick in the second round of the National Basketball Association draft by the Dallas Mavericks. He wound up playing professional ball in Spain during the 1994-95 season.

Illini Lore

On April 24-25, 1994, Monsignor Edward J. Duncan was honored for his 50 years of service as chaplain and director of The Newman Foundation. Among the guests honoring Monsignor Duncan at a gala luncheon included retired General Motors chairman Thomas Murphy and former Illini football great Dick Butkus. During the festivities, University of Illinois Director of Athletics Ron Guenther announced that the Illini football team would institute a special citizenship award to honor its long-time team chaplain. Monsignor Duncan became chaplain at St. John's Catholic Church in 1943.

1994-95

I·L·L·I·N·I M·O·M·E·N·T

LIBERTY BOWL CHAMPS:

Lou Tepper's third full season as head football coach at the University of Illinois was just 22 agonizing points away from being a banner year. And though the painful sting of narrow losses to four Bowl-qualifying teams was eased a bit in the finale when Illinois won the Liberty Bowl, Illini fans couldn't help but think about what might have been during this roller coaster of season. The campaign began disappointingly at Chicago's Soldier Field with a one-point loss to Washington State, 10-9, but Illinois rebounded well by demolishing their next two non-conference foes, Missouri and Northern Illinois, by a cumulative score of 76-10. In week four, the Illini came up 36 inches shy of a victory in the Big Ten opener against Purdue, as the game ended with tight end Ken Dilger stacked up at the one-yard line. Tepper's crew shocked Ohio State in Columbus for a fourth consecutive time the following week, 24-10, helping linebacker Dana Howard live up to his bold prediction of a victory. Illinois then won three of its next four games, sandwiching a difficult 19-14 loss to Michigan between victories over Iowa, Northwestern and Minnesota. The most exciting game of 1994 came November 12 when No. 2-ranked Penn State travelled to Memorial Stadium. A 28-14 halftime lead by the Illini ultimately evaporated into a 35-31 loss to the eventual Rose Bowl champs. A defeat in the regular-season finale at Wisconsin backed the Illini into the Liberty Bowl, and doomsayers weren't optimistic that Illinois could beat pesky East Carolina in the December 31 game at Memphis. However, a dominating offensive performance by quarterback Johnny Johnson and an equally sterling defensive effort from Simeon Rice and company made New Year's Eve especially sweet for the Orange and Blue.

WOMEN'S MILESTONES

Theresa Grentz, the seventh-winningest women's basketball coach in NCAA history and head coach of the 1992 United States Olympic Team, was selected as the University of Illinois' sixth head women's basketball coach on May 15, 1995. The 20-year coaching veteran from Rutgers University replaced Kathy Lindsey, who coached the Fighting Illini for five years. Grentz's coaching career at Rutgers saw the Lady Knights rise toward the top of women's intercollegiate basketball. During her 20 seasons at Rutgers from 1976-95, Grentz's teams compiled a record of 434-150 (.743), including nine consecutive NCAA tournament appearances from 1986-94. Her 1981-82 Rutgers team captured the AIAW national championship with a 25-7 record. Combined with her two seasons at St. Joseph's from 1974-76, Grentz's overall collegiate coaching record was 461-155. Only six other coaches in the history of women's intercollegiate basketball have won more games (461) than Grentz, and only 12 others have a better winning percentage than her .748 success mark. During her collegiate career at Immaculata, Grentz helped establish the first national power in women's collegiate basketball. The Mighty Macs won 74 games and captured three consecutive national titles (1972, '73, '74) during her playing career. Grentz was named a first-team All-American each season, won 1974 AMF Collegiate Player of the Year honors, and had her #12 retired by Immaculata.

ILLINI ITEM

VIRTUALLY DORMANT on the national scene for 37 years, Illinois' wrestling program got the boost it was looking for March 18, 1995 when senior Steve Marianetti (150 pounds) and sophomore Ernest Benion (158) both captured individual NCAA crowns. The dramatic scene took place at the University of Iowa. Although the Hawkeye crowd saw its favorites handily win the national team title, Marianetti's stunning 13-10 victory over Iowa's two-time defending champion Lincoln McIlravy put a damper on their celebration. Illini coach Mark Johnson, in just his third year, led Illinois to a top-ten finish (ninth) for the first time since 1958. It was the first time since 1938 that two UI wrestlers won national titles in the same year.

1995 NCAA wrestling champions Steve Marianetti (left) and Ernest Benion

ILLINI LISTS

KAROL KAHRS' MOST OUTSTANDING WOMEN ATHLETES

Dr. Karol Kahrs, Illinois' long-time associate director of athletics, was recently asked to choose the most outstanding Illini women athletes of the last 20 years. Here are her selections, sport by sport.

Basketball:	Lisa Robinson
Cross Country:	Kelly McNee
Golf:	Renee Heiken
Gymnastics:	Nancy Thies
Swimming & Diving:	Mary Paterson
Tennis:	Lindsey Nimmo
Track & Field:	Tonja Buford
Volleyball:	Mary Eggers

Coach Gary Winckler's 1995 women's track and field squad cruised to championships both indoors and outdoors in Big Ten action, and placed fourth at the NCAA outdoor meet.

ILLINI LEGEND:
DANA HOWARD

Illinois' reputation as "Linebacker U" gained considerable punch on December 9, 1994, when Illini senior Dana Howard earned the Butkus Award as college football's top linebacker. It was the first major individual award ever won by an Illini football player. Presenting the prize that night in Orlando, Florida was its namesake, former UI star Dick Butkus, who was celebrating his 52nd birthday. Said Howard in accepting the award, "I'd like to thank Dick Butkus for bringing that great linebacker tradition to Illinois. It gave me something to measure myself by." Howard's second-consecutive All-America season was highlighted by two memorable events. First was his daring public prediction of victory and his subsequent performance at Ohio State in a 24-10 Illini victory. Howard nailed down the Butkus Award in a 35-31 loss to second-ranked Penn State when he became the Big Ten's all-time leading tackler. No. 40 topped the century mark in tackles all four seasons he played for the Illini, finishing with 595 stops, 23 more than previous record-holder Marcus Marek of Ohio State. Howard was a fifth-round draft pick of the Dallas Cowboys, and now plays for the St. Louis Rams.

Illini Lore

Within a period of just 72 hours, the University of Illinois merged a Springfield-based university into its system, saw the structure of its governing board change, and gained a new president. The tumultuous three-day period began on February 28, 1995, when Governor James Edgar signed legislation to merge Sangamon State University in Springfield with the UI in January of 1996 as well as give the governor power to appoint UI trustees. Two days later, on March 2, UI-Chicago Chancellor James Stukel was named as the University's 15th president, replacing the retiring Stanley Ikenberry.

Epilogue

Next month Illinois opens the 1995 football season against Michigan in Memorial Stadium. As I began to prepare for the play-by-play broadcast of that game on the 60-station Illinois Radio Network, it occurred to me that my love affair with Illini sports began 44 years ago. Same field. Same two teams.

To be specific, it was November 3, 1951. We had driven up from my hometown, Olney, Illinois. It was the first Illini football game I had ever seen. Our seats were in the temporary bleachers at the north end. A 40-mile-an-hour wind blew from the south. It snowed hard. It was a blizzard. In the final five minutes, Tommy O'Connell hit Rex Smith with a short touchdown pass, and Illinois won 7-0 on the way to a 9-0-1 season, including a 40-7 Rose Bowl victory over Stanford.

When we finally found our snow-covered car, I remember plopping into the back seat, listening to the grumbling of my friends about what a lousy day it was, how cold they were, how stupid we were for making the trip. "I loved it," I said. And, I still do. More now than then, more tomorrow than today.

Why do I feel that way? Why do I get chills when Chief Illiniwek dances? Why do I cry when seniors play their last games? Why can't I sleep when the Illini lose a close one? Why will I hug Mike Pearson's book and sit up long after my bedtime remembering the games, players, and coaches that have brought such joy and happiness to my life? Let me explain.

In addition to having been influenced by "just being there," I believe I caught the spirit of Illinois by observing up close those athletes with big hearts. Who can ever forget the competitiveness of Mary Eggers, Kenny Battle, Bill Brown, Dave Scholz, and Craig Virgin? When a kill was needed, when the game was on the line, Eggers took over. Battle was so intense, so dedicated, and so relentless that even his opponents were awed. Brown played hard, played hurt, all out all the time. Scholz set his jaw and willed victory after victory in a memorable 19-5 season in 1968-69. Virgin will be remembered as one of the world's best distance runners despite numerous injuries and illness.

To this day, I can feel the sense of excitement in Memorial Stadium when Dick Butkus lumbered onto the turf to snap the ball and block for the quarterback when it was 4th and short. He did it time after time. We always got the first down. Some will have other memories of Pete Elliott's 1964 Rose Bowl champions, led by Butkus and Jim Grabowski, but to me, it will always be 4th and short with the big guy comin' on to remedy the situation.

Not all memories are on the field. On October 27, 1956, this rookie reporter was a guest at Ray Eliot's Springfield Avenue residence. A few hours earlier, Abe Woodson had taken a Bill Offenbecher screen pass 82 yards for a touchdown keying Illinois' 20-13 upset win over Michigan State. "You like that game, son?" the legendary coach asked. "Yes, sir," I mumbled. He put his hand on my shoulder and said, "Me, too. That's one we won't forget." Ray Eliot is one we won't forget either.

One Monday noon at our Champaign Rotary Club meeting, Mike Hebert was introduced as the featured speaker. He had been named women's volleyball coach at Illinois and his mission now was to educate us. He was trying to drum up some enthusiasm for a game most of us had played at picnics in the park. Hebert's game was to be played by young women in dingy Kenney Gym. It was going to be a tough sell. Mike began his speech by saying, "This is a volleyball." We laughed at that. Then we began to learn. We began to watch. One of the greatest pleasures I've had at Illinois is watching Mike's team rise to national prominence, lead the nation in attendance, and provide thrilling season after season. Mary, Nancy, Kirsten—what a wonderful ride!

Calling the big ones on the air: sports broadcasters live for dramatic endings. Nick Anderson's last-second shot at Indiana amid a five-game victory streak against the Hoosiers ranks very near the top. So do the buzzer beaters of Andy Kaufmann against Iowa and Eddie Johnson against Michigan State. How about the remarkable twin victories over Louisville and Syracuse at Minneapolis on the road to the Final Four in 1989? And, the heroics of the QB's, Dave Wilson, Tony Eason, Jack Trudeau, Jeff George, Jason Verduzco, and Johnny Johnson.

I must say that long after the scores have been forgotten and one season has blended into the next, relationships with players and coaches live on. If there are two more decent human beings teaching young people than Lou Henson and Lou Tepper, I would like to know who they are.

Almost every day I drive from my office north on Route 45 to St. Mary's Road, go under the viaduct, up a little incline, then I look to my left at the Assembly Hall and Memorial Stadium. I never tire of this sight. Sometimes I stop the car and try to imagine where we parked our car that snowy day in 1951.

A guy should never forget exactly where he was the moment he fell in love.

Jim Turpin
August 1995

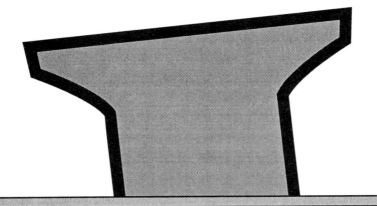

PROUDLY SUPPORTING THE ILLINI
—from legends to future leaders

BUSEY-CARTER TRAVEL
Serving Champaign-Urbana since 1964

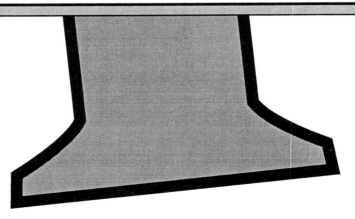

All-Time Fighting Illini Letter-Winner List

Approximately 7,000 men and women have earned varsity letters as athletes in intercollegiate athletics at the University of Illinois from 1878 through the spring of 1995. This list, compiled by author Mike Pearson and UI graduate student Lyn Burgoyne (B.S. '92, M.S. '96), reflects the cumulative information contained within UI's sport summary books. Team managers, who often earned varsity letters, have not been included due to inconsistent information. Female athletes are listed by their maiden names. As with any list of this magnitude, there could be inadvertent errors or omissions. Please contact the UI Sports Information office should you discover a mistake.

KEY TO ABBREVIATIONS

BB - baseball
FB - football
FN- fencing
IHO - ice hockey

MBK - men's basketball
MCC - men's cross country
MGO - men's golf
MGY - men's gymnastics
MSW - men's swimming
MTN - men's tennis

MTR - men's track & field
PO - polo
SOC - soccer
VB - volleyball
WBK - women's basketball
WCC - women's cross country

WGO - women's golf
WGY - women's gymnastics
WR - wrestling
WSW - women's swimming
WTN - women's tennis
WTR - women's track & field

A

Abbot, Richard R.	MTR	1943
Abbott, David	MCC	1927,28
	MTR	1928,29
Abel, Kevin J.	FN	1989,90,91,92
Abell, William A.	FN	1958
Abraham, George E.	FB	1932
Abraham, William	FN	1967,68,69
Abraham, William J.	FN	1947
Abrahamson, Kristen	WCC	1993
Abrams, Jack	MTN	1952
Abromovich, Phil	WR	1951
Acker, Alan S.	FN	1971,72,73,74
Ackerman, Owen	MSW	1957,58,59
Ackermann, Mary	WSW	1991,92,93,94
Acks, Ron	FB	1963,64,65
Adair, Lorrie	WSW	1978,79,80
Adams, Alfred O.	MTR	1933,34
Adams, Earnest	FB	1977,78,79,80
Adams, Neil	MTN	1981,82,83,84
Adams, Paul	FB	1956,57
Adams, Paul	MCC	1975
Adams, Rich	MBK	1975,76,77,78
Adams, Susan	WGY	1988,89,90,91
Adams, William	WR	1934,35
Adamson, Steve	MGY	1981,83,84,85
Ader, Richard F.	SOC	1930,31,32
Adkins, Jason	FB	1994
Adkins, John D.	MGY	1941,42
Adler, Leon	MGY	1917
Adler, M. A.	MGY	1922,23
Adsit, Bertram W.	BB	1899,00,01
	FB	1898,99,00
Adsuar, Natalie	WTN	1995
Agase, Alex	FB	1941,42,46
	WR	1942,43
Agase, Herbert	BB	1950,51
Agase, Louis	FB	1944,45,46,47
	MTR	1945
	WR	1945
Agee, Mel	FB	1987,88,89,90
Agnew, Lester P.	FB	1922
Ahlem, Ted	MSW	1975,76
Ahlsund, Annukka	WSW	1984,85
Ahrens, Carl	BB	1951,52,53
Aihara, Henry K.	MTR	1945
Aina, David F.	FB	1984,85
Ainsworth, Walter W.	MTR	1912
Akers, Todd A.	MTR	1989
Albecker, Walter	MSW	1980
Albers, Daniel P.	FN	1981
Alberts, Dewey V.	MTR	1921
Albrecht, A. J.	FN	1912,13
Albuquerque, Gilberto	MGY	1981,82,84,85
Alcock, Warren	MTN	1948
Alcock, Warren J.	BB	1917
Alcorn, Stanley W.	MSW	1937,39
Alderson, E. W.	MSW	1920
Alexander, Charles	MGO	1970,71,72
Alexander, Jeff	WR	1993
Alexander, Joe	MCC	1993,94
Alexander, Joe W.	BB	1939

Alexander, Robert	WR	1955,56
Allen, Aleck M.	BB	1883
Allen, Art	BB	1965
Allen, Derek	FB	1993,94
Allen, Earl	WR	1981,82
Allen, Guy	WR	1981
Allen, Jae	WBK	1975
Allen, James C.	MTR	1893
Allen, Larry	FB	1970,71,72
Allen, Lawrence T.	FB	1903
Allen, Mike	MGO	1990,91,92
Allen, Robert	FB	1956,57,58
Allen, Robert	MSW	1987,88,89
Allen, Steve	FB	1969
Allen, Susan	WTR	1975
Allen, William	MTR	1974
	MCC	1972,73
Allen, William M.	FB	1965
Alley, Mike	BB	1972
Allie, Glen	FB	1967
Allman, John C.	MTR	1920,21
	MCC	1920
Allman, Omar L.	MTR	1933
Almquist, Robert	MGO	1959,60
Almy, W. H.	MGY	1905
Aloia, Alex	WR	1941,42
Alpert, S. G.	MGO	1930,31,32
Altenberger, Bill	MBK	1955,56,57
Altenberger, Doug	MBK	1983,84,85,87
Altenmeyer, Vern	MBK	1959,60
Althans, Tracey	WGY	1993,94,95
Alwood, Clyde	MBK	1915,16,17
Alyea, Lou	PO	1934
Amaya, Doug	FB	1987,88
Amaya, Manuel	MTN	1973,74
Ambielli, Adam	MTN	1982
Ambler, Basil	WR	1931
Ames, Waldo B.	MTR	1915,16,17
Amico, Mary	WGY	1981
Aminzia, Norbert	FN	1993
Anastasia, Dana	WR	1985
Anderlik, Robert	BB	1945,47,48
Anders, Alphonse	FB	1939
Andersen, Harry E.	MTR	1947,48,49
Anderson, Betty	WBK	1975,76,77
Anderson, Bob	MSW	1968,69,70
Anderson, Daniel C.	MSW	1941,42
Anderson, Darin	WR	1989
Anderson, Darryl	MSW	1966
Anderson, E. J.	MGO	1927
Anderson, Earl	MBK	1918
Anderson, Gary	BB	1971,72,73
Anderson, Harold B.	MSW	1910
	FB	1909
Anderson, John V.	MSW	1938
Anderson, Kai	FB	1965,66
Anderson, Kerry	WR	1967,68
Anderson, Linda	WCC	1980
	WTR	1980,81
Anderson, Lori	VB	1984,85,86,87
Anderson, Neal	FB	1961,62

Anderson, Nick	MBK	1988,89
Anderson, Paul T.	FB	1921
Anderson, Richard	MSW	1966,67,68
Anderson, Richard F.	MSW	1941
Anderson, Samuel	MTR	1952
Anderson, Tom	MSW	1972
Anderson, Truman O.	FN	1984
Anderson, Van	MBK	1948,49,50
Anderson, W. J.	MGO	1926
Anderson, Wilbur H.	SOC	1932,33
Anderson, William W.	FB	1915,16
Anderssohn, Henry	BB	1948,49,50
Andrew, Arthur	WR	1954
Andrew, Philip	MSW	1989
Andrews, Charles	WR	1934,35
Andrews, Donald H.	BB	1927,28,29
Andrews, L. E.	MSW	1917
Andrews, William T.	BB	1879,80,81
Angel, Katherine	WTR	1979,80,81,82
Angel, Wendell W.	MTR	1981
Angelo, Louis	MTR	1991,93
Anger, Edward	PO	1934
Angier, Milton S.	MTR	1922,23,24
Anthonisen, Norman	WR	1942,46,47
Antilla, Arvo A.	FB	1933,34,35
Antonacci, Bill	BB	1995
Antonacci, Rich	FB	1977
Antoniolli, Carl	MGY	1978
Apel, Patti	WSW	1977,78
App, Benjamin R.	MTR	1973,74,75
Applegate, Frank G.	FB	1903
Applegran, Clarence O.	MBK	1916
	FB	1915,19
Appleman, Jim	MTN	1975
Applequist, J. G.	MTR	1899
Aprati, Fred	WR	1964,65,66
Aranda, Ezequiel	MTR	1891
Arbuckle, Leon	BB	1914,15,16
Archer, Arthur E.	FB	1948
	WR	1948
Archer, Corbin	MTN	1995
Arendt, James W.	MGO	1968
Arildsen, Susan	WTN	1982,83,84,85
Arkema, Edward L. S.	SOC	1927
Armstead, Charles	FB	1981,82
Armstrong, Sue	WSW	1979,80,81,82
Armstrong, David T.	FN	1975,76,77
Armstrong, Edward	MTR	1988
Armstrong, James W.	FB	1891,92
	MTR	1893
Armstrong, Jay L.	MTR	1898
Armstrong, Lennox F.	FB	1913,14
Arneborn, Mikael	FN	1992,93
Arneson, Jeff	FB	1991,92,93
Arneson, Paul	BB	1959,60,61
Arnholt, Cheryl	WGO	1984,85,86,87
Arning, Louis H.	MTR	1932
Arnoff, Alison	WSW	1983,84
Arnold, Mark D.	MTR	1982,83,84,85
Arrandale, Matt	BB	1992,93
Arrasmith, William S.	BB	1919

Arrison, Kevin	MSW	1985
Arthur, Ecklund	BB	1945
Arvanitis, George	FB	1984
Ascher, Vernon W.	MTR	1922
Ash, David	FB	1957,58,59
Ash, Homer	MSW	1950,51
Ashley Jr., Richard	FB	1892
Ashley, Robert L.	MTR	1937,38,39
Ashlock, Dennis	FB	1976,77
Ashmore, James N.	BB	1902,03
Asper, Orville W.	MTR	1930
Astroth, Lavere L.	BB	1939,40,42
	FB	1939,40,41
Atherton, George H.	BB	1891,92
	FB	1891,92,93
Atkin, Leonard	FN	1951
Atkins, Kelvin	FB	1979,80,81
Atkinson, Brian	MGO	1994,95
Auclair, Renee-Claude	WSW	1988,89
Aufrecht, Michael	MGY	1960,61,62
Aufrecht, Ronald J.	FN	1965,66,67
Ausich, William I.	FN	1973,74
Austin Jr., Roswell M.	IHO	1943
Austin, Jeffrey	MGY	1952,53,54,55
Avery, Galen	FB	1972
Avery, Mark E.	MTR	1975,77,78
	MCC	1974,75,76,77
Avery, Todd D.	FB	1984,85
Axelrod, David J.	MTR	1974,75
Ayalon, Yuval	MGY	1995
Ayoub, David M.	MTR	1978,79,80,81
Ayres, John	FB	1983,84
Ayres, Robert B.	MTR	1922,23,24
Azinger, Kirk	WR	1985,86,87,88

B

Baader, Richard P.	MTR	1982,83
Babb, Dick	MCC	1970
Babbitt, Richard K.	IHO	1939
Babyar, Chris	FB	1981,82,83,84
Bachman, Bob	MSW	1965,66,67
Bachouros, Peter F.	FB	1950,51,52
Backs, Jason	BB	1988
Badal, Herbert	FB	1954
Baffes, Kathy	WGY	1978,79,80
Bagel, Jean	WGY	1976
Baietto, Michael E.	MTR	1972,73,74,75
Baietto, Robert E.	FB	1954,55
Bailey, Donald	MTR	1940,41
Bailey, Ellen	VB	1980
Bailey, Gordon R.	FB	1931
Baine, Shayla	WTR	1988,89,90,91
Baird, Dave	WR	1984,85,86,87
Baird, William	MTR	1901
Baker, Clarence	FB	1977
Baker, Jerry	BB	1964
Baker, Nicholas	MGY	1990,91,92,93
Baker, Robert	MGO	1933,34
Baker, Yolanda	WTR	1991,92,93
Bakke, Niles	MGO	1970,71,72,73
Balagtas, Lisa	WTR	1987,88,89

Robert (Bo) Batchelder was a three-time football letterman from 1964-66.

Baldrich, Camille	WTN	1992,93,94,95
Bales, Edwards J.	MTR	1926
Balestri, George L.	BB	1943
	IHO	1942,43
Baley, James A.	MGY	1941
Ballantine, Fred	BB	1949
Ballard, Albert D.	FN	1970,71
Ballou, Donald	MGY	1963,64
Balzer, Teresa	WCC	1980
Bane, Frank M.	BB	1914,15
	MBK	1914,15
Banker, Edward H.	BB	1922
Banks, Daniel	MSW	1982,83,85
Banschbach, Edward A.	MTR	1893,94,95
Baranski, Jerome	BB	1951,52
Barasch, Alvin	MGY	1960
Barber, Thomas	MSW	1946
Barbour, Dave	WR	1987,88
Bardo, Stephen	MBK	1987,88,89,90
Bare, Frank	MGY	1952,53,54
Bareis, Barbara	WTN	1982,84,85
Bareither, Charles	FB	1967,68,69
	MTR	1968
Bargo, Ken	FB	1967,68,69
Barker, John K.	FB	1891
Barklage, Oliver F.	BB	1918,19
Barmes, Andy	MTR	1982,83
Barmes, William	MGY	1950
Barnes, David	MSW	1974,75,76,77
Barnes, George H.	MTR	1925,26,27
Barnes, Harvey	WR	1925
Barnes, Jeff	FB	1978
Barnes, Robert A.	BB	1921,22
Barnett, James	MSW	1983,84,85,86
Barnett, Scott	BB	1980
Barnum, Robert V.	MTR	1948,50,51
Baron, Dan	MTR	1974
Barousse, Ignacio C.	FN	1922
Barr, John	MGO	1934
Barr, Ken	MGY	1970,71,72
Barrett, Brad	MGY	1972
Barrett, Jesse L.	MTR	1905,06,07
Barron, James L.	MTR	1911
Barron, Oliver D.	MTR	1913
Barrow, Christine	WGY	1984
Barry, G. W.	MSW	1929
Barszcx, Casey	BB	1957,58,59

Bruce Beckmann was a football letter winner in 1958 and '59.

Barta, Joseph T.	BB	1925
Bartelstein, Alan	MGO	1977,78
Barter, Harold H.	FB	1903
Bartga-Nagy, Rudolfo	FN	1963,64
Barth, Frederic C.	FN	1981
Barth, George B.	MTR	1978
Bartholomew, F. G.	MSW	1930,31,32
Bartholomew, Robert	MBK	1930,31,32
Bartley, Boyd O.	BB	1941,42,43
Bartley, John	WR	1943
Bartulis, Joe	BB	1931
Baskin, Neil	FB	1969
Basolo, Margaret	WTN	1977,78,79
Bass, Mike	FB	1980,81,82
Bass, Rachel	WTR	1983
Bassett, Denman J.	FB	1947
Bassey, Ralph C.	FB	1943
Basson, Michau	MTN	1993,94,95
Batchelder, Robert (Bo)	FB	1964,65,66
Bateman, James M.	FB	1905
Bates, Charles R.	MTR	1903
Bates, Melvin B.	FB	1953,54,55
Bates, Pete	MSW	1965,66,67
Bates, Rob	MSW	1991
Bathke, Kimberly	WGY	1991,92,93,94
Batt, Jaclyn	WTN	1994
Battaglia, Frank	WR	1937,38
Battle, Kenny	MBK	1988,89
Bauer, Craig	MCC	1981,84
	MTR	1985
Bauer, Gene	PO	1936,37,38
Bauer, John A.	FB	1930
Bauer, John R.	FB	1951,52,53
	MTR	1953,54
Bauer, Larry	MBK	1964
Bauer, Ronald	MGY	1966
Bauer, Tom	MTN	1964,65,66
Bauerle, Louis	WR	1929,30
Baughman, James	FB	1951
Baughman, V. Lynn	MCC	1934
	MTR	1934,35
Baughter, George	MSW	1947
Baum, Benjamin F.	FB	1907,08,09
Baum, Harry W.	FB	1893,94,95
	BB	1894,95
Bauman, Frank	FB	1946
Baumann, Erich S.	FN	1991,92,93
Baumgardner, Max	MBK	1951,53
Baumgart, Tom	FB	1970,72
Beach, Becky	WBK	1976,77,78
	WGO	1976,77,78
Beach, Ted	MBK	1950,51
Beadle, J. Grant	BB	1885,86,87,88
Beadle, Thomas B.	FB	1895,97
Beam, Bruce	WR	1973,74,75
Beaman, Bruce	FB	1972,73,74,75
Bear, Ernest R.	MTR	1900,02,03
Beard, Trevor	MGO	1990,91,92
Beary, Matt	MTR	1992,93,94,95
Beastall, Theodore W.	MTR	1959,60
Beattie, Clayton	WR	1963,64,65
Beaumont, G. S.	MTR	1912,13,14
Beaumont, James D.	IHO	1939
Beaver, Daniel	FB	1973,74,75,76
Beavis, Ann-Marie	WSW	1987,88,89,90
Bebak, Arthur P.	FN	1981,82,83
Beck, Bruce	MGO	1970,71,72
Beck, Denver	WR	1970,71,72
Beck, H. Clint	MTR	1909
Beck, Howard W.	MGY	1972,73,74,75
Becker, David L.	MTR	1963,64,65
Becker, Robert	MTN	1934
Becker, Robert H.	FN	1958,59,60
Becker, William	MGO	1962
Beckman, Gary A.	MGO	1969
Beckmann, Bruce N.	FB	1958,59
Bedalow, John	FB	1970,71,72
Bedard, Irvin	MGY	1950,51
Bedell, David T.	MTR	1946,47,48
Bedrosian, Tammy	WGY	1977
Beebe, Charles D.	MTR	1894
	FB	1894,95,96
Beebe, Fred L.	BB	1902,03
Beebe, H. K.	MSW	1923
Beebe, Kenneth J.	FN	1911,12
Beebe, W. E.	MSW	1920,22
Beers, Harley	FB	1902,03
Behan, Paul F.	MTR	1948
Behrensmeyer, George	MTR	1891,92
Beider, David	FN	1978,79
Beile, Charles W.	MTR	1943,47
Beinke, Luann	WSW	1975

Bekermeier, Herbert W.	MTR	1943
Belden, Edgar S.	BB	1888,89,90
Bell, Brian	MSW	1992
Bell, Craig	FN	1963,64,65
Bell, Frank E.	FB	1936,37
Bell, James F.	FN	1953,54,55
Bell, Kameno	FB	1989,90,91
Bell, Oscar C.	MTR	1901
Bell, Richard	MTR	1973
Bellamy, Mike	FB	1988,89
Bellephant, Joe F.	FB	1957
Belmont, Lou	FB	1980,81
Belnap, Nuel D.	MTR	1912,13
Belsole, Bob	BB	1963,64
Belting, Charles H.	FB	1910,11
	MTR	1911,12
Belting, Paul E.	FB	1911
Bemoras, Irvin	MBK	1951,52,53
Benberry, Hershel	MTR	1969,70,71
Bengard, E. Donald	FN	1948,49
Benham, Harold	MBK	1935,36
Benham, Milford J.	FN	1935
Benion, Ernest	WR	1994,95
Benner, Jeffery	MSW	1981
Bennett, Austin H.	FN	1922
Bennett, Basil	MTR	1916,17,20
Bennett, Caslon K.	FB	1930
	MBK	1931,32,33
Bennett, Cleaves	BB	1888
Bennett, F. H.	MGY	1922
Bennett, James	FB	1985
Bennett, Mike	BB	1970
Bennett, Ralph E.	FB	1937,38,39
Bennett, Robert	MBK	1992,93,94,95
Bennett, Sean	BB	1995
Bennett, Theodore (Tab)	FB	1970,71,72
Bennis, Charles W.	FB	1932,33,34
Bennis, William	FB	1937
Bennorth, Robert	MTN	1950,51,52
Benso, Bryan M.	MTR	1987,88
Benson, Cam	FB	1980,81,82,83
Benson, Herschel G.	IHO	1942,43
Benson, Lisa	WTR	1980
Benson, Scott	WR	1994,95
Berbardoni, Edwin	WR	1943
Berg, Howard M.	BB	1935,36
Berg, Kristi	WSW	1993
Berger, Matt	WR	1985,86
Bergeson, Carl H.	FB	1928
	MBK	1930
Berggren, Ashley	WBK	1995
Bergren, Mark	WR	1973,74,75
Bergsma, Bonnie	WSW	1982,83,84,85
Bergstrom, Hugo E.	MTR	1927
Berner, John R.	BB	1938
	FB	1935,36,37
Bernhardt, George W.	FB	1938,39,40
Bernstein, Lionel M.	FN	1942
Bernstein, Louis S.	MBK	1909,10
	FB	1909,10
Bernstein, Matt	WR	1989,92
Berry, Gilbert I.	FB	1930,31,32
Berry, Kenneth	WR	1940,41,42
Berry, Mark	MSW	1981,82
Berry, Rex	BB	1958
Berschet, Marvin W.	FB	1951
	MTR	1950,51,52
Bert Jr., Vernon J.	SOC	1931
Bertelsman, George A.	MTR	1929,31
Berto, Terrie	WGO	1981,82,83,84
Besant, Wilson	MTN	1949,50
Bess, Bob	FB	1968,69
Bess, Ronald W.	FB	1965,66,67
Bessone, Amo	BB	1941
	IHO	1941,42,43
Best, David H.	MTR	1944,45
Beverly, Dwight	FB	1982,83
Beverly, Leticia	WTR	1986,87,88,89
Beyer, George F.	BB	1904,06,07
Beyers, Ben	MTR	1993,94,95
Beynon, Jack T.	MBK	1934,35
	FB	1932,33,34
Bezella, Bruce	MSW	1990,91
Bias, Moe	FB	1982,83
Bickhaus, Dick	BB	1961
Bickhaus, Jim	BB	1954,55,56
Biebinger, Isaac N.	MTR	1896,97
Biehl, Becky	WGO	1992,93,94,95
Biehl, Lia	WGO	1988,89,90,91
Biel, Joseph	BB	1981
Bielefeld, Roger	MTN	1954,55,58
Bierman, Randy	FB	1992,93

Amo Bessone lettered in hockey and baseball at Illinois, then became a Hall of Fame hockey coach at Michigan State.

Bieryzchudek, Anne	WSW	1989,90
Bieszczad, Bob	FB	1968,69
Bigger, Hamilton	MSW	1946
Bihl, Pete	MSW	1977
Bila, Michael S.	MTR	1984,86,87
Billings, Albert F.	MGO	1938,39
Billish, Teresa	WSW	1986,87
Bills, Victor	BB	1982
Bilsbury, Norman	MCC	1988,89
Binder, Richard	BB	1967,68,69
Bingaman, Lester A.	FB	1944,45,46,47
Binkley, Elizabeth	VB	1984,85,86,87
Bird, Patrick	MGY	1958,59,60
Birkhiner, D. James	WR	1941
Birks, John M.	MTR	1919
Birky, David A.	FB	1984,85
Bisbele, Fred B.	BB	1933
Bishop, Danny H.	MGO	1967,68,69
Bishop, David	MSW	1978
Bishop, Dennis	FB	1981,82
Bishop, J. Scott	FN	1986,87
Bishop, Lee	MTN	1951
Bishop, Robert E.	FB	1952,53
Bissell, Lonnie	MCC	1979
	MTR	1980
Bjerknes, Lisa	WTN	1980
Black, Marty	BB	1990,91
Black, Todd	MTN	1979,80,81,82
Black, William	MGY	1905
Blackaby, Ethan	BB	1960
	FB	1959,60
Blackman, E. O.	MSW	1926
Blackman, Ken	FB	1992,93,94
Blackwell, Amanda	WSW	1990
Blackwell, Glynn	MBK	1986,87,88
Blackwell, Mel	MBK	1964
Blahouse Jr., Charles	FN	1955
Blain, Brady	MTN	1995
Blair, Gavin	MGY	1956,63
Blakaslee, James W.	BB	1896
Blakely, David A.	FB	1977
Blanchard, John	MTR	1968,69
Blandy, D. C.	BB	1883
Blanheim, Melvin L.	MTR	1962,63,64

Tonya Booker was the 1994 recipient of the Big Ten Conference Medal of Honor.

Name	Sport	Years
Blankley, Alfred R.	MTR	1905
Blankley, W. H.	MSW	1926,27
Blazek, Frank	MGY	1956
Blazek, James	MGY	1957,58,59
Blazich, John L.	FN	1947
Block, F. L.	MSW	1930
Blom, G. Peter	MTR	1945
Blomfeldt, Allen A.	MTR	1907
Blondell, Jim	FB	1985,86,87
Bloom, Robert J.	FB	1932,33
Blount, Al	WR	1981
Blount, Walter P.	MTR	1919
Blout, Bryon	MBK	1936,37
Bluhm, Ronald	FN	1970
Blum, Daniel	WR	1936,37
Boatman, Tom	MTN	1960,61,62
Boatright, David	FB	1983,84,85
Bobert, Dave	MTR	1968,69,70
Bochte, Sue	VB	1974,75,76
Bock, Brian	BB	1979,80,81,82
Bock, Priscilla	WTR	1976
Bockman, Ted	MSW	1950
Bodden, Shirley	WTR	1986,87
Bodey, Kimberly	WTR	1987,88,90
Bodi, Jane	WTR	1976,77,78
Bodman, Alfred E.	FB	1930,31,32
Bodman, Stanley L.	FB	1930
Boedicker, Charles	MSW	1978,79,80,81
Boehler, Michael	BB	1977
Boeke, Greg	FB	1978,80,81
Boeke, Leroy	FB	1977,78,79,80
Boerio, Charles	FB	1950,51
Bogan, Raki	BB	1995
Bohannon, Edward	WR	1945
Bohaty, Zdenek A.	MGY	1942
Bohm, Ron	FB	1983,84,85,86
Boland, Chester H.	FN	1940,41
Boland, John S.	FN	1936
Bolander, Harold B.	MTR	1912,13,14
	MCC	1913
Bolk, Bill	BB	1956,57,58
Bollman, Keith	WR	1991,92
Bond, Kris	WBK	1995
Boner, Susan	WBK	1976,77,78
Bonk, Bill	BB	1960
Bonner, Bonjiovanna	FB	1978,79
Bonner, Lory T.	FB	1957,58
BonSalle, George	MBK	1955,56,57
Bontemps, Kevin	MBK	1980,81,82,83
Booker, Harry G.	MTR	1970,71,72
Booker, Tonya	WBK	1991,92,93,94
Boor, Alden K.	MSW	1941,42
Bootz, Harold	MGO	1946
Booze, MacDonald C.	FB	1912
Borbeck, Connie	WGO	1985,86,87
Borden, W. T.	MTR	1899
Borg, Gary	BB	1982,83,84,85
Borgialli, Dominic	BB	1978,79
Borland, Harold	WR	1922
Borman, Herbert R.	FB	1951,52,53
Borman, Michael	MSW	1974
Borre, Steven	BB	1977,78
Borri, Robert P.	SOC	1934
Borske, Erin	VB	1994
Borst, G. E.	MSW	1925
Boso, Casper (Cap)	FB	1984,85
Boston, Bill	MSW	1962
Bostrom, Kirk	FB	1979,80
Boswell Jr., Thomas E.	MTR	1947
Bouchard, Mike	MSW	1956,59,60
Boudreau, Louis	MBK	1937,38
	BB	1937
Boughman, James A.	FB	1951
Bourke, Timothy E.	FB	1984,85,86,87
Bouton, Charles S.	BB	1888,89,90,91
Bouton, Peter	MTN	1982,83,84,85
Bowe, Christopher L.	MTR	1986,87,88
	MCC	1985
Bowen, C. L.	MSW	1922,23
Bowen, Herbert L.	BB	1890
	FB	1890
Bower, Ed	WR	1944,45
Bower, Lynn K.	BB	1929
Bowers, James S.	MCC	1957,58,59
	MTR	1958,59,60
Bowers, Stephanie	VB	1988,89,90
Bowker, Susan	WTR	1976
Bowlay-Williams, Victor	FB	1988,89
Bowman, John	WR	1980
Bowman, P. J.	MBK	1989,90
Boyce, Chuck	MSW	1965,67
Boyd, C. N.	BB	1879,80,81
Boyd, Edward P.	MTR	1899,00,01
Boyd, George E.	MTR	1896
Boyd, Jesse	WR	1939,40
Boyer, Darren	FB	1990,91,92
Boykin, Rod	FB	1991,92,93,94
Boyle, Bridget	VB	1986,87,88,89
Boyles, John K.	FN	1954
Boysaw, Greg	FB	1986,88,89
Bozich, John	BB	1956
Brackett, Jerry	BB	1969,70,71
Bradley, Ed	MTN	1950,51
Bradley, James C.	MTR	1897,98,99
Bradley, John J.	FB	1905,06
Bradley, John T.	BB	1914,15,16
Bradley, Kendall R.	FB	1935
Bradley, Lisa	WBK	1985,86,87,88
Bradley, Theron A.	FB	1943
Brady, Edward	FB	1980,81,82,83
Brady, Seth	WR	1994,95
Braid, Ken	FB	1971,72,73
Bralower, Leonard	MGY	1948
Branca, Tom	MSW	1963,64,65
Branch, James M.	FB	1894,95,96
Branch, Robert	MSW	1948,49,50
Brandt, Harry	MTN	1954,55,56
Brandt, Todd	MSW	1982,83,84
Brannan, Jon	WR	1961
Brauer, Liz	WBK	1979,80,81
Braun, Cyril	MTN	1938
Braun, Howard	MBK	1934,35,36
Bray, Edward C.	FB	1943,44,45
Brazas, Steven E.	FB	1984
Brecik, Deann	WSW	1984,85,86,87
Breckenridge, Robert	MTN	1957,58,59
Bredar, James	MBK	1951,52,53
Brede, Erwin C.	MTR	1921
Bredfeldt, Charles	MGY	1920
Breen, Melissa	VB	1975,76,77,78
Brekke, William C.	MSW	1941,42,43
Bremer, Lawrence H.	FB	1908
Brems, Karen	WGY	1981,82,83,84
Breneman, Amos L.	FB	1915
Brennan, James	WR	1939
Brennan, Rich	FB	1969,70
Brennan, Thomas M.	FN	1961,63
Brennan, William	MSW	1975
Brenne, Gary	WR	1968
Brenneman, G. Bruce	MCC	1946
	MTR	1946
Brenton, J. F.	BB	1912
Bresnahan, Neil	MBK	1977,78,79,80
Brewer, Dave	FN	1968
Brewer, Joseph	BB	1951
Brewer, Melvin C.	FB	1937,38,39
Brewer, William R.	BB	1939,41,42
Brewster, Tim	FB	1982,83
Breyfogle, Larry	MBK	1958
Brice, Romero	FB	1987,88,89,90
Brickley, Amy	VB	1991,92,93,94
Bridenthal, C. F.	MGO	1908
Bridges, Dave	MTR	1968
Bridges, Jan M.	MTR	1964,65
	MCC	1963
Bridges, Lee A.	MTR	1986,87,88,89
Bridges, Michael R.	MTR	1975
	MCC	1972,73,74
Bridges, Steve	MTR	1990,92,93,94
Briggs, C. W.	BB	1886,87,88
Briggs, Claude P.	FB	1900
Briggs, John	WR	1980
Briggs, Randy	MGO	1991,93
Briggs, Steve	WR	1977,78,79
Briggs, Thomas	MTR	1949
Briley, Norman P.	FB	1899
Brinck, Per Ake	MSW	1983
Brinkmeyer, Gilbert	MGY	1952,53
Bristol, R. S.	MGO	1921
Brittain, Alpheus	WR	1929
Brittin, John	BB	1943,47
Britton, Earl T.	MBK	1924
	FB	1923,24,25
Brock, J.	MSW	1931,32,33
Brockman, Robert A.	MGY	1975
Brode, Luther D.	MTR	1893,94
Brody, Tal	MBK	1963,64,65
Broerman, Richard	FB	1952
Brokemond, George R.	FB	1958
Brombolich, Kim	WBK	1981,82

Nancy Brookhart earned second-team All-America honors her sophomore, junior, and senior seasons in volleyball.

Bronson, George D.	FB	1902
Brookhart, Nancy	VB	1986,87,88,89
Brookins, Mitchell	FB	1980,82,83
	MTR	1981,83
Brooks, Adrienne	WCC	1985
Brooks, Arvella	MTR	1990,91
Brooks, Carson C.	FB	1966,67,68
Brooks, David	MCC	1971,73
	MTR	1974
Brooks, Eron B.	FN	1925
Brooks, H. M.	MSW	1908
Brooks, Kevin U.	MTR	1984,85,86,87
Brooks, Richard	MTR	1974,75,76
	MCC	1973,74,75
Brooks, Richard A.	BB	1905,06
	FB	1906
Broome, Robert	MGY	1967,68
Brosky, Alfred E.	FB	1950,51,52
Brothers, Bruce	MBK	1954,55,56
Brouder, Cynthia	WTN	1978,79
Brouk, John J.	MSW	1937
Brown, Bob	MBK	1964,66
Brown, Charles A.	FB	1923,24,25
	WR	1925
Brown, Charles E.	FB	1948,49,50
Brown, Christy	WSW	1995
Brown, Darrin I.	FB	1984,85,86
Brown, David	MTN	1947,48,49
Brown, David E.	MTR	1919,20,21
Brown, Donald	BB	1929,30
Brown, Edward W.	MTR	1908,10
Brown, Gary W.	FB	1959,60,61
Brown, Hamilton A.	MTR	1989,90
Brown, Harold J.	MGY	1941
Brown, Horace T.	FB	1909
Brown, James E.	FB	1958,59,60
Brown, James F.	MGO	1942
Brown, James M.	MSW	1941,42,43
Brown, Jana	WTR	1980
Brown, John	MCC	1958
Brown, Joseph A.	FB	1937
	MTR	1937
Brown, Julyon	FB	1988,89,90,91
Brown, Ken	MCC	1960
Brown, Kenneth	MTR	1942
Brown, Kenneth	MTR	1959,60

Brown, Lewis	MTR	1899,00
Brown, Lloyd	MGO	1946,47
Brown, Mekelayaie	WTR	1991,92
Brown, Michelle	WSW	1985,86,87,88
Brown, Neil	MTN	1988,89,90
Brown, Park L.	MTR	1939,40,41
	MCC	1938,40
Brown, Randall	MGY	1966,67
Brown, Thurston	MTN	1962
Brown, Wallace W.	MTR	1919
Brown, William D.	FB	1958,59,60
	MTR	1959,60,61
Brownell, Dean G.	MTR	1923,24,25
Browning, Richard	MGY	1953,54
Brownlee, John J.	FN	1926
Brownlow, Darrick	FB	1987,88,89,90
Brownridge, Enis	WR	1970,71,72
Brownstein, Harold	WR	1956,57,59
Brozek, Gary	BB	1982
Brubaker, James C.	MTR	1967,68,69
Bruce, Ben	MGO	1989,90,91,92
Bruder, Henry L.	MTR	1937
Bruene, Carol	WCC	1985,86
	WTR	1985
Bruin, W. W.	BB	1931
Brundage, Avery	MBK	1908
	MTR	1908,09
Brundage, Martin D.	FB	1901
	MTR	1899,00
Brunkow, N. F.	WR	1912,13
Brunton, Richard W.	MTR	1936,37,38
Brzuszkiewicz, Michael	FB	1976
Buchanan Jr., Gordon	MTR	1920
Buchanan, Lisa	WTN	1980,81
Bucher, E. G.	MGY	1913,14
Buchheit, George C.	MTR	1919
	FB	1918
Buck, P. E.	MGY	1913,14
Buck, Steve	MGY	1977
Bucklin, Robert	FB	1969,70,71
Buenzli, James J.	MGO	1980,81,82,83
Buford, Tonja	WTR	1990,91,92,93
Bujan, George P.	FB	1943,44,45
Bukenas, Dale R.	VB	1974
Bulaw, Adolph	MSW	1935
Bullard, Edward W.	MTR	1911,13
Bullard, Robert I.	MTR	1895,96
Bulow, Dan	FB	1977
Bundy, Herman W.	FB	1901,02
Bunkenberg, Bruce	MBK	1958,59,60
Bunn, Charles M.	BB	1910
Bunning, Walter F.	MTR	1928,29
Bunting, William L.	FN	1923
Bunton, F. L.	BB	1887
Burch, Clarence	MTR	1967,68,69
Burchfield, Brian	FB	1986,87
Burden, Joe	MGO	1970,71,72,73
Burdick, Lloyd S.	FB	1927,28,29
	WR	1930
Burgard, Peter	FB	1980,81,82
Burgener, David B.	MTR	1979,71,72
Burgeson, Lennart B.	MGY	1937
Burgess, Oscar W.	MTR	1916
Burgess, Sandra	WTN	1980,81
Burgess, Sharon	WTN	1979,80
Burghardt, Charles A.	MTR	1945
Burgoon, David W.	MCC	1915
	MTR	1916
Burke, Brigid	WSW	1994
Burke, Christopher J.	FN	1989,90,91,92
Burke, Ralph	MTR	1912,14
Burke, William H.	MTR	1894,95
Burkett, Aspen	WTR	1995
Burkhart, George H.	MTR	1929
Burkholder, Robert	MTN	1967
Burkland, Theodore L.	FB	1896
Burleigh, C. H.	MTR	1898
Burlingame, Keith	FB	1978
Burman, Jon	FB	1988
Burmaster, Jack	MBK	1945,46,47,48
Burns, Bob	FB	1968,69,70
Burns, Bruce	WR	1965,66
Burns, Joesph K.	MTR	1910,11
Burns, Sheila	WTN	1984,85,86,87
Burrell, William G.	FB	1957,58,59
Burris, Merlyn G.	FB	1938
Burroughs, Wilbur G.	FB	1904,05,06
	MTR	1905,06,07
Burton, Gary	MSW	1961,62,63
Burwash, Arthur E.	MTR	1911
Burwell, Bill	MBK	1961,62,63
Burwell, Robert	WR	1945

Busboom, Les M.	MBK	1967,68,69
Buscemi, Joseph A.	FB	1946,47
Busche, Justin	BB	1995
Bush, Alexander T.	MTR	1916
Bush, Arthur W.	FB	1891
Bush, Laura	VB	1987,88,89,90
Bush, Roger	MTN	1940
Bushche, Fred	FN	1965
Bushell, Tim	MBK	1974
Bushnell, Howard	BB	1905,06,07
Bussey, Charles	WR	1926
Buster, William E.	MTR	1945,46,48,49
Butkovich, Anthony J.	FB	1941,42
Butkovich, William	BB	1944,45
	FB	1943,44,45
Butkus, Mark	FB	1980,81,82,83
Butkus, Richard M.	FB	1962,63,64
Butler, Charles	FB	1954,56
Butler, F. L.	BB	1895,96
Butler, Paul L.	MGY	1939
Butt, Harley M.	MTR	1912,13,14
Button, Lyle A.	FB	1947,48,49
Butts, Larry	MGY	1968,69,70
Butzer, Glenn D.	BB	1910,11
	FB	1908,09,10
Buwick, Cynthia	WTN	1977,78,79
Buwick, Eugene	MTN	1949,50,51
Buzick, John W.	MGO	1941
Buzwick, John W.	BB	1908,10
Byars, Mary	WSW	1978
Bye, Gary L.	FN	1975
Byman, Ellis	SOC	1928
Byrd, Darryl	FB	1981,82
Byrd, Rodney	FB	1993,94
Byrne, Lee	MTR	1896,97,98

C

Cabeen, Joshua	MTR	1897
Cabell, Kevin	FB	1976
Cable, Dave	MGO	1991,93,94,95
Cadle, R.	MGY	1932,33
Cadwallader, Douglas P.	MTR	1904
Cady, G. H.	MSW	1930
Cahill, James	BB	1979
Cahill, Leo H.	FB	1948,49,50
Caiazza, Theodore	MTR	1957,58
	MBK	1957
Cajet, Arnold	MSW	1954,55,56
Calabrese, Vanessa	VB	1975,76,77
Calderisi, Michael	FN	1987,88,89,90
Caldwell, Randolph	MTR	1917
Calhoun, Dean	MGY	1966,67
Calisch, Richard W.	MTR	1950,51,52
Callaghan, Richard T.	BB	1963,64,65
	WR	1963,64,65
	FB	1962,63,64
Callahan, John H.	BB	1936,37,38
Callahan, Phil	WR	1982,84,85,86
Calvetti, Joseph A.	MGY	1942,48,49
Calza, Tom	BB	1968,69
Cameron, John K.	FN	1952,53
Camp, William F.	FN	1958
Campbell, Albert	WR	1928
Campbell, Allison	WGO	1975
Campbell, Alvin C.	MTR	1988,89
Campbell, Charles E.	FN	1959,60,61
Campbell, Charles M.	BB	1941,42
Campbell, Laverne C.	MTR	1944
Campbell, Michelle	WGO	1984,85,87
Campbell, Robert	MCC	1942
Campbell, Robert A.	FB	1939
Campbell, Robert S.	MGO	1938
Campbell, Tracy	FB	1973,74
Campoli, Douglas	FN	1983,84,85
Campos, Lou	FB	1984,85,86,87
Canan, Rich	BB	1985
Canino, Toni	WSW	1983,84
Cann, Fremont G.	BB	1928
	MBK	1928
Cannon, James	MGY	1951
Cannon, Ward C.	MTR	1921,22
Cantwell, Francis R.	FB	1934,35
Caparilli, Rich	BB	1986,87,88,89
Capel, Bruce	FB	1962,63,64
Capelle, Mark	MCC	1981
	MTR	1982
Capen, Bernard C.	FB	1902
Caraker, Lori	WSW	1995
Carbonari, Gerald M.	FB	1965,66
Carek, Frank	WR	1934
Carey, Robert	MSW	1955,56

Les Busboom played two seasons under Coach Harry Combes and two under Harv Schmidt.

Carie, Doris	WBK	1987,88,89,90
Carius, Allen B.	MTR	1962,63,64
	MCC	1962,63
Carlini, Perry	FB	1983,84
Carlisle, Amy	WCC	1989
Carlson, Carl E.	FN	1952
Carlson, Clifford E.	BB	1933,34
Carlson, David A.	FN	1970,71
Carlson, Edward H.	IHO	1939
Carlson, Herbert N. R.	MTR	1922
Carlson, Jan	WBK	1975,76
Carlson, Ralph O.	MGO	1937,38,39
Carlson, Roger W.	MGO	1982
Carmichael, Carol	WBK	1977,78,79
Carmichael, Patty	WGY	1977
Carmichael, Tom	MBK	1974,75
Carmien, Tab	FB	1978,80
Carnahan, David H.	BB	1892,93,95,96
Carnahan, Franklin G.	BB	1890,91,92
Carnes, Brian	MSW	1978
Carney, Charles R.	MBK	1920,21,22
	FB	1918,19,20,21
Caroline, J. C.	FB	1953,54
Carpenter, Chris	FB	1986
Carpenter, Hubert V.	BB	1896,97
Carpenter, Kenneth	WR	1934,35,36
Carpenter, Lee	MSW	1968,69,70
Carpenter, Tom	MSW	1972,73,74
Carper, Robert J.	MTR	1977,78,79
Carr Jr., H. Eugene	FB	1958
Carr, Bridget	WGY	1980,81,82
Carr, Chris	FB	1979
Carr, Renee	WTR	1986,87,88,90
Carr, Robert J.	MTR	1928,29,30
Carrington, Michael	FB	1978,79,80,81
Carrison, Henry C.	MTR	1931
Carrithers, Ira T.	BB	1906,07
	FB	1904
	MTR	1905,07
Carroll, Charles	MTR	1918,19
Carroll, Robert C.	MTR	1932,33,34
Carso, L.	WR	1931
Carson, Paul H.	FB	1931
	MTR	1932
Carson, W. Howard	FB	1934,37
Carstensen, Bob	MSW	1988,89,90,91

Darrick Brownlow was a first-team All-American in 1990 for the Illini.

Tony Clements lettered in football and also was a member of the Illini basketball team.

Jack Chamblin, a football letter winner in 1953 and '54, has been a generous contributor to the UI athletic program.

Name	Sport	Years
Carter, Archie	FB	1982,83
Carter, Dale	MTR	1923,24
Carter, Donald H.	FB	1911
Carter, Vincent	FB	1978
Carter, W. E.	MGO	1928
Carter, William S.	MTR	1915,16
Carver, Dorothy	VB	1974,75,76
Carver, Dorothy	WTR	1977,79,80
Cary, M. C.	MSW	1920
Case Jr., John R.	MTR	1912,13
Cashman, Dennis	MGO	1965,66,67
Cashmore, Richard	BB	1948
Caskey, George R.	MTR	1919
Casner, Sidney	MTR	1913
Cason, Robert	MGY	1961
Cassady, Donald	MGO	1951,52,53
Cassell, Charles W.	SOC	1927
Cast, Dick L.	FB	1961
Castator, Alan	MSW	1965,66,67
Castelo, Chip	MGO	1972,74
Castelo, Robert E.	FB	1936,37,38
Castle, Jennifer	WGY	1978
Castles, Bryan	MSW	1980,83
Catalano, Phil	BB	1959,60
Cathrall, Jodi	WTN	1989
Catlett, Stan	WR	1965
Catlin, James M.	FB	1952
Causey, Juan	WR	1978,79
Cavallo, Ernest S.	BB	1938,39
Cave, James A.	MTR	1929,30,31
Cawley, Kevin J.	FN	1977,78,79,80
Cawley, Mitchell	BB	1980
Cayou, F. M.	MTR	1900,01,02
Celaya, Robert	MTR	1931
Cepulis, Wade	MCC	1983,84,85
Cermack, Jerome	MBK	1907
Cerney, Bill	FB	1974,75,76
Cha, Henry	FN	1964
Chadsey, C. P.	MSW	1923,24,25
Chadwick, Michael	MGO	1979,80,81,82
Chaio, Richard	FN	1983,84,85
Chalcraft, Kenneth G.	FB	1961
Chamberlain, Jess	WR	1937
Chambers, Alan R.	MTR	1928
Chambers, Cynthia	WTN	1988,89,90,91
Chambers, Franklin	MTN	1961
Chambers, Robert L.	MTR	1929,30
Chamblin, W. Jack	FB	1953,54
Champagne, Brannon	BB	1984,85,86
Chamy, Luis F.	SOC	1927,28
Chance, W. W.	MGY	1931
Chandler, George A.	MTR	1922
Chaney, Dennis	MSW	1971
Chanowitz, Harry	MTN	1938,39,40
Chapman, E. N.	MSW	1915
Chapman, John	MSW	1963,64
Chapman, Ralph D.	FB	1912,13,14
Chapple, Steve	MGY	1967,68,69
Charles, William W.	FB	1936
Charpentier, Mary	WGY	1978,79,80,81
Charpier, Leonard L.	FB	1916,17
Chase, Dean	MSW	1912
Chase, Morton E.	BB	1879
Chatten, Melville C.	MTR	1893,94
Chattin, Ernest P.	FB	1930
Chaudhuri, Mickey	MTN	1991,92
Check, Robert	WR	1974,75,76,77
Cheeley, Kenneth D.	FB	1940,41
Chen, Yu Hwa	SOC	1927

Name	Sport	Years
Cheney, Howard L.	MTR	1912
Cheriel, Ricardo	MGY	1990,91,92,93
Cherney, Eugene K.	FB	1957,58
Cherot, Anthony	MTR	1969,70
	MCC	1968
Cherry, Robert S.	FB	1940,41
Cherry, W. L.	MGY	1930,31
Chervinko, Paul	BB	1931,32,33
Chester, Guy S.	FB	1894
Chhay, Vuthik	MGY	1991,92,93
Chiappe, Carole	WSW	1978,79
Chiappe, David	MSW	1982,83,84
Chiprin, William	FN	1935,36,42
Chirico, Doug	WR	1975,76
Chirico, Phillip	WR	1975,76
Chirico, Randy	WR	1973
Chiricosta, Anthony	MTN	1976,77,78,79
Cho, David J.	FN	1990,91,92,93
Choi, Charles Y.	FN	1982,83
Christ, G. P.	MSW	1920
Christensen, Bob	BB	1987,88,89,90
Christensen, Paul G.	FB	1916
Christensen, Gary	MSW	1970
Christian, W. A.	MGY	1929,31
Christiansen, Donald W.	BB	1938
Christiansen, Harold A.	MTR	1932,33
Christopher, Ron	BB	1964
Chronis, Tony	FB	1973
Chrystal, Jeff	FB	1973,74,75
Cianciarulo, Howard	WR	1962
Ciaramelli, Robert	BB	1943
Ciccarelli, Nicole	WGY	1994,95
Cies, Jerry B.	FB	1944,45
Cimack, Jeffrey	BB	1975
Ciszek, Ray A. C.	FB	1943,44,45,46
Citron, Abraham	WR	1935
Ciucci, Michelle	WSW	1990
Claar, Elmer A.	MTR	1913,14
Clancy, Timothy	MTR	1987,88,89,90
Clapp, David	BB	1979
Clapper, Kenneth	MTN	1942,43
Clarida, Doug	MBK	1992
Clarida, T. W.	MTR	1915
Clark, A. C.	MTR	1892,93,94,95
Clark, Arthur S.	BB	1883
Clark, George (Potsy)	FB	1914,15
	BB	1915,16
Clark, Howard	MTR	1894,95,96,97
Clark, Keith	MTN	1945
Clark, Robert	FB	1922
Clark, Ronald	FB	1949,50
Clark, Ryan	MTN	1991,92,93
Clark, Shelly	MBK	1994,95
Clark, Tom	MGO	1961
Clarke, Curtis	FB	1983,85
Clarke, Edwin B.	FB	1890
	MTR	1890
Clarke, Frederick W.	FB	1890
	MTR	1890
Clarkson, James F.	BB	1888,89,90
Clasey, Jody	VB	1979,80,81,82
Clatfelter, Jack	MTN	1943
Claycomb, Gordon	MGY	1959
Claypool, Austin	WR	1928,29
Claypool, Mark J.	MTR	1978,79,80,81
Clayton, Clark M.	FB	1898,99
	MTR	1899
Clear, Samuel	FB	1979,80
Cleary, James	MGY	1951
Clements, Chip	MTN	1969,70,71
Clements, John H.	FB	1930
Clements, Jesse (Tony)	FB	1968,69
Clemons, Rennie	MBK	1991,92,93
Clemons, Robert	MSW	1952,53,54
Clery, Colleen	WTN	1976,77
Cleveland, Clarence	MCC	1937
Cline, Dick	MCC	1954
Clinton, Anita	WBK	1993,94
Clinton, Edgar M.	FB	1896
	MTR	1896,97
Clinton, Edgar T.	FN	1928
Clisham, Mary Beth	WGY	1991,92,93,94
Clooney, Donald	MSW	1949,50,51
Close, Greg	WR	1981,82
Close, Tim	MCC	1977,78
Clow, Robert J.	MGY	1940
Coady, Tom	FB	1979,80
Coats, Wayne	MGY	1968,69
Cobb, C. Caton	MGY	1941,42
Cobb, Glenn	FB	1987,88
Cobb, Laurence J.	MTR	1970,71,72
	MCC	1969,70,71

Name	Sport	Years
Cobb, Levi	MBK	1977,78,79,80
Cochran, Phillip	BB	1969
Cochran, R. Bruce	WR	1978,81,82
Cockrell, Paul F.	MGO	1927
Coffeen, Harry C.	FB	1896,97
	MTR	1895,96
Coffey, Lawrence	BB	1984,85
Cogdal, Harry F.	BB	1913,14,15
Coghill, John R.	MGO	1938
Cohen, Larry	MBK	1972
Cohen, Tsafrir	FN	1991,92,93
Cohick, Emmitt	BB	1989,90
Cohn, P. E.	SOC	1933
Cohn, Richard D.	FN	1953,54
Cohn, Stuart L.	FN	1960,61,62
Colangelo, Gerald J.	BB	1960
	MBK	1960,61,62
Colbrese, William L.	MTR	1969
Colby, Greg	BB	1972,73,74
	FB	1971,72,73
Cole, Audrey	WCC	1986
Cole, E. Joseph	FB	1949,50,51
Cole, Jerry	FB	1969,70
Cole, Jewett	FB	1935,36
Cole, Mike	FB	1992,93
Cole, Terry	FB	1980,81,82,83
Coleman, DeJustice	FB	1957,58,59
Coleman, Delbert L.	MTR	1959,60
Coleman, James	FB	1976,77
Coleman, Norris	FB	1969
Coleman, Richard A.	MTR	1950,51,52
Coleman, Roger	FB	1973,74
Collias, Emily	WGY	1984,85,86
Collier, Glenn	FB	1969,70,71
Collier, Steve	FB	1982
Collins, John H.	MTR	1922,23
Collins, John J.	FB	1962
Collins, Michael E.	FB	1976
Collins, Tyrone	FB	1993
Collins, Walter	MBK	1921,22
Collora, N. A.	MSW	1928
Collymore, Karen	VB	1979,80,81,82
Colton, Seth W.	BB	1880
Columbo, J. B.	WR	1911,13
Colwell, Gary	MSW	1978

Jerry Colangelo, president and CEO of the NBA's Phoenix Suns, was an Illini basketball and baseball letterman.

Name	Sport	Years
Combes, Harry	MBK	1935,36,37
Compton, Norton	WR	1952,53
Conda, Reba	WTR	1977
Conda, Rolanda	WTR	1982,83,86
Condon, V. H.	MSW	1922,23
Confer, Warren	MTN	1938
Congreve, George	MSW	1973,74,75,76
Conlan, Jack	MTN	1981,82,83
Conley, Frank C.	BB	1938
Connell, Byron	MGO	1955,56
Conner, Nick	MBK	1971,72,73
Conover, Robert J.	FB	1930
Conrad, Joseph A.	MSW	1941
Conradt, Greg	FB	1988
Conte, Randy	BB	1979,80,81,82
Contratto, James	SOC	1930
Conway, Anne	VB	1989,90,91
Cook, David F.	FB	1931,33
	MTR	1932,33,34
Cook, Ed	MSW	1964
Cook, Eugene	FN	1915
Cook, Gary	BB	1973

Carmel Corbett was selected as the 1995 Big Ten Conference Medal of Honor winner.

Cook, James F.	BB	1900,01,02,03
	FB	1898,00,01,02
Cook, James W.	FB	1891,92
	MTR	1892
Cook, Jeff	MTN	1968,69,70
Cook, Jennie	VB	1994
Cook, Louis P.	BB	1903,04
Cook, William D.	MTR	1947,48
Cooledge, Marshall M.	FB	1925
Cooley, William M.	MTR	1945,46
Cooper Jr., Paul H.	FB	1893,94,95
	BB	1892,94,95,96
Cooper, Norm	FB	1970
Cope, Lorin	WR	1915,16,17
Cope, Walter A.	MTR	1911,12,13
	MCC	1912
Copeland, J. R.	MSW	1925
Copher, Chad	FB	1991,92,93,94
Corbett, Carmel	WTR	1992,93,94,95
Corbitt, Jon	MGY	1995
Corcoran, Maura	WTN	1988
Cordes, Rob	MTN	1993
Cordova, Randy	BB	1971,72,73
Corley, Joseph W.	MTR	1952,53,54
Corneluis, William	MTR	1970
Correll, Charles R.	MGO	1956,57,58
Correll, Walter K.	FB	1941,42
	MTR	1942
Corso, Kara	WGY	1990,91,92,93
Cortesi, Bob	BB	1971,72,73
Cortez, Ralph	WR	1978,80,81
Cortis, Frederic B.	MTR	1911,12,13
Cortis, R. P.	MSW	1923
Cosneck, Barney	WR	1932,33,34
Cossette, Bryan	MTN	1993
Costar, Lloyd	MTR	1912
Costello, Sonya	WSW	1984,85,86,87
Costigan, Carrie	WTN	1986,87,88,89
Coughlin, John A.	MTR	1923
Coulter, Heidi	VB	1994
Counts, John E.	FB	1959
Coupe Jr., Henry J.	IHO	1943
Courter, Anson O.	MTR	1927
Coutchie, Stephen A.	FB	1922,23
Covington, Jim	FB	1981
Cox, Fred	FB	1990,91,92

Cox, Henry R.	BB	1917
Cox, Jeff	MCC	1975
Coxworth, James L.	MTR	1974,75,76
Cozen, Douglas	FB	1978,79
Craig, Hal	MBK	1946
Craig, Herbert W.	FN	1927
Crain, Delmar	MTN	1939,40
Cramer, Curt	MSW	1968,69,70
Cramer, Willard M.	FB	1937,38
Crane, D. W.	MSW	1916
Crane, Donna	WTN	1980
Crane, Dudley	MBK	1914
Crane, Robert L.	MTR	1942,43
Crane, Russell J.	FB	1927,28,29
	WR	1928,29
Crangle, Walter F.	BB	1921
	FB	1919,20,21
Craven, Forest, I.	FB	1932
Cravens, Robert D.	FB	1961
Crawford, David	FN	1972
Crawford, Heath	MGO	1987,88,89,90
Crawford, Ken	BB	1993,94
Crawford, Walter C.	FB	1923
Crawmer, Charly	MTN	1993,94
Crenshaw, Derrick	WR	1990
Cress Jr., John M.	MGY	1939,40
Crews, Randy	BB	1968,69,70
	MBK	1968,69,70
Cronin, Rosanne	WSW	1980,81,82,83
Cronin, Sheila	WSW	1981
Croninger, Carl	PO	1939
Cronk, Howard	MBK	1940
Crosby, F. H.	MSW	1934
Cross, Charles W.	BB	1889,90,91,92
Cross, Gene	MBK	1993,94
Crossley, Clarence F.	BB	1920,22
Crotser, Max	BB	1959,60,61
Crouse, Dave	BB	1964,65,66
Crowe, R. H.	MGO	1930,31,32
Crum, Edward	WR	1933
Crum, Tom	FB	1968
Crumpton, Robert	FB	1991,92,93,94
	MTR	1994
Crutchfield-Tyus, Terra	WTR	1993,94,95
Cruz, Ken	FB	1983,84
Cryer, Henry	MTR	1951,52,55
Cryer, Walter	MGY	1950,52
	MSW	1951,52
Cuchran, Don	BB	1988,89,90
Culbertson, Jon	MGY	1954,55,56
Cullen, Joe	MCC	1980
Cullinan, Duane A.	MTR	1935,36,37
Culp Jr., John D.	MGO	1947,49
Culp, John D.	MTR	1914,15,16
Cummings, Barton A.	FB	1932,33,34
	MTR	1933
Cummins, J. R.	WR	1914
Cundiff, Monica	WBK	1989,90,91,92
Cunningham, Mandy	WBK	1991,92,93,94
Cunningham, Nancy	WTN	1978
Cunningham, Thomas	PO	1941
Cunz, Robert W.	FB	1945,46,47
Curless, Jerry	MBK	1961
Curran, John	FB	1994
Currier, Donald E.	MTR	1914,15
Curry, Jack C.	FB	1943
Curtis, Joe	FB	1980,81,82
Cushing, Matt	FB	1994
Custardo, Fred	FB	1963,64,65
Cutler, John	WR	1912,13,14
Cutter, Robert L.	MSW	1937
Cutter, Scott C.	MTR	1893
Cutter. W. C.	MSW	1910
Cvik, James	BB	1958,59
Cwiklinshi, Ronald	MGO	1957,58,59
Cyboran, John V.	MGO	1982,83
Cyboran, Steve	MGO	1990

D

D'Ambrosio, Arthur L.	FB	1925,26,27
D'Orazio, Vincent T.	FN	1950,51,52
Dadant, Louis C.	MTR	1899,00
Dadant, Maurice G.	FB	1907
	MBK	1906,07,08
Dahl, Andrew W.	FB	1934
	WR	1934,35
Dahlhein, Bruce	BB	1975,76,77
Dahringer, Homer	MBK	1912,13
Dailey, Bo	MTR	1993
Daill, Kris	WSW	1976,77,78
Dalbeck, Leon	BB	1927
Dale, Charlene	WTR	1980,81,82

Mandy Cunningham finished her Illini basketball career as UI's No. 3 all-time leading scorer.

Dalesandro, Mark	BB	1987,88,89,90
Dallenbach, John W.	MGY	1939
Dallenbach, Karl M.	FB	1909
Dammann, James E.	FN	1954,55,56
Dammers, Clifford R.	FN	1962,63,64
Damos, Donn	FB	1970
Damron, Tim	FB	1981,82
Dancisak, Edward J.	BB	1936
Daniel, Cullen	FB	1980
Daniels, Drew	FB	1990
Daniels, Jay	MBK	1982,83
Danke, Cheryl	WGY	1985
Dankert, William	MTN	1952,53
Danner, Richard M.	MGY	1958
Danosky, Anthony J.	FB	1958
Danzer, John	MGY	1929
Danzer, Warren	FN	1958,59,60
Dardano, Rusty	FB	1981
Darlington, Dan	FB	1969,70,71
Daugherity, Russell S.	MBK	1925,26,27
	FB	1925,26
Daugherty, Troy	WR	1983
Daukus, Anthony	BB	1936
Davey, Tim	MSW	1992
David, Amy	WSW	1992,91
Davidson, Marc	MBK	1992,93
Davies, Carl	MBK	1938
Davies, Richard	MGO	1955
Davies, Richard O.	MTR	1965
Davis, Barbara	WTN	1975,76
Davis, Chester W.	FB	1910,11
Davis, Chris	WR	1981,82,83,84
Davis, George F.	MTR	1893
Davis, James O.	BB	1883
Davis, James T.	MTR	1960
Davis, Jared	MTN	1944,45
Davis, John	BB	1951,52
Davis, John E.	BB	1915,16,17
Davis, John	FB	1966,67
Davis, John	MGY	1956,57,58
Davis, John	MGY	1968,69
Davis, John	MGY	1977,78,79
Davis, Oral L.	FN	1940
Davis, Scott	FB	1983,85,86,87
Davitz, Joel	MTN	1944
Daw, Jessie	WTN	1984,85,87
Daw, Joe	MTN	1981,82
Dawson, Bobby	FB	1986,87
Dawson, George	FB	1922
	MGO	1924
Dawson, Jeff	MBK	1973,74
Dawson, James C.	MBK	1965,66,67
	MTN	1965
Dayiantis, George	MGO	1948,50
Dayton, Devin	VB	1975
Dean, Paul	MTN	1939
DeAno, Jon	WR	1962,63
deBeers, James	MTR	1989,90,91,92
	MCC	1990,91
DeBord, James R.	MSW	1967,68,69
Dechert, Douglas R.	MGO	1981,82
Decker, Gene W.	MTR	1950,51
DeDecker, Darrel	FB	1959,60
DeDecker, Jim	MBK	1971,72
Deeken, Dee Dee	WBK	1987,88,89
DeFalco, Steven	FB	1976
Dehner, Lewis (Pick)	MBK	1935,38,39
Deimling, Keston J.	MBK	1926,27,28
	FB	1927,28
dela Garza, Gabriel	FB	1987
Delact, Joan	WGY	1977
Delaet, Thomas E.	FN	1975,76
Delaney, Donald	MBK	1944,45
Delaney, Robert F.	FB	1956,57
Delismon, Ronald J.	FN	1957,58
Deller, Dick	FB	1961,62,63
DeLong, Edward	MTR	1956,57
DeLong, George	WR	1944
Delveaux, Jack	BB	1958,59
	FB	1956,57,58
DeMarco, Vic	WR	1964
Demmitt, Charles R.	BB	1905,06
DeMoss, Clarence W.	MTR	1953
	FB	1952,53
DeMoulin, Ray	MBK	1944
Dempsey, Terry	WSW	1979,80,81,82
Dennett, Kenneth	MSW	1920,21
Dennis, Mark	FB	1983,84,85,86
Dentino, Greg	FB	1980
Denzler, Mike	MSW	1988
DeOliver, Miguel	FB	1981,82
DePaolis, Carl	BB	1978,80

Mark Dalesandro was a first-team All-America selection in 1990 for the Illini baseball squad.

DePew, Daren	BB	1984
Depken, Gerhard C.	BB	1933
Depler, John C.	FB	1918,19,20
Deputy, Donn	MBK	1974
DePuy, Orval C.	MTR	1905,06
Derby, Sylvester R.	FB	1913,14
Des Enfants, Laura	WTR	1979
Des Enfants, Kate	WSW	1986,87
Des Enfants, Robert E.	FB	1954,55
DeSilva, Gayathri	WTN	1980,81,82,83
Deuchler, Gustave H.	MTR	1918
Deuss, E.	MSW	1927,28
Deutschman, Archie	WR	1937,38,39
Deutschman, F. J.	MGY	1902
DeVelde, H. S.	BB	1900,01,02
Devero, James	BB	1946
Devers, Lynn	WGY	1988,89,90,91
Devor, Forest	WR	1958,59,64
DeVore, Adrian	MTN	1991,92
DeVore, Chris	MTN	1994,95
Dewey, C.	MGY	1928
Dezort, Tom	MBK	1970
Dial, Stephanie	WBK	1990
Diamantos, Tony	MSW	1974,75
Diamond, Arthur S.	FN	1976,77,78
Diamond, Robert N.	MGY	1958
Diamond, Scott	MGY	1988
Dick, C. D.	WR	1915
Dicke, Otto A.	BB	1906,07
Dickenson, Roger	MCC	1925
Dickerson Jr., Charles F.	FB	1961
Dickerson, Marianne	WCC	1979,80,81,82
	WTR	1981,82
Dickinson, Charles F.	MTR	1930,31
Dickinson, Richard J.	MTR	1893
Dickinson, Roger F.	MTR	1926
Dickison, Marc	MCC	1991,92,93
	MTR	1994
Dickson, Kerry	MCC	1979,80,81,83
	MTR	1980,81,82,84
Diedrich, Brian	FB	1974,75,76
Diefenthaler, Robert J.	MTR	1937,38,39
Diehl, Harold A.	BB	1919
Dieken, Doug	FB	1968,69,70
Diener, Walter G.	BB	1902,03,04
Dierkes, Alfred	BB	1952

Former Illini swimmer Jim DeBord is now director of the Peripheral Vascular Laboratory at Peoria's Proctor Hospital.

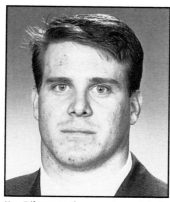

Ken Dilger was the second-round draft pick of the Indianapolis Colts in 1995.

Dietrich, Cathy	WSW	1991,92,93,94
Diettrich, Henry J.	MTR	1942
	MCC	1941
Diewald, Emil	WR	1955
DiFeliciantonio, John	FB	1974,75,76
Diffenbaugh, Harry	BB	1879,80,81
Dilger, Cindy	WBK	1992,93
Dilger, Ken	FB	1991,92,93,94
Dill, Arthur W.	MTR	1893
Dill, Marchoe	WBK	1994,95
Dillavou, Lanny D.	MTR	1986
Dillinger, Harry	FB	1903,04
Dillman, Brian	MTN	1988,89,90
Dillman, Greg	MSW	1988,89
Dillman, Lisa	VB	1987,88,89,90
Dillon, Andrew	MGY	1987,88,89
Dillon, Chester C.	FB	1910,11,12
Dillon, David	FB	1939,40
	MBK	1941
Dillon, Edward	WR	1941
Dillon, Roy H.	MTR	1897
Dilsaver, Carl	MGO	1953,54
Dimit, George	FB	1946
Dimit, Mary	WTR	1976
Dimit, Stacie	WTR	1976
Dintelmann, Robert H.	MTR	1955,56,57
	MCC	1955,56
Dippel, Kathy	VB	1982,83
Dismuke, Mark	FB	1978
Disosway, Mark D.	BB	1907,08
Dittmann, Martha	WSW	1977
Dixon, A.	MGY	1924
Dixon, Michele	WSW	1988,89,90
Dixon, Terence	MSW	1983,84,85,86
Dixon, Wesley	BB	1970,71,72
Dlesk, David C.	MTR	1979,80
Dluzak, Marijo	VB	1974
	WBK	1975,76,77
Dobry, Tim	BB	1994
Dobrzeniecki, Mike	FB	1971
Dobson, Bruce	FB	1971,72,73
Doepel, Robert F.	FB	1920
Dolan, Francis (Frank)	MGY	1949,50,51
Doll, Jill	WSW	1989,90,91,92
Dollahan, Bruce E.	FB	1957,58
Dollins, Matthew	MSW	1989

Bill Edwards served as captain of Coach Harry Combes' Illini basketball team in 1963-64.

Domantay, Gregory	MCC	1982
	MTR	1983
Dombroski, Jack	FB	1975,76
Dombrowski, Robert J.	FB	1984,85
Domitrz, Cheri	WSW	1985,86,87,88
Domko, Joe	WR	1964
Donato, Michelle	WCC	1989,90
Doney, Scott	FB	1979,80
Donnelly, George	FB	1962,63,64
Donnelly, Patrick	FB	1988,89,90
Donnelly, Tyler	FB	1993
Donoghue, R. C.	MTR	1894,99
Donoho, Louie W.	FB	1946
Donohoe, Philip H.	MTR	1920,21
Donohue, John	MSW	1958,59,60
Donohue, Kim	WCC	1994
	WTR	1995
Donovan, Dan	FB	1988,89
Doolen, Bryan	MBK	1926
Dooley, Dick	MSW	1961,62,63
Dooley, Justin	MGY	1985,86
Dooley, Wilbur	WR	1929,30,31
Doolittle, Areal	FB	1986,87
Dorn, Ernest F.	BB	1927,28,29
	MBK	1927,28,29
Dorr, Dick	FB	1964
Doss, Paul C.	BB	1918,19
Dossey, Doug	MTR	1992,93,94,95
Doster, Robert	MBK	1946,47
Doty, Dick	BB	1971,72
Doud, William O.	FB	1901
Dougherty, Floyd C.	BB	1921,22
Douglas, Art	PO	1935
Douglas, Bruce	MBK	1983,84,85,86
Douglass, Paul W.	FB	1949,50
Douglass, Paula	VB	1984,85,86,87
Douthard, Talib (Ty)	FB	1993,94
Dowd, Donald	MSW	1955,56
Dowdeswell, Marla	WSW	1992,93
Dowdy, Chris	VB	1979,80,81,82
Dowell, Wilbur	WR	1932
Dowling, Ralph	MTR	1944
Downey, David J.	MBK	1961,62,63
Downey, William H.	MTR	1948,49
Downs, H. Burton	MTR	1938,39,40
Downs, Robert B.	MTR	1947,48,49,50
	MCC	1947,48,49
Downs, Roger	MTN	1946,47
Doxey, Samuel	FB	1891
Doyle, Russell	BB	1938
Dozier, Benjamin A.	MTR	1970,71,72
Drake, Elmo S.	MTR	1911
Drake, Greg	MSW	1988,89,90,91
Drake, Waldo H.	MTR	1911
Draper, E. L.	MGY	1902
Dray, Don	MGO	1973,74,75,76
Drayer, Clarence T.	FB	1921
Drechsler, Russell E.	BB	1939,40,41
Dressen, Mark	BB	1989,90,91,92
Drew, Earl	MBK	1928,29
Drewes, Elizabeth	WCC	1978
	WTR	1976,77,78,79
Driemeyer, Dan	MSW	1971
Driscoll, Denny	FB	1970
Driscoll, John	MSW	1944
Drish, John W.	MBK	1939,40,41
	BB	1939,40,41
Drummond, Becky	WGY	1994
Drury, Ian	WR	1987,88
Druz, Dave	MSW	1972,74,75
Dubrish, Bob	FB	1973
Ducato, Phil	WR	1987
Dudas, Daniel	BB	1954,55,56
Dudley, Sue	WSW	1975,76,77
Dufelmeier, Arthur J.	FB	1942,46,47
Dufelmeier, Jamie	FB	1969,70
Duffner, John	BB	1934,35,36
Duffy, Robin	WSW	1979,80,81,82
Duffy, Walter	MCC	1979,80,81
Dufresne, Jacques A.	MTR	1933,34,35
	MCC	1932,33,34
Duis, Mike	MBK	1992
Duke, Austin L.	FB	1952
Dulick, Jason	FB	1993,94
Dunbar, Harry B.	MTR	1903
Duncan, Earl J.	MTR	1931
Duncan, James F.	MTR	1926
Dundy, Michael W.	FB	1961,63
	MTR	1962,63
Duner, Sven	MBK	1913,14,15
Dunham, N. C.	MTR	1906,07
Duniec, Brian J.	FB	1962,63,64

Dunlap, Kim	WTR	1983,84,85,86
Dunlap, Ron	MBK	1966,67
Dunlap, Tom	MTN	1968,69,70
Dunn, Clarence L.	MTR	1942,43,47
	MCC	1941,42,46
Dunn, Merle	WR	1952
Dunning, Frank W.	MTR	1905,07
Dupon, Norm	MSW	1962
Dupps, Kris	WBK	1992,93,94,95
Durant, Phillip S.	FB	1921
	BB	1921,23
Durbin, Cathy	WSW	1976
Durdil, Jennifer	WGY	1989,90,92
Durfee, Ted	PO	1934
Durham, Theo	MTR	1995
Durkin, John F.	MTR	1969,70,71
Durkin, Michael K.	MTR	1972,73,74,75
	MCC	1971,72,73,74
Durlacher, Dave	WR	1988,89
Durlacher, Lindsey	WR	1994,95
Durland, Clyde E.	MTR	1903,04
Durrell, Kenneth	FB	1978,79,80
Dusenberry, Paul B.	MTR	1920,21
	MCC	1921
Dusenbury, Marshall V.	FB	1951
Dutcher, James	MBK	1954,55
Dvorak, Gerry	VB	1982
Dvorak, R. F.	MSW	1921
Dwyer, Dave	FB	1979,80,81
Dwyer, Robert	WR	1949,50
Dykstra, Eugene R.	FB	1934,35,36
Dykstra, Greg	MCC	1967,68,69
	MTR	1968,69,70
Dykstra, Larry R.	MTR	1970,71,72
Dysert, Terry	FB	1970
Dystrup, Andrew	BB	1967
Dziedzic, Dave	WR	1993

E

Eads, Robert	BB	1944
Eagerman, Aaron	WR	1995
Earl, Robert	MTN	1976,77,78,79
Eason, Tony	FB	1981,82
East, Warren E.	MTR	1910
Easter, Robert A.	FB	1961,62,63
Easterbrook, James C.	FB	1940
Easterbrook, John W.	FB	1958,59,60
Eastin, Edward M.	MTR	1966
Eaton, Carol	WGO	1979
Eaton, Jane	WGO	1979
Eberhardy, Richard	MSW	1957,58,59,60
Eberle, Mimi	WGY	1980
Eberly, Mike	MTN	1991,92
Echols, Holly	MGY	1949
Echternacht, T. J.	WR	1930
Eckburg, David	MCC	1990,92,93,94
	MTR	1994,95
Eckenroad, Susanne	WSW	1981
Eckert, Vernon M.	MTR	1934,35
Eddleman, T. D. (Dike)	MBK	1947,48,49
	FB	1946,47,48
	MTR	1943,46,47,48,49
Edgren, Thomas	WR	1974,75
Edidin, Norman	MTN	1941
Edison, Markwood	WR	1933
Edwards, Charles	FB	1994
Edwards, Charles F.	MTR	1940,42
Edwards, David	FB	1980,82,83,84
Edwards, Don	MGO	1985,86,87,88
Edwards, James B.	BB	1918,19
Edwards, James F.	MTR	1967,68,69
Edwards, Jason	FB	1993,94
Edwards, Jeffrey	MTN	1977,78,79,80
Edwards, Julie	VB	1991,92,93,94
Edwards, Richard	MGO	1978,80
Edwards, Robert W.	MGY	1937,38
Edwards, Steve	MTR	1973
Edwards, William R.	MBK	1962,63,64
Eggers, Mary	VB	1985,86,87,88
Ehizuelen, Charlton O.	MTR	1974,75,76,77
Ehlers, Norman F.	MTR	1958
Ehnborn, Gustave B.	SOC	1927,28,29
Ehni, Ralph E.	FB	1938,39,40
Eichelberger, Tony	BB	1960,61,62
Eichmeier, Katy	WSW	1976
Eichner, Astrid	WTN	1987,88,90
Eichorn, Greg	FB	1988,89,90,91
Eicken, James H.	MTR	1976,77,78,79
	MCC	1975,76,77,78
Eickholt, Diane	WBK	1980,81,82,83,84
Eickman, Gary	FB	1963,64,65
Eilbracht, Lee P.	BB	1943,46,47

Julie Edwards earned first-team All-Big Ten honors for the Illini volleyball team.

Ekstrom, Lee	MSW	1969
Elbl, Michael	MTN	1967,68
Elder, R. M.	MTR	1903
Elders, Gerald W.	MTR	1940,41
Eldredge, L. E.	MSW	1924,25
Eliason, John	MGY	1964,65,66
Elkin, David	MGY	1993,94,95
Ellerbeck, Ron	MGO	1960
Elliott, John A.	MTR	1984,85,86,87
	FB	1984,85
Ellis, Donald C.	FB	1949
Ellis, Elias L.	MSW	1937,38
Ellis, George H.	BB	1883,84,85
Ellsworth, Sam	FB	1983,84,86,87
Elsen, Virginia G.	WCC	1981
	WTR	1982
Elsner, Bernard W.	FB	1950,52
Elting, Donald N.	FB	1938,39
Elwell, Dan	MBK	1916
Ely, Graham	PO	1941
Ely, Warren G.	MTR	1947,48
Emerick, Bill	BB	1971
Emery, Eugene	MGO	1944,45
Emery, Robert S.	MTR	1918,19,20
Emmons, Bob	WR	1931,32,33
Emmons, David	WR	1939
Emmons, James	WR	1940
Emrich, Jon B.	MTR	1982
Ems, Clarence E.	FB	1917,20
Enck, James A.	MTR	1964,65,66
Engel, Elmer H.	FB	1940,41,42
Engel, Greg	FB	1990,91,92,93
Engelhorn, Rich	MCC	1966
Engels, Donald J.	FB	1949,50,51
England, Joseph	MGO	1960,61,62
Engle, David	BB	1970,71,72
English, E. C.	MTR	1899,00
English, Frank J.	BB	1917,20
Engstrom, DeWayne	MSW	1980
Engvall, Phillip W.	BB	1929
Enochs, Claude D.	FB	1897
	MTR	1896,97,98
Enochs, Delbert R.	MTR	1898
Ensalaco, Robert	MGY	1964
Ensslin, Sabine	WTN	1989,90,91

Don Engels lettered in 1949, '50, and '51 for Coach Ray Eliot's football team.

Deon Flessner was a varsity basketball letter winner in 1966 and '67.

Epkins, Joe	MTN	1958,59,60
Epps, Nick	FB	1982
Epstein, Ralph J.	FN	1932,33,34
Erb, Bruce	FB	1967,68,69
Ericks, John	BB	1986,87,88
Erickson, Carl V.	BB	1925
Erickson, Keith	MSW	1984,85
Erickson, Richard J.	FB	1965,66,67
Erickson, William	MBK	1947,48,49,50
Erlandson, Jim	FB	1981,82
Ernst, Donald W.	FB	1951,52,53
Erwin, Frank K.	MGY	1973,74,75,76
Erwin, John R.	MSW	1936
Essick, Raymond	MSW	1955
Essick, Raymond	MSW	1978,79,80,81
Esslinger, Paul	WR	1922
Estes, Raymond A.	MTR	1975,76,77,78
Estey, Jill	WBK	1990,91,92,93
Etnyre, Roy E.	MTR	1930,32
Etzbach, W. H.	MSW	1930
Evans Jr., Harry	MTR	1923,24,25
Evans, David P.	FN	1964,65,66

Evans, Edwin R.	BB	1907
Evans, John C.	FB	1930,31
Evans, Paul B.	MTR	1930,31
	MCC	1929,30
Evans, Robert H.	MTR	1893,94,95
Evans, Terry L.	MGO	1966,67
Evans, Wendy	WGO	1992,93,94
Everaert, Christine	WSW	1992,93
Evers, Walter A. (Hoot)	BB	1939
	MTR	1940
	MBK	1940
Eyer, Lawrence	BB	1975,76,77

F

Faford, Ann	WTN	1976,77,78
Fairbanks, Jamie	MGO	1991,92,93,94
Faircloth, S. E.	MSW	1917,20
Fairfield, David	MCC	1925,27
	MTR	1927,28
Fairfield, Kevin	MGO	1987,88,89,90
Fairweather, Charles A.	FB	1901,02,03,04
	MTR	1903
Falcon, Dee Dee	VB	1981
Falkenberg, G. V.	MSW	1920
Falkenburg, Fred P.	BB	1900,01,02
Falkenstein, Elry G.	FB	1952,53
Falkenstein, Robert R.	FB	1940
Farmer, Alan	MTN	1952
Farnham, Brad	MBK	1974,75
Farr, Alvin I.	BB	1909
Farrar, Kelli	WGY	1995
Farrington, Charles E.	BB	1938
Fasules, James W.	MTR	1971,72,73,74
Fay, Richard B.	FB	1936,37
Fazzini, Pat	BB	1974,75,76,77
Feagin, Steve	FB	1989,90,91,92
Fearey, Hiram D.	SOC	1928
Fearn, Ronald R.	FB	1961,62,63
Fee, Richard M.	IHO	1939
Feeheley, Tom	FB	1974
Feigenbutz, Vince	BB	1952,53,54
Feinstein, Victor	MGY	1976,77,78,79
Feldman, Ed	MTR	1968
Feldman, Marla	WSW	1975,76
Feldman, Stanley	BB	1948,49

Felichio, Francis (Bud)	BB	1960,61,62
Fell, Milan T.	MTR	1925,26
Felmley, John	MBK	1917,20
Fencl, Fred	MBK	1934
Fencl, George S.	BB	1930,31,32
	MBK	1930,31,32
	SOC	1929,30,31
Fenske, Greg	MGY	1971,72,73
Ferdinand, Ken	MBK	1976,77
Fernandez, Juana	WTR	1985,86,87,88
Ferranti, Louis	IHO	1942
Ferrari, Patrick	WR	1977,78
Ferrari, Ron	FB	1980,81
Ferreira, Al	WR	1983
Ferrill, Dent	WR	1911
Fessenden, Douglas A.	MTR	1922,24
Fessenden, Ralph J.	MTR	1952,53,54,55
Fetherston, J. M.	WR	1913
Feuerbach, William J.	BB	1892
Ffitch, Peter B.	MCC	1980,81
	MTR	1982
Field, David A.	MGY	1939,40
Field, David E.	MTR	1917
Fieldhouse Jr., George	IHO	1939,40
Fieldhouse, Jim	MSW	1970,71,72,73
Fields, David W.	MTR	1921
Fields, Kenneth E.	FB	1928
Fields Jr., Willis E.	FB	1965,66,67b
Fifield, C. W.	MSW	1916
Filippo, Richard	BB	1980,81,82
Filips, Donna	WTR	1975
Fillipan, John	BB	1976
Fina, John	MGY	1948,49
Fina, Joseph	MGY	1947,48,49,50
Fina, Louis R.	MGY	1940,41,42
Fina, Paul	MGY	1939,40,41
Finch, James	FB	1985,86
Finis, Jerry	FB	1974,75,76
Finis, Marty	FB	1980
Finke, Jeff	FB	1987,88,89,90
Finn, Richard G.	BB	1926,27,28
Finn, Robert L.	BB	1941,42
Finney, Bruce	MCC	1971
	MTR	1972
Finney, Damon W.	MTR	1975
Finzer, David	FB	1977,78
Fiore, Phillip J.	MTR	1977
Fiorini, Tim	WR	1978
Firnhaber, Martha	VB	1988
Fischer, George	BB	1947,48
Fischer, John	FB	1934
Fischer, Louis E.	FB	1895,96,97
Fiser, Chuck	MGO	1985,86,87
Fish Jr., C. M.	MGO	1927,28
Fish, Julian L.	MTR	1914
Fisher, Arthur E.	MGY	1935,36
Fisher, Ben	MTN	1948
Fisher, F. L.	MSW	1925,26,27
Fisher, Fred D.	FB	1925
Fisher, Leon	FB	1986
Fisher, Ralph M.	MTR	1933
	MCC	1933
Fisher, Shane	FB	1992,93,94
Fisher, William	FB	1975
Fit, Stan	FB	1985,86,87,88
Fitch, Horatio M.	MTR	1922,23
Fitz, Eugene	WR	1928
Fitzgerald, Joseph	BB	1954,55
Fitzgerald, Richard J.	FB	1963
Fix, John	MSW	1957,58,59
Flachmann, Charles O.	MSW	1933,34,35
Flachmann, John M.	MSW	1941
Flanders, J. A.	MSW	1909
Flannery, James M.	MTR	1977,79
	MCC	1979
Flannigan, Kathy	WBK	1977,78,79,80
Fleager, Clarence E.	BB	1898,99
Fleischer, Kenneth	FN	1970,71,73
Fleischmann, Gayle	WGY	1977,78,79,80
Fleming, John D.	MGO	1965,66,67
Flessner, Deon	MBK	1966,67
Flesvig, Christine	WTN	1983,84,85,86
Fletcher, Charles H.	BB	1912,13
Fletcher, Darrin	BB	1985,86,87
Fletcher, Pete	MGO	1969
Fletcher, Ralph E.	FB	1918,19,20
	MBK	1919
Fletcher, Robert H.	FB	1918,19,20
Fletcher, Rodney	MBK	1950,51,52
	MGO	1950
Fletcher, Tom	BB	1962
Fletemeyer, Richard	MSW	1957,59,60

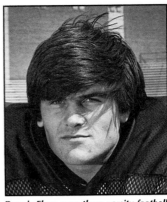

Dennis Flynn won three varsity football letters at Illinois.

Flock, Ward J.	BB	1917
Flodin, Lloyd	BB	1961,62,63
Flood, Gerold	MGO	1950,51
Flood, Paul	WR	1929
Flood, William	MGY	1962,63
Florek, Ray	FB	1946
Floreth, John	SOC	1928,29
Florio, A. E.	SOC	1933
Florio, Dave	MSW	1965,66,67
Flostrom, Victor	WR	1922
Floto, E. C.	MTR	1903
Floyd, Thomas	MTR	1951,52,53
Flynn, Dennis P.	FB	1977,78,81
Flynn, James	BB	1954,57,58
Flynn, Katy	WSW	1979,80,81,82
Flynn, Thomas F.	MTR	1893
Foggey, Erik	FB	1989,90,91,92
Foley, Henry J.	MGO	1959
Foley, Richard	MBK	1947,48,49
Follett, Dwight W.	FB	1924
Follmer, Clive	BB	1952,53
	MBK	1951,52,53
Follmer, Mack	MBK	1950,51
Folts, Thomas	MSW	1980,81,82,83
Fontaine, Simone	WSW	1990,91,93
Foor, Doug	WR	1988
Forbes, Stuart F.	FB	1897
Ford, Brian M.	FB	1974,75
Ford, Jay	WR	1993
Ford, Mary	WTR	1981,82,83
Foreman, Paul L.	MTR	1959,60,61
Forhan, Richard M.	FN	1962
Forman, Hamilton M.	MTR	1908
Forman, Marvin N.	MGY	1939
Fornof, J. R.	MGO	1908
Fornof, John	FN	1963
	MSW	1961
Forsberg, Vernon A.	SOC	1932
Forseman, Eric	FB	1981
Forst, Lawrence H.	FB	1943,45
Forsthoefel, Natalie	WGY	1993,94,95
Forsythe, Robert W.	FN	1948,49,50
Forsythe, William	MSW	1957
Fort, Charles	BB	1952,53,54
Forte, Dominic J.	FB	1976
Foskett, Roy M.	MTR	1903,04,05
Foss, William	BB	1967,68,69
Foster, Alfred B.	MTR	1893
Foster, Bruce	MSW	1969
Foster, Dale W.	FB	1952
	MTR	1952,53,54,55
Foster, Douglas	MGO	1962,63,64
Foster, Duane	MTR	1958
Foster, Greg	FB	1978,79,80
Foster, Jed	MBK	1971,72,73
Fouts, L. H.	FB	1893
	MTR	1892,94,95
Fowler, Charles	MBK	1942
Fox, A. L.	MSW	1922,23
Fox, Charles M.	FB	1949,50
Fox, Wylie B.	FB	1962,63,64
Fracaro, Denise	VB	1982,83,84,85
Francis, Frank D.	FB	1899
Francis, Gary	FB	1954,55,56
Francissen, Vern	MCC	1980
Frandsen, Lee R.	MBK	1959,60
	MTR	1959
Frangos, John	BB	1992
Frank, Joseph	MBK	1938,39,40
Franke, Steven C.	FN	1980,81

Kendra Gantt's 49-point performance vs. Kent State in 1983 still stands as UI's single-game scoring record.

Franklin, Murray	BB	1935,36,37
Franklin, Richard	FN	1976,77
Franks, Bruce	MTN	1974,75,76,77
Franks, Mark	MSW	1992
Franks, Robert D.	FN	1941
Franks, Willard G.	FB	1946,47
	MTR	1946
Fransene, Sarah	WSW	1995
Franz, Frederick W.	MTR	1977,78,79,80
Frary, C. Deane	MTR	1936,37,38
Frase, Robert C.	FN	1964,65
Frazier Jr., Leotis K.	MTR	1956
Frazier, Bruce	BB	1951,52,53
Frazier, Ernest	MSW	1945
Frazier, Scott	MCC	1982
Frederick, E. M.	WR	1915
Frederick, George R.	FB	1935
Fredericks, Brian	FN	1972
Fredericks, W. M.	WR	1933,34
Frederickson, Daniel T.	BB	1894
Frederickson, George	BB	1891,92,93,94
Frederickson, J. L.	MGO	1921,22
Frederickson, William	BB	1886,87,88
Freeland, Chesley B.	MTR	1909
Freeman, Don	MBK	1964,65,66
Frees, Herman	BB	1893,94,96
Freese, John A.	MTR	1902
Fregeau, John	WR	1968,69,70,71
Frei, Tom	MTN	1984,85,86
French, A. Blair	FB	1926,27
Frentz, William	BB	1956
Fretz, Karl	FN	1967,68,69
Freund, Peter	FB	1987,88
Frew, Pete	BB	1994
Frey, Hugh W.	MTR	1935
Fricker, David	WR	1956
Fricker, Donald P.	FN	1957
Friduss, Janvis H.	FN	1941,42
Friedberg, J. Frank	FN	1931
Friel, Marty	FB	1974,75,76
Frighetto, Mark	BB	1975,76
Frillman, James	BB	1955,57
Frink, Frederick F.	BB	1932,33,34
	FB	1931,33
Fritz, Alan	BB	1969,70,71
Fritz, Bill	MCC	1974,75,77
Fritz, Timothy	MTR	1984
Froehlich, Peter	WR	1976,78,79,80
Fronczak, Stan	MBK	1948
Froom, Albert N.	MTR	1906
Froschauer, Frank E.	FB	1932,33,34
	MBK	1933,34,35
Fruin, Leon T.	MTR	1930
Frye, Richard N.	FN	1939
Fulcher, Victoria	WTR	1988
Fulk, Robert T.	FB	1984,85
Fuller, James R.	BB	1887,88,89
Fuller, Michael K.	MTR	1971,72
Fullerton, Theron B.	FB	1913
Fullerton, Thomas C.	MTR	1943,44
Fullerton, Willard	WR	1930
Fulling, B. C.	MSW	1927
Fulton, Clifton	MBK	1943,50
Fulton, G. T.	BB	1892,93
Fulton, Robert B.	BB	1899,00,02
Fulton, W. J.	MGY	1927,28,29
Fulton, William J.	BB	1895,96,97,98
Fultz, Duane E.	FB	1939
	MTR	1940

Funk, Clarence P.	BB	1883
Funk, Mark	MSW	1981,82
Funkhouser, Mark R.	MGO	1982
Furber, William A.	BB	1891
	FB	1890
Furimsky, Paul	FB	1954
Furlong, Mark	WR	1976,77,78
Furness, Carl N.	MTR	1921
Fuzak, William G.	BB	1930,31

G

Gaa, Becky	WGY	1990,91,92,93
Gabbard, Thomas	WR	1957,58,59
Gabbard, William	WR	1956,58
Gabbett, William T.	FB	1961,62
Gabrione, Pete	FB	1992,93,94
Gage, John C.	MTR	1930,31
Gaines, Harry E.	MTR	1936,37,38
	MCC	1935
Galan, Anna	WSW	1988,89
Galbreath, Charles S.	FB	1933,34,35
Gale, E. O.	MSW	1922
Gale, Eli P.	MTR	1901
Galla, George	BB	1963
Gallagher, Joyce	WBK	1979
Gallagher, Thomas B.	FB	1946,47,48
Galland, Michael	MCC	1933,35
Gallivan, Raymond P.	FB	1924,25,26
Gallo, Michael P.	MTR	1964
Gamboa, Renee	WSW	1995
Gandy, Chris	MBK	1994,95
Gann, John	FB	1971,72,73
Gannon, Joseph F.	IHO	1941
Gano, Clifton W.	FB	1935
Gantt, Dave	BB	1959
Gantt, Kendra	WBK	1982,83,84,85
Gantz, Howard S.	MTR	1915,17
Garcia, Joe	WR	1946,47,48,49
Gardiner, Allison	WSW	1986,87,88,89
Gardiner, Lion	FB	1906,07,08
	MTR	1907,08
Gardiner, Robert P.	MTR	1918,19
Gardner, Laura	WGY	1978
Gardner, Morris (Moe)	FB	1987,88,89,90
Gardner, Robert	MTR	1970
	MCC	1969
Gardner, Thomas	MGY	1953,54,55
Garfield, Marvin	MTN	1949
Garland, John	MSW	1955,56,57
Garner, Donald S.	FB	1930
Garret, Roger	FN	1964,65,66
Garrett, Christine	WGO	1992,93,94,95
Garrett, Frank	PO	1938,39
Garrett, Rebekah	WCC	1991,94
	WTR	1994,95
Garrett, Richard P.	MTR	1897,99,00
Garrett, T. C. Scott	FN	1971
Garris, Kiwane	MBK	1994,95
Garrity, Allison	WGY	1984,85,86,87
Gartland, Eileen	VB	1975,76,77
Gartland, Kathleen	VB	1975,76,77,78
Gartrell, Willie	FB	1974,75
Gary, Charles	WR	1992,93,94,95
Gasparich, Stephen J.	SOC	1928
Gasparich, Timothy	BB	1981
Gassmann, Neal M.	MTR	1990
	MCC	1985,86,88,89
Gates, Andrew W.	FB	1890,91
Gates, James	MTN	1942,43,46
Gates, Linda	WTN	1989,90,92
Gates, Markland T.	FN	1964,65
Gates, Ralph	MBK	1912
Gates, William	MBK	1936
Gatewood, Roy	MBK	1950
Gatlin, Anne	WSW	1979
Gaumer, Gilbert	WR	1948,49,50
Gaumer, Wayne	WR	1949,50
Gaut, Robert E.	FB	1892,93,94
Gawron, William	BB	1958
Gay, Pharoah	MTR	1994,95
Gaynor, Allen	MSW	1974,75
Gaynor, Duffy	MSW	1972,73
Gbur, Edward F.	BB	1930,31,32
Gedman, Stacy	FB	1967
Gedvilas, Leo	BB	1944,45,46
	MBK	1945
Gee, Jerry	MBK	1995
Geers, Tim	MBK	1990,91
Geiger, Laura	WTR	1976,77
Geis, Clarence	WR	1925,26
Geissler, Burkhard	MGY	1963,64
Geist, H. F.	MGY	1912

Geist, Harvey	MTN	1934
Gellinger, Terry	BB	1958,59,60
Gelman, Max M.	FN	1938
Gelwicks, Greg	MSW	1988,89
Genis, John E.	FB	1941,42,46
Gentry, Derrick L.	MTR	1981,82,83,84
Gentry, Gretchen	WTR	1984
George, Jeff	FB	1988,89
George, Richard	FB	1978,79,80,81
Georlett, Clem	MGO	1958,59
Geraci, Joseph L.	FB	1959
Gerard, Gregory G.	FN	1977
Gerard, Kenneth C.	MTR	1928
Gerard, Michael R.	FN	1976,77
Gerdes, Ken	WR	1991,93
Gerecke, Herbert	MBK	1951,52
Gerhardt, Tom	MBK	1976,77,78
Gerometta, Arthur L.	FB	1943
Gerometta, Robert	MSW	1947,48
Gerrish, William G.	MTR	1965,66
Gerten, Nicholas	FN	1916
Gfroerer, George	MSW	1952,53,54,55
Giallombardo, Joseph J.	MGY	1938,39,40
Gianacakos, Richard	FB	1990
Gibala, Nick	MGO	1970,71,72
Gibbs, Paul	MBK	1933
Gibbs, Robert	FB	1940,42
Gibson, Alec	FB	1984,85
Gibson, Charles	MTR	1994,95
Gibson, James	WR	1974,75,77
Gibson, Ken	MBK	1990
Gibson, Robert L.	MTR	1978,79,80
Giddings, Mike W.	FB	1984,85
Gilbert, Dwight A.	MTR	1988,89
	MCC	1986,87,88
Gilbertson, Hunter	MTR	1950,51
Gilkerson, Thomas J.	MTR	1904,05
Gill, John S.	MTR	1936
Gill, Kendall	MBK	1987,88,89,90
Gill, Richard J.	MSW	1942
Gillan, John H.	IHO	1940,41,42
Gillen, John	FB	1977,78,79,80
Gillen, Ken	FB	1979,80,82
Gillespie, Gordon	BB	1944
	MBK	1944

Quarterback Jeff George was the NFL's No. 1 draft pick in 1990.

Gillette, Steven M.	FN	1986,87,88,89
Gilliean, Allisa	WTR	1995
Gilliland, William	BB	1887,88,89,90
Gilman, Adam	FN	1993
Gilmore, George	MTN	1957,58,59
Ginay, John	WR	1936,37,38
Gindler, Matt	MGO	1994,95
Ginsburg, Marvin	FN	1956
Givot, Michael	MSW	1985,86,87,88
Gladding, Donald K.	MTR	1942,43
	MCC	1942
Glade, Henry A.	BB	1928
Glade, Jayne	WTR	1981,82,83,84
Gladish, Ronald L.	FN	1963,64
Glass, Doyle	MTN	1954
Glass, Rufus C.	MTR	1928
Glasser, J.	MGY	1931,32,33
Glassgen, Al	WR	1944
Glasson, Steve	FB	1986,87,88,89
Glauser, Glenn L.	FB	1961
Glazer, Herbert	FB	1935
Gleis, Kirsten	VB	1992
Glick, Sanford	WR	1932

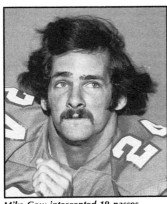

Mike Gow intercepted 19 passes during his Illini career, second only to Al Brosky.

Glielmi, Rob	FB	1982,83,84,85
Glomb, Robert	MGY	1961,62
Glosecki, Andy R.	FB	1936
	MTR	1936,38
Glynn, Kathy	VB	1977,78,79
Gnade, Gail	WSW	1977
Gnidovic, Donald J.	FB	1950,51
Goddard, Robert F.	FN	1928
Godeke, Frank B.	BB	1925
Goecke, Michelle	WTN	1992
Goelitz, Walter A.	FB	1917
Goelitz, William H.	MTR	1913,14,15
Goern, Sandra	WTN	1985,86,87,88
Golaszewski, Paul P.	FB	1961
Goldberg, Jeff	FB	1976
Golden, Craig	FN	1980,81
Golden, Scott	FB	1981,82,83
Goldstein, Charles B.	BB	1933
Goldstein, Jacob	MGO	1995
Goldstein, William J.	MGY	1938,39,40
Goldwater, R. W.	MGO	1929
Gombos, Edward	MGY	1957,58,59
Gongala, Robert B.	FB	1952,54
Gonzalez, Joseph A.	MTR	1951,52
Gonzalez, Marcelino	MTR	1943,44,45,46
Good, Richard, J.	FB	1940,41,42
Goodell Jr., Warren F.	MTR	1943
Goodman, David	MTN	1983,84
Goodrich, John	MGY	1960
Goodspeed, A. C.	MTR	1903
Goodspeed, Wilbur F.	MTR	1901
Goone, David	MGY	1981,82,83
Gordon, James	FB	1986,87
Gordon, Louis J.	FB	1927,28,29
Gordon, Michael J.	PO	1935,36
Gordon, N.	MSW	1931
Gordon, Stephen M.	FB	1976
Gore, Stanley A.	MSW	1944
Gorenstein, Sam	FB	1931
Goretzke, Fritz A.	MTR	1964,65,66
Gorham, Sidney	MTN	1956
Gorin, James C.	FN	1932
Gorzowski, Jacek J.	FN	1990,91,92
Gosier, Harry	FB	1983
Gosnell, Alan	MBK	1958,59,60
Goss, James	BB	1975,76
Gossett, J. E.	MSW	1910,11

Jim Graham was a varsity letter winner in wrestling in 1978.

Gossett, W. P.	MGY	1922
Gotfryd, Peter J.	BB	1943
Gottfried, Charles	FB	1946,47,48,49
	WR	1947,48,49
Gottman, Jay	MTN	1986
Gould, Dennis C.	FB	1961
Gould, Maurice S.	FB	1941
	MTR	1942
Gould, P. N.	MSW	1917
Gould, William C.	MTR	1931
	MCC	1930
Goulding, Bob	MGO	1963,64,65
Goverdare, Paul	WR	1940,41
Gow, Mike	FB	1972,73,74
Grable, Leonard M.	FB	1925,26,27
Grabowski, Jim S.	FB	1963,64,65
Grace, Dale	MGY	1961,62
Grace, Sterling	MGY	1963
Gradman, Harold	WR	1930,31
Graeff, Robert E.	FB	1955
Graff, Dennis	MBK	1974
Graff, Ryan	MGO	1992,93,95
Gragg, Elbert R.	FB	1932,33
Gragg, George L.	MTR	1938,39
Graham, James G.	WR	1978
Graham, John	FB	1970,71
Graham, Paul J.	MTR	1909,10,11
Graham, Walter	FB	1976
Grahl, Carl H.	WR	1934
Granata, William J.	SOC	1927
Grandcolas, Sarah	WSW	1985,86,87,88
Grange, Garland A.	FB	1927
Grange, Harold E. (Red)	FB	1923,24,25
Grant, African	FB	1985,86,87
Grant, Alan S.	BB	1939,40,41
Grant, Kimp	MGY	1991,92,93
Grant, Liz	WSW	1985,86,87,88
Grant, Randy	FB	1983,84
Grant, Wendell E.	MTR	1962,63,64
Graves, Marvin	BB	1953,55
Graves, Perry H.	BB	1914
	FB	1913,14
Gray, Dan	MCC	1985
Gray, J. M	MSW	1917
Gray, J. N.	MGY	1931,32,33
Gray, Reno	MBK	1978,80
Greanias, Evon C.	MTR	1943
Grear, Sidney F.	MTR	1905,06
Greathouse, Forrest	FB	1925
	MTR	1926
Greathouse, Teresa	WGY	1975,76
Greco, Dale	FB	1964,65
Green, Chris	FB	1987,88,89,90
Green, Dorian	MTR	1994,95
Green, Fred	MBK	1946,47,48,49
Green, Gordon	FB	1985
Green, Howard S.	FB	1906,07
Green, Jim	MGO	1974
Green, Jim	MBK	1987
Green, Lonsdale	MSW	1910,11,12
Green, Morris L.	FN	1936,37
Green, Ralph	MSW	1913,14
Green, Richard	WR	1928
Green, Robert K.	FB	1932
Green, Stanley C.	FB	1946
Green, Vivian J.	FB	1922,23
Green, William, J.	FB	1924,25
Greenberg, Scott	MTN	1984,86,87
Greene, Earl B.	FB	1921
Greene, Joe	WR	1995
Greene, Royner	MBK	1934,35
Greene, Steve	FB	1972,73,74,75
Greenleaf, John	MTN	1954,55
Greenwood, Donald G.	FB	1943,44
Gregory, Flint	BB	1968,69,70
Gregory, Gregg	BB	1966,67
Gregory, Melissa	WSW	1978,79,80
Gregus, Dan	FB	1980,81,82
Gregus, Kurt	FB	1986,87,88,89
Greiner, Sue	WTR	1983
Gremer, John A.	FB	1955,59
Grey, N. E	MSW	1916
Gribble, Paul A.	BB	1927
Grider, Chris	MSW	1987
Grieb, Donald L.	MGY	1972,75
Grieb, Linn	WTR	1976,77,78
Grier, Gretchen Y.	WTR	1982,83
Grierson, Ray G.	FB	1941,42,46
Grieshaber, Gary	WR	1973
Grieve, Robert S.	FB	1935,36
	MTR	1935,36,37
Griffin, Donald D.	FB	1941,42

Griffin, J. M.	FN	1912,14
	MSW	1913,14,15
Griffin, James	MBK	1979,80,81,82
Griffith, Howard	FB	1987,88,89,90
Grimes, Michael	MGY	1971,72,73,74
Grimmer, Mike	MSW	1974,75,76,77
Grimmett, Richard	FB	1977
Groh, Harold	MSW	1927,28,29
Groppel, Jack	MTN	1973
Gross II, Richard G.	MTR	1970,71,72
	MCC	1969,70,71
Gross, Chalmer A.	FN	1929,30
Gross, Samantha	WCC	1991,92
	WTR	1992,93
Grossfeld, Abie	MGY	1957,58,59,60
Grossi, George	MGY	1964
Grossman, Jake	MSW	1954,55,56
Grossman, Thomas	FN	1981,82,83,84
Groth, Gene	BB	1965
Grothe, Don	FB	1953,57,58
Groves, James C.	MTR	1904
Gruben, Peter	MSW	1987,89,90,91
Gruenberg. A. A.	MSW	1924
Gruenfeld, Julius J.	MSW	1943
Grumish, Julie	WGO	1989,90,91
Grunwald, Carl	WR	1946
Gryboski, Edward	FB	1933,34,35
Guard, Jason	FB	1986,87,88,89
Gudeman, Gene	MTN	1958
Gueche, Sadri	MTN	1990,92
Guenther, Ronald E.	FB	1965,66
Guercio, Anthony M.	MTR	1983,84
Guerrera, Chris	MSW	1987,88,89
Gugala, John	BB	1947,48,49
Guinn, Deb	WSW	1975
Gulick, Catherine	WTR	1978,79
Gullickson, Jennifer	WSW	1987,88,89
Gumm, Percy E.	FB	1908,09
Gundlach, Norman J.	BB	1926,27,28
Gunkel, Woodward W.	BB	1914,15,16
Gunlock, Virgil	WR	1926,27
Gunn, Charles A.	BB	1891,92
	MTR	1890,91,92
Gunn, Richard	BB	1955,56
Gunning, Delany T.	BB	1905,06,07
Gussis, Lloyd	BB	1967,68,69
Gustafsson, Jon	FB	1991
Guth, Glenn	BB	1971
Guthrie, Russell D.	FN	1958
Gutteridge, Theresa	WSW	1985,86,87,88
Guttschow, Roy	MBK	1934,35
Guyton Jr., Fred F.	FN	1959
Gwillim, Linda	WGO	1976
Gwin, Greg	MSW	1962,63,64

H

Haag, Eileen	WSW	1980
Haake, Eric	BB	1988
Haas, Brian L.	MTR	1988,89,90,91
Haas, Dan	WR	1969
Haas, Raymond C.	BB	1918,20
Hackett, Colleen	WCC	1983,84,85
	WTR	1983,84,85
Hackett, Kady	WSW	1993,94,95
Hackett, Theodore N.	MTR	1936,37
Hackleman, Michael	MGY	1963
Hackler, Sarah	WSW	1995
Hadley, Raymond	MGY	1960,61,62
Hadsall, Harry H.	BB	1896,97
	FB	1895
Haefler, Robert E.	BB	1936,37
Haffner, Scott	MBK	1985
Hagen, Jack L.	SOC	1927
Haier, Otto C.	FN	1929,30
Haig, Thomas	MSW	1981,82
Hailand, Frank	MGY	1956,57,58
Haime, Kevin	MGO	1984,85,86
Haines, Leonard	MBK	1924,25,26
Hainsworth, Joseph	FN	1980,81,82,83
Hairston, Ray	FB	1984,85,86
Haisley, Ernle	MTR	1958,59
Halas, George S.	MBK	1917,18
	BB	1916,17
	FB	1917
Halas, Walter H.	BB	1914,15,16
Hale, Clarence	MGY	1937
Hale, Clyde S.	MTR	1940,41
Hale, Hugh K.	MTR	1926,28
Haley, Arthur F.	MTR	1893
Halik Jr., Edwin J.	MTR	1968,69
Halkin, Daniel	MGY	1979

Tom Haller earned letters in three different sports in 1957, then began a long career in major league baseball.

Hall, Albert L.	FB	1911
	MBK	1910,12
Hall, Albert R.	BB	1899
Hall, Arthur R.	FB	1898,99,00
Hall, Charles V.	BB	1928,30
Hall, Harry A.	FB	1923,24,25
Hall, John	MGO	1961,62,63
Hall, Joseph W.	FB	1950,52
Hall, Melvin E.	MTR	1923,24
	MCC	1923
Hall, Orville, E.	FB	1944
Hall, Pamela	WTR	1982,83,84
Hall, Raymond T.	MTR	1927
Hall, Richard	MTR	1968
	MCC	1967,68
Hall, Richard L.	FB	1923,24
Hall, Seymour E.	MTR	1895
Hallden, John T.	MSW	1937
Halle, David A.	MCC	1984,85,86,87
	MTR	1985,86,87,88
Haller, Thomas F.	BB	1957
	FB	1956,57
	MBK	1957
Hallerud, Dean	MSW	1959
Halstrom, Bernhard C.	FB	1915
Hamann, Carolyn	WSW	1983,84,85,86
Hamann, Suzi	WSW	1981,82,83
Hamer, Charlton P.	MTR	1985,86,87,88
Hamer, Paul E.	MTR	1944,45
	MCC	1944
Hamilton, Gail	WGY	1989
Hamilton, Lowell	MBK	1986,87,88,89
Hamlett, Robert T.	MTR	1927,28
Hamman, James	MGY	1981
Hammel, Jeff	MSW	1975,76
Hammitt, Andrew B.	MTR	1913,14,15
Hammond, James	MTR	1960,61,62
Hamner, Jerry	FB	1987,88,89,90
Hampton, Keith	MTR	1930,31,32
Hamstra, Daniel	BB	1980,82,83,84
Handelman, Hyman	FN	1938
Handlon, Colin	MBK	1938,39,40
Hankenson, Lew	WR	1960,61,62
Hankenson, Steve	WR	1986,87,88,89
Hanley, James T.	MTR	1908,09,10
Hanlon, James A.	MTR	1973,74,75,76
Hanna, Cindi	WBK	1993,94,95

Lowell Hamilton was a member of the Flying Illini's starting five.

Kevin Hardy was a first-team All-Big Ten linebacker for the Illini in 1994.

Hannam, Gail	WGO	1975,76
Hannum, P. E.	FB	1903
Hanschmann, Fred R.	FB	1915,18
Hansen, David	MSW	1955,56
Hansen, Don	FB	1963,64,65
Hansen, Henry F.	MSW	1935,36
Hansen, Jarrett	FB	1994
Hansen, Jay	WR	1993
Hansen, Michelle	WTR	1991
Hansmann, Katie	WSW	1995
Hanson, Eric	MSW	1983
Hanson, Martin E.	FB	1900
Hanson, Michael	BB	1983
Hanson, Rodney	FB	1955,56,57
Hanson, Tim	WR	1983,85
Hanssen, Gustav A.	BB	1887,88,89,90
	MTR	1889
Hapac, William J.	BB	1939,40
	MBK	1938,39,40
Happeny, J. Clifford	FB	1922
	BB	1923
Harbour, Dave	FB	1986,87
Hardacre, G. K.	MSW	1922
Harder, Harold	MGO	1972,73,74,75
Hardy, Dale G.	FB	1976,77,78
Hardy, Kevin	FB	1992,93,94
Harford, Douglas	FB	1965,66
	MTR	1965,66,67
Hargis, Douglas	BB	1981,82
Harkey, Lance	FB	1985,86
Harkins, Eileen	VB	1991
Harkness, Roland	WR	1945
Harmeson, Terry	MSW	1969
Harmon, Ivan G.	FB	1903
Harms, Frederick E.	FB	1965,66,67
Harney, J. M.	MTR	1901
Harold, Robert	BB	1975,76
Harp, Jeff	WR	1985,86
Harpell, Danielle	WCC	1988,89,90,91
	WTR	1989,90,91,92
Harper, Bueford R.	MTR	1929,30
Harper, Charles	MBK	1929,30,31
Harper, Derek	MBK	1981,82,83
Harper, Gordon K.	MTR	1929
Harper, Robert H.	BB	1924
Harper, William	FB	1965

Lorna Henderson earned All-Big Ten honors for the Illini volleyball team in 1991.

Harrington, Peter J.	MGY	1947,48
Harrington, Raymond B.	BB	1928
Harris, Bryan	PO	1941
Harris, David	FN	1959
Harris, Davin	MBK	1993
Harris, Harold E.	MTR	1958,59,60
	MCC	1957,58
Harris, Harvey	FN	1968,69
Harris, Jean	WTN	1975
Harris, Mark	MTR	1976
Harris, Miles	MTN	1970,71,72,73
Harris, Newton M.	BB	1891
Harris, Robert	WR	1941
Harris, Sandra	WBK	1988,89
Harris, Theron	FB	1994
Harrison, Jodie	MBK	1968,69
Harrold, Norman M.	MSW	1942
Harshbarger, John	BB	1977,78
Harshbarger, Terry L.	MTR	1962,63
Harshbarger, Thad	WR	1959
Hart, Brett	WR	1994,95
Hart, Ralph W.	FB	1890,91,92
	BB	1892
Hart, William W.	MTR	1914
Hartenstein, Harvey	MTN	1952
Harter, Charles E.	FN	1965,66,67
Hartley, Frank	FB	1988,89,90
Hartman, Leo P.	MSW	1940,41,42
Hartman, William H.	MTR	1965,66
	MCC	1963
Hartmann, Brad	FB	1990
Harts, D. H.	MTR	1899
Hartz, Sylvester H.	FN	1934,35
Harvey, Allan F.	MGY	1957,58,59
Harvey, Donald	BB	1958,59
Harvey, Ted	BB	1963
Haselwood, John M.	FB	1903,04
Hasenstab, Jeff	FN	1991,92,93,94
Haskell, Howard H.	BB	1893,94,95,96
Haskins, Richard	BB	1952,53
Haslett, James M.	FN	1978,79,80
Haslhuhn, Gerald	FN	1956,57
Hastings Jr., Douglas A.	SOC	1929,30,31
Hatch, Lemoine S.	MGO	1923
Hatfield, Doug	MSW	1969
Hatfield, Joe	FB	1972,73,74
Hathaway, Ralph W.	FB	1938,39
Hatton, Troy	WR	1995
Haubold, Bill	MGO	1986
Haubold, Lois	WTN	1977,78,79,80
Haulenbeck, John	MSW	1945,46
Hauser, Bob	FN	1979
Haviland, William D.	MTR	1939
Hawkins, Burford H.	MGO	1952,53,54
Hawkins, LeShawn	BB	1992,93,94
Hawkins, Leslie L.	WTR	1987
	WCC	1985,86, 87
Hawthorne, Jamison	MTN	1993,94
Hayer, Joseph C.	FB	1949
Hayes, Bannon D.	MTR	1986,87,88,89
Hayes, Bob	FB	1972
Hayes, Edwin R.	SOC	1931,32,33
Hayes, Erik	FB	1992
Hayes, John	WR	1942
Hayes, John C.	MGO	1941
Hayes, Joseph C.	MTR	1945
Haymaker, Chris	MSW	1989
Hayne, Wilbur	MTN	1973,74,75
Haynes, Clint	FB	1982,83
Haynes, Kristen	WBK	1987,88,89,90
Hays, Bill	MSW	1964
Haywood, Nate	FN	1972,73
Hazelett, John	FB	1943
Hazlitt, Albert M.	BB	1897,98
Hazzard, E. M.	BB	1930,31
Heald, Paul J.	FN	1979,80,81
Healy, Keith	WR	1985,86,87,88
Healy, Patrick	MGO	1979
Heaven, Mike	FB	1981,82,83,84
Hebeisen, Kellie	VB	1990,92,93
Heberer, Ronald	BB	1951,52
Hecht, Brian	BB	1995
Heck, Kristen	WSW	1995
Heckert, Monica	WSW	1990
Hedden, Dan	MTN	1963
Hedgcock, Frank M.	MTR	1956,57,58
	MCC	1956,57
Hedges, Elsum G.	MGO	1936
Hedtke, William A.	FB	1931
Hegeler, Edward	MSW	1944
Heiken, Renee	WGO	1990,91,92,93
Heikes, Samuel I.	BB	1920

Heil, Robert	MGY	1957
Heimovics, I.	MGY	1922
Heinrich, F. M. (Mick)	FB	1972,73
Heinrich, Tom	BB	1971,72
Heinsen, Norman K.	MTR	1928
Heise, Jenny	WTR	1995
Heiss Jr., William C.	FB	1944,45,46
Heitmeyer, Troy A.	MTR	1988
Heitz, Angie	WTR	1984,85
Hejnicki, Jennifer	WSW	1992,93
Helbling, James L.	FB	1943
Heldman, Matt	MBK	1995
Helfer, Cheryl	WTR	1976,77,78,79
Helfrich, Kim	VB	1974
Helle, Mark	FB	1980,81,82
Heller, Steve	MTN	1961,62
Hellmich, Hudson A.	MTR	1932,33,34
	MBK	1932,33,34
Hellstrom, Norton E.	BB	1921,22,23
	FB	1920
	MBK	1921,23
Helman, David	WR	1938,39
Helmick, Dave	WR	1981,83
Helmke, Heidi	WGY	1981,82,83,84
Helwig, Kent	MSW	1981,82,83,84
Hemann, Jackie	WBK	1992
Hembrough, Gary	FB	1959,60,61
Henderson, Ann	WBK	1994,95
Henderson, Carrie	WBK	1986
Henderson, Fred	MTR	1912,13,14
Henderson, Lorna	VB	1989,90,91,92
Henderson, Sean	MGY	1990,91,92
Henderson, Tom	MTN	1980,81,82
Henderson, William R.	FB	1956,57,58
Hendrickson, Richard W.	FB	1957
Henkel, Bill	FB	1987,88,89,90
Henriksen, Kristin	VB	1990,91,92,93
Henry, Ann	WTR	1984,85,86
Henry, C. D.	MSW	1911
Henry, Smith T.	MTR	1901,02
Henry, Trisha	WSW	1995
Henry, Wilber L.	MBK	1935,36,37
	BB	1935,36,37
	FB	1934,35,36
Hensley, Timothy T.	FN	1985,86,87,88
Henson, Eric	MCC	1992,93,94
	MTR	1993,94,95
Herman, Jevon	WR	1995
Herning, Lance	MCC	1962
Herr, Rich	FB	1989
Herrick, G. Wirt	MTR	1909,10,11
Herrick, Lyle G.	MTR	1899,02,03
Hertz, Jed	MTN	1968,71
Herzog, Shawn	BB	1994,95
Hesmer, Theodore	WR	1927,28
Hess, G. R.	BB	1913
Hess, Jennifer	WSW	1992,93
Hester, Jack	BB	1952
Hester, Jerry	MBK	1994,95
Hester, John	BB	1953,54
Hestrup, Joel	WR	1976,77
Hewitt, F. E.	MSW	1932,33,34
Hewitt, Ronald	FN	1955,56
Hewitt, Wilfred	WR	1931
Hichhalter, Cheri	WSW	1983
Hickey, James J.	MSW	1935
Hickey, Robert	FB	1957,58,59
Hickman, Robert Z.	FB	1928
Hicks, Bruce	MTN	1935,36
Hicks, Laura	WGY	1985,86
Hicks, Tom	FB	1972,73,74
Higgins, Albert G.	FB	1890
Higgins, Charles H.	BB	1901,02
Higgins, Doug	FB	1987,88,89,90
Higgins, John N.	SOC	1927
Highsmith, Charles	MGY	1955
Hill, Aaron	MTR	1932
Hill, Arthur	MSW	1982,84,85,86
Hill, Arthur H.	BB	1901,04
Hill, Barb	WSW	1984
Hill, Cliff	MTR	1977,81
Hill, David	FB	1990,91
Hill, Elton	MGO	1934,35,36
Hill, Gregory H.	MCC	1984
	MTR	1982,83,84,85
Hill, Herbert	MBK	1929
Hill, Kimbrell	WR	1940
Hill, LeRon W.	FB	1957,58
Hill, Robert	WR	1916
Hill, Sam H.	FB	1922
	MTR	1921,22,23
Hill, Stanley	FB	1912

Peoria Manual High School's Jerry Hester hit a record six three-pointers in the second half of a 1995 victory over Indiana.

Hill, Stephen	MTN	1953,54
Hiller, William C.	MTR	1952,53
Hills, Otto R.	FB	1928,29,30
	MTR	1931
Hills, Stacy R.	BB	1894
Hines, N. W.	MSW	1932,33
Hinkle, Robert S.	FB	1947
	MTR	1944,48,49,50
Hinman, Lawrence D.	MTR	1908
Hinrichsen, George C.	BB	1907
Hinsberger, Mike	FB	1973
Hinton, Larry	MBK	1964,65,66
	MTR	1964
Hinze, Victor H.	BB	1936,37
Hirsch, Alan	MGY	1990,91
Hirsch, Joel S.	MGO	1963
Hiserote, Kim	MCC	1971
Hlinka, Anthony	MGY	1955
Hlinka, Charles	MGY	1950
Hoagland, John	MTR	1895,97,98,99
Hobart, John A.	MGO	1936,37,38
Hobble, Arthur C.	MTR	1899,00
Hobbs, Glenn M.	BB	1890
	MTR	1889,90,91,92
Hochhauser, Daniel	MGY	1970,71,72
Hochstrasser, Ronald	FN	1981,82,83,84
Hocking, William	MBK	1940,41,42
Hodge, John R.	SOC	1932
Hodges, Bill	BB	1970,71,72,73
Hodges, James D.	FB	1937,38
Hoeft, Julius	FB	1932
Hofer, Lance	FB	1980
Hofer, Lori	WBK	1983
Hoffenberg, Earl	BB	1967
Hoffman, Dennis	MSW	1960,61
Hoffman, George O.	BB	1925,26,27
Hoffman, Harold	WR	1920
Hoffman, James H.	FB	1966
Hoffman, Lyle	MGO	1933,34
Hoffman, Robert	MTN	1951,52
Hoffman, Robert W.	FB	1912
Hoffman, Thomas	BB	1949
Hoffman, William	BB	1950,51
Hoffmann, Robert	MBK	1913
Hogan, Dorothy	WTN	1980

Joel Hirsch lettered in golf for Illinois in 1963.

- 237 -

Illinois' Ken Holtzman enjoyed an all-star career in major league baseball.

Hogan, Kelly WGY 1994,95
Hogan, Mickey FB 1967,68
Hogan, Richard FB 1982
Hohm, Harley D. FB 1916
Hohman, Elmo P. MTR 1914,15,16
Hois, William MGY 1977
Holbrook, F. W. MSW 1928,29,30
Holbrook, Jim MSW 1962,63,64
Holbrook, Michael MTR 1963,64
Holcomb, Derek MBK 1979,80,81
Holcombe, Robert FB 1994
Holden, David MTN 1966,67,68
Holecek, John FB 1991,92,93,94
Holland, Pat BB 1962,63
Hollenbach, Jeff FB 1973,74
Hollingsworth, Elbert R. MTR 1931,32
Hollman, E. E. MGY 1912
Hollopeter, Cecil MBK 1925
Holmes, Harold MGY 1961,62,63
Holmes Jr., John A. MGO 1966,67
Holmes, Kam WTN 1976,77
Holmes, Mike FB 1979,80
Holmstrom, John T. MGO 1940,41,42
Holquist, Henry J. MSW 1939,40,41
Holquist, Sue WSW 1975,76
Holtmann, Al MTN 1957,58,59
Holtz, Carla VB 1974
Holtzman, Ken BB 1965
Holveck, Gary MGY 1967
Holzer, Werner WR 1957,58,59
Homoly, Andy MCC 1988,89,91
MTR 1992
Hooper, Jill WSW 1981,83
Hooper, Max BB 1952,53,54
MBK 1952,53,54
Hoover, H. Harold MTR 1899
Hopkins, Brad FB 1990,91,92
Hopkins, Kristine WSW 1984,85,86
Hopkins, Michael FB 1988,89,90,91
Hoppenjans, Mark MTN 1991
Hoppmann, Rita WTN 1981,82,83,84
Hopwood, Milton T. MSW 1937,38,39
Horimura, H. MGY 1916,17
Horn, John FB 1993
Horsely, Robert E. FB 1931
Hortin, Gordon MBK 1944

Illinois lineman Brad Hopkins was a first-round draft choice of the Houston Oilers in 1993.

Horvath, Cheryl WBK 1978,79
Hosfield, Mark MGY 1976,77,78
Hoskins, R. N. MGY 1926
Hotchkin, Robert BB 1935
Hotchkiss, Robert J. BB 1894,95
FB 1894,95
Houcek, Richard MSW 1946,47
Hougham, Kym MGO 1973,74,75,76
Houghton, Eldon WR 1932,33,34
Houser, Edwin MGY 1951
Houston, Edward N. MTR 1960
How, John MBK 1928,29
Howard, Dana FB 1991,92,93,94
Howard, Daniel O. MTR 1920
Howard, Gillian WTR 1991
Howard, Glen MTR 1992,95
Howard, Joseph O. FN 1969,70,71
Howat, Rick MBK 1969,70,71
Howell, Edward WR 1936
Howell, Lisa WGY 1979
Howie, Bill MTN 1953
Howie, Bill MTN 1986,87
Howland, Dennis R. MTR 1969,70,71
Howorth, Ronald MGY 1961
Howse, Kenneth R. MCC 1968,69,70
MTR 1969,70,71
Hrischuk, Amy VB 1994
Hrnyak, Nick BB 1983
Huber, William W. FB 1946
Huddleson, Clyde WR 1912
Huddleston, Thielen B. FB 1930
Hudelson, Clyde W. FB 1912
Hudgins, Lesley WBK 1986,87,88
Huebner, Dave FB 1976
Huebner, Louis H. MSW 1944
Huff, George A. BB 1889,90,91,92
FB 1890,92
Huff, Roger G. BB 1910
Huff, Walter W. BB 1907
Huffman, Shannon WTR 1994,95
Hughes, Edgar O. MGY 1936,38
Hughes, Eric L. MTR 1946
MCC 1945
Hughes, Gaylord MGY 1948,49,50
Hughes, Henry L. FB 1920
Hughes, John WR 1940
Hughes, Robert WR 1943,44
Hughes, Seth M. MTR 1923,24,25
Hugill, William MTR 1939
Huisinga, Larry FB 1970,71,72
Hull, James M. BB 1924
Hull, Thomas F. BB 1942
Hull, W. H. MTR 1912
Hull, Walker F. FB 1908,09
Hull, Wendell WR 1957
Hult, Bernard E. SOC 1930,31
Hult, Richard E. SOC 1930,31
Hulvey, Walter MTN 1953
Humay, Daniel M. BB 1965,66,67
FB 1966
Humbert, Fred H. FB 1927,28,29
Hummel, Glenn MTN 1973,74,75,76
Humphrey, Darryl BB 1986
Humphrey, Dwight MBK 1946,47
Humphreys, Albert WR 1926
Humphreys, John MGO 1923,24,25
Hungate, Eddie FB 1985
Hunsaker, Joe MSW 1957,58,59
Hunsley, Lorne E. MTR 1924,25
Hunt, L. D. MGO 1924,25
Hunt, Paul MGY 1971,72,73
Hunt, Robert MSW 1956,57,58
Hunt, Tyler R. FN 1956,57
Hunter, James A. MTR 1911,12,13
Huntley, Converse R. BB 1879,80,81
Huntley, Osman H. MTR 1936
Huntoon, Harry A. FB 1901,02,03,04
Hunziker, Janae WTR 1977,78,79,81
Hurd, Joyce WTR 1975
Hurley, O. Landis FB 1940
Hurst, Joe MGO 1964,65
Hurtte, Frank FB 1944
Husted, Guy H. MTR 1913
Husted, Merle R. MTR 1916,17
Huston, Paul E. MTR 1948
MCC 1947,48
Huston, William E. FB 1966,67,68
Hutchings, Steven MGY 1990
Hutchinson, Edgar B. MGO 1937,38,39
Hutchinson, Martha WBK 1978,79,80,81
Hutchinson, Scott R. MTR 1987
Hutchinson, Susan WTN 1981,82,83,84

Hutchinson, Thomas W. MTR 1978
Huth, William WR 1939
Huttenlocher, Gail WSW 1985,86,87,88
Huyler, Joe MSW 1959,60,61,62
Hyde, Rich BB 1989,90,91
Hyinck, Clifton F. FB 1931

I

Iantorno, Tony MGO 1974
Iavarone, Greg BB 1982,83,84,85
Iffland, Llewellyn MGY 1963,64,65
Illingworth, Michael MGY 1978
Im, Oscar MGY 1985,86
Imrie, Earl D. MTR 1958
Inch, Christopher A. MTR 1988
MCC 1987,88
Ingalls, Anne WTR 1976,77,78
Ingle, Scott BB 1903
Ingle, Walden M. FB 1938
Ingram, Daniel BB 1974,75,76
Ingrum, Ronald BB 1967,68,69
Ingwersen, Burton A. BB 1918,19,20
FB 1917,18,19
MBK 1918,19,20
Inman, Bridget WBK 1993
Inman, Dave WR 1970
Innis, Brian BB 1982
Innis, Jeffrey BB 1981,82,83
Iovino, Vito J. FB 1956
Irle, Joseph WR 1974
Irons, Louis M. MTR 1947,48,49,50
Irussi, Bruce WR 1979,80
Irwin, Doug BB 1992,93
Isenburg, Orville MTN 1940
Ishu, Albert P. FN 1983,84,85,86
Ittersagen, Jill WGO 1981,82,83,84

J

Jackson, Clifford L. BB 1921,22,23
Jackson, Davis FB 1967,68,69
Jackson, Earl A. FB 1931
Jackson Jr., Edwin WR 1951,54,55
Jackson, Greg MBK 1969,70,71
Jackson, James L. FN 1937
Jackson, Kevin FB 1992,94
Jackson, Mannie MBK 1958,59,60
Jackson, Matt BB 1995
Jackson Jr., Robert V. SOC 1933
Jackson, Trenton BB 1965
FB 1962,65
MTR 1963,64,65
Jacob, Paul WR 1970,71
Jacobs, Jeffrey P. MCC 1982,83,84,86
MTR 1983,84,85,86
Jacobson, John D. MTR 1986,87,88
MCC 1986,87
Jacobson, Ken WR 1962,63,64
Jacques, Virgus FB 1973
Jaeger, Robert O. PO 1939,40,41
Jager, William MSW 1979,80,81
James, Brad FB 1987
James, David FB 1994
Janata, John FB 1981,82
Janecek, Bill FB 1967,68
Janicki, Nick BB 1970
FB 1969
Jankowsky, Alexandre FN 1961,62
Janota, Neil MSW 1972,73,74,75
Jansen, Earl FB 1935
MSW 1934
Janssen, Donald FB 1944
Jarboe, Marcus MTR 1993,95
Jaronik, Frank J. MGO 1941,42
Jaronik, Stanley MGO 1945
Jasper, Thomas BB 1890,91,92,93
Jaworek, Thomas E. IHO 1939,40,41
Jebe, Tod A. FN 1986,87
Jefferson, Harry FB 1954,55,56
Jeffery, Dan WR 1964,66
Jeffery, John WR 1964
Jemsek, Gregory MGO 1947,48
Jenkins, Earl A. MTR 1990,91,92,93
Jenkins, Eddie FB 1971,72,73
Jenkins, Edwin M. MTR 1906,07,08
Jenkins, Jerome J. MTR 1986,87,88,89
Jenkins, Richard H. FB 1951
Jenkins, Terrence D. FB 1984,85
Jenkinson, H. R. MGY 1928,29,30
Jenks, Charles N. FB 1925
Jenner, Kris BB 1983
Jenner, Kyle W. MTR 1982
Jennings, Alpha M. MGY 1935

Walk-on Mike Hopkins eventually earned the Big Ten Conference Medal of Honor for proficiency in athletics and academics.

Jennings, Scott A. MTR 1981,83
Jensen, George MSW 1947
Jensen, Stanley C. FB 1930,31
Jerzak, Edward FB 1957
Jeske, Thomas FB 1971
Jestes, Edmiston R. BB 1924,25
Jewsbury, Walter M. MTR 1949,50,53
MCC 1948,49
Jirele, Jeffrey S. MCC 1975,76
MTR 1976,77
Jirus, Richard MGY 1954,55,56
Jobson, Robert F. FN 1942
Joesten, Holly WSW 1982,83
Johansen, Bob BB 1965
MBK 1965,66,67
Johns, D. C. MSW 1963
Johns, John BB 1944,45
Johnson, A. M. MTR 1900
Johnson, Amy WTN 1991
Johnson, Bob FB 1972
Johnson, Brian MBK 1995
Johnson, Carl FB 1956,57,58
Johnson, Cathryn WTN 1977
Johnson, Clarence E. MTR 1898
Johnson, Dennis BB 1981,83
Johnson, Disa VB 1984,85,86,87
Johnson, Donald T. FB 1944
Johnson, E. Thomas BB 1919,20,21
Johnson, Eddie MBK 1978,79,80,81
Johnson, Filmel FB 1990,91,92,93
Johnson, Frank FB 1973,74,75,76
Johnson, Franklin P. MTR 1922,23,24
Johnson, Gaye WGY 1978,79,80
Johnson, Gerald P. MTR 1950
Johnson, H. M. MSW 1925
Johnson, Harlan MSW 1946
Johnson Jr., Herschel E. FB 1966,68
Johnson, Howard MTN 1939
Johnson, Howard MBK 1974,75
Johnson, Jackie FB 1984,85
Johnson, Janelle WTR 1993,94
Johnson, Jay FB 1976
Johnson, Jennifer WBK 1985,86,87,88
Johnson, Jerry MTN 1965,66

Jerry Johnson, the son of legendary Illini track coach Leo Johnson, earned a varsity letter in track in 1950.

- 238 -

Amy Jones earned four varsity letters in volleyball from 1990-93.

Name	Sport	Years
Johnson, Johnny	FB	1993,94
Johnson, Joseph	MTR	1944,45
Johnson, Julie	WGO	1980
Johnson, Karl E.	FN	1989,90,91,92
Johnson, Ken	FN	1972
Johnson, Kenneth	MTN	1939,40
Johnson, Mike	FB	1982,83
Johnson, Mikki	FB	1993,94
Johnson, Nathan E.	FB	1939,40,41
Johnson, Richard L.	FB	1966,67,68
Johnson, Rick	WR	1976,77,78,79
Johnson, Robert	PO	1936,37,38
Johnson, Ron	BB	1961,62
Johnson, Roy	MSW	1946
Johnson, Scott	WR	1978
Johnson, Steve	FN	1970
Johnson, Tony	BB	1955
Johnson, William M.	FB	1936
Johnston, Allison	WGO	1985,86,87,88
Johnston, Arthur R.	BB	1897,98,99,00
	FB	1897,98,99
Johnston, Charles	MCC	1925
Johnston, Jeff	WR	1983
Johnston, Scott	FN	1969,70
Jolley, Walter	FB	1927,28,29
Jonas, Joel	BB	1964
Jones, Amos I.	FB	1949,50
Jones, Amy	VB	1990,91,92,93
Jones, Anthony M.	MTR	1991,93,94
Jones, Arthur	MTN	1941
Jones, Benton	MSW	1950,51,52
Jones, Bernette	WTR	1991,92
Jones, Billy M.	MSW	1938,39,40
Jones, Bruce L.	MTR	1975
Jones, Carl	BB	1984,85,87
Jones, Cliff	FB	1977
Jones, Douglas	BB	1980,82,83
Jones, Ebon	MTN	1938,39,40
Jones, Gordon E.	MTR	1934
Jones, Henry	FB	1987,88,89,90
Jones, John C.	MSW	1934
Jones, Keith	FB	1985,86,87,88
Jones, Kristen	WTN	1992,93,94,95
Jones, Mark	FB	1981,82
Jones, Martin	FB	1994
Jones, Mike	MBK	1978
Jones, Reese	MSW	1989,90,91
Jones, Rich	MBK	1966,67

Name	Sport	Years
Jones, Richard	FN	1973
Jones, Robert B.	FB	1945
Jones, Rodney	MBK	1990
Jones, Shawn	FB	1986
Jones, Steven	MSW	1982,83,84
Jones, Tom	FB	1969,70
Jones, W. Ray	MTR	1908,09,10
Jones, William N.	MTR	1976
Jonsson, Karl	MCC	1955,56,57
	MTR	1955,56,57
Joop, Lester	FB	1943,44,45
Jordan, Arthur I.	MTR	1910
Jordan, Jerome J.	BB	1925,26
Jordan, Larry C.	FB	1965,66,67
Jordan, Stephen	FB	1987,88
Joudakin, Al	MGY	1961
Joy, Samuel S.	BB	1898
Judson, Howard	BB	1944,45
	MBK	1944,45
Judson, Paul	MBK	1954,55,56
Judson, Phil	BB	1955,56
	MBK	1955,56
Judson, Rob	MBK	1977,78,79,80
Juengert, Steve	MGY	1983,84,86,87
Junghans, Brian	FB	1986
Jurack, Mike	BB	1991,92,93
Jurasevich, John	BB	1958,59,60
Jurczyk, Gary	FB	1975,76,77
Jurgens, Carl	MSW	1971
Juriga, Jim	FB	1982,83,84,85
Jurinek, George	WR	1961,62
Jurtzrock, E. V.	WR	1917
Jutton, Jerry	WSW	1977,78
Jutton, Lee	FB	1901
Juul, Herbert V.	MBK	1906,07
	BB	1906
K		
Kabel, Robert L.	MTR	1953
Kachiroubas, Lou	WR	1946,47,52
Kaczkowski, Thomas H.	MTR	1974,75
Kadota, Paul	FN	1957
Kaemerer, David W.	MTR	1972,73,74
Kagen, Irving	WR	1941,42
Kahon, Don	WR	1966
Kaihatsu, Edward J.	FN	1981,82,83
Kaires, Gerald	BB	1945,46,48
Kaiser, Becky	WTR	1979,80,81,82
Kaiser, John	FB	1969,70
Kaiser, Paul W.	BB	1919
Kakacek, John	WR	1979,81
Kal, Harris	BB	1974,75,76
Kalal, Randy	WGY	1975
Kalin, Gene	MGY	1970,71,72
Kallis, Leonard	BB	1938,40
Kamin, Burt	SOC	1929
Kamin, Mike	MTR	1994,95
Kamm, Albert C.	MTR	1933,34
	MBK	1933,34
Kamm, R. M.	MGY	1914
Kamp, Elbert	MBK	1930,31,32
Kamp, Robert	MBK	1930,31,32
Kamper, Reiner H.	FN	1985,86,87
Kamps, Claire	WTN	1932
Kandel, Bruce	BB	1975,76,77
Kane, Doug	BB	1985,86,87
Kane, John F.	FB	1943
Kane, Laurie	WTN	1990,91
Kanke, Tim	WR	1994,95
Kanosky, John P.	FB	1935
Kaplan, Bruce S.	MTR	1972
Kaplan, Hyman H.	FN	1936
Kaplan, Mark	MGY	1967,68,69
Karacan, Ercument	MTN	1945
Karafotas, Phil	MSW	1962,63,64
Karakas, Thomas J.	IHO	1943
Karich, Sarah	WSW	1987
Kariher, Harry C.	MTR	1898,99
Karkow, Waldemar	MCC	1947
	MTR	1947,48
Karmazin, Karen	WGO	1995
Karnes, T. D.	MBK	1924,25
Karnezis, Phillip P.	FN	1989,90,91
Karnopp, E. B.	MTR	1903
Karpen, William E.	MGY	1972,73,74,75
Karpinchik, Nick	MSW	1954,57
Karras, John	FB	1949,50,51
Karubas, Kari	WGY	1994,95
Kasap, George	FB	1951
Kasap, Mike	FB	1942,46
Kasch, Fred W.	BB	1933,34

Name	Sport	Years
Kasper, Ray	BB	1964,65,66
Kassel, Charles E.	FB	1924,25,26
	MBK	1925,26
Kasten, Frederick W.	FB	1902,03,04
Kastor, Frank	WR	1954,55
Kating, John	BB	1956,57,58
Kats, Jerry H.	MTR	1951
Kats, Judith	WSW	1988
Katz, William B.	FN	1937
Katzman, Jesse	MGY	1994
Kaufman, Larry L.	FN	1954,55,56
Kaufmann, Andy	MBK	1990,91,93
Kaufmann, Eugene H.	IHO	1939
Kautt, Elmer C.	SOC	1927
Kavathas, Sam	FB	1974
Kawal, Edward J.	FB	1929
	MBK	1930
Kay, Charles J.	BB	1913
Kay, Michael	MTR	1970
Kays, William	WR	1977
Kazarian, Stacey	WTN	1985,86
Kearney, Herschel P.	FB	1943
Kearney, Thomas	MTR	1974,75
Keator, Edward O.	MTR	1898,99,00,02
Kee, Dick	FB	1963,64,65
Keen, J. Patrick	MGO	1969,70
Keenan, Donald	MSW	1955,56
Keene, Richard	MBK	1993,94,95
Kehlor, J. M.	MGO	1912
Kehoe, Scott	FB	1983,84,85,86
Keinlen, Tom	MSW	1963,64
Keith, Alvin	FB	1970,71,72
Kell, Dick	MTN	1961
Kellaney, Kenneth	MGO	1975,76,77,78
Kelleher, Elizabeth	WGO	1988,89,90
Kelleher, Rachel	WCC	1992
Keller, Charles	MBK	1986
Keller, Charles I.	MTR	1938
Keller, Thomas O.	MTR	1974,75
Kelley, Benita	WTR	1995
Kelley, Bill	MSW	1991,92
Kelley, Jon	MTR	1990
Kelley, Robert L.	MTR	1942,43,44,45
Kelly, David J.	FB	1976,77,78,79
Kelly, Jennifer	WSW	1987
Kelly, John	MCC	1968,69,70
Kelly, John	WR	1979
Kelly, Mark	FB	1985,86,87,88
Kelly, Maurice (Moe)	FB	1969,70,71
Kelly, Pat	WR	1962
Kelly, Sue	WSW	1980,81
Kelso, E. L.	BB	1879
Kelso, Kevin	MTN	1972,73,74,75
Kemman, Herbert F.	BB	1911
Kemner, Carl A.	FN	1973,74,75
Kempf, George A.	BB	1911
Kennedy, Brian S.	MGO	1982
Kennedy, Dan W.	FN	1963,64
Kennedy, David R.	FN	1959
Kennedy Jr., John H.	FB	1931
Kennesey, George	MSW	1992
Kennett, Greg	MTN	1988,89
Kenney, Gene	WR	1950
Kenney, Harold (Hek)	WR	1924,25,26
Kenney, Wendell L.	MTR	1920
Kennicott, Robert M.	FN	1933
Kent, David	FB	1993
Kerestes, Tim	WR	1969
Kerr, George E.	MTR	1958,59,60
Kerr, John	MBK	1952,53,54
Kerr, John K.	MSW	1943
Kerr, Jonathan	FB	1991,92,93,94
Kerr, Marsha	WSW	1975
Kersulis, Walter T.	MBK	1945,48,49,50
	FB	1944,47,48,49
Kesler, Robert	MSW	1948,49
Kestly, Christie	WTN	1991
Keswick, Bruce	MSW	1970,71,72,73
Ketzle, Henry B.	MTR	1901,02
Keuhl, Doug	WR	1973
Kewney, Kathryn	WTN	1982
Keys, John J.	SOC	1927
Keys, Melvin	MTR	1983,84,85
Khachaturian, Jon	FB	1976
Kieding, Ray	MSW	1928,29,30
Kienlen, Donald L.	MTR	1940,41
	MSW	1939,40,41
Kilbane, James	BB	1946,47,48
Kiler, William H.	FB	1894,95
Killen, Ray T.	IHO	1941,42
Kim, Jin B.	FN	1988,89,90,91
Kim, Sukhoon	FN	1978,79,80,81

Illini basketball's Richard Keene is UI's all-time three-point field-goal leader.

Name	Sport	Years
Kimball, C. B.	MTR	1891
Kimball, Edwin R.	BB	1883,84
Kimball, Jason	MGY	1995
Kimbell, Steve	FB	1965
Kimmel, Lissa	WTN	1992,93,94,95
Kimmel, Lyman B.	MTR	1925,28
Kimpel, Janice	WGO	1975,76,77
Kimpel, Raymond	MGO	1948,49,50
Kincaid, Brian V.	MTR	1990,91,92
Kinderman, Frederick W.	BB	1924,25,26
King, Andrew	MGO	1976,77,78
	WR	1976
King, Harless W.	FB	1891
King, J. W.	FB	1898
King, Nancy	VB	1974
Kingman, Charles D.	BB	1895,96
Kingsbury, Brian G.	FB	1976,77
Kingsbury, F. L.	MGY	1924
Kinkead, David R.	BB	1887,88,89
Kinney, Jeff	FB	1990,91,92
Kinsey, Daniel C.	MTR	1924,25
Kirby, Eugene	MGY	1960,61
Kirby, Marty	BB	1977
Kircher, Helmuth	MBK	1913,14
Kirchner, Peter A.	MGO	1968
Kireilis, Raymond W.	MSW	1939,41
Kirk, Todd	FB	1904,05
Kirk, Walt	MBK	1944,45,47
Kirkland, Alfred Y.	MSW	1939,40,41
Kirkpatrick, Bruce	WR	1968,69,70
Kirkpatrick, Jesse B.	FB	1918
Kirkpatrick, John R.	MTR	1906
Kirschke, John W.	FB	1938,39
Kirwan, Jim	FB	1975,76
Kisner, James W.	FB	1984,85
Kisselburg, B. M.	MGO	1915
Kissinger, Donald K.	BB	1918,19,20
Kissinger, Molly	VB	1983
Kittler, Bud	FB	1973
Kivela, Paul	MCC	1982,84,85,86
	MTR	1984,86
Kjellstrom, Theodore	MSW	1952
Klaas, Palmer	WR	1972,73,74
Klapper, Jessica	WTN	1994,95
Klapperich, Andrew	MSW	1979,80,81,82
Klass, Craig	WR	1973
Klaus, Robert	BB	1957,58,59

Jim Juriga was a three-time All-Big Ten selection for the Illini football team.

Maurice (Moe) Kelly lettered for the Illini football team for three seasons.

Marko Koers set several varsity records as an Illini track performer.

Klausman, Henry	MGY	1960,61,62
Kleber, Doug	BB	1974,75,76,77
	FB	1973,74,75
Kleckner, Bill	FB	1972,73,74
Klein J. Leo	FB	1915,16,17
	BB	1916,17,18
Klein, Jim	FB	1992,93,94
Klein, Kristen	WGO	1988,90,91
Klemm, Frederick	BB	1965,66,67
Klemp, Joseph B.	FB	1937
Klimek, Anthony F.	FB	1948,49,50
Klimek, Josh	BB	1993,95
Kline, William G.	MTR	1903,05,06
Klingel, Martin	MSW	1961,63
Klingler, Vicki	WBK	1991,93,94
Kloepper, Victor F. H.	MTR	1922
Klusendorf, Don	MBK	1984
Kmiec, Kenneth K.	FB	1965,66,67
Kmiec, Tom	FB	1968
Knapp, Clyde G.	FB	1926
Knauff, Lawrence F.	FN	1962,63
Knebelkamp, Kent	BB	1983,84
Kneesi, C. W.	MSW	1927
Knell, Phil D.	FB	1965,66
Knight, E. J.	MTR	1905
Knight, William A.	MTR	1933
Kniss, Steve E.	FN	1967,68
Knop, Nancy L.	WCC	1977,78
	WTR	1976,77,78,79
Knop, Robert O.	FB	1916
Knotts, Tom	BB	1974,75
Knowles, Richard T.	FN	1941
Knowles, Stacey	WTN	1986,87,89
Knowlton, Brett	MTN	1988
Knox, Carl W.	FB	1937
Knox, J. H.	MTR	1905
Knox, Rodney	FB	1974
Knutson, Laura	WGY	1987,88,89,90
Kobylinski, Brian	MGY	1992,93,94,95
Koch, George W.	FB	1919
Koch, Paul	BB	1965,66
Kocian, Frederick M.	MTR	1981,82
Koehnemann, Harry E.	MGY	1939,40,41
Koenig, Thomas E.	MTR	1964,65
	WR	1963

Koers, Marko	MTR	1992,93,94,95
	MCC	1991,92
Koerwitz, Chris	FB	1994
Koester, Kraig	FB	1991,92,93
Koestner, Elmer	BB	1955
Kogut, A. Charles	FB	1971,72,73
Kogut, James K.	FB	1976,77
Kohlhagen, Richard M.	FB	1952,53
Kohr, Charles	MGO	1963,64,65
Kokes, Wilbert J.	MGO	1935,36,37
Kolasa, Richard J.	MTR	1987,89,90,91
Kolb, Gary A.	FB	1959
	BB	1960
Kole, Kathy	WTN	1975,76,77,78
Kolens, S. William	FB	1940,45
Kolfenbach, Edwin J.	FB	1931
Kolloff, Thomas	FB	1977
Komm, J.	MGY	1927
Komm, R.	MGY	1932
Konstant, Anthony	MSW	1945,46
Kontur, Tracy	WGY	1987,88,89,90
Koonz, John C.	MTR	1924
Kopale, Robert	BB	1979,81,82
Kopatz, Jim	BB	1974
	FB	1974,75
Kopel, Howard F.	IHO	1940,41
Koperski, Kevin	MGY	1995
Kopf, Frank A.	MTR	1912
Kopka, John	BB	1949
Kopko, Amy	WTR	1980,81,82,83
Kopp, William K.	BB	1918,19,20
	FB	1918,19
	MBK	1919
Koptik, Bohumil J.	BB	1915,16,17
Kordas, Judy	WBK	1978,79
Korfist, Matt	WR	1990,92
Kortkamp, Andy	BB	1993,94,95
Kosakiewicz, Anthony	MSW	1945
Koshkarian, Kent A.	FN	1983,84,85,86
Koster, Bridget	WTR	1985
Koster, Mark R.	MTR	1969,70,71
Kostick, Andrew	MGY	1957
Kostick, Eugene	MSW	1958
Kott, John H.	SOC	1930,31,32
Kovacic, Ivan	PO	1934,35
Kowalski, August J.	BB	1935
	FB	1932
Kowalski, Charles	MGY	1992,93,94
Kozlowski, Aaron	MSW	1990,91
Kpedi, Andy	MBK	1990,91
Kracen, Scott	MSW	1968,69
Kraft, Don	FB	1955
Kraft, Gerald G.	FN	1940
Kraft, Michael	MGY	1980,81
Kraft, Mike	BB	1989,90
Kraft, Reynold R.	FB	1915,16,17
Krainik, Anthony	MTR	1978,79,80,81
Kraiss, Katherine	WCC	1994
	WTR	1995
Krajewski, Mark	MTN	1989,90,91,92
Krakoski, Joseph	FB	1960
Krakower, Irving	SOC	1929
Kral, Ed	MSW	1961,62,63
Krall, William E.	FB	1945
Kramer, Martin	FN	1958,59,60
Kramer, Mike	MTN	1978,79,80,81
Kraml, Ken	WR	1959
Kramp, Robert	MSW	1952,53,54
Krantz, Louis	BB	1950,51,52
Kranz, Richard	WR	1945
Kratz, A. P.	MGY	1905
Kratz, J. P.	MTR	1899,00
Kratz, Paul	MSW	1950
Krause, Dennis W.	MCC	1965
	MTR	1966
Krebs, Wilbur E.	BB	1914,15,16
Kreidler, Chester J.	MTR	1917,18
Kreitling, Richard A.	FB	1957,58
Krelle, Jim	MBK	1970,71,72
Kriegsmann, Michael	MTR	1990,93,94
Kring, C. W.	MGY	1931,32
Krivec, John J.	MTR	1939,40
Kriviskey, Bruce M.	FN	1960,61,62
Krolik, Ann	VB	1976,77
Krom, Dave	WR	1965
Kronenfeld, Phillip	FN	1970,71,72
Krueger, Bernard E.	FB	1946,47,48,49
Krueger, Kerry	FB	1980,82,83
Krueger, Kurt	FB	1981,83
Krupar, Charles F.	BB	1918
Kruze, John J.	FB	1960,61
Kubala, Tom	MTR	1973

Kucera, Richard K.	BB	1938,40
Kuehl, Edwin C.	BB	1923
Kuehn, Clyde	BB	1968,69,70
Kueker, Brian A.	MTR	1975,76,77,78
Kuenne, Jill	WTR	1979,80,81
Kuhfuss, John D.	FN	1970,71
Kuhlman, Erich	MSW	1991,92
Kuhn, Clifford W.	FB	1933,35,36
Kujawa, Jens	MBK	1986,87,88
Kumerow, Ernie	BB	1959,60,61
Kummerow, Walter	WR	1966
Kunde, Mark	MSW	1988
Kuntstadler, R. H.	MGO	1925,26,27
Kunz, Phil	MBK	1987,88
Kurlak, Peter	MSW	1939,40,41
Kurtock, Buffy	WTR	1977
Kurz, W. C.	MGO	1928
Kushner, Terry	MGY	1969
Kusinski, John	BB	1926,27,29
Kusmanoff, Tony	WR	1963
Kustock, Al	FB	1972,73
Kusz, William	MTR	1937
Kuypers, Bob	MSW	1974,75
Kwasniewski, Eugene S.	FB	1945,46
Kwint, Joseph A.	SOC	1931

L

La Badie, Lee D.	MTR	1970,71,72
	MCC	1969,70,71
La Frank, Samuel E.	MTR	1971,72,73
Laase, F. H.	WR	1924
Lachky, Joe	BB	1972
Laing, George D.	BB	1912
Lakes, Charles	MGY	1983,84,85
Lakin, J. C.	MSW	1931
Lally, J. Richard	MTR	1963,64
	MCC	1962
Lalor, Foster M.	BB	1917,18
Lamb, F. W.	MSW	1925,26
Lamb Jr., Lawton B.	MTR	1950,51,52
	MCC	1949
Lamb, Shane	FB	1986
Lambert, Andre	MTN	1983,84
Lamborn, Denise	WGY	1987,88
LaMere, Dorothy	WSW	1977
Lamoreux, John R.	MTR	1967,68
	MCC	1966,67,68
Land, Susanne	WTN	1947
Landers, Kathleen	WSW	1987
Landmeier, Vernon O.	MCC	1933
	MTR	1934
Landon, R. H.	MGY	1927,28
Landry, Jeremiah	MGY	1992,93,94,95
Landt, Louis	MBK	1959,60
Lane, Randy	MGY	1986,87,88
Lane, Thomas	MSW	1948
Lang, Alvin L.	MTR	1917,18
Lang, Susan	WGO	1981,82,83,84
Langdon, Bill	WR	1963
Lange, Gary	FB	1969
Langhorst, Oliver M.	FB	1928
Langston, Donnell	MTR	1972
Lansche, Oral A.	FB	1913
	MTR	1915
	WR	1915
Lansford, Bob	MTN	1959,60
Lanter, Steve W.	MBK	1977,79
Lanter, Wayne	BB	1957
Lantis, Julie E.	WCC	1982,83
	WTR	1983,84
Lantz, Simon E.	FB	1894
Lanum, Franklin B.	FB	1926,29
Lanum, Harold B.	FB	1910
Lanum, Ralph L.	FB	1918
Lapins, Ron	BB	1973,74,75
LaPlante, Liz	WGY	1978
Lapriore, Chris	MTN	1985
Larimer, Floyd C.	FB	1917,20
Larimer, Mark R.	FN	1948
Larkin, Erik	FN	1990
Larsen, Brett	FB	1992,93,94
Larsen, Eric M.	MSW	1934,35
Larson, Donald	MSW	1955,56,57
Larson, Lambert L.	BB	1913
Larson, Laurie	WGO	1976,77,78,79
Larson, Lyman B.	MTR	1963
Lary, Brad	MSW	1947
Lasater Jr., Harry A.	FB	1936,37
	MBK	1938
LasCasas, Vince A.	MTR	1952
Laster, Tony	FB	1989,90,91
LaSusa, Deanna	WCC	1981

Lat, Paul	MGY	1975,76,77,78
Latham, E. B.	BB	1883
Lattimore, John A.	MTR	1958,59,60
Laurence, Daniel L.	FN	1969
Laurvick, Brett	BB	1994,95
Lavelle, Kenneth E.	FN	1975,76,77,78
Laverman, Petra	VB	1988,89,90
Lavery, Larry B.	FB	1959,60
Law, Glenn	WR	1926
Lawler, William	MGY	1960,61,62
Lawlor, Mike	FB	1983
Lawlor, Sean T.	FB	1984,86
Lawrence, C. G.	MTR	1897,98,99
Lawrence, Cathy	WBK	1983
Lawrence, Cynthia	WTR	1987,88,89,90
Lawrence, Sean	BB	1991
Laws, Joe W.	FN	1975,76,77
Lawton, Brad	MTR	1992,93
Layer, Bruce	WR	1968
Layne, Allen	MSW	1991,92
Laz, Donald R.	FB	1950
	MTR	1949,50,51
Laz, Douglas L.	MTR	1976,77
Lazear, Weston B.	MTR	1907
Lazier, Murney	FB	1947,48
Leach, Todd	FB	1991,92,93
Leach, William F.	MTR	1963
Leasure, Scott	WR	1983
LeBosquet, Maurice	MGO	1921,22
Lechner, Steven	MGY	1978,79,80,81
Leck, Walter C.	MTR	1932
LeCrone, Armand J.	MTR	1959,60,61
LeCrone, Charles M.	MTR	1958,59,60
Ledbetter, George	WR	1934,35
Leddy, George	MBK	1946
Ledvora, Joseph	MGY	1983,84,86
Lee, Gary	FB	1980,81
Lee, Jamie	WR	1994,95
Lee, Jessica	VB	1994
Lee, Joyce L.	WSW	1989,90,91,92
Lee, Omar C.	MTR	1928
Lee, Stanley	WR	1943,48
Lee, Willie	FB	1971
Leech, Rhonda	WGO	1975,76
Leeper, Sam	MBK	1962
Leever, Nicholas J.	FN	1980,81,82,83

A serious knee injury in 1979 ended a promising basketball career for Steve Lanter.

Charles Lakes, an Illini gymnast from 1983-85, was a member of the 1988 U.S. Olympic team.

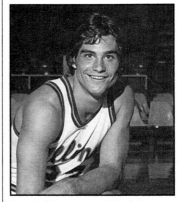

Larry Lubin was one of Coach Lou Henson's first Illini recruits.

- 240 -

Lehman, Fred	MSW	1951,52
Lehmann, J. Dan	FN	1970,72,73,74
Lehmann, Jeffery G.	MTR	1983,84,85
Lehmann, Michael H.	MTR	1979,80,81,82
Lehmann, William	MTR	1936,38
Lehmkuhl, Richard	MSW	1981
Lehnerer, Jim	WR	1964,65
Leigh, William L.	MTR	1979,80
Leighty, Brad	MGO	1986,87
Leighty, Rick	MBK	1976,77
Leiken, Richard W.	FN	1962,63
Leininger, Joseph	MTN	1980
Leischaruring, M. F.	WR	1913
Leishman, Jane	WGO	1983
Leistner, Charles A.	FB	1943
Leitch, Neal M.	FB	1918
Lembeck, Tom	WR	1983
Lempke, Duane A.	FN	1959
Lenich, William	FB	1937,38,39
Lenington, Ernest	MTR	1931,32,33
Lenke, E. H.	MGY	1902
Lennon, J. Patrick	FB	1960
Lenti, Kim	VB	1978,79,80,81
Lentz, Jack	MSW	1938
Lenzini, James R.	MTR	1978,79,80,81
Lenzini, Robert E.	FB	1951,52,53
	MTR	1952
Leo, Herbert T.	MBK	1911,12
	MTR	1910,11,12
Leonard, Berny	BB	1966
Leonard, Bryan	MBK	1981,82,83
Leonard, Marion R.	FB	1924,25
Leonardi, Anthony	BB	1982,83
Lepic, Mike	FB	1974
Lester, Wagner	FB	1989,90
Leuchtmann, Joseph W.	MCC	1986,87
	MTR	1986,87
Leuthold, Donald W.	MTR	1947,48,49,50
Levanti, John	FB	1971,72,73
Levanti, Louis	FB	1947,48,49
	MTR	1946
Levanti, Mike	WR	1970,71,72
Levenick, Stu	FB	1974,75
Levenson, Steve	MTN	1966,67,68
Leverich, Wesley	WR	1939

Levin, M.	MSW	1924
Levine, Bob	MSW	1968,69,70
Levine, Julius	SOC	1932
Levitt, David	MGY	1973
Levitt, Lloyd	FB	1978,79
Levy, Bertram	MTN	1944
Lewers, Richard	MTN	1935,36
Lewin, Maxwell M.	SOC	1928,29
Lewis, Ben C.	BB	1933,34,35
Lewis, Charles M.	MTR	1892,93,94,95,96
Lewis, Chester	WR	1973
Lewis, James W.	FB	1928
Lewis, Joe	FB	1970,71,72
Lewis, Kenneth S.	MTR	1918
Lewis, Norman B.	MSW	1936,37
Lewis, Randy R.	MGO	1981,82,83,84
Lewis, Tom I.	MSW	1942
Lewis, William M.	MTR	1940,41,42
Lewke, Bob	MTN	1965,66
Liberty, Marcus	MBK	1989,90
Lichter, J. P.	MSW	1913
Lifvendahl, Richard A.	FB	1919
	MTR	1919
	MGY	1920
Ligare, Edwardo	BB	1886
Light, Curtis R.	BB	1911
Limestall, Susan	WBK	1975,76,77
Lindall, Fred H.	MTR	1931,32
	SOC	1932
Lindbeck, Emerit (Em)	FB	1953,54,55
	BB	1955,56
Lindberg, Edward F. J.	MTR	1906,07,08,09
Lindberg, Lester L.	FB	1933,34,35
Linde, Gerald H.	MTR	1924
Linden, Frank W.	BB	1898
Linden, O. W.	MSW	1921
Linden, Russell W.	FB	1920
Linder, Raymond	MGY	1947,48,50
Lindgren, Justa M.	FB	1898,99,00,01
Lindner, Paul	MGY	1987,88
Lindsay, Forrest	MBK	1926
Lindy, Donald	WR	1940
Line, Harold E.	MTR	1932
	MCC	1930,31,32
Line, Jerry	FB	1967

Lingner, Adam	FB	1979,80,81,82
Linhart, George	MGY	1990,91
Lipe, Cordon	MBK	1923,24,25,26
Lipe, K. Jack	MBK	1925,26
Lipson, Lee	FN	1948,49
Lirot, Daniel	MGY	1954,55,56
Litt, Leon B.	FB	1907
Littell, David A.	FN	1972,73,74
	MTN	1972
Little, Charles D.	FB	1984,85,86,87
Little, Roger	MTN	1945,48,49,50
Livas, Steve	FB	1969
Lively, Thomas G.	MSW	1938
Livingston, Mary	VB	1974
Llewellyn, Chris	WR	1982,84
Llewellyn, Jon	WR	1988,89,90,91
Lloyd, R. C.	MTR	1901
Loar, Ned	MSW	1955,56,57
Lobb, Andrew	MTN	1986,87
Locascio, Sharon	WCC	1986,87
	WTR	1988
Locascio, Victor	WR	1952
Locke, Seward C.	SOC	1932
Lockwood, W. W.	MSW	1930
Loewe, Richard	WR	1948,50
Loffredo, Bob	WR	1966,67,68
Logan, David	MGO	1948,49,50
Logeman, Ron	FB	1976
Lohr, Lane	MTR	1984,85,86,87
Lollino, Frank V.	FB	1961,62
Lombardi, Vince	MTN	1993
Lonergan, Charles P. A.	FB	1904
Long, Frank B.	BB	1884,85,86,87
Long, Harold D.	MTR	1932
Long, Kelly	WTR	1980
Long, Mark	MTN	1985,86,87,88
Long, Troy L.	MTR	1901,05
Looby, Mary	WTR	1978
Lopater, Dave	MSW	1971
Lopez, John	FB	1979,80,81
Lord, Chester	PO	1941
Lorenz, Bob	BB	1966
Lorenz, Ed	WR	1969
Losito, John	MTN	1984,85
Lothrop, James	MTN	1942,43

Lottes, Jan	VB	1983
	WTR	1983
Lotz, John R.	BB	1898,99,00,01
Lotzer, Joseph J.	IHO	1940,41,42
Loughman, Philip G.	MTR	1971
Louis, Benjamin E.	MTR	1966
	MBK	1966,67,68
Louncey, Linnea	VB	1974,75
Love, John	MBK	1962,64
Lovejoy, Charles E.	FB	1917,18,19
Lovelace, Curtis	FB	1987,88,89,90
Lovelace, Jay	MBK	1962
Lovellette, Lindell J.	FB	1960
Lovin, Christopher	MSW	1983,84,85,86
Lowe, George A.	MSW	1937,38,39
Lowe, Kevin	FB	1974
Lowenthal, Fred	FB	1898,99,00,01
Lowes, Forrest M.	BB	1894,95
Lubeck, Chris	MSW	1988,89,90,91
Lubeck, Kim	WSW	1992
Lubin, Lawrence L.	MBK	1976,77,78,79
Lucas, Anatole	FN	1948,49
Ludington, Lashon	FB	1993,94
Ludlam, John S.	BB	1926
Luhrsen, Paul H.	FB	1952,53
Lukas, Peter	WR	1942
Lukasik Jr., Fred	MGO	1968
Lukaszewski, Don	BB	1955,56,57
Luker, Thomas P.	MTR	1956,57
Luker, Tom	MCC	1954,55,56
Lundberg, Albert J.	FB	1937,38,39
Lundeen, Jeffery	MTR	1964,65
Lundgren, Carl L.	BB	1899,00,01,02
	FB	1899,00
Lundien, Edwin	MGY	1950
Lundine, Dan	BB	1995
Lundquist, Debra	WGY	1977
Lundstedt, Dave	BB	1972,73,74,75
Lunn, Robert J.	FB	1945
Luthringer, Marshall	WR	1924,25
Lutz, Charles	WR	1940
Lutz, Robert	WR	1952,53
Luyando, David	MGY	1984
Lyle, Duane	FB	1994
Lymperopoulous, J.	BB	1928,29,30

Golfer Brenda Macconnachie was a four-time letter winner at Illinois.

Lynch, Clinton FB 1990,91,93
Lynch, George MCC 1950
Lynch, James FB 1985,86
Lynch, James R. FN 1965,66
Lynch, Jennifer WGO 1992,93,94,95
Lynch, Lynn FB 1949,50
Lyon, Daniel R. MTR 1926,27,28
Lyon, F. S. MGO 1929,30,31
Lyons, Thomas E. FB 1909,10

M

Maart, Michelle WGY 1985,86,87,88
MacAdams, Maggie WGY 1976,77,78
MacArthur, John E. FB 1942
Macchione, Rudolph J. FB 1944
Macconnachie, Brenda WGO 1985,86,87,88
MacDonald, Don MTN 1953
MacDonald, J. M. MGO 1917
MacDonald, Mike MBK 1989
MacDonald, Rod MSW 1972,73,74,75
Macedo, Goncalo MGY 1993,94,95
MacGregor, Ellen WSW 1985,86,87,88

MacIntyre, James MTR 1965
Mackay, J. J. MTR 1904,05,06
Mackay, John L. BB 1884,85
Mackie, Chris MSW 1986,87
Mackin, Beth WSW 1987,88
Mackin, James MSW 1987,88,89
MacLean, Dan FB 1979,80
MacLean, William P. SOC 1934
Macomber, Bart WR 1966,67,68
Macomber, F. Bart FB 1914,15,16
Maddux, Scott MCC 1989,90,91,92
MTR 1992
Maddux, Troy MCC 1990
Madej, Diane (Tina) WSW 1976,77
Madix, Bob BB 1958,59,60
Madsen, Harry MSW 1950,51
Madsen, Olav FB 1914
Madsen, Wendy WCC 1993
WTR 1991,92,93
Maechtle, Donald M. FB 1946,47,48
Magas, Barbella WBK 1975,77,78
Maggioli, Archille F. FB 1946,47
Maher, Steve MGY 1984,85
Mahon, John MGO 1985
Maier, George BB 1951
Maier, John MSW 1977,78
Mail, Isaac P. MTR 1941,42,43
Majercik, Larry BB 1970
Major, Charles F. BB 1925,26
Major Jr., Fred FB 1950
Major, John WR 1983,84
Makeever, Samuel J. MCC 1923,29
MTR 1924,25,30
Makielski, Ward MSW 1988
Makovsky, Ed MBK 1953,54
Maksud, Mike BB 1954
Malik, Warren C. FN 1941,42
Malinsky, Robert E. FB 1948
Malley, Robert BB 1946,47
Malmberg, Kenneth MSW 1985,86,87,88
Maloney, Russ MSW 1990,91,92
Malstrom, Gordon MGO 1960
Malz, Peter J. MTR 1951
Manaois, Arnold C. FN 1982,83,85
Mango, Robert J. MTR 1970,71,72,73

Mann, A. S. MGY 1913
Mann, Arthur R. MTR 1895
Mann, Philip MGO 1977,78
Mann, William WR 1947,48,50
Mann, William E. MSW 1944,45,46
Manpearl, David MTN 1994,95
Manzke, Edward MBK 1989
March, Dean FB 1974,76
Marczewski, Jeff MTR 1981,82
Margolis, Ralph BB 1924,25,26
Marianetti, Steve WR 1992,93,94,95
Marinangel, Jim FB 1967
Marine, Gar MSW 1966
Marine, Jennifer S. WCC 1993
Maris, Ronald W. MTR 1957
Markland, Jeff FB 1986,87
Marks, James MBK 1948,49
Marks, John MBK 1951
Markworth, Martin MBK 1936
Marlaire, Arthur G. FB 1940
Marley, James A. MTR 1903,05
Marlin, Ken WR 1946,47,49
Marquardt, Robert MGO 1952
Marrero, Emilio MGY 1988,89,92
Marriner, Lester M. FB 1925,26,27
Marriner, Scott T. FB 1931
Marshak, Sara WTN 1993,94,95
Marshall, Chuck WR 1968,69
Marshall, Douglas G. MGY 1937
Marshall, John MSW 1930
Marshall, Paul FB 1993,94
Marsillo, Paul BB 1977,78,79,80
Martignago, Aldo A. FB 1947,48,49
Martin, Hollie MBK 1926
Martin, James PO 1939,40
Martin, Jeff BB 1993,94
Martin, Jeffery C. FB 1984,85,86
Martin, John FB 1992
Martin, John D. MTR 1946
Martin, Lorenzo E. MTR 1956
Martin, Mike FB 1980,81,82
Martin, Richard S. MGO 1929,30,31
Martin, Robert W. FB 1898
MTR 1899,00,01
Martin, Russel FB 1958
BB 1958,59,60
Martin, Wesley P. FB 1938,39
Marzulo, Sam C. MTR 1923,24
MCC 1923
Masar, Terry FB 1969,70,71
Masek, Albert BB 1934
Mason, Arthur H. MTR 1914,15,16
MCC 1913
Mason, Lou BB 1908
Mason, Melissa WTR 1982
Mason, Richard W. MTR 1958,59
Mason, Taylor FB 1978
Mason, W. T. MGO 1926
Massey, Keith BB 1984,85,86
Masterson, Daniel MTR 1966
Masterson, Donald J. MTR 1966
Mastoris, Helen WCC 1989
WTR 1989,90
Mastrangeli, Al A. FB 1946,47,48
Matejzel, August BB 1968,69,70
Mathers, Manley B. MTR 1913
WR 1911,12
Mathews, Clyde M. BB 1899,00,01,02
FB 1900
Mathieu, Bud MSW 1976,77,78
Mathis, Archie WR 1924,25
Mathis, Mark FB 1985,86
Mathis, William MTR 1946,47
Mathisen, Arthur MBK 1941,42,43
Matiya, Joellyn WGY 1980,81,82
Matlock, Gary WR 1974,75,76,78
Matson, George A. MGY 1942
Matsumoto, Yukio WR 1953,54
Matt, John BB 1960,61,62
Matten, Brad MSW 1968,69,70
Matter Jr., Herbert J. MTR 1942,43,47
Matthei, L. P. MSW 1931
Matthews, Audie MBK 1975,76,77,78
Matthews, Joyce WSW 1985
Mattiazza, Dominic L. FB 1941
Mattison, Steve FB 1994
Mauck, Eugene H. MSW 1936
Mauck, Jeff FB 1985
Mauer, John MBK 1924,25,26
Maurer, Ron BB 1963,64,65
Mautner, Henry MSW 1947
Mauzey, John FB 1968,69

Former Illini football star Larry McCarren starred with the NFL's Green Bay Packers.

Maxwell, Barry MTN 1970,71,72
Maxwell, John R. BB 1893
MTR 1893
Maxwell, Nancy WGO 1977,78,79,80
May, Elbridge MBK 1929,30,31
May, Robert D. FB 1931,32
May, Roger WR 1966,67,68
May, William W. MTR 1906,07,08,09
Mayback, Laurie WCC 1980
Mayer, Bob WR 1970,71,72,73
Mayer, Patricia WTR 1979
Mayer, S. R. MSW 1924
Maynard, Eugene E. MTR 1952,53,54
Mayville, Mike BB 1974,76
Maze, Anthony FB 1936,37
Mazeika, Anthony M. BB 1938,39
Mazikowski, Carol WTR 1980,81,82,83
Mazur, Dan MCC 1991,92,93
MTR 1994,95
Mazzetta, Ozzie MGO 1954
McAfee, Floyd H. FB 1954,55
McArthur, Joan VB 1974
McAvoy, Tim FB 1979,80,81
McBain, Mike FB 1983,84,85
McBeth, Mike FB 1979
McBride, John MBK 1973
McBride, Kevin BB 1977,78,79
McBride, Willis B. MBK 1893
McCabe, Claude P. BB 1933
McCabe, Dennis WR 1972
McCann, Thomas E. BB 1921
McCarren, Larry FB 1970,71,72
McCarron, Dennis WR 1955,56
McCarthy, James P. FB 1941,42
MGO 1942,43
McCarthy, John MGY 1967,68,69
McCarthy, Kathleen WSW 1987,88
McCarthy, Terence MSW 1983,84,85
McCarthy, Tim FB 1969,70
McCartney, Tom FB 1972,73
McCaskill, Arthur FB 1964
McCaskrin, Henry M. MTR 1892,93,94
McClain, Amy WSW 1985,86,87
McClatchey, Angela WTR 1986,87,88,89
McCleery, Ben H. FB 1909
McClellan, Angie WBK 1986,87
McClellan, Lynn FB 1987,88
McClelland, Kim WBK 1989
McCloskey, Pam WGO 1984,85,86
McCloud, Tim FB 1992,93,94
McClure, Brian BB 1993,94,95
McClure, L. Milton MTR 1936
McClure, Ora D. BB 1890
McClure, Ray MBK 1946
McClure, Robert T. FB 1978,79
McClure, William E. FB 1927,28
McCollum, Greg BB 1984,85,86,87
McCollum, Harvey D. BB 1897,98,99,00
McCollum, Tom MTN 1963,64
McConnell, Douglas MSW 1976,77,78,79
McConnell, Thomas M. BB 1937,38,39
McCord, Ralph N. MTR 1908,09,10
McCormick, Olin BB 1892
FB 1892,93
McCormick, Roscoe C. FB 1898
McCown, Wilbur M. MTR 1938,39,40
McCoy, William MTN 1937,38
McCracken, Brian WR 1985,86,87
McCracken, Malcolm B. FB 1975,76

Ernie McMillan, an Illini football letterman from 1958-60, went on to a brilliant NFL career with the St. Louis Cardinals.

McCracken, Rebecca	WTR	1976
McCrackin, Robert	PO	1941
McCraven, Steve	MTN	1988,89
McCray, Michael P.	FB	1976,77
McCulley, C. T.	MTR	1903,04
McCulley, Daniel M.	MTR	1980,81
McCullough, Lawrence	FB	1978,79
McCullough, Thomas M.	FB	1941
McCullum, Al	WR	1964,65,66
McCullum, Thomas	FB	1961
McCully, Matt	BB	1994,95
McCune, Clinton C.	IHO	1941,42
McCune, Henry L.	BB	1880,81,83
McCurdy, Henry H.	BB	1920,21,22
McDade, Richard L.	FB	1958,61
McDermith, Harry	WR	1933
McDermont, Verne A.	MTR	1929,30,31
McDevitt, William	FN	1962,63
McDonald, A. P	MSW	1914,16
McDonald, B. A.	MGY	1925,26
McDonald, James W.	FB	1937,38
McDonald Jr., John	FN	1941
McDonald, John J.	BB	1936,37
McDonald, Ken	FB	1979
McDonald, Mark	FB	1977
	WR	1978
McDonald, Phil	FB	1974,75,76
McDonald, Richard	MTN	1956,57
McDonald, Robert	BB	1980
McDonough, Daren	MTR	1993,94,95
McDonough, Mike	FB	1967,68
McDyer, Dale	MSW	1958,59
McEathron, William J.	BB	1883
McElfresh, Fred M.	MTR	1893,94
McElwee Jr., E. James	MTR	1961,62
	MCC	1960,61
McElwee Sr., Ermel J.	MTR	1926,27,28
	MCC	1925,26,27
McFadzean, John	SOC	1927,28,29
McFarland, P. E.	MGY	1924
	MSW	1924
McGann, David G.	FB	1961
McGann, Mike	FB	1983
McGarry, Shawn	FB	1987,88
McGee, Cindy	WGY	1983

Mel Meyers, a letter winner in 1959 and '60, was one of Big Ten football's first African-American quarterbacks.

McGill, Ruel S.	BB	1897,98
McGinnis, Gordon F.	MTR	1921,22
	MCC	1921
McGlaun, Gregory	MGY	1994,95
McGlone, Catherine	WCC	1980
	WTR	1981
McGovern, Edward F.	FB	1943
McGowan, Mark	FB	1985,86,87,88
McGraw, Arthur C.	MTR	1936
McGregor, John L.	FB	1915,17
McGrone, Bryan	FB	1987
McGufficke, Graeme	MSW	1983,85,86,87
McHose, Joseph C.	MTR	1924
McIlduff, Thomas E.	BB	1879,81
McIllwain, Wallace W.	FB	1922,23,24
McIlvoy, Jack	WR	1935,37
McInich, Nelson	MTN	1935
McIntosh, Hugh	FB	1969
McKay, Ernest	MBK	1917
McKay, Robert	MBK	1927
McKee, Christopher	MGY	1986,87,88,89
McKee, James H.	FB	1895,96
McKeever, Donald	MTR	1927
McKenley, Herbert H.	MTR	1946,47
McKenzie, Nick	MTN	1986
McKeon, Larry	FB	1969
McKeown, Bill	MBK	1964,65
McKeown, John L.	MTR	1913,14,15
McKibbin, Wayne J.	IHO	1940,41
McKinley, George H.	FB	1901,02
McKinley, Robert O.	MSW	1940,41
McKinney, Jerry	BB	1956
McKinney, Norman	MTR	1917
McKinzie, James	MGO	1951,52
McKinzie, Laura	WGO	1976,77
McKissic, Dan	FB	1967,69
McKnight, William A.	FB	1901,02,03
McKown, Robert W.	MTR	1956,57,58
McLane, E. C.	FB	1897,98,99
McLarty, Brandon	MSW	1992
McLellan, Jeffery C.	MTR	1967,68,69
McMahon, John E.	SOC	1933,34
McMillan, Ernest	FB	1958,59,60
McMillen, James W.	FB	1921,22,23
	WR	1923,24
McMillin, Kirk	FB	1969,70
McMillin, Troy	FB	1978,79,81
McMillin, Ty	FB	1972,73,74
McMullen, Rolla	BB	1956,57
	FB	1955,56
McMurchie, Kevin	MGY	1980,81,82,83
McNabb, Lou	MTR	1970
McNally, Andrew	MSW	1920,21
McNamara, Brian	MSW	1991,92
McNamara, Mary	WTN	1975,76,77
McNamara, Maureen	WTN	1981,82,83,84
McNee, Kelly	WCC	1983,84,85
	WTR	1983,84,85,86
McNulty, Joel M.	MTR	1951,52,53
McPartlin, Chris	FB	1994
McPheron, Ron	MSW	1984
McQuinn, Mike	FB	1980,81,82
McRae, Thomas	FN	1993
McRobie, Douglas	BB	1914
McSween, Cirilo A.	MTR	1951,52,54
McSwine, Becky	WSW	1977,78
McVey, Andrew	MSW	1987,88,89
Means, Pam	WBK	1983,84,86
Mechling, Paul	WR	1953,54
Medley, Earl	WR	1970,71
Mee, Julian E.	BB	1920,21
	MBK	1920,21
Meeks, Richard	WR	1952,53,55
Meeland, Tor	MSW	1942,43
Meents, Scott	MBK	1983,84,85,86
Meharry, J. E.	MTR	1899
Mehock, Harry E.	MTR	1925,26
Meier, Joseph	MGO	1979,80
Meier, Mike	MCC	1972
Meislahn, Arthur C.	MTR	1925,26,27
Melin, Carl A.	MTR	1903,04
Melino, Castanzo	BB	1936
Mellen, William	WR	1953,55,56
Melnicove, Gary	MSW	1962,63
Melsek, Daniel	FB	1976
Melton Jr., Albert	MTR	1974,75,76
Mench, Mark	FN	1976
Menke, Ken	MBK	1942,43,47
Menke, Robert	MBK	1946
Menke, Wilbur	FN	1929
Menkhausen, Brian	FB	1986,87,88,89
Meola, Kristi	WTN	1992,93,94

Mercer, Frank	PO	1934,35
Mercer, Lindy	WSW	1995
Merigold, Julian S.	MTR	1925
Meriweather, Michele	WSW	1987,88
Merker, Henry F.	FB	1897
Merrifield, Albert W.	BB	1889,90,91,92
	MTR	1889,90,91,92
Merrill, Stillwell F.	MTR	1900
Merriman, John R.	MTR	1911
	FB	1909,10,11
Mersbach, David	MSW	1953,54
Mershon, Brian	BB	1986,87
Mershon, Mike	BB	1988
Merzian, Chuck	WR	1951
Mesch, Dan	MTN	1959,60
Metcalf, Doug	MSW	1975
Metcalf, Robert L.	MGO	1939
Mettle, Jerry	MBK	1967
Mettler, Charles W.	IHO	1940
Meurisse, Charles	MTN	1975,76,77,78
Meyer, Irwin H.	BB	1929
Meyer, John	FB	1977
Meyer, Matt	MBK	1979
Meyer, Mike	MTN	1983,84,86
Meyer, Ronald H.	FN	1950,51
Meyer, Russ	MSW	1973,74,75,76
Meyer, Wayne	WR	1953
Meyer, Werner	FN	1950,51
Meyers, Curtis	FB	1980
Meyers, Melvin	FB	1959,60
Meyers, William	BB	1945
Meyle, Wendy J.	WTR	1981,82,83,84
Michael, Tom	MBK	1991,92,93,94
Michal, Mary	WCC	1992
Michalak, Tony	BB	1984,85,86,87
Michel, Chris	FB	1985,86
Michelson, Larry	MSW	1960
Mickelson, A. M.	MGO	1935
Middeler, Jenny	WBK	1983,84,85,86
Middleton, George E.	FB	1920
Middleton, James R.	MSW	1942
Mieher Jr., Edward C.	MTR	1924,25
	MCC	1922,23,24
Mierzwa, Fred	MGY	1967,68
Mies, Harold H.	MTR	1938
Migdow, Ben	MTN	1946,47
Milani, Anthony	MSW	1980
Miles, Donna	WTR	1982,85
Miles, Joe	FB	1980,81,82,83
Miles, Kathy	WTR	1980
Miles, Rutherford T.	MTR	1899,1901
Miller, Bob	FB	1982,83,84
Miller, C. Marshall	MTR	1934
Miller, Christine	WTR	1991,92
Miller, Clarence B.	MTR	1907,08
Miller, David H.	FB	1939
Miller, Diane	WGO	1975,76,77,78
Miller, Fred	MBK	1969,70,71
Miller, Fred C.	BB	1900,03
Miller, Harold R.	MCC	1924
	MTR	1925
Miller, Jeff A.	FN	1980
Miller, Jerome	BB	1952,53
Miller, Justi Rae	WGO	1986,87,88,89
Miller, Kenneth R.	FB	1951,52,53
Miller, Lester	BB	1946,47,48
Miller, Phil	WR	1972,73,74,75
Miller, Richard R.	FB	1952,55,56
Miller, Robert F.	IHO	1942
Miller, Robert	MSW	1955,56,57
Miller, Roy A.	FB	1922,23,24
Miller, Stephen	MGO	1979,80
Miller, Terry	FB	1965,66,67
	MTR	1966,67
Miller, Thomas S.	MTR	1928,30
Miller, Jr., V. Ward	MTR	1959
Miller, William G.	MTR	1892
Mills, Allen	FN	1950,51,52
Mills, Coke	MBK	1935
Mills, Douglas C.	BB	1960,61,62
	MBK	1961,62
	FB	1961
Mills, Douglas R.	MBK	1928, 29,30
	FB	1927,28,29
Mills, George A.	BB	1930,31,32
Mills, Morton J.	MTR	1919
Mills, Ralph	MTR	1897,99
Milne, Edward L.	MTR	1895,96,97
Milosevich, Paul	BB	1940,41,42
	FB	1939,40,41
Milstein, Sidney M.	FN	1971,72,73
Mindcock, Laura	WTR	1993,94,95

Basketball's Tom Michael held Illinois' record for three-pointers at one time in his career.

Mingle, David	MGY	1984,85,87,88
Mingle, Michael	MGY	1989
Minicucci, Dominick	MGY	1988,89
Mink, Ely H.	SOC	1930,31,32
Minkus, Marc	MTN	1974
Minnes, Mason	FB	1970,71,72
Minor, James R.	FB	1955,56
Minor, William B.	FB	1962,63,64
Minot, George	WR	1926,29
Minsker, Robert S.	FB	1933
	WR	1934
Mioduski, Moseph	MTN	1939
Missey, Matt	MTR	1993
Mitchell, Bill	FB	1967
Mitchell, George W.	MTR	1892
Mitchell, Jeffrey	MGY	1979,80,81,82
Mitchell, Robert (Bobby)	FB	1955,56,57
	MTR	1957,58
Mitchell, Ronald L.	MTR	1952,54,58,59
Mitchem, Rickie	FB	1975,76,77
Mitizia, Albert M.	MTR	1935,36
Mitter, Todd	BB	1988,89
Mitterwallner, M. H.	FB	1925,27
Mittleman, Benjamin	MBK	1918,19
Mix, M. I.	MSW	1912
Mkchyan, Tigran	MGY	1985,86,87,88
Mobarak, Aaron A.	MTR	1990,91
Modjeska, Eugene F.	MGO	1940,43
Moeck, Peggy	VB	1974,75,76
Moench, R. G.	MSW	1931
Mohan, Edgar H.	FN	1921,22
Mohr Jr., Albert W. T.	FB	1918,19,20,21
Mohr, Scott	BB	1978
Mohr, Scott	FB	1987,88
Molaro, Steve	BB	1959
Moler, Jason	BB	1989,90
Moll, Joe	MTN	1934,35,36
Moll, William D.	FN	1956
Mondie-Milner, Celena	WTR	1987,88,89,90
Mongreig, Louis M.	FB	1917
	MTR	1917
Monk, Marvin E.	MGY	1937
Monson, Jeff	WR	1993
Montero, Kristin	WGY	1995
Montgomery, George	MBK	1982,83,84,85
Montgomery, Lisa	WGY	1982
Moore, Barry	BB	1966

George Montgomery lettered for Coach Lou Henson from 1982-85.

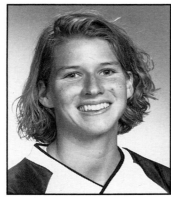

Merrill Mullis was a three-time Academic All-Big Ten selection.

Moore, Christopher	MSW	1982
Moore, Cindy	WGY	1982,83
Moore, Craig	FB	1986,87
Moore, David	WR	1956,57,58
Moore, Henry H.	MSW	1944,45
Moore, Merrill D.	MSW	1945
Moore, Paul	FB	1976
Moore, Robert	BB	1951,52,53
Moore, Ron	FN	1970,72
Moore, Terrance D.	MTR	1985
Moore, Tom	MSW	1991,92
Moore, Vernon	MBK	1932
Moran, Mark A.	MTR	1898,99
Morehouse, Merritt J.	MTR	1889
Morency, Pat	WBK	1979,80,81,82
Moreno, David R.	FN	1983,84,85,86
Morf, F. P.	MGY	1925
Morgan, Octavus	FB	1971,72,73
Morley, George	MSW	1964
Morrey, Kevin	MTN	1971,72,73,74
Morrill, Guy L.	MTR	1910,11,12
Morris, Bill	MBK	1972
Morris, George	MTR	1967,68,69
Morris, Harold H.	FB	1916
Morris, Karen J.	WCC	1990,91,92,93,94
	WTR	1993,94
Morris, Kathy A.	WCC	1992,93
	WTR	1992,94
Morris, LaRue	FB	1936
Morris, Max	FB	1943
Morris, R. Jeffery	MTR	1976
Morrison, Allie	WR	1929,30
Morrison, Heraldo E.	MTR	1986
Morrison, John E.	BB	1907,08
Morrison, R. C.	WR	1928
Morrison, Wayne	MTN	1975
Morrissey, Don	WR	1959,60
Mors Jr., Robert J.	MTR	1960
Morscheiser, Jack	FB	1971
Morse, Roger W.	SOC	1931,33
Morton, Robert	MBK	1944,45
Mosely, Marquis	FB	1993,94
Moses, James	MTN	1949,50,51
Moskiewicz, John	MSW	1954
Moskovitz, Bonnie	VB	1983

Bob Noelke, a native of Glen Ellyn, Illinois, played football at Illinois in the late 1970s.

Mosley, Larry	FB	1980,81
Moss, Larry	MTN	1962,63
Moss, Perry L.	FB	1946,47
Mosser, Keith M.	FN	1984,85,86,87
Most, Fred	MTN	1952,55
Mota, Dan	WR	1983,84,85
Mota, Joseph L.	FB	1961
Mottern, H. M.	MSW	1913
Mottlowitz, Kevin	WR	1987,88,89
Mountjoy, Earl L.	FB	1909
Mountz III, Robert E.	FB	1960,61
Moyer, Carlisle E.	BB	1933,34,35
Moyer, H. Anita	WCC	1977,78,79
	WTR	1976,77,78,79
Moynihan, Charles J.	FB	1903,04,05,06
Mroz, Wallie	BB	1945
	MBK	1946
Mudrock, Mark	MGO	1979,80
Muegge, Louis W.	FB	1925,27
	WR	1928
Mueller, Dave	FB	1963,64
Mueller, Erik	WR	1987,88
Mueller, Kristie	WSW	1993,94,95
Mueller, Richard A.	FB	1948,49,50
Mueller, Roger	MGO	1955,56
Mueller, Steven	FB	1988,90,91,92
Mueller, William	MSW	1983,84,85,86
Muhl, Clarence A. (Stub)	FB	1923,24,25
Muhl, Fred L.	FB	1903
Muirhead, William	BB	1953
Mulcahy, Kourtney	WGO	1994
Mulchrone, John	FB	1979,80
Mulchrone, Pete	FB	1979,81,82
Mullen, R. Patrick	MTR	1964,65,66
Mulligan, Sean	BB	1989,90,91
Mulliken, John W.	MGO	1966,67,68
Mullin, Tom	FB	1972,73
Mullins, George	MSW	1947,48,49
Mullis, Merrill	VB	1990,91,92,93
Mulloy, Chris	MSW	1991,92
Mumaw, Gary	MCC	1975,76
Munch, Donald C.	FB	1930
Mundt, Craig	BB	1964
Munnis, James	MCC	1931
Munro, Dan	MSW	1983,84,85
Munson, Keith E.	FN	1983,84,85,86
Munson, Mike	BB	1985,86,87,88
Murawski, Michael	BB	1967,68,69
Murchison, R. R.	MGY	1905
Murin, Laura	WGY	1981
Murnick, Scott	FB	1987
Murowitz, Herbert	FN	1957
Murphy, Debra	WTR	1976
Murphy Jr., Frank	MGO	1947
Murphy, Frank D.	MTR	1910,11,12
Murphy, Jane	WGO	1980,81,82,83
Murphy, Mary Ellen	WGO	1980,81,82,83
Murphy, Mike	FB	1979,80,81,82
Murphy, Patrick	FB	1960,61
Murphy, Thomas W.	FB	1951,52
Murray, Bill	BB	1966,67,68
Murray, Edward	FB	1973,74
Murray, James	BB	1977,78,79
Murray, John	MTN	1988,89,90
Murray, Lindley P.	FB	1931
Murray, Oscar J.	MTR	1914
Murray, Robert	MGY	1951
Murray, William	MGY	1975
Musch, Tom	MSW	1969,70
Muschler, George	MTR	1974
Musiek, Annette	WSW	1979
Muther, William	WR	1956,57,58
Muti, Joe	FB	1990,91
Mutter, Charles	WR	1936,37,38
Myers, Carl	MTR	1993,94,95
Myers, Les	MCC	1976
Myers, William	BB	1946,47

N

Nagel, Richard	MGY	1971,72
Nagle, James	MTR	1954
Nagle, Perry I.	MTR	1921
Nair, Madhu	MTN	1985,86
Nalls, Alonzo	WR	1987
Naponic, Robert	FB	1966,67,68
Naprestek, Frank J.	BB	1911
Nash, Joseph	BB	1977
Nasser, David	MTN	1989,90,91,92
Nasser, Mark	MTN	1993,94
Nast, Wayne A.	MTR	1951
Naughton, Jr., Frank U.	MTR	1920,21

Nauta, Michael	MTR	1965
	MCC	1963
Navarro, Mike	FB	1970,71,72
Neal, John	BB	1949,50
Neal, Melissa	VB	1994
Neathery, Herbert	FB	1950,51,52
Nedrud, Brad	MSW	1973,74,75
Needham, James	BB	1892
	FB	1891,92
Needler, L. Q.	MGO	1921
Neil, Kathy M.	WTN	1985,86,87,88
Neilson, Dotty	WGY	1983
Neisz, W. Royce	FN	1964
Nelle, Richard S.	MTR	1932
Nelligan, Ryan	BB	1990,91
Nelson, Barbara	WBK	1975
Nelson, Dale	WR	1949
Nelson, Evert F.	FB	1927
Nelson, H. A.	BB	1879,80,81
Nelson, Jesse W.	FB	1914,15
Nelson, John	MSW	1988,89
Nelson, Kenneth J.	FB	1934,35,36
Nelson, Maureen	WTN	1976,77,78,79
Nelson, Ralph W.	FB	1956
Nelson, Robert	BB	1969
Nelson, Steve	FB	1983,84
	WR	1984,85
Nelson, Steve	FB	1989,91
Nemec, Carrie	VB	1978,79,80
Netzel, Denise	WSW	1979
Neufeldt, James	BB	1945,47
Nevels, Charles	MSW	1944
Neverstitch, Lisa	WTR	1979,80
Nevins, Arthur S.	BB	1913
	MTR	1911,12,13
New, Nash	BB	1968
Newcom, Gregory	BB	1980,81
Newell, Bruce	MSW	1964,65
Newell, Lee	MGO	1964,65
Newell, Richard F.	FB	1960,61
Newsome, Collinus	WTR	1995
Neylon, Brian	MSW	1985,86,87,88
Nichols, David C.	MTR	1944,45
Nichols, Mike	WR	1991,92,93
Nichols, Pete	MSW	1960
Nichols, Sidney W.	FB	1917
Nicholson, Garry	BB	1970,71
Nickol, Edgar	FB	1926,28
	MTR	1927,28
Nicoll, Shawn	WR	1980
Nieckula, Aaron	BB	1995
Niedzelski, Clifford T.	FB	1941
Nielsen, Kurt	MSW	1979
Nietupski, Ronald	FB	1956,57,58
Niezgoda, Joe	BB	1962,63
Niezyniecki, Ted	BB	1986,87
Niklewicz, F. T.	BB	1934,36,37
Nilsen, P. J.	MGY	1914,15
Nimmo, Lindsey	WTN	1991,92,93
Nipinak, Michael	MTR	1974
Nisbet, Tom	MBK	1937,38,39
Nitschke, Ray E.	FB	1955,56,57
Niva, George	MGO	1957,58
Niziolek, Frank	MSW	1990,91,92
Noble, Carl	MTN	1956,57,58
Noble, Frank	MTN	1962,63,64
Noble, John	BB	1884
Noelke, Robert J.	FB	1978,79
Nolan, Dan	MCC	1990,93
	MTR	1992
Noonan, Peggy	WSW	1976
Nordmeyer, Richard J.	FB	1955,56,57
Nordquist, Ken	WR	1953
Norman, Bob	WR	1957,58
Norman, Ken	MBK	1985,86,87
Norman, Sandy	WTR	1978
Norman, Tim	FB	1977,78,80
Norris, Joan	VB	1984
Norris, Ralph V.	MTR	1905,06,07
Norton, James M.	MTR	1965,66,67
Norton, John	FB	1977
Norwood, E. E.	MGY	1923,24,25
Nosek, Stephen A.	FB	1951,53,54
Noth, Charles J.	BB	1942
Notree, Bryant	MBK	1995
Novack, Joseph C.	MCC	1926,27
	MTR	1928
Novak, Mike	WR	1990,91,92,93
Novosel, Brett	MSW	1991
Novosel, Scott	MSW	1988,89,90,91
Novotny, A. L.	MGO	1921,22,23
Novotny, Meg	WSW	1992,94

Former Illini baseball player Donn Pall has played for several years in the major leagues.

Nowack, A. J. (Butch)	FB	1926,27,28
Nowack, Carl	MSW	1978,79
Nowack, Steven	MSW	1980
Nowak, Bill	FB	1967,68
Nucci, Sue	VB	1991,92,93,94
Nuhsbaum, M. Tanja	WTR	1991,92
Numrych, Charlene	WGY	1981,82,83,84
Nusspickel, Raymond E.	BB	1930
	FB	1930,31
Nykeil, Theodore	BB	1938

O

O'Bradovich, Edward	FB	1959,60
O'Brien, Dan	WR	1989,90,92
O'Brien, Kelly	WTR	1989,90,92
O'Brien, Kevin	FN	1978,79
O'Brien, Mike	WR	1985,86,87,88
O'Brien, W. C.	MSW	1925,26
O'Connell, James P.	FN	1984
O'Connell, John J.	MTR	1936
	MCC	1935
O'Connell, T. F. (Tim)	MTN	1926,27,28
O'Connell, Thomas B.	FB	1951,52
O'Connor, Forrest E.	BB	1923,24
O'Connor, Kevin	BB	1989,90
O'Grady, John	BB	1928
O'Hare, John	MGY	1966
O'Heron, John	MGY	1947
O'Keefe, Arthur F.	FB	1931
O'Keefe, James A.	BB	1926
O'Laughlin, Mike	WR	1959,61
O'Meara, Allan R.	MTR	1916
O'Neal, Alvin	MBK	1971
O'Neal, George	MTN	1945
O'Neal, Robert	MBK	1941
O'Neal, Robert D.	MGO	1934,35
O'Neal, Ronald D.	FB	1961
O'Neill, Dick A.	FB	1931
O'Neill, Robert J.	FB	1939
Oakes, Bernard F.	FB	1922,23
	MTR	1924
Oaks, John	WR	1972,73
Oberle, Betty	WCC	1978,79
Oberrotman, Alan	FN	1971,72
Ockert, Carl	MTR	1946

Football's Wayne Paulson was a member of Illinois' 1964 Rose Bowl squad.

Oeler, R. C.	MGY	1928,29,30	Orsag, James	BB	1983,84,85	Palekas, Audrey	WSW	1979,80,81	Passmore, Don	FB	1981,82,83,84

Oeler, R. C. — MGY 1928,29,30
Oestreich, John — BB 1992,93,94,95
Offenbecher, Bill — BB 1959
    FB 1956,57
Ofner, Clyde N. — FN 1971,72
Ohl, Don — MBK 1956,57,58
Ohman, Tom — BB 1966,67
Oien, Charles — BB 1979
Olander, Milton M. — FB 1918,19,20,21
Olcott, G. W. — MSW 1924
Oldham, Yvonne — WTR 1983,84,85,86
Olefsky, Jerry — MTN 1962,63
Olesen, Robert J. — MTR 1986,87,89,90
Olin, Jon — MSW 1964,65
Oliver, Alfonso L. — FN 1970,71,72,73
Oliver, Chauncey B. — FB 1909,10,11
Oliver Jr., Percy L. — FB 1954,55,56
Olker, Joseph — BB 1982,83,84
Olsen, C. F. — MGO 1914,15
Olsen, Donald E. — MTR 1940,41,42
Olsen, Hugh H. — MSW 1945
Olsen, R. S. — MSW 1921,22
Olson, Carlton — MGY 1976,78,79,80
Olson, David — FB 1990,91,92,93
Olson, Everette — MBK 1927
Olson, Gail I. — MTR 1979,80,81,82
Olson, Sara — WTN 1981
Olson, William E. — FN 1962,63
Olszewski, John M. — MTR 1978,80
    MCC 1978,79,80
Oltendorf, Kevin — MGY 1981,82,83
Oman, Steve — FB 1967,68
Ontiveros, John — WR 1953,54,55
Oostendorp, Heather — WSW 1989,90
Oostendorp, Kristen — WSW 1988,89,90
Orlovich, Michael G. — MTR 1937
Orlovich, Robert B. — MTR 1927,28,29
Ormsbee, Terry — FB 1974,76
Ornatek, Tony — FB 1968
Oros, James — BB 1977,78,79
Orr, Charles R. — FN 1961,62
Orr, E. E. — MTR 1893,95
Orr, John M. — FB 1944
    MBK 1945
Orr, R. V. — MGY 1914

Orsag, James — BB 1983,84,85
Orsi, Tom — MGO 1957,58,59
Orth, Glen — WR 1932,33
Ortiz, Hector — MTN 1987,88,89,90
Osborn, Harold M. — MTR 1920,21,22
Osby, Vince — FB 1982,83
Osinski, Henry S. — FN 1948,49
Osley, Willie — FB 1970,71
    MTR 1970
Osness, James — FN 1982
Osowski, Jan — WGY 1979,80,81
Ossola, Ken — BB 1970,71,72,73
Ostaszewski, Walter R. — MTR 1932
Osterkorn, Walter — MBK 1948,49,50
Ott, George — MSW 1923
Ott, J. E. — MSW 1916
Otto, Gordon — MBK 1916
Ottoson, Eric R. — MTR 1987,88,89
Ovelman, John W. — FB 1930
Overbee, William B. — MTR 1917
Overman, Warren C. — MSW 1935,36,37
Ovitz, Ernest G. — BB 1906,07,08
Owen, Boyd W. — FB 1930
    MBK 1931,32,33
Owen, Holly — VB 1977,78,79
Owen, Starr H. — IHO 1941
Owens, Isaiah H. — FB 1941,46,47

P
Pace, Dennis — MBK 1967,68,69
Pacini, Michael S. — FN 1978,79,80,81
Pacotti, John B. — BB 1938,40
Paden, J. C. — MTR 1905
Padgett, Christopher — MSW 1983,84,85
Paetau, Gary — MTR 1970
Paetau, Holger — MTR 1972,74
Pagakis, Chris N. — FB 1949,50
Pagoraro, Robert A. — MGO 1969,70,71
Painter, David — MCC 1979,80
Pakutinsky, Frank — WR 1936
Pakutinsky, Pete — WR 1934,35,36
Pala, Steve — MSW 1990,91
Palacio, Bob — BB 1990
Palanca, Paul — FN 1980,81,82
Palazzari, Aldo — IHO 1941,42

Palekas, Audrey — WSW 1979,80,81
Pall, Donn — BB 1983,84,85
Palm, Stacy — WTR 1987
Palma, Gus — FB 1990,91
Palmer, Harry M. — FB 1933
Palmer, Howard — BB 1944
Palmer, Peter — FB 1952,53
Palmer, Ralph W. — FB 1943
Palmer, Richard — MGY 1950,51
Palmer, William — MGY 1964
Paloucek, Keith — WR 1980,81,82,83
Palton, Mary — WSW 1978
Pancratz, Kevin — FB 1975,76,77
    WR 1974,75,76,77
Pangrle, Brian — MGY 1981,82,83
Panique, Ken — BB 1973
    FB 1971
Pannier, Kathy — WTR 1980,81,82
Panozzo, Brad — MGY 1995
Parenti, George — BB 1949,51
Parfitt Jr., Alfred W. — FB 1943
Parham, Earl R. — MTR 1988,89
Parke, Glenn — WR 1969
Parker, Curtis — MBK 1924
Parker, Drew — MTN 1995
Parker, Edwin S. — MBK 1942
    BB 1942,43
Parker, George T. — MTR 1915
Parker, Kenneth — MBK 1943
Parker, Quintin — FB 1986,88,89,90
Parker, Roy S. — BB 1902,03,04
    FB 1901,02
Parker, Walter A. — FB 1891,93
Parkhill, Thomas S. — MGO 1965,66,67
Parola, J. Tony — MTR 1964
    FB 1964
Parola, Jerry F. — FB 1961
Parr, S. W. — BB 1883
Parrilli, Anthony K. — FB 1959,60,61
Parrish, Melissa — VB 1989
Parsons, Wil — BB 1989,90
Pashby, R. W. — MSW 1930
Pasko, Larry — FB 1956
Pasko, William — FB 1961,62,63
Passaglia, Andy — WR 1971,72,73,74

Passmore, Don — FB 1981,82,83,84
Pater, Matt — FB 1987,88
Paterson, James A. — MTR 1928,29,30
Patrick, Gerald J. — FB 1958,59
Patrick, Stanley A. — MBK 1944
    MTR 1944
Patterson, Asa E. — MTR 1991,93,94
Patterson, Bruce — MCC 1921
    MTR 1921,22
Patterson, James A. — SOC 1927,28
Patterson, John D. — FB 1939
Patterson, Mary — WSW 1975,76,77,78
Patterson, Paul L. — FB 1944,46,47,48
    MTR 1944
Pattison, Richard H. — MTR 1923
Patton, Antwoine — FB 1992,93,94
Patton, Herbert R. — MGO 1938,39,40
Patton, Mary Andrea — WSW 1978
Patton, Michael K. — MTR 1982,83,84,85
    MCC 1981,82,83,84
Paul, Earl A. — BB 1927
Paul, James W. — MSW 1974,75,76
Paul, John — MBK 1957,58
Paul, Renae — WCC 1993,94
Paul, Victor — WR 1958
Paulson, Kirsten — WSW 1991,92
Paulson, Wayne D. — FB 1963,64
Pauly, Patrick — MSW 1982,83,84,85
Pavesic, Ray — FB 1977
Pawlow, Richard — BB 1957
Pawlowski, Joseph G. — FB 1940,41,42
Paxton, Albert E. — BB 1925
Payette, Rebecca — WSW 1986,87
Payne, Donnie — BB 1992,93,94
Payton, David — BB 1984,85,86,87
Peach, John W. — BB 1976,77,78
    FB 1976,77
Pearlman, Gavin — FB 1992
Pearlstein, David — MGY 1990,91,92,93
Pearman, Barry — MCC 1993,94
    MTR 1995
Pearne, Gary — MTN 1987,88,89,90
Pearson, Jack — MSW 1950
Pearson, Preston — MBK 1966,67
Pearson, Roland — WR 1961,62

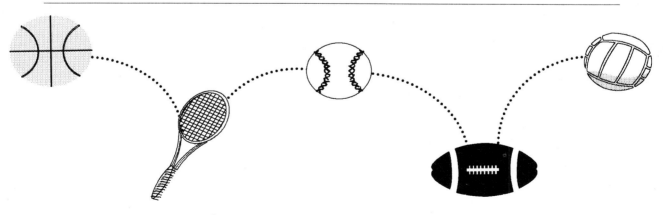

Baseball's Max Pike lettered for the Illini in 1932.

Pearson, W. W.	BB	1889,90
Pechous, Ed	MTN	1954
Peck, Ken E.	MTR	1969,70,71
Pedelty, Amy	VB	1984
Peden, Don C.	BB	1921,22
	FB	1920,21
Pederson, Laurie	WSW	1981,82,83,84
Pedregal, Marianne	WGY	1984,85,86,87
Peebles, Thomas A.	MTR	1904,05,06
Peekel, Rick	BB	1972,73,74
Peirce, Fred D.	BB	1883
Pell, Robert	MGO	1957
Pellant, F. Robert	MTR	1956,57,58
Pelton, Lance	WR	1991,92,93,94
Peltzer, A.	MGY	1927,30
Pendarvis, Harry R.	MTR	1916,17
Pendleton, James K.	MSW	1951,52
Pengilly, H. E.	FN	1911,12,13
Penn, Albert	BB	1908
	MBK	1908
Penn, Henry	BB	1909,10

Peoples, Stephen	MTR	1982
Pepper, Cam	FB	1989,90
Peragine, Tom	MSW	1989,90,91,92
Perdue, Ralph P.	FN	1926
Perdue, Thomas W.	FN	1931
Pereira, Leonard	FN	1929
Perella, E.	FN	1933
Perella, P. J.	FN	1932
Peressini, William	MGO	1975,76,77,78
Perez, Peter J.	FB	1943
Perez, Richard B.	FB	1956,57
Peritz, Ray	PO	1940,41
Perkins, Bernon G.	FB	1931
Perkins, Cecil	FB	1926,27
Perkins, Clyde M.	FB	1943,45
Perlman, S. L.	MGY	1923,24
Perrin, Lonnie	FB	1972,73,75
Perry, Edward	MBK	1958,59,60
Perry, Joe	WR	1967
Perry, Loyd W.	BB	1943
Perry, Michael	FN	1976
Perry, Russell A.	FN	1929
Perry, Thomas	WR	1942,43
Perryman, Alvin	MTR	1977,78,79,80
Pershell, Russell M.	BB	1935
Pertle, J. L.	MSW	1927
Pesek, James	FB	1990,91,92
Petefish, William M.	MTR	1931
	MCC	1930
Peters, Forrest I. (Frosty)	FB	1926,28,29
	MTR	1927
Peters, Scot	MSW	1984
Petersen, Gregory A.	MGO	1981,82,84
Petersen, Neal	MSW	1971,72
Peterson, Anne	WGY	1978,79,80
Peterson, Carl	BB	1962,63
Peterson, Clifford L.	FB	1938,40
Peterson, Daniel E.	FB	1951
Peterson, David	MGY	1981,82
Peterson, Eugene	MGO	1950
Peterson, James H.	MGO	1955
Peterson, James M.	MTR	1961,62
	MCC	1961
Peterson, Karla	WGY	1992,93,95
Peterson, Mark	FB	1972,73,74

Peterson, Michael	MTR	1984
Peterson, Mike	BB	1964,66
Peterson, Ralph	MTR	1954
Peterson, Reuben W.	BB	1917
Peterson, Robert	MBK	1951,52,53
Pethybridge, Frank H.	FB	1914
Petkus, Bob	FB	1965
Petraitis, Luke	FB	1989
Petreshene, Victor	BB	1955,56,57
Petritis, Daniel	MGY	1990,91
Petry, Jack	WR	1946
Petry, Paul	WR	1939,40,41
Pettigrew, James Q.	FB	1906,07,08
	MTR	1908,09
Pettinger, R. G.	MTR	1899,00
Petty, Harold O.	FB	1932
Petty, Lawrence O.	FB	1916,19
Petty, Manley R.	FB	1914,15,16
Pezzoli, Phillip A.	FB	1938
Pfeffer, Frank	BB	1904
Pfeffer, John E.	FB	1892,93,94,95
Pfeifer, Myron P.	FB	1940,41,42
Pfeiffer, Stacey	WBK	1984
Pflager, Miller S.	SOC	1933,34
Phelps, John C.	BB	1912,13,14
	MTR	1912,13
Phelps, Robert L.	MTR	1943,44,45,46
Philbrick, Alvah	BB	1883,84,85,86
Philbrick, Solon	BB	1883,84
Philiotis, Greg	MTN	1985
Phillip, Andrew M.	BB	1942,43,47
	MBK	1942,43,47
Phillips, Charles	MBK	1938
Phillips, Donald J.	MTR	1982,83
Phillips, James E.	FB	1938,39,40
Phillips, Jim (Chubby)	FB	1973,74,75,76
Phillips, Miles D.	FN	1985,86,87
Phillips, Oliver J.	MGY	1942
Phillips, R. J.	MGY	1925
Phillips, Ronnie E.	MTR	1970,71,72
Phipps, Thomas E.	FB	1903
Pianfetti, Brian M.	FN	1990,91,92,93
Piano, Louis J.	SOC	1930,31,32
Piatt, Charles L.	FB	1931,33
Piazza, Sam J.	FB	1948,49,50
Picard, Richard	WR	1949,50,51
Pickering, Michael D.	FB	1969,71
Piel, Mike	FB	1986,87
Pierce, Alfred	FB	1992
Pierce, Charles I.	BB	1889
Pierce, Jack B.	FB	1945,47,48
	MTR	1946
Pierce, Scott	MBK	1991,92
Pierce, Stephen	FB	1985,86
Pierce, Steve	MSW	1985,86
Pierre, Don	WR	1956,58
Pierre-Louis, Gandy	MTR	1995
Pierzynski, Thaddens	MTR	1945,47
Piggott, A.	MSW	1923
Piggott, Bert C.	FB	1946
Pigozzi, Ray	WR	1950,51
Pihera, Otto	MSW	1947
Pike, Albert M.	MTR	1918
Pike, David R.	FB	1962
Pike, Max N.	BB	1932
Pilenyi, Janos A.	FN	1990,91,92
Pillath, Jerry	FB	1968
	WR	1967,69
Pillinger, R. A.	MSW	1908
Pillsbury, Arthur L.	BB	1889
	FB	1890
Pilz, Clifford	MTN	1942
Pinckney, Frank L.	FB	1905,06
Pinder, Cyril C.	FB	1965,66
	MTR	1966
Pineda, Ron	WR	1960
Pinsley, H. H.	SOC	1929
Piotrowski, Mary	WTR	1992
Piper, John	MSW	1928,29
Pirk, Stacey	WGO	1991,92
Pittman Donald C.	FB	1947
Pitts, R. L.	BB	1903,04,05
	FB	1902,03
Pivovar, Greg M.	MTR	1971,72,73
Pixley, Arthur H.	FB	1893,94,95,96
Plain, Henry A.	BB	1949,50
Planert, Edward	BB	1944,45,46
Plankenhorn, James	FB	1961,62,63
Plant, Francis B.	MTR	1899,00
Platt, Damien	FB	1993,94
Platt, Lolita	WBK	1992,93
Plattner, Sharon	WSW	1992,93,94,95

Kip Pope lettered for the Illini swimming team from 1967-69.

Player, John	WR	1923,24
Pletta, D. H.	MGY	1925,26,27
Pleviak, Anthony J.	FB	1966,67,68
Plew, Elmer	MBK	1953,54
Plews, Herb	BB	1948,49,50
Plummer, Ashley	FB	1980,81
Plummer, Lisa	WTR	1980,81,82
Pnazek, Karl	FB	1969
Poat, Raymond W.	BB	1937
Podlecki, Karen	VB	1977
Podmajersky, Paul	FB	1943
Pogue, Bob	BB	1966
Pogue, Harold A.	FB	1913,14,15
	MTR	1914,15,16
Pokorny, Ray	FB	1976
Polakow, A. H.	MTR	1914
Polanek, Eileen	WSW	1980
Polaski, Clarence L.	FB	1936
Polaski, Kenneth	MGY	1964
Polk, Jonelle	WBK	1984,85,86,87
Polkwalski, H.	WR	1912
Pollack, Allyson	WGY	1981,82
Pollak, Mike	BB	1972
Pollard, Ray A.	MTR	1941
Pollensky, Chas	MTR	1935
Pollock, Dino	FB	1989
Polock, Bob	BB	1971,72,73
Poloskey, Michael	FB	1990,91
Polz, Chris	WR	1990
Polz, Jeff	WR	1963,65
Polz, John	WR	1960,61,62
Polz, Laura	WGY	1990,91,92
Ponder, Max	WR	1952
Ponsonby, Charles	MCC	1966
Ponting, Theophilus C.	BB	1925
Pontious, Joyce	WGY	1978,79,80,81
Ponzer, Ernest D.	MTR	1924,25
Ponzer, Howard S.	MCC	1927
	MTR	1927,28
Popa, Elie C.	FB	1950,51
Pope, Jean A.	FB	1904
Pope, Kip	MSW	1967,68,69
Pope, Sally	WGO	1979,80
Popken, Roland	MBK	1922,23,24
Popperfuss, Henry	MBK	1908,09,10
Porter, Horace C.	MTR	1896,97
Porter, Tom	WR	1961
Portman, Crain P.	FB	1933,34
	MTR	1934
Posey, Douglas	MGY	1962
Possehl, Louis	BB	1944
Possehl, Robert	BB	1946
Post, Clarence F.	MTR	1903
Post, Warren M.	FN	1970,71
Postle, D. E.	MSW	1921,22
Postmus, Dave	FB	1987,88
Poston, Emmett	MBK	1909,11
Potter, Glenn	MBK	1922,23,24
Potter, Keith	MSW	1976,77,78,79
Potter, Phil H.	FB	1916
Potter, Richard N.	MGY	1937
Potter, Robert	BB	1952
Pottgen, Jennifer	WSW	1994,95
Powell, Larry D.	FB	1978,79
Powers, John	WR	1983
Powers, John P.	MCC	1985,87,88,89
	MTR	1988,89
Powers, Robert	MSW	1983
Powers, Terri	WGY	1978,79,80

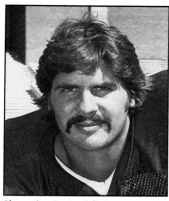

Champaign Centennial's Jerry Ramshaw lettered for the Illini football team in 1977 and '78.

Powers, Tim	BB	1987,88
Powers, Tom	BB	1986,87
Powless, Dave	FB	1963,64
Prather, Paul	MGY	1935,37
Pratt, Margaret	WTN	1975
Pray, Lee	MGO	1933
Preacely, Robbyn	WBK	1993
Preissner, Paul	WR	1994,95
Prentiss, William L.	BB	1943
	IHO	1943
Prescott, John S.	MTR	1919,20,21
Pribil, Martin	MSW	1976
Price, Dale	WR	1940
Price, Henry	WR	1951
Price, Mike	MBK	1968,69,70
Price, Samuel L.	FB	1963,64,65
Prickett, F. W.	MTR	1897
Priddle, George H.	SOC	1932,33
Priebe, Michael	FB	1978,79
Priest, Edwin N.	FN	1976,77
Priest, Eric	FN	1977,78,79,80
Priestley, Gilbert P.	IHO	1941
Priestley, Russell T.	IHO	1942
Primous, Marlon	FB	1988,89,90,91
Prina, Jodi	WBK	1977,78
Prince, David C.	FB	1911
Prince, Eric W.	MTR	1990
Prince, Tom	MGO	1988,89,90
Prindiville, Frank J.	BB	1912,13
Probst, J. S.	MBK	1918
Prochaska, Brad	MGY	1971,72
Prokopis, Alexander	FB	1944
Prout, Charles	WR	1936
Prouty, E. C.	MGO	1912,14
Provenzano, Tony	BB	1961,62,63
Provinse, Jason	WR	1994,95
Pruett, Eugene F.	FB	1913
Prymuski, Robert M.	FB	1946,47,48
Puccetti, Ronald P.	FN	1947
Puchalski, Don	MSW	1959
Puebla, Kevin	WR	1976,77,78,79
Puentes, Rey	MTN	1992
Puerta, Joe	WR	1931,32,33
Pugh, Dwayne	FB	1982,83,84,85
Pulcher, Victoria J.	WTR	1987
Pullen, Robert	BB	1981,82,83,84
Pullman, Cheri	WTN	1993
Pullman, Peggy	WGY	1990,92
Purma, Frank L.	MTR	1931,32
Purvin, Theodore V.	WR	1940,41
Purvis, Charles G.	FB	1939
Pusey, Frank	WR	1911,12
Putnam, Edmund D.	MTR	1966
Pyrz, Anthony C.	BB	1939,40

Q

Quackenbush, B. H.	MSW	1924
Quackenbush, Justin	MGO	1949
Quade, Charles (Chip)	MGY	1979,80
Quade, John C.	FB	1893,94
Qualls, Mark	FB	1988,90
Quarles, Samuel	FB	1975,76
Quayle, Robert H.	BB	1909,10
Quigley, Phillip	MSW	1976,77,78,79
Quigley, Stephanie	WSW	1980
Quinn, Bob	FB	1969,71
Quinn, E. J.	BB	1890,91
Quiros, Jorge L.	FN	1950,51,52

R

Race, Carrie	WCC	1980
Rachmeler, Dale	FN	1970
Raddatz, Russ	FB	1968
Radebaugh, Gus H.	SOC	1934
Radell Jr., Willard W.	FB	1965
	WR	1965
Radford, Norman H.	BB	1927
Radloff, Ronald L.	MTR	1979
Rafaloski, Dennis	MGY	1971
Railsback, Fay D.	FB	1906,07,08
	MTR	1908,09
Raklovits, Richard F.	BB	1950,51
	FB	1949,50
Rakoski, Kristen	WSW	1992,93,94,95
Rakoski, Lisa	WSW	1990,91,92
Ralph, Stanley	FB	1975,77,78,79
Ramein, Robert O.	FB	1982
Ramey, F. W.	MGO	1917
Ramirez, Robin	FN	1991,92,93
Ramsey, R. W.	MGO	1915
Ramshaw, Jerry	FB	1977,78
Randell, Jillian	WSW	1995
Randoll, Melvin	MTN	1946,47,48
Range, Perry	MBK	1979,80,81,82
Rapp, J. H.	MTR	1914
Rascher, Vernon	MGO	1951,52
Rasmussen, Chuck	WR	1959
Rasmussen, Rich	MGO	1974,75
Rathke, Phil	FB	1993
Ray, Hugh L.	BB	1905,06
Rayburn, Cecil C.	MTR	1894,95
Rayburn, Roland	WR	1942,43
Raymond, Edward	MGY	1968,69,70
Rea, Sally	VB	1985,86
Read, E. N.	MTR	1899
Read, Phil	MSW	1969
Read, Richard	WR	1951,52
Reali, Craig	MGY	1977,78,79,80
Reamer, Owen J.	FN	1935
Rear, David	BB	1981,82
Reasoner, Melton	MCC	1930
Reavis Jr., Rudolf W.	MTR	1976,77,78,79
Rebecca, Sammy J.	FB	1950,51
Reber, Dawn	WSW	1995
Rechenmacher, Jayne	WGY	1978,79,80,81
Rechenmacher, Jill	WGY	1986
Reddish, Paul W.	FN	1932
Redhed, William S.	MTR	1909,10
Redington, Nancy	WGO	1980
Redman, Louis	WR	1933
Redman, Matthew	MGY	1994,95
Redmann, Doug	FB	1967,68,69
Redmon, G. Bogie	MBK	1963,64,65
	MTR	1963,64,65
Redmond, John	MGY	1991
Redmond, Stacy	WGY	1995
Reed, Jim	BB	1965,66,67
Reed, Robert	MGY	1965,66
Reed, Ross C.	MGO	1940,41,42
Reed, Scott D.	FN	1975,76
Reeder, James W.	FB	1937,38,39
	MTR	1938
Reese, Jerrold A.	FB	1984,86
Reeves, Harley E.	FB	1892
Rehberg, Robert	MCC	1941
	MTR	1942,46,47
Rehling, C. H.	WR	1915
Rehm, Arthur C.	MTR	1923,25
Rehor Jr., Joseph	MGY	1932,35
Reichle, Richard W.	BB	1920,22
	FB	1919,21
Reid, Connie	WGY	1983
Reif, John P.	MGO	1947,48
Reilly, Edward F.	FN	1975
Reinhart, Freddie A.	BB	1935,36,37
Reinhart, Rick	FB	1973
Reinking, Krista	WBK	1995
Reising, Richard K.	MTR	1939,40
Reiter, E. L.	MGY	1928,29,30
Reitsch, Charles	MSW	1949,50,51
Reitsch, Henry O.	MBK	1921
	FB	1920
Reitsch, Robert	FB	1925,26,27
Reitsch, Robert A.	MGO	1954,55,56
Rekitzke, Philip	BB	1983
Rempert, John	MSW	1982
Renfro, Rick	FB	1983
Renn, Donald D.	FB	1954,55
Rennacker, Roy	MBK	1909
Renner, Jerry	BB	1961,62,63
	MBK	1961

Renwick, F. W.	MGO	1932
Replogle, Vernon L.	MTR	1929
Resner, Peter	WR	1977
Reston Jr., J. B. (Scotty)	MGO	1931,32
	SOC	1929,30,31
Rettinger, George L.	FB	1938,39
Reynolds, Greg	MCC	1981,86
	MTR	1982,87
Reynolds, Kenneth	MBK	1925,26,27
Reynolds, Richard W.	MTR	1951,52
Reynolds, Shelly	WGO	1985
Reynolds, Thomas E.	SOC	1928,29
Rezab, Ray	MSW	1983
Rhodes, Danny	BB	1995
Rhodes, Dusty	BB	1995
Rhodes, Ora M.	FB	1896
Rice, James E.	MTR	1967
Rice, Simeon	FB	1992,93,94
Rich, William	MTN	1936,38
Richards, Debby	WSW	1989,90
Richards, Edward J.	FB	1922,23
Richards, James V.	FB	1908,09
	MTR	1908,09,10
Richards, Jeff	BB	1988,89
Richards, Lloyd	FB	1992,93,94
Richards, Robert E.	MTR	1946,47
Richards, Ronald	BB	1957
Richardson, Brad J.	MTR	1969
Richardson, Chris	FB	1991,92,93,94
Richardson, Quinn	MBK	1981,82,84
Richardson, Timothy	BB	1980,81,82,83
Richardson, William H.	MTR	1905,06,07
Richart Jr., Frank E.	MGO	1939,40,46
Richart, Jane	WSW	1986,87
Richie, James K.	FB	1908
	MTR	1908,09,10
Richman, Harry E.	FB	1927,28
Richmond, Robert	MBK	1939,41
Richter, Gary	MSW	1986,87,88,89
Richter, Lori	WSW	1990
Richter, Padra	WSW	1989,90
Richter, Sandra	WSW	1989,90
Richter, Susan	WSW	1986
Rick, Dickson	MSW	1926
Rickard, Kelley	WTN	1982

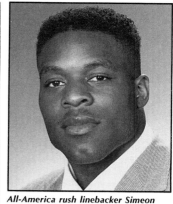

All-America rush linebacker Simeon Rice set the Big Ten record for quarterback sacks.

Ricketts, C. Alan	MTR	1950
Ricketts, Diane	WBK	1982
Rickman, T.	BB	1929
Rideout, Blaine	MCC	1935
Rideout, Wayne	MCC	1935
Ridley, William	MBK	1954,55,56
Riegel, Robert W.	MBK	1935,36,37
	MTR	1935,36
Riehle, John	FB	1968
Riepma, Paul	MTN	1944,45
Riggins, Pat	WTR	1980
Riggins, Paul	WR	1950,51
Riggs Jr., Thomas J.	FB	1938,39,40
Righter, Edwin B.	BB	1908,10
Riley, Dawn	WTR	1993,94,95
Riley, James	MTN	1960,61
Riley, Kate	WBK	1989,90,91,92
Riley, Roy	MBK	1906
Rimar, Jeanne C.	WTR	1993
Rimzdius, Nancy	VB	1975,76,77,78
Rinaker, Lewis	BB	1888
Ring, Wayne	MGO	1945,46,47

Richard Reynolds lettered for the Illini track and field squad in 1951 and '52.

Washington, Illinois' Mel Romani helped quarterback the Illini football team from 1959-61.

Ringquist, Clarence L.	FB	1928
Ringquist, Mauritz E.	MTR	1935
Ripley, C. T.	MGO	1908
Ripskis, Stanley	MCC	1962
	MTR	1962,63
Ritter, Michael G.	MTR	1989
Ritz, John	WR	1926,27
Rizzo, Kenneth	BB	1967,68
Roach, Arlena	WBK	1990,91
Roach, James W.	MSW	1941,42,43
Roberson, Garvin	FB	1971,72,73
	MBK	1972,73
Roberts, Brian	BB	1989,90,91
Roberts, Chester C.	FB	1909,10,11
Roberts, Clifford	FB	1958,59,60
Roberts, Dave	MBK	1973,74,75
Roberts, Gilbert J.	FB	1922,23,24
Roberts, Janet	VB	1975,76,77,78
Roberts, Jennifer	WTN	1982
Roberts, Linda	WBK	1975,76
Roberts, Luann	WGY	1983,84,85,86
Roberts, Melvin	FB	1992,93,94
Roberts, Ralph O.	BB	1903,04
Roberts, Rodney	FN	1967,68,69
Robertson, Currie	WBK	1995
Robertson, Robert	FB	1966,67
Robertson, Thomas	BB	1976
Robinson, Darrell	FB	1969,70,71
	WR	1970
Robinson, Deborah	WGY	1975
Robinson, Frank	WR	1956
Robinson, Herman	MTR	1931,32
Robinson, J. T.	MTR	1936,37,38
Robinson, James O.	MTR	1939,40
Robinson, Lisa	WBK	1979,80,81,82
Robinson, Lynnette	WBK	1979,80,81,82
Robinson, Mark	BB	1984,87
Robinson, Olaf E.	FB	1929,30
Robinson, Roy	FB	1972,73,74
Robinson, William B.	BB	1924
Robisch, Brett	MBK	1995
Robison, Morris W.	FB	1922
Roddick, Lawrence	MSW	1986
Rodgers, Lee	PO	1936,38
Rodgers, Randy	FB	1968
Rodgers, Robert A.	MTR	1928,29,30

Rodgerson, Mike	BB	1965,66,67
Rodman, Charles S.	MTR	1901,02,03,04
Rodriguez, Raul	MGY	1980,81,82,83
Rodriguez, Sandra	WBK	1978
Roemer, John	MGY	1970,71,72
Roettger, Walter H.	BB	1922,23,24
	MBK	1922,23
Rogala, Alexis	WGO	1991
Rogers, Aaron M.	MTR	1989,90,91
Rogers, Greg	BB	1984
Rogers, Rhea A.	WTR	1981
Rogers, Tina	VB	1990,91,92,93
Rohrer, Carl J.	MTR	1909,10,11
Rokusek, Frank E.	FB	1922,23,24
Rolfe, Rial E.	MGO	1922,23,24
Rolle, Glenn L.	IHO	1943
Rollo, Cook	MGY	1966,67,68
Romani, Melvin C.	FB	1959,60,61
Romein, Daniel C.	MTR	1977
Romero, David	MGY	1986,87,89,90
Romersberger, Richard	MTR	1942
Romic, Stephanie	WBK	1983,84,85,86
Rommelman, Douglas	BB	1978,79
Rooks, Thomas	FB	1982,83,84,85
Roos, E. G.	MSW	1916
Roosevelt, Rita	WBK	1977
Root, Clark W.	FB	1930
Root, George H.	FB	1893
	MTR	1894
Ropp, Franklin N.	MTR	1907
Rosborough, Terrill	MTN	1968,69
Roscetti, Erin	WSW	1988
Rosch, Frank	MGY	1980,81,82,83
Rose, Jerry	FB	1968
Rosenbaum, Lee	MSW	1980
Rosenfeldt, H.	BB	1931
Rosenthal, Frank V.	BB	1929,31
Rosenwinkel, Pam	WGY	1975
Roska, Sarah	WGY	1976
Ross, H. A.	MGY	1917
Ross, James E.	FN	1952,53
Ross, Roy	MSW	1950
Ross, Steve	FB	1970,72
Rossetto, Karen	WGY	1989,90,91
Rotblatt, Marvin	BB	1945,46,47,48
Roth, Barb	WSW	1983,84,85
Roth, Michael	WR	1973,75,76
Roth, Robert J.	BB	1942
Roth, Steve	MBK	1992,93,94,95
Rothgeb, Claude J.	BB	1904,05
	FB	1900,02,03,04
	MTR	1902,03,04,05
Rothlisberger, Curt	MTR	1984,86
Rothwell Jr., William F.	MTR	1966
Rotkis, Walter A.	MSW	1937
Rott, Dennis	WR	1967,68,69
Rotteld, Herb	MSW	1971
Rotter, G. E.	WR	1915
Rotzoll, Dan	FB	1970,71
Rounds, William P.	BB	1886,87
Rouse, Eric V.	FB	1976,77,78
Roush, D. William	FB	1928, 29
Rowader, Thomas	MGO	1952,53,54
Rowe, Enos M.	BB	1912
	FB	1911,12,13
Rowe, Robert	MBK	1946
Rowland, E. M.	MTR	1900
Roy, Willie	WR	1963
Royal, T. E.	MSW	1921,22,23
Royer, James M.	MTR	1927
Royer, Joseph W.	FB	1892
Roysdon, William I.	BB	1892,93,94,95
Rozmus, Jerrry	BB	1962
Ruben, Benjamin	MSW	1953
Rubenstein, Allan	MSW	1956,57,58
Rubin, Jacqueline	WGO	1994,95
Rubiner, John	WR	1987
Rucker, Derrick	FB	1990,91,92
Rucker, Douglas	MSW	1948,49
Rucks, Bill	MBK	1974,75
Rucks, Jim	BB	1972,73
	FB	1970,71,72
	MBK	1972
Rudin, Greg	WR	1989,90,91
Rudnicki, Patsy	WGY	1982,83,84,85
Rudolph, David L.	MTR	1961
Rudolph, Leonard	MTR	1937
Rue, Doran T.	MTR	1925,26,27
Rue, Orlie	FB	1913,14
Ruf, Michelle A.	WGY	1985,86,87,88
Ruff, Robert	MTR	1976

Rugg, Robert F.	MGO	1976,77,78,79
Ruholl, Connie	WBK	1991,93
Ruleau, John G.	MTR	1985
Rumana, Henry	SOC	1932,33
Rump, Charles A.	FB	1905
Rumpel, Carol	VB	1985
Rundquist, Elmer T.	FB	1915,16,17
	WR	1916
Runkle, Willard C.	MTR	1926
Runneberg, Elton	WR	1915
Ruppert, Thomas	MGY	1959
Rusackus, Charles J.	MSW	1936
Ruscin, Mark J.	MTR	1989
Rush, Ira L.	BB	1913,14,15
Rush, Scott	FN	1989,90,91,92
Rusk, Steve	WR	1994,95
Russ, Jerald B.	FB	1945
Russell, Brian	MTR	1983
Russell, Charles M.	BB	1880,81
Russell, Dave	WR	1963,64
Russell, David	BB	1966,68
Russell, Donna	WCC	1986,87,88
	WTR	1987,88,89,90
Russell, Eddie L.	FB	1963,64,65
Russell, Frank H.	BB	1935
Russell, James T.	MTR	1985,86
Russell, Mike	FB	1992,93
Russell, W. Hunter	FB	1930,32
	MTR	1934
Russo, Tony	MGO	1989
Rutgens, Joseph C.	FB	1958,59,60
Ruth, Mike	BB	1992
Ruther, Robert E.	MTR	1944,49
Ryan, Amy	WSW	1994
Ryan Jr., Clement J.	FB	1955
Ryan, Dean	WR	1947,48
Ryan, Edward	MBK	1906,07
Ryan, Eric	WR	1995
Ryan, Howard R.	BB	1917,19,20
Ryan, John (Rocky)	FB	1951,52,53
Ryan, Kate	WSW	1995
Ryan, Kristi	WSW	1994
Ryan, Mike	FB	1968,69
Rydberg, Laura	WTN	1994,95
Rykovich, Julius	BB	1943,47
	FB	1946
Ryles, Richard	FB	1982
Rylowicz, Robert A.	FB	1950,51
Ryniec, Al	BB	1972,73,74
Ryniec, Dave	BB	1963,64,65
Ryniec, Louis A.	BB	1959,60,61,62
Ryniec, Tim	BB	1987

S

Sabalaskey, John	BB	1952,53,54
Saban, Joseph P.	FB	1945
Sabin, Beth	WTR	1980
Sabino, Daniel, F.	FB	1950,51,52
Sabo, John P.	MBK	1921,22
	FB	1918,20,21
Sachs, Henry	MBK	1939,40,41
Sader, Melvin	MGY	1935
Sadler, Jenny	WSW	1990,94
Saikley, Frank	MTN	1941,42,43
Sainati, Leo	BB	1938
Sajnaj, Chester B.	FB	1943
Salamone, Kristina	WTN	1975,76,77,78
Salata, Bob	WR	1959
Salemo, Charles	MGY	1981
Salemo, Lloyd	MGY	1980
Salinas, Maria	WGY	1975,76
Salmon, Kalli	WSW	1989,90,91,92
Salmons, Tina	WTN	1975,76,77,78
Salomente, D.	WR	1931
Salter, Cody	BB	1995
Salter, John	MGY	1960,62
Salyers, R.	MTR	1905
Sammons, Donald	MSW	1954
Samojedny, George	FB	1969,71
Sampey, Eileen	WSW	1989,90
Samsten, Kari	MGY	1981,82,83,84
Samuels, Brian	FB	1990,91
Samuels, Jonathan H.	BB	1885,86,87,88
Samuelson, Jill	VB	1983,84,85
Sanches, Gilmarcio	MGY	1981,82,83,84
Sanchez, Gina	VB	1993
Sanchez, Victor	MGY	1964,65,66
Sandeen, John D.	MTR	1966,67,68
Sander, Matt	BB	1992,93
Sanders, Bobby	FB	1993,94
Sanders, Floyd W.	MTR	1929
Sanders, Hope	WTR	1992,93,94,95

Sanders, Ralph L.	MTR	1912,13,14
Sandor, Bela	MSW	1960
Sands, Jennifer	WSW	1995
Sandstrom, James	FN	1954,55
Sanford, Derek	BB	1967
Sanner, J. David	MTR	1968,69
Santini, Veto	FB	1969
Sapora, Allen	WR	1936,37,38
Sapora, Joe	WR	1928,29,30
Sargent, Norbert	WR	1955,56,57
Saric, Robert	WR	1978
Sarkary, Xerxes	MTN	1991
Sarros, James J.	MTR	1978
Sarussi, Marty	MSW	1984,86,87
Sauer, Andrew	WR	1943
Saunders, Chris	MCC	1994
	MTR	1995
Saunders, Don	FB	1964
Sawicki, Tom	MSW	1965,66,67
Sawin, Frank L.	FN	1941
Sawtelle, Stephen E.	MTR	1978
Sayre, C. B.	FN	1911,12,13
Sayre, Elvin C.	FB	1934,35,36
Scamen, Warren	WR	1976
Scanlan, John	MGY	1983,84
Scanlan, Robert W.	FN	1947,48,49
Scarcelli, Tony	FB	1980,81,83
Schacht, Frederick W.	FB	1894,95,96
Schachtman, Milton R.	SOC	1932,33,34
Schaefer, Frank J.	PO	1937,38,39,40
Schaefer, Paul V.	BB	1908,09
Schafer, Tom	MBK	1984
Schalin, Guy	MTN	1981
Schalk, Edward A.	FB	1931
Schanel, James	MSW	1976,77,78,79
Schankin, Arthur A.	FN	1956,57,58
Schantz, Eric	MTN	1985,86
Scharbert, Robert D.	FB	1961,62
Scharf, Albert	BB	1943,46,47
Scheidegger, Bruce	BB	1979,80
Scheirer, Mark	MCC	1988,89,90,91
Schellenberg, Steven	MTR	1977,78
Scherr, Kelly	VB	1993,94
Scherrer, Steve	MSW	1983,84,86
Scherschligt, Barbra	WTN	1985,86
Schertz, Thomas	FB	1986,87

Tina Rogers was Illinois' Female Athlete of the Year in 1994.

Lou Ryniec was a four-time letter winner for the Illini baseball team.

Burt Schmidt, football letter winner from 1947-49, is now a significant contributor to the Fighting Illini Scholarship Fund.

Schertz, Todd	FB	1986
Scherwat, Don	MSW	1947,48,49
Scheuplein, Bret	FB	1994
Schick, A. I.	MSW	1932
Schicker, Blake R.	FN	1986,87
Schicker, Eric	FN	1984,85,86,87
Schicker, Glenn R.	FN	1988,89
Schiene, Martin	MGO	1977,78,79,80
Schierer, Charles	BB	1967,68,69
Schildhauer, Fred J.	MTR	1923,24
Schilke, Renold E.	MTR	1962,63
Schiller, Arthur M.	FN	1952,53
Schiller, Charles L.	BB	1942
Schillmoeller, Renatta	WSW	1983
Schindehette, Russell	MSW	1980,81,82,83
Schinker, Lee	BB	1962,63
Schlansker, D. Lynn	MTR	1932,33
Schlapprizzi, Fred H.	MTR	1921,22
Schlapprizzi, Lester B.	BB	1923,24
Schleizer, Shawn M.	MTR	1990,93,94
Schlicker, P. F.	FN	1929,31
Schlinkman, Jean	VB	1975,76,77
Schlosser, Merle J.	FB	1947,48,49
Schlueter, Bill	BB	1965
Schmeissing, Roy	MGY	1961
Schmidt, Burton J.	FB	1947,48,49
Schmidt, Edward S.	MTR	1961
Schmidt, Gerald, C.	FB	1967
Schmidt, Harv	MBK	1955,56,57
Schmidt, Jon	MCC	1979,80,81
	MTR	1979,80,81,82
Schmidt, Mark S.	MTR	1978,79
Schmidt, Michael	MGY	1976,78,79
Schmidt, Roderick L.	MBK	1973,74,75
Schmitke, Todd	BB	1979,80,81,82
Schnack, Jason	FB	1993
Schneck, Sereno W.	MTR	1894
Schneider, Craig	FB	1986,87,88,89
Schnittgrund, Gary D.	MTR	1968,69
Schober, Max W.	BB	1905
Schobinger, Eugene	FB	1912,13,14
	MTR	1913,14,15
Schoch, Philip F.	MTR	1924,25,26
Schoeller, Julies E.	FB	1905
Schoeninger, Joseph F.	MTR	1934
Schofield, Jane	WSW	1987,88,89,90

Rick Schmidt led the Illini basketball team in scoring in both 1974 and '75.

Scholtens, Sandy	VB	1985,86,87,88
Scholz, Dave	MBK	1967,68,69
Scholz, Mike	BB	1973,74
Scholz, Robert	MSW	1953
Schomer, Susan	WSW	1980
Schooley, Thomas	FB	1977
Schrader, Alfred C.	BB	1883,84,85
Schrader, Charles	FB	1956
Schrader, Henry C.	FN	1939
Schram, Bill	WR	1959
Schreier, Marc	MGY	1995
Schrieder, G. W.	WR	1912
Schroder, Robert	MGO	1944,45
Schroeder, Bill	WR	1971
Schroeder, C. J.	MBK	1972,73,74
Schroeder, G. W.	WR	1913,14
Schroeder, John R.	MGY	1967
Schroeder, Michael	FN	1966,67,68
Schroeder, Rod	MTN	1970,71,72
Schroeder. F. R.	MSW	1928,29,30
Schubert, Wolfgang M.	MTR	1939
Schuckman, Meyers	BB	1937
Schuder, John	MTN	1938
Schuh, Charles R.	MTR	1918,19,20
Schuldt, James	BB	1951
	MBK	1951,53
Schullian, Brian	BB	1992,93,94,95
Schulte, Rick	FB	1981,82,83,84
Schultz, Alfred	WR	1925
Schultz, Arthur F.	FB	1930
	WR	1931
Schultz, Emil G.	FB	1922,23,24
Schultz, Ernest W.	FB	1925,26,27
Schulz, Larry	FB	1974,75,76
Schumacher, Gregg H.	BB	1962
	FB	1962,63,64
Schumacher, Henry N.	FB	1930
Schumaker, Jason	BB	1991,92,94
Schunk, Charles	MTN	1947,48
Schurecht, H. S.	FN	1914
Schustek, Ivan D.	BB	1932,34
	FB	1931,32,33
Schutt, Steve	MGY	1973,74
Schwab, Jennifer	WCC	1992,93,94
	WTR	1992,93
Schwartz, Daniel	FN	1968,69
Schwartz, Debbie	WSW	1994,95
Schwartz, Frank	BB	1956,57,58
Schwartz, Larry	FN	1969,70
Schwartz, Lloyd	BB	1910
Schwartz, Martin	WR	1950,51
Schwartz, Michael	FN	1992,93
Schwartz, Richard	WR	1952
Schwartz, Steven H.	FN	1972,73,74,75
Schwartz, Terry	MSW	1973,74
Schwarz, Chris	VB	1985,86,87,88
Schwarz, Liz	VB	1979,80,81
Schwarz, Margie	VB	1978,79,80,81
Schwarz, Rita	VB	1982,83,84,85
Schwarz, Robert	MTN	1939,40,41
Schwarzentraub, Jeff	FB	1993
Schwitzer, G. B.	MGY	1922,23
Scicougsky, Brooke	WTR	1995
Sconce, Harvey J.	BB	1896
	FB	1894,95
Scott, Bob	FB	1975,76,77
Scott, Donald G.	BB	1893
Scott, Greg	MSW	1973,74,75,76
Scott, J. Russell	MTR	1922,23
Scott, Jay	MGO	1992,93,94,95
Scott, John	FB	1977,78
Scott, Lawson	MTR	1892
Scott, Robert E.	FB	1952
Scott, Russell	MCC	1921,22
Scott, Steve	BB	1974,75,76,77
Scott, Tom	BB	1953,54
Scott, Tom	FB	1968,69,70
Scotty, Brian	MSW	1980,84
Scotty, Matthew	MSW	1985,86,87,88
Scotty, Thomas	MSW	1983,85,86
Scully, Mike	FB	1983,84,85,87
Seabrooke, Theodore	WR	1940,41,42
Seaman, Glen	MSW	1977,78
Seaman, Richard	MSW	1986,87
Seamans, Frank L.	FB	1932
Searcy, Ed	MBK	1960
Searcy, Todd M.	FB	1984,85
Sebring, Bob	FB	1984,85
Secrest, John	BB	1964,65
See, Kelly	VB	1981,82,83
See, Tracy	WSW	1990,91,92,93
Seely, Irving R.	MTR	1933,34,35

Seely, Ralph W.	MTR	1933
Segers, Alicia	WGY	1976
Seib, Robert C.	MTR	1942,43
	MCC	1941,42
Seidler, Burton A.	MSW	1943
Seifert, Dave	BB	1992,93
Seigel, Kenneth E.	FB	1944
Seiler, Otto E.	FB	1909,10,11
	MTR	1910,11
Seiwert, Herb	MSW	1948,49
Seldon, John M.	MTR	1929
	MCC	1928
Self, Bruce	MTR	1967,68,69
Seliger, V. L. (Blinky)	FB	1946,47,48
Semeniuk, Tanya	WGY	1993
Senneff, George F.	FB	1912,13
Sentman III, Lee H.	FN	1957,58
Sentman Jr., Lee H.	MTR	1929,30,31
Sepke, Arnold	MGY	1968,69
Serpico, Ralph M.	FB	1943,44,45,46
Sewall, Luke	FB	1980,81,82,83
Seybold, Harvey	MSW	1974,75,76
Seyler, Jim	MBK	1944,45,46
Seyman, Sandy	WGO	1977,78,79
Shade, Susan	WBK	1975
Shaffer, Jim	FB	1989,90
Shank, Robert	MTR	1988,89,90,91
Shannon, James S.	BB	1887
Shannon, Kathleen	VB	1991,92,93
Shapin, Paul	MGY	1966,67,68
Shapiro, David	WR	1946,47,48
Shapiro, Harold	MBK	1939,40,41
Shapiro, Richard	MTN	1974,75,77
Shapland, Bob	MBK	1970,71
Shapland, Earl P.	FB	1912
Shapland, Mark	MBK	1989
Shapland, Robert	BB	1969,70,71
Sharer, Rock	MSW	1959,60,61
Sharp, John	MGY	1949
Sharp, Sarah	WBK	1988,89,90,91
Shatiko, Basil	WR	1924
Shattuck, W. F.	MSW	1926,27,28
Shattuck Sr., Walt F.	FB	1890
Shavers, Errol	FB	1989
Shaw, Harold	MGY	1966,67,68
Shaw, Joseph E.	BB	1928
Shaw, Kenny	FB	1979
Shaw, Martha	WTR	1978
Shaw, Ward	WR	1925
Shea, Dan	FB	1980
Shea, Jeff	MSW	1963
Sheahan, Tim	WR	1995
Sheean, Frank T.	BB	1899
Sheffield, Jay	FN	1954,56
Shelby, Aaron	FB	1990,91,92,93
Shellander, Nancy	WBK	1984
Shepherd, John W.	MTR	1903
Sheppard, Lawrence D.	FB	1904
Sheppard, Sarah	WGY	1978,79,80
Sherline, Charles H.	MTR	1986,88
Sherrod, Michael	FB	1978,79,80
Sherry, H. Raymond	MTR	1968,69,70
Sheuring, Verland	MCC	1954,55,56
Shewchuk, William	FN	1953,54
Shields, Raymond J.	BB	1908
Shineflug, Bob	MTN	1963,64
Shipka, Ronald B.	FN	1958,59
Shipman, Tracy	VB	1988
Shirley, Alton	MBK	1943
Shively, Bernie A.	FB	1924,25,26
	MTR	1925,26,27
	WR	1926,27
Shively, Bob	WR	1965
Shively, Debbie	WGY	1987,88
Shlaudeman, Harry	BB	1884,85,86
Shlaudeman, Harry R.	FB	1916,17,19
Shoaff, Oliver	MBK	1943
Shockey, Victor E.	MTR	1980,81,82,83
Shoemaker, Kenn	MSW	1975
Shoptaw, Robert	BB	1955,56,57
Short, William E.	FB	1927
Shriner, William	MSW	1961,62,63
Shuler, Hugh M.	BB	1896,97,98
	FB	1897
Shuman, Donald L.	MTR	1946,47,49
Shumway, Horatio G.	BB	1884
Siambekos, Chris	FB	1986,89
Sibbitt, J. P.	MTR	1928
Sidari, John	FB	1990,91,92,93
Siders, Stacey A.	MTR	1951,52,53
Sidlinger, Bruce	MGY	1951
Siebens, Arthur R.	FB	1913

Sandy Scholtens' teams compiled a cumulative record of 136 victories and 17 losses during her volleyball career from 1985-88.

Siebert, Eric	WR	1995
Siebert, Fred W.	FN	1929,30,31
Siebold, Harry P.	FB	1937,40
Siegal, Irving J.	SOC	1927
Siegel, Bill	MCC	1969
Siegel, Jeff	BB	1974,75,76
Siegel, William	MTR	1970
Siegert, Herbert F.	FB	1946,47,48
Siegert, Philip	MSW	1960,61
Siegert, Rudolph	FB	1954,55
Siegert, Wayne	FB	1949,50
Sigerson, Charles W.	IHO	1939
Siglin, Brett	MCC	1993
Sigourney, Chris	FB	1979,81,82,83
Sikich, John	MTR	1939,40,41
	WR	1939,40,41
Siler, R. W.	MTR	1900
Siler, Rich	FB	1981
Siler, Roderick W.	FB	1901
Silhan, William	MGY	1964,66,67
Silkman, John M.	BB	1913
	FB	1912,13
Silva, Dave	BB	1989
Silva, Hugo	FN	1988,89,90,91
Silverman, David	MGY	1969
Silverman, Lawrence	FN	1952,53
Silverman, Leslie	FN	1936
Silverstein, Ralph	WR	1935,36,37
Silverstone, Abbey	FN	1958,59,60
Siml, Art	WR	1961
Simmering, Laura	WCC	1988,89,90,91
	WTR	1989,91,92,93
Simmons, G. E.	MSW	1924
Simmons, Jill	WSW	1979,80
Simon, Donald	MGO	1963,64
Simon, Frank	MTR	1928,29
	SOC	1928
Simon, Joseph V.	MTR	1926,27,28
Simon, Timothy	MTR	1985,86,87,88
Simonetti, Robert	BB	1949
Simonich, Louis J.	BB	1924,25
Simons, Steve	MTN	1965,66
Simpson, Faith	WGY	1991
Simpson, J. M.	MGO	1915,16,17
Simpson, Ken	MSW	1967,68

Sarah Sharp finished her career in 1991 as Illinois' No. 4 all-time leading scorer.

Simpson, Tim	FB	1988,89,90,91
Sims, C. E.	MGY	1915
Sims, Robert	MSW	1992
Sinak, Tom	BB	1993,94,95
Singalewitch, Heather	WGY	1987,88,89,90
Singer, R. B.	MGY	1923,24
Singman, Bruce	FB	1962
Sinnock, Pomeroy	FB	1906,07,08
Sinnock, Pommery	MSW	1932
Sipes, Stanton	BB	1976
Siron, Jon	BB	1973,74,75
Sisco, August C.	BB	1937
Sisson, John	MTN	1963,64,65
Sitko, Leonard J.	MCC	1987,88,89,90
	MTR	1988,89,90,91
Sittig, John F.	MTR	1925,26,27
Sizer, Richard	WR	1941
Skarda, Edward J.	FB	1936,37
Skikas, Norm	BB	1960
Skisak, Chris	WR	1973,74
Skizas, Gus	BB	1949,50
Skizas, Peter	BB	1982
Skorus, Nina	VB	1980,81
Skrna, Mary	WSW	1980
Skubisz, Joe	FB	1987,88
Skudlarek, Mary	VB	1980,81
Skunberg, Craig	MSW	1982
Slack Jr., Jerry	MTR	1950,51
Slater, C. Paul	IHO	1940
Slater, William F.	FB	1890,91,92
Slattery, Edward T.	MGO	1983,84
Slimmer, Louis F.	FB	1923,24
Sliva, Oscar	FB	1969
Slocum, Karl R.	BB	1905
Slogan, John C.	MTR	1975,76,77,78
Slomski, Dennis	WR	1995
Slomski, Dina	WGY	1992,94,95
Slothower, James B.	MGO	1956,57
Slowinski, Art	FB	1991
Slusher, Carroll	BB	1969,70,71
Smaidris, Mike	MCC	1993,94
Small, Andy	BB	1989,90,91,92
Small, Ervin	MBK	1988,89,90
Small, Mike	MGO	1985,86,87,88
Small, William G.	MBK	1961, 62, 63
Smalzer, Joe	FB	1974,75
Smerdel, Matthew T.	FB	1942
	WR	1943
Smid, Jan	FB	1952,53,54
Smidl, E.	MGY	1917
Smiley, Arthur	MBK	1942,43,46,47
Smiley, Jack	BB	1946
Smiley, Larry	MSW	1967,68,69
Smiser, Todd	BB	1991,92,93
Smith, Aimee	WBK	1994,95
Smith, Al	MTR	1971
Smith, Andrew	MSW	1983
Smith, Bobby J.	FB	1976
Smith, C. F.	MTR	1899
Smith, Charles (Bubba)	BB	1989,90,91
Smith, Charles J.	FB	1944
Smith, Claire H. W.	MTR	1905,06,07
Smith, Dale J.	MGO	1956,57
Smith, Daniel N.	BB	1933
Smith, Darrell	FB	1981
Smith, Dave	MBK	1974
Smith, Dave P.	MTR	1988
Smith, Deborah	WTR	1988,89
Smith, Dewitt	MTR	1893
Smith, Donald I.	FB	1950
Smith, Ed	MTR	1983,84
Smith, Eugene R.	FB	1920
Smith, Fred D.	MTR	1903,05
Smith, George	WR	1970
Smith, Gerald	BB	1953,54
Smith, Gerald	MGO	1961,62,63
Smith, Harold R.	MGO	1949,50
Smith, Harvey H.	MTR	1932
Smith, J. Dale	FB	1956,57
Smith, James A.	FB	1939,41,42
Smith, Jan	WTR	1975
Smith, Jerome	BB	1952
Smith, Joyce	VB	1988
Smith, Karen	WGY	1975
Smith, Kevin	FB	1975
Smith, Larry	MBK	1987,88,89,91
Smith, Leonard A.	MTR	1969
Smith, M. Rex	FB	1950,51,52
Smith, Mark	MBK	1978,79,80,81
Smith, Marshall F.	FB	1948
Smith Jr., Maurice	BB	1967
Smith, Mick	BB	1966
	FB	1965,66
Smith, Ronald C.	FN	1962,63
Smith, Russell W.	MTR	1923
Smith, Shari	WGY	1988,89
Smith, Stuyvesant C.	FB	1919
Smith, Suzanne	WTR	1977,78,79
Smith, Terika	WTR	1991,92
Smith, Thomas D.	FB	1965,66
Smith, Timothy C.	MTR	1975,76,77,78
Smith, Warren H.	SOC	1934
Smith, Willie	FB	1969
Smock, Walter F.	FB	1900
Smolensky, Loren	WTN	1987,88
Snavely, Edwin R.	FB	1931
Sneberger, James	MCC	1937
Snook, John K.	FB	1932,33
Snow, Mark P.	FN	1979,80,81,82
Snyder, Ira D.	BB	1929
Snyder, James B.	BB	1906,07,08
Snyder, Ray E.	MTR	1945
Snyder, Ray	WR	1945
Socolof, Joseph D.	FN	1986,87,88,89
Soebbing, Mark H.	FB	1976
Soga, Susumu	WR	1926,27
Sokol, Steven	BB	1978
Solbert, Michael	MSW	1983
Solyom, Andrew	MBK	1928
Somers, Aloysius J.	MTR	1917
Somlar, Scott	FB	1980
Sommer, Chuck	BB	1972,73
Sommer, Joseph	MSW	1961,62,63
Sommers, Scott	MTN	1979,80,81,82
Sommerville, Jessica	WSW	1993
Song, Kenneth K.	FN	1986,87,88,89
Sorey, Revie	FB	1972,73,74
Soucheck, Elizabeth	WSW	1995
Sowa, Nick	FB	1979
Spakowski, Scott	MTR	1988,89
Spangler, Scott	MTR	1983
Sparks, Frank	MGO	1960
Spasott, Tom	MSW	1962
Spaulding, Tony	BB	1991
Speer, Kenneth R.	MTR	1935,36,37
Spencer, James E.	BB	1884,85,86
Sperry, L. B.	MGY	1925
Spiezio, Scott	BB	1991,92,93
Spiller, John	FB	1969
Spink, Phillip M.	MTR	1916,17,20
Sprague, Stanley R.	FB	1945
	MTR	1945
Spreitzer, Fred	MSW	1963
Spreitzer, James	MSW	1961,62,63
Springe, Otto	FB	1909,10,11
	MTR	1910
Spurgeon, A. Lowell	FB	1935,36,37
	MTR	1936,37
Spurlock, Albert C.	MTR	1936
Spurney, Robert	MGY	1975,76,77,78
Squier, George K.	FB	1914,15
Squirek, Jack S.	FB	1978,79,80,81
St. Clair, Tim	MTR	1984
Staab, Jake	MBK	1944,45
Staake, Donald	MTN	1944
Staff, Lawrence M.	MTR	1955,56,57
Stafford, Bruce	MTN	1960,61,62
Stafford, Harold	MTN	1952,53
Stahl, Archie	MGY	1922,23
Stahl, C. N.	FN	1921
Stahl, Cecil	MGY	1922
Stahl, Floyd S.	BB	1926
Stahl, Garland (Jake)	FB	1899,00,01,02
	BB	1901,02,03
Stallings, Dennis	FB	1994
Stammer, Steven E.	FN	1987,88,89
Standring, Bob	FB	1973
Stange, Harold	BB	1946,49
Stangle, Solomon	WR	1926
Stanley, Tim	FB	1982,85
Stanners, Jerry K.	MTR	1955,56,57
Staples, Paul	MSW	1988,89
Stapleton, Christopher	MSW	1986,87,88
Stapleton, John M.	FB	1959
Starck, Robert W.	MTR	1940,41,42
Starghill, Trevor	FB	1994
Stark, Art	MSW	1966,67,68
Starkey, Dean E.	MTR	1986,87,88,89
Starks, Marshall L.	FB	1958,59,60
Starnes, Bob	MBK	1961,62,63

Kurt Steger was a two-sport star for the Illini in the 1970s, earning letters in both football and baseball.

Stasica, Stanley J.	FB	1945
	MGO	1946
Stauner, James P.	FB	1974,75,76
Stead, Charles B.	MTR	1917
Stecyk, Amy	VB	1977,78,79
	WTR	1979
Steele, James	FB	1890,91
Steele, Phil	BB	1886,87
Steers, Fred	MTN	1946,47,48
Stefanski, Steve	FB	1993
Steger, Kurt	BB	1976,77,78
	FB	1975,76,77
Steger, Peter	FB	1978
Steger, Russell (Ruck)	BB	1947,48,49,50
	FB	1946,47,48,49
Stein, Cindy	WBK	1982,83
Steinberg, Philip	MCC	1944
	MTR	1945
Steinhaus, Steve	FB	1994
Steinman, Henry J.	FB	1929
Steinwedell, Carl	BB	1900,01,02,03
Stellner, Frank L.	MTR	1926
	MCC	1925
Stellwagen, Joel	FB	1966
Stelter, Chris	FB	1994
Stelton, Peter	MSW	1960,61,62
Stelzer, Robert	WR	1960
Stephens, Sarah	WSW	1995
Stephenson, Lewis A.	FB	1901
Stephenson, Robert	FN	1933
Stephenson, Roger A.	MTR	1909
Sterba, Tony	MSW	1970,71,72,73
Sterle, Norbert J.	IHO	1941
Stern, Matt	FB	1991
Stern, Simon H.	FN	1933,34
Sternaman, Edward C.	FB	1916,17,19
Sternaman, Joseph T.	FB	1921
Sterneck, Morris	MBK	1954
Sterneman, Ruth	WCC	1981,83,84,85
	WTR	1984,86
Sternfeld, Robert	FN	1937,38
Sterrenberg, Ronald K.	MTR	1977,78
Sterrett, David B.	MSW	1955,56,57
Stetson, Deborah	WCC	1981,84
	WTR	1984,85
Stettensen, Jim	MSW	1970,71,72,73

Stettin, Megan	VB	1992,93,94
Steuernagel, Fred W.	BB	1930,31,32
Stevens, Don	FB	1949,50,51
Stevens, Lawrence J.	FB	1951,52
Stevens, Lisa	WCC	1980
Stevens, Terrence C.	FN	1990,91,92,93
Stevens, Thomas	MTR	1980,81,82,83
	MCC	1980,81,82
Stevenson, Amos M.	MTR	1899,00
Stevenson, Jeff	FB	1985
Stevenson, Nancy	WBK	1975
Stewart, Baird E.	FB	1952,53,54
Stewart, Brian	WR	1991,93,94,95
Stewart, Charles A.	FB	1905,06
	MBK	1906,07
Stewart, Charles M.	IHO	1940
Stewart, D. Larry	MTR	1957,58,59
Stewart, Dave	MTN	1953
Stewart, David L.	FB	1957,58
Stewart, Frank	FB	1914,15,16
Stewart, James R. (Bud)	FB	1926,27
	BB	1926,27,28
Stewart, Lynn	FB	1962,63,64
Stewart, Paul J.	BB	1921,22,23
Stewart Jr., Thomas	BB	1974,75,76
Stewart, Thomas C.	FB	1946,47,48,49
Sticha, Cherie	WSW	1995
Stierwalt, Mitchell	BB	1979,80,81
Stiles, Leroy C.	BB	1915,16
Stillwell, Al	MTR	1974
Stilwell, Leland	MBK	1922,23,24
Stimpfle, Lisa	WSW	1990,91,92,93
Stine, Francis B.	MTR	1927,28,29
	MCC	1927,28
Stine, Mike	FB	1983
Stirton, James C.	MTR	1914,15,16
Stitzel, Clarence M.	MTR	1911,12
Stitzel, Stan	WR	1966
Stluka, Gary	MSW	1970,71,72
Stoddard, David	MTR	1973,74
Stoldt, David J.	MGY	1977,78,79,80
Stoll, Steven G.	FN	1964,65
Stoltz, Christina	WCC	1980
Stoltz, Teresa	WCC	1985
Stone, Clyde E.	FB	1902
Stone, Kenneth	MGY	1954,55,56
Stone, Melissa	WTR	1989
Stone, Richard R.	FB	1965
	MTR	1965,66
Stone, W. W.	MTR	1899
Stonitsch, Mike	WR	1991,92,93,94
Stotlar, James	MTR	1948,49
Stotz, Charles H.	FB	1938
Stotz, James T.	FB	1966
Stotz, Richard A.	FB	1966
Stout, Hiles G.	FB	1954,55,56
	MBK	1955,56,57
Stout, Lorence S.	MTR	1939,40,41
Stout, Susan	WTN	1985,86,87,88
Stout, W. H.	MSW	1928,29
Stovall, David	MTR	1994
Stowe, Bob	FB	1980,81,82,83
Strader, Wayne	FB	1977,78,79,80
Strainis, Frank	BB	1961,62,63
Strange, Rob	MSW	1978,79
Strange, Robert	WR	1949
Strauch, Donald J.	FB	1916
Strauss, Deborah	WTN	1978
Straw, Thomas C.	FB	1931,32,33
Straza, Melissa	WCC	1986,87
	WTR	1987,88
Streed, Jack A.	FN	1942
Streeter, Sean	FB	1988,89,90,91
Stricker, Steve	MGO	1986,87,88,89
Stringfellow, Efrem Z.	MTR	1978,79,80,81
Stroker, Steven	MSW	1979,80,81
Strong, David A.	FB	1936
Strong, H. D.	WR	1914
Strong, Jasper	FB	1992,93,94
Struznik, Mark	WR	1993
Strzepek, Alfred W.	SOC	1933
Studebaker, Adam	BB	1991,94
Studley, Charles B.	FB	1949,50,51
Studwell, Scott	FB	1973,75,76
Studzinski, James D.	MTR	1950
Stuebe, Louis F.	FN	1921
	MGY	1921
Stuebe, Louis M.	FN	1947,48,49
Stuermer, Raymond J.	MGY	1937
Stuessy, Dwight T.	FB	1926,27,28
Sturrock, Tom	FB	1968
Stuttle, Fred L.	MTR	1925,26,27

Illini football star Scott Studwell went on to an All-Pro career with the NFL's Minnesota Vikings.

Styles, Edward B.	MGY	1910,11,12
Su, Kenneth	MGY	1994,95
Suarez, Mike	FB	1993,94
Sublette, Bruce M.	FN	1950,51,52
Suess, Frederica	WSW	1986,87
Suitor, Rick	MGO	1970,71,72,73
Sulaver, Randy	WR	1972,73,74,75
Sullivan, Albert	WR	1977,78
Sullivan, Bruce E.	FB	1965,66
Sullivan, Dave	WR	1992,93,94
Sullivan, Gerry	FB	1971,72,73
Sullivan, Harold F.	MTR	1926
Sullivan, Jeanne	VB	1978,79,80,81
Sullivan, John	FB	1974,75,77,78
Sullivan, Kelcey	WGY	1991
Sullivan, Mike	FB	1974,75
Sullivan, Patricia	WSW	1989,90
Sullivan, Paul	WR	1990,91
Sullivan, Robert	MGY	1951,52,53
	MSW	1953
Sullivan, Robert	WR	1976
Sullivan, Warren	FN	1947
Summers, W. Michael	FB	1961,62,63
Sundahl, Karen	WSW	1987
Sunderlage, Don	MBK	1949,50,51
Suppan, Mike	FB	1974
Suqui, Zeyad	FN	1984
Surdyk, Florian J.	FB	1937
Suritz, Charles S.	FN	1967
Suter, Earl R.	BB	1913
Sutin, L. R.	MGO	1928,29
Sutter, J. H.	MTR	1899
Sutter, Jeremy	MTN	1994,95
Sutter, Kenneth F.	FB	1956
Sutton, Archie M.	FB	1962,63,64
Sutton, Larry	BB	1989,90,91,92
Sutton, M.	MSW	1924
Sutton, Michael G.	FN	1977,78,79
Sutton, Sandy	WGO	1982,83,84
Swakon, Larry	BB	1971,72,73,75
Swank, Roger L.	MTR	1950,51,52
Swann, Leeda	WSW	1994
Swanson, Harold A.	BB	1935,36,37
	MBK	1936,37
Swanson, Mark B.	FB	1930
Swanson, Reuben E.	MTR	1922
	MCC	1921
Swartz, Joel	WR	1960
Swartzendruber, Fred	MTR	1945
Swasney, E. H.	BB	1879,80,81
Swatek, E. T.	MSW	1907
Sweeney, Ira J.	BB	1926,27,28
Sweeney, Marshall J.	MTR	1923,24,25
Sweet, Gayln L.	MTR	1971,74
Sweet, Paul C.	MTR	1921,22,23
Sweetman, Frank	MSW	1924
Sweney, Don	FB	1893,94,95,97
	MTR	1893,94,95,98
Swensen, Charles C.	FN	1950,51
Swienton, Kenneth R.	FB	1952,53,54
Swift, A. Dean	MTR	1938
Swikle, Charles G.	BB	1934,35,36
Switzer, Robert M.	BB	1900
Swonick, Robert	MGY	1970,71
Swoope, Craig	FB	1982,83,84,85
Szabo, Steve	WR	1955,56,57
Szluha, Nicholas	FN	1960,61,62
Szukala, Jerry	BB	1965,66

T

Taaffe, Sabine	WSW	1989,90,92,93
Taber, B. F.	MSW	1911,12,13
Tabor, Hubert B.	FB	1921
	MBK	1922
Tack, Joseph	MSW	1979,80
Tackett, William C.	FB	1892,93
	MTR	1893
Tagart, Mark	FB	1984,85
Tague, Chris	MSW	1977,78,79,80
Tait, Fred	MSW	1952,53
Takata, Chris	WSW	1981
Talbot, Paul	MCC	1993
	MTR	1994
Taliaferro, Mike	FB	1962,63
	FN	1963
Tallmadge, Floyd	MBK	1906
Tangman, Horace J.	BB	1949,50
Tanner, Jim	MSW	1968
Tanner, John	MSW	1972,73,74,75
Tanner, Joseph R.	MSW	1970,71,72
Tanner, Tom	MSW	1977,78,79
Tanous, Jerry	MGO	1961

Archie Sutton was a two-time first-team All-Big Ten selection in football.

Tapping, Charles H.	MTR	1914,15
Tapscott, Robert A.	MGO	1943,48
Tarkoff, Daniel	BB	1978,79
Tarnoski, Paul T.	FB	1905
Tarwain, John	FB	1928
	MBK	1930
Tate, Albert R.	FB	1948,49,50
Tate, Barb	WGO	1981
Tate, Donald E.	FB	1951,52,53,54
Tate, Kyle	FB	1994
Tate, Richard A.	FB	1965,66,67
Tate, William L.	FB	1950,51,52
Taylor, Brooks	MBK	1990,91,92,93
Taylor, C. B.	FN	1915
Taylor, Carooq	FB	1977,80
Taylor, Curtis	MBK	1986
Taylor, Deb	WBK	1980,81
Taylor, Deryck L.	MTR	1961,62,63
Taylor, F. M.	MSW	1925
Taylor, Joseph W.	BB	1904,05,07
	FB	1904
Taylor, Keith	FB	1983,85,86,87
Taylor, Kelli	WSW	1989,90,91,92
Taylor, Kyle	MTR	1993,94,95
Taylor, Paul	MBK	1918,19,20
Taylor, Randall R.	FB	1976,77,78
Taylor, Roger	MBK	1957,58,59
Taylor, Trent	WR	1979,80,81,82
Taylor, W. H.	MSW	1921,22,23
Teach, Jeffrey D.	MTR	1991,93,94,95
Teafatiller, Guy	FB	1984,85
Tedesco, Robert	BB	1957,58
Tee, Darrin	FB	1986,87
Tee, David	FB	1982
Teeman, Hall	PO	1934,35
Tellin, Tracy	WCC	1990,91,93
Temelli, Esra	VB	1982
Temmler, Bernard	WR	1961
Temple, Harry C.	MGY	1934
TenPas, Larry	WR	1954,55,56
Terrien, Molly	WBK	1984,85
Tewksbury, W. J.	MGO	1925,26,27
Tex, Cathy	WGO	1977
	WGY	1975
Thacker, Edgar	WR	1926,27

Former Illini swimmer Joe Tanner became the first UI athlete to go into space.

Track and field's Don Tjarksen was a member of three Illini Big Ten championship teams.

Thanos, Jon D.	MTR	1986,87,88
	MCC	1984,85,86,87
Thatcher, Chris	MTN	1993
Theil, Linda	WSW	1976,77,78,79
Theobald, Nan	WSW	1978,79,80
Theobald, William G.	BB	1933
	MBK	1933
Theodore, James J.	FB	1934
Theodore, John A.	FB	1935
Thiede, John	FB	1977,78
Thienpont, Greg	BB	1984
Thies, Nancy	WGY	1976,77
Thomas, Althea	WTR	1989,90,91
Thomas, Calvin	FB	1978,79,80,81
Thomas, Deon	MBK	1991,92,93,94
Thomas, Derrick	MBK	1995
Thomas, Glen H.	BB	1916
Thomas, Harry	WR	1916
Thomas, Kelly	WBK	1985
Thomas, Ken	FB	1987,89
Thomas, Ranis	MTR	1944
Thomas, Raymond R.	BB	1910,11,12
Thomas, Robert E.	BB	1912,13
Thomas, Stephen K.	FB	1961
Thomas, Tim	BB	1988
Thomases, Robert	FB	1938
Thompson, Andy	BB	1991,92,93,94
Thompson, Darryl	FB	1982,83
Thompson, Earl	WR	1942
Thompson, Edwin	MTN	1967,68,69
Thompson, Frank L.	MTR	1900,01
Thompson, Fred B.	MTR	1898
Thompson, Fred L.	BB	1895,86
Thompson, H. P.	MSW	1912
Thompson, Harwell C.	MTR	1912,13
Thompson, Herbert P.	FB	1911
Thompson, Jett	MSW	1992
Thompson, John	MGO	1974
Thompson, M.	MGY	1928
Thompson, Maurice P.	IHO	1939,40
Thompson, O. H.	MSW	1914
Thompson, Paul W.	FN	1976,77,78
Thompson, T. H.	MSW	1912
Thompson, Thomas	MBK	1908,09,10
Thomson, Willard P.	MTR	1952,53,54,55
Thonn, Ray	BB	1956,57,58
Thorby, Charles H. J.	FB	1895

Track and field's Tama Tochihara was an All-America middle distance runner for the Fighting Illini in the 1990s.

Thoren, Duane (Skip)	MBK	1963,64,65
Thornton, Bruce	FB	1975,76,77,78
Thornton, Robert I.	BB	1897,98
Thorp, Don	FB	1980,81,82,83
Thurlby, Burdette	BB	1948,50
	MBK	1948,49,50
Thurmon, Kimberly	WTR	1991,92
Tibbetts, James D.	FN	1962,63,64
Ticknor, Anthony	MGY	1985,86
Tiedemann, Lance	MSW	1988,89,90,91
Tieken, Theo	BB	1886,87
Tiernan, Terry	WR	1962
Tiffin, Donna	WTR	1976,77
Tilton, Harry W.	FB	1894
Tilton, Leon D.	MTR	1913
Timko, Craig S.	FB	1965,66,67
Timm, Judson A.	FB	1927,28,29
	MTR	1928,29
Timmerhaus, Klaus	MTR	1948
Tingley, Loyal	FN	1969
Tischler, Matthew	FB	1935
Tish, Allen I.	FN	1978,79,80,81
Titus, Rayburn L.	FN	1942
Tjaden Jr., Dean A.	FN	1969,70,71
Tjarksen, Donald E.	MTR	1958,59
Tobin, Marni	WSW	1994,95
Tochihara, Tama	WCC	1993
	WTR	1991,92,93,94
Tocks, John H.	FN	1964,65,66
Tockstein, L. A.	MTR	1929
Todaro, Steven B.	FN	1976
Todd, Josie	WBK	1988
Toerring, Christian J.	MTR	1891
Tofft, Leonard	WR	1935
Tohn, Clarence G.	FB	1943
Tolbert, Roderick L.	MTR	1986,87,88,89
Toliuszis, Mike	MGO	1960,61,62
Tolman, Robert G.	FN	1921
Tolmie, T. W.	MGY	1917
Tomala, Andy	WR	1978
Tomanek, Emil	FB	1944
Tomaras, William	WR	1941,42,46
Tomars, Peter T.	FN	1956
Tomasula, David G.	FB	1965,66,67
Tomlinson, Amy	WCC	1990,91,92,94
	WTR	1992,93,94
Toncoff, Jean	WR	1929,30
Toncoff, John	BB	1933,34
Tonry, Donald	MGY	1956,57,59
Tookey, Bill	BB	1964
Topper, Martin	MCC	1922
Torchia, Meta R.	WSW	1985,86,87,88
Toriani, Keith	BB	1990,91,92,93
Torres, R.	MGY	1934
Tortorelli, Jeanne	WBK	1983
Tosetti, Arthur	WR	1924,25
Toth, Anne	WSW	1995
Toth, Magdalena	WSW	1983,84,85,86
Tothero, Steve	MSW	1989,90,91,92
Townsell, William	WR	1988
Townsend, Rolla E.	MTR	1903
Trabert, M. L.	MGY	1935
Trandel, Eugene J.	MTR	1946
Trapp, Harold F.	MTR	1896
Tratt, Kerrie	WSW	1990
Travis Jr., Foster L.	MTR	1964,65,66
Travis, Lee	WGY	1975,76,77
Travis, Terrence	BB	1983
Travnik, Mary Pat	WBK	1976,77,78,79
Traynham Jr., Floyd	FN	1937,39
Treadman, Jack	WR	1944
Treado, Kristine	WSW	1987,88,89
Tregoning, Wesley W.	FB	1941,45
Trenda, Pamela	WSW	1989,90,91,92
Trenkle, Howard	WR	1922
Treseler, Kristie	WGO	1994
Triebel Jr., Albert	MGO	1936
Trigger, Jeff C.	FB	1966,67,68
Trigger, Tom	MSW	1966,67
Trimble, Leon	MTR	1929
Trimble, Ocie	MTR	1951,52,53
Tripp, Robert S.	FN	1959,60
Trobe, Pete	FN	1968,69,70
Trousil, Tom	WR	1959,60
Trowbridge, Sam	WR	1931
Trudeau, Jack	FB	1983,84,85
True, Bill	BB	1992,93
Trugillo, Glen	BB	1949,50
Trujillo, Oscar	MGY	1994
Trumpy, Bob	FN	1964
Tryban, Edward E.	BB	1930,31,32
Tucker, Craig	MBK	1981,82

Tucker, Derwin	FB	1975,76,77,78
Tucker, Joel	MGY	1986,87,88,89
Tucker, Otho	MBK	1973,75,76
Tumilty, Richard J.	FB	1941
Tupper, James O.	FB	1913
Turek, Jerry	MTN	1994,95
Turek, Joseph J.	FB	1939,40
Turek, Marty	MSW	1992
Turnbow, Charles R.	MGO	1943
Turnbull, David	FB	1937
Turnbull, Jeffrey	MGY	1993
Turner, Bill	WR	1954,55
Turner III, Elbert L.	MTR	1989,90,91
	FB	1988,90,91
Turner, E. Scott	FB	1991,92,93,94
	MTR	1991,92,93,94
Turner, Greg	FB	1986,87,88
Turner, John H.	MTR	1940,41
Turner, Kevin	MBK	1995
Turner, Shawn	FB	1985,86,88
Turner, T. R.	MGO	1985
Tuttle, Will	MBK	1992
Twardock, A. Robert	MTR	1951,52,53
Tweedy, Jennifer	WCC	1990
	WTR	1990,91,92,93
Twist, Clarence C.	BB	1911
Twist, John F.	FB	1908,09,10
Twitchell, Thomas H.	IHO	1942,43
Twomey, John E.	MTR	1946,47
	MCC	1946,47
Twomey, Victor L.	MTR	1946,48,49,50
	MCC	1945,47,48,49
Tyson, Steven M.	MTR	1984,85,86,87

U

Uecker, Bill	FB	1972,73,74
Ulrich Jr., Charles	FB	1949,50,51
Ultes, Ronald	BB	1952,53,54
Umbach, Dana	WBK	1975
Ummel, Kregg	MCC	1989,90,91
Umnus, Leonard	FB	1922,23,24
Unruh, Dan	WR	1979,80,81
Upton, Richard A.	MTR	1949,50
Urbanckas, Alfred	MTR	1956,57
Urbanik, Edward J.	FN	1949
Uremovich, George	FB	1971,72,73
Urso, Philip J.	FN	1952,53
Useman, Ernest M.	MTR	1930
Usher, Darryl C.	MTR	1985,86
	FB	1983,84,85,87
Usinger, William A.	MGO	1940,41
Usrey, Vergil R.	MTR	1924
Utt, Arthur H.	MTR	1918
Utz, George J.	FB	1956,57

V

Vail, Charles	MBK	1918,20,21
Valek, James J.	FB	1945,46,47,48
Valente, John	BB	1986,87,88
Valentino, John	MGY	1974
Valentino, R. Rudolph	FB	1949,51
Van Aken, Harry	FN	1968
Van Dyke, Jos. A.	FB	1932
Van Etten, Gary	MGY	1971
Van Gunter, M. B.	MSW	1933
Van Handel, Kerry	WBK	1987,88,89,90
Van Heltebrake, Jerry	MSW	1971
Van Hook, Forest C.	FB	1906,07,08
Van Hooreweghe, Joseph	BB	1943
Van Inwagen, F.	MTR	1905,06,07
Van Kirk, William K.	MTR	1979,82
Van Matter, Francis	FN	1914,15,16
Van Meter, Vincent J.	FB	1932
	MTR	1934,35
Van Orman, Ellsworth G.	FB	1935
Van Oven, Frederick W.	MTR	1896,97,98
Van Rossen, Donald	MSW	1953
Van Tine, James	MTN	1955,56,57
Van Tuin, J. W.	MSW	1933,35
Vance, Eugene	MBK	1942,43,47
Vandagrift, Carl W.	BB	1905,06,07
Vandersteeg, Jeff	WR	1969,70
Vangundy, Charles P.	BB	1886,87,88
Vangundy, Claude	BB	1910,11
Vanselow, Harold	BB	1968,69
Varrige, Tom	FB	1980,81,82
Vasaune, Steve	FN	1992,93
Vasey, Nicole	WBK	1995
Vaughn, Govoner	MBK	1958,59,60
Vaughn, Jon	WR	1994,95
Vayda, John	BB	1954,55,56
Veatch, David S.	FN	1977,78,79,80

Mary Pat Travnik earned four letters for the Illini women's basketball team.

Veatch, Paul D.	FN	1975
Veercruysee, Bob	WR	1973
Veerman, Beth	WSW	1990
Veirs, David C.	MTR	1899,00,01
Velasco, Herman	FN	1954,55,56
Velasco, Manny	MTN	1986,88,89
Venegoni, John	BB	1978,79
	FB	1978,80,81
Venerable, Terry	WTR	1976
Venkus, Laura	VB	1978,79
Verduzco, Jason	FB	1989,90,91,92
Vermette, Bob	BB	1958,59
Vernasco, Joseph P.	FB	1950,51
Vernasco, Walter L.	FB	1952,53,54
Veronesi, Don	FB	1993
Versen, Walter G.	FB	1944
Vestuto, Paul	WR	1977,78,79
Vial, H. C.	MSW	1917
Vierneisel, Phil	FB	1973,74,75,76
Viernes, Nicole	WGY	1994,95
Vieth, Wayne	MTR	1951
Vincent, Randall	BB	1974,75,76,77
Vinke, Bob	MSW	1973,74,75
Virgin, Craig	MCC	1973,74,75,76
	MTR	1974,75,76,77
Vitacco, Alfred G.	BB	1939
Vitoux, Michael E.	FN	1968,69
Vlach, William P.	SOC	1934
Voelker, Gary	FB	1992,93
Voelkner, Alvin	MSW	1960
Vogel, Margaret	WCC	1983,84,85
	WTR	1982,84,85
Vogel, Michelle	WCC	1981,83,84
Vogel, Otto H.	BB	1921,22,23
	FB	1921
Vogel, Rob	FB	1993
Vogt, Gary	WR	1962,63
Vohaska, William J.	FB	1948,49,50
	WR	1949,50
Vokac, Frank G.	MSW	1935,36
Volkman, Dean E.	FB	1965,66,67
Von Ebers, Donald	MGY	1947,48,49
Von Oven, Fred W.	FB	1896,97
Von Spreckelsen, Ray	MTN	1942,46
Voorhees, George	WR	1944,45
Vopicka, James	MBK	1936,37

Jack Trudeau's 8,725 yards passing still stands as the Illini record.

Vopicka, Jim	BB	1964,65	Walker, Carl	WR	1961,62	Walton, H. R.	MGO	1915	Watson, John W.	FB	1913,14,15

Vopicka, Jim — BB — 1964,65
MBK — 1964,65
Voris, Alvin C. — MTR — 1893
Vorreyer, Richard — BB — 1955,56,57
Vosburgh, William R. — MSW — 1911,12,13
Voss, George — MTN — 1969
Vossen, Michele — WBK — 1981,82,83,84
Voyda, John F. — MGO — 1956,57,58
Vranek, Lee R. — MTR — 1943,47,49
Vukelich, John J. — FB — 1949
Vyborny, Julian — FB — 1969,70

W

Waarich, Herman — MTR — 1949,50,51
Wacaser, Jan — WTR — 1980,82
Wacaser, Lottus — VB — 1979
Wachowski, Theodore J. — MTR — 1927,28
Wachter, John — FB — 1986,88,90
Wack, Rick — MTN — 1970,71,72
Waddell, Barry — MTN — 1981,83
Wadsworth, Albert M. — FB — 1899
Wagaser, Jan — WTR — 1981
Wagner, Alexander — FB — 1912,13,14
Wagner, Bertram E. — MTR — 1950,51
Wagner, David A. — MTR — 1978
Wagner, E. H. — MSW — 1929
Wagner, Mark — MTN — 1977
Wagner, Richard B. — FB — 1922
Wagner, Wayne — MGY — 1963,64,65
Wagstaff, C. D. — MGY — 1917
Wahl, Edward C. — BB — 1931,32
Wahl, Robert T. — BB — 1941
Wahlstrom, Marvin — MSW — 1946
Wailing, Karen — WSW — 1983,84,85,86
Wainwright, Jack — FB — 1964
Wakefield, James — BB — 1945,46,47,48
Wakerlin, Warren — MGY — 1961,62,63
Walch, Leo — MGO — 1952
Waldbeser, Clifford H. — FB — 1951,52,53
Waldinger, Beth — WTR — 1982
Waldo, J. H. — MSW — 1917,20
Waldron, Ralph H. — FB — 1966,68
Walduck, C. L. — MGO — 1912
Walenga, Frank — BB — 1951,52
Walewander, John — BB — 1986,87,88

Walker, Carl — WR — 1961,62
Walker, David R. — FB — 1955,56
Walker, Frank H. — FB — 1927,28,29
Walker, George — MTR — 1945,46,47,48
Walker, George — MCC — 1966,67
— MTR — 1966,67,68
Walker, Harold B. — BB — 1928,29
Walker, John — MGO — 1969
Walker, John — PO — 1939
Walker, John A. — MTR — 1949,50
Walker, Michael L. — FN — 1968,69
Walker, Mike — FB — 1970,72
Walker, Rick — MSW — 1979
Walker, Sharmella — WBK — 1989,91,92
Walker, Thomas — MSW — 1957,58,59
Walker, Thurman — FB — 1960,61,62
Walker, Wesley — MSW — 1980,81,82
Wall, Joe — FB — 1991
Wallace, Douglas A. — FB — 1957,58,59
Wallace, Edward — BB — 1911
Wallace, Henry S. — MTR — 1921,22
Wallace, Oscar — MTR — 1973
Wallace, Robert R. — MGO — 1967,68,69
Wallace, Samuel H. — MTR — 1920,21,22
Wallace, Stanley H. — FB — 1951,52,53
Wallace, William H. — MTR — 1924,25,26
Waller, Mike — FB — 1972,74,75
Waller, William H. — FB — 1934
Wallin, Robert W. — FB — 1940,42
Wallner, Neil — FB — 1986,87
Walquist, Lawrence W. — MBK — 1920,21,22
— FB — 1918,19,20,21
Walser, Herman J. — FB — 1931,32,33
Walsh, George — FB — 1954,55
Walsh, Kevin — WR — 1989
Walsh, L. Ed — FB — 1965
Walter, George — SOC — 1929,30
Walters, David B. — MCC — 1974,76,77,78
— MTR — 1975,76,78,79
Walters, Jay — FB — 1967
Walters, Kathy — WCC — 1977
— WTR — 1979
Walters, Michael W. — MGY — 1956,57,58
Walters, Thom D. — MTR — 1963
Walters, Vicki — WTR — 1983

Walton, H. R. — MGO — 1915
Wanger Jr., David E. — MTR — 1930
Wannemanker, Bob — MSW — 1970,72
Ward, Brian F. — FB — 1982,83,85
Ward, Bruce N. — FN — 1979
Ward, Cheryl — WCC — 1981
— WTR — 1982,83,84,85
Ward, Lindsey — WSW — 1995
Ward, Nicole — WGY — 1992,93,94,95
Ward, Raymond C. — FB — 1943,44
Ward, Richard — MSW — 1980,81
Wardell, Roosevelt — FB — 1988
Wardley Jr., George P. — FB — 1936,37,38
— MBK — 1937,38,39
Ware, J. W. — MTR — 1905
Ware, Paul R. — MTR — 1952
Warfield, Roy M. — BB — 1891
Warford, Dennis — BB — 1980
Warga, F. J. — MGY — 1928,29,30
Warmbier, Kenneth — BB — 1982,83,84,85
Warner, Earl A. — MTR — 1903
— BB — 1904
Warner, Gale A. — MTR — 1925
Warren, James B. — FB — 1962,63
Warren, Kent — MSW — 1990,91
Warshaw, Lawrence — FN — 1979,80,81,82
Washburn, Ludlow J. — MTR — 1908,09,10
Washington, Acquanetta — WBK — 1988
Washington, Beverly — WTR — 1975,76,77,78
Washington, Edward W. — FB — 1962,63,64
Washington, Lester — MTR — 1983,84,85
Washington, Mike — MBK — 1975,76
Washington, Tyrone — FB — 1992,93,94
Wasik, Jon — MGY — 1994,95
Wasser, Norman — MTR — 1947,48,49
Wasserman, Sarah — WGY — 1991,92
Wasson, Roy A. — MTR — 1941
Waters, Alan J. — BB — 1965,66,67
— FB — 1964,65,66
Waters, Sonya — WBK — 1989,90,91,92
Watson, Carl P. — MBK — 1909,10
— FB — 1908
— MTR — 1908
Watson, Chauncey B. — FB — 1911,12
Watson, James — MSW — 1953

Watson, John W. — FB — 1913,14,15
Watson, William A. — MTR — 1966,67
Watters, Laurie — VB — 1981,82,83
Watts, Claude H. — BB — 1911,12,13
Watts, James — WR — 1945
Watts, Larry — WR — 1966,67
Wax, Shawn — FB — 1988,89,90
Wayman, Leonard — MGY — 1934,35
Weatherspoon, Nick — MBK — 1971,72,73
Weatherford, Harold — MSW — 1976
Weaver, Robert — MTN — 1943
Weaver, Scott — FB — 1993,94
Webb, Ashley — WGO — 1995
Webb, Terrence — MTR — 1969,70,71
Weber, Amanda — WSW — 1995
Weber, Charles — MGY — 1965,66,67
Weber, Charles — FB — 1977,78
Weber, Cynthia — WGY — 1975,76,77,78
Weber, Edward W. — BB — 1934,35,36
Weber, Glenn — MSW — 1946
Weber, Nora — WTR — 1994,95
Weber, Ron — WR — 1994,95
Weber, W. Henry — BB — 1910,11,12
Webster, Frederick F. — MTR — 1916,17
Webster, G. A. — MSW — 1928,29,30
Webster, Julie — WGY — 1980
Webster, Ralph — WR — 1926,28
Weddell Jr., Robert W. — FB — 1951,52
Wedding, C. Nugent — MTR — 1938
Wedding, James — BB — 1968
Wedel, John — WR — 1952
Wedell, Mark — WR — 1975
Weedman, Frederick J. — MTR — 1892,93,94
Weems, C. L. — MGO — 1915
Wehling, Fred J. — MTR — 1935,36
Wehrli, Robert J. — FB — 1937,38
Weidner, Karla — WSW — 1986,87
Weiler, W. Richard — MTR — 1946
Weingartner, Harold — FN — 1937,38,39
Weingrad, Mike — FB — 1982,83
Weinstein, David — MTN — 1978
Weintraub, Edward — MGY — 1964
Weirsema, H. A. — MGY — 1913
Weise, Robert W. — MGO — 1942
Weisenborn, Harold — BB — 1963

Forry Wells, Illinois' 1994 Big Ten Conference Medal of Honor winner, earned eight total varsity letters in football and baseball.

Weisman, Jonathan	FN	1982,83
Weiss, G. S.	MSW	1925
Weiss, Joe	MTN	1947,48
Weiss, John N.	MTR	1918,20,21
Weiss, Jon	MTN	1956
Weiss, Raymond	MGY	1938,39,40
Weiss, Richard M.	FB	1978
Weitz, L. J.	WR	1929
Welch, Anthony	MBK	1982,83,85,86
Welch, Wendy	WCC	1990,91,92
	WTR	1992
Welker, Douglas J.	MTR	1977,78
Wells Jr., Edwin S.	MTR	1921,22,23
	MCC	1922
Wells, Forry	BB	1991,92,93,94
	FB	1990,91,92,93
Wells, John	FB	1982
Wells, Mike	FB	1970,71,72
Wells, Terry	BB	1983,84,85
Welsh, Alex	IHO	1939
	MGO	1940,41
Welsh, Jim	FB	1970,71
Welsh, Roger T.	MCC	1912
	WR	1915
Welter, Cullen J.	MTR	1989,90,91
Welty, William R.	MTR	1936
Welyki, Joseph	MCC	1946
Wendryhoski, Joseph S.	FB	1959,60
Wendt, Pat	FB	1991,92
Wenskunas, Mac P.	FB	1942,45,46
Wente, Mike	MBK	1974
Wentink, Nancy	WTN	1975
Wentz, Brad	BB	1986,87,88
Wenzel, Rusty	BB	1979
Werder, Beth	WSW	1979
Werkowski, Amy	WTR	1987,88,89
Werner, Charles D.	MTR	1925,26
Werner, Franklin	WR	1938
Werner, James	MSW	1978,79,80
Werner, Robert	MSW	1979,80,81,82
Wernham, James I.	BB	1897,98,99
Werremeyer, Kit	MSW	1966,67,68
Wertman, Nancy	WTR	1975,76
Wessberg, Tom	MSW	1986,87
Wessels, John	MBK	1959,60,61

West, B. Kenneth	MGO	1952,53,54,55
West, Donald J.	FN	1942
West, Jason D.	MTR	1991,92,93
	MCC	1991,92
West, Kevin	FB	1982
West, Ron	BB	1954
West, William O.	MCC	1931,32,33
	MTR	1932,33
Westberg, Carey	MTN	1979
Westerlind, Dan R.	FB	1978
Westervelt, Kevin	MBK	1980
Westfall, Curtis	MBK	1907
Westhoff, Sue	WSW	1980,81,82,83
Westohoff, Karen	WSW	1981
Weygand, Tricia	WTR	1994,95
Weygandt, Jerry	BB	1962,63,64
Whalin, Brian G.	FN	1973,74,75
Wham, Charles	FB	1910
Wham, Fred L.	FB	1905,07,08
Wham, James B.	MTR	1940
Wham, Richard A.	MTR	1952,53,54
Wharton, Russell F.	MTR	1920,21,22
	MCC	1921
Wheatland, J. Alan	MGO	1962
	FB	1961,63
Wheeler, H. H.	MTR	1904
Wheeler, Missy	VB	1984
Wheeler Jr., Paul A.	FN	1930,31
Wheeler, R. L.	MSW	1922
Wheeler, T. J.	MBK	1992,93,94
Whipple, G. B.	MGY	1928
Whitacre, Andrew	MGO	1984,85
Whitaker, Kim	WSW	1976
White, Brian	BB	1980,81,82,83
White, Charles V.	MTR	1975,76,77,78
	MCC	1975,77,78
White, Chris	FB	1983,84,85
White, David C.	FN	1965,66,67
White, Donald R.	MTR	1978,79
White, Earl A.	FB	1906,07
White, Earl C.	MTR	1926,27,28
White, Edward L.	FB	1984,85,86
White, F. H.	MGO	1914,15
White, Frank	BB	1879
White, H. H.	MGO	1917
White, Harold R.	MCC	1925
	MTR	1926,28,29
White, James	MBK	1911,12,13
White Jr., James E.	MTR	1991
White, John M.	IHO	1939,40
White, Liz	WBK	1983,84,85,86
White, Matthew	MGY	1992,93,94
White, Ronald D.	FB	1975,76
White, Scott	MSW	1972
White Jr., Sylvester	MTR	1989
Whitehead, Chenise	WBK	1983,85,86
Whitehead, Donell	MTR	1984
Whitelatch, Rex	WR	1958,59
Whitelaw, J. C.	MGO	1914,15
Whiteside, Jim	FB	1967,68
Whitlow, Jamey	MCC	1993
Whitman, Doug	FB	1967,68
Whitmore, Harold	BB	1905
Whitney, E. M.	MGY	1935
Whitson, Herman	WR	1920
Whittaker, Dick	MSW	1959
Whittaker Jr., Lorin	MSW	1957,58
Whyte, G. K.	MGO	1928
Wich, Fred	MSW	1975,76,77,78
Wickersham, Don	BB	1971,72
Wickhorst, George N.	FB	1925
Wickiser, Jo	WTN	1983
Wickland, Albert	BB	1947,48
Widdersheim, John	BB	1977,78
Widner, Albert E.	FB	1943
Wiedow, Roy W.	BB	1944,45,46
Wieneke, Mark J.	MTR	1986
	MCC	1985
Wiesenborn, Kurt	WR	1977
Wietz, Leroy J.	FB	1927,28,29
Wilder, Frank S.	BB	1900
Wile, Dan	FB	1955
Wiley, D. F.	MGO	1928,29
Wiley, Francis R.	FB	1903
Wiley, Raymond S.	MTR	1899
Wilkerson, Michael R.	MTR	1985
Will, Larry D.	MTR	1977,78,79,80
Willey, Kristin	WTN	1991
Williams, Anthony	FB	1984,85,86,87
Williams, Brian	FB	1988,89
Williams, Christopher	FB	1976
Williams, David	BB	1955,56,57

Williams, David	FB	1983,84,85
Williams, Derrick	WR	1984,85,86
Williams, Elvie	WR	1976,77
Williams, Gil	MTR	1964,65
Williams, Greg	FB	1973,74
Williams, Janet	WSW	1976
Williams, John	MSW	1974,75,76
Williams, Katherine	WTR	1991,92,93,94
Williams, Marty	WR	1978
Williams, Mary B.	WTN	1990,91,92
Williams, Melvin R.	FB	1984,85
Williams, Milton L.	BB	1929,30
Williams, Nate	MBK	1975,76
Williams, Oliver	FB	1981,82
Williams, R. C.	MGO	1912
Williams, Rick	FB	1973,75
Williams, Scott	FB	1890,91
Williams, Sean	BB	1994,95
Williams, Steven	FB	1985,86,88,89
Williams, Tonya	WTR	1993,94,95
Williams, Tyrone	MTR	1995
Williams, Willie J.	MTR	1952,53,54
Williamson, Esby	MSW	1932
Williamson, J. C.	MSW	1930,31
Williamson, James	FN	1957,58,59
Williford, Edward	MBK	1913,14,15
Willig, Joseph H.	SOC	1932
Willingham, Thomas	MSW	1983
Willis, Norman L.	FB	1960,62
Willis, Stephen I.	MTR	1972
Willis, William W.	FB	1949
Willmann, Dean E.	FB	1954
	WR	1952,53
Wilmarth, George H.	FB	1897,98
Wilmot, Ralph	FN	1939,40
Wilmoth, Fred	FB	1954
Wilson, A. Gordon	SOC	1931
Wilson, Anthony	MSW	1985,86,87
Wilson, Bob	WR	1946
Wilson, Brett	FB	1983
Wilson, Darryl	FB	1979,80,81
Wilson, David C.	FB	1980
Wilson, David D.	FB	1921,22
Wilson, John	FB	1971
Wilson, Joseph W.	FB	1902
Wilson, Kenneth (Tug)	FB	1925
	MTR	1918,19,20
	MBK	1919,20
Wilson, Kirby	FB	1981,82
Wilson, Mary E.	VB	1975,76,77
Wilson, Norman K.	FB	1912,13
	MTR	1912
Wilson, Paul	MSW	1991,92
Wilson, Ray	FB	1983,84,85,86
Wilson, Richard	MCC	1978
Wilson, Robert A.	FB	1941,42
Wilson, Thomas P.	FB	1930,35,36
Wilson, Wendell S.	FB	1925,26
Wiman, Robert L.	BB	1954,55
	FB	1953,54
Windmiller, Robert	MBK	1969,70
	BB	1969,70,71
Windy, Gary	FB	1970
Wine, John	MSW	1984,85,86,87
Wineland, Harold S.	FB	1962
Wing, Roger	BB	1952,53
Winkelman, Susan	WGO	1987,88,89,90
Winsett, Barb	VB	1987,88,89,90
Winship, Harold L.	MTR	1977
	MCC	1977
Winsper, Edwin S.	FB	1930
Winston, Charles S.	BB	1898
Wintermute, Bob	FB	1969,70
Winters, C. P.	MGO	1915
Winters, Efrem	MBK	1983,84,85,86
Wislow, Len	FB	1967,68
Witek, Roger	FB	1987
Withrow, Loretta	WCC	1988,89,90
	WTR	1989,90,91
Witt, Terry	WR	1966
Witte, Theodore C.	BB	1929,30,31
Wiza, John	FB	1970,71,72
Wodziak, Frank S.	FB	1950,51,52
Wohlwend, Dave	BB	1992,93,94
Wojs, Dennis	BB	1966,67,68
Wolf, Fred	FB	1967,68
Wolf, Roger E.	FB	1952,53,54
Wolf, Ty	MCC	1983,84
	MTR	1984,85
Wolff, Gary L.	MTR	1962,63
Wolff, Leon V.	FN	1939
Wolff, Quentin	WR	1969,70,71

Ron White, a two-year letter winner for the Illinois football team, has been a generous supporter since his playing days.

Wolfley, Richard F.	MGO	1941
Wolfson, Robert H.	FN	1966,67
Wolgast, Arnold E.	FB	1927,29
Wollard, Jason	BB	1993,94,95
Wollrab, James C.	MSW	1939,40,41
Wolochuk, Lee	MGY	1988,90,91
Wolochuk, Mark	MGY	1990,91
Wolters, Brett	MSW	1992
Wolters, Mike	BB	1986,87,88
Womick, John P.	MTR	1966
Wood, Arthur	MCC	1940,42
	MTR	1941
Wood, Charles H.	MTR	1904,08
Wood, Gerald A.	FB	1959,60
Wood, Harlington	PO	1941
Wood, Shellie	WGO	1989,90
Woodbury, Ed	MSW	1973,74,75,76
Woodcock, Geoff	WR	1990,92
Woodcock, Greg	WR	1989,90
Woodcock, Scott	MGO	1994
Woodin, D. E.	MTR	1904,05,06
Woods, Conrad	MTN	1954,55
Woods, John T.	MTR	1978
Woods, Ralf	MBK	1915,16,17
Woods, Ray	MBK	1915,16,17
Woods, Stanley W.	MTR	1957
Woods, Toriano	FB	1993,94
Woodson, Abraham B.	FB	1954,55,56
	MTR	1954,55,56
Woodward, Harold C.	FB	1921,22
Woodward, Reggie	MBK	1986
Woody, Frederick W.	FB	1892,93,94
Woolsey, Robert D.	MTR	1931,32,33
	MCC	1930,31,32
Woolston, William H.	MBK	1911,12
	FB	1910,11,12
Wopat, Paula	WSW	1977
Worban, John C.	FB	1940
Worth, Carolyn	WSW	1984,85,86,87
Worth, John C.	BB	1925,26
Worthy, Tyrone	FB	1979,80
Wrenn, John M.	FB	1946,47
Wright, Carolyn	WBK	1980,81
Wright, Dave	FB	1970,71,72

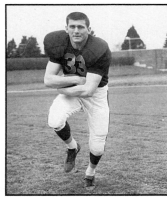

Streator, Illinois' Al Wheatland earned varsity letters in both football and golf in the early 1960s.

Roger Wolf played football for the Fighting Illini from 1952-54.

Jim Wright, long-time Champaign businessman, lettered in basketball and track at Illinois.

Wrobke, Dewey	BB	1918,19,20
Wrobke, Floyd	BB	1932,33
Wuethrich, David	BB	1981,82
Wujek, Kathy	WTN	1975
Wukovits, Victor	MBK	1940,41,42
Wunder, Linda	WBK	1978,79,80,81
Wurtzel, Frederic	MTN	1965,66,67
Wyatt, Arthur R.	MGO	1946,47,48,49
Wyatt, Nathaniel C.	MTR	1977,78,79
Wyatt, R. D.	FB	1906
Wycoff, Eric	FB	1984,85
Wylie, Mary	WSW	1982,83,84,85
Wysinger, Tony	MBK	1984,85,86,87

Y

Yadron, Paul	FB	1973,74
Yahiro, Mark	MGY	1978
Yanuskus, P. J.	FB	1929,30,32
Yarcho, Wayne B.	MTR	1938,39
	MCC	1938
Yario, Sue	VB	1980,81,82,83
Yarnall, Thomas C.	MTR	1925,26
Yasukawa, Steven	MGY	1974,76,77,78
Yates, Howard N.	MTR	1920,21,22
Yates, Michael	WR	1982,83,84
Yates, Robert W.	MTR	1926
Yavorski, Michael T.	MTR	1962,64
	FB	1962
Yeaton, Edward	MTN	1937
Yeaton, F. D.	MGY	1905
Yeaton, Frederick C.	BB	1934
Yeazel, Donald R.	FB	1957,58,59
Yi, Theodore	MGY	1977,78
Yochem, Ron	FB	1955
Yonezuka, Natacha	WGY	1984,85
Yonke, Martha	WTR	1976,77,78,79
York, Pam	WSW	1980,81,82,83
Yoss, Jeanne	VB	1984,85
Young, Aitken F.	SOC	1928,29,30
Young, Al	FB	1975
Young, Amy	WTN	1978,79,80
Young, Claude (Buddy)	MTR	1944
	FB	1944,46

Young, Everett	BB	1944
Young, Herbert T.	FB	1938
Young, Maurice	MTR	1995
Young, Richard	MTR	1944
Young, Roy M.	FB	1904,05
Young, W. Cecil	FB	1961,62
Young, Willie	FB	1981
Younger, Charles	MSW	1961,62
Yount, Amy	WSW	1975,76
Yukevich Jr., Stanley F.	FB	1959,60,61
Yule, John S.	BB	1929,32,33
Yurtis, Barry	BB	1969,70

Z

Zaborac, Thomas F.	FB	1945,46
Zahn, Dene W.	MGO	1936
Zambole, Nicholas	MGO	1979,80,81,82
Zander, Andy	WR	1965,67
Zander, Anthony	MGY	1975,76,77
Zander, John	WR	1960,61,62
Zanetakos, William	WR	1952
Zangerle, Adolph A.	BB	1903,04
Zatkoff, Samuel	FB	1944,46,47
Zavell, Howard	MGY	1986,88,89
Zbornik, Joseph J.	SOC	1932
Zeddies, David	MGY	1986,87,88,89
Zeller, Roger L.	BB	1939
Zenarosa, Rena	VB	1992,93
Zeppetella, Anthony J.	FB	1961
Ziegler, A. W.	MGY	1920,21
Ziemba, Chester J.	BB	1939,41
	IHO	1939,40,41
Zieron, Jason	MTR	1995
	MCC	1994
Zimmerman, Albert G.	MTR	1945
	FB	1945
Zimmerman, Beth	WCC	1980
	WTR	1982
Zimmerman, John H.	MTR	1919
Zimmerman Jr., Kenneth	FB	1961,62
	FN	1962,63
Zimmerman Sr., Kenneth	FB	1936,37,38
Zimmerman, Valerie	WGO	1993

Illini golfer Art Wyatt earned four varsity letters in 1946, '47, '48, and '49.

Zimmerman, Walter H.	FB	1895,96
Zimmerman, Wessel	MSW	1984
Zimner, David	MCC	1988
Zindell, Lee H.	FN	1961
Zinker, Edward	BB	1950,51
Zinzi, Vito	MGY	1947,48
Zirbel, Craig	FB	1980,81,82
Zitnik, Mark	FB	1988,89,90,91
Zitz, John	MSW	1990,91
Zitzewitz, A. F.	MGY	1924
Zitzler, E.	MGY	1931,32
Zobel, Julie	WCC	1986
Zochert, Dave	BB	1969,70,71
Zombolas, Anthony	FN	1953,54
Zopf, William	MGY	1992
Zuidema, Greg	WR	1970,71,72
Zunich, Andreja (Butch)	MGY	1977,78,79,80
Zuppke, Robert E.	FB	1937
Zych, Jon	MTN	1991,93,94

Wright, Ernie	WR	1967
Wright, Frederick W.	PO	1935,36,37,38
Wright, Jack	MTN	1935
Wright, Jr., James W.	MBK	1952,53,54
	MTR	1953,54
Wright Sr., John W.	FB	1965,66,67
	MTR	1966,67
Wright Jr., John W.	FB	1990,91,92
Wright, Laurence S.	MTR	1923,24,25
Wright, Newton A.	MTR	1914,15
Wright, Noel N.	SOC	1927
Wright, Richard	FB	1969,71
Wright, Robert C.	FB	1935
	MTR	1936
Wright, Royal	FB	1890,91,93
	MTR	1889
Wright, Sidney B.	FB	1908
Wright, Wesley E.	MTR	1974,75,76

Year-by-Year Summaries

The following is a year-by-year summary of University of Illinois athletic teams through the 1994-95 season. History has been documented more completely for some sports than others, but an attempt has been made to chart each of the 22 different sports that have attained varsity status. Big Ten championship teams are denoted in bold face.

Baseball

Year	Overall Record	Big Ten Record	Big Ten Finish	Year	Overall Record	Big Ten Record	Big Ten Finish	Year	Overall Record	Big Ten Record	Big Ten Finish
1879	1-0			1918	13-6	7-3	2nd	1957	17-9	7-4	2nd
1880	1-0			1919	13-5	7-4	2nd	1958	18-10	8-6	4th
1881	0-1			1920	16-8	6-4	3rd	1959	22-9	9-6	2nd
1882	No Team			**1921**	**17-3**	**10-1**	**1st**	1960	21-10	6-8	7th
1883	3-0			**1922**	**17-2-1**	**8-2**	**1st**	1961	22-8	9-4	4th
1884	1-1			1923	14-6-1	7-4	2nd	**1962**	**25-6**	**13-2**	**1st**
1885	1-0			1924	10-6-1	4-3-1	5th	**1963**	**18-13**	**10-5**	**1st**
1886	4-2			1925	11-8-0	6-5	5th	1964	9-22	1-14	10th
1887	4-4			1926	16-7-1	7-4	3rd	1965	14-9	8-6	5th
1888	3-4			**1927**	**10-7-3**	**7-3-1**	**1st-T**	1966	14-14	5-7	6th
1889	1-2-1			1928	32-12-5	6-6	NA	1967	17-21	5-11	9th
1890	5-3			1929	13-7-2	6-5	4th	1968	18-19	7-10	6th
1891	8-2			1930	15-5-0	8-2	2nd	1969	22-20	11-7	2nd
1892	8-3			**1931**	**15-4**	**8-2**	**1st**	1970	19-16-1	8-10	6th
1893	14-8			1932	10-5	7-3	2nd	1971	20-16-1	10-7-1	4th
1894	8-6			1933	13-3	8-2	2nd	1972	16-21	5-9	8th
1895	10-4			**1934**	**15-3**	**9-1**	**1st**	1973	21-13	8-10	7th
1896	15-4			1935	12-4	7-3	2nd	1974	27-11	9-7	4th
1897	8-9-1			1936	13-4	10-2	2nd	1975	25-17-1	4-11-1	9th
1898	12-9			**1937**	**14-3**	**9-1**	**1st**	1976	20-22	3-12	10th
1899	13-11	10-4	2nd	1938	8-8	4-4	6th	1977	23-25	8-10	6th
1900	**12-2-1**	**11-2**	**1st**	1939	7-7-2	4-5	8th	1978	25-22-1	6-12	9th
1901	12-7	9-5	2nd	**1940**	**16-5**	**9-3**	**1st-T**	1979	14-30-1	3-15	10th
1902	12-4	8-3	2nd	1941	13-7	7-4	3rd	1980	18-33	6-10	6th
1903	**17-1**	**13-1**	**1st**	1942	9-9	5-7	5th	1981*	35-26	11-3	4th
1904	**23-4**	**11-3**	**1st**	1943	8-6	5-3	3rd	1982	49-23	14-2	4th
1905	14-5	11-5	2nd	1944	9-3-2	5-2-2	3rd	1983	23-24-2	6-9	-
1906	**13-3**	**8-3**	**1st**	1945	10-10-1	6-5-1	3rd	1984	46-21	3-10	-
1907	**10-1**	**7-0**	**1st**	1946	13-8-0	6-3	3rd	1985	46-21	13-4	4th
1908	**11-3**	**11-3**	**1st**	**1947**	**22-6**	**9-3**	**1st**	1986	34-19-2	8-8	-
1909	11-3	9-3	2nd	**1948**	**20-7-1**	**10-2**	**1st-T**	1987	32-24-0	9-7	-
1910	**14-0**	**11-0**	**1st**	1949	9-8-1	6-5-1	5th	1988**	26-20	12-16	7th
1911	**18-2**	**14-1**	**1st**	1950	13-6	6-5	4th	**1989**	**42-16**	**17-11**	**1st**
1912	13-3-1	10-2-1	2nd	1951	16-9	8-3	2nd	**1990**	**43-21**	**19-9**	**1st**
1913	11-5-1	8-4	3rd	**1952**	**20-11-1**	**10-5**	**1st**	1991	26-30	13-15	7th
1914	**11-7-1**	**7-3**	**1st**	**1953**	**17-6**	**10-3**	**1st-T**	1992	36-20	16-12	3rd
1915	**18-1-1**	**9-1-1**	**1st**	1954	16-15	4-11	9th	1993	32-23	12-16	8th
1916	**13-1**	**8-1**	**1st**	1955	14-10	7-6	4th	1994	26-26	12-16	7th
1917	13-7	8-3	2nd	1956	15-18-1	4-11	10th	1995	25-31	14-14	5th-T

* - Conference divided into East and West Divisions, with top two teams from each division competing in playoffs
** - Divisional system eliminated, top four teams advanced to playoffs

Men's Basketball

Year	Overall Record	Big Ten Record	Big Ten Finish	Year	Overall Record	Big Ten Record	Big Ten Finish	Year	Overall Record	Big Ten Record	Big Ten Finish
1906	6-8	3-6	4th	1936	13-6	7-5	3rd-T	1966	12-12	8-6	3rd-T
1907	1-10	0-8	5th	1937	14-4	10-2	1st-T	1967	12-12	6-8	7th-T
1908	20-6	6-5	3rd	1938	9-9	4-8	8th-T	1968	11-13	6-8	7th-T
1909	7-6	5-6	4th	1939	14-5	8-4	3rd	1969	19-5	9-5	2nd-T
1910	5-4	5-4	4th	1940	14-6	7-5	4th-T	1970	15-9	8-6	3rd-T
1911	6-6	6-5	4th	1941	13-7	7-5	3rd-T	1971	11-12	5-9	5th-T
1912	8-8	4-8	5th	1942	18-5	13-2	1st	1972	14-10	5-9	8th-T
1913	10-6	7-6	5th	1943	17-1	12-0	1st	1973	14-10	8-6	3rd-T
1914	9-4	7-3	3rd	1944	11-9	5-7	6th	1974	5-18	2-12	10th
1915	16-0	12-0	1st	1945	13-7	7-5	3rd	1975	8-18	4-14	9th-T
1916	13-3	9-3	2nd-T	1946	14-7	7-5	5th-T	1976	14-13	7-11	7th-T
1917	13-3	10-2	1st-T	1947	14-6	8-4	2nd-T	1977	16-14	8-10	6th
1918	9-6	6-6	4th-T	1948	15-5	7-5	3rd-T	1978	13-14	7-11	7th
1919	6-8	5-7	5th	1949	21-4	10-2	1st	1979	19-11	7-11	7th
1920	9-4	8-4	3rd	1950	14-8	7-5	3rd-T	1980	22-13	8-10	6th-T
1921	11-7	7-5	4th-T	1951	22-5	13-1	1st	1981	21-8	12-6	3rd
1922	14-5	7-5	4th-T	1952	22-4	12-2	1st	1982	18-11	10-8	6th
1923	9-6	7-5	4th-T	1953	18-4	14-4	2nd	1983	21-11	11-7	2nd-T
1924	11-6	8-4	1st-T	1954	17-5	10-4	3rd-T	1984	26-5	15-3	1st-T
1925	11-6	8-4	3rd-T	1955	17-5	10-4	2nd-T	1985	26-9	12-6	2nd
1926	9-8	6-6	5th-T	1956	18-4	11-3	2nd	1986	22-10	11-7	4th-T
1927	10-7	7-5	4th-T	1957	14-8	7-7	7th	1987	23-8	13-5	4th
1928	5-17	2-10	9th-T	1958	11-11	5-9	8th-T	1988	23-10	12-6	3rd-T
1929	10-7	6-6	5th-T	1959	12-10	7-7	5th-T	1989	31-5	14-4	2nd
1930	8-8	7-5	4th-T	1960	16-7	8-6	3rd-T	1990	21-8	11-7	4th-T
1931	12-5	7-5	5th	1961	9-15	5-9	7th	1991	21-10	11-7	3rd-T
1932	11-6	7-5	5th	1962	15-8	7-7	4th-T	1992	13-15	7-11	8th
1933	11-7	6-6	5th-T	1963	20-6	11-3	1st-T	1993	19-13	11-7	3rd-T
1934	13-6	7-5	4th	1964	13-11	6-8	6th-T	1994	17-11	10-8	4th-T
1935	15-5	9-3	1st-T	1965	18-6	10-4	3rd	1995	19-12	10-8	5th-T

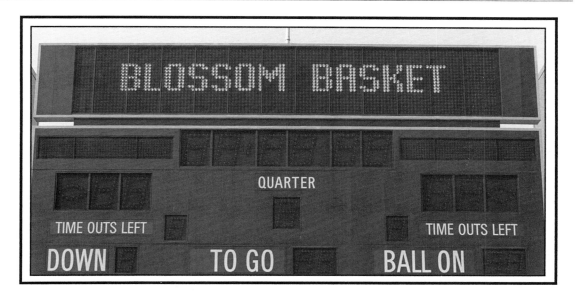

THE FIGHTING ILLINI FLORIST

The Blossom Basket

THE FIGHTING ILLINI FLORIST

1002 North Cunningham Avenue • Urbana • 367-8354

Women's Basketball

Year	Overall Record	Big Ten Record	Big Ten Finish	Year	Overall Record	Big Ten Record	Big Ten Finish
1974-75	10-11			1984-85	13-15	7-11	6th
1975-76	15-10		5th*	1985-86	20-10	12- 6	3rd
1976-77	15- 9		5th*	1986-87	19-10	11- 7	4th
1977-78	9 - 9		5th-T*	1987-88	9-19	3-15	9th
1978-79	9-12		DNP*	1988-89	11-18	6-12	6th-T
1979-80	6-21		5th*	1989-90	11-17	5-13	8th
1980-81	20-11		DNP*	1990-91	9-19	6-12	8th
1981-82	21- 9		2nd*	1991-92	9-19	6-12	8th
1982-83	14-14	9 - 9	6th	1992-93	12-15	7-11	7th
1983-84	12-16	6-12	8th	1993-94	10-17	5-13	10th
				1994-95	10-17	3-13	10th-T

*Tournaments from 1976-82 were not sanctioned by the Big Ten Conference

Men's Cross Country

Year	Dual Meet Record	Big Ten Finish	NCAA Finish	Year	Dual Meet Record	Big Ten Finish	NCAA Finish
1905	—	2nd		1950	0-2	6th	
1906	No team			1951	—	UI did not enter	
1907	No team			1952	—	UI did not enter	
1908	No team			1953	—	UI did not enter	
1909	No team			1954	1-1	3rd	
1910	No team			1955	1-1	2nd	
1911	No team			1956	3-1	2nd	4th
1912	—	7th		1957	3-1	3rd	
1913	1-1	2nd		1958	0-2	4th	
1914	—	3rd		1959	1-0	UI did not enter complete team	
1915	—	5th		1960	0-2	UI did not enter complete team	
1916	0-1			1961	0-2	UI did not enter complete team	
1917	World War I			1962	2-2	4th	
1918	World War I			1963	4-1	5th	
1919	1-1	7th		1964	No team		
1920	1-1	2nd		1965	0-4	7th	
1921	**1-0**	**1st**		1966	3-4	8th	
1922	1-0	4th		1967	4-7	10th	
1923	1-0	2nd		1968	4-5	6th	
1924	0-0-1	5th		1969	9-1	2nd	5th
1925	0-1	3rd		1970	6-1-1	4th	25th
1926	0-1	4th		1971	3-3	5th	
1927	2-0	2nd		1972	5-5	8th	
1928	0-2	7th		1973	4-1-1	4th	
1929	0-1	9th		1974	6-3	3rd	
1930	1-0	3rd		1975	5-1	4th	10th
1931	—	4th		1976	3-1	2nd	5th
1932	—	2nd		1977	5-0	2nd-T	22nd
1933	4-0	No meet held		1978	4-1	5th	
1934	1-2-1	No meet held		1979	2-3	4th	
1935	4-0	No meet held		1980	1-0	3rd	21st
1936	0-5	No meet held		1981	1-0	2nd	
1937	1-2	No meet held		1982	1-1	4th	
1938	1-2	UI did not place		1983	0-2	4th	9th
1939	No team			**1984**	**1-0**	**1st**	**14th**
1940	1-1	UI did not place		1985	1-0	5th	
1941	2-2	4th	10th	1986	1-0	2nd	7th
1942	0-3	2nd	5th	1987	—	2nd	
1943	World War II			1988	—	4th	
1944	0-1	5th		1989	—	2nd	
1945	0-1	4th		1990	—	4th	
1946	—	3rd		1991	—	5th	
1947	**2-0**	**1st**		1992	—	4th	
1948	2-0-1	2nd		1993	0-1	8th	
1949	1-2	2nd	8th	1994	0-1	4th	

Women's Cross Country

Year	Dual Meet Record	Big Ten Finish	Year	Dual Meet Record	Big Ten Finish
1978	5-0	4th*	1987	—	8th
1979	5-1	9th*	1988	—	8th-T
1980	2-1	9th*	1989	—	7th
1981	not available	9th	1990	—	6th
1982	1-1	6th	1991	—	7th
1983	1-0	6th	1992	—	7th
1984	1-0	2nd	1993	—	6th
1985	1-0	3rd-T	1994	1-0	4th
1986	—	7th			

*Championships from 1978-80 were not sanctioned by the Big Ten Conference

Fencing

Year	Dual Meet Record	Big Ten Finish	NCAA Finish	Year	Dual Meet Record	Big Ten Finish	NCAA Finish
1910-11	2-4	1st		1952-53	9-0	1st	6th
1911-12	2-2	1st		1953-54	8-2	1st	8th
1912-13	0-2	1st-T		1954-55	9-2	2nd	5th
1913-14	0-1			1955-56	10-0	1st	1st
1914-15	1-0			1956-57	8-3	2nd	6th
1915-16	1-1			1957-58	8-4	1st	1st
1916-17	2-0			1958-59	8-4	2nd	4th
1917-18	World War I			1959-60	10-1	1st	8th
1918-19	World War I			1960-61	6-5	1st	9th
1919-20	1-0	1st		1961-62	11-1	1st	4th
1920-21	1-0			1962-63	10-2	2nd	8th
1921-22	1-1	1st		1963-64	12-0	1st	7th
1922-23	1-0	3rd		1964-65	13-1	1st	6th
1923-24	2-0			1965-66	7-7	1st	15th
1924-25	2-1	2nd		1966-67	12-3	2nd	12th
1925-26	2-0-1	4th		1967-68	11-6	1st	12th
1926-27	4-0	3rd-T		1968-69	13-4	2nd	14th
1927-28	1-3	2nd		1969-70	18-5	2nd	15th
1928-29	5-0	1st		1970-71	14-4	4th	
1929-30	3-2	1st		1971-72	15-3	1st	6th
1930-31	4-0	1st		1972-73	17-2	1st	8th
1931-32	4-0-1	1st		1973-74	11-3	1st	13th
1932-33	4-0-1	1st		1974-75	8-4	1st	
1933-34	4-3	2nd		1975-76	14-5	4th	
1934-35	5-2	1st		1976-77	15-4	2nd	16th
1935-36	5-4	2nd		1977-78	13-2	3rd	
1936-37	6-1	2nd		1978-79	17-2	2nd-T	23rd
1937-38	4-4	2nd		1979-80	20-4	1st	11th
1938-39	8-2	2nd		1980-81	25-2	1st	15th
1939-40	4-5-1	4th		1981-82	15-3	2nd	13th
1940-41	8-2	3rd	2nd	1982-83	17-2	1st	11th
1941-42	7-3	1st	3rd	1983-84	24-4	3rd-T	20th
1942-43	0-0		1st	1984-85	20-3	2nd	17th
1943-44	World War II			1985-86	15-1	1st*	13th
1944-45	World War II			1986-87	22-1		8th
1945-46	World War II			1987-88	25-0		7th
1946-47	4-3	2nd	6th	1988-89	23-1		11th
1947-48	3-6	2nd	15th	1989-90	27-2		14th
1948-49	7-2	2nd	10th	1990-91	24-2		13th
1949-50	6-3-1	1st	17th	1991-92	17-1		10th
1950-51	9-0	1st	5th	1992-93	22-3		10th
1951-52	8-0	1st	5th				

*Final official championship meet held by Big Ten Conference

Year	Overall Record	Big Ten Record	Big Ten Finish	Bowl	Year	Overall Record	Big Ten Record	Big Ten Finish	Bowl
1890	1-2-0				1922	2-5-0	2-4-0	6th	
1891	6-0-0				**1923**	**8-0-0**	**5-0-0**	**1st**	
1892	9-3-2				1924	6-1-1	3-1-1	2nd-T	
1893	3-2-3				1925	5-3-0	2-2-0	4th-T	
1894	5-3-0				1926	6-2-0	2-2-0	6th-T	
1895	4-2-1				**1927**	**7-0-1**	**5-0-0**	**1st-T**	
1896	4-2-1	0-2-1	6th-T		**1928**	**7-1-0**	**4-1-0**	**1st**	
1897	6-2-0	1-1-0	4th		1929	6-1-1	3-1-1	2nd	
1898	4-5-0	1-1-0	4th		1930	3-5-0	1-4-0	8th	
1899	3-5-1	0-3-0	6th-T		1931	2-6-1	0-6-1	9th-T	
1900	7-3-2	1-3-2	8th		1932	5-4-0	2-4-0	7th	
1901	8-2-0	4-2-0	4th		1933	5-3-0	3-2-0	5th	
1902	10-2-1	4-2-0	4th		1934	7-1-0	4-1-0	3rd	
1903	8-6-0	1-5-0	7th		1935	3-5-0	1-4-0	9th-T	
1904	9-2-1	3-1-1	4th		1936	4-3-1	2-2-1	6th	
1905	5-4-0	0-3-0	6th-T		1937	3-3-2	2-3-0	8th	
1906	1-3-1	1-3-0	5th		1938	3-5-0	2-3-0	7th	
1907	3-2-0	3-2-0	3rd		1939	3-4-1	3-3-0	6th	
1908	5-1-1	4-1-0	2nd		1940	1-7-0	0-5-0	9th	
1909	5-2-0	3-1-0	3rd		1941	2-6-0	0-5-0	9th	
1910	**7-0-0**	**4-0-0**	**1st-T**		1942	6-4-0	3-2-0	3rd-T	
1911	4-2-1	2-2-1	4th-T		1943	3-7-0	2-4-0	6th	
1912	3-3-1	1-3-1	6th-T		1944	5-4-1	3-3-0	6th	
1913	4-2-1	2-2-1	5th		1945	2-6-1	1-4-1	7th	
1914	**7-0-0**	**6-0-0**	**1st**		**1946**	**8-2-0**	**6-1-0**	**1st**	**Rose Bowl**
1915	**5-0-2**	**3-0-2**	**1st-T**		1947	5-3-1	3-3-0	3rd-T	
1916	3-3-1	2-2-1	4th-T		1948	3-6-0	2-5-0	8th	
1917	5-2-1	2-2-1	5th-T		1949	3-4-2	3-3-1	5th-T	
1918	**5-2-0**	**4-0-0**	**1st**		1950	7-2-0	4-2-0	4th	
1919	**6-1-0**	**6-1-0**	**1st**		**1951**	**9-0-1**	**5-0-1**	**1st**	**Rose Bowl**
1920	5-2-0	4-2-0	4th		1952	4-5-0	2-5-0	6th-T	
1921	3-4-0	1-4-0	8th-T		**1953**	**7-1-1**	**5-1-0**	**1st-T**	
					1954	1-8-0	0-6-0	10th	
					1955	5-3-1	3-3-1	5th	
					1956	2-5-2	1-4-2	7th-T	
					1957	4-5-0	3-4-0	7th	
					1958	4-5-0	4-3-0	6th	
					1959	5-3-1	4-2-1	3rd-T	
					1960	5-4-0	2-4-0	5th-T	
					1961	0-9-0	0-7-0	9th-T	
					1962	2-7-0	2-5-0	8th	
					1963	**8-1-1**	**5-1-1**	**1st**	**Rose Bowl**
					1964	6-3-0	4-3-0	4th-T	
					1965	6-4-0	4-3-0	5th	
					1966	4-6-0	4-3-0	3rd-T	
					1967	4-6-0	3-4-0	5th-T	
					1968	1-9-0	1-6-0	8th-T	
					1969	0-10-0	0-7-0	10th	
					1970	3-7-0	1-6-0	9th-T	
					1971	5-6-0	5-3-0	3rd-T	
					1972	3-8-0	3-5-0	6th-T	
					1973	5-6-0	4-4-0	4th-T	
					1974	6-4-1	4-3-1	5th	
					1975	5-6-0	4-4-0	3rd-T	
					1976	5-6-0	4-4-0	3rd-T	
					1977	3-8-0	2-6-0	8th-T	
					1978	1-8-2	0-6-2	9th	
					1979	2-8-1	1-6-1	9th	
					1980	3-7-1	3-5-0	6th-T	
					1981	7-4-0	6-3-0	3rd-T	
					1982	7-5-0	6-3-0	4th	Liberty Bowl
					1983	**10-2-0**	**9-0-0**	**1st**	**Rose Bowl**
					1984	7-4-0	6-3-0	2nd-T	
					1985	6-5-1	5-2-1	3rd	Peach Bowl
					1986	4-7-0	3-5-0	6th-T	
					1987	3-7-1	2-5-1	8th	
					1988	6-5-1	5-2-1	3rd-T	All-American Bowl
					1989	10-2-0	7-1-0	2nd	Citrus Bowl
					1990	**8-4-0**	**6-2-0**	**1st-T**	**Hall of Fame Bowl**
					1991	6-6-0	4-4-0	5th	John Hancock Bowl
					1992	6-5-1	4-3-1	4th	Holiday Bowl
					1993	5-6-0	5-3-0	4th-T	
					1994	7-5-0	4-4-0	5th-T	Liberty Bowl

Year	Dual Meet Record	Big Ten Finish	NCAA Finish	Year	Dual Meet Record	Big Ten Finish	NCAA Finish
1908	1-0			1973	—	3rd	
1909	No team			1974	—	8th	
1910	No team			1975	—	5th-T	
1911	No team			1976	—	7th	
1912	1-0			1977	—	6th	
1913	—			1978	—	7th	
1914	1-0			1979	—	5th	
1915	1-0			1980	—	8th	
1916	2-0			1981	—	8th	
1917	1-0			1982	1-0	3rd-T	
1918	World War I			1983	1-1	7th	
1919	World War I			1984	1-1	5th	28th
1920	—	3rd-T		1985	2-1	10th	
1921	1-2	3rd-T		1986	1-0	2nd	
1922	0-3	4th		1987	2-0	4th	
1923	**5-0**	**1st**		**1988**	**—**	**1st**	**23rd-T**
1924	5-0	3rd		1989	—	2nd	
1925	2-2	4th		1990	—	2nd	
1926	2-2	2nd		1991	—	4th	
1927	**3-2**	**1st**		1992	—	9th	
1928	3-2	3rd		1993	—	6th	
1929	4-2	*		1994	—	8th	
1930	**6-0**	**1st**		1995	—	5th	
1931	**6-0**	**1st**	5th				
1932	2-1	4th					
1933	1-3-1	6th					
1934	2-3-1	4th					
1935	3-1	6th					
1936	3-3	3rd					
1937	3-3-1	3rd					
1938	4-2	4th					
1939	5-2	6th					
1940	**5-2**	**1st**	4th				
1941	**7-1**	**1st**	4th				
1942	3-3-1	5th					
1943	5-2	5th					
1944	1-5	7th					
1945	1-1	5th					
1946	3-5	9th					
1947	3-4	5th					
1948	5-6	6th					
1949	0-9	8th					
1950	4-7	6th	7th				
1951	3-9	9th					
1952	1-9	9th					
1953	4-5	8th					
1954	3-8	5th					
1955	5-6-1	8th					
1956	5-6-1	6th-T					
1957	8-3	8th					
1958	7-6-2	7th					
1959	4-8	10th					
1960	2-5-1	10th					
1961	3-6	10th					
1962	1-11	6th					
1963	4-5	7th-T					
1964	5-3	9th					
1965	1-1	10th					
1966	2-2	9th					
1967	0-1	8th					
1968	4-4	8th					
1969	1-1	8th					
1970	2-1-1	7th					
1971	4-2	4th-T					
1972	—	6th					

*Did not compete in Big Ten Championship due to conflict with final exams

Women's Golf

Year	Dual Meet Record	Big Ten Finish	Year	Dual Meet Record	Big Ten Finish
1975	2-0	4th*	1985	—	5th
1976	—	2nd*	1986	—	5th
1977	—	4th*	1987	—	6th
1978	—	8th*	1988	—	5th
1979	—	8th*	1989	1-0	5th
1980	—	9th*	1990	1-0	6th
1981	—	7th*	1991	—	6th
1982	—	4th	1992	—	3rd
1983	—	5th	1993	—	3rd-T
1984	—	6th	1994	—	3rd-T
			1995	—	3rd

*Championships from 1975-81 were not sanctioned by the Big Ten Conference

Men's Gymnastics

Year	Dual Meet Record	Big Ten Finish	NCAA Finish	Year	Dual Meet Record	Big Ten Finish	NCAA Finish
1898	—			1952	4-1	1st	3rd
1902	—			1953	5-2	1st	2nd
1905	—	3rd		1954	6-0	1st	2nd
1910	0-1	2nd		1955	7-1	1st	1st
1911	1-0	1st		1956	4-3	1st	1st
1912	1-0	1st		1957	11-0	1st	2nd
1913	0-1	4th		1958	10-1	1st	1st
1914	0-1	3rd		1959	10-1	1st	2nd
1915	1-1			1960	8-3	1st	3rd
1916	0-2	4th		1961	7-2	2nd	5th
1917	0-2	4th		1962	7-0	3rd	4th
1918	World War I			1963	1-8	6th	11th-T
1919	World War I			1964	3-6	5th	
1920	0-1	3rd		1965	1-8-1	6th	
1921	0-1	4th		1966	6-2	3rd	4th
1922	0-1	4th		1967	8-2	4th	4th
1923	0-2	5th		1968	8-4	4th	
1924	0-2	5th		1969	4-6	3rd	
1925	0-3	7th		1970	6-3	3rd	
1926	0-3	7th		1971	7-3	3rd	
1927	3-1	3rd		1972	2-7	6th	
1928	2-1	3rd		1973	2-12	6th	
1929	4-0	1st		1974	8-9	4th	
1930	3-1	2nd		1975	10-8	4th	
1931	3-0	3rd		1976	5-8	3rd	
1932	3-0	3rd		1977	6-5	2nd	
1933	3-1	3rd		1978	9-6	2nd	
1934	3-3	3rd		1979	8-7	4th	
1935	3-0	1st		1980	10-5	4th	
1936	4-1	3rd		1981	7-3	1st	8th
1937	4-3	3rd		1982	9-6	2nd	11th
1938	4-2	2nd		1983	9-1	1st-T	6th
1939	6-0	1st	1st	1984	8-3	4th	9th
1940	5-0	2nd	1st	1985	5-5	4th	11th
1941	6-0	1st	1st	1986	11-3-1	3rd	12th
1942	5-1	1st	1st	1987	8-3	4th	12th
1943	World War II			1988	11-0	1st	2nd
1944	World War II			1989	7-1	1st	1st
1945	World War II			1990	1-3	4th	
1946	World War II			1991	4-4	5th	
1947	1-1	2nd		1992	4-3	3rd	13th
1948	4-3	2nd	3rd	1993	9-1	4th	6th
1949	4-0	2nd	3rd	1994	3-4	6th	
1950	7-1	1st	1st	1995	4-5	5th	
1951	7-0	1st	2nd-T				

Women's Gymnastics

Year	Dual Meet Record	Big Ten Finish	Year	Dual Meet Record	Big Ten Finish
1974-75	—	4th*	1985-86	12-6	5th
1975-76	**7-1**	**1st***	1986-87	11-6	4th
1976-77	**4-4**	**1st***	1987-88	5-3	3rd
1977-78	3-5	3rd*	1988-89	9-5	4th
1978-79	3-5	2nd*	**1989-90**	**7-2**	**1st**
1979-80	4-2	2nd*	1990-91	3-8	4th-T
1980-81	1-3	4th	1991-92	2-14	6th
1981-82	2-3	6th	1992-93	2-14	7th
1982-83	8-7	3rd	1993-94	4-14	7th
1983-84	2-4	4th-T	1994-95	6-12	5th
1984-85	2-5	5th			

*Championships from 1975-81 were not sanctioned by the Big Ten Conference

Ice Hockey

Year	Overall Record	Big Ten Record
1938	0-4	0-3
1939	3-7	0-6
1940	3-11	1-7
1941	17-3-1	6-1-1
1942	10-4-2	4-0
1943	10-2	5-1

Soccer

Year	Overall Record
1927	1-1
1928	3-0
1929	3-0
1930	4-0-1
1931	7-0-1
1932	4-2-3
1933	5-2-1
1934	5-2
1935	2-3-1

Polo

Year	Overall Record
1934	0-7
1935	4-5
1936	2-2
1937	3-2
1938	7-4-1
1939	9-5
1940	8-6
1941	5-7

Year	Dual Meet Record	Big Ten Finish	Year	Dual Meet Record	Big Ten Finish
1910-11	2-1	1st	1934-35	3-2	2nd
1911-12	2-2	1st	1935-36	2-3	4th
1912-13	3-2	1st	1936-37	2-3-1	5th
1913-14	1-3	2nd	1937-38	1-5	6th
1914-15	2-2	3rd	1938-39	5-0	4th
1915-16	2-2	3rd	1939-40	2-4	6th
1916-17	0-3	3rd	1940-41	3-4	6th
1917-18	World War I		1941-42	3-5	8th
1918-19	World War I		1942-43	3-2	8th
1919-20	2-2	3rd	1943-44	2-1	8th
1920-21	2-2	3rd	1944-45	3-3-1	7th
1921-22	2-2	4th	1945-46	4-4	6th
1922-23	4-2	4th	1946-47	0-6-1	8th
1923-24	1-4	8th	1947-48	1-6	8th
1924-25	2-1	5th	1948-49	2-4	9th
1925-26	3-2	6th	1949-50	4-2	9th
1926-27	3-3	5th	1950-51	2-7	9th
1927-28	6-0	4th	1951-52	1-5	10th
1928-29	5-0	3rd	1952-53	1-6	8th
1929-30	6-0	4th	1953-54	8-2	4th
1930-31	2-2	6th	1954-55	7-3	8th
1931-32	2-1	5th	1955-56	6-4	7th
1932-33	5-1	3rd	1956-57	8-1	5th
1933-34	3-2	4th	1957-58	10-2	5th
			1958-59	7-2	6th
			1959-60	6-2	6th
			1960-61	5-4	7th
			1961-62	4-5	8th
			1962-63	7-4	10th
			1963-64	1-7	10th
			1964-65	1-8	9th
			1965-66	10-5	9th
			1966-67	5-3	7th
			1967-68	4-4-1	7th
			1968-69	3-6	8th
			1969-70	5-6	7th
			1970-71	2-5	7th
			1971-72	3-5	8th
			1972-73	7-3	8th
			1973-74	7-3	5th
			1974-75	6-5	6th
			1975-76	5-5	5th
			1976-77	3-4	6th
			1977-78	3-1	8th
			1978-79	4-5	7th
			1979-80	4-2	8th
			1980-81	4-4	8th
			1981-82	4-5	9th
			1982-83	4-2	7th
			1983-84	6-2	5th
			1984-85	7-4	5th
			1985-86	8-3	5th
			1986-87	1-7	7th
			1987-88	2-5	9th
			1988-89	2-4	9th
			1989-90	4-7	8th
			1990-91	1-8	10th
			1991-92	1-9	11th
			1992-93	4-8	11th

Women's Swimming

Year	Dual Meet Record	Big Ten Finish	Year	Dual Meet Record	Big Ten Finish
1974-75	not available	6th*	1985-86	5-4	8th
1975-76	7-4	6th*	1986-87	4-3	5th
1976-77	3-9	7th*	1987-88	1-5	9th
1977-78	3-5	10th*	1988-89	2-5	9th
1978-79	3-2	9th*	1989-90	2-7	9th
1979-80	6-3	10th*	1990-91	1-7	9th
1980-81	7-5	10th*	1991-92	2-6	11th
1981-82	3-3	7th	1992-93	0-9	10th
1982-83	3-3	6th	1993-94	3-9	10th
1983-84	2-4	9th	1994-95	9-3	8th
1984-85	5-7	8th			

*Championships from 1975-81 were not sanctioned by the Big Ten Conference

Men's Tennis

Year	Dual Meet Record	Big Ten Finish	Year	Dual Meet Record	Big Ten Finish
1904	0-1		1943	4-0	2nd
1905	1-2-1		1944	3-3	7th-T
1906	1-0-1		1945	4-2-1	7th
1907	—				
1908	0-3				
1909	2-1				
1910	—				
1911	—				
1912	—				
1913	1-0				
1914	2-2	2nd			
1915	3-3				
1916	3-2				
1917	**2-0**	**1st**			
1918	World War I				
1919	World War I				
1920	4-1-1				
1921	3-4				
1922	**6-2**	**1st**			
1923	4-4				
1924	4-0-3	2nd			
1925	3-1-1				
1926	**5-0**	**1st**			
1927	**4-1**	**1st**			
1928	**4-1**	**1st**			
1929	3-1				
1930	4-1				
1931	5-3				
1932	**8-3**	**1st**			
1933	9-1-2				
1934	4-5-2	5th			
1935	4-1-1	3rd			
1936	4-3	5th-T			
1937	2-8	8th			
1938	5-5	5th-T			
1939	9-2	4th			
1940	8-2	5th-T			
1941	3-8	Did not enter			
1942	7-4	4th			

Men's Tennis (cont.)

Year	Dual Meet Record	Big Ten Finish	Year	Dual Meet Record	Big Ten Finish
1946	**10-0**	**1st**	1971	12-6	5th
1947	9-1	2nd	1972	17-5	4th
1948	9-2	4th	1973	13-4	5th
1949	3-2	5th-T	1974	19-5	6th-T
1950	8-1	2nd	1975	16-11-1	5th
1951	9-1	4th-T	1976	13-5-1	5th
1952	3-5	6th	1977	7-7	5th
1953	1-5	7th	1978	8-10	10th
1954	7-3	5th	1979	5-16	9th
1955	12-2	3rd	1980	21-17	10th
1956	5-4	5th	1981	18-12	7th
1957	14-2	4th	1982	18-12	5th
1958	16-1	2nd	1983	16-16	5th
1959	12-3	2nd	1984	23-9	2nd
1960	8-4	4th	1985	20-16	3rd
1961	7-4	5th	1986	12-20	6th
1962	5-5	4th	1987	16-13	3rd
1963	4-8	7th	1988	11-13	10th
1964	9-10	7th	1989	11-16	8th
1965	9-4	5th	1990	8-17	7th
1966	15-5	4th	1991	10-13	10th
1967	9-12	6th	1992	11-11	6th
1968	15-6	8th	1993	4-23	11th
1969	4-12	5th	1994	13-15	5th
1970	7-7	5th	1995	18-10	7th

Women's Tennis

Year	Dual Meet Record	Big Ten Finish	Year	Dual Meet Record	Big Ten Finish
1974-75	6- 0	5th*	1985-86	16-16	7th
1975-76	5- 3	9th*	1986-87	12-18	7th
1976-77	7- 8	9th*	1987-88	10-17	10th
1977-78	6- 6	10th*	1988-89	6-22	7th
1978-79	5-11	10th*	1989-90	15-14	8th
1979-80	18- 9	10th*	1990-91	19 -9	5th
1980-81	21-21	10th*	1991-92	16- 8	4th
1981-82	22-16	8th	1992-93	14- 6	3rd
1982-83	16-21	8th	1993-94	13- 9	5th
1983-84	15-18	7th	1994-95	14-10	6th
1984-85	17-20	5th			

*Championships from 1975-81 were not sanctioned by the Big Ten Conference

Men's Track

Year	Big Ten Indoors	Big Ten Outdoors	NCAA Indoors	NCAA Outdoors	Year	Big Ten Indoors	Big Ten Outdoors	NCAA Indoors	NCAA Outdoors
1901	-	5th	-	-	1949	3rd	4th	-	36th
1902	-	5th	-	-	1950	3rd	2nd-T	-	-
1903	-	5th-T	-	-	1951	1st	1st	-	14th
1904	-	5th	-	-	1952	1st	1st	-	6th-T
1905	-	5th-T	-	-	1953	1st	1st	-	2nd
1906	-	4th	-	-	1954	1st	1st	-	2nd
1907	-	1st	-	-	1955	4th	2nd	-	29th
1908	-	3rd	-	-	1956	5th	7th	-	-
1909	-	1st	-	-	1957	10th	4th	-	18th-T
1910	-	1st	-	-	1958	1st	1st	-	6th
1911	2nd	2nd	-	-	1959	2nd	1st	-	9th
1912	1st	1st	-	-	1960	2nd	1st	-	10th
1913	1st	1st	-	-	1961	4th	3rd	-	24th-T
1914	1st	1st	-	-	1962	5th	7th	-	-
1915	2nd	3rd	-	-	1963	6th	5th	-	-
1916	1st	2nd	-	-	1964	6th	3rd	-	9th
1917	2nd	2nd	-	-	1965	5th	7th	25th-T	-
1918	4th	2nd	-	-	1966	7th	7th	39th-T	-
1919	3rd	3rd	-	-	1967	9th	8th	-	-
1920	1st	1st	-	-	1968	9th	5th	-	-
1921	1st	1st	-	1st	1969	5th	6th	-	-
1922	1st	1st	-	4th	1970	7th	4th	-	-
1923	2nd	2nd	-	6th	1971	7th	3rd	44th-T	33rd-T
1924	1st	1st	-	10th	1972	2nd	2nd	7th-T	20th
1925	4th	5th	-	10th	1973	5th	7th	24th-T	25th-T
1926	4th	2nd	8th	-	1974	2nd-T	5th	6th	18th-T
1927	5th	1st	-	1st	1975	2nd	1st	20th	11th
1928	1st	1st	-	3rd	1976	3rd	4th	4th	25th
1929	2nd	1st	-	3rd	1977	1st	1st	4th	7th
1930	2nd	2nd	-	6th	1978	5th-T	4th	-	-
1931	2nd	2nd	-	3rd	1979	6th	5th	-	40th
1932	4th	4th	-	7th	1980	3rd	3rd	46th-T	-
1933	3rd	3rd	-	18th	1981	1st	3rd	27th-T	24th-T
1934	3rd	1st	-	19th	1982	4th	4th	14th-T	38th-T
1935	5th	7th	-	32nd	1983	6th	3rd	-	58th-T
1936	4th	5th	-	32nd	1984	5th	5th	-	56th-T
1937	5th	4th	-	32nd	1985	2nd	3rd	27th-T	58th-T
1938	6th	6th	-	-	1986	2nd	2nd	21st-T	51st
1939	9th	7th	-	17th	1987	1st	1st	17th-T	8th
1940	5th	5th	-	-	1988	1st	1st	2nd	7th
1941	4th	6th	-	14th	1989	1st	1st	14th	51st-T
1942	2nd	2nd	-	15th	1990	3rd	3rd	-	-
1943	3rd	2nd	-	7th	1991	2nd	2nd	51st	71st
1944	2nd	2nd	-	1st	1992	6th	5th	30th-T	43rd
1945	2nd	1st	-	2nd	1993	2nd	2nd	15th-T	21st-T
1946	1st	1st	-	1st	1994	3rd	1st	17th-T	17th-T
1947	1st	1st	-	1st	1995	2nd	2nd	4th	41st
1948	2nd	3rd	-	4th					

Women's Track and Field

Year	Big Ten Indoors	Big Ten Outdoors	NCAA Indoors	NCAA Outdoors
1975	—	—		
1976	—	4th*		
1977	—	3rd*		
1978	4th*	6th*		
1979	9th*	6th*		
1980	8th*	8th*		
1981	6th*	7th*		
1982	7th	6th	7th	
1983	8th	4th		
1984	8th	10th		
1985	8th	9th		
1986	4th	3rd		
1987	5th	2nd	46th	
1988	**3rd**	**1st**	**14th**	**17th**
1989	**1st**	**1st**	**13th**	**7th**
1990	2nd-T	2nd	40th-T	—
1991	2nd	2nd	—	27th-T
1992	**1st**	**1st**	**—**	**13th-T**
1993	**1st**	**2nd**	**16th-T**	**21st-T**
1994	2nd	2nd	12th-T	29th-T
1995	**1st**	**1st**	**24th**	**4th**

*Championships from 1976-81 were not sanctioned by the Big Ten Conference

Volleyball

Year	Overall Record	Big Ten Record	Big Ten Finish	NCAA Finish
1974	19-9			
1975	15-14-1		2nd*	
1976	25-14		5th*	
1977	38-17-6		5th-T*	
1978	28-14		3rd*	
1979	18-20		5th-T*	
1980	22-32		5th*	
1981	17-27		9th*	
1982	17-20	8-5	3rd-T	
1983	5-25	2-11	10th	
1984	18-15	6-7	6th	
1985	39-3	16-2	2nd	9th-T
1986	**36-3**	**18-0**	**1st**	**5th-T**
1987	**31-7**	**17-1**	**1st**	**3rd-T**
1988	**30-4**	**18-0**	**1st**	**3rd-T**
1989	27-8	13-5	2nd	5th-T
1990	21-12	11-7	4th	
1991	19-10	14-6	4th	
1992	**32-4**	**19-1**	**1st-T**	**5th-T**
1994	18-13		14-6	3rd-T

*Championships from 1975-81 were not sanctioned by the Big Ten Conference

Year	Dual Meet Record	Big Ten Finish	NCAA Finish	Year	Dual Meet Record	Big Ten Finish	NCAA Finish
1911	**0-1**	--		1958	8-3-1	2nd	6th
1912	0-2	--		1959	4-7-1	5th	25th-T
1913	**2-0**	T-1st*					
1914	1-0	--		1960	3-11	9th	
1915	2-0-1	4th		1961	10-1	5th	21st-T
1916	1-2-1	4th		1962	6-6	8th	19th-T
1917	**4-0**	1st		1963	6-6-2	10th	40th-T
1918	Did not compete in intercollegiate wrestling			1964	7-6-1	7th	46th-T
1919	Did not compete in intercollegiate wrestling			1965	3-11	4th	22nd-T
				1966	2-11	10th	
1920	**3-0**	1st		1967	2-10	9th	
1921	2-1	5th		1968	1-9	8th	
1922	**6-0**	1st		1969	9-11-1	7th	
1923	4-2	--					
1924	**5-0**	1st-T		1970	6-8	9th	
1925	**5-0**	1st-T		1971	2-13	10th	
1926	**4-2**	1st		1972	3-9	10th	
1927	**6-0**	1st		1973	8-8	10th	
1928	**7-0**	1st		1974	7-13	7th	
1929	6-1	2nd		1975	10-9-1	7th	
				1976	10-8-1	9th	
1930	**6-0**	1st		1977	3-11	9th	
1931	6-1	--		1978	8-8	9th	
1932	**5-0**	1st-T		1979	12-10	6th	24th-T
1933	5-3-1	--					
1934	7-2-1	2nd		1980	8-12	8th	
1935	**5-1**	1st	3rd-T	1981	7-9-1	10th	
1936	5-2	3rd		1982	9-8	9th	
1937	**6-2**	1st		1983	1-13-1	8th	
1938	7-2	3rd	2nd	1984	4-8	9th	
1939	6-3	2nd-T	4th-T	1985	11-10	6th	
				1986	5-8	8th	38
1940	6-4	4th-T		1987	13-7	4th	40th-T
1941	6-6	2nd-T		1988	3-9	7th	33rd
1942	8-0	2nd-T	8th	1989	3-10	10th	28th
1943	4-1	3rd-T					
1944	4-3	4th-T		1990	3-9	10th	19th
1945	4-1	3rd		1991	3-11	10th	19th
1946	**4-4**	1st	3rd	1992	2-11	8th	54th-T
1947	**6-2-1**	1st	6th	1993	9-4	8th	23rd-T
1948	4-4	2nd-T	3rd	1994	7-5-1	9th	37th-T
1949	6-1-2	5th	10th-T	1995	13-2	4th	9th
1950	8-2	9th	10th				
1951	5-4-1	4th					
1952	**5-5-2**	1st					
1953	7-5-2	4th					
1954	7-5	6th	12th-T				
1955	11-2	3rd	9th				
1956	6-6-1	8th	8th-T				
1957	6-3-1	4th	6th-T				

* - Team championships were determined in the "Western Intercollegiate Wrestling, Gymnastics and Fencing Association," an open meet, from 1912-1921. From 1922 -1933 team championships were based on dual meet records. In 1926 the conference sponsored its own meet, but only individual champions were named until 1934, when a point system was adopted to name a team champion in that meet.

Personnel History of the Division of Intercollegiate Athletics (Athletic Association) University of Illinois

This personnel history was compiled through research of University of Illinois souvenir athletic programs, its athletic summary books, UI staff directories and the Big Ten Conference record book. Some of the lists are incomplete due to insufficient information.

Please contact the UI Sports Information office should you discover errors.

Faculty Representatives
1896-98	Henry H. Everett
1898-99	Jacob K. Shell
1899-1906	Herbert J. Barton
1906-29	George A. Goodenough
1929-36	Alfred C. Callen
1936-49	Frank E. Richart
1950-59	Robert B. Browne
1959-68	Leslie A. Bryan
1968-76	Henry S. Stillwell
1976-81	William A. Ferguson
1981-89	John Nowak
1981-87	Alyce T. Cheska
1988-	Mildred B. Griggs
1989-	David L. Chicoine

Directors of Athletics
1892-94	Edward K. Hall
1894-95	Fred H. Dodge
1895-98	Henry H. Everett
1898-1901	Jacob K. Shell
1901-36	George A. Huff
1936-41	Wendell S. Wilson
1941-66	Douglas R. Mills
1966-67	Leslie Bryan (interim)
1967-72	E.E. (Gene) Vance
1972	Charles E. Flynn (interim)
1972-79	Cecil N. Coleman
1979	Ray Eliot (interim)
1980-88	Neale R. Stoner
1988	Ronald E. Guenther (interim)
1988	Dr. Karol A. Kahrs (interim)
1988-91	John Mackovic
1991-92	Robert Todd (interim)
1992-	Ronald E. Guenther

Ron Guenther
Director of Athletics

Associate/Assistant Athletic Directors
1958-67	Melvin Brewer
1960-78	Raymond Eliot
1973-78	Richard P. Tamburo
1973-79	Lynn J. Snyder
1974-	Dr. Karol A. Kahrs
1975-84	R. William Sticklen
1976-79	George A. Legg
1977-79	T. Dwight (Dike) Eddleman
1978-	Thomas D. Porter
1979-80	Edie Borg
1980-89	Vance Redfern
1983-89	Edward Swartz
1984-87	John Koenig
1984-	Dana Brenner
1987-	Rick Allen
1989-92	Robert Todd
1993-	Terry Cole
1994-	Warren Hood
1994-	William Yonan
1994-	Debbie Richardson

Sports Information Directors
1922-43	L.M. (Mike) Tobin
1943-56	Charles E. Flynn
1956-70	Charles M. Bellatti
1970-74	Norman S. Sheya
1974-89	Theodore A. (Tab) Bennett
1980-85	Lani Jacobsen (women's SID)
1985-87	Thomas Boeh (women's SID)
1987-89	Mary Fowler (women's SID)
1989-	Michael G. Pearson

Athletic Trainers
Pre-1913	William (Willie) McGill
1913-16	Dr. Samuel Bilik
1916-47	David M. (Matt) Bullock
1947-51	Elmer (Ike) Hill
1951-57	Richard Klein
1957-69	Robert Nicollette
1969-73	Robert Behnke
1973-83	John (Skip) Pickering
1975-78	Dana Gerhardt (women's)
1978-80	Ellen Murray (women's)
1980-	Karen Iehl-Morse (women's)
1983-	Al Martindale

Business Managers
1922-27	Frank D. Murphy
1927-30	Carl Lundgren
1930-42	Charles E. (Chilly) Bowen
1943-50	Clyde W. (Bud) Lyon*
1950-69	Henry Thornes

1969-74	R. William Sticklen
1975-76	Carl W. Freeman
1977-84	Thomas Johnson
1984-86	Terry Hearne
1986-87	Julie Frichtl
1987-	Tim Tracy

*On leave of absence for war service from 1944-46

Equipment Managers
1913-46	David M. (Matt) Bullock
1946-72	Paul Schaede
1973-81	Carl V. Rose
1981-85	Marion Brownfield
1985-	Andy Dixon

Facilities Director
1923-38	Ben Crackel
1938-47	Fred Brunner
1948-66	Fred J. Stipe
1966	William Hagerman
1966-73	Russell Mace
1973-87	Robert L. Wright
1987-94	John O'Donnell
1994-	Allan Heinze

Fighting Illini Scholarship Fund Directors
1969-92	T. Dwight (Dike) Eddleman
1981-83	Carl Meyer (Chicago Operation)
1981-89	Wayne Williams (St. Louis Operation)
1983-89	Ronald E. Guenther (Chicago Operation)
1989-93	John Southwood (Chicago Operation)
1991-	Steven Greene (Chicago Operation)
1993-	Ken Zimmerman Jr. (Champaign Operation)

Team Physicians
1933-71	Dr. Leland M.T. Stilwell, M.D.*
1942-45	Dr. Irwin W. Bach, M.D. (acting)
1971-74	Dr. David Hamilton, M.D.
1975-78	Dr. L.M. Hursh, M.D.
1978-83	Dr. David Hamilton, M.D.
1983-	Dr. Robert Gurtler, M.D.
1983-	Dr. Stephen H. Soboroff, M.D.
1993-	Dr. Michael Gernant, M.D.

*On leave of absence for war service from 1942-45

Richard (Itch) Jones
Baseball

Lou Henson
Men's Basketball

Theresa Grentz
Women's Basketball

Ticket Managers

1924-27	L.M. (Mike) Stohrer
1927-42	Charles E. (Chilly) Bowen
1942-47	Clyde W. (Bud) Lyon*
1944-46	Jane Geiler (acting)
1947-75	George A. Legg
1976	Paul J. Foil
1977-89	Paul Bunting
1989-	Mike Hatfield

*On leave of absence for war service from 1944-46

Baseball Coaches

1878-91	Student coaches appointed
1892-94	Edward K. Hall
1895	Student coach appointed
1896-1919	George A. Huff
1920	George (Potsy) Clark
1921-34	Carl L. Lundgren
1935-51	Walter H. Roettger
1952-78	Lee P. Eilbracht
1979-87	Thomas Dedin
1988-90	Augie Garrido
1991-	Richard (Itch) Jones

Basketball Coaches - Men's

1906	Elwood Brown
1907	F.L. Pinckney
1908	Fletcher Lane
1909-10	Herbert V. Juul
1911-12	T.E. Thompson
1913-20	Ralph R. Jones
1921-22	Frank J. Winters
1923-36	J. Craig Ruby
1937-47	Douglas R. Mills
1948-67	Harry Combes
1967-74	Harv Schmidt
1974-75	Gene Bartow
1975-	Louis R. Henson

Basketball Coaches - Women's

1974-76	Steven Douglas
1976-79	Carla Thompson
1979-84	Jane Schroeder
1984-90	Laura Golden
1990-95	Kathy Lindsey
1995-	Theresa Grentz

Cross Country Coaches - Men's

1938-60	Leo T. Johnson
1961	Edward Bernauer
1962-63	Phillip Coleman
1965-66	Robert C. Wright
1967-	Gary Wieneke

Cross Country Coaches - Women's

1977-81	Jessica Dragicevic
1981-83	Mary Beth Spencer
1984-85	Patty Bradley
1985-91	Gary Winckler
1992-93	Mary Beth Spencer-Dyson
1994-	Gary Winckler

Diving Coaches

1975-93	Fred Newport

Fencing Coaches

1911	R.N. Fargo
1912	K.J. Beebe
1913-16	H.E. Pengilly
1917-21*	A.J. Schuettner
1922-23	R.G. Tolman
1924-28	Waldo Shumway
1929-38	Herbert W. Craig
1939-40	James L. Jackson
1941-72**	Maxwell R. Garret
1973-93	Arthur Schankin

*Intercollegiate Fencing suspended from 1918-19 due to World War I
**Suspended from 1944-46 due to World War II

Football Coaches

1890	Scott Williams
1891	Robert Lackey
1892-93	Edward K. Hall
1894	Louis D. Vail
1895-96	George Huff
1897-98	Fred L. Smith
1899	Neilson Poe
1900	Fred L. Smith
1901-02	Edgar G. Holt
1903	George Woodruff
1904	Arthur R. Hall, Justa M. Lindgren, Fred Lowenthal, Clyde Mathews
1905	Fred Lowenthal
1906	Justa M. Lindgren

Gary Wieneke
Men's Cross Country/Track & Field

Gary Winckler
Women's Cross Country/Track & Field

Lou Tepper
Football

Ed Beard
Men's Golf

Paula Smith
Women's Golf

Yoshi Hayasaki
Men's Gymnastics

1907-12	Arthur R. Hall
1913-41	Robert C. Zuppke
1942-59	Raymond Eliot
1960-66	Peter Elliott
1967-70	James Valek
1971-76	Robert Blackman
1977-79	Gary Moeller
1980-87	Mike White
1988-91	John Mackovic
1991-	Louis Tepper

Golf Coaches - Men's

1922-23	George Davis
1924	Ernest E. Bearg
1925-28	D.L. Swank
1929-32	J.H. Utley
1933	Robert Martin
1934	F.H. Renwick
1935-38	J.H. Utley
1939-43	W.W. Brown
1944-66	Ralph Fletcher
1967-71	Richard Youngberg
1972-80	Ladd Pash
1981-	Ed Beard

Golf Coaches - Women's

| 1974-78 | Betsy Kimpel |
| 1978- | Paula Smith |

Gymnastics Coaches - Men's

1898	Adolph Kreikenbaum
1902	Adolph Kreikenbaum
1905	Leo G. Hana

1910-13	Leo G. Hana
1914-17*	R.N. Fargo
1921	A.J. Schuettner
1922	S.C. Staley
1924-25	J.C. Wagner
1926-29	R.C. Heidloff
1930-42**	Hartley D. Price
1947-48	Hartley D. Price
1949-61	Charles Pond
1961-62	Pat Bird (acting)
1962-73	Charles Pond
1973-93	Yoshi Hayasaki
1993-95	Don Osborn

*Intercollegiate gymnastics suspended from 1918-19 due to World War I
**Suspended from 1944-46 due to World War II

Gymnastics Coaches - Women's

1974-75	Kim Musgrave
1975-77	Allison Milburn
1977-93	Beverly Mackes
1993-	Lynn Crane

Ice Hockey Coaches

| 1938-39 | Raymond Eliot |
| 1940-43 | Victor Heyliger |

Polo Coaches

| 1934 | Pepper Clay |
| 1935-39 | Clifford B. Cole |

| 1940 | Alfred J. DeLorimer |
| 1941 | Philip R. Danley |

Soccer Coaches

1910	W.S. Strode
1927-33	Hartley D. Price
1934-35	King J. McCristal

Strength & Conditioning Coaches

| 1980-88 | William Kroll |
| 1988- | Leo Ward |

Swimming Coaches - Men's

1906-09	W.H. Hockmeister
1910-11	George B. Norris
1912-17*	Edward J. Manley
1920-52	Edward J. Manley
1953-70	Allen B. Klingel
1971-93	Donald Sammons

*Intercollegiate swimming suspended from 1918-19 due to World War I

Swimming Coaches - Women's

1974-75	Jeanne Hultzen
1975-80	Ann Pollack
1980-93	Donald Sammons
1993-	James Lutz

Tennis Coaches - Men's

1908-13	P.B. Hawk
1914	W.A. Oldfather
1915-17*	Student coaches appointed
1920-24	E.E. Bearg

Lynn Crane
Women's Gymnastics

Jim Lutz
Women's Swimming

Jennifer Roberts
Women's Tennis

Craig Tiley
Men's Tennis

Mike Hebert
Volleyball

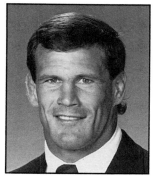

Mark Johnson
Wrestling

1925	B.P. Hoover
1926-29	A.R. Cohn
1930	E.A. Shoaff
1931-34	C.W. Gelwick
1935	Gerald Huff
1936-37	Casper H. Nannes
1938-42	Howard J. Braun
1943-46	Ralph Johnson
1946-64	Howard J. Braun
1965	Bob Lansford (acting)
1966-72	Dan Olson
1972-73	William Wright
1973-77	Bruce Shuman
1977	John Avallone Jr. (acting)
1978-81	Jack Groppel
1981-85	Brad Louderback
1986-92	Neil Adams
1992-	Craig Tiley

*Intercollegiate tennis suspended from 1918-19 due to World War I

Tennis Coaches - Women's

1974-75	Peggy Pruitt
1975-78	Carla Thompson
1978-81	Linda Pecore

1981-87	Mary Tredennick
1987-	Jennifer Roberts

Track and Field Coaches - Men's

1895	Harvey Cornish
1896-98	Henry H. Everett
1899-1900	Jacob K. Shell
1901-03	H.B. Conibear
1904-29	Harry L. Gill
1930	C.D. Werner
1931-33	Harry L. Gill
1934-37	Don C. Seaton
1938-65	Leo T. Johnson
1965-74	Robert C. Wright
1974-	Gary Wieneke

Track and Field Coaches - Women's

1974-75	Jerry Mayhew
1975-81	Jessica Dragicevic
1981-84	Mike Shine
1984-85	Patty Bradley
1985-	Gary Winckler

Volleyball Coaches

1974-75	Kathleen Haywood

1975-77	Terry Hite
1977-80	Chris Accornero
1980-83	John Blair
1983-	Mike Hebert

Wrestling Coaches

1911	R.N. Fargo
1912-13	Alexander Elston
1914	Theodore Paulsen
1915-17*	Walter Evans
1921-28	Paul Prehn
1929-43	Harold E. (Hek) Kenney
1944-46	Glenn C. Law
1946-47	Harold E. (Hek) Kenney
1948-50	Glenn C. Law
1950-68	B.R. Patterson
1968-73	Jack Robinson
1973-78	Thomas Porter
1978-83	Greg Johnson
1983-92	Ron Clinton
1992-	Mark Johnson

*Intercollegiate wrestling suspended from 1918-19 due to World War I

Don Osborn
Men's Gymnastics

Photo Credit List

Decade Page: UI Sports Information

1895-96
Moment: The Palmer House Hilton
Birthdays: UI Sports Information
Item: UI Sports Information
Lists: UI Sports Information
Legend: UI Sports Information
Lore: UI Archives

1896-97
Moment: UI Sports Information
Birthdays: UI Sports Information
Item: UI Sports Information
Lists: UI Sports Information
Legend: UI Illio
Lore: UI Sports Information

1897-98
Moment: UI Sports Information
Birthdays: UI Sports Information
Item: UI Sports Information
Lists: UI Sports Information
Legend: UI Sports Information

1898-99
Moment: UI Sports Information
Birthdays: UI Sports Information
Item: Mark Jones
Lists: UI Sports Information
Legend: UI Sports Information
Lore: UI Sports Information

1899-1900
Moment: UI Sports Information
Birthdays: UI Sports Information
Item: UI Archives
Lists: UI Sports Information
Legend: UI Sports Information
Lore: UI Newspaper Library

1900-01
Moment: UI Sports Information
Birthdays: UI Sports Information
Item: Univ. of Tennessee Sports Information Dept.
Legend: UI Illio
Lore: UI Illio

1901-02
Moment: UI Sports Information
Birthdays: UI Sports Information
Item: UI Sports Information
Lists: UI Sports Information
Legend: UI Sports Information
Lore: UI Archives

1902-03
Moment: UI Sports Information
Birthdays: UI Sports Information
Item: Mrs. Red Grange
Lists: UI Illio
Legend: UI Sports Information
Lore: UI Sports Information

1903-04
Moment: UI Sports Information
Birthdays: UI Sports Information
Item: UI Sports Information
Lists: UI Sports Information
Legend: UI Sports Information
Lore: UI Archives

1904-05
Moment: UI Sports Information
Birthdays: UI Sports Information
Item: UI Sports Information
Lists: UI Sports Information
Legend: UI Sports Information

Decade Page: UI Archives

1905-06
Moment: UI Sports Information
Birthdays: UI Sports Information
Item: UI Archives
Legend: UI Archives
Lore: UI Archives

1906-07
Moment: UI Sports Information
Birthdays: UI Sports Information
Item: UI Sports Information
Lists: UI Sports Information
Legend: UI Sports Information

1907-08
Moment: UI Sports Information
Birthdays: UI Sports Information
Item: UI Sports Information
Lists: UI Sports Information
Legend: UI Sports Information
Lore: UI Sports Information

1908-09
Moment: UI Sports Information
Birthdays: Pacific & Atlantic Photos, Inc.
Item: UI Sports Information
Lists: UI Illio
Legend: UI Sports Information
Lore: UI Newspaper Library

1909-10
Moment: UI Sports Information
Birthdays: UI Sports Information
Item: UI Sports Information
Lists: UI Sports Information
Legend: UI Archives
Lore: UI Sports Information

1910-11
Moment: UI Sports Information
Birthdays: UI Sports Information
Item: UI Sports Information
Lists: UI Sports Information
Legend: UI Sports Information
Lore: UI Archives

1911-12
Moment: UI Sports Information
Birthdays: UI Sports Information
Item: UI Sports Information
Lists: UI Sports Information
Legend: UI Sports Information

1912-13
Moment: UI Sports Information
Birthdays: UI Sports Information
Item: UI Sports Information
Lists: UI Illio
Legend: UI Sports Information
Lore: UI Sports Information

1913-14
Moment: UI Sports Information
Birthdays: UI Sports Information
Item: UI Sports Information
Lists: UI Sports Information
Legend: UI Sports Information
Lore: UI Illio

1914-15
Moment: UI Sports Information
Birthdays: Sportspix Chicago
Item: UI Sports Information
Lists: UI Illio
Legend: UI Sports Information
Lore: UI Archives

Decade Page: UI Archives

1915-16
Moment: UI Sports Information
Birthdays: UI Sports Information
Item: UI Sports Information
Lists: UI Sports Information
Legend: UI Sports Information
Lore: UI Archives

1916-17
Moment: UI Newspaper Library
Birthdays: UI Illio
Item: UI Sports Information
Lists: UI Sports Information
Legend: UI Sports Information
Lore: UI Archives

1917-18
Moment: UI Archives
Birthdays: UI Sports Information
Item: UI Sports Information
Lists: UI Sports Information
Legend: UI Sports Information

1918-19
Moment: UI Sports Information
Birthdays: UI Sports Information
Item: UI Sports Information
Lists: UI Sports Information
Legend: UI Sports Information
Lore: UI Archives

1919-20
Moment: UI Sports Information
Birthdays: UI Sports Information
Item: UI Sports Information
Lists: UI Sports Information
Legend: UI Sports Information
Lore: UI Sports Information

1920-21
Moment: UI Sports Information
Birthdays: UI Sports Information
Item: UI Sports Information
Lists: UI Sports Information
Legend: UI Sports Information
Lore: UI Sports Information

1921-22
Moment: UI Sports Information
Birthdays: UI Sports Information
Item: UI Sports Information
Lists: UI Sports Information
Legend: UI Sports Information
Lore: UI Archives

1922-23
Moment: UI Sports Information
Birthdays: UI Sports Information
Item: UI Sports Information
Lists: UI Sports Information
Legend: UI Sports Information
Lore: UI Archives

1923-24
Moment: UI Sports Information
Birthdays: UI Sports Information
Item: UI Sports Information
Lists: UI Sports Information
Legend: UI Sports Information

1924-25
Moment: UI Sports Information
Birthdays: UI Sports Information
Item: UI Sports Information
Legend: UI Sports Information

Decade Page: Mark Jones

1925-26
Moment: UI Sports Information
Birthdays: UI Sports Information
Item: DuPage County Heritage Museum, Wheaton, IL
Lists: UI Sports Information
Legend: UI Sports Information
Lore: UI Sports Information

1926-27
Moment: UI Sports Information
Birthdays: Champaign-Urbana Evening Courier
Item: UI Sports Information
Lists: UI Sports Information
Legend: UI Sports Information
Lore: UI Archives

1927-28
Moment: UI Sports Information
Birthdays: UI Sports Information
Item: UI Sports Information
Lists: UI Sports Information
Legend: UI Sports Information
Lore: Courtesy of St. John's Catholic Church

1928-29
Moment: UI Sports Information
Birthdays: UI Sports Information
Item: UI Sports Information
Lists: UI Sports Information
Legend: UI Sports Information
Lore: UI Sports Information

1929-30
Moment: UI Sports Information
Birthdays: UI Sports Information
Item: UI Sports Information
Lists: UI Sports Information
Legend: UI Sports Information
Lore: UI Sports Information

1930-31
Moment: UI Sports Information
Birthdays: UI Sports Information
Item: UI Sports Information
Lists: UI Sports Information
Legend: UI Sports Information
Lore: UI Archives

1931-32
Moment: UI Sports Information
Birthdays: UI Illio
Item: UI Sports Information
Legend: UI Sports Information
Lore: UI Sports Information

1932-33
Moment: UI Sports Information
Birthdays: UI Illio
Item: UI Sports Information
Lists: UI Sports Information
Legend: UI Archives

1933-34
Moment: UI Sports Information
Birthdays: Gliessman Studios
Item: UI Sports Information
Lists: UI Sports Information
Legend: UI Sports Information
Lore: Associated Press

1934-35
Moment: UI Sports Information
Birthdays: UI Illio
Item: Univ. of Michigan Athletic Public Relations
Lists: UI Sports Information
Legend: UI Sports Information

Decade Page: Mark Jones

1935-36
Moment: UI Sports Information
Birthdays: UI Illio
Item: UI Sports Information
Legend: UI Sports Information

1936-37
Moment: UI Sports Information
Birthdays: UI Sports Information
Item: UI Sports Information
Lists: Champaign-Urbana Evening Courier
Legend: UI Sports Information
Lore: UI Archives

1937-38
Moment: UI Sports Information
Birthdays: UI Sports Information
Item: UI Sports Information
Legend: UI Sports Information
Lore: UI Sports Information

1938-39
Moment: UI Sports Information
Birthdays: UI Sports Information
Item: UI Sports Information
Lists: UI Sports Information
Legend: UI Sports Information
Lore: UI Sports Information

1939-40
Moment: UI Sports Information
Birthdays: UI Illio
Item: UI Sports Information
Legend: UI Sports Information
Lore: UI Archives

1940-41
Moment: Champaign-Urbana Evening Courier
Birthdays: UI Sports Information
Item: UI Sports Information
Lists: UI Sports Information
Legend: UI Sports Information

1941-42
Moment: UI Sports Information
Birthdays: UI Sports Information
Item: UI Sports Information
Legend: UI Sports Information

1942-43
Moment: UI Sports Information
Birthdays: UI Sports Information
Lists: Mark Jones
Item: UI Sports Information
Legend: UI Sports Information

1943-44
Moment: UI Sports Information
Birthdays: UI Sports Information
Item: UI Sports Information
Legend: Gliessman Studios
Lore: UI Archives

1944-45
Moment: UI Sports Information
Birthdays: UI Sports Information
Item: UI Sports Information
Lists: UI Sports Information
Legend: UI Sports Information
Lore: UI Sports Information

Decade Page: Mr. and Mrs. Gene Vance

1945-46
Moment: UI Sports Information
Birthdays: UI Sports Information
Item: UI Sports Information
Lists: UI Sports Information
Legend: UI Sports Information
Lore: UI Archives

1946-47
Moment: UI Sports Information
Birthdays: UI Sports Information
Item: Champaign-Urbana Evening Courier
Lists: UI Sports Information
Legend: UI Sports Information
Lore: UI Archives

1947-48
Moment: Press Association
Birthdays: UI Sports Information
Item: UI Sports Information
Lists: UI Sports Information
Legend: Gliessman Studios

1948-99
Moment: UI Sports Information
Birthdays: UI Sports Information
Item: UI Sports Information
Lists: UI Sports Information
Legend: UI Sports Information

1949-50
Moment: UI Sports Information
Birthdays: UI Sports Information
Item: UI Sports Information
Legend: UI Sports Information
Lore: UI Sports Information

1950-51
Moment: UI Sports Information
Birthdays: UI Sports Information
Item: UI Sports Information
Lists: UI Sports Information
Legend: UI Sports Information
Lore: UI Alumni Association

1951-52
Moment: UI Sports Information
Item: Associated Press
Legend: UI Sports Information
Lore: ABC, Inc.

1952-53
Moment: UI Sports Information
Birthdays: UI Sports Information
Lists: UI Sports Information
Item: UI Sports Information
Legend: UI Sports Information

1953-54
Moment: UI Sports Information
Birthdays: UI Sports Information
Item: UI Sports Information
Legend: Champaign-Urbana Evening Courier
Lore: UI Archives

1954-55
Moment: UI Sports Information
Item: UI Sports Information
Lists: Gliessman Studios
Legend: Gliessman Studios
Lore: UI Archives

Decade Page: Mark Jones

1955-56
Moment: UI Sports Information
Item: Gliessman Studios
Legend: Gliessman Studios

1956-57
Moment: UI Sports Information
Item: UI Sports Information
Legend: UI Sports Information
Lore: UI Archives

1957-58
Moment: Gliessman Studios
Item: Green Bay Packers
Lists: Gliessman Studios
Legend: UI Sports Information
Lore: UI Alumni Association

1958-59
Moment: Gliessman Studios
Item: UI Sports Information
Lists: Gliessman Studios
Legend: UI Sports Information

1959-60
Moment: UI Sports Information
Item: UI Sports Information
Legend: UI Sports Information
Lore: UI Sports Information

1960-61
Moment: Gliessman Studios
Item: UI Sports Information
Legend: UI Sports Information
Lore: UI Archives

1961-62
Moment: UI Sports Information
Item: UI Sports Information
Legend: UI Sports Information
Lore: UI News Bureau

1962-63
Moment: UI Sports Information
Item: UI Sports Information
Legend: UI Sports Information
Lore: UI Sports Information

1963-64
Moment: UI Sports Information
Item: Lester Nehamkin
Lists: Notre Dame Sports Information
Legend: UI Sports Information
Lore: UI Archives

1964-65
Moment: UI Sports Information
Item: UI Sports Information
Lists: United Press International
Legend: UI Sports Information
Lore: UI Archives

Decade Page: Mark Jones

1965-66
Moment: Gliessman Studios
Item: UI Sports Information
Lists: UI Sports Information
Legend: UI Sports Information
Lore: UI Alumni Association

1966-67
Moment: UI Archives
Item: Champaign-Urbana Evening Courier
Lists: Baltimore Colts
Legend: UI Sports Information

1967-68
Moment: UI Sports Information
Item: UI Sports Information
Legend: Mr. and Mrs. Robert Wright
Lore: UI News Bureau

1968-69
Moment: UI Sports Information
Item: UI Sports Information
Lists: UI Sports Information
Legend: Champaign-Urbana Evening Courier

1969-70
Moment: UI Sports Information
Item: Mark Jones
Lists: UI Sports Information
Legend: UI Sports Information

1970-71
Moment: UI Sports Information
Item: UI Sports Information
Lists: UI Sports Information
Legend: UI Sports Information
Lore: UI Archives

1971-72
Moment: Champaign-Urbana Evening Courier
Item: UI Sports Information
Lists: UI Sports Information
Legend: UI Sports Information
Lore: UI Archives

1972-73
Moment: UI Sports Information
Item: UI Sports Information
Lists: UI Sports Information
Legend: UI Sports Information
Lore: UI Archives

1973-74
Moment: Phil Greer
Item: UI Sports Information
Lists: H.F. Duncan
Legend: UI Sports Information
Lore: UI Alumni Association

1974-75
Moment: UI Sports Information
Women's Milestones: UI Sports Information
Item: Michael Smeltzer
Legend: UI Sports Information

Decade Page: Mark Jones

1975-76
Moment: UI Sports Information
Women's Milestones: UI Sports Information
Item: UI Sports Information
Lists: MSU Sports Information
Legend: UI Sports Information

1976-77
Moment: UI Sports Information
Women's Milestones: UI Sports Information
Item: UI Sports Information
Lists: UI Sports Information
Legend: Mark Jones

1977-78
Moment: UI Sports Information
Women's Milestones: UI Sports Information
Item: UI Sports Information
Lists: University of Minnesota
Legend: UI Sports Information
Lore: UI Sports Information

1978-79
Moment: UI Sports Information
Women's Milestones: UI Sports Information
Item: UI Sports Information
Legend: UI Sports Information
Lore: Fabian Bachrach

1979-80
Moment: UI Sports Information
Women's Milestones: UI Sports Information
Item: UI Sports Information
Lists: UI Sports Information
Legend: UI Sports Information
Lore: UI Sports Information

1980-81
Moment: UI Sports Information
Item: UI Sports Information
Lists: UI Sports Information
Legend: UI Sports Information

1981-82
Moment: Curt Beamer
Item: UI Sports Information
Lists: Mark Jones
Legend: UI Sports Information

1982-83
Moment: Memphis Press
Women's Milestones: Mark Jones
Item: UI Sports Information
Lists: UI Sports Information
Legend: UI Sports Information

1983-84
Moment: UI Sports Information
Women's Milestones: UI Illio
Item: Michael Smeltzer
Lists: UI Sports Information
Legend: UI Sports Information

1984-85
Moment: UI Sports Information
Women's Milestones: McCandless Photography
Item: UI Sports Information
Lists: Michael Smeltzer
Legend: Darrell Beachy
Lore: UI News Bureau

Decade Page: Mark Jones

1985-86
Moment: UI Sports Information
Women's Milestones: McCandless Photography
Item: UI Sports Information
Lists: Mark Jones
Legend: UI Sports Information

1986-87
Moment: Michael Smeltzer
Women's Milestones: McCandless Photography
Item: UI Sports Information
Lists: UI Sports Information
Legend: UI Sports Information

1987-88
Moment: UI Sports Information
Women's Milestones: David Ghent
Item: UI Sports Information
Lists: UI Sports Information
Legend: UI Sports Information
Lore: UI News Bureau

1988-89
Moment: Mark Jones
Women's Milestones: UI Sports Information
Item: Mark Jones
Lists: Mark Jones
Legend: UI Sports Information

1989-90
Moment: Mark Jones
Item: McCandless Photography
Lists: Mark Jones
Legend: Mark Jones
Lore: UI News Bureau

1990-91
Moment: Mark Jones
Women's Milestones: Mark Jones
Item: UI Sports Information
Legend: UI Sports Information

1991-92
Moment: Mark Jones
Item: Mark Jones
Lists: UI Sports Information
Legend: Mark Jones
Lore: Mark Jones

1992-93
Moment: Mark Jones
Women's Milestones: UI Sports Information
Item: UI Sports Information
Lists: Mark Jones
Legend: UI Sports Information
Lore: Bill Wiegand

1993-94
Moment: Mark Jones
Women's Milestones: UI Sports Information
Item: Mark Jones
Lists: UI Sports Information
Legend: UI Sports Information
Lore: Mark Jones

1994-95
Moment: Mark Jones
Women's Milestones: UI Sports Information
Item: Mark Jones
Legend: Butkus Award Committee

**Red Grange: An Original
Superstar**

Pg. 72
All photos: UI Sports Information

Pg. 73
All photos: UI Sports Information
except—
middle left: DuPage County
Heritage Gallery
Middle right: Mark Jones
Bottom right: Associated Press

**All-time Fighting Illini
Letter-Winner List**

Pg. 228
Batchelder: UI Sports
Information
Beckmann: UI Sports Information
Bessone: UI Sports Information
Booker: Mark Jones

Pg. 230
Brookhart: UI Sports Information
Brownlow: Mark Jones
Busboom: UI Sports Information
Clements: UI Sports Information

Pg. 231
Chamblin: UI Sports Information
Colangelo: UI Sports Information

Pg. 232
Corbett: UI Sports Information
Cunningham: UI Sports
Information
Dalesandro: UI Sports
Information
DeBord: UI Sports Information

Pg. 233
Dilger: UI Sports Information
Edwards, Bill: UI Sports
Information
Edwards, Julie: Mark Jones
Engels: UI Sports Information

Pg. 234
Flessner: UI Sports Information
Flynn: UI Sports Information

Pg. 235
Gantt: UI Sports Information
George: Mark Jones

Pg. 236
Gow: UI Sports Information
Graham: UI Sports Information
Haller: UI Sports Information
Hamilton: UI Sports
Information

Pg.237:
Hardy: UI Sports Information
Henderson: UI Sports
Information
Hester: Mark Jones
Hirsch: UI Sports Information

Pg. 238
Holtzman: UI Sports Information
Hopkins, Brad: UI Sports
Information
Hopkins, Mike: Mark Jones
Johnson: UI Sports Information

Pg. 239
Jones: UI Sports Information
Juriga: UI Sports Information
Keene: Mark Jones
Kelly: UI Sports Information

Pg. 240
Koers: Mark Jones
Lakes: UI Sports Information
Lanter: UI Sports Information
Lubin: UI Sports Information

Pg. 242
Macconnachie: UI Sports
Information
McCarren: UI Sports Information

Pg. 243
McMillan: UI Sports Information
Meyers: UI Sports Information
Michael: UI Sports Information
Montgomery: UI Sports
Information

Pg. 244
Mullis: UI Sports Information
Noelke: UI Sports Information
Pall: UI Sports Information
Paulson: UI Sports Information

Pg. 246
Pike: UI Sports Information
Pope: UI Sports Information

Pg. 247
Ramshaw: UI Sports
Information
Rice: UI Sports Information

Pg. 248
Reynolds: UI Sports
Information
Rogers: UI Sports Information
Romani: UI Sports Information
Ryniec: UI Sports Information

Pg. 249:
Schmidt, Burt: UI Sports
Information
Schmidt, Rick: UI Sports
Information
Scholtens: UI Sports
Information
Sharp: UI Sports Information

Pg. 251
Steger: UI Sports Information
Studwell: UI Sports Information
Sutton: UI Sports Information
Tanner: NASA

Pg. 252
Tjarksen: UI Sports Information
Tochihara: Mark Jones
Travnik: UI Sports Information
Trudeau: UI Sports Information

Pg. 253
Washington: UI Sports
Information
Weddell: UI Sports Information

Pg. 254:
Wells: Mark Jones
Wheatland: UI Sports
Information
White: UI Sports Information
Wolf: UI Sports Information

Pg. 255
Wright: Champaign-Urbana
Courier
Wyatt: UI Sports Information

Personnel History

All photos: UI Sports
Information